THE BIBLICAL RESOURCE SERIES

General Editors

ASTRID BECK

DAVID NOEL FREEDMAN

Editorial Board

JOHN HUEHNERGARD, *Ancient Near Eastern Languages*

PETER MACHINIST, *Hebrew Bible*

SHALOM PAUL, *Hebrew Bible*

JOHN MEIER, *New Testament*

STANLEY PORTER, *New Testament and Greek*

ADELA COLLINS, *New Testament*

THE BIBLICAL RESOURCE SERIES

Available

Frank Moore Cross, Jr., and David Noel Freedman,
Studies in Ancient Yahwistic Poetry

S. R. Driver, *A Treatise on the Use of the Tenses in Hebrew
and Some Other Syntactical Questions*

Roland de Vaux, *Ancient Israel: Its Life and Institutions*

Ancient Israel

Its Life and Institutions

Roland de Vaux, O.P.

Translated by
John McHugh

WILLIAM B. EERDMANS PUBLISHING COMPANY
GRAND RAPIDS, MICHIGAN

DOVE BOOKSELLERS
LIVONIA, MICHIGAN

First published in French in two volumes under the title
Les Institutions de l'Ancien Testament
© 1958, 1960 Les Editions du Cerf, Paris

English translation © 1961 Darton, Longman & Todd Ltd
1 Spencer Court
140-142 Wandsworth High Street
London SW18 4JJ

This edition published jointly 1997 in the United States of America by
Wm. B. Eerdmans Publishing Co.
255 Jefferson Ave. S.E., Grand Rapids, Michigan 49503
and Dove Booksellers
30633 Schoolcraft Road, Suite C, Livonia, Michigan 48150

All rights reserved

Printed in the United States of America

01 00 99 98   5 4 3 2

Library of Congress Cataloging-in-Publication Data

Vaux, Roland de, 1903-1971.
[Institutions de l'Ancien Testament. English]
Ancient Israel : its life and institutions / Roland de Vaux :
translated by John McHugh.
p.   cm.
Previously published: London : Darton, Longman & Todd, 1961.
Includes bibliographical references and index.
ISBN 0-8028-4278-X (paper : alk. paper)
1. Jews — Social life and customs — To 70 A.D.
2. Judaism — History —To 70 A.D.   I. Title.
DS112.V313   1997
306'.089'924 — dc21   97-4938
                                             CIP

TO THE STUDENTS OF THE ÉCOLE BIBLIQUE

WITH WHOM I HAVE LEARNED

WHAT THIS BOOK CONTAINS

PREFACE

INSTITUTIONS are the various forms in which the social life of a
people finds expression. Some it will take for granted as a matter of custom; others it will adopt of its own choice; and yet others will be imposed
upon it by an authority. Individuals are subject to the nation's institutions,
but the institutions themselves exist, ultimately, for the sake of the society
whose welfare they promote, whether the society be small as a family, or
large as a state or religious community. Again, the institutions of a society
will vary with time and place, and will depend, to some extent, on natural
conditions such as geography and climate, but their distinguishing characteristic is that they all proceed, in the end, from the human will.

The institutions of a people with a long past are therefore closely bound up
not only with the territory in which it has lived but with history. They will
be made to suit that people, and will bear the mark of its psychology, of its
ideas on man, the world and God. Like its literature, its art, its science and
religion, its institutions too are an element in, and an expression of, its civilization. In order to understand and describe these ancient witnesses to the life
of a people, the historian has to take into account all the traces of the past.
Clearly, written documents have pride of place, but the things which survive,
even the humblest remains of man's labour, cannot be passed over. Everything is grist which will enable us to reconstruct the conditions and the
setting of the people's social life.

Because of these various relations with other sciences, the institutions of
Israel have usually been studied as part of a larger whole. Long treatises have
been devoted to them in the classic historical works, the *Geschichte des Volkes
Israel* by Rudolf Kittel, and especially in Schürer's *Geschichte des jüdischen
Volkes* for the last period of the Old Testament. Conversely, the recent
studies by J. Pirenne on *Les Institutions des Hébreux*[1] follow the historical
development. Formerly, institutions were treated under the heading of
Antiquitates Hebraicae, but nowadays they are associated with archaeology, and
are thus presented by I. Benziger in *Hebräische Archäologie*, 3rd edition, 1927,
by F. Nötscher in *Biblische Altertumskunde*, 1940, and by A. G. Barrois in
Manuel d'Archéologie Biblique, I, 1939; II, 1953. Ample space is devoted to
them in histories of civilization, such as A. Bertholet, *Kulturgeschichte
Israels*, 1919, and J. Pedersen, *Israel, its Life and Culture*, I-II, 1926; III-IV,
1940.

1. *Archives d'Histoire du Droit Oriental*, IV, 1949, pp. 51-76; V, 1950, pp. 99-132; *Revue Internationale
des Droits de l'Antiquité*, I, 1952, pp. 33-86; II, 1953, pp. 109-149; III, 1954, pp. 195-255.

All these works are excellent and have constantly been used in the preparation of this book, but it has been felt that Old Testament institutions could well form the subject of a special study. For this the main source is evidently the Bible itself. Except in the legislative and ritual sections, the Bible does not treat directly of these questions, but the historical, prophetical and wisdom books contain much information, all the more interesting because it tells us what actually did happen and not what ought to have happened. To make use of all these texts calls for accurate exegesis, and before we can draw conclusions, literary criticism must assign dates to the various passages, for the development of institutions followed the course of history. Archaeology, in the strict sense, *i.e.* the study of the material remains of the past, is only an auxiliary science, which helps us to reconstruct the actual setting in which the institutions functioned: but it reveals to us the houses in which families lived, the towns administered by the elders of the people or the king's officials, the capitals where the court resided, the gates where justice was administered and the merchants set up their stalls, with their scales and the weights they kept in their purses. It shows us the ramparts which armies defended, the tombs at which the funeral rites were performed, and the sanctuaries where the priests directed worship. Finally, if we wish to have a real understanding of the institutions of Israel, we must compare them with those of its neighbours, with Mesopotamia, Egypt and Asia Minor, where information is plentiful, and with the little states of Syria and Palestine, where it is scanty. But it was among the latter that Israel carved out for itself a homeland; many of them were founded about the same time, and Israel had constant contact with them throughout its long history.

The present book offers only the conclusions of all this research. Nomadic customs and tribal organization left traces on the life of Israel long after the settlement in Canaan; hence the book begins with an introductory study of nomadism. Next come family institutions, then civil and political institutions. The second volume[1] will deal with military and religious institutions. This book, however, is not intended for specialists in biblical studies; rather, it is meant to help towards an intelligent reading of the Bible. Consequently, there are many references to biblical texts, but the author has deliberately refrained from over-technical discussions and from loading the pages with erudite footnotes. Many of the suggestions or statements advanced here need to be more fully supported and are based on findings of textual, literary or historical criticism which are open to debate. He can only hope that his readers will have confidence in him. Those who wish to check his statements and to form their own judgment will find the necessary material in the bibliographical notes which are grouped according to the chapters. This bibliography, however, is not meant to be complete; it contains only such older works as have not been superseded, and those more recent studies

1. This English edition contains both volumes together.

which seem most useful and from which the author has drawn his information. In quoting them, he wishes to acknowledge his debt to those who have studied these questions before him, but he is also providing weapons against himself, for many of these works put forward solutions very different from those he has finally adopted. The inquiring reader may look and choose for himself.

The subject-matter of the book is restricted by its title to the Old Testament period, and the New Testament period is called as witness only by way of clarification or addition. In the study of the Old Testament itself, institutions occupy a subordinate place, and the reader may sometimes feel that he is very far from the spiritual and doctrinal message he seeks for in the Bible. Nevertheless, he is always on the border-land of biblical religion, and often n direct contact with the message it enshrines. Family customs, funeral rites, the status of foreigners, of slaves, the notions of personality and the rôle of the king, the connection between the law—even profane law—and the Covenant with God, the manner of waging war—all these reflect religious ideas, and these same ideas find conscious expression in worship and liturgy. The institutions of the Chosen People prepare the way for, and indeed foreshadow, the institutions of the community of the elect. Everything in this sacred past matters to us, for the Word of God is a living thing, and a man is better able to hear its tones if he listens to it in the actual surroundings in which it was first given to mankind.

Jerusalem, June, 1957.

TRANSLATOR'S NOTE

THIS book is a translation of *Les Institutions de l'Ancien Testament*, published in two volumes by *Les Editions du Cerf*, Paris; the first volume was published in 1958, the second in 1960. The translation has been made from this first edition of the French original, but it incorporates a number of additions and corrections which Fr de Vaux wishes to see inserted in the text; he has also brought the entire bibliography up to date to the beginning of 1961. The principal additions will be found on pp. 37, 58, 82 130 and 208, and the main corrections on pp. 147, 183 and 203.

The spelling of proper names follows that to be adopted in the forthcoming *Jerusalem Bible*,[1] the English edition of the *Bible de Jérusalem*,[2] but biblical names have been registered in the index under the spelling given in the Authorized Version as well. Biblical references are in every instance to the original text (Hebrew, Greek or Aramaic); where the numeration of verses differs among the various translations, it would have been cumbersome to refer to all the numerations in both Catholic and non-Catholic versions. The references have therefore been left as they stand, but they can always be found by referring to the *Bible de Jérusalem*. The index has been rearranged and expanded; in particular, the longer entries (*e.g.* Abraham) have been broken down into sub-headings, and the main references have been given first.

It only remains for me to thank Fr de Vaux for the interest he has taken in this translation, for the promptness with which he has answered all my queries, and for enabling us to include so much new material, especially in the Bibliography.

Ushaw College, Durham
Easter, 1961

1. London: Darton, Longman & Todd Ltd; New York: Doubleday & Co. Inc.
2. Paris: Les Editions du Cerf.

NOTE ON NOMENCLATURE OF SOME
BOOKS OF THE BIBLE AND APOCRYPHA

FOR the convenience of readers who are not familiar with the nomenclature adopted in this book, the lists below show the equivalents in the Authorized/King James Version, and in Douai-Challoner and Knox, where differences occur.

A.V./K.J.	In this book	D-C., Knox
Joshua	Josue	Josue
1 Samuel	1 Samuel (1 S)	1 Kings
2 Samuel	2 Samuel (2 S)	2 Kings
1 Kings	1 Kings (1 K)	3 Kings
2 Kings	2 Kings (2 K)	4 Kings
1 Chronicles	1 Chronicles (1 Ch)	1 Paralipomena
2 Chronicles	2 Chronicles (2 Ch)	2 Paralipomena
Ezra	Esdras (Esd)	1 Esdras
Nehemiah	Nehemias (Ne)	2 Esdras
1 Esdras	3 Esdras	——
2 Esdras	4 Esdras	——
Tobit	Tobias	Tobias
Ecclesiastes	Qoheleth (Qo)	Ecclesiastes
Solomon	Canticle (Ct)	Canticle of Canticles (D-C.)
		Song of Songs (Knox)
Ecclesiasticus	Sirach (Si)	Ecclesiasticus
Hosea	Osee (Os)	Osee
Obadiah	Abdias (Abd)	Abdias
Micah	Michaeas	Michaeas
Zephaniah	Sophonias (So)	Sophonias
Haggai	Aggaeus	Aggaeus
Revelation	Apocalypse (Ap)	Apocalypse

CONTENTS

PART II

CIVIL INSTITUTIONS

PART III

MILITARY INSTITUTIONS

CONTENTS

PART IV

RELIGIOUS INSTITUTIONS

INTRODUCTION

Nomadism and its Survival

1. *The Background*

AT the beginning of their history the Israelites, like their ancestors before them, lived as nomads or semi-nomads, and when they came to settle down as a nation, they still retained some characteristics of that earlier way of life. Consequently, any study of Old Testament institutions must begin with an investigation into nomadism. The biblical records preserve many ancient traditions about the early life of the Israelites, and these are of first importance in our study; but since this evidence has been to some extent systematized by later editors of the books, great care is needed in interpreting these records. We have other sources of information too: texts about the Arabs in pre-Islamic times, and ethnographical studies about the Arabs of to-day. These nomad Arabs, by race and country, are closely related to the Israelites, and what we know of pre-Islamic, modern and contemporary Arab life can help us to understand more clearly the primitive organization of Israel. On the other hand, one must beware of hasty comparisons which may overlook essential differences.

The fact is, that even in the comparatively small area of the Middle East, there have always been different types of nomads, and what is true of one type is not necessarily true of another. Even to-day, these differences persist (though one wonders how much longer any form of nomadism can survive).

(1) The real nomad, or true Bedouin (the word means 'man of the desert') is a camel-breeder. He can live in, or at least traverse, regions which are strictly desert, *i.e.* where the annual rainfall is less than 4 inches. He travels enormous distances with his herds in search of grazing, and has very little contact with settled people.

(2) A nomad, however, may breed only sheep and goats, and these flocks are not so hardy; they need to drink more often and cannot survive on the rough pastures which are sufficient for camels. This type of Bedouin lives mainly in the half-desert region (where the rainfall is 4-10 inches), and the distances he travels from one grazing ground to the next are necessarily shorter. Sometimes he does cover considerable ground, but then he must follow a route where the watering-places are not too distant from one another. He has far more contact with the settled regions, for his grazing lies along their borders.

(3) Once he begins to raise cattle as well as flocks, the shepherd ceases to be a true nomad. He settles in one place, begins to cultivate the land and to build houses. Among the group, however, some will continue to live in tents with the flocks, at least during the winter and the spring. Depending on the extent to which he is tied to the land, such a man is either half a nomad or half a settler.

In and between these main types of society there are of course intermediate stages and hybrid forms. A camel-breeding tribe may possess flocks of sheep also, or even land at the far ends of the track of its migration, or oases culti-vated by serf-labour.

Neither the Israelites nor their ancestors were ever true Bedouin, that is, camel-breeders. Their fathers kept sheep and goats, and when we first meet them in history, the Patriarchs are already becoming a settled people. This is one factor which puts limits on the comparisons which can be drawn from the Bedouin whom ethnographers have studied.

These modern writers have also studied sheep-breeding tribes who are beginning to settle down. The latter represent the same social type as the earliest Israelite groups, and here the comparison has greater truth in it. But again there is a difference. The sheep-breeders of to-day, half nomad or half settler, were formerly camel-breeders. They no longer wander so far afield for pasture, and are now gradually settling down, but they retain the memory and some of the customs of that life of liberty in the open desert. The Israel-ites had no such memories, because neither they nor their ancestors had ever known this life. Besides, in their time, there was no real 'desert civilization' to lay down codes of behaviour; in their eyes the desert was the refuge of outlaws, the haunt of brigands, the home of demons and wild beasts. We shall return to this subject when discussing what has been called the 'nomadic ideal' of the Old Testament.

Nevertheless, the fact remains that the Israelites or their ancestors did live for a time in the desert as nomads or semi-nomads. Naturally, such a life entails a distinct pattern of society, and enjoins a code of behaviour all of its own; we are therefore justified in using, with due reservation, the organiza-tion and customs of the Arabs for comparison.

In the desert, the unit of society must be compact enough to remain mobile, yet strong enough to ensure its own safety; this unit is the tribe. In the desert, an individual who is separated from his own group must be able to count without question on a welcome from the groups through which he passes or which he joins. Anyone may have need of this help, and therefore everyone must give it; this is the basis of the law of hospitality and asylum. Finally, in the desert there is no police force or court of justice with authority over the tribes; consequently, the group as a whole is held responsible for crime, and liable for its punishment—the law of blood-vengeance. These three sociological facts, which are the most obvious characteristics of nomad-ism, must now claim our attention for a time.

2. Tribal Organization

(a) The constitution of a tribe

A tribe is an autonomous group of families who believe they are descended from a common ancestor. Each tribe is called by the name or surname of that

ancestor, sometimes, but not always, preceded by 'sons of'. Arab examples
are innumerable. In the Bible, the descendants of Amalek, Edom and Moab
are called Amalek, Edom and Moab without the addition of 'sons of'. On
the other hand, we find both 'Israel' and 'sons of Israel', both 'Judah' and
'sons of Judah' and so on, but always 'sons of Ammon' (except in two
instances, one of which is textually uncertain). Instead of 'sons' we may find
'house', in the sense of family or descendants: 'the house of Israel', for
example, and especially 'the house of Joseph'. Assyrian texts follow the same
usage in references to Aramaean groups who lived in conditions similar to
those of the first Israelites: *bit* (house of) *Yakin* and *mar* (sons of) *Yakin*, or *bit*
Adini and *mar Adini*; the terms are even used, long after the settlement, for
Israelites in the northern kingdom after Omri: *bit Humri* and *mar Humri*.

What unites all the tribesmen, then, is this blood-relationship, real or
supposed; they all consider themselves 'brothers' in a wide sense. Abimelek
says to the entire clan of his mother, 'Remember that I am of your bones and
of your flesh' (Jg 9: 2). All the members of David's clan are, in his eyes, his
'brothers' (1 S 20: 29), and he goes so far as to tell all the elders of Judah, 'You
are my brothers, you are of my flesh and of my bones' (2 S 19: 13). Every
tribe has its traditions, too, about the ancestor from whom it claims descent.
These traditions are not always historically true, but whatever their value,
the important fact is that the nomad believes he is of the same blood as the
rest of his tribe, and that the relationship between different tribes is also explained in terms of kinship. In his eyes, the whole social organization of the
desert is summed up in a genealogy.

It was this idea which, in the early days of Islam, led to the composition of
those great genealogies catalogued by Wüstenfeld. Each tribe descends from
a single ancestor, and two allied tribes descend from two ancestors who were
brothers in the strict sense. These genealogies, however, though they may be
accurate for a small group, inevitably become arbitrary and artificial once an
attempt is made to extend them in space and time. In the Mid-Euphrates
region there is a group of small sheep-breeding tribes called the 'Agêdât, *i.e.*
'Confederates', whose name signifies clearly enough just how the group was
formed; but this political and economic union has since been expressed in a
genealogical table. This procedure leads to the invention of eponymous
ancestors. We know of a tribe called the Khoza'a ('Separated'), because it
separated from the Azd at the time of the great Yemenite dispersion, but the
genealogists have assigned it a personal ancestor, whom they call Khoza'a.
Similarly the Kholoj ('Transported') are so called because Omar I transferred them from the 'Adwan to the Al-Harith, whereas, according to the
genealogists, Kholoj is a surname of Qais, the son of Al-Harith.

In practice, other factors besides common descent may help to constitute a
tribe. The mere fact of living in the same region leads groups of families to
join together. Weak elements are absorbed by stronger neighbours;

alternatively, several weak groups combine to form a body capable of remaining autonomous, that is, of standing up to attack. Individuals, too, can be incorporated into a tribe either by adoption into a family (as often happens with freed slaves), or through acceptance by the sheikh or the elders.

But even here the principle is safeguarded, for the newcomer is attached 'in name and in blood' to the tribe; this means that he acknowledges the tribe's ancestor as his own, that he will marry within the tribe and raise up his family inside it. The Arabs say that he is 'genealogized' (root: *nasaba*). With a whole clan the fusion takes longer, but the result is the same, and the new-comers are finally considered as being of the same blood. A text of Al-Bakri puts it neatly: 'And the Nahd ben Zaïd joined the Bené al-Harith, became confederate with them and completely united with them; and the Jarm ben Rabbân joined the Bené Zubaïd, attached themselves to them and lived together, and the whole tribe with its confederates was attached to the same ancestor (*nusibat*).'

The tribes of Israel were not exempt from such changes, and they absorbed groups of different origin. Thus the tribe of Judah eventually welcomed to its own ranks the remnants of the tribe of Simeon, and incorporated foreign groups like the Calebites and Yerahmeelites. The Bible gives a clear picture of the process in its references to the Calebites. They were originally outside the Israelite confederation, for Caleb was the son of Yephunneh the Qeniz-ite (Nb 32: 12; Jos 14: 6, 14; comp. Gn 15: 19; 36: 11), but they had contact with Israel from the time of the sojourn at Qadesh, where Caleb was named as Judah's representative for the exploration of Canaan (Nb 13: 6). Their integration into this tribe is recorded in Jos 15: 13; cf. Jos 14: 6-15, and in the end Caleb is genealogically attached to Judah. The son of Yephunneh becomes the son of Hesron, son of Peres, son of Judah (1 Ch 2: 9, 18, 24) and brother of Yerahmeel (1 Ch 2: 42), another foreign group (1 S 27: 10) also attached to the line of Judah (1 Ch 2: 9). There can be no doubt that simi-lar fusions took place frequently, especially in early days, and that the very concept of the 'Twelve Tribes' contains some elements of systematic arrange-ment, though one cannot say precisely how far this system is artificial. In any case, the number and order of the tribes, sometimes even their names, vary from text to text, and these variations prove that the system which finally prevailed was not reached straightaway.

(b) The union, division and disappearance of tribes

The Twelve Tribes of Israel were a federation, and parallel examples are found among Arab tribes. Sometimes it is merely an association of small tribes which unite to present a common front against powerful neighbours, like the 'Agêdât, the 'Confederates' of the Mid-Euphrates, mentioned above. At other times, a tribe may be compelled to split up when its numbers become too great; these new groups, all originating from the common stock, then become autonomous, though the extent of their independence may vary. Nevertheless, they do retain a feeling of family solidarity; when they unite for common enterprises, such as migrations or wars, they recognize a chief to be obeyed by some or all of the groups. These patterns of society can be studied in our own day in the two great rival federations of the Syrian desert, the 'Anezeh and the Shammar. During its years of wandering in the desert and its struggle for the conquest of Canaan, Israel lived in similar conditions, conditions which persisted after the settlement, in the period of the Judges. The system of the Twelve Tribes has been compared with the amphictyonies which united a number of Greek cities round a sanctuary. The comparison, though interesting, should not be pressed too far, for, unlike the amphictyonies, the Twelve Tribes were not ruled by a permanent body, and, in their system, were not subject to the same measure of effective political control. The importance of the Israelite confederation was primarily religious; it was not only the feeling of kinship, but also their common faith in Yahweh, whom they had all agreed to follow (Jos 24), which united the tribes around the sanctuary of the Ark, where they assembled for the great feasts.

On the other hand, when a nomad group becomes too numerous to continue living together on the same grazing grounds, it sometimes divides into two groups which then live quite independently of one another. This was the reason why Abraham and Lot separated (Gn 13: 5-13). But the claims of kinship still hold good, and when Lot was carried off a prisoner by the four victorious kings, Abraham went to his help (Gn 14: 12-16).

The numbers of a tribe may, however, diminish instead of increasing until it finally disappears. Thus Reuben grows weaker (cf. Gn 49: 3-4 and Dt 33: 6), and the civil tribe of Levi disappears (Gn 34: 25-30; 49: 5-7), to be replaced by the priestly tribe 'dispersed throughout Israel' (cf. Gn 49: 7). Simeon disappears, and at an early date the remnants were absorbed by Judah (Jos 19: 1-9; Jg 1: 3f.); it is no longer mentioned in the Blessings of Moses (Dt 33), which may perhaps be earlier than the reign of David.

(c) *The organization and government of a tribe*

A tribe, though it forms a single unit, has an internal organization which is also founded on blood-ties. Among nomadic Arabs, the limits and names of these sub-divisions fluctuate somewhat. The basic unit is naturally the family ('ahel), a concept which has a fairly wide meaning. Several related families constitute a clan, or fraction of a tribe, called, according to the locality, either hamûleh or 'ashireh. The tribe itself is called a qabileh, but formerly it was called a batn or a hayy, two words expressing that unity of blood on which the tribe is founded.

The Israelites had a very similar organization. The bêth 'ab, the 'house of one's father', was the family, which comprised not only the father, his wife or wives and their unmarried children but also their married sons with their wives and children, and the servants. Several families composed a clan, the *mishpaḥah*. The latter usually lived in the same place, and its members always met for common religious feasts and sacrificial meals (1 S 20: 6, 29). In particular, the clan assumed the responsibility for blood-vengeance. Each clan was ruled by the heads of its families, the *z'qenîm* or 'elders', and in time of war it furnished a contingent, theoretically a thousand strong, commanded by a chief, *śar*. In Jg 8: 14 the 'chiefs' of Sukkoth are distinguished from the 'elders'. In Gn 36: 40-43 there is a list of the chiefs of the clans of Edom, who bore the special name of *'allûph*, perhaps etymologically connected with *'eleph* ('a thousand'), A group of clans, of *mishpaḥôth*, formed a tribe, *shebeṭ* or *maṭṭeh*, two words with the same meaning, which also denote the commander's staff and the royal sceptre. The tribe therefore embraced all those who obeyed the same chief.

The hierarchy of the three terms, *bêth 'ab*, *mishpaḥah* and *shebeṭ*, is clearly expressed in Jos. 7: 14-18, but one term may sometimes be used for another, as in Nb 4: 18 and Jg 20: 12 (Hebrew text). Similarly, Makir and Gilead, which are clans of Ephraim, are mentioned in the Song of Deborah on a par with the other tribes (Jg 5: 14-17).

Among the Arabs a tribe is governed by a sheikh, who acts in conjunction with the principal heads of its families. This authority generally stays in the same family, but does not always pass to the eldest son, for the Arabs set great store by personality and character, and expect their sheikh to be prudent, courageous, noble-hearted . . . and rich.

It is difficult to say who, among the Israelites, corresponded to the sheikh, or what title he bore. Possibly it was the *nasî'*. This is the name given to the leaders of the Twelve Tribes during the time in the desert (Nb 7: 2), with the further detail that they were 'the chiefs of their fathers' houses, the leaders of the tribes' (cf. Nb 1: 16, etc.). The same word denotes the chieftains of Ishmael (Gn 17: 20; 25: 16), and the Ishmaelites had twelve *nasî'* for as many tribes (the parallel with Israel is obvious). The same word is used of Midianite leaders in Nb 25: 18 and Jos 13: 21. One could object that these texts belong to the Priestly tradition, which is generally held to be the most recent of all, and that the same word frequently recurs in Ezechiel; but it is also found in texts which are certainly ancient (Gn 34: 2; Ex 22: 27). It has also been suggested that the word denoted the deputy of a tribe to the Israelite amphictyony, but that is assigning to it a religious sense which is not apparent in the passages just referred to. On the other hand, if such an organization existed and was ruled by some kind of council, the tribes would naturally have been represented in it by their chiefs. One should note, however, that the word was not employed exclusively for the chief of a tribe, but was used for the leaders of smaller sections too. The Arabs use the word 'sheikh' with the same freedom.

(d) *Tribal territory. War and raiding*

Each tribe has a territory recognized as its own, inside which the cultivated land is generally privately owned, and pasture land is held in common. Boundaries are sometimes ill defined, and groups belonging to different tribes sometimes live side by side in very fertile regions, if their tribes are on friendly terms. But the tribe which has the primary right of possession can lay down conditions and demand some form of payment for grazing rights.

This lack of precise law easily gives rise to disputes, especially over the use of wells or cisterns. Everyone in the desert is bound to know that such and such a watering-place belongs to such and such a group, but from time to time a title may be disputed and quarrels break out between shepherds. It has always been so: Abraham's herdsmen quarrel with Lot's (Gn 13: 7); Abimelek's servants seize a well dug by Abraham (Gn 21: 25); Isaac is hard put to it to maintain his rights over the wells he himself had dug between Gerar and Beersheba (Gn 26: 19-22).

If quarrels about routes of migration, grazing lands and watering-places are not settled amicably, as in the biblical examples just mentioned, they lead to war. The sheikh takes the decision, and all the men must follow him. As a rule, the booty is shared between the fighting men, but the chief has a right to a special share, which was originally fixed at one quarter of the total captured, but later was left to the chief's discretion. In Israel, in the time of David, the booty was divided equally between the combatants and those who stayed at the rear, one portion being reserved for the chief (1 S 30: 20-25). Nb 31: 25-30 dates this institution back to the period in the desert, and the chief's portion is there considered as a tribute for Yahweh and the Levites.

Every Arab tribe has its war-cry and its standard. In addition, it carries into battle a decorated litter, called *'utfa*, or, more recently, *merkab* or *abu-Dhur*. Nowadays, the litter is empty, but in days gone by the most beautiful girl in the tribe rode in it to spur on the fighting men. Israel, too, had its war-cry, the *t'rû'ah* (Nb 10: 5, 9; 31: 6; Jos 6: 5, 20; Jg 7: 20-21; 1 S 17: 20, 52; cf. Am 1: 14; 2: 2; So 1: 14, 16, etc.). This war-cry formed part of the ritual of the Ark of the Covenant (1 S 4: 5; 2 S 6: 15), which was the palladium of Israel; its presence in battle (1 S 4: 3-11; 2 S 11: 11) reminds us of the sacred litter of the Arabs. Perhaps, too, the tribes in the desert grouped themselves, in camp and on the march, under standards, *'ôth* (Nb 2: 2).

When several tribes join together to form a confederation, they adopt a common standard, like the flag of the Prophet unfurled at Mecca and Medina. Here again we may find a parallel with the Ark of the Covenant and the name 'Yahweh-Nissi' ('Yahweh is my banner') given to the altar which Moses erected after his victory over the Amalekites (Ex 17: 15).

Raiding is different from war, for its object is not to kill but to carry off plunder and to escape unharmed. It is the desert's 'sport of kings'; it involves the use of racing camels and of thoroughbred mares, and has its own clearly-defined rules. Ancient Israel knew nothing quite like this. The nearest approach is to be found in those incursions of the Midianites and 'sons of the East' in the days of the Judges: these invaders were mounted on camels (Jg 6: 3-6). On a smaller scale, one might point to David's expeditions into the Negeb during his stay with the Philistines (1 S 27: 8-11).

3. The Law of Hospitality and Asylum

Hospitality, we have said, is a necessity of life in the desert, but among the nomads this necessity has become a virtue, and a most highly esteemed one. The guest is sacred: the honour of providing for him is disputed, but gener-ally falls to the sheikh. The stranger can avail himself of this hospitality for three days, and even after leaving he has a right to protection for a given time. This time varies from tribe to tribe: among some it is 'until the salt he has eaten has left his stomach'; in big tribes like the Ruwalla of Syria it is for three more days and within a radius of 100 miles.

Old Testament parallels spring to mind. Abraham gives a lavish reception to the three 'men' at Mambre (Gn 18: 1-8), and Laban is eager to welcome Abraham's servant (Gn 24: 28-32). Two stories show to what excesses the sentiment of hospitality could lead: that of the angels who stayed in Lot's house at Sodom (Gn 19:1-8), and the story of the crime at Gibeah (Jg 19: 16-24). Both Lot and the old man of Gibeah are ready to sacrifice the honour of their daughters in order to protect their guests, and the reason is stated in both cases: it is simply because the latter have come under their roof (Gn 19: 8; Jg 19: 23).

Nomad life also gives rise, invariably, to a law of asylum. In this type of society is is impossible and inconceivable that an individual could live iso-lated, unattached to any tribe. Hence, if a man is expelled from his tribe after a murder or some serious offence, or if, for any reason whatever, he leaves it of his own free will, he has to seek the protection of another tribe. There he becomes what modern Arabs call a *daḥil*, 'he who has come in', and what their forefathers called a *jâr*. The tribe undertakes to protect him, to defend him against his enemies and to avenge his blood, if necessary. These customs are reflected in two Old Testament institutions, that of the *ger* (which is the same word as the Arabic *jâr*) and that of cities of refuge.[1]

4. Tribal Solidarity and Blood-Vengeance

The bond of blood, real or supposed, creates a certain solidarity among all the members of a tribe. It is a very deep-rooted feeling, and persists long after the settlement in Canaan. The honour or dishonour of every member affects

---

1. Cf. pp. 74-76 and 160-163.

the entire group. A curse extends to the whole race, and God visits the sins of the fathers on the children to the fourth generation (Ex 20: 5). A whole family is honoured if its head is brave, while the group is punished for a fault of its leader (2 S 21: 1).

This solidarity is seen above all in the group's duty to protect its weak and oppressed members. This is the obligation which lies behind the institution of the *go'el*, but as this is not confined to the nomadic state it will be treated along with family institutions.[1]

The most solemn responsibility of the Israelite *go'el* was to enforce blood-vengeance, and here we encounter another law of the desert, the *târ* of the Arabs. The blood of a kinsman must be avenged by the death of the one who shed it, or, failing him, by the blood of one of his family. Blood-vengeance does not operate within the group, but the guilty man is punished by his group or expelled from it. The Arabs say, 'Our blood has been shed.' In primitive times this duty devolved on all the members of the tribe, and the extent of it served to determine the limits of the tribal group. In recent times, however, the obligation has become more restricted and does not extend beyond the family circle, taken in a fairly wide sense. Moreover, to avoid a series of assassinations, they try to substitute for the *târ* some compensation which the victim's family are compelled to accept, whatever their feelings about blood-vengeance.

The same law existed in Israel. It is expressed with savage ferocity in the song of Lamek (Gn 4: 23-24):

> 'I have killed a man for a wound,
>   A child for a bruise.
> The vengeance for Cain may be sevenfold,
>   But for Lamek, seventy-sevenfold!'

Lamek is the descendant of Cain, who was condemned to live in the desert. And Cain bears a 'sign', which is not a stigma of condemnation, but a mark which shows he belongs to a group in which blood-vengeance is ruthlessly exacted. This story (Gn 4: 13-16) states clearly the social basis for the institution. It is not simply to obtain compensation, 'man for man, woman for woman', as the Koran puts it; rather, it is a safeguard. Where society is not centralized, the prospect of the blood-debt which will have to be paid is a deterrent which restrains both individuals and the group.

The custom persisted after the tribes had settled in Canaan. Thus Joab kills Abner (2 S 3: 22-27 and 30) to avenge the death of his brother (2 S 2: 22-23). Legislation, however, endeavoured to mitigate this vengeance by the introduction of a system of justice. Though the laws about cities of refuge (Nb 35: 9-34; Dt 19: 1-13) sanction blood-vengeance, they hold it in check to some extent by requiring a preliminary judgment on the guilt of the accused and

1. Pp. 21-22.

by excluding cases of involuntary manslaughter.[1] In contrast with Bedouin law, however, Israelite legislation does not allow compensation in money, alleging for this a religious motive: blood which is shed defiles the land in which Yahweh dwells, and must be expiated by the blood of him who shed it (Nb 35: 31-34).

The law of blood-vengeance, we have said, does not operate inside the group itself. There appears to be a single exception, in 2 S 14: 4-11. To obtain the recall of Absalom, banished after the murder of Amnon, the woman of Teqoa pretends that one of her sons has been killed by his brother, and that her clansmen want to put the latter to death; the woman begs David to intervene so that the 'avenger of blood' may not slay her son. But the decision of the clan is normal if we understand it as the punishment of the guilty, just as the banishment of Absalom was normal: it is the exclusion of the guilty from the family. In this passage only the term 'avenger of blood' is abnormal, and it may be used here in a loose sense.

5. The Later Development of Tribal Organization in Israel

Though analogies from the life of Arab nomads may throw useful light on the primitive organization of Israel, it is important to realize that nowhere in the Bible are we given a perfect picture of tribal life on the full scale. The traditions about the Patriarchs concern families, or, at the most, clans; and no one can deny that in the accounts of the desert wanderings and of the conquest the characteristic profile of each tribe has been to some extent subordinated to the wider interest of 'all Israel'. Quite the most rewarding period to investigate is that of the Judges, where we read of tribes living, and taking action, sometimes independently of one another, and sometimes in association with one another. But this is precisely the time when the tribes have no individual chiefs; it is the elders who wield authority, and one senses that the clan, the mishpahah, is becoming the most stable unit of society. In short, tribal organization is beginning to crumble. It is the price to be paid for becoming a settled people; a tribe gradually turns into a territorial group, which itself continues to sub-divide.

Such an evolution is in fact commonplace. The Caliph Omar I complained that the Arabs who had settled in Iraq had begun to call themselves by the names of their villages instead of their ancestors. In our own day, certain half-settled Bedouin in Palestine are called after their present homes, e.g. the Belqaniyeh of the Belqa, the Ghoraniyeh of the Ghôr, etc.; or after their place of origin, like the Haddadin of Ma'în, who come from Kh. Haddad. Similarly, in the Song of Deborah (Jg 5: 17), the 'tribe' of Gilead takes its name from its homeland, and some authors ascribe a geographical meaning to the names of other Israelite tribes. We may note, too, that the Blessings of

1. Cf. pp. 160f.

Jacob (Gn 49) and of Moses (Dt 33) frequently allude to the territory occupied by the tribes.

This territorial disposition of the tribes was itself modified by the administrative organization under the monarchy. True, everyone remembered to which tribe he belonged, but the unit of society which survived, and which to some extent retained the ancient customs, was the clan. In practice, after the settlement, the village stood for the clan, and in many of the genealogies of Chronicles, names of villages replace names of ancestors.

6. Relics of Nomadism

Amid these new surroundings, certain ancient customs survived, and the comparisons we have drawn with Arab nomadism often held good long after the settlement. Blood-vengeance is a desert law, but it became a permanent institution, and the solidarity of the clan never disappeared.

Language is more conservative than custom, and Hebrew retained several traces of that life of years gone by. For example, generations after the conquest, a house was called a 'tent', and not only in poetry (where it is frequent) but also in everyday speech (Jg 19: 9; 20: 8; 1 S 13: 2; 1 K 8: 66). Disbanded soldiers return 'every man to his own tent' (1 S 4: 10; 2 S 18: 17). 'To your tents, Israel' was the cry of revolt under David (2 S 20: 1) and after the death of Solomon (1 K 12:16). On the other hand, this expression did not last, for shortly afterwards we read how every man returned 'to his house' (1 K 22: 17) or 'his town' (1 K 22: 36). Again, to express 'leaving early in the morning', a verb is often used which means 'to load the beasts of burden' (Jg 19: 9; 1 S 17: 20, etc.); nomads use the word to say 'striking camp at dawn'. These expressions continued in use long after Israel had settled in Canaan, and when their ideal was to live a quiet life 'every man under his vine and his fig-tree'.

Though it is less significant, the frequent use, in Old Testament poetry, of metaphors borrowed from nomadic life should not pass unnoticed. Death, for example, is the cut tent-rope, or the peg which is pulled out (Jb 4: 21), or the tent itself which is carried off (Is 38: 12). Desolation is represented by the broken ropes, the tent blown down (Jr 10: 20), whereas security is the tent with tight ropes and firm pegs (Is 33: 20). A nation whose numbers are increasing is a tent being extended (Is 54: 2). Lastly, there are countless allusions to the pastoral life, and Yahweh or his Messiah are frequently represented as the Good Shepherd (Ps 23; Is 40: 11; Jr 23: 1-6; Ez 34, etc.).

7. The 'Nomadic Ideal' of the Prophets

In spite of these surviving traces, our oldest biblical texts show little admiration for the nomadic life. The story of Cain (Gn 4: 11-16) is a condemnation of outright nomadism. Cain is driven into the desert in punishment for the murder of Abel; he will be a wanderer and a vagabond, marked with a sign, the *wasm* of the desert nomad. Doubtless, Abel was a herdsman (Gn 4: 2), and has all the narrator's sympathy, but the text makes it clear that it was sheep and goats that he looked after; in other words, he is supposed to have led the same sort of life as the Hebrew Patriarchs, on the border of the real desert. Before his crime Cain was a farmer (Gn 4: 2). So, in this story, the desert is presented as the refuge of disgraced settlers and outlaws, as in fact it was before the rise of the large camel-breeding tribes who founded a desert civilization, one which had its greatness indeed, but which the Israelites never knew.

The same unfavourable tone recurs in the story of Ishmael: 'His hand will be against everyone, everyone's hand will be against him; he will settle down away from his brethren' (Gn 16: 12). The desert is the home of wild beasts, monsters and demons (Is 13: 21-22; 34: 11-15), and the scapegoat is driven out there, loaded with all the sins of the people (Lv 16).

On the other hand, we do encounter what has been called the 'nomadic ideal' of the Old Testament. The Prophets look back to the past, the time of Israel's youth in the desert, when she was betrothed to Yahweh (Jr 2: 2; Os 13: 5; Am 2: 10). They condemn the comfort and luxury of urban life in their own day (Am 3: 15; 6: 8, etc.), and see salvation in a return, at some future date, to the life of the desert, envisaged as a golden age (Os 2: 16-17; 12: 10).

There is, in this attitude, a reaction against the sedentary civilization of Canaan, with all its risks of moral and religious perversion. There is also a memory of, and a nostalgia for, the time when God made a Covenant with Israel in the desert, when Israel was faithful to its God. But nomadism itself is not the ideal; rather, it is that purity of religious life and that faithfulness to the Covenant, which was associated in Israel's mind with its former life in the desert. If the Prophets speak of a return to the desert, it is not because they recall any glory in the nomadic life of their ancestors, but as a means of escape from the corrupting influence of their own urban civilization. We shall encounter this mystique of the desert again in the last days of Judaism, among the sectaries of Qumran, when Christian monasticism still lies in the future.

8. *The Rekabites*

The ideal which the Prophets exalted, but never tried to put into practice, was actually carried out by a group of extremists, the Rekabites. We know of them chiefly through Jeremias. To give an object lesson to the people, the prophet invited the members of Rekab's family to the Temple, and offered them a drink of wine. They refused it, saying that their ancestor Yonadab, son of Rekab, had given them this command: 'Neither you nor your sons shall ever drink wine, and you must not build houses, or sow seed, or plant vines, or own property. On the contrary, you are to dwell in tents all your life, so that your days may be long in the land where you live as aliens (gerîm).' This age-old fidelity to the commands of their ancestor is held up as an example to the Jews who do not obey the word of Yahweh (Jr 35).

It is interesting to compare this passage with a remark of Jerome of Cardia about the Nabateans at the close of the fourth century B.C. 'It is a law among them not to sow corn or to plant fruit-trees, not to drink wine or to build a house; whoever does so is punished with death' (cited in Diodorus Siculus XIX, 94). In these two passages, so curiously alike, we have the essential contrast between nomadic life and the life of a settled farmer. The Rekabites had chosen to live far away from urban civilization, and only exceptional circumstances account for their presence in Jerusalem; they had taken refuge there to escape from the Chaldeans (Jr 35: 11).

Normally they lived as nomads, unattached to the land. But at the same time they were fervent worshippers of Yahweh: all the Rekabite names we know are Yahwistic names (Jr 35: 3). Jeremias holds them up as examples, and Yahweh promises them his blessing (Jr 35: 19). Like nomads, they are organized as a clan; they are the b'nê Rekab and form the bêth Rekab, but they also constitute a religious sect, and their ancestor Yonadab is a religious legislator.

This Yonadab ben Rekab is known to us for his part in Jehu's revolution (2 K 10: 15-24). Jehu, on his way to exterminate the cult of Baal at Samaria, takes Yonadab with him to witness his 'zeal for Yahweh' (v. 16). Yonadab, then, must have been a convinced Yahwist, and his uncompromising faith must have been known to all. This incident allows us to date the origin of the Rekabites about 840 B.C., and, according to Jeremias, they were still faithful to the same way of life 250 years later.

Some would go even further, and connect the Rekabites with the Qenites, that group of non-Israelite origin which lived a semi-nomadic life on the borders of Israel, or in its midst (Jg 1: 16; 4: 11; 5: 24; 1 S 15: 4-6; 27: 10), and from whom, according to some authors, the Israelites first learned the name of Yahweh. This connection between the Rekabites and the Qenites depends on two texts in Chronicles (1 Ch 2: 55 and 4: 12). From the critical point of view, these texts are uncertain, yet it is strange that they mention Rekab or the bêth Rekab but not Yonadab. At the best, they mean that the Chronicler has used the fiction of a genealogical link to connect two communities who lived more or less the same kind of life.

Our history of the Rekabites begins under Jehu and ends in the time of Jeremias. We are not justified in regarding them as survivors of an age when Israel led a nomadic life, and the Bible states explicitly that their rule was established by Yonadab only in the ninth century B.C. It was not a survival of earlier days but a reactionary movement.

PART I

FAMILY INSTITUTIONS

CHAPTER ONE

THE FAMILY

1. Of what type was the Israelite family?

ETHNOGRAPHERS distinguish several types of family. In a *fratriarchate*, for example, the eldest brother is the head of the family, and this authority is handed on, along with the property, from brother to brother. Evidence of this type of society has been found among the Hittites and Hurrites in Assyria and Elam. It has been claimed that there are traces of it in the Old Testament, *e.g.* in the institution of the levirate (which will be discussed under marriage[1]), in the action of Jacob's sons to avenge the rape of their sister Dinah (Gn 34), and in the part Laban plays in the arrangement of the marriage of his sister Rebecca (Gn 24). Though none of these examples seems conclusive, we must admit the possibility of Assyrian and Hurrite influence on the customs of Aram Naharaim; and among these two peoples the existence of a fratriarchate, in early times, is now admitted, at least as a hypothesis. We cannot, therefore, exclude the possibility of its influence on the levirate institution, and there may be traces of it in the story of Rebecca.

As a type of family, *matriarchate* is much more common in primitive societies. The characteristic mark of this type of society is not that the mother exercises authority (this is rare), but that a child's lineage is traced through the mother. The child belongs to the mother's family and social group, and is not considered as related to its father's connections; even rights of inheritance are fixed by maternal descent. According to the ethnographical school of Graebner and Schmidt, a matriarchate is associated with small-scale cultivation, while pastoral civilization is patriarchal.

Many authors, however, following Robertson Smith, believe that a matriarchal regime was the original form of the family among the Semites. Certain Old Testament customs and stories, they hold, indicate the presence of this regime among the Israelites. In Gn 20: 12 Abraham is excused for passing off Sarah as his sister, because she was in fact his half-sister, whom he had married. Similarly, 2 S 13: 13 gives us to understand that Amnon and Tamar could have been married, because, though both were David's children, they were born of different mothers. Marriage with one's step-sister, either on the father's or mother's side, is forbidden by the laws of

1. Pp. 37-38.

Lv 18: 9; 20: 17; Dt 27: 22; cf. Ez 22: 11, but the last two texts indicate that this had not always been so; and from this the above-mentioned authors conclude that consanguinity was originally reckoned only through the mother. They point out, too, that the name of a baby was generally decided by the mother,[1] and that the two sons of Joseph, who were born of Egyptian wives, were not acknowledged as children of Israel until they had been adopted by Jacob (Gn 48: 5).

These arguments do not prove the point at issue. The passage about Joseph's children has not the meaning they attribute to it, as the next verse shows (Gn 48: 6). The texts about Sarah and Tamar prove only that marriage with a half-sister was not yet forbidden. Thirdly, it was not always the mother who gave the child its name (Gn 16: 15; 17: 19; 38: 29-30).

Some would also see in the Bible, especially in the marriage of Samson to Timna (Jg 14), a rare type of marriage in which the wife does not leave her clan but brings her husband into it; this, too, would be a relic of a matriarchate. The question will be treated under marriage.[2]

Prehistoric Israel is to us a closed book; but whatever may be true of that epoch, there is no doubt that from the time of our oldest documents, at any rate, the Israelite family is *patriarchal*. The proper word to describe it is *bêth 'ab*, the 'house of one's father'; the genealogies are always given in the father's line, and women are rarely mentioned; and the nearest relation in the collateral line is the paternal uncle (cf. Lv 25: 49). In the normal type of Israelite marriage the husband is the 'master', the *ba'al*, of his wife. The father had absolute authority over his children, even over his married sons if they lived with him, and over their wives. In early times this authority included even the power over life and death: thus Judah condemned to death his daughter-in-law Tamar when she was accused of misconduct (Gn 38: 24).

The family consists of those who are united by common blood and common dwelling-place. The 'family' is a 'house'; to found a family is 'to build a house' (Ne 7: 4). Noah's family includes his wife, his sons and their wives (Gn 7: 1 and 7); Jacob's family comprises three generations (Gn 46: 8-26). The family included the servants, the resident aliens or *gerîm*[3] and the 'stateless persons', widows and orphans, who lived under the protection of the head of the family. Jephthah, an illegitimate son expelled by his brothers, still claimed to belong to his 'father's house' (Jg 11: 1-7).

Again, the term *bêth* or 'house', like the word 'family' in modern languages, is very flexible and may even include the entire nation (the 'house of Jacob' or the 'house of Israel'), or a considerable section of the people (the 'house of Joseph' or the 'house of Judah'). It may denote kinship in the wide sense: Yaazanyah, the descendant of Rekab, his brothers and all his sons form the *bêth Rekab* (Jr 35: 3); the heads of 'families' in the Chronicler's lists some-

---

1. P. 43.   2. Pp. 28-29.
3. On the *gerîm*, cf. pp. 74-76.

times stand as the heads of very numerous groups (1 Ch 5: 15, 24; 7: 7, 40; 8: 6, 10, 13; 9: 9; 23: 24; 24, 6, etc.); and the heads of 'families' who return from Babylon with Esdras are each accompanied by anything from twenty-eight to three hundred men (Esd 8: 1-14).

In this wide sense, the family was the same group as the clan, the *mishpahah*. The latter concentrated in one area, occupying one or more villages according to its size, like the *mishpahah* of the Danites at Soreah and Eshtaol (Jg 18: 11); alternatively, several *mishpahôth* might live together within a city, like the groups from Judah and Benjamin listed in the census of Jerusalem by Nehemias (Ne 11: 4-8) and by the Chronicler (1 Ch 9: 4-9). The clan had common interests and duties, and its members were conscious of the blood-bond which united them: they called each other 'brothers' (1 S 20: 29).

On the religious level, too, the family played its part as a unit of society. The Passover was a family festival kept in every home (Ex 12: 3-4, 46), and year by year Samuel's father took the whole family on pilgrimage to Shiloh (1 S 1: 3f.).

2. Family solidarity. The go'el

The members of the family in this wider sense had an obligation to help and to protect one another. There was in Israel an institution which defined the occasions when this obligation called for action; it is the institution of the *go'el*, from a root which means 'to buy back or to redeem', 'to lay claim to', but fundamentally its meaning is 'to protect'. The institution has analogies among other peoples (for example, the Arabs), but in Israel it took a special form, with its own terminology.

The *go'el* was a redeemer, a protector, a defender of the interests of the individual and of the group. If an Israelite had to sell himself into slavery in order to repay a debt, he would be 'redeemed' by one of his near relations (Lv 25: 47-49). If an Israelite had to sell his patrimony, the *go'el* had priority over all other purchasers; it was his right and duty to buy it himself, to prevent the family property from being alienated. This law is codified in Lv 25: 25, and it was in his capacity as *go'el* that Jeremias bought the field of his cousin Hanameel (Jr 32: 6f.).

The story of Ruth is yet another illustration of this custom, but here the purchase of the land is rendered more complicated by a case of levirate. Naomi had some property which, because of her poverty, she was forced to sell; and her daughter-in-law Ruth was a childless widow. Boaz was a *go'el* of Naomi and Ruth (Rt 2: 20), but there was a closer relative who could exercise this right before him (Rt 3: 12; 4: 4). This first *go'el* would have bought the land, but he would not accept the double obligation of buying the land and marrying Ruth, because the child of this union would bear the name of the deceased husband and inherit the land (Rt 4: 4-6). So Boaz bought the family property and married Ruth (Rt 4: 9-10).

This story shows that the right of the *go'el* followed a certain order of kinship, an order which is specified in Lv 25: 49: first, the paternal uncle, then his son, then other relations. Further, the *go'el* could renounce his right or decline his duty without blame. By taking off one shoe (Rt 4: 7-8) a man proclaimed that he was forgoing his right; Dt 25: 9 describes a similar action in the law of levirate, but there the procedure is meant to bring the brother-in-law into disgrace. Comparison of this law with the story of Ruth seems to indicate that the obligation of the levirate was at first undertaken by the clan, like the redemption of the patrimony, but was later restricted to the brother-in-law.[1]

One of the gravest obligations of the *go'el* was blood-vengeance, but we have already examined this in connection with tribal organization, because it is rooted in desert custom.[2]

The term *go'el* passed into religious usage. Thus Yahweh, avenger of the oppressed, and saviour of his people, is called a *go'el* in Jb 19: 25; Ps 19: 15; 78: 35; Jr 50: 34, etc., and frequently in the second part of Isaias (Is 41: 14; 43: 14; 44: 6, 24; 49: 7; 59: 20, etc.).

3. *The later development of family customs*

The firmness of these family ties was an inheritance from tribal organization. The transition to settled life, and still more the development of town life, brought about social changes which affected family customs.

The family ceased to be self-sufficient, because the standard of material welfare rose, and the development of industries led to a specialization of activities. Still, blood will have its say, and crafts were probably handed on, just as in Egypt, from father to son; the reservation of the priesthood to families of the tribe of Levi was, no doubt, only an extreme instance of a general practice. There can be no doubt, also, that certain villages were composed of woodworkers or ironfounders (1 Ch 4: 14; cf. Ne 11: 35), while other villages specialized in linen (1 Ch 4: 21) or pottery (1 Ch 4: 23). These guilds of artisans were ruled by a 'father', and were called *mishpaḥôth*, implying that their members were united by kinship, or at least that they were grouped like families.[3]

Of those great patriarchal families which united several generations around one head, few, if any, remained. Living conditions in the towns set a limit to the numbers who could be housed under one roof: the houses discovered by excavation are small. We rarely hear of a father surrounded by more than his unmarried children, and, when a son married and founded a new family, he was said to 'build a house' (Ne 7: 4). The prologue to the book of Job is a pastiche of a patriarchal story, but it betrays its period when it describes Job's

1. On the levirate, cf. p. 37.
2. P. 11.
3. Cf. p. 77.

sons as attending feasts by turns in one another's houses (Jb 1: 4, 13, 18).
Amnon and Absalom, too, had their own homes, away from the palace
where David lived with their unmarried sister Tamar (2 S 13: 7, 8, 20).

Slaves were still counted as members of the family, but they were not so
numerous; instead, another social class made its appearance—that of wage-
earners. A world which consisted merely of family groups, where the servants lived with the master of the house, passed away, and in its place there
arose a society divided into king and subjects, employers and workmen, rich
and poor. This transformation was complete, both in Israel and Judah, by the
eighth century B.C.

By then the authority of the head of the family was no longer unlimited.
A father could no longer put his son to death, and judgment—even on
offences against a father or mother—was reserved to the elders of the town
(Dt 21: 18-21). Even in David's day, a member of a clan had a right of appeal
from the judgment of his clan to the king himself (2 S 14: 4-11).

So, as the feeling of solidarity grew weaker, the individual person began to
emerge from the family group. The principle of individual responsibility is
stated in Dt 24: 16 and applied in 2 K 14: 6; it is confirmed in Jr 31: 29-30 and
developed in Ez 14: 12-20; 18: 10-20. At the same time, however, the duty
of mutual assistance was neglected by relatives, and the prophets had to plead
the case of the widow and orphan (Is 1: 17; Jr 7: 6; 22: 3). The obligation of
the levirate was no longer as binding as it appears in the story of Judah and
Tamar (Gn 38), and the law of Dt 25: 5-10 shows that this obligation could
be rejected. Even the practice of blood-vengeance was circumscribed by the
advent of forensic justice and by the legislation on cities of refuge (Nb 35: 9-29;
Dt 19: 1-13).

CHAPTER TWO

MARRIAGE

1. Polygamy and monogamy

THE story of the creation of the first two human beings (Gn 2: 21-24) presents monogamous marriage as the will of God. The patriarchs of Seth's line (*e.g.* Noah in Gn 7: 7) are said to be monogamous, and polygamy first appears in the reprobate line of Cain, when Lamek takes two wives (Gn 4: 19). Such was the traditional story of the origins of man.

In the patriarchal age, Abraham had at first only one wife, Sarah, and it was because she was barren that he took her handmaid Hagar, at Sarah's own suggestion (Gn 16: 1-2). Abraham also married Qeturah (Gn 25: 1), but since this is related after the death of Sarah (Gn 23: 1-2), Qeturah could have been his lawful, wedded wife. (Against this view, however, Gn 25: 6, which speaks of Abraham's concubines in the plural, seems to refer to Hagar and Qeturah.) Similarly, Nahor, who had children by his wife Milkah, also had a concubine, Reumah (Gn 22: 20-24); and Eliphaz, son of Esau, had both a wife and a concubine (Gn 36: 11-12).

In all this the patriarchs are following the customs of the time. According to the Code of Hammurabi (about 1700 B.C.), the husband may not take a second wife unless the first is barren, and he loses this right if the wife herself gives him a slave as concubine. The husband can, however, himself take a concubine, even if his wife has borne him children; but the concubine never has the same rights as the wife, and he may not take another concubine unless the first is barren. In the region of Kirkuk, in the fifteenth century B.C., the same customs obtained, but it seems that there the barren wife was under an obligation to provide a concubine for her husband.

In all these instances there is relative monogamy, for there is never more than one lawful, wedded wife. But other examples show that these restrictions were not always observed. Jacob married the two sisters Leah and Rachel, each of whom gave him her maid (Gn 29: 15-30; 30: 1-9), and Esau had three wives who were of equal rank (Gn 26: 34; 28: 9; 36: 1-5). It would seem that the patriarchs followed a less stringent code of conduct than that which prevailed in Mesopotamia at the same time, but the latter too was soon relaxed. At the end of the second millennium B.C., the Assyrian Code of Law assigns an intermediary place, between the wife and the concubine who is a slave, to the *esirtu*, or 'woman of the harem'; a man may have several *esirtu*, and an *esirtu* may be raised to the rank of wife.

In Israel, under the Judges and the monarchy, the old restrictions fell into disuse. Gideon had 'many wives' and at least one concubine (Jg 8: 30-31). Bigamy is recognized as a legal fact by Dt 21: 15-17, and the kings sometimes kept a large harem.[1]

There was, it seems, no limit to the number of wives and concubines a man might have. Much later, the Talmud fixed the number of wives at four for a subject and eighteen for a king. In practice, however, only royalty could afford the luxury of a large harem, and commoners had to be content with one wife, or two at the most. Samuel's father had two wives, one of whom was barren (1 S 1: 2); and, according to 2 Ch 24: 3, the priest Ychoyada had chosen two wives for King Joas. It is hard to say whether bigamy of this kind, referred to in Dt 21: 15-17 also, was very common, but it was probably no more frequent than with the Bedouin and fellahs of modern Palestine, who, for all the liberty allowed by Moslem law, are rarely polygamous. Sometimes self-interest leads a man to take a second wife, for he thus acquires another servant; more often, it is the desire for many children, especially when the first wife is barren, or has borne only daughters. There is also the fact that the Eastern woman, being married very young, ages quickly. The same motives played their part, no doubt, in ancient Israel.

The presence of several wives did not make for peace in the home. A barren wife would be despised by her companion (*e.g.* Anna and Peninnah, in 1 S 1: 6), even if the latter were a slave (cf. Sarah and Hagar, in Gn 16: 4-5); and the barren wife could be jealous of one with children (as Rachel was of Leah, Gn 30: 1). The husband's preference for one of his wives could make this rivalry more bitter (Gn 29: 30-31; 1 S 1: 5), until eventually the law (Dt 21: 15-17) had to intervene to prevent the children of his favourite from receiving more than their fair share of the inheritance. The attitude has left its mark on the language, which calls the wives of one man 'rivals' (1 S 1: 6; cf. Si 37: 12).

It is clear, however, that the most common form of marriage in Israel was monogamy. It is noteworthy that the books of Samuel and Kings, which cover the entire period of the monarchy, do not record a single case of bigamy among commoners (except that of Samuel's father, at the very beginning of the period). The Wisdom books, too, which provide a picture of society in their age, never mention polygamy. Except for the text of Si 37: 11, just cited, which might be interpreted in a wider sense, the many passages in these books which speak of a wife in her home all yield a better meaning against the background of a strictly monogamous family (cf., for example, Pr 5: 15-19; Qo 9: 9; Si 26: 1-4 and the eulogy of a perfect wife which closes the book of Proverbs, Pr 31: 10-31). The book of Tobias, a family

1. Cf. p. 115.

tale, never refers to any but monogamous families, that of the elder Tobias, that of Raguel, and that founded by the younger Tobias and Sarra. The image of a monogamous marriage is before the eyes of those prophets who represent Israel as the one wife chosen by the one and only God (Os 2: 4f.; Jr 2: 2; Is 50: 1; 54: 6-7; 62: 4-5), and Ezechiel develops the same metaphor into an allegory (Ez 16). It is true that the same prophet compares Yahweh's dealings with Samaria and Jerusalem to a marriage with two sisters (Ez 23; cf. also Jr 3: 6-11), but this is merely to adapt the allegory of chapter 16 to the historical conditions which prevailed after the political schism.

2. The typical Israelite marriage

Just as the unmarried woman was under the authority of her father, so the married woman was under the authority of her husband. The Decalogue (Ex 20: 17) lists a wife among a man's possessions, along with his servants and maids, his ox and his ass. The husband is called the *ba'al* or 'master' of his wife, just as he is the *ba'al* of a house or field (Ex 21: 3, 22; 2 S 11: 26; Pr 12: 4, etc.); a married woman is therefore the 'possession' of her *ba'al* (Gn 20: 3; Dt 22: 22). Indeed, 'to marry a wife' is expressed by the verb *bâ'al*, the root meaning of which is 'to become master' (Dt 21: 13; 24: 1).

The question immediately arises, whether this usage indicates that the wife was really considered as her husband's property; in other words, had she been bought by him? It has often been suggested that the Israelites practised a form of 'marriage by purchase' (ethnographers have certainly shown its existence among other peoples). The argument is based partly on the vocabulary employed, and partly on the story of Rachel and Leah (who complain that their father has sold them, Gn 31: 15). But one need not give a formal, juridical sense to words spoken by women in a moment of anger. However, the supporters of the purchase-theory appeal above all, and with more reason, to the custom of the *mohar*.

The *mohar* was a sum of money which the fiancé was bound to pay to the girl's father. The word occurs only three times in the Bible (Gn 34: 12; Ex 22: 16; 1 S 18: 25). The amount could vary; it depended on the girl's father (Gn 34: 12), and on the social standing of the family (1 S 18: 23). For a compulsory marriage after a virgin had been raped, the law prescribed the payment of fifty shekels of silver (Dt 22: 29). But, since this was a penalty, the ordinary *mohar* must have been less. Besides, fifty shekels is roughly the sum paid by the Pharaoh Amenophis III for the women of Gezer destined for his harem. According to Ex 21: 32, thirty shekels was the indemnity due for the death of a female servant, but this too was a penalty. The law on the fulfilment of vows (Lv 27: 4-5) valued a woman at thirty shekels, and a girl under twenty years of age at ten shekels.

A fiancé could compound for the payment of the *mohar* by service, as

Jacob did for both his marriages (Gn 29: 15-30), or by accomplishing an appointed task, as David did for Mikal (1 S 18: 25-27) and Othniel for Caleb's daughter (Jos 15: 16=Jg 1: 12).

This obligation to pay a sum of money, or its equivalent, to the girl's family obviously gives the Israelite marriage the outward appearance of a purchase. But the *mohar* seems to be not so much the price paid for the woman as a compensation given to the family, and, in spite of the apparent resemblance, in law this is a different consideration. The future husband thereby acquires a right over the woman, but the woman herself is not bought and sold. The difference becomes clear if we compare the *mohar* marriage with another type of union, which really was a purchase: a girl could be sold by her father to another man who intended her to be his own, or his son's, concubine; she was a slave, and could be re-sold, though not to an alien (Ex 21: 7-11). Furthermore, it is probable that the father enjoyed only the usufruct of the *mohar*, and that the latter reverted to the daughter at the time of succession, or if her husband's death reduced her to penury. This would explain the complaint of Rachel and Leah against their father, that he had 'devoured their money' after having 'sold' them (Gn 31: 15).

A similar custom, with the same name (*mahr*), is found among the Palestinian Arabs of to-day. The *mahr* is a sum of money paid by the fiancé to the girl's parents. Its amount varies from village to village, and according to the family's income; the amount depends, too, on whether the girl is marrying within her kin or outside the clan, whether she is of the same village or from some other place. Those concerned do not regard this payment as a real purchase, and part of the sum goes towards the bride's trousseau.

A parallel, though not identical, custom existed in ancient Babylonian law: the *tirḫatu*, though not a necessary condition of the marriage, was usually paid over to the girl's father, and sometimes to the girl herself. The amount varied greatly, from one to fifty shekels of silver. This sum was administered by the father, who enjoyed the usufruct of it; but he could not alienate it, and it reverted to the wife if she was widowed, or to her children after their mother's death. In Assyrian law, the *tirḫatu* was given to the girl herself. It was not a purchase price, but, according to two very probable theories, either a compensation to the girl for the loss of her virginity, or a dowry intended to assist the wife if she lost her husband. There is a close parallel in the marriage-contracts found in the Jewish colony at Elephantine; there the *mohar* is counted among the wife's possessions, though it had been paid to the father.

The gifts presented by the bridegroom on the occasion of the wedding are quite different from the *mohar*: the two things are clearly distinguished in Gn 34: 12. These presents offered to the girl and her family were a reward for their accepting the proposal of marriage. So, as soon as Rebecca's marriage had been agreed on, Abraham's servant brought out jewels and dresses for the girl, and rich presents for her father and mother (Gn 24: 53).

The same custom is found in Mesopotamia. According to the Code of Hammurabi, the bridegroom distributed presents to the girl's parents, and if they broke off the engagement, they had to restore twice what they had received. By Assyrian law, where the *tirḫatu* was a gift of money made previously to the bride, the man gave her ornaments also and made a present to her father.

Was there, in addition, a dowry, a contribution on the part of the bride at the time of the marriage? It is difficult to reconcile any such custom with the payment of the *mohar* by the bridegroom. In fact, there is no mention of any *mohar* in those texts which mention what seems like a dowry: the Pharaoh gave Gezer as a wedding gift to his daughter when Solomon married her (1 K 9: 16); and when Tobias married Sarra, her father gave Tobias half of his fortune (Tb 8: 21). Solomon's marriage, however, follows Egyptian custom, and he is above convention, while the story of Tobias is set in a foreign land. Besides, since Sarra was an only child, this grant appears to be an advance of the inheritance. In Israel, parents might give presents to their daughter at her wedding—a slave, for example (Gn 24: 59; 29: 24, 29), or a piece of land (Jos 15: 18-19), though the latter present was made after the wedding. In general, the custom of providing a dowry never took root in Jewish territory, and Si 25: 22 seems even to repudiate it: 'A woman who maintains her husband is an object of anger, of reproach and of shame.'

In Babylonian law, however, the father gave the young bride certain possessions, which belonged to her in her own right, the husband having only the use of them. They reverted to the wife if she were widowed or divorced without fault on her part. Assyrian law seems to contain similar provisions.

By marriage a woman left her parents, went to live with her husband, and joined his clan, to which her children would belong. Rebecca left her father and mother (Gn 24: 58-59), and Abraham would not allow Isaac to go to Mesopotamia unless the wife chosen for him agreed to come to Canaan (Gn 24: 5-8). A few marriages mentioned in the Bible seem, however, to be exceptions to this general rule. Jacob, after marrying Leah and Rachel, continued to live with his father-in-law, Laban; when he stole away, Laban reproached him for taking away Leah and Rachel, protesting that they were 'his' daughters and their children 'his' children (Gn 31: 26, 43). Gideon had a concubine who continued to live with her family at Shechem (Jg 8: 31), and her son Abimelek asserted the relationship which united him to his mother's clan (Jg 9: 1-2). When Samson married a Philistine woman of Timnah, the woman continued to live with her parents, where Samson visited her (Jg 14: 8f.; 15: 1-2).

Some think these marriages are a type of union in which the wife does not leave her father's house; instead, the husband takes up residence in her home, and severs his connections with his own clan. Ethnographers call it a *beena* marriage, from its name in Ceylon, where their research has been principally centred. But the comparison is not exact. Jacob's fourteen years of service were equivalent to the *mohar*. He stayed a further six years with his father-in-law (Gn 31: 41) simply because he was afraid of Esau's vengeance (Gn 27: 42-45) and because he had a contract with Laban (Gn 30: 25-31). It was not, in fact, on the plea of matrimonial law that Laban opposed Jacob's departure with his wives (Gn 30: 25f.); he merely blamed him for running away secretly (Gn 31: 26-28). He would have spoken differently if Jacob, by his marriage, had become a member of his own clan. As for Gideon, the text stresses that the woman was a concubine. The story of Samson's marriage is more to the point, but it must be noted that Samson did not stay at Timnah with his wife; he only came to visit her, and he was not incorporated into her clan, so that this too is not a *beena* marriage.

Gideon's marriage should be compared, rather, with the *ṣadiqa* union of the ancient Arabs. It is not so much a marriage as a liaison sanctioned by custom: *ṣadiqa* means 'lover' or 'mistress'. Samson's marriage has close similarities with a form found among Palestinian Arabs, in that it is a true marriage but without permanent cohabitation. The woman is mistress of her own house, and the husband, known as *jôz musarrib*, 'a visiting husband', comes as a guest and brings presents. Ancient Assyrian law also provided for the case where a married woman continued to live with her father, but it has not been proved that this kind of marriage (called *erebu*) constitutes a special type of marriage.

3 Choosing the bride

The Bible gives no information about the age at which girls were married. The practice of marrying the eldest first was not universal (Gn 29: 26). On the other hand, it seems certain that girls, and therefore presumably boys too, were married very young; for centuries this has been the custom of the East, and in many places it still obtains to-day. The books of Kings, however, usually give the age of each king of Judah at his accession, followed by the length of his reign and the age of his son (normally the eldest) who succeeded him. From these figures we can deduce that Joiakin married at sixteen, Amon and Josias at fourteen; but the calculations are based on figures which are not all reliable. In later days the Rabbis fixed the minimum age for marriage at twelve years for girls and thirteen for boys.

Under these circumstances it is understandable that the parents took all the decisions when a marriage was being arranged. Neither the girl nor, often, the youth was consulted. Abraham sent his servant to choose a wife for Isaac, and the servant arranged the contract with Rebecca's brother, Laban (Gn 24: 33-53).[1] Her own consent was asked only afterwards (vv. 57-58), and, if

1. The mention of Bethuel, Rebecca's father, in v. 50, is an addition. Bethuel was dead, and Laban was the head of the family (cf. vv. 33, 53, 55, 59).

we interpret this by analogy with certain Mesopotamian texts, her consent was asked only because her father was dead, and because her brother, not her father, had authority over her. When Abraham expelled Hagar from his camp, she took a wife for Ishmael (Gn 21: 21), and Judah arranged the marriage of his first-born (Gn 38: 6). Alternatively, the father might guide his son's choice, as, for example, when Isaac sent Jacob to marry one of his cousins (Gn 28: 1-2). Hamor asked for Dinah as a wife for his son Shechem (Gn 34: 4-6), and Samson, when he fell in love with a Philistine woman, asked her parents for her (Jg 14: 2-3). Even the independent-minded Esau took his father's wishes into account (Gn 28: 8-9). Caleb decided on his daughter's marriage (Jos 15: 16), as did Saul (1 S 18: 17, 19, 21, 27; 25: 44). At the end of the Old Testament, the elder Tobias advised his son on the choice of a wife (Tb 4: 12-13), and the marriage of young Tobias with Sarra was agreed on with the father of Sarra, in her absence (Tb 7: 9-12).

Once the proposal of marriage had been put to the girl's parents, they discussed the conditions, especially the amount of the *mohar* (Gn 29: 15f.; 34: 12). In short, even in those days marriageable daughters caused as much anxiety to their parents as to-day (Si 42: 9).

Nevertheless, parental authority was not such as to leave no room for the feelings of the young couple. There were love marriages in Israel. The young man could make his preferences known (Gn 34: 4; Jg 14: 2), or take his own decision without consulting his parents, and even against their wishes (Gn 26: 34-35). It was rarer for the girl to take the initiative, but we do read of Saul's daughter Mikal falling in love with David (1 S 18: 20).

Actually, young people had ample opportunity for falling in love, and for expressing their feelings, for they were very free. 2 M 3: 19, it is true, speaks of the young girls of Jerusalem being confined to the house, but this text refers to the Greek period and to an exceptional state of affairs. The veiling of women came even later. In ancient times young girls were not secluded and went out unveiled. They looked after the sheep (Gn 29: 6), drew the water (Gn 24: 13; 1 S 9: 11), went gleaning in the fields behind the reapers (Rt 2: 2f.) and visited other people's houses (Gn 34: 1). They could talk with men without any embarrassment (Gn 24: 15-21; 29: 11-12; 1 S 9: 11-13).

This freedom sometimes exposed girls to the violence of young men (Gn 34: 1-2), but the man who seduced a virgin was bound to marry his victim and to pay an enhanced *mohar*; and he forfeited the right to divorce her (Ex 22: 15; Dt 22: 28-29).

It was the custom to take a wife from among one's own kith and kin; the custom was a relic of tribal life. So Abraham sent his servant to find Isaac a wife among his own family in Mesopotamia (Gn 24: 4), and Isaac in turn sent Jacob there to find a wife (Gn 28: 2). Laban declared that he would rather give his daughter to Jacob than to a stranger (Gn 29: 19), and Samson's father was saddened because his son did not choose a wife from his own clan

(Jg 14: 3); Tobias, too, advised his son to choose a wife within his tribe (Tb 4: 12).

Marriages between first cousins were common, *e.g.* the marriage between Isaac and Rebecca, and those of Jacob with Rachel and Leah. Even to-day such marriages are common among the Arabs of Palestine, where a young man has a strict right to the hand of his cousin. According to Tb 6: 12-13 and 7: 10, Tobias' request for Sarra's hand could not be refused, because he was her nearest kinsman; it is 'a law of Moses' (Tb 6: 13; 7: 11-12). The Penta-teuch, however, contains no such prescription. The text in Tobias must refer either to the accounts of the marriages of Isaac and Jacob (cf. especially Gn 24: 50-51), or perhaps to the law requiring heiresses to marry within their father's clan, to preclude the alienation of family property (Nb 36: 5-9), for Sarra was Raguel's only daughter (Tb 6: 12). The same considerations of patrimony and blood-relationship were the basis of the obligation of the *levir* towards his widowed sister-in-law.[1]

Marriages did take place, however, between persons of different families, and even with foreign women. Esau married two Hittite women (Gn 26: 34), Joseph an Egyptian (Gn 41: 45) and Moses a Midianite (Ex 2: 21). Naomi's two daughters-in-law were Moabites (Rt 1: 4); David had a Caleb-ite and an Aramaean among his wives (2 S 3: 3), and Solomon's harem included, 'besides the pharaoh's daughter, Moabites, Ammonites, Edomites, Sidonians and Hittites' (1 K 11: 1; cf. 14: 21). Achab married Jezabel, a Sidonian (1 K 16: 31). Israelite women, too, were married to foreigners, Bathsheba to a Hittite (2 S 11: 3), and the mother of Hiram the bronze-worker to a Tyrian (1 K 7: 13-14).

These mixed marriages, made by kings for political reasons, became com-mon among subjects also, after the settlement in Canaan (Jg 3: 6). They not only tainted the purity of Israel's blood, but also endangered its religious faith (1 K 11: 4), and were therefore forbidden by law (Ex 34: 15-16; Dt 7: 3-4). An exception was made for women captured in war, whom Israelites could marry after a ceremony symbolizing the abandonment of their country of origin (Dt 21: 10-14). Scant respect was paid to these prohibitions, how-ever, and the community which returned from the Exile continued to contract mixed marriages (Ml 2: 11-12); Esdras and Nehemias both had to take strict measures, which, it seems, were not always very effective (Esd 9-10; Ne 10: 31; 13: 23-27).

Within the family, marriages with very close relations were forbidden, because one does not unite with 'the flesh of one's body' (Lv 18: 6), affinity being held to create the same bond as consanguinity (Lv 18: 17). These bans amount to the prohibition of incest. Some are primitive, others represent later additions to the law; the main collection of precepts is found in Lv 18. An impediment of consanguinity exists in the direct line between father and

1. See p. 38.

daughter, mother and son (Lv 18: 7), father and granddaughter (Lv 18: 10), and in the collateral line between brother and sister (Lv 18: 9; Dt 27: 22). Marriage with a half-sister, which was permitted in the patriarchal age (Gn 20: 12) and even under David (2 S 13: 13), is forbidden by the laws of Lv 18: 11; 20: 17; marriage between a nephew and aunt, like that from which Moses was born (Ex 6: 20; Nb 26: 59), is prohibited by Lv 18: 12-13; 20: 19. The impediment of affinity exists between a son and his step-mother (Lv 18: 8), between father-in-law and daughter-in-law (Lv 18: 15; 20: 12; cf. Gn 38: 26), between mother-in-law and son-in-law (Lv 20: 14; Dt 27: 23), between a man and the daughter or granddaughter of a woman he has married (Lv 18: 17), between a man and his uncle's wife (Lv 18: 14; 20: 20), between brother-in-law and sister-in-law (Lv 18: 16; 20: 21). Marriage with two sisters, which might seem to be authorized by the example of Jacob, is forbidden by Lv 18: 18.

Members of the priestly line were subject to special restrictions. According to Lv 21: 7, they could not take a wife who had been a prostitute, or divorced by her husband. Ez 44: 22 adds also widows, unless they were widows of a priest. The rule was even stricter for the high priest: he could marry only a virgin of Israel.

4. Engagements

Engagement, or betrothal, is a promise of marriage made some time before the celebration of the wedding. The custom existed in Israel, and Hebrew has a special word for it, 'araś, which occurs eleven times in the Bible.

The historical books provide little information. The engagements of Isaac and Jacob are rather peculiar. Though Rebecca was promised to Isaac in Mesopotamia, the wedding took place only when she joined him in Canaan (Gn 24: 67); Jacob waited seven years before marrying, but he had a special contract with Laban (Gn 29: 15-21). The story of David and Saul's two daughters is clearer. Merab had been promised to him, but 'when the time came' she was given to another man (1 S 18: 17-19); Mikal was promised to David on payment of a hundred foreskins from the Philistines, which he brought 'before the time had passed' (1 S 18: 26-27). On the other hand, Tobias married Sarra as soon as the terms of the marriage contract were agreed (Tb 7: 9-16).

Legal texts, however, show that engagement was a recognized custom with juridical consequences. According to Dt 20: 7, a man who is engaged, though not yet married to a girl, is excused from going to war. The law of Dt 22: 23-27 makes provision for the case in which a betrothed virgin is violated by a man other than her fiancé. If the crime was committed in a town, the girl is stoned along with her seducer, because she should have cried for help; if she was assaulted in the country, only the man is put to death, because the woman might have cried without being heard.

The gloss in 1 S 18: 21 probably preserves the formula spoken by the girl's father to make the engagement valid: 'To-day you shall be my son-in-law.' The amount of the *mohar* was discussed with the girl's parents at the time of the engagement, and was no doubt paid over at once if, as usually happened, it was paid in money.

The custom existed in Mesopotamia also. An engagement was concluded by the payment of the *tirḫatu*, the equivalent of the *mohar*, and it entailed juridical consequences. A certain interval elapsed between the engagement and the marriage, during which either party could withdraw, but at the price of a forfeit. Hittite law contained similar provisions.

5. *Marriage ceremonies*

It is interesting to note that both in Israel and in Mesopotamia, marriage was a purely civil contract, not sanctioned by any religious rite. Malachy, it is true, calls the bride 'the wife of thy covenant' (*b'rîth*: Ml 2: 14), and *b'rîth* is often used for a religious pact; but here the pact is simply the contract of marriage. In Pr 2: 17 marriage is called 'the covenant of God', and in the allegory of Ez 16: 8 the covenant of Sinai becomes the contract of marriage between Yahweh and Israel.

The texts just cited may well allude to a written contract; apart from these references, the Old Testament mentions a written marriage contract only in the story of Tobias (Tb 7: 13). We possess several marriage contracts originating from the Jewish colony at Elephantine in the fifth century B.C., and the custom was firmly established among the Jews in the Graeco-Roman era. How far back it dates is hard to say. The custom existed in very early times in Mesopotamia, and the Code of Hammurabi declares that a marriage concluded without a formal contract is invalid. In Israel, acts of divorce were drawn up before the Exile (Dt 24: 1-3; Jr 3: 8), and it would be surprising if contracts of marriage did not exist at the same time. Perhaps it is merely by accident that they are never mentioned in the Bible.

The formula pronounced at marriage is given in the Elephantine contracts, which are made out in the name of the husband: 'She is my wife and I am her husband, from this day for ever.' The woman made no declaration. An equivalent formula is found in Tb 7: 11, where Sarra's father says to Tobias: 'Henceforth thou art her brother and she is thy sister.' In a contract of the second century after Christ, found in the desert of Judah, the formula is: 'Thou shalt be my wife.'

Marriage was, of course, an occasion for rejoicing. The chief ceremony was the entry of the bride into the bridegroom's house. The bridegroom, wearing a diadem (Ct 3: 11; Is 61: 10) and accompanied by his friends with tambourines and a band (1 M 9: 39), proceeded to the bride's house. She was richly dressed and adorned with jewels (Ps 45: 14-15; Is 61: 10), but she wore a veil (Ct 4: 1, 3; 6: 7), which she took off only in the bridal chamber. This explains why Rebecca veiled herself on seeing Isaac, her fiancé (Gn 24: 65), and how Laban was able to substitute Leah for Rachel at Jacob's first marriage (Gn 29: 23-25). The bride, escorted by her companions (Ps 45: 15), was conducted to the home of the bridegroom (Ps 45: 16; cf. Gn 24: 67). Love songs were sung in praise of the bridal pair (Jr 16: 9), examples of which survive in Ps 45 and in the Song of Songs, whether we interpret them literally or allegorically.

The Arabs of Palestine and Syria have preserved similar customs—the procession, the wedding songs and the veiling of the bride. Sometimes, during the procession, a sword is carried by the bride or in front of her, and sometimes she performs the dance of the sabre, advancing and retiring before it. Some have compared this with the dance of the Shulamite in Ct 7: 1. In some tribes the bride pretends to escape from the bridegroom, and he has to make a show of capturing her by force. It has been suggested that these games are a survival of marriage by abduction; the story of the men of Benjamin and the girls who danced in the vineyards of Shiloh would be an example from the Old Testament (Jg 21: 19-23). There seems to be little foundation for these comparisons. The brandishing of the sword is symbolic: it cuts away bad luck and drives off evil spirits. There is nothing to suggest that the Shulamite's dance was a sabre-dance, and the incident at Shiloh is explained by exceptional circumstances which are recorded in the story.

Next came a great feast (Gn 29: 22; Jg 14: 10; Tb 7: 14). In these three passages the feast took place at the home of the bride's parents, but the circumstances were exceptional. As a general rule it was certainly given at the bridegroom's house (cf. Mt 22: 2). The feast normally lasted seven days (Gn 29: 27; Jg 14: 12), and could even be prolonged for two weeks (Tb 8: 20; 10: 7). But the marriage was consummated on the first night (Gn 29: 23; Tb 8: 1). The blood-stained linen of this nuptial night was preserved; it proved the bride's virginity and would be evidence if she were slandered by her husband (Dt 22: 13-21). The same naïve custom still obtains in Palestine and other Moslem countries.

6. *Repudiation and divorce*

A husband could divorce his wife. The motive accepted by Dt 24: 1 is 'that he has found a fault to impute to her'. The expression is very vague, and in the Rabbinical age there was keen discussion on the meaning of this text. The rigorist school of Shammai admitted only adultery and misconduct as grounds for divorce, but the more liberal school of Hillel would accept any reason, however trivial, such as the charge that a wife had cooked a dish badly, or merely that the husband preferred another woman. Even before this

age, Si 25: 26 had told the husband: 'If thy wife does not obey thee at a
signal and a glance, separate from her.'

The form of divorce was simple: the husband made out a declaration con-
tradicting that which had sealed the marriage contract: 'She is no longer my
wife and I am no longer her husband' (Os 2: 4). In the colony at Elephantine
he pronounced in front of witnesses the words: 'I divorce my wife' (literally:
'I hate my wife'). In Assyria he said: 'I repudiate her' or 'You are no more
my wife.' But in Israel, Mesopotamia and Elephantine, the husband had to
draw up a writ of divorce (Dt 24: 1, 3; Is 50: 1; Jr 3: 8) which allowed the
woman to remarry (Dt 24: 2). A writ of divorce dating from the beginning
of the second century of our era has been found in the caves of Murabba'at.

The law laid few restrictions on the husband's right. A man who had
falsely accused his wife of not being a virgin when he married her could
never divorce her (Dt 22: 13-19), nor could a man who had been compelled
to marry a girl he had violated (Dt 22: 28-29). If a divorced wife remarried,
and later regained her liberty by the death of her second husband or by
divorce from him, the first husband could not take her back (Dt 24: 3-4; cf.
Jr 3: 1). Osee's double marriage (Os 2-3)—if, as it seems, he did take back a
wife he had divorced—is not forbidden by this law, for in the meantime she
had not remarried, but had become a prostitute. Nor did the law apply to
Mikal, first married to David, then given to another man and finally taken
back by David (1 S 18: 20-27; 25: 44; 2 S 3: 13-16), because David had never
divorced her.

We do not know whether Israelite husbands made much use of this right,
which seems to have been very far-reaching. The Wisdom books praise
conjugal fidelity (Pr 5: 15 19; Qo 9: 9), and Malachy teaches that marriage
makes the two partners one person, and that the husband must keep the oath
sworn to his partner: 'I hate divorce, says Yahweh, the God of Israel' (Ml 2:
14-16). But not until New Testament times do we find the proclamation, by
Jesus, of the indissolubility of marriage. He uses the same argument as
Malachy: 'what God has joined together, let no man separate' (Mt 5: 31-32;
19: 1-9 and parallels).

Women, on the other hand, could not ask for a divorce. Even at the
beginning of the Christian era, when Salome, the sister of Herod, sent her
husband Kostabar a letter of divorce, her action was held to be against Jewish
law. If the Gospel envisages the possibility of a woman divorcing her husband (Mk 10: 12, but not in the parallels), it is certainly with reference to
Gentile customs. The Jewish colony of Elephantine, which was subject to
foreign influence, did allow a woman to divorce her husband. In Palestine
itself the custom is attested in the second century of our era by a document
from the desert of Judah.

In Mesopotamia, according to the Code of Hammurabi, the husband could
divorce his wife by pronouncing the appropriate formula, but he had to pay

her compensation, varying according to the circumstances. The wife could obtain a divorce only after a judicial decision recognizing the husband's guilt. In Assyrian law the husband could repudiate his wife without any compensation, but the wife could not obtain a divorce at all. The situation revealed by Assyrian marriage contracts is still more complicated, for they often stipulate still more onerous conditions for the husband: when arranging the marriage, the wife's parents might protect her interests by special clauses.

Though the Old Testament makes no mention of them, it is likely that in Israel too, certain financial conditions were attached to divorce. According to the marriage contracts of Elephantine, the husband who repudiated his wife could not reclaim the *mohar*; he paid the 'price of divorce'. Similarly, the wife who separated from her husband paid the same 'price of divorce', but took away her personal property, which presumably included the *mohar*.

7. *Adultery and fornication*

The condemnation of adultery in the Decalogue (Ex 20: 14; Dt 5: 18) is placed between the prohibitions of murder and stealing, among acts which injure one's neighbour. In Lv 18: 20 it is ranked among sins against marriage: it makes a person 'unclean'. In Israel, then, as everywhere in the ancient East, adultery was a sin against one's neighbour, but the text of Lv 18: 20 adds a religious consideration, and the stories of Gn 20: 1-13; 26: 7-11 represent adultery as a sin against God.

If a man commits adultery with a married woman, both the partners in crime are put to death (Lv 20: 10; Dt 22: 22), and, on this count, a girl engaged to be married is treated exactly like a woman already married (Dt 22: 23f.), for she belongs to her fiancé in exactly the same way as a married woman belongs to her husband. According to Dt 22: 23f.; Ez 16: 40 (cf. Jn 8: 5), the penalty was death by stoning, but it is possible that in ancient times it was death by burning. Judah condemned his daughter-in-law Tamar to be burned alive (Gn 38: 24), because he suspected she had given herself to a man at a time when she was the widow of his son Er, and, by the law of levirate, promised to his other son Shelah.

The latest collection of Proverbs (Pr 1-9) often puts young men on their guard against the seductions of a woman who is unfaithful to her husband. She is called the 'strange woman', meaning simply the wife of another man (Pr 2: 16-19; 5: 2-14; 6: 23-7: 27). Such love leads to death (2: 18; 5: 5; 7: 26-27), but this 'death' is generally synonymous with moral perdition: it appears once as the revenge of the injured husband (6: 34), never as the legal punishment of adultery.

The older parts of Proverbs rarely refer to adultery (Pr 30: 18-20) but they rank it side by side with prostitution (23: 27). The man who goes after prostitutes dissipates his wealth and loses his strength (Pr 29: 3; 31: 3), but he commits no crime in the eyes of the law. Judah, for example, is not blamed for taking his pleasure with one whom he thinks is a prostitute (Gn 38: 15–19); his only fault is in not observing the law of levirate towards his daughter-in-law (Gn 38: 26).

The husband is exhorted to be faithful to his wife in Pr 5: 15-19, but his infidelity is punished only if he violates the rights of another man by taking a married woman as his accomplice.

In contrast with the licence which the husband enjoyed, the wife's mis-conduct was punished severely: it is the 'great sin' mentioned in certain Egyptian and Ugaritic texts, the 'great sin' which the king of Gerar almost committed with Sarah (Gn 20: 9; cf. the metaphorical use of the same term with reference to idolatry, in Ex 32: 21, 30, 31; 2 K 17: 21). Her husband could, indeed, pardon her, but he could also divorce her, and her punishment entailed disgrace (Os 2: 5, 11-12; Ez 16: 37-38; 23: 29). We have no information about unmarried women, except that a priest's daughter who turned to prostitution was to be burned alive (Lv 21: 9).

8. *The levirate*

According to a law of Dt 25. 5-10, if brothers live together and one of them dies without issue, one of the surviving brothers takes his widow to wife, and the first-born of this new marriage is regarded in law as the son of the deceased. The brother-in-law can, however, decline this obligation, by making a declaration before the elders of the town; but it is a dishonourable action. The widow takes off his shoe and spits in his face, because 'he does not raise up his brother's house'.

This institution is called levirate, from the Latin *levir*, translating the Hebrew *yabam* ('brother-in-law'). Only two examples of it occur in the Old Testament, both of them difficult to interpret and only imperfectly corres-ponding to the law in Deuteronomy: the stories of Tamar and Ruth.

Judah's first-born son, Er, dies without having a child by his wife Tamar (Gn 38: 6-7). It is the duty of his brother Onan to marry the widow, but Onan does not want to have a child who would not be, in law, his own son, so he frustrates his union with Tamar; for this sin, Yahweh brings about his death (Gn 38: 8-10). Judah ought now to give Tamar his youngest son Shelah, but he shirks this duty (38: 11); so Tamar tricks her father-in-law into having intercourse with her (38: 15-19). This story of ancient times presents the obligation of the levirate as much stricter than in the law of Deuter-onomy; the brother-in-law may not decline the duty, and it passes to all the surviving brothers in turn (cf. Mt 22: 24-27). Tamar's intercourse with Judah may be a relic of a time when the duty of levirate fell on the father-in-law if he had no other sons, a practice which is found among some peoples.

More probably, it is the desperate act of a woman who desires children of the same stock as her husband.

The story of Ruth combines the custom of the levirate with the duty of redemption which fell on the go'el.[1] The law of Dt 25 does not apply, for Ruth had no more brothers-in-law (Rt 1: 11-12). The fact that some near relative must marry her, and that this obligation proceeds in a certain order Rt. 2: 20; 3: 12), no doubt indicates a period or a *milieu* in which the law of levirate was a matter for the clan rather than for the family in the strict sense. In any case, the intentions and effects of the marriage were those of a levirate marriage, for it was made 'to perpetuate the name of the dead' (Rt 4: 5, 10; cf. 2: 20), and the child born of it was considered the son of the deceased (Rt 4: 6; cf. 4: 17).

There are parallels to this custom among other peoples, and especially among Israel's neighbours. Though the Code of Hammurabi does not mention it, the Assyrian laws devote several articles to it. Though they do not expressly state that the widow had to be childless, this may be due to a gap in the text. On the other hand, they treat engagement, for this purpose, in just the same way as a consummated marriage; if a betrothed man dies, his fiancée must marry the dead man's brother. Some of the Hittite laws also mention the levirate, but they are less detailed. The custom also existed among the Hurrites of Nuzu and perhaps in Elam, and there is evidence of it at Ugarit also.

Discussion about the purpose of the levirate seems to be endless. Some have regarded it as a means of perpetuating ancestor-worship, others as an indication of a fratriarchal society. But, whatever may be true of other nations, the Old Testament gives its own explanation, which seems sufficient. The essential purpose is to perpetuate male descent, the 'name', the 'house', and therefore the child (probably only the first child) of a levirate marriage was considered the child of the deceased man. It was not mere sentiment, but an expression of the importance attached to blood-ties. A secondary, but similar, purpose was to prevent the alienation of family property. This consideration appears in Dt 25: 5, which makes it a condition of the levirate that the brothers should be living together, and it explains why, in the story of Ruth, the right of redeeming the land is linked with the duty of marrying the widow. The same motive is found in the legislation about the Jubilee (Lv 25), and in the law about daughters who are heiresses (Nb 36: 2-9).

1. See p. 21.

CHAPTER THREE

THE POSITION OF WOMEN: WIDOWS

IT has already been said that the wife called her husband *ba'al* or 'master'; she also called him *'adôn* or 'lord' (Gn 18: 12; Jg 19: 26; Am 4: 1); she addressed him, in fact, as a slave addressed his master, or a subject his king. The Decalogue includes a man's wife among his possessions, along with his house and land, his male and female slaves, his ox and his ass (Ex 20: 17; Dt 5: 21). Her husband can repudiate her, but she cannot claim a divorce; all her life she remains a minor. The wife does not inherit from her husband, nor daughters from their father, except when there is no male heir (Nb 27: 8). A vow made by a girl or married woman needs, to be valid, the consent of father or husband and if this consent is withheld, the vow is null and void (Nb 30: 4-17).

For all this, the wife of an Israelite was by no means on the level of a slave. A man could sell his slaves, or even his daughter (Ex 21: 7), but he could never sell his wife, even though he had acquired her as a captive in war (Dt 21: 14). The husband could divorce his wife, but she was protected by the letter of repudiation, which restored her freedom. Most probably, the married woman kept, if not the use, at least the ownership, of part of the *mohar* and of whatever she received from her parents (cf. Jos 15: 19; Jg 1: 15).

All the hard work at home certainly fell to her; she looked after the flocks, worked in the fields, cooked the food, did the spinning, and so on. All this apparent drudgery, however, far from lowering her status, earned her consideration. Sometimes, in exceptional circumstances, a woman could even take part in public affairs. Israel honoured Deborah and Jael as heroines (Jg 4-5), Athaliah reigned over Judah for several years (2 K 11); Huldah the prophetess was consulted by the king's ministers (2 K 22: 14f.); and the books of Judith and Esther tell how the nation was saved by a woman.

Within the family, respect for a wife increased on the birth of her first child, especially if the child were a boy (Gn 16: 4 and Gn 29: 31—30: 24; note the explanation of the names which Leah and Rachel gave to their children). Her husband became more attached to her, and her children owed her obedience and respect. The law condemned the faults of children against their mother as much as offences against their father (Ex 21: 17; Lv 20: 9; Dt 21: 18-21; 27: 16), and the Decalogue (Ex 20: 12) commanded equal honour to be given to father and mother (cf. Lv 19: 3). The Wisdom books insist on the respect due to one's mother (Pr 19: 26; 20: 20; 23: 22; 30: 17; Si 3: 1-16). And those rare passages which give us a glimpse into the intimacy of family life show that an Israelite wife was loved and listened to by her husband, and treated by him as an equal: Samuel's mother, for example (1 S 1: 4-8, 22-23), and the woman of Shunem (2 K 4: 8-24), or the two aged couples in the book of Tobias. And there is no doubt that this was the normal picture. It was a faithful reflection of the teaching enshrined in Genesis, where God is said to have created woman as a helpmate for man, to whom he was to cling (Gn 2: 18, 24); and the last chapter of Proverbs sings the praises of a good housewife, blessed by her children, and the pride of her husband (Pr 31: 10-31).

The social and legal position of an Israelite wife was, however, inferior to the position a wife occupied in the great countries round about. In Egypt the wife was often the head of the family, with all the rights such a position entailed. In Babylon she could acquire property, take legal action, be a party to contracts, and she even had a certain share in her husband's inheritance.

In the colony at Elephantine, under such foreign influence, the Jewish wife acquired certain civil rights. We have already said that she could obtain a divorce. She could also own property, and thereby became liable to taxation (in a long list of taxpayers, there are thirty-two names of women). Deeds of exchange and donations, etc., also survive, in which the contracting parties were women.

The position of widows calls for some special remarks. A vow made by a wife continued to bind her after her husband's death (Nb 30: 10). By the levirate law, a childless widow could continue as part of her husband's family. If there were no levir, she could re-marry outside the family (Rt 1: 9), spending the interval before her second marriage with her own father and mother (Rt 1: 8; Gn 38: 11; cf. Lv 22: 13). The story of Tamar, however, shows that even during this period her father-in-law retained authority over her (Gn 38: 24). The widow wore mourning, at least for a time (Gn 38: 14; 2 S 14: 2; Jdt 8: 5; 10: 3). How long the period of mourning lasted is not known, but to spend more than three years mourning, as Judith did, seems exceptional (Jdt 8: 4).

Judith was a rich widow. More commonly widows, especially those with children to support, were in a piteous condition (1 K 17: 8-15; 2 K 4: 1-7; cf. the widow in the Gospel, Mk 12: 41-44; Lk 21: 1-4). They were therefore protected by religious law and commended to the charity of the people, together with orphans and resident aliens—all those, in fact, who no longer had a family to assist them (Ex 22: 21, and emphatically in Deuteronomy 10: 18; 24: 17-21; 26: 12-13; 27: 19; cf. Is 1: 17; Jr 22: 3; note in contrast Is 1: 23; Jr 7: 6; cf. also Jb 29: 13). God himself is their protector, according to Ps 146: 9.

CHAPTER FOUR

CHILDREN

1. *Attitude to children*

AT a peasant or Bedouin wedding in modern Palestine, a pomegranate is sometimes split open on the threshold of the house or at the opening of the tent: its grains symbolize the many children their friends wish them.

In ancient Israel, to have many children was a coveted honour, and the wedding guests often expressed the wish that the couple would be blessed with a large family. As Rebecca leaves her family, she is blessed with the words: 'O sister of ours, become the mother of thousands of ten thousands' (Gn 24: 60). When Boaz marries Ruth, the wish is expressed that his young wife may be 'like Rachel and Leah, the two who built up the house of Israel' (Rt 4: 11-12). First Abraham and then Isaac received the promise that their posterity would be countless as the stars in the sky (Gn 15: 5; 22: 17; 26: 4). God promised Hagar, too, that her posterity would be past counting (Gn 16: 10). Children are 'the crown of man' (Pr 17: 6), and sons are 'olive plants around the table' (Ps 128: 3), 'a reward, like arrows in the hand of a hero; happy the man who has his quiver full of them' (Ps 127: 3-5).

Sterility, on the other hand, was considered a trial (Gn 16: 2; 30: 2; 1 S 1: 5) or a chastisement from God (Gn 20: 18), or a disgrace, from which Sarah, Rachel and Leah all tried to clear themselves by adopting the child which their maids bore to their husbands (Gn 16: 2; 30: 3, 9).

All these texts show that the Israelites wanted mainly sons, to perpetuate the family line and fortune, and to preserve the ancestral inheritance. Daughters were held in less regard; they would leave the family when they married, and so the strength of a house was not measured by the number of its daughters.

Among the sons, the eldest enjoyed certain privileges. During his father's lifetime, he took precedence of his brothers (Gn 43: 33). On his father's death he received a double share of the inheritance (Dt 21: 17) and became the head of the family. With twins, the first to see the light was reckoned the elder (Gn 25: 24-26; 38: 27-30; although Zerah's hand was seen first. Peres was the elder—cf. 1 Ch 2: 4—because he was the first to emerge from his mother's womb). The eldest could lose his right of primogeniture for a grave offence, as Reuben did by his incest (Gn 35: 22; cf. 49: 3-4 and 1 Ch 5: 1), or he could surrender it, as Esau did by selling his birth-right to Jacob (Gn 25: 29-34). But the eldest son was protected by law against favouritism on the part of his father (Dt 21: 15-17).

Nevertheless, the displacing of the elder son by a younger one is a theme which often recurs in the Old Testament. Apart from Jacob and Esau, Peres and Zerah, many other examples could be quoted. Isaac inherits, not Ishmael; Joseph is his father's favourite, then Benjamin; Ephraim is preferred to Manasseh; David, the youngest in his family, is chosen from among all his brothers and leaves his kingdom to Solomon, his youngest son. Some would treat these instances as signs of a custom opposed to the right of the firstborn; such a custom does exist among some peoples, and is known as ultimogeniture, because the inheritance and the father's rights pass to the youngest son. But the examples quoted from Israelite history are exceptions to the ordinary law, and merely emphasize the tension between juridical custom and the love which tended to make a father most fond of a son born in his old age (cf. Gn 37: 3; 44: 20). Moreover, the Bible states explicitly that these stories stress the fact that God's choice is absolutely unmerited and quite gratuitous: he accepted Abel's offering and rejected that of his elder brother Cain (Gn 4: 4-5); he 'loved Jacob and hated Esau' (Ml 1: 2-3; Rom 9: 13; cf. Gn 25: 23); he pointed out David (1 S 16: 12) and gave the kingdom to Solomon (1 K 2: 15).

The firstborn, because he was the first-fruits of marriage, belonged to God. The firstborn of a flock were sacrificed, but those of mankind were redeemed (Ex 13: 11-15; 22: 28; 34: 20), for the God of Israel abhorred the sacrifice of children (Lv 20: 2-5, etc., and cf. the sacrifice of Isaac in Gn 22). Instead, the Levites were consecrated to God as substitutes for the firstborn of the people (Nb 3: 12-13; 8: 16-18).

2. Birth

According to a rather obscure text in Ex 1: 16, a woman in labour perhaps sat on two stones placed at a slight distance from each other; these stones would be the equivalent of the chair of childbirth, mentioned in Rabbinical times and still used in some parts of the East. In Gn 30: 3, Rachel asks Bilhah to give birth on her knees; Gn 50: 23 says that 'the children of Makir, son of Manasseh, were born on the knees of Joseph'; and Job, cursing the day of his birth, bewails the fact that he found two knees to receive him (Jb 3: 12). From this some authors have concluded that childbirth sometimes took place on the knees of another person, a midwife or a relative, and this custom is in fact found outside Israel. But there is probably a simpler explanation: the texts about Rachel and Joseph must be referring to adoption (cf. Gn 48: 12[1]), and Job 3: 12 refers to the knees of a mother who is suckling her child. From Ex 1: 19 we might deduce that the women of Israel had easy

1. Cf. p. 51.

delivery, as so often occurs among the peasants and Bedouin of Palestine to-day. But this isolated text carries little weight when set side by side with the curse pronounced against woman in Gn 3: 16: 'I will multiply thy sorrows when thou art with child; in sorrow thou shalt bring forth children.' This was the common experience, and the pains of childbirth are frequently used, in a metaphorical sense, by the prophets (Is 13: 8; 21: 3; 26: 17; Jr 4: 31; 6: 24; 13: 21; 22: 23; 50: 43; cf. also Ex 15: 14; Is 37: 3; 2 K 19: 3; Os 13: 13; Ps 48: 7). The mother was assisted by a midwife (Gn 35: 17; 38: 28) and Ex 1: 15 shows that there were professional midwives. According to Jr 20: 15 (cf. Jb 3: 3), the father was not present at the birth.

The baby was washed, rubbed with salt—Palestinian peasants still say 'it makes them strong'—and wrapped in swathing cloths (Ez 16: 4; cf. Jb 38: 8-9). As a general rule, it was suckled by its mother (Gn 21: 7; 1 S 1: 21-23; 1 K 3: 21; 2 M 7: 27), but sometimes a child would be entrusted to a nurse (Gn 24: 59; 35: 8; Ex 2: 7-9; Nb 11: 12; 2 S 4: 4; 2 K 11: 2), as was the custom in Mesopotamia and Egypt.

The child was weaned much later than nowadays (cf. for Samuel 1 S 1: 20-23); according to 2 M 7: 27 a child was weaned at the age of three; this was the custom in ancient Babylon also. Isaac's weaning was celebrated by a feast (Gn 21: 8).

3. *The name*

The child was given a name immediately after birth. This name was usually chosen by the mother (Gn 29: 31—30: 24; 35: 18; 1 S 1: 20), but sometimes by the father (Gn 16: 15; 17: 19; Ex 2: 22; cf. Gn 35: 18). The custom of postponing the naming until circumcision, eight days later, is not recorded until New Testament times (Lk 1: 59; 2: 21).

Among primitive peoples, and throughout the ancient East, the name denotes the essence of a thing: to name it is to know it, and, consequently, to have power over it. In the earthly paradise, when God allowed men to name the animals (Gn 2: 19-20), it was a sign that he was putting them under man's power (cf. the parallel story in Gn 1: 28). To know the name of a person is to be able to hurt him (hence 'taboo names' among primitive peoples, and secret names among the Egyptians), or to be able to do him good (*e.g.* Moses, whom God knew by name, Ex 33: 12, 17). This is the reason why it is so important for the believer to know the true name of his God (Ex 3: 13-15; cf. Gn 32: 30), and this is a feature found in all Eastern religions. Finally, since the name defines the essence, it reveals the character and destiny of the bearer. The name becomes the expression of a hope, or a symbol which men try to decipher by rough etymologies.

Sometimes a particular circumstance of the birth provided the inspiration for a child's name. It might concern the mother who bore the child: Eve called her firstborn Cain (*Qaïn*) because she had 'acquired' (*qanah*) a man

(Gn 4: 1). The names of Jacob's sons tell a similar story (Gn 29: 31—30: 24): Rachel, dying in childbirth, called her son Ben-Oni, 'son of my sorrow', but Jacob changed this name of ill omen to Benjamin, 'son of the right hand' (Gn 35: 18). Less often, the name concerns the father: Moses called his son Gershom, because he was born when Moses was a *ger*, living in a foreign land (Ex 2: 22). The child himself might provide the occasion: Jacob was so called because, while still in his mother's womb, he grasped the heel, *'aqeb*, of his twin (Gn 25: 26), whom he displaced, *'aqab* (Gn 27: 36; Os 12: 4); Peres was born by opening a breach, *peres* (Gn 38: 29). Finally, the circumstance may be an event contemporary with the birth: the wife of Phinehas, hearing that the Philistines have captured the Ark, brings to birth a son whom she calls Ikabod, meaning 'Where is the glory?' (1 S 4: 21). We may compare with the last example the symbolic names which Osee and Isaias gave to their children (Os 1: 4, 6, 9; Is 7: 3; 8: 3).

In the explanation of these names, the Bible often gives a popular etymology, made up after the event and justified by some imaginary feature of the person named. This is certainly true of a number of examples, but it is not always and necessarily so. The same custom of calling a child after the circumstances of its birth obtains among many peoples, including present-day Arabs. Thus a woman who had borne only daughters called the fourth Za'uleh ('Irritating'), and the eighth Tamâm ('Enough!'), and a man whose daughter was born on a morning of heavy dew called her Endeyeh ('Full of dew'). Names taken from a child's physical appearance are quite rare: Nahor means 'the snorer', Qareah 'the bald' and Paseah 'the lame'. With these we may compare a modern example: a woman from the district of Jerusalem exclaimed, on seeing her son, 'But this child's a negro (*habash*)!' So they called him Habash.

Names of animals were commonly used, especially in the early ages: Rachel means 'sheep', Deborah 'bee', Yona 'dove', Aiiah 'vulture', Shephuphan 'viper', Caleb 'dog', Nahash 'serpent', Eglah 'heifer', Akbor 'mouse' and so on. Some authors have maintained that these were originally names of clans, and that the names are evidence of primitive totemism. In fact, however, they are names of individuals, not of clans, and date from an epoch when no other trace of totemism is found. Moreover, similar names were known among the ancient Arabs and are found among the Bedouin to-day. Some are descriptive, or expressive of a wish: a girl called Deborah will be as busy as a bee, a boy called Caleb, Shephuphan or Aiiah will be strong or terrible to his enemies, like a dog, a viper or a vulture. Again, a child may be called after the first animal seen at the time of its birth; the custom still obtains with modern Bedouin.

Names taken from plants are much rarer: Elôn means 'oak-tree', Zeitan 'olive', Qôs 'thorn' and Tamar 'palm-tree'. These names are to be explained in the same way as names of animals.

The most important category of names is the 'theophoric', *i.e.* those which contain some divine name or title. Some are formed with 'Baal'; this may at times be an epithet of Yahweh, for *ba'al* means 'master', but it is often the name of the Canaanite God. The proportion of these names is especially high in the ostraka of Samaria, which date from a period when the religion of the northern kingdom was corrupted by syncretism. They disappear after the monarchical period. Under the influence of Yahwism, some of these names were altered in the texts, 'Baal' being replaced by 'El' or 'Yahweh'; alternatively, they might be emended for the purpose of public reading, as when Ishbaal was changed into Ishbosheth, Yerubbaal into Yerubbosheth, and Meribbaal into Mephibosheth.

But far more common than these are names derived from Israel's national God, denoted by his names of El or Yahweh (in shortened forms) or by some epithet or attribute. The names are composed of this divine word and a verb (or, less frequently, a noun or an adjective). They express a religious idea, the power or the mercy of God, the help expected from him, the feeling of kinship with him. No doubt the everyday use of these names tended to weaken their significance, but they became much more common in periods of religious revival, and some reflect the particular religious situation of an age, for example, that of the Exile or the Return. These facts prove that their real significance had not been forgotten.

Theophoric names could be abridged, the divine element being understood ('hypochoristic words'): *e.g.* Nathan, 'he has given', instead of 'Nathanyahu', 'Yahweh has given'; Mattan 'Gift', instead of Mattanyahu, 'Gift of Yahweh'.

At the close of biblical times there arose the custom of giving a patronymic name, *i.e.* the child was called after its grandfather (less often its father), greatgrandfather, or uncle. There is evidence of it first at Elephantine, then in Judaea in the third century B.C., and it seems to have been common at the beginning of the Christian era (cf. Lk 1: 59).

Occasionally, Israelites or Jews by birth have foreign names, not only in the colonies outside Palestine, but in Palestine itself. Aramaic names appear after the Exile and are very common in the New Testament period: Martha, Tabitha, Bar-Tolomai, etc.

In the Graeco-Roman period a person might have a Greek or Roman name in addition to a Jewish one: *e.g.* Salome Alexandra, John Mark. Sometimes the name was translated into Greek (Mattanyah became Theodotos), or the Semitic name given a Greek form (such as Jesus or Maria).

A person could change his name when he grew up. The Bible ascribes some of these changes to divine intervention. Jacob's name was changed to Israel for wrestling with God (Gn 32: 29; cf. 35: 10). The names of Abram and Sarai were changed into Abraham and Sarah (Gn 17: 5, 15); these are only dialect forms of the same names, but if one recalls the significance of names discussed above, a change of name would mark a change in the person's destiny (cf. Gn 17: 6, 16). We have also observed that to name a person is to assert one's authority over him, and this explains the changes of name imposed by a master. The pharaoh gave Joseph the name of Saphenath-Paneah (Gn 41: 45). The chief eunuch changed the names of Daniel, Ananias, Misael and Azarias into Baltassar, Shadrak, Meshak and Abed Nego (Dn 1: 6-7). When the pharaoh installed Elyaqim as king of Judah, he made him take the name of Joiaqim (2 K 23: 34), and similarly Nabuchodonosor changed the name of Mattanyah, whom he set on the throne, to Sedecias (2 K 24: 17). These last examples involve the problem of the coronation name in Israel, a subject which will be considered in connection with the king.[1]

4. Circumcision

Circumcision is the removal of the foreskin. The ceremony was to be performed on the eighth day after birth, according to the law of Lv 12: 3 and the Priestly account of the covenant with Abraham (Gn 17: 12). The same tradition says it was actually on the eighth day after his birth that Isaac was circumcised (Gn 21: 4). According to Ex 4: 25 and Jos 5: 2-3, flint knives were used, which shows how ancient the custom is; later, however, metal instruments came into use.

The operation was carried out by the father (Gn 21: 4), in the exceptional case of Ex 4: 25 by the mother, or, in later times, by a physician or a specialist (1 M 1: 61). There was no ruling about the place where it was to be performed, but it was never done in the sanctuary or by a priest. With adults, the wound healed only after several days of rest (Gn 34: 25; Jos 5: 8).

The Israelites were commanded to circumcise not only their children, but also their servants, both native and foreign (Gn 17: 12-13). Only circumcised foreigners, whether servants or resident aliens, could share in the Passover, the feast of the Israelite community (Ex 12: 43 :49). According to the biblical narrative, circumcision was first practised by Abraham's clan after its entry into Canaan; God ordered it as a sign of the covenant he had made with Abraham (Gn 17: 9-14, 23-27). The Patriarchs continued to observe the custom (Gn 34: 13-24), and Jos 5: 4-5 tells us that it was maintained throughout the sojourn in Egypt. On the other hand, Moses was not circumcised, according to the story of Ex 4: 24-26. The custom was forgotten in the desert, but resumed on entering the Promised Land (Jos 5: 4-9).

It is difficult to determine the extent of the practice of circumcision in the ancient East, for the available evidence is uncertain and contradictory. In Egypt, bas-reliefs bear witness to the custom from the third millennium B.C., texts mention it, Herodotus speaks of it, and yet some of the mummies are not circumcised. It certainly seems to have been obligatory for the priests.

1. Cf. pp. 107-108.

Yet Jos 5: 9 appears to describe uncircumcision as 'the disgrace of Egypt'. On the other hand, Jr 9: 24-25 mentions the Egyptians, along with Judah, Edom, Ammon, Moab and the Arabs as being circumcised in the flesh but uncircumcised in heart. Ez 32: 21-30 consigns Pharaoh and his army to Sheol with the uncircumcised, along with the Assyrians, the Elamites, the hordes of Meshek and Tubal, the Edomites, all the princes of the North and all the Sidonians. Flavius Josephus says that the Idumeans (Edomites) were compelled to accept circumcision by John Hyrcanus. But, if we are to believe Herodotus, all the Phoenicians and Syrians of Palestine were circumcised; Aristophanes asserts the same of the Phoenicians. According to the pre-Islamic poets, the ancient Arabs were circumcised, and the Pseudo-Bardesanus says that the Romans tried to forbid this practice in Arabia.

Among the peoples with whom the Israelites had direct contact in Palestine, the Philistines were uncircumcised (1 S 18: 25; cf. Jg 14: 3; 1 S 17: 26, 36) and the term 'uncircumcised' (without any addition) is sometimes enough to describe them (Jg 15: 18; 1 S 14: 6; 31: 4). This distinguishes them from the Canaanites, who are never so described, and must therefore have been circumcised. There is, of course, the episode of the Shechemites who were compelled to circumcise themselves in order to marry Israelite maidens (Gn 34: 13-24), but, according to Gn 34: 2, the Shechemites were 'Hivvites' ('Horites' in the Greek text); this implies that they constituted a non-Semitic enclave among the population.

It seems, then, that the Israelites were not distinguished from the Semitic population which they displaced, or with whom they mingled in Palestine, by the fact of their circumcision. On the contrary, they appear to have adopted this custom when they settled in Canaan (cf. Gn 17: 9-14, 23-27; Jos 5: 2-9), but with them the practice took on a particular religious significance.

Originally, and as a general rule, circumcision seems to have been an initiation-rite before marriage; consequently, it also initiated a man into the common life of the clan. This is certainly true of many African tribes which practise it to-day, and very probably true of ancient Egypt, where it was performed at the age of puberty. The custom must originally have had the same purpose in Israel: the story of the Shechemites expressly connects it with marriage (Gn 34); the obscure episode of Ex 4: 24-26 seems to refer to marriage also, for the pretence of circumcising Moses makes him a 'bridegroom of blood'. We may add that the Hebrew words for bridegroom, son-in-law and father-in-law are all derived from the same root, ḥatan, which means in Arabic 'to circumcise'.

The metaphorical uses of the word confirm this interpretation: the 'uncircumcised heart' (Jr 9: 25) is a heart which does not understand (contrast Dt 10: 16; 30: 6; Jr 4: 4). The 'uncircumcised ear' is an ear which does not listen (Jr 6: 10); 'uncircumcised lips' are those which cannot speak (Ex 6:

12, 30). Circumcision, therefore, is regarded as that which makes a man fit for normal sexual life; it is an initiation to marriage.

This significance must have died out when the operation was performed soon after birth. Above all, religion gave the rite a more lofty significance. It was a sign of incorporation into the life of the group, into the community of Israel (cf. Gn 34: 14-16; Ex 12: 47-48). Hence it is prescribed as an obligation, and as a sign of the covenant which God made with Abraham and his descendants (Gn 17: 9-14: from the Priestly tradition).

The religious importance of circumcision, however, gained ground only gradually. The laws of the Pentateuch make only passing references to it, in connection with the Passover (Ex 12: 44, 48), with the purification of women after childbirth (Lv 12: 3) and as a term of comparison with the first fruits of trees (Lv 19: 23). It was only during the Exile that circumcision became the distinctive mark of a man who belonged to Israel and to Yahweh. The explanation is not hard to find: the exiles lived among peoples who did not practise it, while, at the same time, apparently, the custom was being progressively abandoned among the nations surrounding Palestine. This would account for certain ancient references: Ez 32: 30 counts the Sidonians among the uncircumcised; so also were the Ammonites, according to Jdt 14: 10; and according to Josephus, John Hyrcanus compelled the Idumeans to circumcise themselves. The same author adds that in his time, the first century of our era, the Jews were the only inhabitants of Palestine who had themselves circumcised.

The importance of circumcision as a sign of the covenant with God was therefore all the more strongly emphasized. Proselytes were obliged to accept it (cf. the first Jewish-Christian controversies, Ac 15: 5f.; 16: 3; Gal 2: 3). The first references to pagans being circumcised when they accepted the Jewish faith are found in Jdt 14: 10 and Est 8: 17 (Greek), both late documents. In New Testament times the duty of circumcision took precedence of the law of the sabbath (Jn 7: 22, 23).

This custom aroused the scorn of the pagans (Martial, Persius, Horace) and had to contend with the invasion of Greek conventions, which did not accept it. Antiochus Epiphanes forbade it in Palestine, and inflicted cruel punishment on those who resisted his orders (1 M 1: 60-61; 2 M 6: 10). Indeed, Jews who followed Hellenistic fashions tried to hide the marks of their circumcision (1 M 1: 15; cf. 1 Cor 7: 18).

5. Education

During his early years a child was left to the care of his mother or nurse, even after he had been weaned (2 S 4: 4) and was learning to walk (Os 11: 3). The little Israelite spent most of his time playing in the streets or squares with boys and girls of his own age (Jr 6: 11; 9: 20; Za 8: 5; Mt 11: 16). They sang and danced, or played with little clay models, samples of which have been found in excavations; little girls, it would seem, have always played with dolls.

It was the mother who gave her children the first rudiments of education, especially of their moral formation (Pr 1: 8; 6: 20). She might continue to advise her children even in adolescence (cf. Pr 31: 1), but as the boys grew up to manhood, they were usually entrusted to their father. One of his most sacred duties was to teach his son the truths of religion (Ex 10: 2; 12: 26; 13: 8; Dt 4: 9; 6: 7, 20f.; 32: 7, 46) and to give him a general education (Pr 1: 8; 6: 20, and especially Si 30: 1-13). The whip and the rod played their part in this training (Pr 13: 24; 22: 15; 29: 15, 17; cf. Dt 8: 5; 2 S 7: 14; Pr 3: 12; Si 30: 1).

Writing was in common use at an early date. Besides the professional scribes, like those employed at the court for administration (2 S 8: 17; 20: 25; 1 K 4: 3, etc.), and private secretaries like Baruch (Jr 36: 4), members of the ruling class could write, judging by the stories of Jezabel (1 K 21: 8) and of Isaiah (Is 8: 1). But these were not the only ones: a young man of Sukkoth was able to give Gideon, in writing, the names of all the chiefs of his clan (Jg 8: 14), and the commandment of Dt 6: 9; 11: 20 presumed that every head of a family could write.

Most teaching, however, was done by word of mouth. The teacher told his story, gave explanations and asked questions; the pupil repeated the story, and asked or answered questions (Ex 13: 8; Dt 6: 7, 20f.; Ps 78: 3-4, etc.). This method of teaching continued under the Rabbis, and obtains even to-day in Koranic schools.

The content of the instruction was very general. The father handed on to his son the national traditions (which were also religious traditions), and the divine commands given to their forefathers (Ex 10: 2 and the other texts just quoted). Children were also taught literary passages, such as David's lament over Saul and Jonathan (2 S 1: 18), which was still being recited in the days of the Maccabees (1 M 9: 20-21).

The father also gave his son a professional education; in practice, trades were usually hereditary, and the crafts were handed down in the family workshop. A Rabbi was to say: 'He who does not teach his son a useful trade is bringing him up to be a thief.'

This educational rôle of the father explains why the priests, whose mission was to teach, are called 'father' (Jg 17: 10; 18: 19). It also explains how Joseph, who became the pharaoh's counsellor, was like a 'father' to him (Gn 45: 8), and how Aman, vizier to Assuerus, could be called his 'second father' (Est 3: 13 or 8: 12). Similarly, the relationship between teacher and pupil was expressed by the words 'father' and 'son' (2 K 2: 12, compared with 2 K 2: 3; cf. the frequent use of 'my son', 'my sons' and 'Hear, my son' in the book of Proverbs).

Apart from the education he received at home, the young Israelite had ample opportunity for learning. In the caravans and by the wells, he heard men sing of the 'justices of Yahweh' (Jg 5: 10-11). At the village gates he would listen to the palavers of the elders, to the settlement of lawsuits, and to the arrangement of commercial transactions. The child accompanied his parents to the sanctuaries (1 S 1: 4, 21) or to the temple at Jerusalem (cf. Lk 2: 41f.), where he would hear the chanting of the Psalms and the recounting of those historical episodes which were connected with each great festival. As in the Middle Ages, the liturgy was a powerful medium of religious instruction.

Certain men had a special mission to instruct the people. First of all came the priests, guardians and teachers of the Law, the *Tôrah*, which by etymology means 'directive', 'instruction'. Some didactic teaching was probably given at an early date in the centres of worship: the boy Samuel was entrusted to Eli the priest (1 S 2: 21, 26), and Joas was instructed by the priest Yehoyada (2 K 12: 3).

The prophets, too, had a mission to instruct the people; this was at least as much a part of their task as foretelling the future. And prophetic inspiration lent to their preaching the authority of a word of God. It is certain that under the monarchy the prophets were the religious and moral teachers of the people; and, we may add, the best of all their teachers, if not always the most heeded. Along with them 'wise men' taught men how to live a good life; their influence increased after the Exile, when wise men and scribes became identical terms, and moral education was combined with study of the Law. Their teaching was handed down in the gatherings of the elders (Si 6: 34), in the conversation at festive meals (Si 9: 16), in the open air, at the city gates, in the streets and at the cross-roads (Pr 1: 20f.; 8: 2 f.) They expressed their teachings in epigrams, which were preserved in oral tradition and later preserved in written collections (Pr 10: 1; 22: 17; 25: 1, etc.).

Apart from this teaching, given, as it were, when occasion offered, and from which anyone could benefit, the prophets and teachers of wisdom gathered pupils around them to whom they gave a more continuous training (Pr 8: 32; Is 8: 16; 50: 4). It is probable, too, that schools for scribes existed at an early date in the two capitals, where the civil servants were trained; similar training-schools existed in Mesopotamia, in Egypt and among the Hittites. There is, however, no proof of an organized system of schools until a late period. The word 'school' (*bêth-midrash*) occurs for the first time in the Hebrew text of Si 51: 23. According to a Jewish tradition, it was only in A.D. 63 that the high priest Joshua ben Gimla decreed that every town and village should have a school which all children would have to attend from the age of six or seven. This tradition is contested by some scholars who date the institution of public instruction from the time of John Hyrcanus, about 130 B.C.

The preceding paragraphs concern only the education of boys. Girls remained under the control of their mothers, who taught them what they needed to know for their duty as wives and housekeepers.

6. *Adoption*

Adoption is an act by which a man or woman acknowledges a person of different blood as his or her son or daughter, with the legal rights and duties of a true child. Adoption was practised in Mesopotamia from a very early time. Its object was to secure for barren couples the benefit of children, and thus to provide them with help and support in their old age. In the middle of the second millennium B.C., at Nuzu, in the region of Kirkuk, contracts of fictitious adoption were used to cover all manner of economic transactions.

The Old Testament laws contain no directives about adoption. The historical books record no example of adoption in the strict sense, *i.e.* the legal acknowledgement of one born outside the family as having the rights of a child born into the family. Thus we cannot regard as real adoptions the instances of Moses, who was treated as a son by Pharaoh's daughter (Ex 2: 10), or of Genubath, who was brought up among Pharaoh's children (1 K 11: 20), or of Esther, to whom Mardochai gave a home when she had no father or mother (Est 2: 7, 15). Moreover, these three examples all occur on foreign soil. The story of Abraham's planning to leave his goods to his servant because he had no child (Gn 15: 3) has been explained as the adoption of a slave, in conformity with a custom attested by the Nuzu texts; if this explanation is correct, it reveals the influences of a Mesopotamian custom in the patriarchal age, but it does not prove that the custom took root in Israel, and the Bible itself does not represent the act as an adoption.

Some other examples are clearer. Rachel gives Jacob her servant Bilhah, so that Bilhah may bear a child on her knees, and that Rachel may thus have a child, through Bilhah: Bilhah's two children are, in fact, named by Rachel and regarded as her sons (Gn 30: 3-8). Jacob considers Joseph's two sons, Ephraim and Manasseh, as his own (Gn 48: 5) and puts them 'between his knees' (Gn 48: 12). We are told, too, that the children of Makir, Manasseh's son, 'were born on Joseph's knees' (Gn 50: 23). Finally, Naomi takes Ruth's newborn child to her breast and says: 'A son is born to Naomi' (Rt 4: 16-17). We are almost bound to see in all these cases one and the same rite expressing adoption: the child was laid on or between the knees of the man or woman who adopted it. But these are not adoptions in the full sense, for they all take place within the family and in the direct line, the child being 'adopted' by its stepmother (cf. without any mention of the rite Gn 16: 2; 30: 1-13), its grandfather or its grandmother. The legal consequences of such an adoption are therefore not far-reaching.[1]

We might see a reflection of customs of adoption in those passages where the relations between Yahweh and Israel are expressed as those of father and son (Ex 4: 22; Dt 32: 6; Is 63: 16; 64: 7; Jr 3: 19; 31: 9; Os 11: 1, etc.), but these are hardly more than metaphors, in which the idea of divine fatherhood

1. But cf. p. 53.

fades into background before that of God as Master and Creator. Only in the New Testament will it be brought into full relief. More significant is Nathan's prophecy about the king of David's line: 'I shall be a father to him, and he shall be a son to me' (2 S 7: 14, with the other passages dependent on it, 1 Ch 17: 13; 22: 10; 28: 6; Ps 89: 27). Only one text is explicit, that of Ps 2: 7, 'Thou art my son; to-day I have begotten thee', which certainly seems to be using a formula of adoption.[1]

We may conclude that the notion of adoption, in the juridical sense, was known in Old Testament times, but had little influence on daily life; it was unknown in later Jewish law.

1. Cf. pp. 112-113.

CHAPTER FIVE

SUCCESSION AND INHERITANCE

IN ancient Israel there was no such thing as a written will or testament. But before he died, a father used to 'set his house in order' (2 S 17: 23; 2 K 20: 1; Is 38: 1), *i.e.* he gave verbal instructions about the distribution of his property (cf. Dt 21: 16; Si 14: 13; 33: 24). However, he had to conform to law and custom. Only two legislative texts refer to inheritance (Dt 21: 15-17 and Nb 27: 1-11, taken in conjunction with Nb 38: 6-9), and they concern particular cases. They need to be supplemented by incidental information from the biblical narratives, and these narratives are not always easy to interpret.

The fundamental rule is that sons alone have a right to the inheritance. Among the sons, the eldest had a privileged position[1] and received a double share of his father's goods (Dt 21: 17; cf. 2 K 2: 9, metaphorically). The same provision is made in the Assyrian laws, at Nuzu and at Mari. The law safeguards the right of the eldest by forbidding the father to show favour to the son of the wife he prefers at the expense of the eldest son (Dt 21: 15-17). (This law retrospectively condemns Abraham for expelling Ishmael [Gn 21: 10f.] and David for preferring Solomon to Adonias [1 K 1. 1/, cf. 2: 13].) Probably only the movable chattels were shared, and the house, with the ancestral holdings, would be allotted to the eldest, or at least not divided. This would keep the family property intact, and might explain the text of Dt 25: 5 about brothers who 'live together'.

In the early days of Israel, and, indeed, as a general rule in Mesopotamian law-codes, the sons of concubines who were slaves had no share in the inheritance, unless their father had given them equal rank with the sons of free-born wives, by legal adoption. Sarah did not want Ishmael, the son of the slave-woman, to share the inheritance with her son Isaac (Gn 21: 10), and in the event Abraham left his goods to Isaac, and only made presents to the sons of his concubines (Gn 25: 5-6). But Sarah pretended she had forgotten her promise that Hagar's children should be recognized as her own (Gn 16: 2): Ishmael therefore, had a right to the inheritance, and Abraham was downhearted at sending him away (Gn 21: 11). The sons of the slave-women Bilhah and Zilpah were given equal rank with those of Rachel and Leah (Gn 49: 1-28) and had an equal share with them in the land of Canaan, which

---

1. On the rights of the eldest son, see pp. 41-42.

was Jacob's inheritance. But the reason is that they had been adopted by Rachel or by Leah (Gn 30: 3-13). Later usage seems to have been less strict. The case of Jephthah, excluded from his father's inheritance by his half-brothers, is sometimes quoted (Jg 11: 2), but Jephthah was an illegitimate son, born of a prostitute and not of a concubine (Jg 11: 1).

Daughters did not inherit, except when there were no male heirs. This precedent was established at the instance of the daughters of Selophehad (Nb 27: 1-8), but with the proviso that they were to find husbands from a clan of their father's tribe, and so prevent the family property from passing to another tribe (Nb 36: 1-9). Under this law the daughters of Eleazar married their cousins (1 Ch 23: 22), and this, too, is probably that 'law of Moses' to which Tb 7: 11 refers.

There is one notable exception. Job's three daughters received a share of the inheritance along with their seven brothers (Jb 42: 13-15). This may represent later custom, for the book of Job is post-Exilic, or perhaps it was then imagined that in patriarchal times, in which the story is set, the father had absolute freedom in the distribution of his property. Indeed, perhaps the purpose was to show the enormous wealth of Job and the ideal happiness of a family in which all the children were treated equally.

If a man died without issue, the property passed to his male kinsmen on his father's side, in the following order: his brothers, his father's brothers, his nearest relative in the clan (Nb 27: 9-11). His widow had no right to the inheritance. By contrast, Babylonian law and the usage of Nuzu both laid down that a widow did have a share in the inheritance, or at least that she was to keep what she had contributed to the marriage and the gifts she had received from her husband. The contracts of Elephantine allow a childless widow to inherit from her husband. In Israel, a childless widow either returned to her father (Gn 38: 11; Lv 22: 13; Rt 1: 8), or remained a member of her husband's family by a levirate marriage.[1] If a widow had grown-up children, they provided for her support. If the children were still young, she may have managed the property left to them as their trustee (this would explain 2 K 8: 3-6). The money owned by Mikayehu's mother (Jg 17: 1-4) was perhaps her own personal property, distinct from the legacy left by her husband. The case of Naomi, offering for sale a piece of land which had been the property of her deceased husband (Rt 4: 3, 9) is difficult to explain, but we should at least notice that in Rt 4: 9 the land is regarded as the joint property of her two sons, Kilyon and Mahlon. These two were also dead, and Naomi appears to be acting as the guardian of their rights. Judith had received from her husband quite a fortune, including both movable and immovable goods (Jdt 8: 7), and she disposed of it quite freely before her death (Jdt 16: 24); this story, however, dates from an age when custom had grown much more liberal, and when the way was already being prepared for

1. Cf. pp. 37-38 and 40.

that recognition of a widow's rights which was eventually sanctioned by Jewish law.

The episode of Naboth (1 K 21: 15) has led some writers to conclude that the property of men condemned to death reverted to the king; but it may simply be an instance of arbitrary confiscation. Some late passages show that the father could make advances of the inheritance long before his death (Tb 8: 21; Si 33: 20-24; cf. Lk 15: 12).

CHAPTER SIX

DEATH AND FUNERAL RITES

THE distinction between soul and body is something foreign to the Hebrew mentality, and death, therefore, is not regarded as the separation of these two elements. A live man is a living 'soul' (*nephesh*), and a dead man is a dead 'soul', a dead '*nephesh*' (Nb 6: 6; Lv 21: 11; cf. Nb 19: 13). Death is not annihilation. So long as the body exists and the bones at least remain, the soul exists, like a shade, in a condition of extreme weakness, in the subterranean abode of Sheol (Jb 26: 5-6; Is 14: 9-10; Ez 32: 17-32).

These ideas account for the care bestowed on the corpse and the importance of honourable burial, for the soul continued to feel what was done to the body. Hence to be left unburied, a prey to the birds and the wild beasts, was the worst of all curses (1 K 14: 11; Jr 16: 4; 22: 19; Ez 29: 5). Yet the corpse which was doomed to corruption, and the tomb which contained it, were both considered unclean, and conveyed uncleanness to those who touched them (Lv 21: 1-4; 22: 4; Nb 19: 11-16; Ag 2: 13; cf. Ez 43: 7).

1. *Treatment of the corpse*

In Gn 46: 4 there is an allusion to the custom of closing the eyes of the dead; this almost universal custom is perhaps simply explained by the resemblance of death to sleep. The nearest relatives embraced the body (Gn 50: 1). It is probable that it was then prepared for burial, but we have no information earlier than the New Testament (Mt 27: 59 and parallels; Jn 11: 44; 19: 39-40). The pins and other ornaments found in excavated tombs show that the dead were buried fully clothed. Samuel came up from Sheol with his cloak around him (1 S 28: 14), and Ez 32: 27 tells us that soldiers were laid to rest in their armour, with their swords under their heads and their shields under their bodies.

Embalming was never practised in Israel: the two examples known, those of Jacob and Joseph, are explicitly ascribed to Egyptian custom (Gn 50: 2-3). The corpse was not placed in a coffin (cf. 2 K 13: 21), but carried on a bier (2 S 3: 31; cf. Lk 7: 14). Joseph's body was placed in a coffin; but it is the only example recorded, and this also is to be explained by Egyptian custom (Gn 50: 26).

2. *Burial*

We do not know the interval which elapsed between death and burial. The seventy days' mourning before the transfer of Jacob's body is exceptional, for the Egyptians accorded the Patriarch a royal funeral. The precept of Dt 21: 22–23 concerns only the bodies of those who had been executed: they had to be removed before nightfall. The delay was probably very short, as it still is in the East; it is probable that, as a general rule, burial took place on the day of death.

There is no evidence that corpses were cremated in Palestine, except in days long before the coming of the Israelites, or among groups of foreigners; the Israelites never practised it. On the contrary, to burn a body was an outrage, inflicted only on notorious criminals (Gn 38: 24; Lv 20: 14; 21: 9), or upon enemies a man wanted to annihilate for ever (Am 2: 1). There remains one difficult instance: the people of Yabesh in Gilead burnt the bodies of Saul and his sons before burying their bones (1 S 31: 12); it seems to have been a departure from traditional usage, and the parallel passage in 1 Ch 10: 12 omits this point. In addition we must not confuse with cremation the references given in Jr 34: 5; 2 Ch 16: 14; 21: 19, which speak of a fire being lit at the death of a king who died in peace with God: this is certainly not cremation, but incense and perfumes were burned near the body.

The normal type of Israelite tomb is a burial chamber dug out of soft rock, or making use of a natural cave. The entry is a narrow passage opening on one of the sides: on the other three sides are ledges on which the bodies were laid. There is sometimes a cavity in which the bones of skeletons were placed, to make way for new burials. These tombs are, in fact, common tombs, used by a family or clan over a considerable period. There does not seem to have been any fixed rule about the position of the bodies. Some personal belongings and pottery were put beside the corpse. These funeral offerings, intended for the use of the dead, are not so numerous or rich as in the Canaanite period, and, at the end of the Israelite period, are confined to a few vases or lamps. Men's ideas on the fate of the dead had progressed, and their offerings had only symbolic value.

In the Hellenistic period a new type of tomb appears; instead of ledges, narrow niches are cut perpendicularly into the wall, and the corpses placed inside. For at least two hundred years, from 100 B.C. to A.D. 100, the bones were laid to rest in coffers of soft limestone: great numbers of these ossuaries have been discovered in the neighbourhood of Jerusalem. In Palestine, other methods of burial, such as shafts opened in the rock, stone sarcophagi and wooden or leaden coffins, are later than Old Testament times.

Not every family could afford the expense of owning and maintaining such tombs. The poor were simply laid to rest in the ground, and at Jerusalem, in the Kedron valley, there was a 'tomb of the sons of the people', a common trench, where the bodies of 'stateless persons' and condemned criminals were thrown (Jr 26: 23; cf. 2 K 23: 6). The rich, on the other hand, provided themselves during life with burial-places worthy of their rank (Is 22: 16; cf. Jb 3: 14), and the remains of well-tended tombs, belonging to important persons in Jerusalem, can still be seen at Shiloah. The necropolis of the kings of Judah, where David and his successors until Achaz were buried, lay inside the ramparts, in the old city of David (1 K 2: 10; 11: 43; 14: 31, down to 2 K 16: 20, but cf. 2 Ch. 28: 27). Excavations have brought to light two galleries in the rock, which may be the remains of these tombs; they have been opened several times, and were later wrecked by quarrying.

The site of a tomb might be marked by a pillar: thus, Jacob set up a stele over Rachel's tomb (Gn 35: 20), and Absalom, who had no son 'to make his name remembered', had a stele prepared for himself near Jerusalem (2 S 18: 18). Some stelae were definitely funeral monuments, and stelae were also erected on the high places, the bamôth; this raises the question whether a cult of the dead was not practised on the high places. This suggestion can claim the support of a few biblical texts which have been corrupted or badly understood. Is 53: 9 should read, according to the Qumran manuscript: 'They set his grave among the wicked, and his bamah (here: the place of his tomb) with the rich (or: with evil-doers)'; Jb 27: 15, with a very simple change of vowels, reads: 'Their survivors will be buried in bamôth, and their widows will not weep for them'; Ez 43: 7 needs no correction: 'Never again will they defile my holy name with their prostitutions, and with the funeral stelae (pégér) of their kings in their bamôth.' But the construction of a monument over the tomb or in connection with it is a late practice. The first written mention of it occurs in connection with the tomb of the Maccabees at Modin (1 M 13: 27, 30). The tombs in the Kedron valley which have monuments over them (the so-called tombs of Absalom, Josaphat, St James and Zacharias) all date from the end of the Greek or the beginning of the Roman period, according to the experts.

Except for the kings of Judah, there is no evidence that the dead were buried inside the towns. The tombs were scattered over the surrounding slopes, or grouped in places where the nature of the soil was favourable. The tomb was family property, whether it stood on land belonging to the family (Jos 24: 30, 32; 1 S 25: 1; 1 K 2: 34), or in a piece of land bought as a burying place (Gn 23). It was thus that family tombs were established: the cave of Macpelah, which Abraham bought for the burial of Sarah (Gn 23) became in later days the tomb of Abraham himself (Gn 25: 9-10), of Isaac and Rebecca, of Jacob and Leah (Gn 49: 29-32; 50: 13). It was normal for a man to be buried 'in the tomb of his father' (Jg 8: 32; 16: 31; 2 S 2: 32; 17: 23); they hoped for it during life (2 S 19: 38), and David made this gesture as a last tribute to the bones of Saul and his descendants (2 S 21: 12-14). Conversely, to be excluded from the family tomb was a punishment from God

(1 K 13: 21-22). The expressions 'to sleep with one's fathers' and 'to be re-united with one's own', which record the deaths of great Old Testament figures, patriarchs and kings of Israel or Judah, perhaps referred originally to this custom of a family tomb; but the original meaning later took on a deeper sense, and the words became a solemn formula signifying death, and at the same time emphasizing that the ties of blood reached beyond the grave.

3. *Mourning rites*

The deceased person's relatives, and those present at the death and funeral, went through a certain ritual, many items of which were customary on occasions of great sorrow, in public calamities and in seasons of penance.

At news of the death, the first action was to tear one's garments (Gn 37: 34; 2 S 1: 11; 3: 31; 13: 31; Jb 1: 20). Then 'sackcloth' was put on (Gn 37: 34; 2 S 3: 31); it was a coarse material, usually worn next to the skin, around the waist and below the breast (cf. 2 K 6: 30; 2 M 3: 19). (The 'nakedness' of Mi 1: 8 means this rudimentary garment, in spite of the parallel of Is 20: 2-4.) The mourners took off their shoes (2 S 15: 30; Ez 24: 17, 23; Mi 1: 8) and headdress (Ez 24: 17, 23). Yet, on the other hand, a man covered his beard (Ez 24: 17, 23) or veiled his face (2 S 19: 5; cf 15· 30). It is probable that to put one's hands on one's head was a regular sign of mourning: the Bible speaks of this gesture as an expression of sorrow or shame (2 S 13: 19; Jr 2: 37), and it is the pose of weeping women in certain Egyptian bas-reliefs and on the sarcophagus of Ahiram, king of Byblos.

The mourner would put earth on his head (Jos 7: 6; 1 S 4: 12; Ne 9: 1; 2 M 10: 25; 14: 15; Jb 2: 12; Ez 27: 30); he would roll his head (Jb 16: 15), or even his whole body (Mi 1: 10) in the dust, and lie or sit among a heap of ashes (Est 4: 3; Is 58: 5; Jr 6: 26; Ez 27: 30).

Mourners would also shave their hair and beard, at least partly, and make cuts on their bodies (Jb 1: 20; Is 22: 12; Jr 16: 6; 41: 5; 47: 5; 48: 37; Ez 7: 18; Am 8: 10). These rites, however, are condemned by Lv 19: 27-28; cf. 21: 5, and by Dt 14: 1, for the taint of heathenism they preserve. Lastly, mourners refrained from washing and using perfumes (2 S 12: 20; 14: 2; Jdt 10: 3).

4. *Rites concerning food*

David kept a day's fast for Saul and Jonathan (2 S 1: 12) and also for Abner (2 S 3: 35), and people were surprised that he did not fast for his dead child (2 S 12: 20-21). After burying the remains of Saul and his sons, the inhabit-ants of Yabesh fasted for seven days (1 S 31: 13), the usual period of strict mourning (Gn 50: 10; Jdt 16: 24; Si 22: 12; but cf. 38: 17). The fact that Judith continued to fast, except on feast days, throughout her widowhood, is noted as something exceptional (Jdt 8: 5-6).

Neighbours or friends brought mourning bread and the 'cup of consolation' to the relatives of the deceased (Jr 16: 7; Ez 24: 17, 22; cf. Os 9: 4), for the uncleanness which was attached to the house of the dead prevented food from being prepared there.

On the other hand, some texts mention, though in mockery, the making of food-offerings to the dead person (Ba 6: 26), which might be placed on his tomb (Si 30: 18 [Greek: in Hebrew 'before an idol']). Excavations show that there was a time when the Israelites followed the Canaanite custom of depositing food in the tomb. In Tb 4: 17 the elder Tobias counsels his son to be lavish with bread and wine on the tomb of the just, but this precept is taken from the pagan book entitled *The Wisdom of Ahiqar*, and, in the immediate context of the book of Tobias, could be interpreted of alms given on the occasion of a funeral . Whatever be the true interpretation of this text, such and similar customs continued for a long time, and still do continue in parts of the Christian world; they indicate nothing more than a belief in survival after death and a feeling of affection towards the dead. They are not acts of worship directed towards the dead, for that attitude never existed in Israel. Prayer and sacrifice of expiation for the dead (both incompatible with a cult of the dead) appear at the very end of the Old Testament, in 2 M 12: 38-46.

Perhaps we should explain the very awkward text of Dt 26: 14 by reference to the same customs. The Israelite there declares that he has taken nothing as mourning food, nor made any offering to the dead, out of the tithe, which is holy and reserved to the poor (v. 13); either use would have made the entire tithe unclean.

5. The funeral lamentations

The chief funeral ceremony was the lamentation for the dead. In its simplest form it was a sharp, repeated cry, compared in Mi 1: 8 to the call of the jackal or the ostrich. They cried, 'Alas, alas!' (Am 5: 16), 'Alas, my brother!' or, 'Alas, my sister!' (1 K 13: 30), or, if it were a member of the royal family, 'Alas, Lord! Alas, Majesty!' (Jr 22: 18; 34: 5). A father would call on his son by name (2 S 19: 1, 5). For the death of an only son, the lamentation was particularly heart-rending (Jr 6: 26; Am 8: 10; Za 12: 10). These cries were uttered by the men and women in separate groups (Za 12: 11-14); it was the duty of close relations (Gn 23: 2; 50: 10; 2 S 11: 26), though everyone present joined in (1 S 25: 1; 28: 3; 2 S 1: 11-12; 3: 31, etc., where to 'make mourning' means 'to perform the lamentation').

These exclamations of sorrow could be developed into a lament, a *qînah*, composed in a special rhythm (2 S 1: 17; Am 8: 10). The oldest and finest is that sung by David for the death of Saul and Jonathan (2 S 1: 19-27). David wrote one for Abner, too (2 S 3: 33-34). But these laments were usually composed and sung by professionals, men or women (2 Ch 35: 25; Am 5: 16), especially women (Jr 9: 16f.; cf. Ez 32: 16). It was a trade or profession which they taught their daughters (Jr 9: 19). There were fixed forms, and a stock number of themes, which the wailers then applied to the individual. Thus the lament over Judas Maccabee, the beginning of which is quoted in 1 M 9: 21, repeats the words of the lament over Saul and Jonathan. The mourners praised the qualities of the dead man and bewailed his fate, but it is a most striking fact that the examples preserved in the Bible never have a religious content. In the elegy on Saul and Jonathan, for example, there is deep human emotion, but not a word of religious feeling.

In the Prophets we find imitations of these funeral hymns, which they use to depict the misfortunes of Israel, of its kings and of its enemies (Jr 9: 9-11, 16-21; Ez 19: 1-14; 26: 17-18; 27: 2-9, 25-36; 28: 12-19; 32: 2-8; Am 5: 1-2). The best example of all is the book of *Lamentations*.

6. *Interpretation of these rites*

These funeral rites have sometimes been explained as evidence for a cult of the dead. Sometimes the argument is that the deceased person was feared, and that the living therefore wanted to protect themselves from him, or to secure his goodwill; at other times, it is argued that the living attributed a kind of divinity to the dead. There is no foundation for either opinion in the Old Testament.

At the other extreme, it has been held that these rites were merely the expression of sorrow at the loss of a dear one. It is true that many of these rites were used in times of great sorrow and national disaster; they were not, then, restricted to funeral services. But to say that the rites are merely the expression of sorrow is not sufficient, for some of them (wearing sackcloth, for example, or fasting) are found as penitential rites, and can therefore have a religious meaning. The self-mutilation and shaving of the head which the Law condemned (Lv 19: 27-28; Dt 14: 1) certainly had a religious signifi- cance, even though we cannot now define it. The food-offerings express, at the very least, belief in a life beyond the grave. Finally, these ceremonies were regarded as a duty which had to be paid to the dead, as an act of piety which was their due (1 S 31: 12; 2 S 21: 13-14; Tb 1: 17-19; Si 7: 33; 22: 11- 12). For children, these rites formed part of that duty to their parents enjoined by the Decalogue. We conclude that the dead were honoured in a religious spirit, but that no cult was paid to them.

PART II

CIVIL INSTITUTIONS

CHAPTER ONE

POPULATION

IT would help to a better understanding of the institutions of Israel, if we could determine the size of its population. A demographic survey is essential for any sociological research, but, as usually happens when ancient civilizations are the subject, the lack of accurate statistics makes the problem complex.

There is, of course, some numerical information in the Bible, but it is not very helpful. According to Ex 12: 37-38, 600,000 foot-soldiers came out of Egypt, besides their families and a mixed multitude who went with them. Before the departure from Sinai (Nb 1: 20-46), a detailed count of the tribes gives 603,550 men over twenty years of age (cf. Ex 38: 26); the Levites are counted separately, and there are 22,000 over a month old (Nb 3: 39), and 8,580 between the ages of thirty and fifty years (Nb 4: 48). In the plains of Moab (Nb 26: 5-51), the total strength of the tribes is 601,730 men over twenty, and there are 23,000 Levites over a month old (Nb 26: 62). There is no great discrepancy between these various figures, but they presuppose a total population of several millions leaving Egypt and living in the desert, which is impossible. They are merely the expression of the way in which men of a much later age imagined the wonderful increase of the people, and the relative importance of the original tribes. In particular, Judah is the strongest and Simeon the smallest.

Another census is recorded, for the time of David (2 S 24: 1-9). This is a record of the kingdom at its widest extent, when it included Transjordan and stretched as far as Tyre and Sidon and the Orontes. It lists 800,000 men liable for military service in Israel, and 500,000 in Judah. In the parallel passage (1 Ch 21: 1-6) the Chronicler has put the figure for Israel even higher, though he excludes non-Israelite territories. The lower total, in 2 S, is still far too high: 1,300,000 men of military age would imply at least five million inhabitants, which, for Palestine, would mean nearly twice as many people to the square mile as in the most thickly populated countries of modern Europe. Moreover, to interpret these figures (or those of Numbers) as including the women and children is to go against the explicit statements of the text. We must simply acknowledge that these figures are artificial.

More reliable evidence is found in 2 K 15: 19-20. In 738 B.C. Tiglath-Pileser III imposed on Israel a tribute of a thousand talents of silver; in order to pay it, Menahem levied a tax of fifty shekels each from all the *gibbôrê ḥaïl* of his kingdom. If we reckon three thousand shekels to the talent,[1] this means that there were in Israel, at that time, sixty thousand heads of families who enjoyed a certain prosperity.[2] This would give us, with their wives and children, between three and four hundred thousand souls. To them must be added the lower classes, the artisans and the poor (their number is uncertain, but they were fewer than the *gibbôrê ḥaïl*), foreigners and slaves (also uncertain, but fewer still). The grand total, then, would not amount to 800,000 inhabitants for the whole kingdom of Israel, and would scarcely pass the million mark even with the addition of Judah, for the latter was only one-third as large as Israel, and much of it was more sparsely populated.

This estimate of the population of Judah may be confirmed by a non-biblical document from approximately the same date. The Annals of Sennacherib record that in the campaign of 701 against Ezechias, forty-six towns and innumerable villages were captured, and that 200,150 men, women and children were taken from them as prisoners of war. If this referred not to a deportation of captives, but to a census of the defeated enemy, the number would give us the total population of Judah except for Jerusalem, which was not captured. Unfortunately the text, as in parallel passages of the Annals, is clearly referring to captives carried off as prizes by the victors, and the number is then too high. The inscription is probably an error for 2,150.

The 'towns' of the Bible were not large. It is astonishing to see from excavations just how small they were. Most of them could easily be fitted into Trafalgar Square, and some would scarcely fill the courtyard of the National Gallery. The Annals of Tiglath-Pileser III give a list of the towns in Galilee conquered in 732; the number of captives varies between 400 and 650—and this king used to deport entire populations. They were, then, villages like those of to-day, and no bigger. Certain centres were larger, of course. According to the estimate of its excavator, Tell Beit-Mirsim, the ancient Debir, contained two or three thousand inhabitants during the time of its greatest prosperity, and it was a relatively important city.

For Samaria and Jerusalem other sources of information are available. Sargon II says that he carried off 27,290 persons from Samaria. This deportation affected mainly the capital, and was wholesale, but it must have included those who had taken refuge there during the siege. The archaeologists who have excavated it also assert that the town must have contained about thirty thousand inhabitants.

For Jerusalem, the figures of Nabuchodonosor's deportations are difficult; they are difficult to establish, and difficult to interpret, for the texts have preserved varying traditions. According to 2 K 24: 14, ten thousand men of rank and station, with all the blacksmiths and locksmiths, were exiled in 597, but

1. Cf. p. 204.
2. On the *gibbôrê ḥaïl* cf. p. 70.

the doublet in 2 K 24: 16 reckons only seven thousand persons of quality and a thousand blacksmiths and locksmiths. Finally, according to Jr 52: 28-30, Nabuchodonosor deported 3,023 'Judeans' in 597 B.C., 832 citizens of Jerusalem in 587, and 745 'Judeans' in 583, making 4,600 in all. This last list, which is independent, no doubt concerns special classes of captives. The figures given in 2 K 24: 14 and 16 should not be added together, and are roughly equal: about ten thousand were deported. These represent only part of the population, but, on the other hand, they may include outsiders who had merely taken refuge inside the city walls. This makes all calculation precarious. Nor can we rely on 2 M 5: 14, according to which Antiochus Epiphanes put to death 40,000 in Jerusalem and sold as many again as slaves. The figures of the population of Jerusalem given by the Pseudo-Hecataeus and Josephus are still more exaggerated. At a reasonable estimate, in our Lord's time the city had about twenty-five or thirty thousand inhabitants. A few years ago this was just the population of the Old City within the walls, and in roughly the same space. The population cannot have been much bigger in Old Testament times.

The population of the country must have varied from time to time. It is certain that the territorial conquests and the assimilation of Canaanite enclaves which took place under David, and still more the economic prosperity of Solomon's reign, produced a sharp rise in population; this continued during the following two centuries, thanks to the progress of commerce, industry and agriculture. Even so, at the height of this prosperity, in the first half of the eighth century B.C., the total population of Israel and Judah cannot have been much more than one million. By way of comparison, we may note that at the British census of 1931, before the great Zionist immigration, Palestine had 1,014,000 inhabitants. It is questionable whether the country could ever have supported many more people in ancient times, without the assistance of those artificial resources which modern economy provides.

Chapter Two

THE FREE POPULATION: ITS DIVISIONS

1. *Social evolution*

IN a nomad civilization there are simply families. They may be rich or poor, but the tribe is not divided into different social classes. Some tribes are 'nobler' than others, but all Bedouin regard themselves as 'noble' compared with the settled cultivators. Even slaves do not constitute a class apart: they form part of the family. From all that we can discover it was the same with Israel so long as it led a semi-nomad life.

Settlement on the land, however, brought about a profound social transformation. The unit was no longer the tribe but the clan, the *mishpaḥah*, settled in a town which was usually no more than a village. Social life became a life of small towns, and it is relevant to note that the old, and basic, framework of Deuteronomy is largely municipal law: *e.g.* the rules about the cities of refuge (Dt 19), unknown murderers (21: 1-9), rebellious sons (21: 18-21), adultery (22: 13-28), and the levirate (25: 5-10). This organization, based on the clan, survived to some extent under the monarchy,[1] and was still a living force at the return from the Exile (Ne 4: 7; Za 12: 12-14).

The centralization of the monarchy, however, brought about important changes.

The king's officials, civil or military, whether grouped in the two capitals or posted in the provinces as representatives of authority, formed a kind of caste, detached from, and sometimes opposed to, municipal interests. Above all, the play of economic life, business deals and the sale of land, destroyed the equality between families, some of whom became very rich while others sank into poverty. But it would be a mistake to see in ancient Israelite society the contrasts found in other societies, past or present, between 'nobles' and 'plebeians', 'capitalists' and 'proletariat'. In Israel, there never really existed social classes in the modern sense of groups conscious of their particular interests and opposed to one another. It is to avoid such misleading comparisons that we prefer to speak here of 'divisions of the population'. But it is not so easy to define them, owing to the variety and uncertainty of the vocabulary in use.

1. Cf. p. 138.

2. *The men of rank and influence*

In the texts from Deuteronomy quoted above, municipal affairs are in the hands of the *z*ᶜ*qenîm*. Some think this term means all the adult men—those who wore a beard, *zaqan*—gathered in popular assembly. It is much more likely that they are the 'elders' (the corresponding adjective means 'old'), the heads of families, who form a sort of council in every village (1 S 30: 26-31).

In Nb 22: 7 and 14 and in Jg 8: 6 and 16 they appear alternately with the *śarîm*, the 'chiefs'. The same two words appear side by side, as synonyms, in Jg 8: 14, where we learn that there were seventy-seven of them at Sukkoth. The two words appear to be synonyms in Is 3: 14 also. The same word *śarîm* denotes the heads of families, explicitly in Esd 8: 29 and probably in Esd. 8: 24f. In Jb 29: 9 the *śarîm* sit at the gate of the town, like the 'elders' of Pr 31: 23. The two terms are therefore to some extent equivalent.

Śarîm may have this meaning in some other texts too, but it often clashes with another sense. The *śarîm* are sometimes the officers or officials of the king, both in foreign kingdoms (Gn 12: 15; Jr 25: 19; 38: 17f.; Est 1: 3; 2: 18; Esd 7: 28) and in Israel. Often they are military officers, commanders of a unit or of the whole army (1 S 8: 12; 17: 18, 55; 2 S 24: 2, 4; 1 K 9: 22; 2 K 1: 14; 11: 4, etc.). Often too they are civil officials, such as Solomon's ministers (1 K 4: 2), governors (1 K 20: 14; 22: 26; 2 K 23: 8), or officials in general (Jr 24: 8; 26: 10f.; 34: 19, 21, etc.).

In relation to the king, these officers were merely 'servants' (2 K 19: 5; 22: 9, etc.).[1] But among the people they enjoyed a privileged position. The king sometimes gave them lands (1 S 8: 14; 22: 7).

They were specially numerous in the capitals, Samaria and Jerusalem, where they formed a powerful body with which the king had to reckon (Jr 38: 24-25), for they might even plot against their master (2 K 21: 23). They were men of influence, and in many cases are indistinguishable from the heads of the great families, from whose ranks they were often recruited.

In Nb 21: 18 and Pr 8: 16, *śarîm* alternates with *n*ᵈ*dîbîm*, the 'excellent' men. These had a seat of honour in the assemblies (1 S 2: 8; Ps 113: 8); they were rich and powerful (Ps 118: 9; 146: 3; Pr 19: 6).

In Is 34: 12 and Qo 10: 17 the *śarîm* are parallel with the *ḥorîm*, and in Jr 27: 20 *ḥorîm* takes the place of *śarîm* in the corresponding text of 2 K 24: 14. This word, always used in the plural, is quoted alongside *z*ᶜ*qenîm* in 1 K 21: 8, 11, and alongside *gibbôrê ḥail* (see below) in 2 K 24: 14. According to the root and its derivatives in languages related to Hebrew, these are 'free men', 'men of good birth'.

These words are therefore almost synonymous and denote the ruling class of the monarchical period, administrators and heads of influential families—in

1. Cf. p. 120.

short, the men of position. In other texts, they are simply called the 'great', the *g^edolîm* (2 K 10: 6, 11; Jr 5: 5; Jon 3: 7).

After the Exile other names appear, denoting the same group. In Jb 29: 9-10, the *n^egîdîm* are equated with the *sarîm*, and in 1 and 2 Ch the two are in practice equivalent. But the pre-exilic texts use only the singular, *nagîd*, and apply it to the king appointed by Yahweh (1 S 9: 16; 10: 1; 2 S 5: 2; 7: 8; 1 K 14: 7; 16: 2; 2 K 20: 5). On the other hand, we have the *s^eganîm* mentioned with the *horîm* in Ne 2: 16; 4: 8, 13, and with the *sarîm* in Esd 9: 2, and this word is frequently used in the Memoirs of Nehemias for the influential people. One feels that in his vocabulary this word replaces *z^eqenîm*, 'the elders', which he does not use. But in the earlier texts the word means 'governor' and is borrowed from the Babylonian.

These men of influence and position can no doubt be called 'nobles' in a broad sense, but they do not form a nobility in the proper sense of a closed class to which one belongs by birth, which enjoys certain privileges and owns a large part of the land.

Some authors used to regard the *gibbôrê haïl* as a class of landed proprietors, a sort of squirearchy. They relied mainly on 2 K 15: 20, where Menahem taxes the *gibbôrê hail* of his kingdom in order to pay tribute to the Assyrians. But it seems that this term meant originally (and often does mean in the Chronicles) the valiant men, the brave warriors, the gallant knights, like *gibbôrîm* on its own, even if they possess no property of their own (Jos 8: 3; Jg 11: 1).

The term was then applied to those who were bound to armed service and, having to provide their own equipment, enjoyed a certain standard of living. This is the sense which best answers the text of 2 K 15: 20, where there are sixty thousand of them, of 2 K 24: 14, where they are contrasted with the poorest people of the land, and of Rt 2: 1, where Boaz is simply a man of substance, like Saul's father in 1 S 9: 1.

3. The 'people of the land'

The texts often speak of the 'people of the land', *'am ha'ares*, an expression which has been interpreted in several ways. Many believe it means the lower social class, the common people, the plebs as opposed to the aristocracy, or the peasants as opposed to the townsfolk. Others, on the contrary, see them as the representatives of the people in the government, a sort of Parliament or House of Commons. Others, again, regard them as the body of free men, enjoying civic rights in a given territory.

Examination of the texts shows that the last explanation is the only one which can be accepted for the earliest period, but that the meaning of the term gradually changed.

First, let us consider the texts where it refers to non-Israelites. In Gn 23:

12-13, 'the people of the land' means the Hittites, the citizens of Hebron, by contrast with Abraham, who is only a resident stranger there.

In Gn 42: 6 it means the Egyptians, in contrast with the sons of Jacob; in Nb 14: 9 it means the Canaanites who are masters of the land, in contrast with the Israelites (cf. the parallel from Nb 13: 28, 'the people who dwell on the land'). Ex 5: 5 seems to contradict this interpretation, for in the Massoretic text the Pharaoh calls the Hebrews 'the people of the land'. This would justify translating it by 'the common people', but it is very tempting to adopt the Samaritan reading: 'they are more numerous than the people of the land'.

Turning now to Israel, three periods may be discerned in the use of this expression. Before the return from the Exile, it was used principally by 2 K, Jr and Ez. The 'people of the land' are distinguished from, or contrasted with, (a) the king or the prince, 2 K 16: 15; Ez 7: 27; 45: 22; (b) the king and his servants, Jr 37: 2; (c) the chiefs and the priests, Jr 1: 18; 34: 19; 44: 21; (d) the chiefs, the priests and the prophets, Ez 22: 24-29. They are never contrasted with another class of the people.

According to 2 K 24: 14, Nabuchodonosor left 'only the poorest of the people of the land' in Jerusalem, and the qualification inserted indicates that the term itself does not stand for the poorer classes (cf. also Es 22: 29). This emerges also from the texts just quoted, e.g. Jr 1: 18: '. . . against this whole land, against the kings of Judah, their chiefs (*śarîm*) their priests and all the people of the land'.

The law of Lv 4 distinguishes the sin-offerings which have to be offered: v. 3 for the high priest, v. 13 for the whole community of Israel, v. 22 for a chief, v. 27 for anyone of 'the people of the land'. The obligation of punishing certain offences rests upon all the 'people of the land' (Lv 20: 2-4).

The 'people of the land', then, stands for the whole body of citizens. That is why the expression, applied to the kingdom of Judah, is used as an alternative for the 'people of Judah': compare 2 K 14: 21, 'All the people of Judah chose Ozias' with 2 K 23: 30, 'The people of the land chose Joachaz.' In the same way, the 'people of the land' punished the murderers of Amon and proclaimed Josias king, 2 K 21: 24. In 2 K 11: 14, 18, 'all the people of the land' acclaimed Joas and destroyed the temple of Baal: this was a national revolution, directed against Athaliah and her foreign entourage. It is true that v. 20 contrasts the 'people of the land' with the city, that is, with Jerusalem. But the reason for the distinction is that the court resided in Jerusalem, with all the officials and supporters of the regime which had been overthrown. The contrast in v. 20, therefore, implies no more than the distinction between the people of Judah and the inhabitants of Jerusalem in Jr 25: 2. Nowhere does the expression mean a party or a social class.

At the return from the Exile it continued to be used in this general sense (Ag 2: 4; Za 7: 5), and it is found even in Dn 9: 6, where the enumeration of

'our kings, our princes, our fathers, all the people of the land' recalls those of
Jeremiah and Ezechiel. But the meaning changes in Esd and Ne. The term
is used in the plural, 'the peoples of the land' or 'of the lands', Esd 3: 3; 9: 1,
2, 11; 10: 2, 11; Ne 9: 30; 10: 29, 31, 32. Here it denotes the non-Jewish
inhabitants of Palestine, who hinder the work of restoration, hinder the
observance of the sabbath, and with whom mixed marriages are made. The
'peoples of the land' are contrasted with the 'people of Judah' in Esd 4: 4,
and with the 'people of Israel' in Esd 9: 1. It is a complete reversal of the
pre-exilic use, and again the explanation lies in the basic meaning of the
expression: the community of the Return are *not* the 'people of the land'
because they do not enjoy the political status accorded to the Samaritans,
the Ammonites and the Moabites. It is these latter who are the 'people of the
land' or of 'the lands'.

Thus the way was prepared for a third meaning. In the Rabbinical period
the 'people of the land' are all those who are ignorant of the law or do not
practise it.

4. *Rich and poor*

In the early days of the settlement, all the Israelites enjoyed more or less the
same standard of living. Wealth came from the land, and the land had been
shared out between the families, each of whom guarded its property jealously
(cf. once more the story of Naboth in 1 K 21: 1-3). Commerce, and the buying and selling of real estate for profit, were as yet unimportant factors in
economic life. There were, of course, exceptions: Nabal, for instance, was a
rich stock-breeder in the highlands of Judah: he had 3,000 sheep and 1,000
goats and, in order to appease David, his wife Abigail could send 200 loaves,
100 bunches of dried grapes, 200 fig cakes, with skins of wine, bushels of
parched grain and dressed mutton, 1 S 25: 2, 18. Job's wealth was even
greater: 7,000 sheep, 3,000 camels, 500 pair of oxen, 500 she-asses, Jb 1: 3;
but the story portrays Job after the manner of a great sheikh of the patriarchal
age (cf. Abraham in Gn 12: 16; 13: 6; 24: 35). In contrast, the first two kings
of Israel came from only moderately well-to-do families. Saul's father was a
gibbôr ḥail (cf. above), but he sent his son to look for the lost she-asses, 1 S 9:
1f., and Saul ploughed the fields himself (1 S 11: 5). David looked after the
flocks (1 S 16: 11, cf. 17: 20, 28, 34f.), and his father sent him off to his
brothers in the army, with a measure of parched corn, ten loaves and ten
cheeses (1 S 17: 17). According to another tradition, when David was called
into the king's presence, he brought a present of five loaves, a skin of wine
and a kid (1 S 16: 20). All this represents a very modest standard of living,
and we do not hear of any other families in the same circles being any
better off.

Excavations in Israelite towns bear witness to this equality in standards of
living. At Tirsah, the modern Tell el-Farah near Nablus, the houses of the
tenth century B.C. are all of the same size and arrangement. Each represents

the dwelling of a family which lived in the same way as its neighbours. The contrast is striking when we pass to the eighth century houses on the same site: the rich houses are bigger and better built and in a different quarter from that where the poor houses are huddled together.

Between these two centuries, a social revolution had taken place. The monarchical institutions produced, as we saw, a class of officials who drew a profit from their posts and the favours granted them by the king. Others, by hard work or good luck, made vast profits from their lands. Prosperity was the order of the day. In Os 12: 9, Ephraim (Israel) says: 'Yes, I have become rich, I have amassed a fortune', and Is 2: 7 says: 'The land is full of silver and gold, and treasures past counting.' The prophets condemn their contemporaries for their luxury in building (Os 8: 14; Am 3: 15; 5: 11), in entertainment (Is 5: 11-12; Am 6: 4) and in dress (Is 3: 16-24). They condemn the buying up of the land by those 'who add house to house and join field to field till there is no room left' (Is 5: 8). The wealth of the day was in fact badly distributed and often ill-gotten: 'If they covet fields they seize them; if houses, they take them', Mi 2: 2. The rich landlords would speculate and defraud others (Os 12: 8; Am 8: 5; Mi 2: 1f.), the judges took bribes (Is 1: 23; Jr 5: 28; Mi 3: 11; 7: 3), and the creditors knew no pity (Am 2: 6-8; 8:6).

On the other side we have the weak, the small men, the poor, who suffered from these burdens. The prophets took their cause in hand (Is 3: 14-15; 10: 2; 11: 4; Am 4: 1; 5: 12; cf. Ps 82: 3-4), and the law too protected them. In days gone by, there had been the precepts of Ex 22: 24-26; 23: 6, but Deuteronomy reflects the social conditions of its period. It promulgates the duty of almsgiving (Dt 15: 7-11), says that when a debtor is poor, his security must be given back to him before sunset (Dt 24: 12-13, supplementing the law of Ex 22: 25-26), and protects the hired labourer (Dt 24: 14-15).

It was well understood that the poor would always be with them (Dt 15: 11, cf. Mt 26: 11), but there were regulations which aimed at preventing pauperism and restoring a certain equality between Israelites, though it is hard to say how far they were actually put into practice.[1] In every sabbatical year, the produce of the land was left for the destitute (Ex 23: 11), and debts were cancelled (Dt 15: 1), 'so that there may no longer be any poor man among you' (Dt 15: 4). In the Jubilee year a general emancipation was to be proclaimed and every man was to have his ancestral land restored to him (Lv 25: 10, with the commentaries in the rest of the chapter).

The rich were found mostly among the influential people, and many passages in the Prophets condemn the two together. But the poor did not form a separate social class in contrast with them: the poor were individuals, and precisely because they were isolated, they were defenceless.

In themselves, the words 'rich' and 'poor' carry no moral or religious

1. Cf. pp. 173-177.

connotation. But they acquire moral overtones in two opposed lines of thought. On the theory of earthly rewards, wealth is a reward of virtue and poverty is a punishment; this we find in texts like Ps 1: 3; 112: 1-3; Pr 10: 15-16; 15: 6, a line against which Job protests. Another line of thought starts from the more common experience of life and from the facts denounced by the prophets: there are wicked, impious rich men who oppress the poor, but the poor are beloved by God (Dt 10: 18; Pr 22: 22-23), and his Anointed will do them justice (Is 11: 4). Thus the way was prepared for the spiritual transposition of vocabulary which begins in Sophonias: 'Seek Yahweh, all you humble of the earth' (So 2: 3, cf. 3: 12-13). The spirituality of the 'poor' was developed in the second part of Isaias and the post-exilic Psalter, but by then the terms for poverty had lost their sociological associations: neither before nor after the Exile were the poor a religious party or a social class.

5. Resident aliens

Besides the free citizens of Israel who formed the 'people of the land', and travelling foreigners who could count on the customs of hospitality but were not protected by law (Dt 15: 3; 23: 21), part of the population consisted of resident foreigners, the gerîm.

Among the ancient Arab nomads, the jar was the refugee or lone man who came seeking the protection of a tribe other than his own.[1] In the same way the ger is essentially a foreigner who lives more or less permanently in the midst of another community, where he is accepted and enjoys certain rights.

The word may be used of individuals or groups. Abraham was a ger at Hebron (Gn 23: 4), and Moses in Midian (Ex 2: 22; 18: 3). A man of Bethlehem went with his family to settle as a ger in Moab (Rt 1: 1). The Israelites were gerîm in Egypt (Ex 22: 20; 23: 9; Dt 10: 19; 23: 8). The people of Beeroth had taken refuge in Gittayim, where they lived as gerîm (2 S 4: 3).

When the Israelites had settled in Canaan, they considered themselves the legitimate owners of the land, the 'people of the land'; the former inhabitants, unless they were assimilated by marriage or reduced to slavery, became gerîm, and to these were added immigrants. The ancient texts considered an Israelite who went to live among another tribe as a ger: a man of Ephraim was a ger at Gibeah, where the Benjaminites live (Jg 19: 16).

Levites in general were in the same class, because they had no land of their own (Jg 17: 7-9; 19: 1), and the laws for the protection of society class Levites and gerîm together (Dt 12: 12; 14: 29; 26: 12).

From the social point of view these resident aliens were free men, not slaves, but they did not possess full civic rights, and so differed from Israelite citizens. They may be compared with the perioikoi of Sparta, the original inhabitants of the Peloponnese, who retained their freedom and could own

1. Cf. p. 10.

property, but had no political rights. The *gerîm* of Israel, however, were in the beginning less fortunate. Since all landed property was in Israelite hands, the *gerîm* were reduced to hiring out their services (Dt 24: 14), as the Levites did for their own profession (Jg 17: 8-10). As a rule they were poor, and are grouped with the poor, the widows and the orphans, all the 'economically weak' who were recommended to the Israelites' charity. The fallen fruit, the olives left behind on the tree, the leavings of the grapes, the gleanings after the harvest were to be left for them (Lv 19: 10; 23: 22; Dt 24: 19-21, etc., cf. Jr 7: 6; 22: 3; Ez 22: 7; Za 7: 10). Like the rest of the poor, they were under the protection of God (Dt 10: 18; Ps 146: 9; Ml 3: 5). The Israelites were to help them, remembering that they themselves had once been *gerîm* in Egypt (Ex 22: 20; 23: 9; Dt 24: 18, 22), and for the same reason they were charged to love these aliens as themselves (Lv 19: 34; Dt 10: 19).

They were to share in the tithe collected every third year (Dt 14: 29), and in the produce of the Sabbatical year (Lv 25: 6), and the cities of refuge were open to them (Nb 35: 15). In legal actions they were entitled to justice just like the Israelites (Dt 1: 16), but were liable to the same penalties (Lv 20: 2; 24: 16, 22). In everyday life there was no barrier between *gerîm* and Israelites. Some *gerîm* acquired a fortune (Lv 25: 47; cf. Dt 28: 43), and Ezechiel foretold that in the Israel of the future they would share the land with the citizens (Ez 47: 22).

From the religious point of view, though Dt 14: 21 says that a *ger* may eat a dead carcase, Lv 17: 15 forbids this to *gerîm* as well as to Israelites. Otherwise they are subject to the same laws of cleanness (Lv 17: 8-13; 18: 26; Nb 19: 10). They must observe the sabbath (Ex 20: 10; Dt 5: 14), and fast on the day of Atonement (Lv 16: 29). They can offer sacrifices (Lv 17: 8; 22: 18; Nb 15: 15, 16, 29), and they take part in religious festivals (Dt 16: 11, 14). They can even celebrate the Passover with the Israelites, provided that they are circumcised (Ex 12: 48-49; cf. Nb 9: 14).

It is noteworthy that nearly all these passages were written shortly before the Exile: Deuteronomy, Jeremias and the Law of Holiness in Leviticus. Thus it seems that at the end of the monarchy the number of *gerîm* in Judah had increased, and provision had to be made for them. There had probably been an influx of refugees from the former northern kingdom.

The assimilation of these *gerîm*, akin in race and of the same faith, was easy, and must have helped to hasten the assimilation of *gerîm* of foreign birth. This paved the way for the status of proselytes, and it was by this Greek word that the Septuagint translated the Hebrew word *ger*.

Sometimes the term *tôshab* occurs alongside that of *ger* (Gn 23: 4; Lv 25: 23, 25; 1 Ch 29: 15; Ps 39: 13). The *tôshab* appears also with the wage-earning workmen in Ex 12: 45; Lv 22: 10; 25: 40, with the slaves, the workmen and 'all those who dwell with you' in Lv 25: 6. From these texts it seems that the status of the *tôshab* was like that of the *ger*, though not exactly the same. He seems less assimilated, socially and religiously (Ex 12: 45; cf. Lv 22: 10), less firmly rooted in the land and also less independent: he has no house of his own, but is some man's *tôshab* (Lv 22: 10; 25: 6). It is a later word, appearing mostly in texts edited after the Exile.

6. *Wage-earners*

Besides the slaves, who will be the subject of the next chapter, there were paid workers, free men who hired themselves for a definite job, for a certain time, at an agreed wage. Resident or travelling foreigners also hired out their services in this way (Ex 12: 45; Lv 22: 10; Dt 24: 14), as Jacob had done with Laban (Gn 29: 15; 30: 28; 31: 7). As time went on, some families grew poorer and lost their lands, and so an increasing number of Israelites were obliged to work for wages (cf. Dt 24: 14). In early days it was mostly agricultural labourers who were hired in this way. They worked as herdsmen (Am 3: 12), as harvesters or grapepickers (perhaps Rt 2: 3f.; 2 K 4: 18; cf. Mt 20: 1f.). They could be hired by the day, like modern 'day-labourers' (Lv 19: 13; Dt 24: 15; cf. Mt 20: 8), or by the year (Lv 25: 50, 53; Is 16: 14; 21: 16; Si 37: 11).

The Old Testament gives no direct information on the amount of their wages. In Mesopotamia, workmen were paid either in money or in kind. According to the Code of Hammurabi they were paid one shekel of silver a month during the season of hard work, and rather less for the rest of the year; but some contracts fixed much smaller sums. The same code presumes that the yearly wage will amount to ten shekels or thereabouts, and perhaps this may explain Jg 17: 10 and the difficult text of Dt 15: 18. Its meaning would then be that a slave who has served for six years has repaid his master double his own worth, at the rate of a paid man, since the value of a slave was thirty shekels (Ex 21: 32). The labourers in the Gospel (Mt 20: 2) earn a denarius, which represents much more, but it would be pointless to compare values between two such distant periods.

The fact remains that the condition of the wage-labourers was far from enviable (Jb 7: 1-2; 14: 6), and unjust masters did not even give them their due (Jr 22: 3; Si 34: 22). Yet the law did make some effort to protect them. Lv 19: 13 and Dt 24: 14-15 lay down that workmen must be paid every evening (cf. Mt 20: 8), and the prophets were their champions against oppression (Jr 22: 13; Ml 3: 5; Si 7: 20).

7. *Craftsmen*

Apart from labourers, economic progress and the development of urban life multiplied the number of independent craftsmen. Many trades are mentioned in the Old Testament: millers, bakers, weavers, barbers, potters, fullers, locksmiths, jewellers, etc. A more general term, *ḥarash*, denotes a worker in wood or stone, and especially in metals, *i.e.* a smith, founder or carver. They worked on the system of the family workshop, where the father handed on the craft to his son, sometimes assisted by a handful of workmen, slaves or paid men.

The craftsmen of one trade lived and worked together in a certain quarter or street, as they do in Eastern towns to-day; again, a village would specialize in one industry. Geographical and economic circumstances accounted for these concentrations, *e.g.* the presence of the raw material, ore, clay or wool, or of the means of production, such as supplies of water or fuel, or good sites for ventilating the furnaces, etc. These groupings were also founded on tradition, for the crafts were, as a general rule, hereditary. Thus we learn that textiles were made at Beth-Ashbea in the south of Judaea (1 Ch 4: 21), and that the Benjaminites worked in wood and metal in the regions of Lod and Ono (Ne 11: 35). Excavations indicate that weaving and dyeing were flourishing industries at Debir, the modern Tell Beit-Mirsim. At Jerusalem there was a 'Bakers' Street' (Ne 3: 31-32), a 'Fuller's Field' (Is 7: 3), a 'Gate of the Potsherds' near which the potters worked (Jr 19: 1f.), and a 'Goldsmiths' Quarter' (Jr 37: 21). This specialization was carried still further in the Graeco-Roman and Rabbinical periods.

These craftsmen who worked side by side gradually organized themselves into guilds. There is clear evidence of this after the Exile, when the craft guilds, following the model of the family system from which they had sprung, called themselves families or clans, *mishpaḥoth*.[1] At Beth-Ashbea there are *mishpaḥoth* of linen-makers (1 Ch 4: 21). The head of the guild is called a 'father', *e.g.* Yoab, 'father' of the Valley of the Smiths, 1 Ch 4: 14, and the journeymen are called 'sons'. Uzziel is a 'son' of the goldsmiths (Ne 3: 8), that is, a journeyman goldsmith, like Malkiyyah of the same corporation (Ne 3: 31), and Hananyah, a perfumer by trade (Ne 3: 8). In Judaism these guilds were to be given legal status, and to make rules for the protection of their members. Sometimes they would even have their own places of worship: there was a weavers' synagogue in Jerusalem. The influence of the professional organizations in the Graeco-Roman world must have hastened this development, but the passages quoted, and the older parallels from Mesopotamia, show that these guilds originated long before. Perhaps they may date back to the monarchical period, if we admit that certain signs often engraved on the pottery, are, if not the owner's name, trade-marks of a corporation, not of a family workshop. It is difficult to decide, but in any case, during this pre-exilic period, all important enterprises were in the hands of the king. The foundry at Esyon Geber under Solomon, excavated some years ago, was a state factory. According to 1 Ch 4: 23, the potters of Netayim and Gedarah worked in the royal workshop. It was from these

1. Cf. pp. 8 and 21.

workshops that those jars with an official stamp came; the stamp was presumably meant as a guarantee of their capacity.[1]

8. *Merchants*

The Israelites did not take to commerce until late in their history. Foreign trade, or big business, was a royal monopoly. With the help of Hiram of Tyre, Solomon equipped a fleet on the Red Sea (1 K 9: 26-28; 10: 11, 22), which was to barter the products of the Esyon Geber foundry against the gold and wealth of Arabia. A similar enterprise was planned under Josaphat but did not succeed (1 K 22: 49-50). Solomon also traded with desert caravans (1 K 10: 15), and ran a forwarding agency; his agents bought horses in Cilicia and chariots in Egypt and then re-sold them both (1 K 10: 28-29)— but this interpretation of the text is not certain.

Achab signed a commercial agreement with Benhadad, by which he could set up bazaars in Damascus, as the Syrian king could in Samaria (1 K 20: 34); this is yet another royal concern. This kind of business went on all over the Near East in ancient times. Solomon's counterparts were the king of Tyre (1 K 5: 15-26; 9: 27; 10: 11-14), and the queen of Sheba (1 K 10: 1-13). And the tradition was of great antiquity. In the third millennium B.C. and again under Hammurabi, the kings of Mesopotamia owned caravans; in the Amarna period the kings of Babylon, Cyprus and other lands had merchants in their service; in the eleventh century B.C. the Egyptian story of Wen-Amon tells us that the prince of Tanis had a merchant navy and that the king of Byblos kept a register of the business he did with the pharaoh.

Private citizens in Israel did business only in their own locality. In the town or village square, where the market was held (2 K 7: 1), craftsmen sold their wares, and peasants the produce of their fields and herds. This business was on a very small scale and the producer sold direct to the consumer without any middleman; hence there was no merchant class. Real commerce was in the hands of foreigners, especially the Phoenicians, who were the universal agents of the East (cf. Is 23: 2, 8; Ez 27), and (according to Na 3: 16) the Assyrians also. Even after the Exile the Jews brought agricultural products to Jerusalem, but the Tyrians sold imported goods there (Ne 13: 15-16). Perhaps the first Israelite merchants we know of in Palestine itself are those who worked under Nehemias when he was restoring the ramparts (Ne 3: 32); on the other hand, these too may have been Tyrians, for, according to Ne 13: 16, some of them lived in the city.

This state of affairs is reflected in vocabulary; a 'Canaanite' means a 'merchant' in Jb 40: 30; Pr 31: 24; Za 14: 21. Other words describe the merchant as 'one who travels around', or by a root connected with the verb 'to walk'. They were foreigners, caravan drivers like the Midianites of

---

1. Cf. pp. 126 and 202-203.

Gn 37: 28, or merchants on foot who toured the country, selling their imported rubbish and buying the local products for export.

It was in the Diaspora and by force of necessity that the Jews became merchants. In Babylonia the descendants of those exiles who did not take part in the Return are found as clients or agents of big commercial firms. In Egypt, in the Hellenistic period, we know from the papyri that some were traders, bankers or brokers. The Palestinian Jews gradually followed suit, but the wise men, and later the Rabbis, were far from approving of it. Though Ben-Sirach says that the profits of commerce are legitimate (Si 42; 5), he also observes that a merchant cannot live without sin (Si 26: 29; 27: 2).

CHAPTER THREE

SLAVES

1. *The existence of slavery in Israel*

CERTAIN writers, and especially Jewish scholars, have denied that real slavery ever existed in Israel; at least, they maintain, Israelites were never reduced to slavery. There is a semblance of justification for this view if we compare Israel with classical antiquity; in Israel and the neighbouring countries, there never existed those enormous gangs of slaves which in Greece and Rome continually threatened the balance of social order. Nor was the position of the slave ever so low in Israel and the ancient East as in republican Rome, where Varro could define a slave as 'a sort of talking tool', '*instrumenti genus vocale*'. The flexibility of the vocabulary may also be deceptive. Strictly speaking '*ebed* means a slave, a man who is not his own master and is in the power of another. The king, however, had absolute power, and consequently the word '*ebed* also means the king's subjects, especially his mercenaries, officers and ministers; by joining his service they had broken off their other social bonds. By a fresh extension of meaning, the word became a term of courtesy. We may compare it with the development of its equivalents 'servant' in English or 'serviteur' in French, both derived from *servus*, a slave. Moreover, because a man's relations with God are often conceived on the model of his relations with his earthly sovereign, '*ebed* became a title for pious men, and was applied to Abraham, Moses, Josue or David, and finally to the mysterious Servant of Yahweh.

By 'slave' in the strict sense we mean a man who is deprived of his freedom, at least for a time, who is bought and sold, who is the property of a master, who makes use of him as he likes; in this sense there were slaves in Israel, and some were Israelites. The fact is proved by some early texts which speak of slaves in contrast with free men, wage-earners and resident foreigners, or which speak of their purchase for a sum of money; and the existence of slavery is presupposed also by the laws about emancipation.

2. *Slaves of foreign origin*

Throughout antiquity, war was one of the chief sources of supply for the slave-market, for captured prisoners were generally sold as slaves. The custom obtained in Palestine, too. In the days of the Judges, Sisera's army, had it been victorious, would have shared out the spoil: 'a damsel, two damsels, to every warrior' (Jg 5: 30). After the sack of Siqlag, the Amalekites carried off all the inhabitants into captivity (1 S 30: 2-3). Yahweh will judge the nations who 'have drawn lots for my people; they have traded boys against harlots; for wine they have sold the maidens' (Jl 4: 3). In the Hellenistic age, slave-traders followed the armies of Antiochus Epiphanes in order to buy the Jews whom they would take prisoner (1 M 3: 41; 2 M 8: 10-11). Later, Hadrian sold the prisoners taken in the Second Revolt.

All these are examples of Israelites enslaved by foreign enemies. But the Chronicler records that Peqah, king of Israel, in his war against Judah, took 200,000 prisoners, women, boys and girls, who were set free at the protest of a prophet (2 Ch 28: 8-15). It is uncertain what credence should be given to this story, which has no parallel in the Books of Kings; the figure, at least, is suspect. But it does show that the enslavement of prisoners of war who were brothers by race was not unheard of, though the custom was abhorred by right-thinking men. On the other hand, the presence in Israel of foreign prisoners as slaves is presumed by two laws of Deuteronomy. Dt 21: 10-14 considers the case of a female prisoner whom her captor takes as wife: he may later divorce her, but he may never sell her. This implies that he could have sold her, if he had not married her. The story of Nb 31: 26-47, which relates the sharing of the spoil after the war with Midian, is a parallel example: the virgins were shared among the combatants and the whole community, all the rest having been put to death to carry out the anathema (Nb 31: 15-18).

The law of Dt 20: 10-18 deals with the conquest of towns. If a town stands on the land assigned by God to Israel, it is to be totally destroyed and no living thing may be left in it. When a town outside the Holy Land is attacked, it must be given the chance to surrender. If it agrees, the whole population is condemned to forced labour; if it refuses and is captured, all the men are put to death and the women and children are reckoned as booty. In its present form, this law breathes the spirit of Deuteronomy (cf. the parallel in 7: 1-6), but it is unreal: the age of territorial conquest and foreign wars was long past. It reflects the memory of the ancient curses (Jos 6: 17-21; 8: 26; 10: 28f., etc.; 1 S 15: 3; cf. Dt 2: 34; 3: 6), of the obstacles to total conquest (Jos 17: 12-13; Jg 1: 28, 30, 33, 35), and of David's wars (2 S 8: 2; 12: 31), which provided the State with its first slaves.[1]

The slave traffic was general throughout the ancient East. In Am 1: 6 and 9, Gaza and Tyre are condemned for dealing in prisoners. According to Ez 27: 13, Tyre bought men in Asia Minor, and Jl 4: 6 says she sold Judaeans there. These Phoenicians, who were the chief traders in Israel, must also have been slave-dealers. The law allowed Israelites to buy slaves, men and women, of foreign birth, or born of resident aliens (Lv 25: 44-45; cf. Ex 12: 44; Lv 22: 11; Qo 2: 7).

1. Cf. pp. 88-90.

Slaves who had been bought for money are distinguished from those born in the house (Gn 17: 12, 23, 27; Lv 22: 11; cf. Jr 2: 14): *yʿlîd bayth*. It is possible, however, that the expression does not refer only to those born in the house; it may include all those who are attached to a house as slaves, and who have certain obligations to the master of the house when it is necessary to take up arms. This would explain the 318 *yʿlîdê bayth*, who were the 'partisans' of Abraham (Gn 14: 14), and the use of *yalîd* when referring to war (Nb 13: 28; 2 S 21: 16, 18). A master could buy married slaves, or marry off those he had; the children belonged to the master (cf. Ex 21: 4), and were a cheap addition to his domestic staff. If they had been brought up in the family, they would be more attached to it and would be better treated, but they had the same social status as those who had been bought.

3. *Israelite slaves*

We know for certain that there were slaves of foreign origin; but were Israelites ever reduced to slavery? We have just mentioned the text of 2 Ch 28: 8-15, which condemns this practice, and it is forbidden by Lv 25: 46 which, after speaking of foreigners, adds: 'You may have them as slaves, but none of you shall ever exercise such absolute power over your brethren, the children of Israel.' Yet Lv 25: 39-43 speaks of an Israelite who is 'sold' to another Israelite; he must be treated as a paid worker or a visitor, and not as a slave. On the other hand, Lv 25: 47-53 deals with the case of an Israelite who has 'sold' himself to a resident alien: he can be redeemed by his kin or can redeem himself, and must be treated with consideration. Whether their master is Israelite or foreign, these slaves are to be set free in the jubilee year (Lv 25: 40).

The Israelites, then, could not become slaves permanently; but the law does allow them to be 'sold' as real slaves, though only for a limited time, and under certain safeguards. It is difficult to say whether this law was ever applied. In Nehemias' time the Jews bewailed the fact that they had had to sell their sons and daughters as slaves, and Nehemias implored the people to cancel their debts and to free persons who had given themselves as security (Ne 5: 1-13). There is no allusion to the law of Lv 25.

It seems, then, that this law is later than the time of Nehemias, and even if this argument from silence is not pressed, the law must be late, since it is a substitute for earlier laws. In Dt 15: 12-18, if a 'Hebrew', man or woman, is sold to one of his brethren, he must serve him for six years and be set free in the seventh year. If he declines to be freed, he becomes a slave for life. This is the law referred to in Jr 34: 14, concerning the liberation of 'Hebrew' slaves under Sedecias.

The law of Ex 21: 2-11 is much older. A 'Hebrew' slave who has been 'bought' is to serve six years and to be freed in the seventh year; if he refuses his freedom he becomes a slave for life. These provisions are identical with those of Dt 15 : 12-18, but they apply only to male slaves. Girls sold as slaves, to become concubines of their master or his son, are not freed, and their status is similar to that of female prisoners of war (Dt 21 : 10-14, cf. above).

It is interesting that in the texts quoted from Ex, Dt and Jr, these slaves are called 'Hebrews', a term which, except in one late text (cf. Jon 1 : 9), is applied to Israelites only in certain conditions. It has been suggested that the word means those Israelites who forfeited their freedom by a semi-voluntary slavery. The theory can be supported from 1 S 14 : 21, where the Israelites who entered the service of the Philistines are called 'Hebrews', and by the analogy of documents from Nuzu, in which the *ḥapiru* sell themselves as slaves. The biblical texts would preserve traces of an archaic usage, but they certainly refer to Israelites.

The only reason why an Israelite was ever reduced to slavery was his own, or his relatives', poverty. Usually, if not always, they were defaulting debtors, or persons given as security for the repayment of a debt.[1] This is presumed in the laws of Lv 25 and Dt 15 : 2-3, and confirmed by the other passages. Eliseus performs a miracle to help a woman whose two children are about to be taken as slaves by a money-lender (2 K 4 : 1-7). In Is 50 : 1, Yahweh asks the Israelites : 'To which of my creditors have I sold you?' Nehemias' contemporaries sell their sons and daughters into slavery as securities for the payment of debts (Ne 5 : 1-5). This explains why such slavery was not permanent; it ended once the debt was paid or cancelled (Lv 25 : 48; 2 K 4 : 7; Ne 5 : 8 and 11). The laws of Ex 21 and Dt 15 fixed a maximum duration of six years. (According to the Code of Hammurabi, certain slaves-for-debt could not be kept for more than three years.) But these laws were not obeyed, as Jr 34 shows. It is because of this difficulty that the ideal law of Lv 25 allows for an extension which may amount to fifty years, but puts the master under the obligation of treating his slave like a wage-earner or a guest.

There were, then, Israelite slaves under Israelite masters. In addition to those who had been reduced to this state by poverty or debt, there were thieves who could not clear themselves and were sold to repay the cost of their theft (Ex 22 : 2). On the other hand, the laws of Ex 21 : 16 and Dt 24 : 7 prescribe the death penalty for abducting an Israelite in order to exploit or sell him as a slave. Possibly the prohibition in the Decalogue (Ex 20 : 15; Dt 5 : 19), which is clearly distinguished from the very detailed commandment about crimes against justice (Ex 20 : 17; Dt 5 : 21), condemns this particularly hateful seizure of a free person.

4. *The number and value of slaves*

We have very little information about the number of domestic slaves in Israel. Gideon took ten of his servants to demolish the sanctuary of Baal (Jg 6 :

1. Cf. p. 172.

27). Abigail, wife of the wealthy Nabal, had an unstated number of slaves, and when she went to marry David, she took five maidservants with her (1 S 25: 19, 42). After Saul's death, the property of the royal family was valued by Siba, a steward, who had fifteen sons and twenty slaves of his own (2 S 9: 10). Some large landowners in the days of the monarchy may have had a comparatively large household, but they were exceptions. The census of the community on its return from the Exile (Esd 2: 64; Ne 7: 66), records 7,337 slaves of both sexes as compared with 42,360 free persons. The situation is therefore utterly different from that in Greece or Rome, but has its parallel in Mesopotamia, where a family of substance had one or two slaves in the earliest periods, and from two to five in the Neo-Babylonian era: in Assyria the figures were a little higher.

Evidence about the value of slaves is equally scanty. Joseph was sold by his brethren for twenty pieces of silver (Gn 37: 28), and that was also the average price of a slave in ancient Babylon. It was the same as the price of an ox. Prices doubled in the Neo-Babylonian age and rose even higher under the Persians. In the middle of the second millennium B.C. the market price of a slave was thirty shekels of silver at Nuzu, forty at Ugarit (Ras Shamra). In Israel a slave cost thirty shekels according to Ex 21: 32, and this is the sum given to Judas to betray Jesus (Mt 26: 15). But by the Greek period, prices had risen: when Nicanor promised the traders ninety captives for a talent, that is, about thirty-three shekels a head (2 M 8: 11), he was asking an absurdly low price, compared with those indicated in contemporary papyri, for he hoped to attract the traders by the prospect of an enormous profit.

5. The position of slaves

Strictly speaking, the slave is a chattel, belonging to his master by right of conquest, purchase or inheritance; the master makes use of him as he wills and can sell him again. The ancient laws of Mesopotamia presume that he is branded, like cattle, with tattoo marks or a brand made with hot iron or by some kind of label attached to his body. In practice, not all slaves bore these marks of identity, but they were commonly applied to runaway slaves who had been recaptured and to those who might be tempted to run away. The Rabbis allowed a slave to be marked in order to discourage him from running away, but the practice is not clearly attested in the Old Testament. A slave who declined to be freed had his ears pierced (Ex 21: 6; Dt 15: 17), but this was not a brand inflicted on him; it was a symbol of his attachment to the family. The nearest analogy to this is the name of Yahweh written on the hands of the faithful in Is 44: 5 to signify that they belong to God, like the name of the Beast marked on his followers in Ap 13: 16-17, or the tattoo marks of the Hellenistic cults.

Yet in the ancient East no one ever quite forgot that the slave was a human being: slaves had their rights. True, the Code of Hammurabi punished cruelty only against another man's slave, because the slave was his master's property; similarly, Ex 21: 32 states that if a slave is gored by a neighbour's bull, the owner of the bull owes compensation to the slave's master. Still, even in Mesopotamia slaves had legal remedy against unjust violence, and in Israel the laws protected them even more explicitly. A man who blinded his slave or broke his tooth was bound to set him free in compensation (Ex 21: 26-27). If a man should beat his slave to death, he was to be punished (Ex 21: 20), but if the slave survived for one or two days the master was exonerated, for 'it was his money' (Ex 21: 21). Obviously, they thought that the master had been sufficiently punished by the loss he had incurred, but this clause shows that even in Israel the slave was thought of as his master's chattel.

In Mesopotamia and in Rome the slave could save money of his own, carry on business and have his own slaves. We cannot be sure that this was so in Israel. Lv 25: 49 certainly allows a slave to redeem himself if he has the means, but the text does not give any more detail. Other cases are sometimes quoted: the servant who went with Saul had a quarter of a shekel in his pocket (1 S 9: 8). Gehazi, servant of Eliseus, persuaded Naaman to give him two talents of silver, with which, Eliseus says, he would be able 'to buy gardens, oliveyards and vineyards, flocks and herds, menservants and maid-servants' (2 K 5: 20-26). Siba, steward to Saul's family, had twenty slaves (2 S 9: 10). But the master retained supreme control over his slave's property: 2 S 9: 12 states clearly that 'all who lived with Siba were in the service of Meribbaal'. But these cases do not afford conclusive proof, for here the Hebrew word is not 'ebed, 'slave', but na'ar, 'young man', and so 'servant', 'assistant', probably always a free man, attached to a master's service.

In everyday life the lot of a slave depended largely on the character of his master, but it was usually tolerable. In a community which attached such importance to the family, in which work was scarcely conceivable outside the framework of the family, a man on his own was without protection or means of support. The slave was at least assured of the necessities of life. More than that, he really formed part of the family, he was a 'domestic' in the original sense of the word. (That was why he had to be circumcised, Gn 17: 12-13.) He joined in the family worship, rested on the sabbath (Ex 20: 10; 23: 12), shared in the sacrificial meals (Dt 12: 12, 18), and in the celebration of religious feasts (Dt 16: 11, 14), including the Passover (Ex 12: 44), from which the visitor and the wage-earner were excluded. A priest's slave could eat the holy offerings (Lv 22: 11), which visitors and wage-earners could not (Lv 22: 10). Abraham's relations with his servant (Gn 24), show how intim-ate master and slave could be. Pr 17: 2 says: 'Better a shrewd servant than a degenerate son' (cf Si 10: 25). He could share in his master's inheritance (Pr 17: 2), and even succeed to it in the absence of heirs (Gn 15: 3). We know of one slave who married his master's daughter (1 Ch 2: 34-35). In these last two cases, obviously, the slave was *ipso facto* emancipated.

The slave had of course to obey and to work, and the wise men advised masters to treat them harshly (Pr 29: 19, 21). Firmness there had to be, but it was to the master's interest to combine with it justice and humanity (Si 33: 25-33). Devout men added a religious motive: Job protests that he has not neglected the rights of his servant and his handmaid, for, like him, they are God's creatures (Jb 31: 13-15).

Leviticus prescribes that a slave of Israelite birth is to be treated favourably: he is to be like a visitor or a wage-earner and is not to be made to do the work of a slave (Lv 25: 39-40). Commenting on this text, the Rabbis laid down that he should not be given tasks which were too exacting or too degrading, like turning the mill (cf. Jg 16: 21), or taking off his master's shoes or washing his feet (cf. 1 S 25: 41). Hence in the New Testament, when John the Baptist protests that he is not worthy to untie the sandals of the one he announces (Mt 3: 11 and parallels), he means he is less than a slave. Peter recoils when Jesus wants to wash his feet (Jn 13: 6-7), because that is a task only for a slave.

6. Female slaves

We have already had occasion to note that female slaves formed a special category. They attended to the personal needs of the mistress of the house (Gn 16: 1; 30: 3, 9; 1 S 25: 42; Jdt 10: 5, etc.), or nursed the children (Gn 25: 59; 2 S 4: 4; 2 K 11: 2). The master arranged their marriages at his discretion (Ex 21: 4). He might take a slave-woman as his concubine, and her lot was then improved. Abraham and Jacob, for example, took slaves as concubines, at the request of their childless wives. But they kept their status as slaves (cf. Gn 16: 6) unless their master freed them (cf. Lv 19: 20). The ancient law of Ex 21: 7-11 allows an Israelite father who is poor or in debt to sell his daughter to be the slave-concubine of a master or his son. She is not freed in the seventh year like the male slaves. If her master is not satisfied, he may re-sell her to her family, but may not sell her to a stranger. If he takes another wife, he must leave intact all the rights of the first. If he intends her to be his son's wife, he must treat her as a daughter of the family.

The Deuteronomic law makes similar provisions for female prisoners of war who are married by their captors (Dt 21: 10-14). But unlike Ex 21, Dt makes no distinction between men and women in the treatment of Israelite slaves: the woman is freed in the seventh year like the man, and like him she can refuse her freedom (Dt 15: 12 and 17). Similarly Jr 34 makes no distinction between male and female slaves. This seems to mean that by this period there were no slave-concubines. The later law of Lv 25 makes no mention of them, and Ne 5: 5 speaks of the violation of Israelite girls by their master, but does not mention their being taken as concubines.

7. Runaway slaves

As a rule, the slave's only way of escaping from his master's cruelty was flight (Si 33: 33), and even if he were well treated he might be tempted to run away, if only to enjoy that freedom to which every man has a right. Nabal was a man of wealth and selfishness and must have known something about this: 'There are too many slaves running away from their masters nowadays', he tells David's messengers (1 S 25: 10). Two of Shimei's slaves fled to Gath (1 K 2: 39). It was the same everywhere. The Code of Hammurabi prescribes the death penalty for aiding and abetting a runaway slave, refusing to give him up, or merely hiding him. Other Mesopotamian laws were less strict; at Nuzu anyone who harboured a fugitive slave paid a fine.

To deal with slaves who took refuge abroad, some treaties between states provided extradition clauses. Thus Shimei was able to recover his two slaves who fled to the king of Gath (1 K 2: 40, cf. also 1 S 30: 15).

Israelite law contains only one article on runaway slaves. Dt 23: 16–17 forbids anyone to hand over a slave who has escaped from his master and sought refuge; he is to be welcomed and well treated, in the town he has chosen. This provision has no parallel in ancient law and is difficult to interpret. It does not seem to apply to an Israelite slave deserting an Israelite master, for he would naturally return to his family or clan. For the same reason it does not apply to an Israelite slave fleeing from a foreign master. It seems then that the law must deal with a foreigner coming from abroad and admitted to Israel as a ger or a tôshab. Extradition would be refused and all the Holy Land would be considered a place of refuge, in the spirit of Is 16: 3–4.

8. The emancipation of slaves

The master obviously had the right to free his slave if he so willed, and further, certain cases are provided for by law. If a man took a female prisoner of war as his wife, she ceased to be a slave (Dt 21: 10–14). Liberation could also occur as compensation for a bodily injury (Ex 21: 26–27); note that the unconditional wording of this text does not allow us to restrict it to Israelite slaves. But, generally speaking, foreign slaves were bound to slavery for life, and were bequeathed with the rest of the inheritance (Lv 25: 46).

The enslavement of Israelites, however, was in theory temporary. Male slaves (according to Ex 21: 2–6) and female slaves as well (according to Dt 15: 12–17), had to be set free after six years of service. They could refuse this freedom, and no doubt often did so, for fear of falling into poverty once more: this, after all, was precisely what had led them to sell themselves. The present which they received from their master (Dt 15: 14) was only a meagre insurance for the future. They had still more cause to remain if their master had given them a wife, for the wife and children remained his property (Ex

21 : 4). In such a case the slave had his ear pierced against the doorpost or lintel, as a symbol of his final attachment to the house, and he became a slave for life. These laws do not seem to have been strictly observed. According to Jr 34: 8-22, which is explicitly based on Deuteronomy, the people of Jerusalem had liberated their 'Hebrew' slaves, during the siege under Nabuchodonosor; but when the siege was raised for a while, they seized them again. The prophet denounces this as felony against their brethren and transgression of a law of God.

The provisions already quoted from Lv 25 concern the liberation of Israelite slaves, in connection with the jubilee year.[1] In this year both they and their children are to go free (Lv 25: 41, 54). Before this period they can be redeemed or can redeem themselves, counting the years left before the jubilee at the price of a hired man for each year (Lv 25: 48-53). These provisions seem somewhat Utopian: a slave who began his term of service soon after the beginning of a jubilee period might well die before seeing the end of it, or become too old to earn his living as a free man. The price of his freedom, unless the jubilee year was very near, would have cost him very dear, for three years' wage was enough to cover the price of a slave. We saw that a slave was valued at thirty shekels (according to Ex 21: 32), and that a workman earned about ten shekels a year, according to the Code of Hammurabi, and perhaps Dt 15: 18.[2] There is, however, no evidence that the law was ever applied, either before or after Nehemias, who makes no reference to it when he orders a remission of debts, involving the liberation of persons held as security (Ne 5: 1-13).

A freed slave is called *hofshi* in the laws of Ex 21 and Dt 15, and in Jr 34 (cf. also Lv 19: 20; Is 58: 6; Jb 3: 19). The word is never used in any context but that of the liberation of slaves, except, figuratively, in Jb 39: 5, and in 1 S 17: 25 (where it means exemption from taxes and forced labour). The only possible translation is, therefore, 'freed'. But there is nothing in the Old Testament to suggest that these freed persons formed a special class of society. This conclusion could only be derived from non-Biblical analogies: at Alalakh and Nuzu, in the Amarna letters and the Ras Shamra texts, in the Assyrian laws and the later Assyrian documents, *hupshu* denotes a class of the population, midway between the slaves and the landowners. They seem to have been serfs, farmers and sometimes craftsmen. In these different social backgrounds the same word has many different connotations, and it is unreasonable to apply one or other of these meanings to Israel, where there were no well-defined social classes. On his liberation the slave belonged once more to the 'people of the land'.

9. State slaves

Prisoners of war provided the states of the ancient East with the servile manpower they needed for the sanctuaries and the palace, for public works

1. Cf. p. 175.   2. Cf. pp. 76 and 84.

and the big commercial or industrial enterprises which were the monopoly
of the king. Though the Old Testament laws deal only with domestic slaves,
it seems that in Israel there were also State slaves.

After the capture of Rabbah, David 'set the population handling the saw,
picks and iron axes, and employed it on the making of bricks, and so he did
for all the towns of the Ammonites' (2 S 12: 31). For a long time it was
thought that this text described a strange massacre of the inhabitants, carried
out with workmen's tools; but the translation just given makes perfect sense,
and there is no need to assume any such massacre. The only question is
whether it means reduction to slavery for the service of the State, or simply
subjection to forced labour. Under Solomon, the work in the mines of the
Arabah and the foundry at Esyon Geber, in remote regions and under appalling conditions, must have caused fearful mortality, and it required a slave
population in the king's service. It is unthinkable that free Israelites could
have been conscripted for it, at least in any number. The Ophir fleet, which
exported the half-finished products of the factory at Esyon Geber, had
'Solomon's slaves' for crews, working alongside the slaves of Hiram of Tyre
(1 K 9: 27; cf. 2 Ch 8: 18; 9: 10). It is possible that these State slaves of foreign
birth worked also on Solomon's large buildings (1 K 9: 15-21). The text uses
the term mas 'obed, 'servile levy', to signify these labourers, who were
recruited from the descendants of the Canaanites; the addition of 'servile'
may be to distinguish this levy from that to which the Israelites were subjected.[1] We may question this distinction, by which the redactor tries to
exempt the Israelites from a burden (cf. v. 22) to which they had in fact been
subjected, according to the early documents of 1 K 5: 27; 11: 28. But the
important point is that he adds (1 K 9: 21) that the Canaanites remained
slaves 'until this day'. In his time, therefore, at the end of the monarchy, there
were State slaves, whose institution was ascribed to Solomon.

Now after the Exile we find 'descendants of the slaves of Solomon' who
had returned from Babylon and lived in Jerusalem and its suburbs (Esd 2:
55-58; Ne 7: 57-60; 11: 3). But their connections had changed. They are
mentioned along with the n'thinim, the 'given', and counted with them (Esd
2: 43-54; Ne 7: 46-56). These 'given' lived on mount Ophel, near the
Temple (Ne 3: 31; 11: 21). They formed the less important personnel of the
sanctuary and were at the service of the Levites (Esd 8: 20). To some extent
their names betray a foreign origin. Though the term does not appear in pre-
exilic texts, there was a similar institution in existence, at least at the end of
the monarchy: Ez 44: 7-9 reproaches the Israelites for introducing foreigners
into the sanctuary and entrusting part of their duties to them. It is even likely
that slaves of foreign origin were attached to Israelite sanctuaries from the
beginning, as was the practice in all the temples of the ancient East, of Greece
and of Rome. The editor of the book of Josue was already acquainted with

1. On the levy, cf. pp. 141-142.

Gibeonites who cut wood and carried water in the Temple (Jos 9: 27), saying that their fathers had been condemned to this task by Josue, for deceiving Israel (Jos 9: 23). It is such foreigners who are alluded to in Dt 29: 10. Esd 8: 20 ascribes the institution of the *n'thinîm* to David, but, in reaction against this employment of foreigners, Nb 3: 9; 8: 19 emphasizes that it is the Levites who were 'given' to the priests for the service of the sanctuary.

Under the monarchy, then, as in neighbouring countries, there were two classes of State slaves, the king's slaves and the Temple slaves, both of foreign origin, and usually prisoners of war or their descendants. After the Exile, with the disappearance of royal institutions, the 'slaves of Solomon' were merged with the 'given', and all were attached to the service of the Temple.

CHAPTER FOUR

THE ISRAELITE CONCEPT OF THE STATE

1. Israel and the various Eastern notions of the State

WHEN the Israelites conquered Canaan, the land was divided into a host of principalities. Jos 12: 9-24 records the defeat of thirty-one kings by Josue, and this list is not a complete inventory of the towns on the political map of Palestine. Two centuries earlier the Amarna letters reflect the same state of affairs and show that Syria too was divided into principalities. It was the form the Hyksos domination took in these regions, but it dates back still further: Egyptian decrees of banishment witness to it at the beginning of the second millennium B.C. These political units are confined to a fortified city with a small surrounding territory. Each was ruled by a king, who at the time of the Hyksos and in the Amarna period, was often of foreign birth, relying on an army drawn from his own people and reinforced by mercenaries. Succession to the throne was normally on the dynastic principle. The same idea of the State is found in the five Philistine principalities on the coast. It is true that these formed a federation (Jos 13: 3; Jg 3: 3; 1 S 5: 8), but this was true of the four Gibeonite towns also (Jos 9: 17), without counting the apparently *ad hoc* alliances between the Canaanite kings (Jos 10: 3f.; 11: 1-2).

In contrast with these pygmy states, there were vast empires: the Egyptian, which for centuries counted the petty kings of Palestine and Syria as its vassals, then the Assyrian, the Neo-Babylonian and the Persian Empires. These were highly organized states, uniting heterogeneous populations across vast territories won by conquest. National feeling was hardly developed at all, and the army which defended the territory and made the conquests was a professional army embodying mercenary formations. The authority was monarchical and the succession, in theory, hereditary.

At the end of the second millennium B.C. some national states made their appearance. They bore the names of peoples—Edom, Moab, Ammon and Aram. They were confined to the territory where the nation lived, and at first made no attempt to spread by conquest. The country was defended, not by a professional army, but by the nation in arms, by calling to arms all the menfolk in time of danger. The government was monarchical, though not necessarily hereditary. From the list of the first kings of Edom (Gn 36:31-39), it appears that the kings owed their power to the fact that they had been either chosen or accepted by the nation. If, later on, the dynastic principle was established, the change was no doubt due to a natural evolution or to the influence of the great neighbouring states.

According to one Biblical tradition, the Israelites asked for a king in order to be 'like the other nations' (1 S 8: 5). But they did not imitate the Canaanite principalities whom they had dislodged. Such a conception of the State never held sway in Israel.

Attempts were made, but they came to nothing: it was this type of royal rank, with hereditary succession, which Gideon refused (Jg 8: 22f.), and the short-lived kingdom of Abimelek at Shechem was based on non-Israelite elements (Jg 8: 31; 9: 1f.). It has recently been maintained that both Jerusalem (a Jebusite town conquered by David) and Samaria (a new town founded by Omri on land bought by him) had the status of city-states of the Canaanite type inside the kingdoms of Judah and Israel, but this conclusion seems to go beyond the texts on which its claims are based.

Nor were the original Israelites inclined to adopt their ideas on the State from the great Empires with which they had been in contact, particularly in Egypt. It was only at the end of David's reign and under Solomon that an attempt was made to realize the idea of empire. But its success was short-lived and all that remained were some features of administrative organization copied from Egypt.

The notion of the State in Israel is in fact closer to that of the Aramaean kingdoms of Syria and Transjordania. First Israel, then Israel and Judah, were, like them, national kingdoms; like them they bore the names of peoples, and like them they did not at once accept the dynastic principle. The parallel could no doubt be pursued further if we knew more about the early history and organization of these kingdoms. It is certainly noteworthy that these national states were formed about the same time as Israel, after a semi-nomadic existence. These states emerged as the result of the solidarity of the tribes which eventually settled down in a limited territory.

2. The Twelve Tribes of Israel

In the first stage of its settlement in Canaan, Israel consisted of a federation of twelve tribes. Parallels to this system are known, and precisely in those related peoples who had passed through the same stage of social evolution. According to Gn 22: 20-24, Nahor had twelve sons, who gave their names to the Aramaean tribes. Similarly the sons of Ishmael are 'twelve chiefs of as many tribes' (Gn 25: 12-16). Again, there were twelve tribes of Esau's descendants established in Transjordan (Gn 36: 10-14, to which v. 12 adds Amalek).

At Shechem the twelve Israelite tribes joined in a pact which sealed their religious unity and established a certain form of national unity between them (Jos 24). This organization has been compared to the amphictyonies in which Greek cities were grouped around a sanctuary: there they joined in common worship and their representatives took counsel together. The comparison is helpful, provided we do not press it too far and try to find all the features of the Greek amphictyonies in the Israelite federation. The twelve tribes were conscious of the bonds which united them, they shared the same name, and together they formed 'all Israel'.

They acknowledged one and the same God, Yahweh (Jos 24: 18, 21, 24), and celebrated his feasts at the same sanctuary, around the Ark, the symbol of Yahweh's presence in their midst. They shared a common statute and a common law (Jos 24:25) and they assembled to condemn violations of this customary or written law (Jos 24: 26), the 'infamies', the 'things which are not done in Israel' (Jg 19: 30; 20: 6, 10; cf. 2 S 13: 12).

The punishment of the outrage of Gibeah (Jg 19-20) shows us the tribes acting in concert to chastise a particularly odious crime. Apart from such an extreme case, perhaps they settled disputes and points of law by appealing to a judge whose authority was generally recognized: the list of 'lesser' judges (Jg 10: 1-5 and 12: 8-15) would be evidence of this institution.[1]

This may well be true, but the theory that there was a council of tribal representatives is far less probable. The narratives in the Book of Judges present the federation of tribes as a body without any organized government and lacking real political cohesion. The members formed one people and shared one worship, but they had no common head, and the oldest tradition never mentions any personality comparable to Moses or Josue. The editor of Judges has divided out the period between chiefs who are supposed to have reigned successively over all Israel, after liberating it from foreign oppression, but it has long been recognized that this is an artificial presentation. Their activity did sometimes involve a group of tribes (e.g. Gideon, and especially Deborah and Baraq), but this was quite unusual. Nothing is said about their actual functioning as rulers; only their military achievements are recorded and Gideon expressly refused a permanent authority (Jg 8: 22-23). The reign of Abimelek (Jg 9) was an isolated episode which affected only the Canaanite town of Shechem and a few Israelite clans.

However much these 'judges' differed from each other, they had one trait in common: they were chosen by God for a mission of salvation (Jg 3: 9, 15; 4: 7; 6: 14; 13: 5), and they were endowed with the spirit of Yahweh (Jg 3: 10; 6: 34; 11: 29; 13: 25; 14: 6, 19). The only authority manifest in Israel at that time was charismatic. This is an aspect which it is important to note, for it will reappear later.

1. See below, p. 151.

3. *The institution of the monarchy*

The related kingdoms of Ammon, Moab and Edom had been in existence for many decades when the Israelite federation was still politically shapeless. Suddenly it formed itself into a state, with Saul as the first king of Israel.

The Books of Samuel have preserved two parallel narratives of the institution of the monarchy, one of which is favourable to it (1 S 9: 1-10, 16; 11: 1-11, 15, continued in cc. 13 and 14, except for some additions). The other is opposed to it (1 S 8: 1-22; 10: 18-25, continued in cc. 12 and 15). According to the first account, the initiative came from God, who chose Saul as the liberator of his people (1 S 9: 16); according to the second, the people themselves demanded a king to be 'like the other nations' (1 S 8: 5, 20; cf. Dt 17: 14).

This development was hastened by the danger from Philistia, which threatened all Israel and made common action imperative. The first tradition is to this extent justified. In it Saul appears as one who continues the work of the Judges: like them he is a saviour appointed by God (1 S 9: 16; 10: 1); he receives the spirit of Yahweh (1 S 10: 6, 10; 11: 6); like them he effectively delivers his people (1 S 11: 1-11; cc. 13 and 14). But for the first time in Israel's history, the whole people respond to this choice by God: on the day after his victory over the Ammonites, Saul is acclaimed as king (1 S 10: 6). The 'charismatic leader', the *nagîd*[1] (1 S 9: 16; 10: 1), becomes the *melek*, the king (1 S 11: 15).

This is something quite new. The Israelite federation became a national state, and in the end took its pattern from the related kingdoms beyond the Jordan. This is where the imitation of other nations comes in, as the other tradition tells us. For this state had to have institutions. The 'law of the king' proclaimed by Samuel (1 S 8: 11-17) and written down (1 S 10: 25) is a warning against this imitation of foreign ways. The dynastic principle was no more readily accepted in Israel than in Edom (Gn 36: 31-39): no provision was made for the succession to Saul, and only Abner's personal authority made Ishbaal a puppet king (2 S 2: 8-9), while the men of Judah anointed David (2 S 2: 4). As in the national states, Saul summoned the militia to arms (1 S 11: 7; 15: 4; 17: 2; 28: 4), but against the Philistine commandos he sent troops of the same type, less numerous than the militia, but more experienced in battle (1 S 13: 2, 15; 14: 2); these he recruited specially (1 S 14: 52) with a corps of officers (1 S 18: 5, 13) whom he rewarded with fiefs (1 S 22: 7). It was the beginning of a professional army, a career open to foreign mercenaries (*e.g.* Doeg the Edomite, 1 S 21: 8; 22: 18). Ishbaal inherited his father's bodyguard (2 S 2: 12) and his two troop leaders from Gibeon, Baanah and Rekab (2 S 4: 2).

The institution of the monarchy had sprung from the tribal federation;

---

1. Cf. p. 70.

under Saul it was still in embryonic form. We do not know what authority Saul exercised apart from his military office. Except for his army commander, Abner (1 S 14: 50), none of his officers are known to us by name. There was no central government, and the tribes, or rather the clans, retained their administrative autonomy. A new and decisive stage was to open with the reign of David.

4. *The dual monarchy*

One tradition portrays David's kingdom as the continuation of Saul's, with the same charismatic aspect. God, who had rejected Saul, chose David as king over his people (1 S 16: 1). Hence David was anointed by Samuel (1 S 16: 12-13), as Saul had been; the spirit of Yahweh took hold of David (1 S 16: 13) as it had done of Saul. This tradition expresses the deep religious sense always attached to power in Israel; but it bears no direct relation to actual history. David's royal rank, both in its origins and in its developments, was very different from Saul's. David was a captain of mercenaries, at first in Saul's pay (1 S 18: 5), then on his own (1 S 22: 2), and then in the service of the Philistines, who made him prince of Siqlag (1 S 27: 6). After Saul's death he was anointed king, not by a prophet, but by the men of Judah (2 S 2: 4).

From the beginning Judah had had a history of its own. Together with Simeon, the Calebites and the Qenites, it had conquered its own territory, with no assistance from the House of Joseph (Jg 1: 3-19). In the days of the Judges, the Canaanite enclaves (Jerusalem, the Gibeonite towns, Gezer and Ayyalon, Jg 1: 21, 29, 35) formed a barrier between Judah and the northern tribes. This did not prevent religious and personal contacts (Jg 17: 7-8; 19: 1f.), but it did keep Judah apart from the communal life of the tribes: Judah is not even mentioned in the Hymn of Deborah (Jg 5), which praises the tribes taking part in the battle and blames those who did not come.

The rôle ascribed by Jg 20: 18 to Judah as leader of the coalition against Benjamin is an addition, based on Jg 1: 1-2. There was a *rapprochement* in the reign of Saul, who lived close by, in Benjamin, and had a certain authority over Judah (cf. especially 1 S 23: 12, 19f.; 27: 1). Yet Judah retained its separate identity and the division reappeared after Saul's death (2 S 2: 7 and 9). Indeed, to all appearances, David continued to be the vassal of the Philistines at the beginning of his reign in Hebron. Saul, to begin with, had relied on the general militia; David never did. He relied on a guard of mercenaries, even for the capture of Jerusalem (2 S 5: 6f.). Thus David's first kingship was very different from Saul's, and time did not alter the personal character of David's rule. After the murder of Ishbaal and in face of the Philistine menace, the men of Israel acknowledged David as their king, but they did not rally to the kingdom, already established, of Judah, nor was Judah absorbed by the more populous Israel. Just as the men of Judah had anointed David king over the House of Judah (2 S 2: 4), so the elders of Israel anointed him king over

Israel (2 S 5: 3). 2 S 5: 4-5 states clearly that David had reigned seven years and six months over Judah and thirty-three years 'over all Israel *and* over Judah'. When David named Solomon as his successor, he appointed him chief 'over Israel *and* over Judah' (1 K 1: 35). The kingdom of David and Solomon had, of course, a real unity, in the sense that the authority of the same sovereign was acknowledged everywhere, but it comprised two distinct elements. The list of Solomon's prefectures, 1 K 4: 7-19a, omits the territory of Judah, which had a separate administration; it is the 'land' of v. 19b.[1] The same distinction held good in military matters. When David ordered his census of the people for the general levy, two lists were compiled, one for Israel, the other for Judah (2 S 24: 1-9). At the siege of Rabbah, Israel *and* Judah were encamped (2 S 11: 11). The unity of the regime proceeded from the fact that the two states had one and the same sovereign: it was a United Kingdom like England and Scotland before the Act of Union, a Dual Monarchy like the old Austria-Hungary or, to take an example less remote in time and place, a double state like the kingdom of Hamath and La'ash, which is known to us from a Syrian inscription of the eighth century B.C.

Furthermore, the kingdom of David and Solomon was no longer merely a national kingdom. Though some authors have perhaps exaggerated the political influence of those Canaanite enclaves which were subjugated by David and Solomon, David's wars of aggression did bring into his kingdom non-Israelite populations, Philistines, Edomites, Ammonites, Moabites and Aramaeans (2 S 8: 1-14); sometimes their kings were left to rule as vassals (2 S 8: 2; 10: 19; 1 K 2: 39), at other times governors were set over them (2 S 8: 6, 14).

The notion of a national state gave way to that of an empire, which aspired to fill the place left vacant by the decline of Egyptian power. Its success was short-lived and its conquests were partly lost by David's successor (1 K 9: 10f.; 11: 14-25), but the idea of empire persisted, at least as an ideal, under Solomon (1 K 5: 1; 9: 19), who gave it practical expression by large commercial enterprises and by the external splendour of Israel's culture (1 K 9: 26-10: 29). This evolution involved an administrative development which was begun by David (2 S 20: 23-26), and completed by Solomon (1 K 4: 1-6 and 7-19); it was modelled, it seems, on the Egyptian administration.[2]

5. *The kingdoms of Israel and Judah*

This Dual Monarchy and this attempt at empire lasted only two generations. On Solomon's death, Israel and Judah parted company, and formed two national states, with their external provinces ever diminishing. But the notion of the State was rather different in the two kingdoms. In Israel the charismatic aspect of Saul's period was revived. The throne was promised

1. Cf. p. 135.   2. Cf. pp. 127ff.

to the first king, Jeroboam, by a prophet speaking in the name of Yahweh
(1 K 11: 31, 37); later, Jeroboam was acknowledged by the people (1 K 12:
20). In the same way Jehu was named as king by Yahweh (1 K 19: 16),
anointed by a disciple of Eliseus (2 K 9: 1f.), and acclaimed by the army
(2 K 9: 13). God himself made and unmade the kings of Israel (1 K 14: 7f.;
16: 1f.; 21: 20f.; 2 K 9: 7f.; cf. Os 13: 11). But Osee also accuses the people
of having made kings without God's sanction (Os 8: 4). The principle
of hereditary succession was never recognized in Israel before Omri,
and the dynastic principle was never taken for granted. Omri's dynasty
lasted some forty years, Jehu's a century, thanks to the long reign of
Jeroboam II, after which six kings, four of whom were assassinated,
succeeded each other in twenty years; and then the kingdom was conquered
by Assyria.

The kingdom of Judah presents a striking contrast. There the dynastic
principle was admitted from the outset, and sanctioned by divine intervention: the prophecy of Nathan promised David a house and kingdom which
would endure for ever (2 S 7: 8-16). God's choice, which in the days of the
Judges, and at intervals in Israel, picked out an individual, here lights on a
particular family; and once the choice was made, the succession followed
human rules. There is no dispute round David's deathbed about the dynastic
principle, but only as to which of David's sons is to succeed him, and it is
David himself, not Yahweh, who names Solomon (1 K 1: 28-35). Later on,
Judah, in contrast to Israel, accepts Roboam, Solomon's son, without dispute
(1 K 12: 1-20). There were palace revolutions in plenty in Judah, but the
Davidic line was always maintained, thanks to the loyalty of the 'people of
the land', the nation (2 K 11: 13-20; 14: 21; 21: 24; 23: 30).

It is probable that if our information about the two kingdoms was fuller
and more balanced, other institutional differences would come to light. One
fact at any rate is very clear: Israel and Judah are sometimes allies, sometimes
enemies, but they are always independent of each other, and other nations
treat them as distinct entities. This political dualism, however, does not prevent the inhabitants feeling themselves to be one people; they are brethren
(1 K 12: 24; cf. 2 Ch 28: 11), they have national traditions in common, and
the Books of Kings, by their synchronized presentation of the history of
Judah and Israel, claim to tell the story of one people. This people is united
by its religion. Like a man of God before him, who came from Judah (1 K 13:
1f.) Amos the man of Judah preached at Bethel, in spite of the opposition of
Amasias, who wanted to send him back to Judah (Am 7: 10-13). In the
Temple of Jerusalem, worship was offered to 'Yahweh, the God of Israel'.
Political conditions may frequently lead writers to contrast 'Israel', i.e. the
northern kingdom with 'Judah'; but 'Israel' always retained its wider
connotation and Is 8: 14 speaks of the 'two houses of Israel'. Thus, all through
the political separation of the monarchy, there survived the religious idea of

the federation of the Twelve Tribes, and the Prophets looked forward to its reunion in the future.

6. The post-exilic community

The fall of Jerusalem marked the end of Israel's political institutions. Henceforth Judaea was an integral part of the successive empires, Neo-Babylonian, Persian and Seleucid, which subjected it to the customary law of their provinces; even when the Hasmonaeans laid claim to the title of king, they were still vassals. Old customs were maintained, no doubt, at a municipal level, by the clans, *mishpaḥoth*, and their elders, *zᵉqenîm*, who represented the people before the authorities (Esd 5: 9; 6: 7), but there was no longer any idea of a State. Within the limits of what cultural and religious autonomy was left to them, the Jews formed a religious community, ruled by its own religious law under the government of their priests. It was a theocratic regime, and here again an ancient idea was reaffirmed and restated: Israel had God for king (Ex 15: 18; Nb 23: 21; Jg 8: 23; I S 8: 7; 12: 12; I K 22: 19; Is 6: 5). The idea was often expressed during and after the Exile, in the second part of Isaias (Is 41: 21; 43: 15; 44: 6) and in the Psalms about the reign of Yahweh (Ps 47; 93; 96-99). The kings who had governed Israel were only his viceroys (1 Ch 17: 14; 28: 5; 2 Ch 9: 8). The Chronicler, reviewing the history of his people, saw in the reign of David the realization of this kingdom of God on earth (1 Ch 11-29), and believed that the Jewish community of the Return, that of Zorobabel and Nehemias, approximated to that ideal (Ne 12: 44-47).

7. Was there an Israelite idea of the State?

Clearly we cannot speak of *one* Israelite idea of the State. The federation of the Twelve Tribes, the kingship of Saul, that of David and Solomon, the kingdoms of Israel and Judah, the post-exilic community, all these are so many different regimes. We may even go further and say that there never was any Israelite idea of the State. Neither the federation of the Tribes nor the post-exilic community were states. Between the two, the monarchy, in its varying forms, held its ground for three centuries over the tribes of the North, for four and a half over Judah, but it is hard to say how far it penetrated or modified the people's mentality. The post-exilic community returned to the pre-monarchical type of life with remarkable ease; this suggests some continuity of institutions at the level of clan and town. This municipal life is also the only aspect of public life considered by the legislative texts. There is indeed the 'law of the king' (Dt 17: 14-20), and the 'rights of the king' in 1 S 8: 11-18 (cf. 10: 25), but these in no way resemble political charters. These texts accept the fact of kingship as something tolerated by Yahweh (1 S 8: 7-9) or as subordinate to his choice (Dt 17: 15); they warn against imitating aliens (1 S 8: 5; Dt 17: 14), and the evil which kingship entails (1 S 8: 11-18; Dt 17: 16-17). And that is all. To study royal institutions we must glean what occasional information we can from the historical books.

One current of opinion was hostile to the monarchy. It can be seen in one of the traditions about the institution of the kingdom (1 S 8: 1-22; 10: 18-25), in the omissions in Dt 17: 14-20, in the denunciations of Osee (Os 7: 3-7; 8: 4, 10; 10: 15; 13: 9-11), and Ezechiel (Ez 34: 1-10; 43: 7-9), who allots only a very obscure rôle to the 'prince' (he avoids the word 'king') in his programme of future restoration (Ez 45: 7f., 17, 22f.). The Deuteronomic editor of the Books of Kings condemns all the kings of Israel and nearly all those of Judah.

On the other hand there is a stream of thought which is favourable to it; it finds expression in the other tradition on the institution of the kingdom (1 S 9: 1-10: 16; 11: 1-11, 15) in all the passages glorifying David and his dynasty, from Nathan's prophecy onwards (2 S 7: 8-16), in the royal psalms (Ps 2; 18; 20; 21, etc.), and in all the texts on the royal Messiah, which proclaim that the future Saviour will be a descendant of David, a king after the image, idealized, of the great king of Israel (Is 7: 14; 9: 5-6; 11: 1-5; Jr 23: 5; Mi 5: 1; cf. the Messianic adaptation of the royal psalms).

But these two opposite convictions are inspired by the same conception of power, one which is fundamental to Israelite thought, the conception of theocracy. Israel is Yahweh's people and has no other master but him. That is why from the beginning to the end of its history Israel remained a religious community.

It was religion which federated the tribes when they settled in Canaan, as it was to gather the exiles on their return from Babylon. It was religion which preserved the unity of the nation under the monarchy, in spite of the division of the kingdoms. The human rulers of this people are chosen, accepted or tolerated by God, but they remain subordinate to him and they are judged by the degree of their fidelity to the indissoluble covenant between Yahweh and his people. In this view of things the State, which in practice means the monarchy, is merely an accessory element; in actual fact Israel lived without it for the greater part of its history. All this should warn us against the tendency of a certain modern school of thought to attach too much importance, in the study of Israel's religion, to what is called 'the ideology of kingship'.

CHAPTER FIVE

THE PERSON OF THE KING

THE fact remains that, for a period of several centuries, Israel lived under a monarchy, and this is precisely the period when its political organization is best known. Moreover, royal institutions had an undeniable influence on some of Israel's religious conceptions, though this influence may have been exaggerated by a recent school of exegesis. We must therefore devote some attention to them. Unfortunately our information is one-sided; it is mainly about Judah, from which most of our documents have come, and we have just seen that Israel held another view of the royal power. Moreover, it is incomplete, because the Biblical writers were not specially interested in studying institutions. We can of course make good this deficiency by examining the organization of the neighbouring countries, which is sometimes better known; this can be very helpful, but then we run the risk of attributing to Israel ideas or customs which were foreign to it.

1. Accession to the throne

We have seen that while the dynastic principle was never really accepted in the northern kingdom, it was always observed in Judah. Even in Judah, however, accession to the throne implies a divine choice: a man is 'king by the grace of God', not only because God made a covenant with the dynasty of David, but because his choice was exercised at each accession. If the kingdom descended to Solomon and not to his elder brother Adonias, it was 'because it came to him from Yahweh' (1 K 2: 15; cf. 1 Ch 28: 5), and, as we shall see, every enthronement meant a renewal of the Davidic covenant and an adoption of the new sovereign by Yahweh. This idea of divine choice is universal in the ancient East. It is affirmed in Mesopotamia, even when a king succeeds his father, as was the ordinary rule, and at all periods, from Gudea, who is 'the shepherd designed by Ningirsu in his heart', down to Nabonidus, whom 'Sin and Nergal chose to reign when he was yet in his mother's womb', and Cyrus, of whom a Babylonian document says, 'Marduk chose his name for the kingdom over the world.' With this we naturally compare Is 44: 28, 'It is I (Yahweh) who say to Cyrus: My shepherd', and Is 45: 1, 'Thus says Yahweh to Cyrus his anointed.' The idea is carried to extremes in Egypt, where every king is held to be a son of Ra, the sun-god. In the

Aramaean kingdoms of Syria, Zakir, king of Hamath and La'ash, says: 'Ba'al Shamaïn called me and stood by me, and Ba'al Shamaïn has made me king.' This Zakir was a usurper, but Bar-Rekub, king of Senjirli, was a legitimate heir, yet he said: 'My master Rekub-el has made me sit on the throne of my father.'

The dynastic principle does not necessarily involve primogeniture, but this was probably the rule among the Hittites, though not, apparently, in the Aramaean kingdoms of Syria. In Egypt and Assyria the father was usually, though not always, succeeded by his eldest son. The king appointed the heir-apparent and took him as a partner in the government during his lifetime. Similarly, at Ugarit the king appointed the heir from among his sons. In Israel too, primogeniture was a title to the succession, but appointment by the king was also required (2 Ch 21: 3), for the king was not bound to choose his eldest son. Though Adonias, the eldest surviving son of David, hoped to be king (1 K 2: 15 and 22), and was supported by a whole party (1 K 1: 5-9; 2: 22), a rival party supported Solomon (1 K 1: 10). It lay with David to choose his successor (1 K 1: 20, 27), and he chose the younger son, Solomon (1 K 1: 17, 30). Joachaz succeeded Josias, although he had an elder brother, who was later placed on the throne by the Pharaoh and given the name Joiaqim (2 K 23: 31 and 36). It is possible that this choice between the sons took place only if the first-born, the normal heir, was dead: with Solomon this would be Amnon, and with Joachaz it was the Yohanan mentioned in 1 Ch 3: 15, of whom nothing is said at the time of the succession. This seems to have been the custom also in Assyria. But the situation was complicated when a king had several wives: Roboam preferred Maakah, although she was not his first wife (compare David and Bathsheba) and he gave Abiyyah, Maakah's eldest son, precedence over his brothers, in the hope that he would be king (2 Ch 11: 21-22).

Solomon was anointed king during the lifetime of his father (1 K 1: 32-40), who did not die until some time later (1 K 2: 1-10). Similarly Yotham assumed power when his father Ozias became a leper (2 K 15: 5), but we are not told that he was at once anointed. These are the only two co-regencies expressly mentioned in the Bible, though there may have been others not mentioned. Some modern historians list a whole series of them: Josaphat, Ozias and Manasseh in Judah, and Jeroboam II in Israel, are all said to have reigned at the same time as their fathers. But these are only hypotheses whose main purpose is to harmonize the discordant data of Biblical chronology. In the two certain cases, Solomon and Yotham assumed power because their fathers were too old or too ill to rule; the term co-regency is therefore somewhat inaccurate, and the situation is not quite the same as in Egypt or Assyria.

Women were excluded from the succession. In the kingdom of Israel, Joram succeeded his brother Ochozias because the latter died without male descendants (2 K 1: 17; cf. 3: 1). In Judah, Athaliah seized power on the death of her son and reigned for seven years, but her reign was regarded as unlawful and was terminated by a revolution (2 K 11).

2. *The coronation rites*

We possess two fairly detailed accounts of an enthronement, concerning Solomon (1 K 1: 32-48) and Joas (2 K 11: 12-20). Both situations are exceptional: Solomon's accession was the last event in a long intrigue and took place in his father's lifetime, while the accession of Joas brought to an end the usurpation of Athaliah. Though a century and a half passed between the two coronations, the two rites are so similar that they must represent the general custom, at least in Judah. There were two parts to the ceremony, the first of which was performed in the sanctuary, and the second in the royal palace. It included the following: investiture with the insignia (not mentioned for Solomon), anointing, acclamation, enthronement, homage of the high officials (not mentioned for Joas). We shall consider these points in order.

(a) *The setting: the sanctuary*. Solomon was consecrated at Gihon, the spring of Jerusalem. Is it because water played a part in the ceremonies, as in the rites of purification before the coronation of the Pharaoh? Some authors, interpreting Ps 110 as a coronation psalm, point to the allusion in v. 7: 'He drinks of the brook by the wayside', but it is a most flimsy theory. It is much more likely that Solomon was consecrated at Gihon because the sanctuary of the Ark was there. We are in fact told that when Sadoq came to Gihon he took the horn of oil 'in the tent' and anointed Solomon (1 K 1: 39): this, then, would be the tent which David had erected for the Ark (2 S 6: 17), and the 'tent of Yahweh' where Joab sought refuge (1 K 2: 28), and near it would be the altar at which Adonias (who was quite near by, at the Fuller's spring, 1 K 1: 9) took refuge on hearing that Solomon had been enthroned in the palace (1 K 1: 49-50). Joas was consecrated in the Temple, where, we presume, the consecration of the other kings of Judah after Solomon took place.

According to 2 K 11: 14, during the ceremony Joas remained 'standing near the pillar, as the custom was'. We may compare this with 2 K 23: 3, which shows us Josias 'standing near the pillar' during the reading of the law: the parallel passage 2 Ch 34: 31 merely says 'in his place'. Writing of Joas, 2 Ch 23: 13 adds the detail that this place was 'near the entrance'. So we may connect it with the 'king's dais' (in Greek) and the 'entrance for the king', which Achaz took out of the Temple to gratify the king of Assyria (2 K 16: 18). This dais is perhaps the one which Solomon erected in the middle of the court, according to 2 Ch 6: 13. This detail is illustrated by two stelae, one from Ras Shamra and one of Egyptian origin, which show the king (or a worshipper?) standing on a pedestal before an image of the God. We may then ask ourselves whether, in 2 K 11: 14; 23: 3 and 2 Ch 23: 13, we should not translate 'on the dais' instead of 'near the pillar'. One fact is certain, that a special place was reserved for the king in the Temple, just as there was a place for the Pharaoh in the Egyptian temples; the new king stood in this place during the ceremonies of consecration.

(b) *The investiture with the insignia.* According to 2 K 11: 12, the priest Yehoyada gave Joas the *nezer* and the *'edûth.* The meaning of *nezer* is certain: it is the diadem or crown, which is the royal emblem par excellence (2 S 1: 10; Jr 13: 18; Ez 21: 30-31; Ps 89: 40; 132: 18). The word *'edûth* is more difficult: it means 'testimony' or 'solemn law', and is usually corrected to *s⁽e⁾adôth,* 'bracelets'. And in fact, in 2 S 1: 10, Saul's diadem and bracelets, which would have been royal insignia, are brought to David. But perhaps in the sacring rite we ought to keep *'edûth.* We find that Ps 89: 40 gives 'diadem' as a parallel to the 'covenant', *b'rîth;* now *b'rîth* is sometimes synonymous with *'edûth.* Another synonym is *ḥôq,* 'decree'; Ps 2: 6-7 speaks of the sacring of the king and the 'decree' of Yahweh. We may compare it with the 'protocol' mentioned by Egyptian enthronement rites, which was supposed to have been written by the hand of the god: *e.g.* Thutmoses III says: 'He has put my diadem on me and established my protocol', which would be a good parallel to 2 K 11: 12. This protocol contained the Pharaoh's coronation names, the affirmation of his divine sonship and power; it was an act of legitimation. It may be that the new king of Judah was given a similar testimony affirming his adoption by God and promising him victory over his enemies, in the manner of Yahweh's 'decree' in Ps 2: 7-9, or recalling the covenant between Yahweh and the house of David (2 S 7: 8-16; Ps 89: 20-38; 132: 11-12, where the word *'edûth* occurs).

In Egypt it was the bestowal of the crowns and sceptres of Upper and Lower Egypt which made a man Pharaoh. In Assyria, the crown and sceptre were placed on cushions in front of the god; the priest crowned the king and handed him the sceptre. The Israelite accounts of enthronement do not mention a sceptre: it is not an exclusively royal emblem, there is no special name for it, and when it is carried by the king it seems to signify his executive power (Ps 2: 9; 110: 2) and his functions as judge (Ps 45: 7).

(c) *The anointing.* The coronation or imposition of the diadem does not appear in Solomon's sacring, as it does in that of Joas, but the two accounts agree on the essential rite of anointing (1 K 1: 39; 2 K 11: 12). It is mentioned from the beginning of the monarchy, for Saul (1 S 9: 16; 10: 1), for David as king of Judah (2 S 2: 4), then as king of Israel (2 S 5: 3), in addition to the special tradition in 1 S 16: 13. Apart from Solomon and Joas, it recurs in the story of Absalom's usurpation (2 S 19: 11); it is recorded of Joachaz in the kingdom of Judah (2 K 23: 30), and of Jehu in Israel (2 K 9: 3, 6). But it is certain that all the kings of Judah were anointed, and it is probably true of all the kings of Israel. The prophet Samuel anointed Saul (1 S 10: 1) and David (according to the tradition of 1 S 16: 13). Jehu was anointed by a disciple of Eliseus. A priest anointed Solomon, according to 1 K 1: 39 (though v. 34 speaks of Sadoq and Nathan, a priest and a prophet) and Joas (2 K 11: 12). In the other instances the texts use a plural verb, but the rite was obviously performed by a single officiant, who was a religious personage. There can be no doubt that all the kings of Judah were consecrated in the Temple and anointed by a priest.

Anointing is a religious rite. It is accompanied by a coming of the Spirit: we would say that it confers a grace. Thus the spirit of God took hold of Saul after he was anointed (1 S 10: 10), and in the story of David the link between the two is even more direct according to 1 S 16: 13. The king is the Anointed of Yahweh (1 S 24: 7, 11; 26: 9, 11, 16, 23; 2 S 1: 14, 16 (Saul); 2 S 19: 22 (David); Lm 4: 20 (Sedecias); cf. 1 S 2: 10; 12: 3, 5; 2 S 22: 51; Ps 18: 51; 20: 7; 84: 10; 89: 39, 52; 132: 10). The king, a consecrated person, thus shares in the holiness of God; he is inviolable. David refuses to raise a finger against Saul because he is Yahweh's Anointed (1 S 24: 7, 11; 26: 9, 11, 23), and he executes the man who had dared to lift his hand against the king (2 S 1: 14, 16).

The anointing of a king is not, however, a rite peculiar to Israel. Yotham's fable about the kingship of Abimelek (Jg 9: 8, 15), shows that the rite existed in Canaan before the establishment of the Israelite monarchy, and the command to Elias to go and anoint Hazael as king of Aram (1 K 19: 15), may indicate that the rite was practised at Damascus, though this is not borne out either by the account of Hazael's accession (2 K 8: 9-15) or by the non-biblical documents. Concerning Canaan, extra-biblical documents do exist, though they are not all equally convincing. There is a text from Ras Shamra which may contain an allusion to the anointing of Baal as king, but the text is mutilated and its meaning uncertain. One of the Amarna letters tells us that the kings of Syria and Palestine were anointed as vassals of the Pharaoh, and an Egyptian balsam vase found in one of the royal tombs at Byblos may have served for such an investiture. These facts suggest an Egyptian practice rather than a native custom: we know from other sources that the high officials in Egypt were anointed on appointment to office, but the Pharaohs were not. The kings in Mesopotamia do not seem to have been anointed: the only text which might be quoted is of doubtful value: it is a mutilated passage of the Assyrian royal ritual, which may refer to anointing. Hittite kings, on the other hand, were anointed with 'the holy oil of kingship', and in their titles these sovereigns are styled, 'Tabarna, the Anointed, the Great King, etc.'

Was anointing, in Israel, a strictly royal rite? In 1 K 19: 15-16 God commands Elias to go and anoint Hazael, Jehu . . . and Eliseus. Hazael was to be king of Syria, Jehu would be anointed king of Israel by a disciple of Eliseus, but we hear nothing of the anointing of Eliseus or of any other prophet. Here the word was demanded by the context and is used metaphorically. In Is 61: 1, 'anointed' is used figuratively and signifies the prophet's consecration to Yahweh (cf. Jr. 1: 5). The same figurative use is found in Ps 105: 15 = 1 Ch 16: 22, where the Patriarchs are called 'anointed' and 'prophets'.

Many passages, however, say that priests were anointed, and according to Ex 40: 12-15, it was this anointing which conferred on them the priesthood in perpetuity, from generation to generation. These passages all belong to the Priestly tradition, and in them we can distinguish two parallel series of texts: in one, anointing is reserved to the high priest alone (Ex 29: 4-9; Lv 4: 3, 5, 16; 6: 13 (retaining the singular), 15; 8: 12; 16: 32), while in the other it is received by all priests (Ex 28: 41; 30: 30; 40: 12-15; Lv 7: 35-36; 10: 7; Nb 3: 3).

Everyone admits that all these texts were edited after the Exile. Before this the historical and prophetical books never mention the anointing of priests, not even of the high priest. It is therefore possible that, after the disappearance of the monarchy, the royal anointing was transferred to the high priest as head of the people, and later extended to all the priests. One should note, however, that, apart from these texts from the Pentateuch, there is no certain evidence for the anointing of priests before the Hellenistic period. Za 4: 14, it is true, speaks of the 'two sons of the oil', who are probably Josue and Zorobabel, the spiritual and temporal heads of the community; but even if we grant that this unusual expression refers to an anointing (which is a moot point), it is certain that Zorobabel was never anointed, and consequently we cannot conclude that the high priest Josue was ever anointed either. There remains the uncertain text of 1 Ch 29: 22, which mentions an anointing of Sadoq as priest, along with that of Solomon as king. This text only tells us how the practice of former times was then pictured (cf. the texts just quoted from the Pentateuch referring to Aaron), but it is no evidence of contemporary practice. On the contrary, the 'anointed prince' of Dn 9: 25 is probably the high priest Onias III, and the 'race of anointed priests' in 2 M 1: 10 is apparently that of the high priests. But the custom of anointing priests had ceased by the Roman era, and the Rabbis even thought that it had never been practised throughout the period of the Second Temple. Hence it is hard to say at what period the high priest or the priests in general were anointed, though it is clear that it was not under the monarchy.[1] In those days the king was the only Anointed One.

We have stressed somewhat this problem of anointing, because of its religious implications. Anointing, as we shall see, made the king a sacred person and empowered him to perform certain religious acts. Further, 'Anointed' and 'Messiah' are synonyms, being respectively the translation and the transliteration of the same Hebrew word, *mashiah*. The reigning king is therefore a Messiah, and we shall see that he is also a saviour.

These elements were to combine in the expectation of a future saviour who

1. Cf. pp. 399-400.

would be the Messiah King. But it was only in the last century before Christ, in the apocryphal Psalms of Solomon, that this combination became explicit and that the long-promised, long-expected saviour was called the Anointed, the Messiah.

(d) *The acclamation*. After the anointing, the new sovereign was acclaimed. The horn or the trumpet was sounded, the people clapped their hands and shouted: 'Long live the king!' (1 K 1: 34, 39; 2 K 11: 12, 14; cf. 2 K 9: 13). It is the same shout which the rebels must have raised at the banquet of Adonias (1 K 1: 25), and which greeted the appointment of Saul at Mispah (1 S 10: 24). This was the cry of Hushai when he pretended to go over to Absalom (2 S 16: 16).

This acclamation does not mean that the people chose the king, but that the people accepted the choice made by Yahweh and made effective by the anointing: the shout of 'Long live the king!' is not a wish, it is an acquiescence (cf. 'Jehu is king' after the anointing and the sounding of the horn in 2 K 9: 13). Men recognize the king's authority and submit to it. The same meaning must be given to similar expressions such as the greeting: 'May the king live for ever!' (1 K 1: 31), or the oaths by the life of the king (1 S 17: 55; 2 S 14: 19). This oath is sometimes coupled with one by the life of Yahweh (2 S 11: 11; 15: 21), and this double formula makes the king's authority parallel to that of God.

(e) *The enthronement*. After the acclamation all left the sanctuary and entered the palace, where the new king took his seat on the throne (1 K 1: 46, Solomon; 2 K 11: 19, Joas). This action marks the assumption of power, and 'to sit on the throne' becomes a synonym for 'to begin to reign' (1 K 16: 11; 2 K 13: 13). The same expressions recur in other Eastern cultures and in our modern languages. Thus the throne becomes the symbol of royal power (Gn 41: 40; Ps 45: 7), and is sometimes almost personified (2 S 14: 9). It is still called the throne of David, when speaking of his successors the kings of Judah (1 K 2: 24, 45; Is 9: 6; Jr 13: 13; 17: 25), to mark the permanence of the Davidic dynasty promised by Nathan's prophecy, 'Your throne shall be established for ever' (2 S 7: 16; cf. Ps 89: 5; 132: 11-12).

Solomon's throne of gold and ivory is described in 1 K 10: 18-20 as one of the wonders of the world; its back was surmounted by bulls' heads, two standing lions served as arm-rests and it was approached by six steps flanked by figures of lions. The thrones of gods or kings which archaeologists have unearthed provide analogies which illustrate this description, and there is no need to look for a cosmic symbolism, as some have done.

As Yahweh was held to be the true king of Israel,[1] the royal throne is called 'the throne of Yahweh' (1 Ch 29: 23), and more explicitly, 'the throne of the kingship of Yahweh over Israel' (1 Ch 28: 5). This throne of Yahweh had Justice and Right for its supports (Ps 89: 15; 97: 2). The king's throne, too,

---

1. Cf. p. 98.

was firmly established on justice (Pr 16: 12; 25: 5; 29: 14; cf. Ps 72: 1-2), or on right and justice (Is 9: 6).

(f) *The homage.* When the king had taken possession of his throne, the high officials came to do him homage (1 K 1: 47). This homage is mentioned only in the account of Solomon, but it must have taken place at every accession: the ministers made acts of obedience and the new sovereign confirmed them in their offices. Here the Assyrian royal ritual had a picturesque ceremony: the officials laid their insignia before the king, and then ranged themselves round in any order, without regard for precedence. The king then said: 'Let every man resume his office', and every one resumed his insignia and his place in the hierarchy.

3. *The coronation name*

At the coronation of the Pharaoh his full set of titles was proclaimed, comprising five names, of which the last two were the names of accession and of birth, each inscribed on a cartouche. In ancient Mesopotamia an old coronation text of Uruk says that the goddess Ishtar takes away the king's 'name of lowliness' and calls him by his 'name of lordship'. But the Assyrian royal ritual says nothing of a change of name, and one must not draw too sweeping a conclusion from expressions like those of Assurbanipal in his inscriptions: 'Assur and Sin have pronounced my name for power.' This is probably no more than a way of signifying predestination by God; we may compare a Babylonian text about Cyrus: 'Marduk has pronounced his name, Cyrus of Anshan, and has appointed his name for kingship over the world.' Consequently, it is not proved that the kings of Assyria took a new name at their coronation. Assarhaddon certainly received a new name when he became heir-apparent, but this name was hardly ever used in his reign. There remain three instances which are clearer: Tiglath-Pileser III took the name of Pulu when he became king of Babylon (cf. the Pul in the Bible, 2 K 15: 19; 1 Ch 5: 26), Salmanasar V reigned at Babylon under the name of Ululai, and Assurbanipal called himself Kandalanu at Babylon; perhaps they were conforming to a custom of Lower Mesopotamia. Several Hittite kings were known by two names, but as both names are used in official texts dating from their reigns, they cannot be birth and coronation names.

In Israel, the Messianic titles given to the child, probably the Emmanuel, whose birth is foretold in Is 9: 5, have been compared with the five names of the Egyptian protocol: there are in fact four double names, and perhaps the trace of a fifth. This is very probably a literary imitation of an Egyptian custom, but it does not justify the conclusion that the kings of Israel were given a similar set of titles at their accession.

On the other hand there are two certain instances of a change of name. When the Pharaoh made Elyaqim king, he gave him the name of Joiaqim (2 K 23: 34), and Mattanyah, placed on the throne by the king of Babylon, was named Sedecias (2 K 24: 17). The two cases are similar in that each time a foreign suzerain intervenes, whereas Joiakin came to the throne between these two kings without his suzerain intervening and with no mention of a change of name. The change might then be a mark of the bond of vassalage, except that one would expect the Pharaoh to give his vassal an Egyptian name (cf. Gn 41: 45), and the king of Babylon a Babylonian name (cf. Dn 1: 7), whereas the new names of these two kings are just as Hebrew and even Yahwist as those they had before. It is therefore possible that the change was an Israelite custom accepted by the foreign master.

If this is so, the kings of Judah—we find nothing similar in Israel—may have been given a coronation name or a reigning name, and this conclusion seems to be confirmed by other texts. Besides general expressions like 2 S 7: 9; 1 Ch 17: 8 (literally, 'I will make you a [great] name'), which have their equivalents in Egypt, certain facts are significant. To begin with the most cogent, the son and successor of Josias is called Joachaz in 2 K 23: 30, 31, 34, but Shallum in Jr 22: 11, and the list of Josias' sons in 1 Ch 3: 15 contains no Joachaz but does contain a Shallum. May this not be the birth name, and Joachaz the reigning name? We know that the successor of Amasias is some-times called Ozias and sometimes Azarias in the accounts of 2 K 14: 21—15: 34, but the prophets always call him Ozias (Is 1: 1; 6: 1; 7: 1; Os 1: 1; Am 1: 1; Za 14: 5), and so does 2 Ch 26, every time, in the account of his reign. Yet he is called Azarias in the genealogy of 1 Ch 3: 12. We may therefore conclude that Azarias was his birth name and Ozias his coronation name. According to 2 S 12: 24-25 the child of David and Bathsheba received the name of Solomon from his mother, but the prophet Nathan called him Yedidyah. It is curious that this latter name never appears again: could it have been his birth name, displaced by his reigning name? A still more hazardous conjecture is to consider David as the coronation name, in fact a royal title, of the first king of Israel, whose birth name was Elhanan: the same Elhanan who slew Goliath according to 2 S 21: 19, and the same as that Baalhanan, who, according to Gn 36: 38-39, reigned over Edom after a certain Saul.

If we have no more or no clearer examples, the reason may be that the reigning name, the only official one, almost always completely displaced the name given at birth, so that it was no longer even remembered. But in every instance we are still in the realm of hypothesis: the most one can say is that it is probable, though not certain, that the kings of Judah took a new name when they succeeded to the throne.

4. *The enthronement psalms*

The crowning of the king was accompanied by popular demonstrations. Besides the cry of 'Long live the king!' there was cheering, and playing on the flute and trumpet (1 K 1: 40; 2 K 11: 13-14). This music and cheering evidently provided an accompaniment to songs praising the new ruler, as in such demonstrations in the East to-day. Some of the 'royal' psalms may have been composed and sung in this most solemn of settings, as Ps 45 was composed for a royal wedding. The question concerns chiefly Ps 2 and 110, which seem to allude to the rites of enthronement.

In Ps 2, in reply to the princes of the earth who have conspired against Yahweh and his Anointed (v. 2), Yahweh declares that it is he who has established his king in Sion (v. 6). The king (or the cantor) then proclaims the decree, the *ḥôq*, of Yahweh: on this day of sacring he adopts him as his son and promises him dominion over all the land (vv. 7-9). Then the kings pay homage to him (v. 12). In this psalm, then, we find the anointing, the 'decree' (which is the equivalent of the 'testimony' delivered to Joas, 2 K 11: 12, and of the 'covenant' with the house of David, 2 S 7: 8-16[1]), and finally the homage. The supposed revolt of the vassal kings is understandable at the time of a change of reign, and has a parallel in the sham fight which was performed in Egypt at coronation feasts. The question of adoption will be considered later.[2]

In Ps 110, Yahweh seats the king on his right hand (v. 1), promises him the sceptre of power (v. 2), declares that he has begotten him (v. 3, according to the Greek, the text being corrupt and disputed), and declares him a priest after the order of Melchisedech (v. 4); the king slays his enemies, he is 'arbiter of the nations' (vv. 5-6). Here again we see the enthronement, the investiture, the promises and probably the adoption. The allusion to the priesthood of Melchisedech will be discussed later.[3]

These two psalms are therefore close akin and would be appropriate to a sacring feast. Against this it may be objected that the New Testament uses them as Messianic psalms, and that part of the Jewish tradition and all Christian tradition interpret them as such. Some writers point out that the psalmist could not promise universal empire to the human king of the little kingdom of Judah, and that he certainly could not address him as Yahweh's son. Yet there is nothing here which goes beyond the expressions of court etiquette, or the ideas the Israelites held about their king. On the first point, there are numerous parallels from other Eastern sources, but we need only recall the 'Psalm of David' (2 S 22= Ps 18), in which the king sings of his victories over all his enemies in terms very like those of Ps 2 and 110, or the expressions of the royal wedding song in Ps 45, which also allude to the sacring, or the good wishes expressed at the accession of Solomon (1 K 1: 37 and 47). The title of 'son' is found in Nathan's prophecy (2 S 7: 14), where the primary reference is to the human king descended from David, as the next words (vv. 14b-15) show. Moreover, the terms of this prophecy are applied explicitly to Solomon by 1 Ch 17: 13; 22: 10; 28: 6. The two aspects

1. Cf. p. 103.   2. Cf. p. 111.   3. Cf. p. 114.

of universal dominion and divine adoption are combined in the commentary on this prophecy given in Ps 89: 20-38.

Other psalms, too, may have been sung on this occasion, even though they did not contain express references to the ceremonies of the day. Ps 72, for example, prays that the king may reign in justice and foretells that he will rule to the ends of the earth, and Ps 101 draws a portrait of the righteous prince.

It has been maintained that Ps 2, 72 and 110 were at first royal psalms, and were modified after the Exile in a Messianic sense; but it is very hard to say what the revisions were. It is more reasonable to suppose that these psalms, like Nathan's prophecy and other texts referring to royal Messianism, had a twofold meaning from the moment of their composition: every king of the Davidic line is a figure and a shadow of the ideal king of the future. In fact, none of these kings attained this ideal, but at the moment of enthronement, at each renewal of the Davidic covenant, the same hope was expressed, in the belief that one day it would be fulfilled. All these texts, then, are Messianic, for they contain a prophecy and a hope of salvation, which an individual chosen by God will bring to fulfilment.

5. The king as saviour

The king is *ipso facto* a saviour. It is a common idea among primitive peoples that the king embodies the good estate of his subjects: the country's prosperity depends on him, and he ensures the welfare of his people. The idea is common in Eastern countries, too. In Egypt, to cite only two examples, there is a hymn about Senusret III which reads: 'He has come to us, he has brought the people of Egypt to life, he has done away with their afflictions.' Another hymn describes the reign of Ramses IV in these words:

Those who had fled returned to their towns, those who had hidden showed themselves again;

those who had been hungry were fed, those who had been thirsty were given drink;

those who had been naked were clad, those who had been ragged were clothed in fine garments;

those who were in prison were set free, those who were in bonds were filled with joy . . .

In Mesopotamia, Assurbanipal says: 'From the moment that Assur, Sin, etc., placed me on the throne, Adad made his rain fall, Ea opened her springs, the corn grew five cubits high, the harvest of the land has been abundant.' Adad-shum-usur, a priest, wrote to the same king: 'Shamash and Adad . . . have destined for my lord the king . . . good government, days of justice, years of righteousness, abundant rains, powerful floods, good com-

merce . . . ; those who have been ill for many days are cured. The hungry are
satisfied, the starved grow fat. . . . Women give birth, and in their joy tell
their children: our lord the king has given you life.'

It is not surprising, then, to find similar developments of thought in
Israel. So we read in Ps 72:

> He will judge the lowly among the people with justice,
>> he will prove himself a saviour to the children of the poor,
>> and will crush their oppressors.

> He will come down like gentle rain upon grass,
>> like the showers which soften the earth.
> In his days justice shall blossom forth,
>> and widespread peace, until the moon be no more.

> He will set free the poor who call for help,
>> and the lowly, who stand helpless, alone;
> he will show mercy to the weak and the poor,
>> and will save the life of the poor.

> Abundance of wheat on the earth,
>> even on the tops of the hills!
> Abundance like Lebanon's, when its fruit is awaking,
>> and its flowering, like grass over the earth!

Just as in former times the Judges had been 'saviours' (Jg 3: 9, 15), so
under the monarchy the king delivered the nation from its enemies (2 S 19:
10); he was a 'saviour' (2 K 13: 5), whom men called to their aid (2 K 6: 26).

6. Divine adoption

Some recent writers go further, and speak of the king's divine character, of
a divine kingship, or of a divinization of the king, in Israel. Here too they
appeal to Eastern parallels, but not all of them are equally convincing. It is
clear enough that the Pharaoh was considered a god: he is called, without
qualification, 'the god', or 'the good god': he is the son of Ra the creator
god; during his life he is an incarnation of Horus and after his death he is
assimilated to Osiris. This divine character is expressed in the royal titles, in
religious literature, in the rites of coronation and in art, which represents the
Pharaoh with divine attributes and more than human stature.

In Mesopotamia, it was from time to time acknowledged, in very early
days, that the king had a divine character. Among the Babylonians and
Assyrians, however, this is far less apparent. Despite the fiction of divine sonship and the fact that a certain supernatural power was ascribed to him, the
king still remained a man among men. It was quite a different concept from

that which the Egyptians had. Among the Hittites the king was deified after his death, but during his lifetime he was not recognized as a 'god'.

The limited evidence available from Palestine and Syria, apart from Israel, does not allow us to conclude that the kings were deified. In the Amarna letters, when the vassal kings address the Pharaoh as 'my Sun (god)' or 'my god', they are conforming to the Egyptian manner of expression, which need not necessarily be a true expression of their own thought. The Aramaean inscriptions seem to exclude the notion of the king's divinity by representing him as definitely subordinate to the god. The historical and ritual texts from Ras Shamra say nothing of any divinization of the king, and it is only by a forced interpretation that the mythological poems can be invoked as witnesses to it.

It is not true then, to say that the idea of a divine king was shared by all the peoples of the ancient Near East. And when we turn our attention to Israel, the arguments adduced are extremely flimsy. It is true that the anointed king stood in a special relationship to Yahweh.[1] David knew everything, 'like an angel of God' (2 S 14: 17, 20), but the very words of this flattery exclude the idea that he was a god (cf. 1 S 29: 9). The idea of any king-worship, whereby the king, on certain feasts, took the place of God, is based on mere conjectures. Thus, some writers appeal to Ps 45: 7, rendering it as 'Thy throne, O Elohim, endures for ever and ever.' Other possible interpretations have been suggested, such as 'divine throne', 'throne like that of God', but even if the text calls the king an Elohim, we must remember that the term 'Elohim' is applied not only to God but to beings of superhuman power or nature. Thus, for example, it is used of members of the court of heaven (Jb 1: 6; Ps 29: 1; 89: 7), of the shade of Samuel (1 S 28: 13), and even of exceptional men such as princes or judges (Ps 58: 2; 82: 1, 6). The Israelite idea is that while the king is not just a man like other men, he is not a god (cf. 2 K 5: 7 and Ez 28: 2, 9).

This leaves the affirmations of divine sonship in Ps 2: 7 and 110: 3 (Greek). The word of Yahweh in Ps 2: 7, 'Thou art my son, to-day I have begotten thee', is best understood as a formula of adoption. According to the Code of Hammurabi, when someone adopted a person, he said to him, 'You are my son', and if the latter wanted to break the bond thus created, he would say, 'You are not my father' or 'You are not my mother.' Such declarative formulas were used in Israel for engagements: 'To-day you shall be my son-in-law' (1 S 18: 21), for marriage: 'Henceforth you are her brother and she is your sister' (Tb 7: 11), and for divorce: 'She is no longer my wife' (Os 2: 4). In the same way, in Ps 2: 7, Yahweh declares that on this day of consecration, 'to-day', he acknowledges the king as his son; he adopts him. This brings us back to Nathan's prophecy: 'I shall be his father, and he shall be my son' (2 S 7: 14). It is no valid objection to say that the text speaks of the adoption

1. Cf. pp. 103-105.

of the entire Davidic dynasty, for this adoption, obviously, had to be made effective for each sovereign; thus the text is applied to Solomon by 1 Ch 22: 10 and 28: 6.

Granted that the king is adopted by Yahweh, this does not by any means imply that he is equal to him or deified. Ps 89: 27, commenting on Nathan's prophecy, makes the necessary distinction: 'He will call unto me, Thou art my father, my God, the Rock of my salvation.' Israel's religion, indeed, with its faith in Yahweh as a personal God, unique and transcendent, made any deification of the king impossible. Nor can it be said that this represents only the official religion, for if the popular religion or the royal ideology had accepted such a divine character of the king, we should find traces of it in the Prophets, who are anything but lenient towards unfaithful kings. They accuse the kings of many crimes, but never of claiming divinity. Israel never had, never could have had, any idea of a king who was a god.

7. The king and worship

The fact remains that the king, sanctified by his anointing and adopted by Yahweh, is a sacred person and seems thereby to be empowered to perform religious functions. One often hears of the royal priesthood in Israel. We recall that the kings of Egypt, Assyria and Phoenicia were priests. In the Bible, Melchisedech is both king of Salem and priest of El-Elyon (Gn 14: 18). And it is precisely Ps 110: 4, which we have interpreted as an enthronement psalm, which says: 'Thou art a priest for ever in the order of Melchisedech.'

In the historical books, the king appears several times as the leader in acts of worship. David sets up the first altar for Yahweh in Jerusalem (2 S 24: 25); it is David, too, who conceives the project of building him a temple (2 S 7: 2-3), and, according to 1 Ch 22-29, plans in detail how this is to be served. It is Solomon who actually builds the temple directly opposite his own palace, and who dedicates it (1 K 5-8). It is Jeroboam who founds the sanctuary in Bethel, recruits its clergy and arranges its calendar of feasts (1 K 12: 26-33); hence it is a 'royal sanctuary' (Am 7: 13). The chief priests are officials nominated and dismissed by the king (2 S 8: 17; 20: 25; 1 K 2: 26-27; 4: 2). Joas publishes ordinances concerning the Temple (2 K 12: 5-9), and Josias supervises their enforcement (2 K 22: 3-7). The same Josias takes the initiative in the reform of worship and directs it in person (2 K 23). The priest Uriyyah carries out the modifications introduced by Achaz in the sanctuary and its worship (2 K 16: 10-18).

But the kings go even further: the historical texts show them personally performing priestly acts. They offer sacrifices: e.g. Saul at Gilgal (1 S 13: 9-10), David at Jerusalem (2 S 6: 13, 17-18; 24: 25), Solomon at Gibeon (1 K 3: 4, 15), at Jerusalem for the dedication of the Temple (1 K 8: 5, 62-64), and then at the three great feasts of the year (1 K 9: 25). Some of these texts can, of course, be taken in a factitive sense, that the king 'had sacrifice offered', but not all are capable of this meaning. And other texts in fact exclude it: in 2 K 16: 12-15, Achaz goes up to the new altar he has had made, offers the first sacrifice, and then commands the priest to continue the liturgy there; in 1 K 12: 33 it is said that Jeroboam 'went up to the altar to offer sacrifice' (cf. 13: 1f.). Again, David and Solomon bless the people in the sanctuary (2 S 6: 18; 1 K 8: 14), which is a rite reserved to the priests by Nb 6: 22-27 and 1 Ch 23: 13. Solomon consecrates the middle of the court (1 K 8: 64). David wears the loincloth which is the vestment of officiating priests (2 S 6: 14). Neither the prophets nor the historical books before the exile make any protest against these intrusions by the king into liturgical worship. It is only after the end of the monarchy that they become a stumbling-block, and 2 Ch 26: 16-20 says that Ozias was struck with leprosy because he had dared to burn incense at the altar, thus usurping a privilege of the sons of Aaron (2 Ch 26: 18, cf. Nb 17: 5; 1 Ch 23: 13).

All this evidence calls for a carefully balanced solution. The part played by the king in the regulation and supervision of worship or the nomination of the clergy does not mean that he was himself a priest; it does not exceed the prerogatives which the head of State may have over the State religion. It is quite another thing when he performs actions which are properly sacerdotal. But we must note that the instances where the king's personal action is beyond question are all very special or exceptional: the transference of the Ark, the dedication of an altar or a sanctuary, the great annual festivals. Ordinarily, the conduct of worship was left to the priest (2 K 16: 15). Anointing did not confer on the king a priestly character, since, as we have seen,[1] priests were not anointed in the days of the monarchy; but it did make him a sacred person, with a special relationship to Yahweh, and in solemn circumstances he could act as the religious head of the people. But he was not a priest in the strict sense.

But, it may be objected, Ps 110 is a royal psalm, and it calls the king a 'priest'. It has recently been suggested that this verse (Ps 110: 4) was addressed, not to the king, but to the priest whom the newly enthroned king (vv. 1-3) was confirming in his functions, and that these words were originally addressed to Sadoq, the psalm being composed in David's reign. It is an interesting hypothesis, but without foundation. The text can be explained otherwise: it could mean that the king was a priest, but in the only way in which an Israelite king could be: that is, in the way we have described. He was a priest in the same way as Melchisedech, who, it was thought, had been king and priest in that same Jerusalem where the new king was being enthroned. It was the starting-point of the Messianic interpretation to be given to the verse in He 5: 6.

1. Cf. p. 105.

CHAPTER SIX

THE ROYAL HOUSEHOLD

1. *The harem*

IN a society which tolerated polygamy, the possession of a large harem was a mark of wealth and power. It was also a luxury which few could afford, and it became the privilege of kings. Saul had at least one concubine (2 S 3:7), and elsewhere there is mention of his 'wives' (2 S 12:8). Even when David was reigning only in Hebron, he already had six wives (2 S 3: 2-5), and in Jerusalem he took more concubines and wives (2 S 5: 13; cf. 2 S 19: 6), including Bathsheba (2 S 11: 27). When he fled from Absalom he left ten concubines in Jerusalem (2 S 15: 16; 16: 21-22; 20: 3). According to 2 Ch 11: 21, Roboam had eighteen wives and sixty concubines. Abiyyah had fourteen wives according to 2 Ch 13: 21. According to 2 Ch 24: 3 Joas had at least two wives and so had Josias (cf. 2 K 23: 31, 34, 36). Den-hadad called on Achab to surrender his wives (1 K 20: 3-7), and Nabuchodonosor deported Joaikin and his wives (2 K 24: 15). The same fate befell the wives of Joram (2 Ch 21: 14, 17) and of Sedecias (Jr 38: 23). Sennacherib, according to his Annals, accepted the women of Ezechias' harem as tribute. The 'king' in the Song of Songs has sixty queens and eighty concubines (Ct 6: 8). But all these are eclipsed by the fabulous harem of Solomon, who had, according to 1 K 11: 3, seven hundred wives and three hundred concubines. Whatever we may think of these last figures, Dt 17: 17 had good cause to warn the king against possessing too large a harem.

Things were probably much the same in the small states bordering on Israel, though we are poorly informed about them. In the Amarna period we learn, incidentally, that the king of Byblos had at least two wives, and the king of Alasia (Cyprus) speaks of his 'wives'. In the eighth and seventh centuries B.C., however, the Assyrian Annals attribute to the kings of Ascalon, Sidon and Ashdod only one wife each, who may have been the queen consort; this would still leave room for other wives and concubines.

We are better informed about the great empires. Among the Hittites there was only one queen consort, but the king had a harem of wives (free women) and of slave concubines also. Similarly, in Assyria, the king had other wives besides the queen, the 'Lady of the Palace'; often they were princesses from vassal countries. In Egypt the Pharaoh had only one 'great royal spouse'. Five persons, no doubt in succession, held this title in the very long reign of

Ramses II, but his one hundred and sixty-two children prove that he did not restrict himself to his official spouses. According to the Amarna letters, a Pharaoh's harem was the nearest approach to that attributed to Solomon: the princess from Mitanni whom Amenophis III married arrived with 317 young maidens, and the same Pharaoh ordered from the king of Gezer forty 'beautiful women' at forty shekels of silver each. The Pharaoh received thirty young girls as a present from the king of Mitanni, twenty-one from the king of Jerusalem and twenty or thirty from a Syrian prince.

Foreign women were often introduced into these harems to serve not only the king's pleasures but also his policy. Such marriages set the seal on alliances, maintained good relations and guaranteed the loyalty of subject countries. We saw that Amenophis III married a princess of Mitanni: he also married a sister of the king of Babylon. Thutmoses IV before him had married a daughter of the king of Mitanni, and after him Ramses II married a daughter of the Hittite king. Another Hittite king gave his daughter to Mattiwaza of Mitanni; Asarhaddon of Assyria gave his to a Scythian king. A daughter of the king of Amurru became queen at Ugarit, and such cases could be multiplied.

In the same way, David married Maakah, daughter of the Aramaean king of Geshur (2 S 3: 3). Solomon became the Pharaoh's son-in-law (1 K 3: 1), and if he took wives from among the Moabites, the Ammonites, the Edomites, the Sidonians and the Hittites (1 K 11: 1, cf. 14: 21), his motive was to strengthen the bonds with his allies and tributaries. The marriage of Achab with Jezabel, daughter of the king of Tyre (1 K 16: 31), was arranged by his father Omri, in order to strengthen his alliance with the Phoenicians.

From some passages it appears that the king's harem, at least in the early days of the monarchy, used to pass to his successor. In 2 S 12: 8, Nathan says that it was Yahweh himself who, by establishing David as king of Israel, had given him the wives of his master Saul. Absalom publicly approached the concubines whom David had left in Jerusalem: it was a way of asserting that he was now king (2 S 16: 21-22), for possession of the harem was a title to the throne. Ishbaal's anger against Abner, who had taken one of Saul's concubines (2 S 3: 7-8), is easy to explain if she had passed by inheritance to Ishbaal, for Abner's action would imply that he was disputing the power with him. Adonias desired to have Abishag, who had belonged to David's harem (although, according to 1 K 1: 4, he had not had carnal knowledge of her) and had entered Solomon's harem. But when Adonias persuaded Solomon's mother to present his request to the king, Solomon answered: 'Ask me to give him the kingdom, too!' (1 K 2: 13-22). No evidence has yet been found of any such custom among Israel's immediate neighbours, but we may note that it existed among the Persians: Herodotus (III, 68) records that the false Smerdis had usurped both Cambyses' throne and all his wives. Among the ancient Arabs, wives formed part of the inheritance, and the custom was not abolished at one stroke by the Koran's prohibition. In Israel, too, the voice of religion was raised in protest against this incestuous practice: Reuben lost his pre-eminence because he had taken his father's concubine (Gn 35: 22; 49: 3-4), and the laws of Lv 18: 8; Dt 23: 1; 27: 20 were meant for the king as well as the rest of the people; only he did not always observe them (cf. Ez 22: 10).

Among the ladies of the harem, one held the king's preference. This was evidently the privilege of Bathsheba under David, of Jezabel under Achab, of Athaliah under Joram, and it is explicitly stated of Maakah that Roboam 'loved her more than all his other wives and concubines' (2 Ch 11: 21). But the king's favour was not enough to give this wife official title and rank. It is remarkable that the Old Testament only once uses the word 'queen', the feminine of *melek*, 'King', in connection with Israel, and that is in a poetical passage and in the plural, to describe the 'queens' of the 'King' in the Song of Songs, as distinct from his concubines (Ct 6: 8). Elsewhere the singular is used of foreign queens: the queen of Sheba (1 K 10), the queen of Persia (Est *passim*, especially Est 2: 17: the king preferred Esther before all the other women—cf. 2 Ch 11: 21—'and chose her as queen'—nothing similar in 2 Ch 11).

2. *The Great Lady*

On the other hand, at the court of Judah, official rank was accorded to the *g'bîrah*. In ordinary speech the word means 'mistress' as opposed to servant, and corresponds to *'adôn*, 'lord', the feminine of which is not used in Hebrew (2 K 5: 3; Is 24: 2; Ps 123: 2; Pr 30: 23). In 1 K 11: 19 it is applied to the Pharaoh's wife and consort, but it is never used of the wife of a king of Judah; under Asa, the *g'bîrah* is his grandmother Maakah (1 K 15: 13; 2 Ch 15: 16). The *g'bîrah* carried into captivity in Jr 29: 2 is the king's mother, according to the parallel in 2 K 24: 15. The sons of the *g'bîrah* mentioned in 2 K 10: 13 along with the sons of the king must be distinct from them: they are the sons of the queen-mother (and therefore the king's brothers). In Jr 13: 18 the king and the *g'bîrah* are Joiakin and his mother. Etymology and usage suggest that the title should be rendered as Great Lady.

This title implied a certain dignity and special powers. Bathsheba was certainly *g'bîrah* under Solomon; he receives her with great honour and seats her on his right hand (1 K 2: 19). The power of the Great Lady did not proceed merely from the influence of a mother over her son, as with Bathsheba; it was much more extensive, and for abusing it, Maakah was deprived by Asa of her dignity of Great Lady (1 K 15: 13). This authority of the queen-mother explains how Athaliah could so easily seize power on the death of Ochozias (2 K 11: 1f.); the queen-mother had an official position in the kingdom, and hence the Books of Kings always mention the name of the king's mother in the introduction to each reign in Judah—except in the cases of Joram and Achaz, where no woman is named, and of Asa, where his grand-mother's name takes the place of his mother's. It is possible that the Great Lady was accorded her rank on the accession of her son, which would explain the career of Hamital, wife of Josias, who was queen-mother under Ioachaz, was set aside under Joiaqim and Joiakin, and returned under Sedecias, the brother of Joachaz (2 K 23: 31, 36; 24: 8, 18). It is also possible that the mother became *g'bîrah* as soon as her son was designated heir to the throne, as is suggested by 2 Ch 11: 21-22. The story of Bathsheba does not enable us to decide this point, since Solomon's sacring took place immediately after his nomination; but it does at least prove that before this nomination Solomon's mother had not the dignity which she subsequently enjoyed (cf. 1 K 1: 15-16, 31 and 2: 13-19). Bathsheba was the first Great Lady in Israel. On the other hand it seems that the Great Lady could keep her position after her son's death: Maakah, wife of Roboam, was still *g'bîrah* under her grand-son Asa, after the short reign of her son Abiyyam (1 K 15: 13). From the same passage we see that the *g'bîrah* could be dismissed by the king: Maakah had favoured the cult of Asherah.

Hittite parallels may help to elucidate this rather complicated question. The *tavannana* was the lawful queen, the mother of the heir-apparent, and played an important part in policy and religion. If she survived the king she retained the same position during the reign of her son (or sons, if two brothers succeeded to the throne); and only on her death did the dignity pass to her daughter-in-law, the wife of the reigning king. Like Maakah, she could be dismissed for a serious offence against the king or the state; but, as in Judah, this seems to have been exceptional. The queen-mother must have held a similar position in Ugarit, where several official letters are addressed to the king's mother, also called the *'adath*, which is the feminine of *'adôn*, and there-fore the equivalent of *g'bîrah*. The Akkadian texts of Ras Shamra indicate that this queen-mother intervened in political affairs, and they also mention a Great Lady of Amurru. For Assyria the evidence is less clear, but we should remember the part played by the queens Sammuramat and Naqi'a during the reigns of their husbands and then of their sons. This tradition is preserved in the Greek legends of Semiramis and Nitokris. One may also point to the influence of Adad-guppi', the mother of Nabonidus.

There is no direct evidence of the existence of a Great Lady in the northern kingdom. In the introductions to the reigns of Israel, the name of the king's mother is never given. 2 K 10: 13 mentions a *g'bîrah* who can only be Jezabel, but the word is put in the mouth of the princes of Judah. The institution, moreover, presupposes a dynastic stability which was not usually found in the kingdom of Israel. But we must draw attention to a rare term, which is per-haps the Israelitic equivalent of the *g'bîrah* of Judah. In Ps 45: 10, the *shegal* is mentioned as standing on the right hand of the king; she is not classed with the other women of the harem, for she is the queen consort. Now Ps 45 has been interpreted as a wedding-hymn composed for a king of Israel. It is also very tempting to restore the word *shegal* at the end of Jg 5: 30 in the Hymn of Deborah, in place of the impossible *shalal*, 'booty'. The word is parallel to Sisera, and would denote the queen or queen-mother, cf. v. 28. Once again, the Hymn of Deborah is a composition of northern Israel. The only other examples of the term in the Old Testament, Ne 2: 6 (the queen of Persia) and Dn 5: 2, 3, 23 (the Aramaic plural form: the wives of Balthazar) do not prove that the word was an official term in Judah before the Exile.

3. *The royal children*

Our only information on the position of the king's daughters comes from the story of Tamar, the daughter of David. From this we may conclude that the princesses lived in the palace until their marriage, under the care of women (2 S 13: 7). They wore a distinctive dress (2 S 13: 18-19), probably a long-sleeved robe like that given by Jacob to his favourite son Joseph (Gn 37: 3, 23, 32). Their father would give them in marriage to his senior officers (1 K 4: 11, 15) or to friendly kings (2 K 8: 18).

The king's sons were brought up in the palace by nurses (2 K 11: 2), then entrusted to tutors chosen from the leading men of the city (2 K 10: 1, 6f., cf. 1 Ch 27: 32). We are told that Achab had seventy sons. The figure is no doubt symbolic of a large family (cf. Jg 8: 30; 9: 2, 5), but this parallel shows that we must take 'sons' in the literal sense and not interpret it as descendants in general or as more distant relatives. We know besides that Achab had a harem (1 K 20: 2, 5, 7), which may have been a large one. In the same way, in the story of Absalom and Amnon, the 'king's sons' are certainly the sons of David (2 S 13: 23-38). Again, 2 K 10: 13 speaks of the sons of the king and the sons of the Great Lady; there is no good reason to interpret these terms as honorific titles instead of taking them in the strict sense. When they had grown up and, no doubt, married young, the king's sons led an independent life and were provided for by their father (2 Ch 21: 3; cf. Ez 46: 16). Amnon resided outside the palace (2 S 13: 5), and Absalom had his own house (2 S 13: 20; 14: 24) herds and lands (2 S 13: 23; 14: 30). But even when they were adults these sons were still subject to the authority of their father the king (2 S 13: 27).

Apart from the heir-apparent, who had special prerogatives (2 Ch 11: 22), the king's sons could perform certain duties at the court (2 S 8: 18; 1 Ch 18: 17). The expression *ben hammelek*, 'son of the king', is, however, used several times in contexts which seem to imply that it does not mean a son in the proper sense. In 1 K 22: 26-27=2 Ch 18: 25-26, the 'king's son' Yoash is named after the governor of the city, and both are ordered to put the prophet Micheas in prison. In Jr 36: 26, the 'king's son' Yerahmeel, and two other men are commanded to seize Baruch and Jeremias. In Jr 38: 6, Jeremias is thrown into the cistern of the 'king's son' Malkiyyahu. In 2 Ch 28: 7 the 'king's son' Maaseyahu is killed along with two of the king's officers. None of these men appear elsewhere as a member of the royal family. It seems therefore that in these four instances the title 'king's son' denotes an office. This conclusion is perhaps confirmed by two discoveries in Palestine, one of a seal, the other of a stamp from a signet-ring: both have a proper name, followed by 'king's son' in the place where other seals mention their owner's office. These officials were not of very high rank; Yoash is named after the governor of the city and in three instances out of four their intervention is connected with prisoners. Probably, therefore, the *ben hammelek* was a police officer. The explanation may be that this officer was perhaps chosen originally from among the king's sons.

A parallel from Egypt may be noted: 'royal son of Kush' is the title of the viceroy of Ethiopia, who was never a descendant of the Pharaoh, except perhaps for the first holder of that title, who would have been a grandson of the founder of the Eighteenth Dynasty.

4. *The king's attendants*

The royal family was surrounded by a court of officials and household servants (1 K 10: 4-5). All, whatever their office, were called the king's 'servants', from the soldiers of the guard (1 K 1: 33; 2 S 11: 9, 13; 20: 6), to the highest officials (1 K 11: 26; 2 K 19: 5; 22: 12; 2 Ch 34: 20; and for foreign courts cf. 2 K 5: 6; 25: 8; 2 Ch 32: 9).

The question has been raised whether the expression 'king's servant', *'ebed hammelek*, when used in the singular, may not sometimes denote a special office. For example the *'ebed hammelek* Asayah is named together with the secretary Shaphan (2 K 22: 12= 2 Ch 34: 20). Further, we possess a number of seals bearing a proper name followed by *'ebed hammelek* or by *'ebed* with the name of a king. Seals of the same type, but of Phoenician, Ammonite, Edomite and perhaps Philistine origin, have also been discovered. Now it is true that the title stands in the place where an office is usually mentioned, but this does not prove that it denotes a particular office. As a matter of fact the title is given to Nebuzaradan (2 K 25: 8) who at the same time is called the commander of Nabuchodonosor's guard. Finally, the number of seals which have survived would be surprisingly large, if all their wearers had occupied the same office. We should rather conclude that it was a general title, borne by several officials who used their seals to stamp official documents. The corresponding Assyrian expression also covered different functions.

At the time of the capture of Jerusalem in 587 B.C., the Chaldaeans took prisoner five men 'who saw the king's face' (2 K 25: 19; in the parallel of

Jr 52: 25 there are seven). This is sometimes translated as 'counsellors', and in fact in Est 1: 14, the same words denote the seven members of the royal council of Persia. In itself, however, the expression has a general sense: it means those who are admitted to the king's presence (cf. 2 S 14: 24, 28, 32), just as the expression 'to go to see the face of Yahweh', means 'to go to the Temple' (Dt 31: 11; Ps 42: 3). The term then includes the king's personal servants, and also his friends and courtiers, all who 'stand before the king' (1 S 16: 21f.; Jr 52: 12; cf. the angels in Mt 18: 10). The expression is found in Assyrian with the same vague meaning. The king would naturally seek advice from his courtiers (1 K 12: 6; cf. the heavenly court in 1 K 22: 19f.; Jb 1: 6f.; 2: 1f.). The formal title of 'counsellor', *yô'es* was given to Ahitophel under David (2 S 15: 12; cf. 15: 31 and its sequel) and to David's uncle in 1 Ch 27: 32-33. The title is found under Amasias also (2 Ch 25: 16).

1 S 8: 15 mentions, along with the king's servants, the *sarîsîm*. They are named among the men of rank in Jr 34: 19, and among the men of war, the women and the children in Jr 41: 16. A *sarîs* is sent by Achab to the prophet Micheas ben Yimlah (1 K 22: 9=2 Ch 18: 8); another is charged with restoring her goods to the Shunamite (2 K 8: 6). Two or three *sarîsîm* join in throwing Jezabel down from the window (2 K 9: 32). The *sarîsîm* of Joiakin are sent into captivity (2 K 24: 12, 15; Jr 29: 2). The *sarîs* Nathan-Melek had a room in the Temple (2 K 23: 11). At the capture of Jerusalem a *sarîs* was in command of the men of war (2 K 25: 19; Jr 52: 25). It is usually translated by 'eunuch', and it certainly has this sense in other passages (Is 56: 3-5; Si 30: 20, and perhaps in 2 K 20: 18=Is 39: 7, probably in Est 1 and 2, *passim*, and Dn 1, *passim*). But it is more than doubtful whether this sense holds good in the texts quoted earlier, where the *sarîsîm* figure simply as officials or courtiers. Outside Israel, the Bible uses this word to denote the captain of the guard, the chief cupbearer and the chief baker of the Pharaoh (Gn 37: 36; 39: 1; 40: 2); it mentions the chief *sarîsîm* of Sennacherib (2 K 18: 17 omitted in the parallel of Is 36: 2), and of Nabuchodonosor (Jr 39: 3, 13), both of whom took part in military expeditions.

The word itself is borrowed from Assyrian: it is transcribed *sha-reshi*, 'he at the head', simply a dignitary, a courtier, who goes before the king, one of his confidential advisers. For certain tasks, such as the supervision of the harem or the royal children, eunuchs were chosen, and the word acquired this meaning, as several cuneiform inscriptions show. This evolution in meaning also explains all the Biblical uses. The word passed into Egyptian at a late date, in the form *srs*, to signify Persian officials.

The king maintained male and female singers to entertain himself and the court. David, who was called to play the harp before Saul, is rather an exceptional figure anyway (1 S 16: 14-23; 18: 10; 19: 9), but Barzillai says he is too old to accept David's invitation to come and listen to the male and female singers at the palace (2 S 19: 36). The memory of Solomon's musicians is preserved in Qo 2: 8. Sennacherib mentions in his Annals the singers, male and female, of Ezechias, who were given to him in tribute.

These singers, men and women, used to enliven banquets. It was a signal mark of favour to be admitted to the royal table 'as one of the king's sons' (2 S 9: 7, 13; 19: 29, 34; cf. Lk 22: 30). Solomon's table was renowned for its lavish service and the high quality of its menu (1 K 10: 5), though the abundant victuals which reached it (1 K 5: 2-3, 7) supplied not only the king's own table but all the inmates of the palace and the king's pensioners, like the descendants of Barzillai (1 K 2: 7), and (later) the hundreds of prophets who 'ate at Jezabel's table' (1 K 18: 19, cf. Daniel and his companions, Dn 1: 5-15, and the table of Nehemias, Ne 5: 17-18). The great monarchies of the East had officials in charge of the king's table, cupbearers, bakers and carvers, just as the French monarchy had its *officiers de bouche*. The Old Testament speaks of the Pharaoh's chief cupbearer and chief baker (Gn 40: 1f.) and Sennacherib's chief cupbearer (2 K 18: 17f.; Is 36: 2f. where the context shows that such titles could be honorary and associated with other duties, as is abundantly confirmed by Assyrian documents). Nehemias, on the other hand, who was cupbearer to the king of Persia, did serve at the king's table (Ne 1: 11; 2: 1). The small courts of Israel and Judah may have had similar offices, but they are not mentioned in the Bible; in 1 K 10: 5=2 Ch 9: 4, the word usually translated 'cupbearers' really means a 'drinking service'.

The king, who had military duties and often went to war himself, had a squire. At first, he was called the king's 'armour-bearer': this was David's title when he was attached to Saul (1 S 16: 21), and another of Saul's squires took part in the battle of Gilboa (1 S 31: 4-6). Abimelek, king of Shechem, had his squire (Jg 9: 54), and the senior officers of course had theirs (1 S 14: 6f.; 2 S 23: 37). When Solomon began to use chariots, the squire was called the *shalîsh*, literally the 'third man'. The Hittite, Israelite and Assyrian chariots were in fact mounted by three men, the driver, the fighting man and the *shalîsh*, who carried the buckler and the weapons. (He was called in Assyrian the *shalshu*.) In Ex 14: 7; 15: 4, the word is extended to the Egyptian army, whose chariots carried only two men. Every Israelite charioteer had his *shalîsh*, but the king's squire was an important personage, his orderly officer or aide-de-camp; he was the man 'on whose arm the king leaned' (2 K 7: 2, 17, 19; cf. 2 K 5: 18). We hear of Jehu's squire (2 K 9: 25), and Peqahyah's, that Peqah who assassinated his master and reigned in his stead (2 K 15: 25). The word is twice employed in the plural, and in both texts the king's guards are mentioned too (1 K 9: 22; 2 K 10: 25). The name and the office disappeared when there were no more chariots, *i.e.*, at the fall of Samaria in the northern kingdom, and after Sennacherib's invasion in the kingdom of Judah.

Under David, Hushai is called the king's 'friend' (2 S 15: 37, also in v. 32, according to the Greek; 16: 16). The name has been taken as the name of an office by 1 Ch 27: 33, which includes Hushai among David's principal officials, and in fact the list of Solomon's officials also includes a 'friend' (1 K 4: 5). This word re'eh is generally explained as a different form of re'a, 'companion', which is the word used in 1 Ch. 27: 33. But the two words may be unconnected, and re'eh may be a word borrowed from abroad. In the Amarna letters the king of Jerusalem proclaims himself the ruḫi of the Pharaoh. Now there is an Egyptian title rḫ nsw.t, the man 'known by the king', a title of nobility given to men whom the Pharaoh wished to honour. The Hebrew word may be a transcription of this, via the Canaanite language. If so, 2 S 16: 16 is making a play on the words: Hushai is the re'eh, the man 'known by' David, and Absalom asks him why he has not departed with his re'a his 'friend'. The title carried with it no special function and it is not found after Solomon. Possibly it was replaced by a translation of this Egyptian expression; this would explain the 'known' or familiar men of Achab's court, the m'yudda'im (2 K 10: 11). The equivalent mûdû is by then found at Ugarit.

5. The royal guard

David had a corps of foreign mercenaries, the Kerethites and the Pelethites, recruited in Philistia and the neighbouring regions. They were under a separate command from the army raised in Israel (2 S 8: 18 = 1 Ch 18: 17; 2 S 20: 23). The part played by these mercenary troops in war (cf. 2 S 20: 7) will be examined in connection with military institutions, but they also formed the king's bodyguard. They accompanied David on his flight from Absalom (2 S 15: 18), and formed the escort to Solomon on the day of his sacring (1 K 1: 38, 44). They are those 'servants of My Lord' (2 S 20: 6; 1 K 1: 33), who lodged at the palace gate (2 S 11: 9, 13). They are never again mentioned after Solomon's accession, but other foreign mercenaries, the Carites, were in the service of the Palace at the time of the revolt against Athaliah (2 K 11: 4, 19).

On this occasion the Carites are mentioned along with the raṣîm, the 'runners'. The latter furnished the escort platoon which ran before the king's chariot. Absalom, and later Adonias, in their attempts to seize the throne, provided themselves with a chariot-team and fifty runners (2 S 15: 1; 1 K 1: 5), for this was part of royal ceremonial. The runners appear in the reign of Saul (1 S 22: 17), where the context implies that they were recruited from the Israelites. We learn from 1 K 14: 27-28 = 2 Ch 12: 10-11, that their guardroom stood at the entrance to the Palace, and that they kept there the bronze bucklers worn when they accompanied the king to the Temple. There were six hundred of these; they had replaced the golden bucklers which Solomon made and which he had stored in the Gallery of the Forest of Lebanon (1 K 10: 16-17). This suggests that this gallery was the guardroom of Solomon's Palace. These runners kept watch by roster over the Palace and the Temple and they took a leading part in the deposition of Athaliah and the enthronement of Joas (2 K 11). The kings of Israel, too, had their guard: Jehu's accompanied him to Samaria and took part in the extirpation of the worship of Baal (2 K 10: 25).

6. The royal estate

All the kings of the ancient East were large landowners. The lands they owned were administered directly, or rented, or granted as fiefs in return for rents or personal services. This is especially true of Egypt, where the greater part of the land belonged to the king or the temples, and the statements of Gn 47: 20-26 are amply confirmed by the documents of the country. It is also true, though not to the same extent, of Mesopotamia, where the Code of Hammurabi, the Nuzu documents and those of the Kassite period all stress the importance of fiefs, and the texts of all periods mention royal possessions. It is also true of the little kingdoms of Syria, as is proved by the recently discovered archives of Alalakh and Ugarit.

It was equally true of Israel. Samuel warned the Israelites that the king they wanted would make his subjects till and harvest his fields, and would take their vineyards and olivegroves to give them to his servants (1 S 8: 12, 14). This happened as early as Saul's day. Before he became king he had only a small family property (1 S 9: 1f.; 11: 5), but afterwards he was able to distribute fields and vineyards to his officers (1 S 22: 7), and at his death he left a vast amount of property (2 S 9: 9-10). There was no clear distinction between the king's personal possession and the crown's, and everything passed to his successor, even if he were not of the family of the late king. David inherited Saul's harem and also his 'house' (2 S 12: 8). It was only as a favour that he 'restored' to Meribbaal the lands of his grandfather (2 S 9: 7) and he reserved his rights over them: he controlled their administration (2 S 9: 9-10), withdrew them from Meribbaal (2 S 16: 4), and then divided them between Meribbaal and Siba (2 S 19: 30). This power of the king over the estate of his predecessor certainly remained in force in the northern kingdom, where usurpations were frequent. In Judah, where the dynastic succession was uninterrupted, the transmission of the royal estate presented no problem.

This estate could be formed and increased in many ways. The king would acquire lands, as David bought the threshing-floor of Araunah (2 S 24: 24), and Omri the hill of Samaria (1 K 16: 24). Achab tried to buy Naboth's vineyard or to obtain it by exchange (1 K 21: 2). The rest of the story of Naboth could mean that the goods of men condemned to death were forfeit to the king (1 K 21: 15). It is also possible that the king took possession of property left vacant by their owners leaving the country: this would explain the story of the Shunamite (2 K 8: 1-6, especially vv. 3 and 6). It is clear too that an unjust king had no scruples about confiscating his subjects' goods: this had been foretold by 1 S 8: 14, and would itself be sufficient explanation of the story of Naboth. The king could also receive presents. Gezer, the wedding gift of the Pharaoh's daughter (1 K 9: 16), remained crown property, which is why its territory is omitted in the administrative organization of the revenues (1 K 4: 8-19, where one would expect mention of it in v. 9). The Arabs sent flocks to Josaphat (2 Ch 17: 11). The income which Solomon derived from his commercial enterprises certainly favoured the extension and exploitation of the royal estate. In Qo 2: 4-7 Solomon is represented as saying: 'I have planted vineyards for myself, laid out gardens and orchards, and placed in them every kind of fruit tree. I have dug out pools to water what I have planted, bought servants and maid-servants. I have owned men and flocks, cattle and sheep in abundance.' According to 2 Ch 26: 10 (which is confirmed by archaeological observations), Ozias had built towers in the desert and dug cisterns; he had many cattle, many labourers and vine-dressers. 2 Ch 32: 28-29 says that Ezechias had granaries for his grain, wine and oil, grazing grounds for his herds, many flocks and cattle. The king's estate is again mentioned in 2 Ch 31: 3; 35: 7. It is very significant that Ezechiel, in his plan for the future, reserves the prince's portion and makes regulations about it (Ez 45: 7; 46: 16-18; 48: 21). He was still dominated by the age-old tradition of the royal estate.

We are not very well informed about the administration of this estate. The Chronicler gives a list of the overseers of David's property (1 Ch 27: 25-31; cf. 28: 1): there are overseers for the grain crops and the vineyards, for the wine and the oil, for the herds and the flocks, the camels and the she-asses. This list is not invented, as is proved by the non-Israelite proper names in it, but we can verify neither the details nor the date.

The general administration of the estate was in the hands of a special official. He is apparently the man who is 'over the king's house', 'asher 'al habbayth, the master of the palace. This is the title conferred on Joseph by the Pharaoh (Gn 41: 40; cf. 45: 8), and Joseph's duties were in fact concerned with the royal estate (47: 20-26) and its revenues (41: 48-49, 55-56; 42: 6f.). Achab set out during the drought with Obadyahu, his master of the palace, to find forage for his horses, mules and livestock (1 K 18: 5). But the functions of the master of the palace far exceeded those of a royal steward, as is shown by the rest of the story of Joseph and other texts on the subject. He was also major-domo and he ended by becoming the king's first minister.[1] There is perhaps another title to indicate the estate manager. Siba, who is the steward of Saul's property, is called his na'ar, or the na'ar of his house (2 S 9: 9; 19: 18). Boaz too had a na'ar who supervised his harvesters (Rt 2: 5f.). Three seal-impressions have also been found, dating from the end of the monarchy, with the

1. Cf. pp. 129-130.

name of Eliakim, *na'ar* of the king. As the title does not appear in the texts which mention the highest officials of the realm, it may perhaps have been reserved for the steward of the estate.

This information may perhaps be completed by reference to some archaeological discoveries. Some seventy inscribed potsherds have been unearthed in the ruins of the royal palace at Samaria: they are delivery notes for wine or oil, with the name of the receiver and the deliverer, and often an indication of the place of origin. They are administrative receipts dating from the reign of Jeroboam II. It is very likely that they concern the administration of the royal estates near the capital: similar documents have been found in Egypt. It is much less likely that the Judaean jars which are stamped on the handles with *lammelek*, 'to the king', are connected with the management of the estate: obviously they could have been used for the delivery of revenue, but it is simpler and less hazardous to explain the stamp on them as a hall-mark of the royal workshop.[1]

1. Cf. pp. 77-78.

CHAPTER SEVEN

THE PRINCIPAL OFFICIALS OF THE KING

THE king was assisted in the administration of the kingdom by a number of high-ranking officials who lived close by and formed his government; they were his ministers. They are called the king's 'servants', but in relation to the people they are 'chiefs', *śârîm*[1] (1 K 4: 1); they are referred to by their office, or by the title 'set over' such and such a charge. As with other Eastern courts, their functions are sometimes difficult to define, and the Bible does not give a complete picture of this central administration.

1. *The ministers of David and Solomon*

We possess two lists of David's senior officials and one of Solomon's. They are certainly derived from documents preserved in archives, but they have been re-edited and their text has suffered to some extent.

The first list (2 S 8: 16-18 = 1 Ch 18: 14-17) is given after Nathan's prophecy and the summary of David's victories, and before the long story about the succession to the throne. Consequently, it represents the final and definitive arrangement after the foundation of the kingdom. The military command was shared between Joab, commander of the army, and Benayahu, commander of the guard. Yehoshaphat was herald, Serayah (or Shawsha in Ch) was secretary. Sadoq and Ebyathar were the priests, but at the end of the list is added: 'the sons of David were priests'. The order as we have it seems haphazard: commander of the army, heralds, priests, commander of the guard and finally the sons of David. Joab and Benayahu, Sadoq and Ebyathar, all figure in the same offices in the history of the reign. Neither Yehoshaphat the herald nor the sons of David play any part in it.

The mention of the latter is strange: their names, which one would think essential in a document of this kind, are not given, and their status as 'priests' is enigmatic. The most we can presume is that they assisted or did duty for their father in those sacerdotal functions which were occasionally performed by the king.[2] The parallel in 1 Ch 18: 17 has: 'and the sons of David held the first rank next to the king', which is proof of a Levite's scruple, but it does not clarify matters. The text about the two legitimate priests is doubtful. The Hebrew reading is 'Sadoq son of Ahitub and Ahimelek son of Ebyathar'; this must be corrected at least to 'and Ebyathar son of Ahimelek', according to the Syriac (1 S 22: 20 and 2 S 20: 25). Perhaps we should even restore 'Sadoq and Ebyathar son of Ahimelek son of Ahitub', according to 2 S 22: 20; this would make Sadoq a newcomer, without Israelite ancestry. These questions will be dealt with in connection with the history of the priesthood.[1] Here it is enough to note that the religious leaders are included among the royal officials.

The second Davidic list (2 S 20: 23-26), which has no parallel in Chronicles, is given at the very end of David's reign. The same names are here arranged in a more logical order: commander of the army, commander of the guard, herald, secretary (here called Sheya or Shewa), and the priests. But before the herald it adds Adoram, the officer in charge of forced labour; and at the very end, instead of the sons of David who were 'priests', it gives Ira the Yairite, 'priest of David'. This repetition of a list of high officials is easily explained after the return of Joab to the post from which he had been dismissed (2 S 19: 14; 20: 22), and after the suppression of the revolt of Sheba (2 S 20: 1-22); but it is not so easy to account for its new features. It is doubtful whether Adoram, who was still in office after Solomon's death (1 K 12: 18), could already have been in charge of forced labour under David, for this post does not seem to have been instituted until the reign of Solomon (1 K 5: 27; 9: 15). The mention of a 'priest of David' along with Sadoq and Ebyathar is puzzling. According to one reading of the Greek, this Ira the Yairite might be a doublet of Ira the Yattirite, who is one of David's warriors, according to 2 S 23: 38. It is not impossible that this list presents a true account of the state of administration at the end of David's reign; it is also possible that the passage is a subsequent compilation.

The list for Solomon's reign (1 K 4: 1-6) raises some difficult problems of literary and textual criticism, to which no satisfactory solution has yet been found. Examination of external witnesses and the weight of internal evidence would suggest suppressing v. 4 on Benayahu, Sadoq and Ebyathar, and adding to v. 6 the mention of Eliab, son of Joab, as army commander. It would then read as follows (with the proper names often uncertain): the priest Azaryahu, son of Sadoq; the secretaries Elihoreph or Elihaph and Ahiyyah, who are sons of Shisha, evidently David's secretary; Yehoshaphat the herald; the chief prefect Azaryahu or Adoniyahu, son of Nathan; the king's friend, Zabud or Zakkur, another son of Nathan (to whom a gloss has added the title of 'priest'); the master of the palace, Ahishar or Ahhiyah (or 'his brother'?), with no mention of his father's name; the army commander, Eliab, son of Joab; the chief over the levy, Adoniram or Adoram, son of Abda.

The continuity with the Davidic administration is evident. Solomon employs the same herald as his father, the son of one of his priests, both the sons of his secretary, the son of his army commander and at least two sons of

[1] Cf. pp. 372-374.

the prophet Nathan, who had been an adviser of David and had favoured the accession of Solomon. On the whole, it represents a new generation coming to power; this proves that the list does not date from the beginning of Solomon's reign. This is confirmed by the appearance of new posts: there is a chief prefect, a fact which presumes the existence of the organization described in 1 K 4: 7-19, and an officer in charge of forced labour, the introduction of which is recorded in 1 K 5: 27 (with the reservation noted above about the second Davidic list).

It is noteworthy, too, that some of these high officials, or their fathers, have non-Israelite names, names which have puzzled the copyists or the translators: Adoram has a Phoenician name, like his father Abda. The names of Shisha or Shawsa (1 Ch 18: 16) and his son Elihoreph or Elihaph may be Egyptian or Hurrite. In fact it was to be expected that the young Israelite kingdom should recruit some of its officials from the neighbouring countries, which had an administrative tradition. Even for its organization it had to copy models abroad. Study of some offices suggests the influence of Egyptian institutions, but it does not enable us to decide whether this influence was direct, or whether it came indirectly to Israel from the Canaanite states which Israel displaced. Direct influence seems the more likely, for the kingdom of David and Solomon was far bigger than any of the little city-states of Canaan.

The king's 'friend' is rather an honorary title, probably Egyptian in origin[1]; he is perhaps an intruder in this list of officials. The rôles of army commander and commander of the guard will be studied under military institutions[2]. The officer in charge of the prefects, and the officer in charge of forced labour will be discussed in connection with the services they directed[3]; in any case they do not appear after Solomon. There remain three ministers whose functions continued until the end of the monarchy and who are again mentioned together in an important crisis, Sennacherib's invasion in 701 (cf. 2 K 18: 18): they are the master of the palace, the secretary and the herald. These three deserve to be studied on their own.

2. The master of the palace

In Solomon's list, Ahishar is *'asher 'al habbayth*, the master of the palace. The same title is given to Arsa, who had a house at Tirsah under Elah, king of Israel (1 K 16: 9); to Obadyahu, who was minister under Achab (1 K 18: 3); to Yotham, when he succeeded his sick father, the king Ozias (2 K 15: 5); and to Shebna, who was master of the palace under Ezechias (Is 22: 15), and later succeeded by Elyaqim (Is 22: 19-20); it was this Elyaqim who held the discussion with Sennacherib's envoy under the walls of Jerusalem (2 K 18: 18= Is 36: 3). Outside the Bible, the title appears in the inscription of a tomb in Siloam (the name is incomplete: could it be the tomb of Shebna? cf. Is 22:

---

1. Cf. pp. 122-123.   2. Cf. pp. 220-221.   3. Cf. pp. 134 and 142.

16), and on a seal-impression in the name of Godolias, doubtless the man whom Nabuchodonosor installed as governor of Judah after the capture of Jerusalem (2 K 25: 22; Jr 40: 7). He would formerly have been master of the palace under Sedecias, the last king of Judah. It has recently been suggested that the post was hereditary, and that Godolias was a descendant of Elyaqim, who was master of the palace under Ezechias; but there is no sufficient evidence for this suggestion in the texts. In the vocabulary of Chronicles, the equivalent is perhaps the *n'gîd habbayth*, the chief of the palace, a title given by Achaz to a certain Azriqam (2 Ch 28: 7).

The exact semantic equivalent in Assyrian and Babylonian is *sha pân êkalli* and in Egyptian *mr pr*. They were high officials, but their authority seems to have been restricted to the administration of the royal palace: they were the king's stewards or majordomos. In Israel the powers of the master of the palace were far more extensive and the similarity between his functions and those of the Egyptian vizier is even more important than the verbal resemblances. This vizier used to report every morning to the Pharaoh and receive his instructions. He saw to the opening of the 'gates of the royal house', that is, of the various offices of the palace, and then the official day began. All the affairs of the land passed through his hands, all important documents received his seal, all the officials were under his orders. He really governed in the Pharaoh's name and acted for him in his absence. This is obviously the dignity which Joseph exercised, according to Genesis. He had no one above him except the Pharaoh, and he was appointed over the whole land of Egypt; he held the royal seal (Gn 41: 40-44), and to describe his dignity the Bible says that the Pharaoh 'put him in charge of his house'; he made him, in fact, his master of the palace (Gn 41: 40; 45: 8).

The master of the palace had similar functions at the court of Judah. Announcing the promotion of Elyaqim, Is 22: 22 says:

> I lay the key of the house of David
>   upon his shoulder;
> If he opens, none will shut;
> If he shuts, none will open.

The Egyptian vizier's instructions are described in a very similar fashion. Every morning 'the vizier will send someone to open the gates of the king's house, to admit those who have to enter, and to send out those who have to go out'. One is reminded of our Lord's words to Peter, the Vizier of the Kingdom of Heaven (Mt 16: 19). Like the Egyptian vizier, the master of the palace was the highest official in the state: his name comes first in the list of 2 K 18: 18; he alone appears with the king in 1 K 18: 3; and Yotham bears this title when he acts as regent of the kingdom (2 K 15: 5), as the vizier did in the absence of the Pharaoh.

It seems, however, that the master of the palace only gradually came to be the first minister, and perhaps in the early days of the monarchy he was only the steward of the palace and of the royal estate.[1] This would account for his title and for the fact that he is not named among David's senior officials, and does not head the list of Solomon's civil servants. Under David and Solomon the secretary and the king's herald were the immediate representatives of the king: there was no place for a vizier.

In Is 22: 15 Shebna, the master of the palace, is called the *soken*. This word is found in the form *zukinu* in two Canaanite glosses of the Amarna letters, to denote the Pharaoh's commissary. In Akkadian, *shaknu* denotes first the prefect of Assur (*shakîn mâti*), then the governors of the conquered countries; and the term was adopted by the Pharaohs in their Akkadian correspondence. At Ras Shamra, however, the *skn* (in alphabetical script) or the *shakîn mâti* (in Akkadian) was an official at Ugarit, apparently the highest in the land; this corresponds to the position held in Judah by Shebna, *soken* and master of the palace.

3. *The royal secretary*

We have seen that the list of David's high officials included a secretary, whose two sons held the same office under Solomon. An edict of Joas, king of Judah, entrusted to the royal secretary the duty of collecting the contributions given for the repair of the Temple (2 K 12: 11; cf. 2 Ch 24: 11), and it was while performing this duty a century later that Shaphan the secretary learned of the discovery of the Book of the Law (2 K 22: 3, 8-10, 12; 2 Ch 34: 15, 18, 20). Shebna the secretary was one of the three ministers who held the discussion with Sennacherib's envoy (2 K 18: 18, 37; 19: 2; Is 36: 3, 11, 22). We know the names of the last secretaries under the monarchy: we have just said that Shaphan held the post in 622; he was succeeded by Elishama in 604 (Jr 36: 12, 20), and in 588 the secretary was Yehonathan (Jr 37: 15, 20).

This official, an indispensable link in the chain of power from the time of David, was both the king's private secretary and secretary of state. He was responsible for all correspondence, internal and external, and for the Temple collections (2 K 12: 11); he played a considerable part in public affairs. He ranked below the master of the palace (Shebna, who held the latter post, Is 22: 15, was demoted to that of secretary, Is 36: 3, etc.), but he comes immediately after the master of the palace in 2 K 18: 18f.; Is 36: 3f., and the fate of the kingdom hung on the mission they performed together. Shaphan the secretary brought to the king the Book of the Law discovered in the Temple, read it to him and went to consult Huldah the prophetess for him; this was the beginning of the religious reformation (2 K 23). The senior officials held a conference in the house of Elishama the secretary, and there prophecies of Jeremias were read to them (Jr 36: 11-20). The 'secretary's room' where they met (Jr 36: 12, 20, 21) was evidently his office, the state

1. Cf. pp. 125-126.

chancery. During the siege of Jerusalem the home of Yehonathan, the secretary, became a public prison (Jr 37: 15).

In Egypt, under the New Empire, the title 'royal scribe' occurs frequently, both on its own and in combination with other functions. There were innumerable clerks, but above them certain royal scribes had functions of the highest importance and were involved in all affairs of state. The 'scribe of the royal documents' was one of the four holders of the seal during the XIIIth Dynasty; the 'royal scribe', together with the vizier and the herald, conducted the enquiry into the pillage of the tombs in the time of Ramses IX. The same official transcribed the great edict of Horemheb at the dictation of the Pharaoh himself. There can hardly be any doubt that the Israelite post was a copy, on a reduced scale, of that which existed at the Egyptian court.

4. The royal herald

During the reigns of David and Solomon, Yehoshaphat was *mazkîr* and the post continued until the end of the monarchy, since we know of Yoah, the *mazkîr* of Ezechias, 2 K 18: 18, 37; Is 36: 3, 11, 22; and of another Yoah, *mazkîr* to Josias, according to 2 Ch 34: 8. He was not the king's annalist or archivist, as it is often translated. From the meaning of the root, and its causative (Hiphil) form, the *mazkîr* is the man who calls, names, reminds, reports. The exact equivalent is found in the Egyptian scheme of titles: the *whm.w* is 'he who repeats, calls, announces', *i.e.*, the Pharaoh's herald. He was in charge of the palace ceremonies and introduced people to audiences, but his duties far surpassed those of a modern Lord Chamberlain. He reported to the king on what concerned the people and the country, but also passed on to the people the commands of their sovereign. He was the Pharaoh's official spokesman. When the Pharaoh went abroad, he accompanied him, watched over his person, and prepared quarters for each stage of the journey.

In Israel too the herald was a very high official. The mission which received Sennacherib's envoy, himself a high ranking official, consisted only of the master of the palace, the secretary and the king's herald (2 K 18: 18). It is remarkable that in the very serious matter of the violation of the royal tombs under Ramses IX, the three corresponding Egyptian officials, the vizier, the royal scribe and the herald, are named in the same order as alone presiding over the enquiry. This parallelism confirms the connections we have noted, and underlines the Egyptian influence in the organization of the kingdom of Judah.

CHAPTER EIGHT

THE ADMINISTRATION OF THE KINGDOM

1. *The kingdom of David*

WE know nothing about the administration of the kingdom under David apart from the fact already noted,[1] that Israel and Judah remained distinct entities. It is true that 1 Ch 26: 29-32 names some Levites engaged in secular affairs under David, as civil servants or judges, and attributes to this king the establishment of a police force, also composed of Levites, who supervised all the affairs of Yahweh and the king on both sides of the Jordan; but what these statements mean, or from what period they date, cannot be decided.

It is also true that 1 Ch 27: 16-22 names the chiefs who commanded the tribes under David, but this list is obviously artificial. It follows the order of the sons of Jacob as given in 1 Ch 2: 1-2, it retains Simeon and Levi (not to mention Reuben) which under David were no longer autonomous tribes; it then divides Joseph into three (Ephraim and the two halves of Manasseh) and omits the last two names on the list, Gad and Aser, so as not to exceed the number of twelve. It is still probable, however, that in the strictly Israelite territory David retained the tribal organization as he found it established, and as we find it described, with only slight variations, in Gn 49 and Dt 33. Beyond these frontiers the subject lands were laid under tribute and administered by governors (2 S 8: 6, 14), or else left under their vassal kings (2 S 8: 2; 10: 19).

2. *The administration under Solomon*

In contrast to this, a most important document has survived from the reign of Solomon. It is a list of twelve prefects, *niṣṣabîm*, with the description of the lands they governed (1 K 4: 7-19). Five of them are named only by their patronymic, 'son of X', and it has been suggested that the redactor had before him an old document from the archives, the edge of which was damaged: this would account for the absence of certain personal names. On the other hand, the administrative lists of Ugarit show that this designation by patronymic alone was the rule for certain families, which served the king from father to son. The twelve prefectures are given in the following order:

1. Cf. pp. 95-96.

I. The hill-country of Ephraim, probably including part of the territory of Manasseh.

II. The former country of the Danites, augmented by the districts annexed from the Canaanites and Philistines.

III. The plain of Sharon, from Philistia in the south to the next district on the north.

IV. The prefecture of Dor, continuing from the plain of Sharon and bounded on the east by the ridge of Carmel.

V. The former Canaanite territories in the plain of Esdraelon and the region of Beisan.

VI. On the other side of the Jordan, with Ramoth-Gilead as its capital, what was formerly Eastern Manasseh, and what remained of David's Aramaean conquests.

VII. In Transjordan, the prefecture of Mahanaim, lying to the south of the last-named territory.

VIII. The territory of Nephthali, to the north of the Lake of Tiberias.

IX. The territory of Aser, lying between Nephthali and the Phoenician possessions along the coast.

X. The territory of Issachar, to the south of the Aser and Nephthali prefectures.

XI. The territory of Benjamin.

XII. The territory of Gad (following the Greek text, instead of Gilead) on the other side of the Jordan.

This list dates from the second half of Solomon's reign, as two of the prefects are the king's sons-in-law. The order followed is not always geographical, but follows a logical arrangement: the house of Joseph (I), to which are attached the former Canaanite territories (II, III, IV, V), then the conquests in Transjordan (VI, VII), the Northern tribes (VIII, IX, X), and finally Benjamin (XI) and Gad, facing it on the other side of the Jordan (XII). According to 1 K 4: 7; 5: 7-9, each of the twelve districts supplied on a monthly rota the provisions needed by the Palace (by which is meant the whole staff in the king's service) and the forage for the horses and draught animals. The whole system was under the central control of an officer who held authority over the prefects, Azaryahu son of Nathan, who was a member of Solomon's ministerial cabinet (1 K 4: 5). Mesopotamian documents provide evidence of a vaguely similar organization in the Neo-Babylonian period, and Herodotus (I, 192) states that under Cyrus the victualling of the court and the army was allotted to the provinces according to the month of the year, four months being imposed on Babylonia because of its exceptional wealth.

The avowed object of the Israelite system was to ensure the raising of the revenue. The rôle of the prefects was of course wider than that: they were the governors of their districts, which represented the administrative divisions of the kingdom. But one must remember that in Eastern monarchies, both ancient and modern, the essential task of the administrators, apart from the maintenance of order, is the collection of the taxes and tithes. It will be noticed that six of the prefectures are described by the names of tribes. Evidently Solomon did not try to destroy the administrative units which existed before him; in fact he preserved them when he could, but he had to integrate the Canaanite enclaves conquered by David into the old tribal territories, or group them with each other. He also had to ensure a measure of equality between the districts, since they had to take turns in providing the needs of the State for a month at a time. In point of fact we do not know how the system worked in practice, and it is doubtful whether the small district of Benjamin, for example, was obliged to provide as much as the whole of Ephraim.

It is still more surprising that Judah does not figure in this list. Some exegetes, in fact, have been so surprised that they have modified the text in order to bring Judah in. None the less, Judah is implicitly mentioned: it is 'the land' which, according to 1 K 4: 19b, had a governor of its own (in the same way, in Assyrian, matu, 'the land', means the central province of the empire). But this mention comes after the end of the list of the twelve prefectures; Judah, then, was not incorporated in this system. It would be rash to conclude that it was exempted from all taxation, but one must at least admit that it had an administration of its own. Perhaps the reason why the organization of Judah is not described is that Solomon did not modify it, because he had no new territories to integrate in this region. But this difference of treatment emphasizes the dualist nature of Solomon's monarchy.[1]

We do not know how Solomon administered his external possessions. The allusions to the tribute of the vassal kingdoms (1 K 5. 1), and to what was paid in by the 'pashas of the land' (1 K 10: 15b), occur in glosses added to the text, and in any case give us no details. As far as he could, Solomon must have preserved the organizations created by his father, in the regions which he succeeded in retaining (1 K 2: 10-14; 11: 14-25).

3. The districts of Judah

We have just said that nothing is known about the organization of Judah under Solomon, but we are perhaps better informed on the situation after the schism. In Jos 15: 21-62 (excepting vv. 45-47, which are later insertions) there is a list of the towns of Judah, forming eleven groups introduced by geographical titles.

A list of the towns of Benjamin (Jos 18: 21-28) makes a twelfth group; this list has been separated from the previous list to furnish names of towns in the territory of Benjamin, whose boundaries, like those of the other tribes, are described in accordance with a premonarchical document. It is less certain

1. Cf. p. 96.

that we should include in this list the groups of towns of Simeon (Jos 19: 2-8), and of Dan (Jos 19: 41-46), which have been inserted here accidentally, and are of composite origin. We thus obtain a picture of twelve districts, covering the whole kingdom of Judah. The administrative centres are not indicated; from the towns mentioned we have chosen whichever seems to be the most important, or which gives the best indication of the geographical position of the district.

In the Negeb:
    I. Beersheba (Jos 15: 21-32).

In the Plain:
    II. Azeqah (Jos 15: 33-36).
    III. Lakish (Jos 15: 37-41).
    IV. Mareshah (Jos 15: 42-44).

In the Hill-country:
    V. Debir (Jos 15: 48-51).
    VI. Hebron (Jos 15: 52-54).
    VII. Maon (Jos 15: 55-57).
    VIII. Beth-Sur (Jos 15: 58-59a).
    IX. Bethlehem (Jos 15: 59b Greek; missing in Hebrew).
    X. Qiryath-Yearim (Jos 15: 60).
    XI. Gibeon (to be taken from Jos 18: 25-28).

In the desert:
    XII. Engaddi (Jos 15: 61-62).

This table reveals an organization similar to that of Solomon's twelve prefectures, and no doubt designed, like the former, to ensure the collection of the taxes. In this connection we may recall the governors and the collecting centres established by Josaphat (2 Ch 17: 2, 12). An organization of this kind may have existed even under David and Solomon, but if so, we have no knowledge of it, and according to 1 K 4: 19b, the 'Land', i.e. Judah, was administered by a single governor (the word is different from that used for Solomon's prefects, and the same as that in 2 Ch 17: 2). In any case, the organization we have reconstructed from the lists in Josue is certainly later than the schism, since it includes a part of Israel's two most southerly prefectures under Solomon. But it is impossible to decide how late we should date the list. One authoritative opinion has it that these lists represent the state of the kingdom under Josias, but good arguments have recently been brought forward in favour of an earlier date, viz. the reign of Josaphat, in the ninth century. It is hard to decide, because the document was revised either before, or when, it was inserted into the book of Josue. It is enough for our purpose that it gives us the scheme of an administrative division of the kingdom of Judah.

4. *The districts of the kingdom of Israel*

For the kingdom of Israel we have nothing like this. One is tempted to apply the same method to the lists of towns given by the book of Josue for the northern tribes, but these lists are a medley of points vaguely marking the tribal frontiers and filled with names of towns borrowed from other Biblical lists. We can only presume that the northern kingdom preserved the system of Solomon's prefectures in so far as it retained control over their territory. There is casual mention in 1 K 20: 14-20 of the chiefs of districts, here called *m'dînôth*, the word used in the Book of Esther for the satrapies of the Persian empire.

The ostraka from Samaria, which have already been quoted in connection with the royal estate,[1] provide some details about the central region of the kingdom. Certain geographical names appear as those of districts, each comprising several villages: Abiezer, Heleq, Shechem, Shemida, Noah, Hoglah, Soreq. Except for the last, these districts are given as the clans of Manasseh in Jos 17: 2-3, along with several other names which probably correspond to administrative divisions. This is certainly true of Tirsah, the ancient capital, for the excavations at Tell el-Farah have proved that it retained its importance until the eighth century B.C. Naturally these ostraka do not provide a complete picture, for it is sheer chance that has preserved them, and it seems that they all refer to the management of the royal estate. All these districts were dependent on Samaria, where these ostraka were found: Samaria was both the capital of the kingdom and the administrative centre of a province. It has been suggested, with less probability, that they cover all the territory left to Joachaz of Israel after the incursions of the Aramaeans and the men of Judah.

5. *Local administration*

Mesopotamian documents, especially for the time of Hammurabi, provide ample information about their internal administration of the provinces, and about the numerous duties of their governors and the staff which assisted them; but very little of the kind survives about Israel.

We learn incidentally that the two capitals, Jerusalem and Samaria, each had a governor. He bore the title of *śar ha'îr*, 'chief of the town', or (once) *'asher 'al ha'îr*, 'he who is over the town'. The 'town' suffices to describe the capital, as in 2 K 11: 20; Is 66: 6; Ez 7: 23. It is Amon, governor of Samaria, who is ordered by Achab to put the prophet Michaeas ben Yimlah in prison (1 K 22: 26). An unnamed governor of Samaria appears, together with the master of the palace and the Elders, in the time of Jehu (2 K 10: 5). Under Josias there was at Jerusalem a 'gate of Joshua, governor of the town' (2 K 23: 8), but one of his successors was by then in charge, called Maaseyahu,

1. Cf. p. 126.

according to 2 Ch 34: 8, where he is mentioned with the royal secretary and the herald. He was evidently an important person, nominated by the king. Much earlier, in the abortive attempt at monarchy at Shechem, a governor of the town is mentioned (Jg 9: 30); he had been appointed by Abimelek (Jg 9: 28). We have no proof that there was a similar post in towns other than the capitals. There may perhaps be an indication to the contrary: in 2 K 10: 5, the governor of Samaria, with the master of the palace and the Elders, replies to a message addressed to them by Jehu; but when Jezabel plots the death of Naboth she writes only to the Elders and notables of Yizreel, and no governor of the town appears in the story, though as an official appointed by the king he would have had a major part to play in it (1 K 21: 8-11). In Assyria and Babylonia we know there was a head of the town (*rab âli*), and that there were mayors (*ḥazânu*) in the small towns; there is also evidence for these in the kingdoms of Mari on the Euphrates. But at Ugarit the burgo-master (*ḥazanu* or *ḥazan âli*) seems to have been the governor of the capital, where he had authority over all the inhabitants except those who had been ennobled by the king. This is certainly the nearest parallel with the *śar ha'îr* of the Bible.

Outside the two capitals, local affairs were, it seems, left in the hands of the Elders, the *z^eqenîm*.[1] They formed a sort of municipal council. They are the men who take action under the laws of Dt 19; 21: 1-9, 18-21; 22: 13-21; 25: 5-10. At the end of Saul's reign, David sent messages and gifts to the Elders of the different towns of Judah (1 S 30: 26-31). Jezabel wrote to the Elders of Yizreel (1 K 21: 8) and Jehu addressed himself to the Elders of Samaria and to the royal officials (2 K 10: 1, 5). The Elders of Judah and Jerusalem were convened by Josias to hear the reading of the Law (2 K 23: 1). In Mesopotamia, from the archives of Mari in the eighteenth century B.C. down to the royal correspondence of the Sargon dynasty in the eighth, the Elders appear as the people's representatives and the defenders of their interests, but without any administrative functions. In the Hittite empire, however, municipal affairs seem to have been left to the council of the Elders, which also settled local disputes in co-operation with the commander of the garrison. The Phoenician towns also had their assemblies of Elders, attested, for Byblos and Tyre, by non-Biblical documents, and cf. Ez 27: 9. In Israel the Elders had a similar rôle; under the monarchy they continued to regulate the life of the clans, thereafter identified with the towns and villages.[2] They survived the collapse of the royal institutions; we meet them again during the Exile (Ez 8: 1; 14: 1; 20: 1, 3), and after the Return (Esd 10: 8, 14).

1. Cf. p. 69.   2. Cf. p. 13.

CHAPTER NINE

FINANCE AND PUBLIC WORKS

1. *Royal revenues and State revenues*

LITTLE is known about the fiscal system of Israel or the resources at the disposal of the State. First of all, it must be admitted that there was no distinction between the king's revenues and those of the kingdom. A sovereign's wealth was the expression of his own power and of that of the kingdom he ruled (cf. 1 K 10: 23; 2 Ch 17: 5; 26: 8). The king bore all the expenses (the upkeep of the administration and the army, national defence and public works), but he also enjoyed absolute control of the entire revenue. Similarly, there was only a theoretical distinction between the national and religious treasuries (cf. 1 K 14: 26). The king might deposit in the sanctuary booty taken from the enemy (cf. Jos 6: 19) and his personal gifts (2 S 8: 11; 1 K 7: 51; 15: 15; 2 K 12: 19); his officials too were in charge of the offerings made by the people (2 K 12: 10f.; 22: 3-4); but to meet urgent demands he would draw on both the Temple and Palace treasuries (1 K 15: 18; 2 K 12: 19; 16: 8; 18: 15; cf. even Jg 9: 4).

The king had at his disposal the produce of the royal estate,[1] the profits of his commercial and industrial enterprises,[2] the import or transit taxes paid by the caravan merchants (1 K 10: 15), and the tribute of the vassal states. This last source was an abundant one under David (2 S 8: 2, 6) and under Solomon (according to 1 K 5: 1), but shrank as the external possessions were lost. Mesha king of Moab, before he shook off the yoke of Israel, paid a tribute in kind for which 2 K 3: 4 gives some fantastic figures: 100,000 lambs and the wool of 100,000 rams. According to 2 Ch 17: 11, the Philistines paid tribute to Josaphat, and the Arabs brought him in tribute or gifts 7,700 rams and 7,700 goats. The Ammonites paid tribute to Ozias, according to 2 Ch 26: 8.

2. *'Voluntary' or exceptional contributions*

In addition there were the presents brought by foreign embassies. All the kings of the earth, it was said, wished to be received by Solomon, and each brought his gift (1 K 10: 24-25), but none surpassed the queen of Saba in

1. Cf. pp. 124-125.   2. Cf. p. 78.

lavishness (1 K 10: 2, 10). Before this the king of Hamath had sent gold, silver and bronze to David (2 S 8: 10), and Merodak-Baladan sent a present to Ezechias (2 K 20: 12=Is 39: 1). But these transactions were scarcely profitable, since the king of Israel had to return these courtesies with an equally lavish gesture (1 K 10: 13). The custom was in fact general among the kings of the East.

The sovereign made a clearer profit from the presents which had to be offered by all who presented themselves at court. When David was admitted to Saul's presence he brought only a modest offering (1 S 16: 20), but when Naaman was sent by his master to the king of Israel, his present was a princely one (2 K 5: 5). On the occasion of the king's coronation, custom obliged men to make presents to the king when they swore him fidelity (1 S 10: 27). Such more or less voluntary contributions are also mentioned in Ugaritic documents.

In grave circumstances the king would decree an exceptional tax. Menahem, for example, levied a thousand talents of silver on all the men of rank in Israel, at the rate of fifty shekels a head, in order to buy the favour of Tiglath-Pileser III (2 K 15: 19-20). Joiaqim raised the hundred talents of silver and ten talents of gold demanded by the Pharaoh by taxing the people of Judah, according to their wealth (2 K 23: 33-35).

3. Tithes

Some exegetes have argued that, apart from these occasional contributions, the Israelites were not subject to regular taxation, but this is contradicted by several facts. Solomon's prefectures[1] presuppose a system of revenues in kind which did not derive solely from the royal estates, and when 2 Ch 17: 5 says that all Judah brought its tribute to Josaphat, this is best understood as an annual tax, like the tribute of the vassal states. Though Gn 47: 13-26 describes the land system of Egypt as something strange, owing its origin to Joseph, what surprises the redactor is not that revenues are paid to the Pharaoh but that all the lands, except those of the temples, belong to him and that all the Egyptians are serfs of the crown, in contrast with the system of private property prevailing in Israel.

In particular, 1 S 8: 15, 17 predicts that the king will levy the tithe on the fields, the vineyards and the herds. This is what went on in the neighbouring kingdoms, as is clearly proved by the Ugarit texts. The Bible states that the king may leave this revenue to his officers; this custom is attested by Ugaritic documents also, and there is perhaps an allusion to this practice in Am 5: 11, where the prophet rebukes the men of rank for crushing the poor man by extorting tribute from his corn.

The king seems to have had a right over the first mowing of the meadows

1. Cf. pp. 133-135.

(Am 7: 1), similar, perhaps, to the right of pasturage exercised by the sovereign of Ugarit. Both there and in Israel an individual or his family could be exempted, by the king's favour, from tithes and forced labour (1 S 17: 25).

It is on the model of this institution of the monarchical period that Ezechiel, over and above the estate he reserves for the prince of Israel, fixes the revenue which all the people of the land will owe him, in wheat, barley, oil and live-stock (Ez 45: 13-16); in return for this, and in accordance with the ideals of theocracy envisaged by Ezechiel, the prince will be responsible for all the public sacrifices and oblations (Ez 45: 17).

A final stage was reached when the theocracy was actually set up after the return from the Exile; the people solemnly undertook to pay into the Temple a third of a shekel annually, the first fruits of the earth and the flocks, a tithe on the soil and certain offerings of wood (Ne 10: 33-40). Trustworthy men were charged with collecting, storing and distributing these revenues (Ne 12: 44-47; 13: 10-13). These measures can no doubt be interpreted as the fulfil-ment of the Priestly laws about the tithe due to the sanctuary and its ministers, but whatever be the date of these regulations, it can scarcely be doubted that this religious legislation is the parallel to, or the memory of, a similar civil institution.

4. Forced labour

Forced labour was universal in the ancient East. There is evidence of it in Lower Mesopotamia from the earliest times down to the Neo-Babylonian period. The Assyrian laws condemn certain criminals to a period of forced labour for the king. The Israelites preserved a harrowing memory of the tasks imposed on their ancestors in Egypt (Ex 1: 11-14; 5: 4-19; cf. Dt 26: 6), though their lot had been no worse than that of all the Pharaoh's subjects. Forced labour is also mentioned in the documents of Syria and Palestine before the Israelite settlement.

In Israel it was not organized till after the institution of the monarchy; it was one of the disadvantages foretold by 1 S 8: 12, 16-17. David imposed it on the Ammonites (2 S 12: 31), unless this means that they were reduced to utter slavery.[1] A defeated enemy, if he survived, became liable to this levy (Is 31: 8; Lm 1: 1). At the end of his reign, David is said to have had a minis-ter set over the levy (2 S 20: 24), but this statement is not certain.[2] In any case it is under Solomon that the institution appears in its full development. The great works undertaken by the king, the building of the Temple and the Palace, the fortification of Jerusalem and the garrison towns (1 K 9: 15-19), required a considerable labour force. Solomon of course had state slaves at his disposal, whom he used on the Red Sea fleet and in his factory at Esyon-Geber,[3] and they probably worked also on the great buildings of his reign. The text of 1 K 9: 20-22 implies that all the men employed on them were

1. Cf. p. 89.   2. Cf. p. 128.   3. Cf. p. 89.

descendants of those Canaanites who had escaped extermination and that the Israelites furnished only soldiers and officers for the king. This information, however, does not come from an early document; the text is in the style of Deuteronomy and reflects an opinion from the end of the monarchical period. The same opinion recurs in Chronicles (2 Ch 2: 16-17; 8: 7-9), where it is explicitly stated that only resident aliens had been employed on these buildings.

But the earlier texts are equally explicit in stating that Israelites were involved. It was in 'all Israel' (1 K 5: 27) that Solomon raised the men for the levy, *mas*, and he had 30,000 workmen, of whom 10,000 went in their turn to the Lebanon to cart the wood cut by the king of Tyre's woodcutters (1 K 5: 20, 23, 27-28). Further, it is said, he had 70,000 porters and 80,000 quarry-men employed at Jerusalem with Hiram's masons and carpenters (1 K 5: 29-32). The 'levy of the house of Joseph' over which Jeroboam was placed (1 K 11: 28) was made up of Israelites. It was in fact this burden laid on the Israelites which incited Jeroboam to revolt (1 K 11: 26f.), and after Solomon's death it is given as the main cause of the political schism (1 K 12: 4-16).

The levy was staffed by supervisors and officers (1 K 5: 30; 9: 23; 11: 28), under the orders of the chief of the levy, Adoram, son of Abda, apparently a Phoenician, who was one of Solomon's ministers (1 K 4: 6; 5: 28).[1] It was this Adoram, whom Roboam, through stupidity or for provocation, sent to subdue the rebels of Israel, and who was stoned to death by them (1 K 12: 18).

Later history contains no mention of any other chief of the levy, and it would appear that this ceased to be a regular institution after Solomon's reign. Yet from time to time the kings of Israel and Judah must have resorted to it for the building programmes attributed to them; there is explicit evidence for this in the reign of Asa, who called up every single man in Judah to fortify Geba and Mispah (1 K 15: 22). But popular sentiment regarded this forced labour as an exaction, and Jeremias denounces Joiaqim for building his palace with no respect for justice, making men work without pay (Jr 22: 13). This explains the reluctance of the redactors of the Books of Kings and Chronicles to admit that Solomon had used free Israelites in the levy. Under Nehemias the walls of Jerusalem were rebuilt by teams of volunteers; the writer merely observes that the leading men from Teqoa refused to take part in it (Ne 3: 5).

1. Cf. p. 128.

CHAPTER TEN

LAW AND JUSTICE

1. Legislative codes

THE Law, *Tôrah*, means in the first place a teaching, a doctrine, a decision given for a particular case. Collectively, the word means the whole body of rules governing men's relations with God and with each other. Finally the word comes to mean the first five books of the Bible, the Pentateuch, containing God's instructions to his people, the prescriptions which his people had to observe in their moral, social and religious life. All the legislative codes of the Old Testament are found in the Pentateuch.

(a) *The Decalogue* contains the 'Ten Words' of Yahweh, the essential precepts of morality and religion. It is set out twice (Ex 20: 2-17 and Dt 5: 6-21) with some significant variants, but the two texts stem from a shorter primitive form which may justifiably be assigned to the Mosaic Age.

(b) *The Code of the Covenant* (Ex 20: 22-23: 33) is a composite collection, in which one can easily distinguish a central portion (Ex 21: 1-22: 16), where 'sentences' or 'judgments', *mishpatîm*, of civil and criminal law are grouped together: it is a law for a community of shepherds and peasants. The present context (cf. Ex 24: 3-8) connects it, like the Decalogue which precedes it, with the Sinaitic Covenant, but the directions about slaves, cattle, fields, vineyards and houses can only apply to an already settled population. This code has obvious connections with the curses of Dt 27: 15-26, the 'law' (Dt 27: 26) which was to be proclaimed on Mount Ebal (or Garizim?) after the entry into Canaan (Dt 27: 11-14). This command of Moses was carried out by Josue, according to Jos 8: 30-35, the opening words of which recall in turn the law of the altar with which the Code of the Covenant begins (Ex 20: 24-25). But this passage in Jos 8 does not fit in with its present context nearly so well as with the assembly at Shechem, where Joshua gave the people a law (*mishpat*) written in a 'book of the law' (Jos 24: 25-26). We cannot be certain that the Code of the Covenant, in the form in which it has come down to us, is the actual law promulgated by Josue at Shechem, but we can say that internal evidence and the witness of tradition agree in dating this Code from the early days of the settlement in Canaan, before the organization of the State. It is the law of the tribal federation.

(c) *Deuteronomy*, in its legislative part (Dt 12-26), forms another code which brings together, in ill-defined order, some short collections of laws which may have originated in different ways. Some of them repeat the directions of the Code of the Covenant, others, *e.g.* the laws on the one sanctuary and on the slaves, modify them, and many others are added. This code seems designed to replace the old code by taking account of a whole social and religious evolution; it also reveals a change of spirit by its appeals to the heart and by the tone of exhortation in which its prescriptions are often couched. Fundamentally, it is certainly the 'law' discovered in the Temple in the time of Josias (2 K 22: 8f.). It contains ancient elements which seem to stem, at least in part, from the Northern kingdom, but it is difficult to say how long before the reign of Josias they were collected and completed. One plausible hypothesis is that they were brought to Judah after the fall of Samaria and put together under Ezechias.

(d) *The Law of Holiness* (Lv 17-26) is also a compilation, containing a number of doublets. But it constitutes a unity which, like Deuteronomy, begins with rules about sacrifices and ends with blessings and curses. It differs from it by its strong preoccupation with rites and the priesthood, and its constant reminders of the holiness of Yahweh and his people. It may represent the customs in vogue at the end of the monarchy, originating in a different *milieu* from that of Deuteronomy, and codified during the Exile. It may well have received some additions before or after its inclusion in the Pentateuch.

(e) *The Priestly Code.* The rest of Leviticus is composed of other collections: laws about sacrifices (Lv 1-7); the ritual for the installation of priests (Lv 8-10); the law of purity (Lv 11-16), to which must be added the legislative texts scattered throughout Ex and Nb and associated with events of the desert period. The sum total of these enactments and the narratives in which they are set, together with the Law of Holiness, form what critics call the Priestly Code. It contains some rules which are very ancient and others which are much more recent, and it received its final form only in the Jewish community after its return from Exile.

This brief survey is enough to make clear how inorganic was the legislation of Israel, how it varied with the background and time, and how much more closely connected it was with religious than with civil life. These are points to which we shall have to return, but before embarking on them we must compare this body of law with those of the other peoples in the ancient East.

2. Eastern law in ancient times

It is a remarkable fact that Egypt, where there was so much writing and so much litigation, has left us no body of laws (the Edict of Horemheb is only an administrative document); nor is there any record of any Egyptian king's having been a law-giver, apart from some traditions collected at a very late date by Diodorus of Sicily (I 94), which we cannot check. It was a foreign conqueror, Darius, who issued the only codification recorded by an Egyptian text. Egypt seems to have felt no need for a written law because it had a living law, the Pharaoh, son of Ra, a god upon earth, whose word laid down the law. The language has no word to denote law as such. The nearest term is *ma'at*, which covers the concepts of truth and justice and is an attribute, itself divine, of the Pharaoh. The judges gave their decisions according to the principles of this 'truth which is justice' and by applying the unwritten customs or the directive of the sovereign.

Babylonia, on the other hand, has bequeathed several collections of laws ascribed to the initiative of a king or placed under his name, and they are very ancient. The Code of Ur-Nammu or Ur is to be dated about 2050 B.C., that of Lipit-Ishtar of Isin, about 1850; the law of the city of Eshnunna was promulgated by an unknown king long before Hammurabi and perhaps before Lipit-Ishtar; lastly, the Code of Hammurabi of Babylon, issued about 1700, was the first to be discovered and is the most complete. These are not, strictly speaking, 'codes' in our modern sense, *i.e.* bodies of law to which the judge is obliged to refer in giving judgment. It is noteworthy that in Mesopotamian texts we never come across expressions like 'by application of the law' or 'in virtue of such and such a law'. There is not even any word meaning 'law' in general. The king governs and the judges decide according to 'justice' (*mesharu*) or 'the truth' (*kittu*), following the accepted custom in similar cases. The practice was therefore not very different from that in Egypt, but in Mesopotamia this legal tradition or jurisprudence was, in certain circumstances, collected and put into writing, rather for the benefit of the people, it seems, than for that of the judges. These 'codes', however, were not binding texts, as is evident from the number of divergent solutions given to the same cases by contemporary juridical acts.

The Collection of Assyrian Laws, compiled about 1100 but making use of older material, has long been recognized as a book of law, a manual of jurisprudence, but it covers only certain fields, and does not attempt to set forth the general law of the State. It is perhaps the work of a private jurist, but even if it was compiled for the use of the judges by an official authority, it would still be a reference-book rather than an authoritative code.

The Hittite laws are preserved in copies probably dating from the thirteenth century B.C., but they were compiled, apparently, about 1500. They frequently contrast 'what must be done' now with 'what was done formerly', the change being usually a reduction of the penalty. They are based, then, on an older customary law. They do not constitute a code; they form an even looser collection than that of the Assyrian laws. They refer mostly to very particular cases, the presumption being that ordinary cases will be settled by simple and generally accepted rules.

No similar collection is forthcoming from Syria or Palestine, where juridical texts are extremely rare, apart from the two lots recently discovered in northern Syria, at Ras Shamra and Alalakh. Their principal characteristic is the special place assigned to the king, acting as representative of public authority: judgment is represented as his personal act, without reference to a law of the State. Their usages and formularies have certain peculiar features, but on the whole they have little which is not found in some other province of the ancient East, whether in Asia Minor, Babylonia or more distant Elam.

This fundamental unity of Eastern law is of greater importance than the variations to be found between regions and epochs. It is the expression of a common civilization, in which the application of the same juridical principles has produced a similar customary law.

3. *The sources of Israelite law*

The civil legislation of the Old Testament belongs to the same ancient world, though it certainly has an originality which will be emphasized later. The very close connections and even the occasional identity of expression which we find between Israelite law and the Code of Hammurabi, the Assyrian Collection or the Hittite laws, is not to be explained by direct borrowing but by the influence of a single widespread customary law.

The legislative codes of the Old Testament are collections of particular rules, like the Eastern 'codes', and they are even less unified than the latter. They are also more heterogeneous; ethical, religious or ritual prescriptions are found side by side with articles of civil or criminal law. The laws fall into two groups according to their style. There are laws in casuistical form, in which the conjunction 'if' or 'supposing that' introduces a typical case, followed by the solution. 'If you take a man's cloak as security, you must return it to him at nightfall' (Ex 22: 25). 'Supposing that a bull gores a man . . . that bull shall be stoned' (Ex 21: 28, etc.). Other laws are in an apodictic form and lay down commands or prohibitions in the second person future. 'You shall not allow a witch to live' (Ex 22: 17). 'You shall not boil a kid in its mother's milk' (Ex 23: 19; Dt 14: 21, etc.). The casuistic form is used chiefly for secular law, the apodictic form chiefly for laws covering worship. But we must observe that the distinction of styles and their use is less rigid than is usually thought.

What was the origin of these forms? A theory at present in favour holds that 'casuistic' law is a wholesale borrowing from the Canaanite legislation which the Israelites encountered when they settled in the land, and that the 'apodictic' law represents the strictly Israelite tradition. It is mere guesswork to speculate about the formulation of Canaanite law so long as we possess none of the legislative texts which embodied it, and the juridical texts of Alalakh and Ras Shamra suggest that it hardly differed at all from other Oriental laws. The fact remains that the Mesopotamian codes are compiled in casuistic form, and part of the Israelitic law closely resembles them in style.

Like these codes, the legislative collections of Israel bring together customary decisions.

The apodictic form is not found in these codes. But the originality of Israel in this respect is less striking if we compare it with the treaties imposed by the Hittite kings on their vassals. The treaties very frequently contain clauses introduced by 'if', and also imperative clauses, as for example: 'You shall keep the land which I have given you and shall not covet any territory of the land of Hatti.' The form is like that of the Decalogue: 'You shall not covet your neighbour's house, etc.' (Ex 20: 17). We also have the remains, though badly damaged, of three Assyrian treaties of vassalage, and an important part of a treaty in Aramaic, found at Sfiré near Aleppo; and a treaty of vassalage imposed by Asarhaddon on certain princes of Media has recently been discovered. The essential points of the Hittite treaties are also found in these Assyrian ones; the texts date from the first millennium and may be compared with the legislation of the Old Testament. The structure of Old Testament legislation, however, is much closer to that of the Hittite documents, which date from the second half of the second millennium. In addition, Ras Shamra has yielded fragments of treaties which were imposed on the king of Ugarit by a Hittite sovereign.

4. Characteristics of Israelite law

These resemblances are not accidental. The Covenant between Yahweh and his people had to be sealed by a treaty, and between God and men this could only be a treaty of vassalage. The ancient legal codes of Israel do in fact read like the clauses of such a treaty. The Decalogue is the deed of the Sinaitic covenant, inscribed on large stones entrusted by God to Moses (Ex 24: 12), which are the tables of the law ('edûth: Ex 31: 18), or the tables of the covenant (b'rîth: Dt 9: 9). The Code of the Covenant, as we have seen, may be connected with the pact at Shechem, where Josue concluded a covenant between Yahweh and the people, and gave the people a statute and a law (Jos 24: 25-26). The Code of Deuteronomy is also the expression of a pact: it is set forth as the sum total of the conditions accompanying the gift of the Holy Land (Dt 12: 1; cf. 11: 31-32), and after the curses and blessings it culminates in these words: 'These are the words of the covenant which Yahweh commanded Moses to make with the children of Israel, in the land of Moab, in addition to the covenant he had made with them at Horeb' (Dt 28: 69); the Deuteronomic law is thus connected with the Decalogue, by-passing the Code of the Covenant, which it professes to replace. Under Josias, this Deuteronomic law was accepted by the king and the people as a covenant with Yahweh (2 K 23: 2-3). The fiction of a treaty is still maintained in the Law of Holiness, which ends by recalling the covenant (Lv 26: 42-45), and concludes: 'These are the customs, rules and laws which Yahweh established between himself and the Israelites' (Lv 26: 46).

If this is granted, other points of resemblance appear between the legal codes of the Old Testament and Oriental treaties. The latter begin with a historical introduction, sometimes fairly long, recalling the events leading up to the treaty. Similarly, the two promulgations of the Decalogue are introduced by a very short summary of previous facts (Ex 20: 1; Dt 5: 4-5). This is more developed in the narrative of the pact at Shechem (Jos 24: 2-13), to which we assigned the Code of the Covenant; in the first chapters of Deuteronomy it becomes a record of the entire history of the people. Oriental treaties end with formulas of cursing and blessing, as sanctions for the keeping or breaking of the engagements undertaken. So too the Law of Holiness and the Code of Deuteronomy conclude with blessings and curses (Lv 26: 3-41; Dt 28). The Code of the Covenant has no similar conclusion in its present context, but this context is not the original one, and if we were right in associating this Code with the pact at Shechem, it too involved curses and blessings (cf. Jos 8: 34; Dt 11: 26-29; 27: 12-13): the curses would then be those recorded in Dt 27: 15-26, which, as we have already noted, were closely connected with the Code of the Covenant.

Oriental treaties were inscribed on tablets, or engraved on a stele, and placed in a sanctuary in the presence of the gods. The Decalogue was engraved on two tablets and deposited in the sacred tent, in the Ark 'of the Covenant' or 'of the Law'. The pact at Shechem was written in a book, according to Jos 24: 26, on stones according to Jos 8: 35; Dt 27: 2-4, and the record of this pact was preserved in the sanctuary of Yahweh (Jos 24: 26-27). Again, the 'book of the law', Deuteronomy, was discovered in the Temple at Jerusalem (2 K 22: 8).

Finally, several Hittite treaties order the text to be read periodically before the vassal king and his people. So too Dt 31: 10-13 prescribes a public reading of the law every seven years. It is very likely that such readings actually took place, perhaps even more often, *e.g.* in connection with an annual ceremony for renewing the Covenant, similar to that recorded by the Dead Sea scrolls among the Qumran sect. The historical books have recorded only readings which took place in certain exceptional circumstances, at the reform of Josaphat (2 Ch 17: 9), after the discovery of the Deuteronomy (2 K 23: 2), and after the promulgation of the law by Esdras (Ne 8: 4-18).

But since these pacts governed the relations of Israel's dependence on Yahweh, not on a human suzerain, the Israelite law, for all its resemblances in form and content, differs radically from the clauses of the Oriental 'treaties' and the articles of their 'codes'. It is a religious law. It established the principles of the Covenant with Yahweh: its aim was to ensure that this Covenant remained in force. It is perfectly true that the Hittite and Assyrian treaties invoke their gods as guarantors, and that in the prologue and epilogue of their codes Lipit-Ishtar purports to be the interpreter of Enlil, and Hammurabi to be 'the king of justice to whom Shamash has entrusted the law'; but God was not merely a guarantor of the Covenant, he was a party to it, and no Oriental code can be compared with the Israelite law, which is ascribed in its entirety to God as its author. If it contains, and often mingles, ethical and ritual prescriptions, this is because it covers the whole field of the divine Covenant, and because this Covenant governed the relations of men with one another as well as their relations with God.

The law was the charter of the covenant with God; hence it contained the obligations undertaken by the people, but it was also a body of teaching directed to them. From this notion another characteristic of Israelite legislation proceeds. Unlike all other Eastern laws, its prescriptions are often supported by a justifying motive. This may be a simple explanation based on common sense: if a man has violated an already betrothed girl in the town, both are put to death, 'the girl because she did not call for help, the man because he has abused his neighbour's wife' (Dt 22: 24). Alternatively, the motive may be moral: in judicial actions, gifts must not be accepted 'because gifts blind the eyes of the clear-sighted' (Ex 23: 8). Often it is a religious motive, as in the Decalogue itself: idolatry is forbidden, 'for I, Yahweh your God, am a jealous God' (Ex 20: 5): this is often found in the Law of Holiness, where the prescriptions are punctuated with the refrain, 'I am Yahweh, your God.' Finally, it may be an appeal to history, especially the remembrance of the deliverance from Egypt (Ex 23: 9; Lv 19: 36; Dt 5: 15; 24: 18, etc.). The examples quoted show that these motives are attached to apodictical and casuisitical laws alike and are found in different collections. They are proportionately more numerous in Deuteronomy and the Law of Holiness, but they are found as early as the Decalogue and the Code of the Covenant, and they are certainly a primitive feature of the law in Israel.

This connection between the law and religion explains one last characteristic of Israelite legislation. Because it is designed to safeguard the Covenant, it enjoins severe penalties for all crimes against God, idolatry and blasphemy, and for crimes which tarnish the holiness of the chosen people, e.g., bestiality, sodomy and incest. But it is further distinguished from other Eastern codes (even the Hittite, which is the most lenient) by the humaneness of its sentences. Bodily mutilation is exacted only in one very special case (Dt 25: 11-12) which the Assyrian law punishes in the same way. Flogging is limited to forty strokes, 'lest the bruises be dangerous and your brother be degraded' (Dt 25: 3). Certain dispositions in the Code of the Covenant, more developed in Deuteronomy, protect the stranger, the poor, the oppressed, the widow and the orphan, even the personal enemy (Ex 22: 20-26; 23: 4-9; Dt 23: 16, 20; 24 passim). Exemptions from military service are very generous (Dt 20: 5-9). The law of retaliation, however, the lex talionis, is expressed in all its crudeness: 'life for life, eye for eye, tooth for tooth, hand for hand, foot for foot, burning for burning, bruise for bruise, wound for wound' (Ex 21: 23-25; cf. Lv 24: 19-20; Dt 19: 21). But this formula seems to have lost its force, merely asserting the principle of proportionate compensation. In the oldest text, that of Exodus, it is in fact followed immediately by a law which orders the liberation of a slave in compensation for the loss of an eye or a tooth (Ex 21: 26-27), and it is preceded by a law which, for a wound inflicted in a fight, orders only the payment of compensation and medical expenses (Ex 21: 18-19). Only in one case is strict retaliation exacted: the guilty murderer must die and cannot buy his freedom. This rigour is justified by a religious reason: the blood which has been shed has profaned the land in which Yahweh dwells (Nb 35: 31-34). Thus again we meet the religious sanctions mentioned in the beginning of this paragraph.[1] The Israelites could repeat with pride these words of Deuteronomy: 'What great nation is there whose laws and customs are so just as all this Law?' (Dt 4: 8).

5. The king's legislative and judicial powers

The 'codes' which have come down to us from Mesopotamia are all attributed to a king. As we have seen, they were rather collections of customary law than laws of the State, decreed by the sovereign, but they were at least promulgated by royal authority In Israel, granted the religious nature of the law and its connection with the Covenant, nothing of the sort was possible, and in fact the historical books never allude to any legislative power of the king. The nearest example is the order said to have been given by David, to share the booty between the combatants and those who had been left to guard the baggage, which became 'a rule and a custom' for Israel (1 S 30: 24-25). But David was not then king: as commander, he decided a particular case and his decision became a custom. During the siege of Jerusalem, Sedecias ordered that all slaves should be freed; but this was after he had consulted the people—he did not act on his own authority (Jr 34: 8). The king had of course an extensive administrative authority; he organized his kingdom, appointed his officials and made decrees, but he did not enact law. It is remarkable that the two 'laws of the king' (1 S 8: 11-18; Dt 17: 14-20) make no allusion to any power of the king to lay down laws. On the contrary, the first warns the people against his arbitrary acts, and the second orders him to have a copy of the divine law and obey it to the last detail. It is also noteworthy that apart from this passage the king is nowhere mentioned in the Deuteronomic Code. When Josaphat reformed the administration of justice, he told his judges to apply the law of Yahweh (2 Ch 19: 5-7), and his envoys were to take with them, and to explain everywhere, not a law of the king, but 'the law of Yahweh' (2 Ch 17: 9). The king was not even in the full sense the promulgator of this law, as if it became the law of the State by his authority. That is not the meaning to be ascribed to the reading of Deuteronomy by Josias in the Temple (2 K 23: 1-2). Josias was the

1. Cf. also p. 12.

human intermediary in the covenant between God and his people; he published its clauses and watched over its observance. He performed the same function as Moses on Sinai (Ex 24: 7-8), as Josue at Shechem (Jos 24: 25-26), and Esdras in days still to come at Jerusalem (Ne 8). But the king could add nothing to the authority of a law to which he himself was subject (Dt 17: 19; 1 K 8: 58; 2 K 23: 3). There was no such thing as State law in Israel, and it was only under the foreign rule of Artaxerxes that 'the law of God brought by Esdras' was imposed as 'the law of the king' (Esd 7: 26).

On the other hand, the king was a judge, and held judicial power. This is an essential function of the chief: every sheikh wields it in his tribe and Moses exercised it in the desert (Ex 18: 16). Josue, Moses' successor at the head of the people, 'was filled with the spirit of wisdom' and everyone obeyed him (Dt 34: 9; cf. Nb 27: 18-23). He acted as a judge in condemning Akan (Jos 7: 19-25). This was, of course, an exceptional case, but it was natural that the man who determined the law of the people (Jos 24: 25) should also see to its enforcement. Between the death of Josue and the institution of the monarchy came the period of the 'Judges'. This title has been wrongly extended to the heroes who saved some part of the people from oppression, but it seems to belong properly to the 'lesser' Judges, whose names are given in Jg 10. 1-5, 12: 8 15, along with whom we should count at least Jephthah (cf. Jg 12: 7), who combined this rôle with that of a great 'saviour' Judge. It seems that these Judges were a permanent institution of the tribal federation: instead of a political head, it had a judge to whom all could appeal. Samuel performed the same function when he judged Israel at his home-town, Ramah, and also at Bethel, Gilgal and Mispah (1 S 7: 16-17); he claimed that no one could accuse him of denying any man justice or taking bribes (1 S 12: 3-5). In his old age he appointed his two sons as judges at Beersheba, but they 'accepted gifts and bent justice to their own ends' (1 S 8: 1-3).

It was then that the Israelites begged Samuel to give them a king, 'that he may be our judge' (1 S 8: 5). There is no reason to suspect this passage, which represents the king as heir to an office which already had a long history in Israel. The same passage says that the people asked for a judge-king 'to be like other nations'. Among the texts lately discovered at Ras Shamra and Alalakh there are, in fact, judgments given by the king and contracts guaranteed by his seal. On a wider scale, the preambles of Mesopotamian codes, the poems of Ras Shamra, and Aramaean and Phoenician inscriptions all demand as the first quality of a king the virtue of justice. In Israel, too, men prayed that the king might be given justice (Ps 72: 1-2), the foundation of his throne (Pr 16: 12; 25: 5; 29: 14; cf. Is 9: 6).[1] The list of David's senior officials (2 S 8: 15) is introduced with these words: 'David reigned over all Israel, doing right and justice to all his people', which seems to reserve the administration of justice to the sovereign. In the same way, the list of Solomon's

1. Cf. p. 107.

senior officials (1 K 4: 1–6) is immediately preceded by the story of the famous judgment which proved to all that there was in the king 'a divine wisdom for doing justice' (1 K 3: 28) *i.e.* both to settle quarrels and to assist every man to obtain his rights. This was the wisdom for which Solomon had prayed, to 'judge the people' (1 K 3: 9). Thus 'to judge' was almost a synonym for 'to govern' (cf. again 2 K 15: 5), and 'governors' could be called 'judges' (Ps 2: 10; 148: 11). It is the king who is called the 'judge of Israel' in Mi 4: 14, following what is still the likeliest interpretation.

When Absalom exclaimed: 'Ah! who will make me judge in this land?' If everyone who had a lawsuit and a judgment were to come to me, I would do them justice' (2 S 15: 4), he was coveting the crown itself. The whole story shows that there was at Jerusalem a king's court, to which every man in Israel could appeal. So too, Solomon's palace contained a 'porch of judgment' where the king administered justice (1 K 7: 7). The real or fictitious cases recorded in the historical books show that appeal was made to the king even in cases which we should leave to lower courts: the theft of a sheep (2 S 12: 6), a family blood feud (2 S 14: 4–11), the substitution of a child (1 K 3: 16–28), the recovery of a house and land (2 K 8: 3). The woman of Teqoa is supposed to be appealing from a judgment given by her clan (2 S 14: 4–11), and the king here appears as the judge in the final court of appeal, which he certainly was, but the other examples presume that recourse could also be made to him in the first instance.

6. Judges and courts of law

In practice the majority of cases went to judges other than the king, and increasingly so as institutions developed. It was said that Moses himself was unequal to this task and, on the advice of his father-in-law, Jethro the Midianite, he appointed chiefs to administer justice, reserving to himself only the most difficult cases (Ex 18: 13–26; cf. Dt 1: 9–17).

We are by no means so well informed on the courts of Israel as on those of Mesopotamia, the composition and procedure of which are described in many cuneiform documents. They reveal some interesting parallels with what the Old Testament tells us about the administration of justice. Like ancient Babylonia, Israel had three different jurisdictions, though it is hard to define what was the precise competence of each: the communal jurisdiction of the Elders, the jurisdiction of the king and that of the priests.

In every town disputes and trials were settled by the Elders, that is, the heads of families in the clan, the leading citizens of the place.[1] They sat at the gate of the town, where all the community's affairs were discussed (cf. Gn 23: 10, 18; Jb 29: 7; Pr 24: 7; 31: 23). These are the courts to which the prophets refer when they demand respect for justice 'at the gate' (Am 5: 10, 12, 15; Za 8: 16). The Deuteronomic law describes 'the Elders at the gate of the

1. Cf. pp. 68 and 138.

town' (Dt 21: 19; 22: 15), or 'the Elders of the town' (Dt 19: 12; 21: 3, 8; 25: 7f.) as judges in certain causes. An actual example of the working of these courts is provided by Rt 4: 1-12. Boaz sits at the gate of the town, stops the kinsman who has the right of redemption over Naomi's field and chooses ten Elders. They take their places beside him. The case is stated and discussed between the parties, the man renounces his right and Boaz calls the Elders and all the people to witness it. When the judgment involves a penalty, the Elders impose it (Dt 22: 18-19). When it is the death penalty, it is immediately carried out by the witnesses present (Dt 21: 18-21). The practice is illustrated by the story of Naboth. The Elders and the leading citizens summon Naboth to appear before them, and two false witnesses accuse him of cursing God and the king, a crime which incurs the death penalty (cf. Ex 22: 27; Lv 24: 14). Then 'they took him out of the city, they stoned him and he died' (1 K 21: 11-13). The members of these popular courts are addressed in the exhortations of Ex 23: 1-3, 6-8; cf. Lv 19: 15, 35: they must not bear false witness nor follow the majority in defiance of justice, nor accept gifts; they must acquit the innocent and condemn the guilty. In the Mesopotamian courts the Elders had a definite rôle; and among the Hittites they administered justice under the presidency of a royal official.

But there were also professional judges in Israel, instituted by an authority which can only have been the king's. They could claim as their prototypes the competent laymen appointed by Moses to dispense justice (Ex 18: 13-26). Among the collections of laws, the Deuteronomic Code is the only one which refers to them. It commands that judges and registrars, or scribes, be appointed in every town, and that they are to give just judgments (Dt 16: 18-20). According to Dt 19. 16-18, the false witnesses in a religious trial must appear before the priests and the judges then in office, and they are to conduct the enquiry. According to Dt 25: 2, when a judge finds a man guilty, the flogging is to take place in his presence. Dt 17: 8-13 orders the Elders or the local judge to refer cases they cannot decide to a higher court. They must go to 'the place chosen by Yahweh', that is, to Jerusalem, and submit the case to the priests and the officiating judge (v. 9) or to the priest (singular) and the judge (v. 12). Their judgment is without appeal. There was then at Jerusalem a final court of appeal, both religious and secular. The text hesitates between one priest and several, but is definite in denoting one secular judge. In this legal context, it is not the king who can be called 'judge', as in Mi 4: 14, but an official appointed by the king.

The directions of Dt 16: 18-20 and 17: 8-13 should be compared with Josaphat's reform as described in 2 Ch 19: 4-11. This king appointed 'in every town, in each walled town', judges who were to show themselves incorruptible. At Jerusalem he established a court of priests, Levites, and the heads of Israelite families, who were to act as a court of first instance for the inhabitants of Jerusalem (according to the Greek) and as a court of appeal for cases referred to them from other towns. This court was presided over by Amaryahu, the high priest, for all matters touching Yahweh, and by Zebed-yahu, chief of the house of Judah, for all the king's matters; the Levites served as notaries. The literary expression of this text may have been influenced by Deuteronomy and may reflect certain special interests of the time of the Chronicler, but there is no reason to suspect its basic accuracy. It will then be admitted that under Josaphat, at the beginning of Judah's monarchy, there was a judicial reform which established a royal jurisdiction alongside the communal jurisdiction and which relieved the king of his office of supreme judge. The texts from Deuteronomy which we have just analysed probably refer to the same institution.

With these measures of Josaphat's we may compare the Edict of Pharaoh Horemheb in the fourteenth century B.C. It concerns a reorganization of the courts of justice: the inhabitants of every town are to be judged by the priests of the temples, the priests of the gods and the magistrates appointed by the sovereign. These are men of discernment who are forbidden to respect persons or to accept bribes. The parallel is striking. But whereas the god-king of Egypt had simply 'taken counsel of his heart' in order to dictate to the scribe these 'excellent dispositions', and his judges had to apply 'the words of the Palace and the laws of the Throne-room', Josaphat's measures form part of his religious reform (2 Ch 19: 4; cf. 17: 7-9), and his magistrates 'judge not in the name of men but in the name of Yahweh' (2 Ch 19: 6). In the administration of justice as in everything else, the difference between the royal ideology of Israel and that of Egypt is conspicuous.

In Josaphat's ordinance (2 Ch 19: 8, 11) and in Dt 17: 9, 12; 19: 17, priests are mentioned along with judges. There is no ground for disputing the existence of this priestly jurisdiction; it is found in Mesopotamia, and also in Egypt, as we have just seen from the Edict of Horemheb. It was almost inevitable in Israel, where there was no distinction between civil and religious law, and where all legislation emanated from God. Moses brought the people's disputes 'before God' (Ex 18: 19). The fact that Samuel exercised his judicial functions in three sanctuaries, Bethel, Gilgal and Mispah (1 S 7: 16) and that his sons were judges at Beersheba, another place of worship (1 S 8: 2) is not an irrelevant detail. In certain cases the Code of the Covenant prescribes a procedure 'before God' (Ex 21: 6; 22: 6-8); the law of Dt 21: 1-9 on murder by a person unknown prescribes a ritual act. All this presupposes that the priest took a certain part in judicial affairs. The problem is to know exactly what their competence was. The priests gave *tôrôth*, 'decisions' in the name of God, and according to Dt 33: 10 (reading, probably, the plural) it was their exclusive privilege. According to Lv 13-14, it is the priest who decides whether a man, a garment or a house are infected with 'leprosy' or are clear of it. In Ag 2: 11f., the priests are asked for a *tôrah* on the conditions in which cleanness and uncleanness are passed on. In Za 7: 3 they are asked whether the fast in commemoration of the ruin of the Temple is still of obligation. It would seem, then, that the priests' rôle was only to distinguish between the sacred and the profane, clean and unclean, and this is certainly the function assigned to them in Lv 10: 10 and Ez 44: 23. But Lv 10: 11 extends their competence to 'any law whatever', and Ez 44: 24 adds 'they shall be judges in quarrels; they shall judge according to my law', while Dt 21: 5 says 'that it is their office to pronounce on all disputes and all assaults'. But in the absence of any concrete examples no certain conclusion can be drawn. It seems that the priests were the authentic interpreters of the law, that they judged all strictly religious matters, the 'affairs of Yahweh' (2 Ch 19: 11), and intervened in civil cases at least when these involved some religious law or religious procedure. Their competence was perhaps extended with time. When we read in 1 Ch 23: 4, cf. 26: 29, of 6,000 Levites who were clerks and judges under David, it is evidently the idealized projection into the past of a later situation, probably after the Exile. In New Testament times the Sanhedrin included priests, laymen and scribes; it was presided over by the high priest and it acted as the supreme court of justice.

According to 2 Ch 19: 11, the tribunal instituted by Josaphat at Jerusalem employed Levites as *shôṭ'rîm*. The root *shṭr* means, in Akkadian and several other Semitic languages, 'to write', but the *shôṭ'rîm* were not mere scribes, for they are distinguished from them in 2 Ch 34: 13. They seem to have been clerks of the court, and more generally, clerks attached to the judges (cf. Dt 16: 18; 1 Ch 23: 4; 26: 29). 'Clerk' would also be a good translation of the other uses of the word, which denotes the officials in charge of forced labour (Ex 5: 6f.; perhaps 2 Ch 34: 13), and also the administrative officers of the army (Dt 20: 5f.). To complete this review of the judicial authorities, we may remember that there was a person at the king's court called 'the king's son', who seems to have been a police officer.[1]

7. Procedure

The legislative codes tell us little about judicial procedure, but the process of a trial can be reconstructed by piecing together the allusions in other books of the Bible and by making use of passages which represent God's disputes with men as a formal trial, especially in Job and the second part of Isaias.

Justice was administered in public, at the gate of the town (Dt 21: 19; Am 5: 10), in a holy place or a sanctuary (Ex 21: 6; 22: 7; Jg 4: 5; 1 S 7: 16; Jr 26: 10). The king gave his judgments in the porch of judgment (1 K 7: 7), which was open to all. As a general rule the action, *rîb*, was brought by a private person who appeared as plaintiff (Dt 25: 7, 8; Jb 9: 19; 13: 18; 23: 4; Pr 25: 8; Jr 49: 19; cf. Mt 5: 25). In certain religious cases, such as idolatry (Dt 17:

1. Cf. pp. 119-120.

2–5) or blasphemy against God and the king (1 K 21: 10f.), the tribunal took cognisance of the case after a denunciation.

During the arguments the judge was seated (Is 16: 5; Dn 7: 9-10; 13: 50; cf. Jb 29: 7), but he stood up to pronounce sentence (Is 3: 13; Ps 76: 10). The parties remained standing (Is 50: 8, literally, 'let us stand up together'; cf. 41: 1) and 'to stand before the judge' (Dt 19: 17) means 'to appear in court'. The accuser was the 'adversary', the *śaṭan*; he stood on the right of the accused (Ps 109: 6; Za 3: 1). The defender also stood on the right (Ps 109: 31; cf. 16: 8; 142: 5), but he was rather a witness for the defence than an advocate, for which there is no word in Hebrew. Nor was there any public prosecutor: each party pressed or defended his own case.

In the majority of cases the accusation was presented orally, but Jb 21: 35b–36 indicates that it could be done in writing (cf. Is 65: 6; Dn 7: 10). The accused was heard (Dt 17: 4; Jb 13: 22; Is 41: 21; cf. Jn 7: 51), but Jb 31: 35a does not prove that he did or could present a written defence. The examination of the case then began (Dt 13: 15; 17: 4; 19: 18).

Both parties called witnesses. There were witnesses for the prosecution, like the accusers of 1 K 21: 10, 13, like the hills and the mountains on which Yahweh calls in the action he brings against his people (Mi 6: 1), and witnesses for the defence (Pr 14: 25; Is 43: 9, 10, 12; Jr 26: 17). Otherwise the rôles were not very clearly defined. The accuser gave evidence (1 K 21: 10, 13; Mi 1: 2), and in actions heard by the Elders the latter could be witnesses as well as judges; Is 5: 3 and Mi 6: 1 can be understood in either sense. For a death sentence the law required at least two witnesses for the prosecution (Nb 35: 30; Dt 17: 6; cf. 1 K 21: 10; Dn 13: 34; Mt 26: 59-60; He 10: 28), and possibly for every case, according to Dt 19: 15; cf. Is 8: 2. These witnesses accepted responsibility for the sentence, which is why they had to throw the first stones if the condemned party were stoned (Dt 17: 7; cf. 13: 10; Jn 8: 7). But their evidence had to be verified by the judges, and false witnesses were condemned to the punishment which would have befallen the accused (Dt 19: 18-19; cf. Dn 13: 62). This prospect does not seem to have prevented miscarriages of justice (Ps 27: 12; 35: 11; Pr 6: 19; 12: 17; etc., and cf. the trials of Naboth in 1 K 21: 10f., of Susanna in Dn 13: 28f., of our Lord in Mt 26: 59f., and of Stephen in Ac 6: 11f.). According to the historian Josephus, women and slaves could not give evidence; if the rule is ancient, Israel's practice differed from that of Mesopotamia.

Proofs of fact were produced before the judges: the herdsman accused of losing a beast had to produce the remains of the animal if it had been mangled by a wild beast (Ex 22: 12; cf. Gn 31: 39; Am 3: 12). The wife accused by her husband of having lost her virginity before her marriage presented the bed-linen of the wedding-night, showing the signs of her virginity (Dt 22: 13-17). Tamar, accused before Judah, made him acknowledge the signet, the cord and the staff she had received from him (Gn 38: 25).

When everything had been thoroughly examined, the court 'declared guilty' or 'declared just, innocent', that is, gave its verdict of condemnation or acquittal (Ex 22: 8; Dt 25: 1; 1 K 8: 32; Pr 17: 15). The rôle of the judge, however, was not so much to impose a sentence as to settle a dispute while respecting justice. He was more a defender of right than a punisher of crime. He was a just arbitrator (Jb 9: 33).

8. The judgment of God

When no decision could be reached after the examination, or if the accused could not produce witnesses for the defence, they had recourse to an oath. In the Code of the Covenant, several cases are grouped together (Ex 22: 6-10): if an object entrusted to someone disappears and the thief is not found, the trustee goes to Elohim to attest that he has not taken another man's goods; if a dispute arises over a lost object, the matter is brought before Elohim, and he decides who is responsible; if a beast entrusted to someone's care dies or is wounded or is stolen unseen, an oath by Yahweh decides whether the keeper is at fault or not. The last case clearly presumes a judicial oath, so the two former cases must be interpreted in the same way, giving 'Elohim' its regular sense of 'God', not of 'judges', as some ancient versions and several modern expositors take it, or of 'domestic idols' (teraphim) as has lately been suggested. It may be associated with another method of religious test, where the oath is perhaps understood. When a murder has been committed in the country by some person unknown, the Elders of the nearest town kill a heifer near a stream and wash their hands over the animal, saying: 'Our hands have not shed this blood and our eyes have seen nothing.' They are then covered against blood-vengeance (Dt 21: 1-8).

The judicial oath by the gods or the king was also practised in Babylonia, in Assyria, at Nuzu and in the Jewish colony of Elephantine, especially when property rights were in question; as in the cases quoted from the Code of the Covenant, an oath terminated the action. A man might refuse the oath, but that was to own himself guilty: he feared that if he perjured himself he would be stricken by the curse accompanying the oath. It is to such a refusal that Qo 9: 2 alludes, speaking of 'him who swears an oath' and 'him who fears to swear an oath'. It was therefore an imprecatory oath, as in Nb 5: 21.

The oath itself is therefore an ordeal, a judgment of God (cf. 1 K 8: 31). In Nb 5: 11-31 it is only one action of a fuller ritual. The husband who suspects his wife of misconduct presents her to the priest. The priest sprinkles some of the dust of the sanctuary over a vessel of water, proffers the oath to the woman, dissolves the writing containing the words of the oath into the water, and then makes the woman drink the mixture. If she is guilty this water becomes for her a 'water of bitterness and cursing' which makes her barren for ever, a fearful example to all. It will be observed there is here no question of bringing an action, and that the priest is not acting as a judge but as the minister of a rite. We may connect it with the last part of the story of the golden calf in Ex 32: 20: the idol is ground to a fine powder which the Israelites are made to swallow in water; the conclusion is doubtless to be found in v. 35: 'And Yahweh chastised the people.' The story of the massacre by the Levites (vv. 25f.) would come from another tradition.

This ordeal of bitter waters has no analogy in the ancient East. On the other hand, Israel knew nothing of the judicial ordeal by throwing the accused into a river. It was practised in Babylonia, in Assyria, in Elam, east of the Tigris at Nuzu, and on the banks of the Euphrates at Mari and Carchemish. If it is not found in Palestine, this may simply be because, apart from the Jordan, the country has no river in which anyone could possibly be drowned.

Another form of the judgment of God is the drawing of lots. 'The lot puts an end to quarrels and decides between the mighty' (Pr 18: 18). It serves to pick out one guilty man from a group, as with Akan (Jos 7: 14-15), and Jonathan (1 S 14: 38-42). In the latter case it is stated that the sacred lots were used, the *urim* and the *thummim*, which only a priest could handle. The high priest's breastplate, which contained the lots, is called for that reason the 'breastplate of judgment' (Ex 28: 15). Aaron bears on his breast the 'judgment of the children of Israel' (Ex 28: 30). But again we should note that the procedure here is extra-judicial, and the priest is acting only as the minister of the divine oracle.

9. Penalties

The death penalty is laid down for the following crimes:

Intentional homicide (Ex 21: 12; Lv 24: 17; Nb 35: 16-21) for which monetary compensation is never accepted (Nb 35: 31; Dt 19: 11-12); the abduction of a man in order to make him a slave (Ex 21: 16; Dt 24: 7).

Grave sins against God: idolatry (Ex 22: 19; Lv 20: 1-5; Dt 13: 2-19; 17: 2-7; cf. Nb 25: 1-5); blasphemy (Lv 24: 15-16); profanation of the sabbath (Ex 31: 14-15; cf. Nb 15: 32-36); sorcery (Ex 22: 17; Lv 20: 27; cf. 1 S 28: 3, 9); prostitution by a priest's daughter (Lv 21: 9).

Grave sins against parents (Ex 21: 15, 17; Lv 20: 8; Dt 21: 18-21); abuses of sexual relations: adultery (Lv 20: 10; Dt 22: 22); different forms of incest (Lv 20: 11, 12, 14, 17); sodomy (Lv 20: 13); bestiality (Lv 20: 15-16).

Thus Israelite law, unlike other Eastern laws, limits capital punishment to offences against the purity of worship, against the sanctity of life and the sources of life, and this religious motive is usually expressed in the laws. It is a consequence of the peculiar character of Israel's legislation.[1]

1. Cf. p. 149.

As to the execution of the penalty, the murderer was handed over to the avenger of blood, who employed whatever means he chose. Stoning is ordered for idolaters (Dt 13: 10-11; 17: 5-7), for blasphemers (Lv 24: 14, 23), for a woman who concealed the fact that she was not a virgin at the time of her marriage (Dt 22: 21), for the guilty fiancée and her accomplice (Dt 22: 24), for the rebellious son (Dt 21: 21) and the man who profaned the sabbath (Nb 15: 35-36). A man who disobeyed an order of extermination and one who was guilty of lese-majesty were also stoned, according to Jos 7: 25 and 1 K 21: 10. It was the normal method of execution and it must also be presumed when the text does not state it precisely (cf. Jn 8: 5 for the woman taken in adultery). The condemned person was taken out of the town (1 K 21: 10, 13; cf Lv 24: 14; Nb 15: 36). The witnesses for the prosecution cast the first stones and the people continued till death ensued. The collective character of communal justice was thus expressed to the end.

The penalty could be increased by exposure of the bodies of the condemned. They were 'hung on the gibbet', but had to be taken down before night (Dt 21: 22-23; cf. Jos 8: 29; 10: 27). This was not the punishment of hanging, for the condemned had already been executed (cf. in particular Jos 10: 26; 2 S 4: 12). It was a mark of infamy and an example. We should probably interpret the texts of Nb 25: 4 and 2 S 21: 9 in this way and understand that the corpses of the guilty were impaled.

Death by crucifixion was a punishment unknown in the Old Testament. It is attested among the Persians (impalement or crucifixion), sporadically among the Greeks, frequently among the Romans. The first mention of it in Palestine occurs in Flavius Josephus, writing of the persecution under Antiochus Epiphanes.

Death by burning is prescribed in the law for two cases only: prostitution by a priest's daughter (Lv 21: 9) and the incest of a man who weds both mother and daughter (Lv 20: 14). The same mode of death is ordered in the Code of Hammurabi for similar cases. According to Gn 38: 24, the same punishment was inflicted in ancient times on an adulterous wife.

The punishment of flogging seems to be applied by Dt 22: 18 to the man who has slandered his wife, and by Dt 21: 18 to a disobedient son, according to the parallels in 1 K 12: 11, 14 and Pr 19: 18, where the same verb is employed. According to Dt 25: 1-3, the judge could impose up to forty strokes of the whip (or rod?) on the guilty man, who was stretched on the ground before him (cf. Jr 20: 2). By a legalistic scruple, later Jewish custom restricted the number to 'forty save one' (cf. 2 Co 11: 24).

Bodily mutilation as a consequence of the *lex talionis* is fairly common in the Code of Hammurabi and the Assyrian laws, but it is found in Israelite law only in the special case of Dt 25: 11-12, where it is a symbolic retaliation.[1]

Strictly speaking, there are no pecuniary penalties, in the sense of fines

1. Cf. p. 149.

payable to the State or the community. The money paid to the priests in satisfaction for a crime or sin (2 K 12: 17) is not in the nature of a fine and arises from religious institutions. On the other hand, a wrong done to an individual in his goods or rights is equitably redressed, and this compensation has a penal aspect, as it is generally larger than the damage caused. A man who has slandered his wife pays her father a hundred pieces of silver, which is much more than he had paid in order to marry her (Dt 22: 19). A seducer pays damages to his victim's father (Ex 22: 16). A man who has let his beasts graze in the field or vineyard of another reimburses him on the basis of his best harvest (Ex 22: 4). One who is responsible for a fire which has spread to his neighbour's land and destroyed his crop compensates him for what the fire has destroyed (Ex 22: 5). A man who has caused the death of an animal by leaving a pit open pays the price of it to the owner (Ex 21: 34). A man who has stolen a beast and slaughtered it must pay compensation, fivefold for cattle, fourfold for sheep or goats (Ex 21: 37; cf. 2 S 12: 6; Lk 19: 8). The 'sevenfold' claimed in Pr 6: 31 and 2 S 12: 6, in the Greek, is not to be taken literally and simply means perfect restitution.

Imprisonment by judicial order does not appear till after the Exile, in Esd 7: 26, as an application of a foreign legislation. But there were prisons, in which accused persons were kept pending a decision (Lv 24: 12; Nb 15: 34), and suspects were shut up by police action, often arbitrarily (1 K 22: 27; Jr 37: 15-18). Putting a man in the pillory or the stocks was a further punishment (2 Ch 16: 10; Jr 20: 2; 29: 26). Bodily restraint of one sentenced to make restitution or of a defaulting debtor (Mt 5: 25-26; 18: 30; Lk 12: 58-59) is something borrowed from Hellenistic law. Under ancient legislation, thieves who could not make restitution were sold as slaves (Ex 22: 2) and an insolvent debtor would sell himself or his dependents into slavery to discharge his debt (Lv 25: 39f.; Dt 15: 2f.).[1]

10. *Private vengeance and Cities of Refuge*

The very ancient custom of blood-vengeance, carried out by the *go'el*,[2] never disappeared and was recognized by law. But the same law tried to limit the abuses which could easily arise from this exercise of private justice. It did so by distinguishing between voluntary and involuntary homicide, and by establishing places of refuge where an involuntary killer could find safety.

The principle is laid down in the Code of the Covenant: the man who has killed without premeditation may take refuge in a place which God will appoint, but the wilful murderer must be dragged from the altar itself to be put to death (Ex 21: 13-14). The 'place' thus denoted is evidently a sanctuary, where there is an altar, apparently any lawful sanctuary of Yahweh, but first

1. Cf. pp. 82-83.   2. Cf. pp. 11 and 21-22.

and foremost the central sanctuary of the tribal federation, that of the Ark. There Adonias took refuge (1 K 1: 50-53), and Joab after him. But Joab, who had murdered Abner and Amasa, was not protected by the law of asylum and was put to death in the sanctuary itself, which he refused to leave (1 K 2: 28-31). There is no other actual example of this recourse to a sanctuary as a place of refuge, though certain expressions in the Psalms seem to refer to it. Thus the Temple is a shelter against enemies and anyone dwells there in safety (Ps 27: 2-5); there one is covered by the wings of Yahweh (Ps 61: 4-5), but the wicked are not allowed in (Ps 5: 5).

A more stable institution is that of the Cities of Refuge. Unfortunately the texts describing them are hard to interpret. In the order of the books of the Bible they are as follows:

Nb 35: 9-34: the Israelites are ordered by God to have cities where an involuntary killer can take refuge from blood-vengeance. There are to be three cities of refuge in Transjordan and three west of the Jordan, but they are not indicated by name. Asylum is granted only to the involuntary killer: the wilful murderer may not be received and must die at the hands of the avenger of blood. The community decides the question of guilt, rejects the murderer and watches over the involuntary killer, who must not leave the city of refuge till the death of the high priest.

Dt 4: 41-43, unconnected with its context: Moses chooses three cities of refuge across the Jordan: Beser, Ramoth of Gilead, Golan.

Dt 19: 1-13: after the conquest, the land must be divided into three regions and three cities chosen, which are not named (vv. 8-9, an obvious addition, orders that if the land should become greater still, three other cities shall be added). They are to welcome the involuntary killer, but the murderer is to be rearrested by the Elders of his city and handed over to the avenger of blood.

Jos 20: 1-9: at Yahweh's command and in pursuance of the instructions given to Moses, Josue chooses the cities of refuge where an involuntary killer will be protected from blood-vengeance. It is the Elders of these cities who admit the fugitive after inquiry. He remains there till he has been judged by the community, till the death of the high priest. The list of these towns is given in vv. 7-8: Qedesh of Galilee in the hill-country of Nephthali, Shechem in the hill-country of Ephraim, Hebron in the hill-country of Judah; on the other side of the Jordan, Beser on the plateau, Ramoth in Gilead, Golan in Bashan.

These passages show us the development of the institution in apparent conformity with the course of events recorded in the Pentateuch. The command of Nb 35, associated with the period on the steppes of Moab, fixes the rules but states neither the number nor the names of the cities: the land is not yet conquered. In Dt 4, Moses chooses three cities in the territory already occupied by the Israelites on the far side of the Jordan. Dt 19 provides for three cities in the land of Canaan, which has still to be conquered, but does not name them; the additional verses, 8 and 9, provide for three other unnamed cities in order to complete the traditional number of six, without seeing that the three missing cities are those of Dt 4. Finally, when the conquest is complete, Jos 20 recalls the rules proclaimed earlier and at last gives the names of the six cities with their geographical positions.

The picture is changed, however, if we examine and compare the vocabulary and context of the various texts. The latest of all is obviously Nb 35: the rôle accorded to the religious community, the 'edah, and the mention of the high priest, whose death is the occasion for a general amnesty, show that it was edited after the Exile. This late date and the absence of precise details about the towns show that it was never actually in force. Dt 19 and Jos 20: 4 and 9a, on the contrary, which allot a rôle to the Elders of the murderer's town or of the city of refuge, and which also preserve the primitive idea of blood-vengeance, are ancient. But Jos 20: 6 and 9b, at least, are later retouchings, which mention the community and the high priest in order to bring the text into line with Nb 35, and even so they do not avoid all incoherence. On the other hand, Dt 19 was never a real law, for the towns are not named, which would be necessary for the law to be applicable. But this passage prescribes three cities and three territories in Canaan, which are given, with their names, in Jos 20: 7. If no city in Transjordan is provided for by Dt 19, that is because the land was no longer in Israelite hands. The addition in vv. 8-9, however, shows that the tradition of six cities of refuge was still remembered. Dt 19 thus appears as a project of reform which was never carried out: this reform presumes that the institution described in Jos 20: 7-9a is known, and maintains its principles, but adapts it to new circumstances and secularizes it by taking away from certain towns a privilege which they owed, as we are about to explain, to the existence of a sanctuary, now condemned by the law on centralization of worship. The oldest element in all this documentation is therefore Jos 20: 7-9a, which guarantees the existence of cities of refuge, with the motives and rules for their institution (cf. Jos 20: 4 and Dt 19: 11-12). The list of cities of refuge in Transjordan in Dt 4 come in its turn from Jos 20: 8.

All the towns mentioned in Jos 20 are mentioned elsewhere as Levitical towns. The list is not invented: Beser and Golan do not appear apart from these two contexts, but Beser is mentioned as an Israelite town by the stele of Mesha, and the name of Golan is still preserved in the Bashan region. Further, among the six towns named, Qedesh was captured by Tiglath-Pileser in 734 B.C. and Beser was conquered by Mesha about 850. Ramoth of Gilead, before being finally severed from Israel, was a town over which Israel and the Aramaeans disputed in the first half of the ninth century. Golan and its region were lost soon after the death of Solomon. It is difficult to trace the list back beyond Solomon to the tribal federation, or even to the reign of David, for the towns are chosen and determined by their geographical situation, not by their attachment to a tribe; the mention of Reuben, Gad and Manasseh in connection with the three towns in Transjordan simply gives a second geographical designation and must be considered as secondary. The institution is therefore independent of tribal organization, and does not antedate the reign of Solomon. One may wonder whether it remained long in force and how it developed, but there are no sufficient grounds for asserting that it was a late invention to which nothing corresponded in reality.

Qedesh, the 'holy town', Shechem, hallowed by the memory of Abraham and Jacob, by the tomb of Joseph and the covenant under Josue, and Hebron, which possessed the tomb of the Patriarchs, had each its famous sanctuary. Very probably the three cities across the Jordan were also holy places. Thus the institution of the Cities of Refuge is linked with the right of asylum recognized at the sanctuaries. But it appears on the other hand as the secularizing of an originally religious custom (cf. Ex 21: 13-14). The prerogatives of the sanctuaries and their ministers were in the end transferred to the Cities and their councils of Elders.

Chapter Eleven

ECONOMIC LIFE

1. *Landed property*

IN Egypt all the land belonged to the Pharaoh or the temples, and the Israelites were astonished at this land system which was so different from their own (Gn 47: 20-26). In Mesopotamia, though, the king and the sanctuaries owned large estates, but the oldest texts show that communities, families and individuals already had certain lands, which the king could acquire only by purchase from the owners. With these and other lands of his estates, the king used to found fiefs. A fief is a grant of immovable property, made to an individual in return for the obligation to render personal services. This feudal system was very widespread in the Near East. The Code of Hammurabi and the Hittite Code devote several articles to it and it is frequently alluded to in the Nuzu and Ugarit documents. These texts span the second millennium B.C. At first the fief appears as an inalienable charge, to which personal services are attached. Gradually it took on the character of heritable property, of which a man might freely dispose, and the feudal services attached to it became attached to the property, not to any person or persons.

This development of the fief was already far advanced when Israel first appeared as a people. It was even later that this people became a centralized state, and apparently they never experienced a feudal regime. Those rare texts where some have tried to see an allusion to fiefs are capable of another interpretation. For example, 1 S 8: 14 predicts that the king will seize fields and vineyards and give them to his officers; according to 1 S 22: 7, this was already happening in Saul's time, but these lands were given as gifts rather than fiefs, for there is no mention of any service attached to them. When Saul promises to exempt the family of the man who slays the Philistine champion (1 S 17: 25), the reference is to exemption from taxes or forced labour rather than enfranchisement from the service of a fief. Only once is there an unmistakable reference to feudal services: David received the town of Siqlag from the Philistine prince of Gath on condition that he ensured the policing of the desert and followed his suzerain to war (1 S 27: 6, 10; 28: 1); it was a military fief, but we are on Philistine territory.

Nevertheless, the feudal idea was found in Israel, though transferred on to the theological plane. As Yahweh is the only true king of Israel (Jg 8: 23;

1 S 12: 12), so he is the sole lord of the soil.[1] The Holy Land is the 'domain of Yahweh' (Jos 22: 19), the 'land of Yahweh' (Os 9: 3; cf. Ps. 85: 2; Jr 16: 18; Ez 36: 5). It is the land he had promised to the Fathers (Gn 12: 7; 13: 15; 15: 18; 26: 4; Ex 32: 13; Dt 1: 35-36), the land he has conquered and given to his people (Nb 32: 4; Jos 23: 3, 10; 24: 11-13; Ps 44: 4). This property-right which God retains over all lands was invoked as the basis of the law of Jubilee (Lv 25: 23).[2] It is also in virtue of God's supreme dominion that religious law limits the rights of the human occupants: hence the duty of leaving gleanings of corn and vines for the poor (Lv 19: 9-10; 23: 22; Dt 24: 19-21; cf. Rt 2); the right of every passer-by to satisfy his hunger when passing through a field or a vineyard (Dt 23: 25-26); the annual tithe due to Yahweh (Lv 27: 30-32), to be eaten in Yahweh's presence (Dt 14: 22-27), given to the Levites (Nb 18: 21-32); the tithe every third year for the poor (Dt 14: 28-29; 26: 12-15), and the law about fallow ground in the sabbatical year (Ex 23: 10-11; Lv 25: 2-7;).[3]

In the second millennium B.C., at Nuzu and in Assyria, the fiefs were distributed by drawing lots; in the same way, the Promised Land, at Yahweh's command, was shared by lot between the tribes, according to Jos 13: 6; 15: 1; 16: 1; 17: 1; 18: 6—19: 49, *passim*: Jg 1: 3. This 'sharing out' by lot of the 'plots' in which the tribes were in fact already settled, or which they had still to conquer, is the expression of God's sovereign dominion over the land, in actual fact the tribes acquired their territories by the hazards of a conquest which is schematized in Jos 6-12, and represented in Jg 1 as still incomplete. But probably the drawing of lots among the Tribes for the Holy Land is only an imaginative extension to the whole people of what in fact took place at the level of the clan and the family. In the nomadic system, pastures and watering places are the common property of the tribe.[4] When the tribe becomes settled, the same system may be applied to the arable land. This idea of common property still survives in modern times, and it is interesting to find it attested in ancient Mesopotamia, from the Kassite period onwards; it is particularly noticeable among the Aramaean tribes on the Tigris banks, whose social structure was like that of the earliest Israelites. These communal lands are often mentioned in the *kudurrus*, land-survey documents which were used to authenticate the purchase of a tribal property by the king and its transfer to an individual or a temple.

The use of these common lands, however, is divided among the members of the group, each member of which cultivates a part for his own benefit. There has been a similar system in modern Palestine, traces of which still remain. Outside the village and its immediate surroundings, which were private property (*mulk*), the rest was Government land (*miri*) and allotted to the village as common land (*mesha'*). This was divided into plots which were distributed in rotation, generally every year, or drawn for by lot among the

1. Cf. p. 98.   2. Cf. pp. 175-177.   3. Cf. p. 173.   4. Cf. p. 9.

heads of families. Except for its temporary nature, this is the same division by lot between clans and families as that prescribed by Nb 26: 55-56; 33: 54; 36: 2; cf. 27: 7; this too is what Ezechiel foretold for the future Israel (Ez 45: 1; 47: 22). The same word *gôral*, originally 'a pebble', means both the 'lot' which was drawn and the 'plot' assigned by the lot. According to Is 34: 17, Yahweh himself 'drew by lot the portion of each one', and 'divided the land to them by line'; in Mi 2: 5, the monopolizers will be despoiled and 'will have none to cast the line for them on a plot in the assembly of Yahweh'; according to Ps 16: 5-6, the faithful man has Yahweh for his plot, the line marks out for him a choice portion. The use of such figures would have no meaning unless there existed an actual custom similar to the modern practice, and perhaps a partition of this kind is alluded to in Jr 37: 12.

2. Family property and large estates

This communal property, the temporary use of which was divided among a number of families, is far less in evidence than family property, which, it seems, was the normal system in Israel. In our texts the word *gôral*, 'lot' and 'plot', alternates with *heleq*, 'portion' and *nahalah*, 'heritage'. This ancestral estate often contained the family tomb (Jos 24: 30, 32; 1 S 25: 1; 1 K 2: 34; cf. Gn 23). It was defined by boundaries which it was strictly forbidden by law to remove (Dt 19: 14; 27: 17; cf. Jb 24: 2; Pr 22: 28; 23: 10; Os 5: 10). The peasant was deeply attached to the piece of ground he had inherited from his fathers: Naboth refused to surrender his vineyard at Yizreel to Achab, and the king could not legally force him to do so (1 K 21). The social ideal was that every man should live 'under his vine and under his fig-tree' (1 K 5: 5; Mi 4: 4; Za 3: 10).

Public feeling and custom took care that this patrimony was not alienated, or that at least it should not pass out of the family. It is probable that when land was inherited it was not shared like the other property but passed to the eldest son or remained undivided.[1] If a man dies without male heirs, the land is bequeathed to his daughters (Nb 27: 7-8), but they must marry within their tribe, so that their portion may not be transferred to another tribe (Nb 36: 6-9). If the owner dies childless, the inheritance reverts to his brothers, his uncles or his nearest kinsman (Nb 27: 9-11). If the Law of Levirate binds a man to marry his widowed and childless sister-in-law, the object is no doubt to raise up descendants to the deceased, but it is also to prevent the alienation of the family property.[2]

Sometimes, however, an Israelite was obliged by poverty to sell his patrimony. One of the duties of the *go'el*[3] was to buy the land which his near relation had to abandon. Hence Jeremias buys the field of his cousin Hanameel (Jr 32: 6-9), and Boaz, in place of the nearest *go'el*, buys the land of

1. Cf. p. 53.   2. Cf. p. 38.   3. Cf. pp. 11 and 21-22.

Elimelek, which Naomi, his widow, was offering for sale (Rt 4: 9). Note that in these cases there is no question of the repurchase of a property already sold, but of a prior right to purchase a property offered for sale, and that the land is not restored to the impoverished kinsman, but becomes the property of the *go'el*. These are the only concrete cases recorded in the Bible and it is in their light that the law of Lv 25: 25 must be interpreted: if an Israelite falls into distress and has to sell his land, his nearest *go'el* comes 'to his house' (generally omitted by translators) and buys what he has to sell. The aim of this institution is to keep for kinsfolk the property which the head of a family cannot keep for himself and his direct descendants; it thus links up with the laws on the marriage of heiresses and inheritance in the collateral line. But in Lv 25 this ancient arrangement is recalled in a different context: the object of the Law of Jubilee is in fact to restore property to the individual or family which used to possess it, not merely to retain it in the clan; compared with the institution of the *go'el*, it is something new and, as we shall see, Utopian.

But the *go'el* did not always exercise his right of pre-emption and the economic development of the first centuries of the monarchy[1] hastened the break-up of family properties in favour of rich landlords. Is 5: 8 curses 'those who add house to house and join field to field, until there is no room left for anyone else'; Mi 2: 2 condemns those 'who covet fields and seize them, houses and they take them'. These *latifundia* (large estates) were worked by slaves (2 S 9: 10), or by paid workmen.[2] The system of rent-holding or *métayage*, land tenure in which the farmer pays a part (usually half) of the produce as rent to the owner, who furnishes stock and seed, was apparently never practised in Israel in early days, though it was known in Mesopotamia, and was later provided for in the Rabbinic period. Am 5: 11 blames the rich for taking tribute from the corn of the poor, which could be an allusion to a *métayage*, but it may refer to the tithe, the collection and profits of which were left by the king to his officers (cf. 1 S 8: 15). The first mention of the renting of lands is found in the parable in Mt 21: 33-41, and the earliest documents are the contracts of *métayage* discovered in the caves of Murabba'at, datad A.D. 133.

Finally, it will be recalled that the king owned large estates.[3] The royal estate was managed by stewards (1 Ch 27: 25-31), and worked by the labour of State slaves and the levy of free men (1 S 8: 12).

3. *Conveyances and similar formalities*

The sale of a property was recorded by a contract. This might be simply an oral contract, made in the presence of witnesses in a public place, at the town gate: thus Boaz acquires the property of Naomi and the right to marry her daughter-in-law (Rt 4: 9-11). Abraham's purchase of the field of Ephron is

1. Cf. pp. 72-73. 2. Cf. p. 76. 3. Cf. pp. 124-125.

also represented as an oral transaction, made in the sight of all who passed through the gate of the town (Gn 23: 17-18). But its terms are as precise as a legal deed and comparable to the contracts on cuneiform tablets: a description of the land acquired, the names of the contracting parties and the witnesses. Mention of the gate of the town recalls the clause in certain contracts at Nuzu, drawn up 'after proclamation at the gate'. The transaction at Hebron may well have been concluded by the drawing up of such a contract.

The use of written contracts, which had long existed in Canaan and all the Near East, was certainly widespread in Israel. Two cuneiform tablets found at Gezer contain contracts of sale made under Assyrian rule in the seventh century B.C. and drawn up in Assyrian. It is mere chance that the Bible speaks only once of a written contract, but it does so in great detail (Jr 32: 6-14). Jeremias buys the field offered for sale by his cousin Hanameel. The contract is drawn up, sealed and signed by the witnesses; the money is weighed out. The deed is made out in duplicate; one document is sealed, the other 'open'. All is done 'according to the prescribed rules' and the two copies are given to Baruch to be preserved in an earthen vase. This has been compared with the duplicate documents of Mesopotamia: the tablet of the contract was wrapped in a sheath of clay on which the same text was reproduced. But in Jeremias' time this custom no longer survived in Mesopotamia, and moreover his deed of purchase, drawn up in Hebrew, would be written on papyrus or, less probably, on parchment. This is the earliest evidence of a type of document of which there are many examples in Egypt, from the Hellenistic period onwards; some, dating from the beginning of the second century of our era, have lately been discovered in Palestine. On the same sheet of papyrus two copies of the contract were written, separated by a blank space. The first copy was rolled up and sealed, the other rolled up but not sealed: this is the 'open' copy of which Jeremias speaks. It could be consulted at will but was liable to be falsified; if a dispute arose the sealed copy was opened. Baruch was to put the contract in an earthen vessel: the custom of preserving family archives in this way is attested by many archaeological finds.

The Old Testament tells us little about the value of land. Abraham buys the field and cave of Macpelah for 400 shekels (Gn 23: 15). Jacob pays a hundred qeṣitah (value unknown) for the land of Shechem (Gn 33: 19; Jos 24: 32). David buys the threshing-floor and oxen of Araunah for fifty shekels (2 S 24: 24). Omri pays two talents of silver (6,000 shekels) for the hill of Samaria (1 K 16: 24); Jeremias' field costs him seventeen shekels (Jr 32: 9). These statements give us a certain order of values but nothing exact, since we know neither the area of the lands nor the exact weight of the shekel, nor the purchasing power of silver at the different periods. According to Lv 27: 16 the value of a field is calculated at fifty shekels for every *homer* of barley produced.

In early days the transfer of property was ratified by a symbolic action. According to Rt 4: 7, it was once the custom in Israel to validate all transactions in this way: one of the parties removed his sandal and gave it to the other. This action, performed before witnesses, signified the abandonment of a right. Naomi's first *go'el* in this way renounces his right of pre-emption in favour of Boaz (Rt 4: 8); the brother-in-law who declines the moral obligation of the levirate has his shoe removed (Dt 25: 9-10); he is dispossessed of the right he had over his brother's widow.[1] The shoe seems to have served as a probative instrument in transfers of land: in Ps 60: 10 = 108: 10, the phrase 'over Edom I cast my sandal' implies taking possession. At Nuzu, the seller lifted his foot off the ground he was selling, and placed the buyer's foot on it. Here, too, a pair of shoes (and a garment) appears as a fictitious payment to convalidate certain irregular transactions. This may explain, in Am 2: 6; 8: 6, the poor man who is sold, or bought, for a pair of sandals: he has been unjustly dispossessed, while the exaction has been given a cloak of legality. The same meaning would then be found in the Greek of 1 S 12: 3, confirmed by Si 46: 19; Samuel has not taken a pair of sandals from any man, that is, he has not twisted the law to make an illicit profit.

4. *Deposit and hiring*

Deposit is a free contract by which a man places an object in the safe keeping of another, who does not make use of it and gives it back on demand. The Code of the Covenant (Ex 22: 6-12) provides for the deposit of money, movable objects and animals. If the thing deposited disappears or is damaged through no fault of the depositary, he may exonerate himself by taking an oath; otherwise he owes compensation. The law of Lv 5: 21-26 adds that if he makes a false declaration he must restore the deposit and one fifth. The Babylonian law of Eshnunna and the Code of Hammurabi contain similar provisions, and the latter requires the deposit to be made before witnesses and registered by a contract. A late example of this procedure occurs in the Book of Tobias (Tb 1: 14; 4: 1, 20; 5: 3; 9: 5). The elder Tobias deposited ten talents of silver with Gabael in sealed bags. The deposit was confirmed in writing, signed by the depositor and the depositary, each of whom kept half of the document. On presentation of the document the representative of Tobias was given back the deposit.

A deposit involves no charge on either of the parties. This is not true of hiring, but this form of contract—apart from the hiring of services from wage-earners[2]—was scarcely known among the Israelites. There is only the text of Ex 22: 14, which, if interpreted in the light of the Hittite law, may refer to the hiring of a beast. We have already said that Am 5: 11 contains only an uncertain allusion to the hiring of lands. The hiring of money and

1. Cf. p. 37.   2. Cf. p. 76.

foodstuffs, on the other hand, was developed in the form of loans at interest, in spite of legal prohibitions.

5. Loans

When an Israelite fell on hard times and was reduced to borrowing, he should have found help among his clan or tribe. Lending to the poor is a good deed (Ps 37: 21; 112: 5; Si 29: 1-2; cf. Mt 5: 42). But many refused because the borrowers did not honour their obligations and did not discharge them, even when they were able to (Si 29: 3-7; cf. 8: 12).

All this concerns loans without interest, the only kind of loan allowed by the Code of the Covenant (Ex 22: 24), which contemplates only loans between Israelites. This provision is developed by the law of Dt 23: 20; one may not take interest on money, food or anything whatever lent to one's brother, and the same precept is found in Lv 25: 35-38; but one may lend at interest to a foreigner (Dt 23: 21; cf. 15: 6). Lending at interest was in fact practised by all Israel's neighbours.

Interest is called in Hebrew *neshek*, literally, 'a bite', and *tarbîth*, literally, 'increase'. The former word is found alone in the laws of Ex and Dt and in Ps 15: 5. In later texts it is always used along with the second, and it is hard to distinguish between them. Possibly *neshek* at first referred to any kind of loan (cf. Dt 23: 20) and was later restricted to loans of money, *tarbîth* then applying to loans in kind (cf. Lv 25: 37, where we have, as an exception, the cognate form *marbîth*). In that case the Aramaic of Elephantine, in the fifth century B.C., would give us the final stage in the development: here *marbîth* is the only word used for interest, even in money. Possibly, too, the vocabulary reflects an evolution in the system of lending: either the borrower signs a receipt for sixty shekels and only receives forty (*neshek*, a bite) or else he signs a receipt for forty shekels and undertakes to pay sixty on maturity (*tarbîth*, increase). Alternatively, *tarbîth* may be an increase provided for in case of non-execution, or finally an increment to take account of the depreciation of the provisions borrowed in winter and restored after the harvest, when prices stand lower. Information is so scarce that we can only guess.

Economic development and example from abroad led to frequent violation of these laws. The just man does not lend at interest, says Ps 15: 5, but the wicked does so (Pr 28: 8; cf. Ez 18: 8, 13, 17). It is one of the sins for which Jerusalem is condemned (Ez 22: 12). Things were no better after the Exile, and in Ne 5: 1-13 we find the people burdened with debts. Lending at interest, at rates which strike us as usury, was practised by the Jews at Elephantine. From Rabbinic sources it appears that the Jerusalem Temple itself lent at interest, and the parable in Mt 25: 27; Lk 19: 23 presumes that the custom was common and accepted. The Greek papyri of Egypt, however, show that the Jews did not take to these strictly banking operations till a late period.

The annual rate of interest in the ancient Near East was very high: in Babylonia and Assyria it was generally a quarter or a fifth for money loans, a third for loans in kind, and often much more. In Upper Mesopotamia and in Elam, the interest on money was higher—up to one-third or a half, but the interest on loans of corn was the same as in Babylonia. In Egypt the rate dropped in the Ptolemaic period and seems to have been twelve per cent per annum at Elephantine; this was also the maximum permitted rate at Rome at the beginning of our era. We do not know what the practice was in Israel. The Massoretic text of Ne 5: 11 was interpreted by the Vulgate, in the light of Roman usage, as meaning an interest of one per cent a month, but this text is corrupt.

6. Securities

To guard against his debtor's defaulting, the creditor could demand a security. In Gn 38: 17-18, Judah gives Tamar his signet, cord and staff as pledge, 'erabôn (whence, through Greek and Latin, comes the English 'an earnest'), of her fee. According to 1 S 17: 18, when David was sent to his brothers he had to bring back to his father a pledge, 'arubbah, as proof that he had fulfilled his errand. In credit operations the pledge is a surety, an object in the possession of the debtor which he hands over to the creditor as guarantee for his debt.

A movable pledge is called ḥăbol, ḥăbolah, or 'ăbôt, 'abtît, and the cognate verbs mean 'to engage'. In spite of attempts to distinguish between their meanings, these words seem to be synonymous (cf. the identical prescriptions of Ex 22: 25-26, ḥbl, and Dt 24: 12-13, 'bt). These pledges were sureties accepted when the loan was granted: they remained the property of the debtor and there is nothing to show that the creditor had the right to realize them in order to recoup himself: the pledge must be returned (Ez 18: 12, 16; 35: 15). According to Dt 24: 10-11, the creditor may not enter the debtor's house to take his pledge for himself; it must be handed to him outside, no doubt in order to avoid all appearance of seizure. It was forbidden to accept as sureties objects which are means of livelihood, such as the mill or the millstone (Dt 24: 6). The pledge was often a garment, a substitute for the person, but the Code of the Covenant says that the poor man's garment must be given back to him at dusk, because it is all he has to cover himself with at night (Ex 22: 25-26; the law is repeated in Dt 24: 12-13; cf. Jb 22: 6; 24: 9 (corr.); Am 2: 8). This garment, which the creditor was forbidden to keep except in the daytime, was not a real pledge, proportionate in value to the credit, but a symbolic instrument, a probative pledge, which seems to have been generally true of movable pledges in Israel. But the orphan's ass and the widow's ox (in Jb 24: 3) are real sureties, which can even be used to profit.

Only once is there any question of immovable pledges: according to Ne

5: 3 the Jews pledged their fields, vineyards and houses in order to get corn. It is more than a mortgage, for the creditors were already installed in these properties (v. 5) and Nehemias demanded restitution (v. 11). It is at least a profit-bearing surety, the revenue from which goes to pay off the debt; it is perhaps an alienation pure and simple, since the property 'belongs to others' (v. 5), a fact which contradicts the notion of a pledge.

It is possible that movable pledges, especially garments, were only probative instruments of a weightier guarantee, the pledge of a man's own person. According to Dt 24: 10, the man who lends against security (*mashsha'ah*) must not go into the debtor's house to seize the pledge ('*abôt*) which, according to vv. 12-13, is a garment. Now in Dt 15: 2 the *mashsheh* is a person who works for the creditor, and this is also the sense which must be given to *mashsha'* in Ne 10: 32, referring to the sabbatical year, like Dt 15. The context again allows us to understand it as a personal pledge in Ne 5: 7, 10, 11 (corr.), where the same word is used. The debt contracted on this guarantee is called *mashsha'ah* (Dt 24: 10; Pr 22: 26).

The person who stood as security was handed over to the creditor only when the debt matured and in case of non-payment. He passed into the service of the creditor, who employed him to recover the interest and, if necessary, the principal. This is clear from the story in 2 K 4: 1-7: the lender against security, the *nôshe'*, comes to take the widow's two sons to make them his slaves, but they are still with her, and thanks to the miracle of Eliseus she redeems her pledge (*n'shî*) and keeps her children. The same passage shows us that the pledge was someone dependent on the debtor and not the debtor himself. In Ne 5:2 (corr.) and 5, the Jews pledge their sons and daughters, who are handed over into slavery (cf. Is 50:1: Yahweh has not sold his children, the Israelites, to lenders on pledge). Such men easily made themselves odious through the exercise of their rights. The Code of the Covenant rebukes the practice (Ex 22: 24) and Nehemias was bitterly angry at it (Ne 5: 6f.; cf. 1 S 22: 2; Ps 109: 11).

If he had no personal pledge the defaulting debtor had to enter the service of his creditor, or sell himself to a third party so as to repay his debt (Dt 15: 12; Lv 25: 39, 47). Insolvency was the main cause of Israelites being reduced to slavery.[1]

7. Sureties and bail

The seizure of the pledged person or the actual debtor could be prevented by entering bail or surety. In Biblical law the surety is the person who, when the debt matures, 'intervenes' (the root '*rb*), in favour of the insolvent debtor and assumes responsibility for the payment of the debt, either by obtaining it from the debtor or by substituting himself for him. The collections of laws do not mention it, but there are many allusions to it in the Sapiential books,

1. Cf. p. 83.

and the texts in Pr 11: 15; 17: 18; 20: 16=26: 13, which belong to the 'Salomonic' collections, show that the practice was not of late date in Israel. There is very early evidence of it in Mesopotamia.

The surety intervened by the symbolic gesture of 'striking the hands', that is, shaking hands (Pr 6: 1; 11: 15; 17: 18; 22: 26; Jb 17: 3). In Mesopotamia he 'struck the forehead' of the debtor, but the resemblance between the actions is probably only outward. The surety had to try to free himself by importuning the debtor till he paid up (Pr 6: 3-5); otherwise he himself became liable to seizure (Pr 20: 16=27: 13; 22: 27). The Book of Proverbs warns rash men against thus going surety for their friends or for strangers. Sirach is less unfavourable to the practice: a good man goes surety for his neighbour, but his beneficiary is not always grateful, and going surety has brought many to their ruin; in any case, one must not go surety beyond one's means (Si 29: 14-20; cf. 8: 13).

8. The sabbatical year

Alienation of family property and the development of lending at interest led to the growth of pauperism and the enslavement of defaulting debtors or their dependants. This destroyed that social equality which had existed at the time of the tribal federation and which still remained as an ideal. Religious legislation attempted to remedy these evils by two institutions, the sabbatical year and the jubilee year.

The Code of the Covenant provided that an Israelite slave should not be kept more than six years: he was set at liberty in the seventh year, unless he preferred to stay with his master (Ex 21: 2-6).[1] This passage apparently means that the six years are counted from the time a man enters into service. According to the Code of the Covenant again, the fields, vineyards and olive groves are to lie fallow every seventh year and their produce is to be left for the poor (Ex 23: 10-11). The text does not say whether this reckoning varies with each field and owner, or whether the law orders a general measure, applicable at a fixed date. The latter solution is favoured by the following verse, which refers to the sabbath day and is formulated in the same way (Ex 23: 12).

There is no such uncertainty in the law of Deuteronomy (Dt 15: 1-18). The 'remission' (sh'miṭṭah) occurs every seventh year, and then all persons who have been enslaved for non-payment of a debt are set free (vv. 1-6). Verses 12-28, which repeat the law of Ex 21: 2-6 in this new context, are an invitation to interpret that law in the same manner: the slaves are insolvent debtors who have 'sold' themselves or have been 'sold', and setting them free involves writing off the debt. Vv. 7-11, however, prove that this remission is general and happens at fixed dates: no one may refuse a loan to his poorer brother, thinking: 'Soon it will be the seventh year, the year of remission.'

1. Cf. p. 87.

The general and periodic nature of this institution is confirmed by Dt 31: 10-11, which orders the reading of the Law 'every seven years, the time fixed for the year of remission'.

The law of Ex 23: 10-11 about land, not found in Deuteronomy, is repeated by Lv 25: 2-7: every seventh year the land is to have its sabbatical rest, according to a cycle which is reckoned to begin, by a sabbath year, from the people's entry into the Promised Land. God pledges his blessing for the sixth year, the produce of which will enable them to live through the year of fallow and the next year too, till the harvest (Lv 25: 18-22).

From all these provisions it appears that the sabbatical year was marked by a rest for the land and the setting free of Israelite slaves, signifying the abandonment of debts. The cycle of seven years is obviously inspired by the week of seven days, ending in the sabbath rest, whence the use of the same word 'sabbath' to denote both this year of rest and the whole period (Lv 25: 8; 26: 34, 35, 43). The seven-year periods recur in other Biblical contexts (Gn 41: 25-36; Dn 9: 24-27), and in Oriental literature. But no exact parallel has been found for the remission in the sabbatical year; a Ptolemaic papyrus remitting a debt contracted seven years earlier does not necessarily imply either the same practice or Jewish influence.

In the Bible itself there is scarcely any evidence for the institution apart from the legislative texts. It is very unlikely that the 'sign' given by Isaias (2 K 19: 29= Is 37: 30) refers to the sabbatical (or jubilee) year, in spite of the analogies of the text with Lv 25: 21-22. The freeing of the slaves under Sedecias is an exceptional measure, in connection with which Jeremias quotes Dt 15: 12-13, but complains that the law is not observed. According to the tradition of Lv 26: 35-36, 43; cf. 2 Ch 36: 21, the Holy Land was never able to 'enjoy its sabbaths' till the Jews were deported. After the Exile, Nehemias made them promise to give up in the seventh year the produce of the soil and persons held as sureties, which obviously refers to the prescriptions of the sabbatical year (Ne 10:32). Though Ne 5: 1-13 makes no allusion to it, this does not mean that the law was then unknown, nor even that it was known but not observed, for the social crisis demanded an immediate solution (cf. v. 11) without waiting for the sabbatical cycle.

It is not, however, till the Hellenistic period that we find clear proof that the law was applied, at least in leaving land fallow: in 163-162 B.C. the Jews lacked provisions, 'for it was a sabbatical year granted to the land' (1 M 6: 49, 53). Other historical data are provided by the historian Josephus; these, if they were more reliable, would allow us to trace this observance down to the beginning of the reign of Herod the Great. For the reign of Herod we have another piece of evidence that the law existed and was a source of embarrassment to lenders. During this period Hillel invented a way of circumventing the law by the *prosbol*: a clause was inserted in the contract by which the debtor renounced the advantage he would have gained from the sabbatical year. An acknowledgment of a debt containing such a clause has been discovered at Murabba'at. The land, too, was given rest: it is significant that contracts of *métayage* found in the same place are concluded up to the next sabbatical year (*sh'miṭṭah*). They are dated in February, A.D. 133, which would mark the beginning, more or less, of a sabbatical period, the time when contracts of land tenure would be renewed.

The sabbatical year is therefore an ancient institution, but it is hard to say how faithfully the Israelites observed it. Positive evidence is rare and late, and comes from periods of national and religious fervour.

9. The Jubilee Year

In Lv 25 prescriptions about the sabbatical year are combined with those on the jubilee year (Lv 25: 8-17, 23-55, several parts of which apply equally to both). This text raises some difficult problems. The jubilee (*yôbel*) is so called because its opening was announced by the sound of the trumpet (*yôbel*). It recurred every fifty years, at the end of seven weeks of years. It was a general emancipation (*d'rôr*) of all the inhabitants of the land. The fields lay fallow: every man re-entered his ancestral property, *i.e.* the fields and houses which had been alienated returned to their original owners, except for the town houses, which could only be re-purchased in the year after their sale. Consequently, transactions in land had to be made by calculating the number of years before the next jubilee: one did not buy the ground but so many harvests. Finally, defaulting debtors and Israelite slaves were set free, so the purchase price of these slaves was reckoned from the number of years still to elapse before the next jubilee. Religious grounds are given for these measures: the land cannot be sold absolutely, for it belongs to God; Israelites cannot be cast into perpetual slavery, for they are the servants of God, who brought them out of Egypt.

The practical application of this law seems to encounter insuperable obstacles. Unless we arbitrarily suppose, against the evidence of vv. 8-10, that this fiftieth year was really the forty-ninth, the last of the sabbatical years, the lands must have been left fallow for two consecutive years. The law presumes that the transfer of property, loans at interest and enslavement for debt are current practice, and such was indeed the case in the period of the monarchy. But in such a developed society it is hard to suppose that there was a general return of lands and real property to their original owners or their heirs. Secondly, the directions on the redemption or liberation of the slaves would be ineffective in themselves[1] and are in contradiction to the law of the sabbatical year, which provides for their liberation every seventh year.

There is no evidence that the law was ever in fact applied. Two legislative passages refer to it (Lv 27: 16-25 and Nb 36: 4) but they belong to the final

1. Cf. p. 88.

revision of the Pentateuch and clearly depend on Lv 25. No historical text mentions it, even when it seems to be required by the context. On the subject of the liberation of the Hebrew slaves, Jr 34: 14 quotes Dt 15, but not Lv 25. Nehemias makes the people promise to observe the sabbatical year, but says nothing about the jubilee year (Ne 10: 32). In the prophetical books, Ez 46: 17 apparently refers to it: if the prince makes a gift from his domain to one of his servants, the gift reverts to the prince 'in the year of emancipation' (*d°rôr*), as in Lv 25: 10. But Ezechiel's directions are for a future time, and moreover this particular text is generally considered to be an addition. Another even less probable allusion may be found in Is 61: 1-2, where the prophet proclaims a year of grace and emancipation (*d°rôr*) for the captives; but this text is post-Exilic.

The Law of Jubilee thus appears to set out an ideal of justice and social equality which was never realized. It is difficult to say when it was thought out. It forms part of the Code of Holiness (Lv 17-26), which is the oldest section of Leviticus and may have been compiled by the priests at Jerusalem at the end of the monarchy: but the Law of Jubilee is an addition to the Code of Holiness. It is set forth as a development of the sabbatical law, and is still unknown in the time of Jeremias. It might have been written during the Exile, in which case Ez 46: 17 would reflect the same preoccupations, if this passage is the work of Ezechiel. Or it might have been written after the Exile, even after Nehemias, for he does not refer to it.

Some arguments, on the other hand, would favour a much earlier date. The inalienable nature of the patrimony, which this law safeguards, is an ancient idea. The seven sabbatical years, followed by the jubilee of the fiftieth year, have their parallel in the seven sabbaths between the presentation of the first sheaf and the Feast of Weeks, celebrated on the fiftieth day, Pentecost (Lv 23: 15-16). Now the cycles of fifty days are the basis of an agricultural calendar which may have been used in Canaan and which still survives to some extent among the peasants of Palestine.[1] But we must note that nowhere outside the Bible is the fiftieth year marked by a redistribution of the land or a remission of debts and of persons taken as sureties; nor is there any evidence whatever of such a general liberation, at any time whatever. Some have appealed to the evidence of cuneiform tablets which mention that the tablets (of contracts) have been broken, but this action merely signifies the repudiation or annulment of an agreement, or its invalidation for a legal flaw, or the fulfilment of the obligation. A connection has been suggested with the Akkadian word *a(n)duraru* or *duraru*, meaning exemption, emancipation or declaration of a state of freedom, which is obviously related to the Hebrew *d°rôr*: but this term never denotes a general and periodical remission of obligations.

Taking all these elements into account, one may advance the hypothesis

1. Cf. p. 180.

that the Law of Jubilee was a late and ineffective attempt to make the sabbatical law more stringent by extending it to landed property, and at the same
time to make it easier to observe, by spacing out the years of remission. It was
inspired by ancient ideas, and made use of the framework of an archaic
calendar, which had not lost all its value in rural practice and in the religious
sphere. But it was a Utopian law and it remained a dead letter.

CHAPTER TWELVE

DIVISIONS OF TIME

1. *Ancient Eastern calendars*

WE read in Gn 1: 14 that God created the sun and the moon 'to divide the day from the night and to serve as signs, for feasts and for the days and the years', and time is in practice reckoned by the courses of these two bodies. The day is measured by the apparent revolution of the sun round the earth, the month by the moon's revolution round the earth, the year by the earth's revolution round the sun. The day, the easiest unit to observe, which regulates all life, public and private, has necessarily been taken as the basic unit by all systems, but the lunar month does not equal an integral number of days, and twelve lunar months amount to 354 days, 8 hours and a fraction, whereas a year based on the sun has 365 days, 5 hours and a fraction. The lunar year is therefore nearly eleven days shorter than the solar year. In a primitive society these differences are of little importance and only need to be corrected from time to time by empirical readjustments. But very early in the East, the development of civil and religious institutions, the taxes periodically due to the State, religious festivals, contracts between individuals, all made it necessary to fix past and future dates, in short, to establish an official calendar. These systems varied in different times and places, and the ancient history of the calendar is very complicated.

The Egyptians adopted at first a lunar calendar, adjusted to ensure that the heliacal rising of Sirius (Sothis)—whose feast had to fall in the last month of the year—should mark the year's end. In order to keep this agreement between the lunar and solar years a lunar month was added from time to time. This calendar regulated the seasonal religious feasts throughout the whole of Egyptian history. At the beginning of the third millennium B.C., to avoid these arbitrary readjustments and to meet the needs of civil life, a solar year was decreed, with twelve months of thirty days each, *plus* five supernumerary days, making 365 days, starting from the heliacal rising of Sirius. It was the nearest possible number of days to the natural year, but the latter dropped a day behind the civil year every four years. The Egyptians took a long time to deal with this, and the civil year gradually drew apart from the natural year: the first day of the first month could not fall on the heliacal rising of Sirius for another 1460 years (Sothiac period). After a century or two of the 'New' civil calendar, the discrepancy between the civil and natural year had become too flagrant; but since they did not dare to touch the civil year, they duplicated it by a new lunar calendar, in which a supplementary month was intercalated, according to a simple rule founded on a twenty-five-year cycle. The right solution would have been to add a day to every fourth civil year, but this was not proposed till 237 B.C., by the decree of Canopus, which remained a dead letter. It was only applied by the reform of Julius Caesar instituting a leap year, the system which is still with us.

Mesopotamia was faithful to a lunar calendar from very early days: the year comprised twelve months of 29 or 30 days without fixed order, the next month beginning on the evening when the new crescent moon was sighted. The names of the months varied at first in different regions, but from the time of Hammurabi the calendar of Nippur gradually won favour. The Nuzu calendar, however, in the middle of the second millennium, has a high proportion of Hurrite names, and Assyria had several calendars concurrently down to Tiglath-Pileser I, who had the Babylonian calendar adopted. In this, the year began in the spring, on the first day of Nisanu, and ended on the last day of Addaru. The discrepancy of eleven days between this lunar year and the solar year was corrected every two or three years by the addition of a thirteenth month, called second Ululu (the sixth month), or second Addaru (the twelfth month). Public authority decided the years in which intercalation was to be made. Thus Hammurabi wrote to one of his officials: 'This year has an intercalary month. The coming month must then be called second Ululu.' This was still the practice in the Persian period. Babylonian astronomers were well aware that the two years coincided at the end of nineteen years if seven lunar months had been intercalated, but it was only at the beginning of the fourth century B.C. that rules for intercalation within this cycle were fixed.

The Moslem calendar, which follows a non-rectified lunar year, in which the months do not remain constant with the seasons, is not primitive. It is a rather practical innovation of Islam. The pre-Islamic Arabs followed a lunar year, adapted to the natural year by intercalary months, and the names of their months were partly connected with agricultural operations.

We still know little about the ancient calendar of Syria and Palestine. They were subject to various influences under the stress of invasions and foreign rule. When the Egyptians were masters they introduced their own reckoning, at least for official documents: an inscription of the thirteenth century B.C. found at Tell ed-Duweir (Lakish) mentions deliveries of wheat in the second and fourth months of the flooding (of the Nile), one of the three seasons of the Egyptian year. In Northern Syria the Hurrite names of months appear side by side with Semitic names, and the nomenclature is in every case different from that of Mesopotamia. Inscriptions reveal a certain number of Phoenician month-names, but do not enable us to determine their order. The general impression is one of great confusion, but it is probable that a rectified lunar calendar was followed everywhere, for this is the only one based on the observance of the months which preserves a year related to the rhythm of agricultural operations. There is no proof that a real solar calendar was used, apart from the superficial and temporary influence of the Egyptian system.

There has recently been an attempt to prove the existence of an entirely different system in ancient Mesopotamia. The theory is that the Assyrian merchants who traded in Cappadocia at the beginning of the second millennium B.C. divided the year into seven periods of fifty days, each fifty comprising seven weeks, *plus* a day of festival. As seven fifties make only 350 days, and since the needs of both agriculture and commerce required agreement with the natural year, a period of sixteen days (the *shapattum*) was added at the end of this year. This calendar, it is claimed, was used in Cappadocia concurrently with that of the rectified lunar year. The system could be extended to longer periods, and they reckoned by periods of seven years and fifty years (the *dârum*). About the same time in Babylonia, there is evidence of a reckoning by seven-year periods. But this hypothesis rests on weak arguments; the key argument is the word *ḥamushtum*, translated by 'a fifty' of days, but the word means far more probably a period of five days or a fifth of a month. Besides, the use of this reckoning in Assyria and Babylonia must have been restricted to the first centuries of the second millennium B.C. However, we have traces of a similar system in the institution of the Jubilee[1] and the festal calendar of Israel.[2] The calendar of the Qumran sectaries enumerates agricultural feasts which were celebrated approximately every fifty days. A partial application of this quinquagesimal system is found also in the calendar of Nestorian Christians and, through this Christian adaptation, in the calendar of Palestinian peasants, who reckon seven fifties of days, going from one feast to another.

2. *The Israelite calendar. The day*

The same complexity is found in Israel, which stood at the crossroads of several civilizations and was subjected to varied influences in the course of its history. But no one can deny that the complexity has been increased by the contradictory hypotheses of modern scholars, and it seems that a simpler and more coherent solution can be found than those which have recently been proposed.

As everywhere, the basic unit is the solar day. The Egyptians reckoned it from one morning to the next and divided it into twelve hours of day time and twelve of night; the hours varied in length with the latitude and the season. In Mesopotamia the day was reckoned from one evening to the next; it was divided into twelve *bêru* of two hours each, and each *bêru* had thirty units of four minutes each. The night and the day were divided into six

1. Cf. pp. 175 177.   2. Cf. p. 493.

watches, each lasting for two *bêru*, or four hours. Thus there was, as in Egypt, a difference between the seasonal hour and the real hour, but they were able to fix tables of concordance for the different months.

In Israel, the day was for a long time reckoned from morning to morning. When they wanted to indicate the whole length of a day of twenty-four hours, they said 'day and night' or some such phrase, putting the day first: scores of references could be quoted (Dt 28: 66-67; 1 S 30: 12; Is 28: 19; Jr 33: 20, etc.). This suggests that they reckoned the day starting from the morning, and it was in fact in the morning, with the creation of light, that the world began; the distinction of day and night, and time too, began on a morning (Gn 1: 3-5, cf. 14, 16, 18). The opposite conclusion has been drawn from the refrain which punctuates the story of Creation: 'There was an evening and there was a morning, the first, second, etc., day'; this phrase, however, coming after the description of each creative work (which clearly happens during the period of light), indicates rather the vacant time till the morning, the end of a day and the beginning of the next work.

In the latest books of the Old Testament the expression 'day and night' is reversed: Judith praises God 'night and day' (Jdt 11: 17); Esther asks for a fast of three days 'night and day' (Est 4: 16); Daniel speaks of 2,300 'evenings and mornings' (Dn 8: 14). The same form is found in texts which are not so late but certainly post-Exilic: Ps 55: 18, 'at evening, at morning and at noon'; Is 27: 3, 'night and day', Is 34: 10, 'neither night nor day'. This order is found in only two pre-exilic passages, 1 K 8: 29 and Jr 14: 17, but the parallel of 2 Ch 6: 20 in the former case and the readings of the ancient versions in both cases suggest that the Massoretic text should be corrected. On the contrary, where we find the order 'day and night' in late passages, it is explained by the importance, in the context, of the day as opposed to the night (Za 14: 7; Qo 8: 16), or by the survival of a formula rooted in the spoken language.

The same conclusions clearly emerge from certain biblical stories. Thus in the story of the daughters of Lot: 'The next day the elder said to the younger, Last night I slept with my father; let us make him drink wine again to-night' (Gn 19: 34). In the story of the Levite of Ephraim: he stays three days with his father-in-law and stops the night there. The fourth day, he wakes and wants to depart. He is detained and again stops the night. The fifth day, the father-in-law says to him: 'Behold, the day is far advanced towards evening. Spend the night here again. . . . To-morrow, early in the morning, you will depart. . . .' (Jg 19: 4-9). Saul's henchmen arrive at night to take David by surprise, and Mikal says to him: 'If you do not escape to-night, to-morrow you are a dead man' (1 S 19: 11). In the house of the witch of Endor, Samuel appears to Saul during the night and says to him: 'To-morrow, you and your sons will be with me' (1 S 28: 19). Other passages could be quoted, but they are less decisive (Jg 21: 2-4; 1 S 5: 2-4).

Nehemias, on the other hand, to prevent the merchants breaking the sabbath, orders the gates of Jerusalem to be shut at nightfall, before the sabbath, and not to be opened till after the sabbath (Ne 13 : 19). Here the day seems to begin at sunset.

The same duality is found in the liturgical texts, but it is more difficult to argue from them since their dates are uncertain. According to Lv 7: 15 and 22: 30, the meat of sacrifices must be eaten the same day, not leaving anything to be eaten to the morning of the next day. Had the day begun in the evening the wording would have ordered the meat to be eaten before the evening. The Passover is celebrated on the fourteenth day of the first month, after sunset; the feast of the Unleavened Bread, which lasts seven days, begins on the fifteenth day (Lv 23: 5-6: cf. Nb 28: 16) and this fifteenth day is the day after the Passover (Nb 33: 3; cf. Jos 5: 10). All this presumes that the day began in the morning. But the other reckoning appears clearly in the date of the day of Atonement, 'the evening of the ninth day of the month, from this evening to the next evening' (Lv 23: 32), and in Ex 12: 18, in which Unleavened Bread must be eaten from the evening of the fourteenth day to the evening of the twenty-first. These two passages belong to the final redaction of the Pentateuch. This method of reckoning is used in New Testament times and under later Judaismfor the sabbath, the religiousfeastsand civillife.

The change of reckoning must therefore have taken place between the end of the monarchy and the age of Nehemias. One could date it more precisely if it were certain that in Ez 33: 21-22 the evening and the morning of v. 22 both applied to the fifth day of v. 21. This would bring us to the beginning of the Exile; unfortunately the text is not explicit.

The day was divided without precision according to natural phenomena: the morning and the evening (Ex 18: 13, etc.), mid-day (Gn 43: 16, 25; 1 K 18: 29, etc.), dawn (Gn 19: 15; Jos 6: 15; 1 S 30: 17), the setting of the sun (Gn 15: 12, 17), the breeze which blows before sunrise (Ct 2: 17; 4: 6), the evening breeze (Gn 3: 8), the hottest time of the day (Gn 18: 1; 1 S 11: 11; 2 S 4: 5). Sometimes reference was made to the ritual: the time of the evening sacrifice is an indication of time in 1 K 18: 29; Esd 9: 4, 5; Dn 9: 21. Certain religious actions had to be performed 'between the two evenings' (Ex 12: 6; 16: 12; 29: 39, 41; 30: 8; Nb 9: 3, 5, 11; 28: 4, 8). This expression denotes the time between the sun's disappearance and nightfall, that is to say, twilight, which in the East is very short. So the Samaritans continued to interpret it: the Pharisees explained it as the time preceding sunset.

The night was divided into three watches: the first watch (perhaps Lm 2: 19), the midnight watch (Jg 7: 19), and the last or morning watch (Ex 14: 24; 1 S 11: 11). This was on the whole the Mesopotamian practice, but by New Testament times the Egyptian and Roman custom of four night watches had been adopted (Mt 14: 25; Mk 13: 35).

We know of no terms for the smaller divisions of time. The word *sha'ah*, which later meant 'hour', is only employed in the Aramaic of Daniel, in the vague sense of a moment or instant (Dn 4: 16; cf. 3: 6, 15; 4: 30; 5: 5). But the Israelites had ways of telling the hours of the day. In Mesopotamia and Egypt water-clocks and gnomons were used from the second millennium B.C. and an Egyptian sundial of the thirteenth century has been found at Gezer. The 'degrees of Achaz' on which the sun receded six degrees at the prayer of Isaias (2 K 20: 9–11 = Is 38: 8) are not a gnomon, but a stairway built by Achaz, perhaps in connection with the 'high chamber' mentioned in a gloss in 2 K 23: 12. The miracle in question is not that of a 'clock' going forwards or backwards, but of the sudden movement of a shadow on a stairway.

3. The month

As the Egyptians reckoned the day from morning to morning, so they reckoned the lunar month to start from the morning when the last quarter of the preceding moon disappeared. The Babylonians, who reckoned the day from one evening to the next, made the month begin from the appearance of the crescent new moon at sunset. As long as the Israelites counted the day from morning to morning, they probably followed the Egyptian custom to fix the beginning of the month, but this cannot be stated for certain. If it could, the detailed story in 1 S 20: 18–35 would be more easily understood, and the transfer of the beginning of the feast of the Unleavened Bread from the fifteenth day (Lv 23: 6) to the fourteenth (Ex 12: 8), and its being joined with the Passover, could be explained by a change of reckoning; the Babylonian method of reckoning the day had replaced the Egyptian one.

What is certain in any case is that the Israelites followed a lunar month. Like the Canaanites, they called the month *yerah*, which also means the moon: the month is a lunation. But very soon, too (cf. Ex 23: 15; 34: 18; 1 S 6: 1; 10: 27; 1 K 4: 7) and more often thereafter, they called the month *hodesh*, which means primarily the new moon. In 1 K 6: 38 and 8: 2 the word *yerah*, with the Canaanite name of the month, is glossed by the word *hodesh* with the number of the month.[1]

As a lunation takes 29 days, 12 hours and a fraction, the lunar months had 29 and 30 days alternatively. At first they were given Canaanite names, which were connected with the seasons; Abib, the month of the ears of corn (Ex 13: 4; 23: 15; 34: 18; Dt 16: 1); Ziv, the month of flowers (1 K 6: 1, 37); Etanim, the month in which only the permanent water-courses still flow (1 K 8: 2); Bul, the month of the great rains (1 K 6: 38). The last three names are found with others in Phoenician inscriptions: Abib has not yet been attested there, but has been deciphered in the proto-Sinaitic inscriptions, though the reading is uncertain.

This Canaanite nomenclature was long preserved, since it was still used in Deuteronomy, which fixes the feast of the Passover in the month of Abib (Dt 16: 1), and it is only by chance that the names do not appear in the historical

1. Cf. p. 185.

books after Solomon. It was an official calendar, and it seems that in daily life other names were used. A limestone tablet has been discovered at Gezer, which has an inscription attributed to the tenth century B.C. The text was certainly drawn up by an Israelite. It is a calendar, giving the following table:

Two months: *'sp*	= Ingathering
Two months: *zr'*	= Seedtime
Two months: *lqsh*	= Late seedtime
One month: *'ṣd psht*	= Flax gathering
One month: *qṣr s'rm*	= Barley harvest
One month: *qṣr wkl*	= Harvest (of wheat) and accounting(?)
Two months: *zmr*	= Pruning
One month: *qṣ*	= Summer fruits

This is not a memorandum of tasks to be carried out in the different months of the year, but a concordance table between twelve lunations (the months of the official year, listed here without their proper names) and the periods of the agricultural year, which the peasants called after the tasks they performed in them. The Old Testament uses several of these terms to mark dates. In the oldest liturgical calendars, Ex 23: 16 orders the feast of the Harvest, *qaṣîr*, to be observed, and that of the Ingathering, *'asîph*; Ex 34: 22 prescribes the feast of Weeks at the wheat harvest and the feast of Ingathering. Ruth and her mother-in-law arrive at Bethlehem 'at the beginning of the barley harvest' (Rt 1: 22). Reuben goes out 'at the time of the wheat harvest' (Gn 30: 14). Samson comes to visit his wife 'at the time of the wheat harvest' (Jg 15: 1). In 1 S 12: 17, 'the wheat harvest' is an indication of the season, like 'the barley harvest' in 2 S 21: 9-10. Amos sees the locusts swarming 'at the time when the late growth, *leqesh*, begins to shoot' (Am 7: 1). Much later, the Rule of the Qumran sect, naming the four seasons borrowed from the Greeks, gave them names drawn from agriculture, *qaṣîr*, harvest; *qayṣ*, summer fruits; *zera'*, seedtime; *deshe'*, tender shoots. The first three were already in the Gezer calendar, but here they are matched with the Greek seasons and the order is that of a year beginning in the spring. There seems to be evidence that this same Qumran community had a more complete agricultural calendar, comparable to the 'fifties' of the modern Palestinian peasants.[1]

In the official calendar the Canaanite names of the months were at some time replaced by the ordinal numerals: they were then counted from the first to the twelfth month. As an argument for the antiquity of such a system, one might quote the Egyptian practice of numbering the months of the three annual seasons from one to four, or Mesopotamian passages such as these: 'From the beginning of the year to the fifth month, and from the sixth month to the end of the year' (in the Code of Hammurabi), or 'I have taken the omens . . . for the sixth month' (in the archives of Mari) or 'In the sixth month I shall send' (in the Amarna letters). But the Egyptian division of the year into three seasons never penetrated into Israel, and the Akkadian expressions just quoted are exceptional and do not form part of genuine dating formulae

There is in fact no evidence of this system in the historical books before the account of the capture of Jerusalem by Nabuchodonosor (2 K 25=Jr 52). The other passages (Jos 4: 19 and 1 K 12: 32f.) are from the hand of the redactor, and in 1 K 6: 38 and 8: 2 the numeral of the month is a gloss, explaining the Canaanite name. In the Book of Jeremias, the practice appears under Joiaqim (Jr 36: 9, 22), under Sedecias (Jr 28: 1, 17; 39: 1, 2; cf. 1: 3), and after the fall of Jerusalem (Jr 41: 1). The change was made, then, after the reign of Josias, and this is confirmed by Deuteronomy, which still uses the old name of the month Abib (Dt 16: 1). As we shall see, the change coincided with the adoption of the Babylonian year, beginning in the spring.

But the Babylonian month-names were not accepted at first, probably because of their association with heathen worship, and the ordinal numbers were substituted for them. Two cuneiform tablets of the seventh century B.C., found at Gezer, are dated with the Babylonian name of the month, but they are written in Assyrian and under Assyrian rule. Reference to the months by the ordinal numbers remains the regular practice in Ezechiel and, after the Exile, in Aggaeus. In the Book of Zacharias, the eleventh month is explained as being the month of Shebat (Za 1: 7), the ninth as being the month of Kisleu (Za 7: 1), but these are later glosses. The Babylonian names are used in the Aramaic document of Esd 6: 15 and in the memoirs of Nehemias (Ne 1: 1; 2: 1; 6: 15), which is not surprising, since the Persians had adopted the Babylonian calendar[1]. But the redactor of Esdras and Nehemias and Chronicles never uses any but the ordinal numbers. The Book of Esther always refers to the months by an ordinal, followed, with one exception, by the Babylonian name. In the Books of Maccabees, the ordinal number is sometimes given alone (1 M 9: 3, 54; 10: 21; 13: 51) and sometimes followed by the Babylonian name (1 M 4: 52; 16: 14; 2 M 15: 36), but the Babylonian name in its Greek form is generally given alone. These variations show that the Babylonian names were only introduced long after the Exile and did not become current till very late. Apocryphal works like the Book of Jubilees and the Qumran literature show what obstinate resistance there was in some religious circles. In spite of it, however, the Babylonian month-names were in the end accepted by orthodox Judaism. We give here their order in the year, beginning in the spring, with their approximate equivalents in our calendar:

I. Nisân	March–April	
II. Iyyar	April–May	
III. Siwân	May–June	

[1] And also, at the same period, and for the same reason, in the papyri of Elephantine.

IV. Tammuz	June–July
V. Ab	July–August
VI. Elul	August–September
VII. Tishri	September–October
VIII. Marheshwân	October–November
IX. Kisleu	November–December
X. Tebeth	December–January
XI. Shebat	January–February
XII. Adar	February–March

From the Hellenistic period onwards the Macedonian names of months were introduced into official usage. A man of letters like the historian Josephus uses this system, but it never became familiar to the Jews. In the Greek Old Testament we encounter only the months of Xanthicus and Dioscurus (?) in the foreign documents of 2 M 11: 21, 30, 33, 38, and the month of Dystros in Tb 2: 12.

4. The week

In the Egyptian civil calendar the month of thirty days was divided into three decades. Some think they can find traces of a similar reckoning in the Old Testament. The mourning for Moses and that for Aaron each lasted thirty days (Nb 20: 29; Dt 34: 8), and it may be compared with the mourning of the captive woman which lasted a month (Dt 21: 13; cf. also Est 4: 11; Dn 8: 13). Ten days is a unit of time in Gn 24: 55; 1 S 25: 38. The tenth day of the month appears as the date of a feast or an event (Ex 12: 3; Lv 16: 29 (parallels: 23: 27; 25: 9; Nb 29: 7): Jos 4: 19; 2 K 25: 1 (parallels Jr 52: 4; Ez 24: 1); Ez 20: 1; 40: 1); the twentieth day is mentioned less frequently (Nb 10: 11; 11: 19). At Tell el-Farah in the south, and at Tell ed-Duweir bone tablets have been found, pierced with three parallel lines of ten holes each. These are perhaps 'calendars' for counting the days of the month: they date from the beginning of the monarchy.

All this does not amount to proof. Since the lunar months had alternately twenty-nine and thirty days, one can speak in round terms of thirty days as a month, and if the little 'calendars' found in excavations had to serve for all the months, they would have needed thirty holes. The fact that a feast was celebrated or that an event took place on the tenth of the month proves nothing about the month's division in time. The context of Gn 24: 55 and of 1 S 25: 38 show that this 'decade' is only a rough reckoning, 'ten days or so'.

The only unit less than the month for which there is good evidence is the period of seven days (shabû'a), the week. The origins of this institution, so familiar to us, are very obscure. In a lunar calendar the month would naturally be divided according to the moon's phases. The most obvious division is that marking the full moon in the middle of the month, and in fact the fifteenth day was of special importance in the Assyro-Babylonian calendar: it was the *shapattu*. Now there are certain passages in the Old Testament (2 K 4: 23; Is 1: 13; 66: 23; Os 2: 13; Am 8: 5) in which the *shabbath* is coupled with the new moon as a festal day. Ps 81: 4, in an identical context, employs the very rare word *kese'* ('full moon') so that *shabbath* may possibly have the same sense in the preceding passages as *shapattu* has in Akkadian. It must be remembered that the two great Israelite feasts, the Passover and Tents, were celebrated on the fourteenth-fifteenth days of the first and seventh months respectively, that is, at the full moon; the later feast of Purim was also fixed at the full moon, in the twelfth month.

The division of the month into four according to the moon's quarters is much less evident in the texts. It is true that in the Babylonian Poem of Creation the moon is assigned the function of marking the periods of the month by its phases, and that the Babylonian calendar, at least from the seventh century B.C., picks out as 'unlucky days' the 7th, 14th (19th), 21st and 28th days, which correspond with the lunar phases; but the Assyro-Babylonian calendar, at least till the eleventh century B.C., noted several other unlucky days. If a division into weeks is indicated by the later calendar— which is far from proved—the cycle was interrupted at the end of each month, which comprised twenty-nine or thirty days, and started again at each new moon. In Egypt there seems to have been a division of the months into seven, eight, eight and seven days, with lunar names, but it is obvious that the number of days is not constant, a fact which contradicts the very idea of the week.

Some novel explanations of the week have recently been proposed. According to one author, the seven days of the week are derived from the seven winds which blew from the seven directions, according to the most ancient Babylonian cosmology. Another says that the *ḥamushtu* of the Cappadocian texts being interpreted as a fifth of the month,[1] a 'week' of six days in the old Assyrian calendar was supplemented by the Israelites with a seventh day, reserved for rest. A discussion of these hypotheses would be to little purpose: it will be more useful to recall the sacred and symbolic value of the number seven and the seven-day periods which recur in the Babylonian poem of Gilgamesh and the poems of Ras Shamra. One of the passages in the Gilgamesh poems has an exact parallel in the story of the Flood (Gn 8: 10-12) and seven-day periods are often found in the Old Testament: for marriage celebrations (Gn 29: 27; Jg 14: 12), for mourning (Gn 50: 10), for the condolences of Job's friends (Jb 2: 13); for banquets (Est 1: 5), for a long march (Gn 31: 23; 2 K 3: 9, etc.). These expressions have no formal connection with the calendar, but their frequency makes it probable that from an early date the period of seven days was a calendar-unit.

If such a reckoning is uniformly applied, it is independent of the lunar months, since these are not exactly divisible into weeks. It is possible that the

1. Cf. p. 180.

idea of the week arose from rough observation of the moon's phases, but it became the element of a cycle of its own, overriding those of the months and the years. This in itself distinguishes the Israelite week from the Egyptian and the Babylonian 'weeks'. There are more important differences: the week is marked by the repose of the seventh day, the sabbath, which is an ancient religious institution, peculiar to Israel. We shall deal with it at greater length in connection with religious institutions[1] and would here note only one consequence; the reckoning by weeks—not merely the indication of seven-day periods, as in the passages just quoted—is only found in liturgical texts, except for the late passages in Dn 10: 2 and 9: 24-27 (where they are weeks of years).

The calendar of one religious group in Judaism is entirely governed by the week. It is found most clearly in the apocryphal Book of Jubilees: fifty-two weeks make a year and 364 days, divided into quarters of thirteen weeks, that is, of ninety-one days; seven years make a week of years (as in Daniel), seven weeks of years form a jubilee. This same calendar is found in a part of the Apocrypha ascribed to Henoch, and in the Qumran literature. The purpose of this reckoning is to make the same feasts fall every year on the same days of the week. The liturgical days are the first, fourth and sixth days of the week; the sabbath is the day of rest. The originators of this calendar do not seem to have been concerned over the divergence between this year of 364 days and the real year of $365\frac{1}{4}$ days. But this discrepancy must have appeared very soon, and this calendar cannot have been followed for long, unless there were periodical adjustments not mentioned in any text. The recent attempt to connect this with an ancient priestly calendar, whose influence may be found in the redaction of the Pentateuch, is still no more than a hypothesis. We shall now see, moreover, that the Pentateuch gives evidence of another reckoning.

5. *The year*

The 364-day year of this calendar of Jubilees is a solar year, only less accurately reckoned than the Egyptian year of 365 days. The latter was evidently known to the Israelites and appears in two passages of Genesis. According to Gn 5: 23, the patriarch Henoch lived 365 years. If we remember that according to later tradition Henoch was favoured with revelations on astronomy and the calculation of time, we realize that 365 represents a perfect number, that of the days in a solar year. The chronology of the Flood is even more convincing: the disaster begins on the seventeenth day of the second month (Gn 7: 11) and ends on the twenty-seventh day of the second month of the next year (Gn 8: 14). Hence it lasted twelve months and eleven days, the exact period required to equate the year of twelve lunar months, 354 days, with the solar year of 365 days. The redactor wanted to say that the Flood lasted exactly one solar year. In the same context, compari-

1. Cf. pp. 475-483.

son of Gn 7: 11, 24 with Gn 8: 3-4 indicates that five months make a total of 150 days, that is, five Egyptian months of thirty days. This passage is of late redaction; it appears as a scholar's note to show the correspondence between the solar year and the rectified lunar year, or lunisolar year, which regulated daily life and the liturgy. But in this lunisolar year the feasts did not fall each year on the same days of the week. The calendar of the Jubilees, mentioned above, must have been a reform aimed at tying the feasts to fixed days of the week.

Apart from these scholarly calculations and abortive attempts, there is no proof that a truly solar year ever prevailed in Israel. The intentional chronology of Gn 7: 11; 8: 15 itself emphasizes that the description of the months by the ordinal numbers belonged to a lunar reckoning. We noted earlier that the ordinal system had done away with the use of Canaanite names. These names, being drawn from seasonal events, can only fit a year which is at least approximately adjusted to the natural year; this might be either a solar year or a lunisolar year with an intercalary month. This latter solution is indicated by the Canaanite word for a month (yeraḥ, meaning the moon) and by Mesopotamian analogy. There is no reason to doubt that it was the same in ancient Israel, where the same word stood for the month and the moon, and the beginning of the month was marked by the new moon.

The intercalary month, however, is never mentioned in the Old Testament, except at the very end, for a non-Israelite calendar: the Macedonian month of Dioscorus (2 M 11: 21) is perhaps an intercalary month. The sacred writers invariably speak of only twelve months (1 K 4: 7; 1 Ch 27: 1-15; cf. Jr 52: 31; Ez 32: 1; Dn 4: 26) and we saw that the Gezer calendar too reckoned twelve months. But in 1 K 4: 7 one would have expected the intercalary month to be mentioned: Solomon's twelve districts had each to supply the king and his household for a month of the year; and in 1 Ch 27 each of David's stewards was on duty for a month. What happened when the year had thirteen months? The uncertainty arises from our lack of information: these passages only tell what happened in ordinary years.

In any case, the intercalation of a supplementary month was, for a long time, made in an empirical manner. Even at the end of the first century of our era, the Rabbi Gamaliel II was writing to the communities of the Diaspora: 'The lambs are still too weak and the chickens too small: the grain is not ripe. Therefore it has seemed good to us and our colleagues to add thirty days to this year.' In the end, the Babylonian cycle of nineteen years was adopted, with intercalations at fixed dates. The duplicated month was Adar, the last month of the year; there is no proof that a second Elul month was sometimes intercalated, as in Babylonia.

The year was divided into two seasons, the winter, ḥoreph, and summer, qayṣ, corresponding roughly to the cold and hot seasons, to seedtime and harvest (Gn 8: 22; cf. Ps 74: 17; Is 18: 6; Za 14: 8). Kings and the rich had their summer and winter houses (Am 3: 15; Jr 36: 22). This simple division corresponds to the climate of Palestine, where the hot, dry season and the cold, wet season succeed each other fairly quickly, leaving no distinct sensation of spring and autumn, as in more temperate countries. The Egyptians had three seasons, governed by the rise of the Nile and its effects: Flooding, Seedtime and Harvest. The Greeks at first had three seasons and later four, by the addition of autumn. They were defined by the spring and autumn equinoxes and the summer and winter solstices. This division was introduced among the Jews in the Hellenistic period. We have noted earlier that it appeared in the Qumran documents, with agricultural names. Later, the seasons were called after those months which included the equinoxes and solstices.

6. *The beginning of the year*

The two oldest liturgical calendars (Ex 23: 14-17 and 34: 18-23) list three great annual feasts: Unleavened Bread, Harvest and Ingathering. As the Unleavened Bread was celebrated in the month of Abib, later called Nisan, one might see in this order the indication of a year beginning in the spring, if a date were not defined for Ingathering. According to Ex 23: 16, it falls *b'se'th hashshannah*, at the 'going out' of the year, which most probably means the beginning of the year, as the same word elsewhere means the rising of the sun (Jg 5: 31; Is 13: 10) or of the stars (Ne 4: 15). According to Ex 34: 22, the feast of the Ingathering marks the *t'qûphath hashshannah*, etymologically the 'revolution' of the year, but strictly the end of this revolution (cf. 1 S 1: 20; Ps 19: 7, and the use of the corresponding verb in Jb 1: 5), and therefore the end of the year. We must not introduce into these ancient texts the notion of solstice and equinox which later Judaism gave to *t'qûphah*. How the feast was fixed, whether at the beginning or at the end of the year, is a problem which will claim attention under religious institutions[1]: here it is enough to show that the two calendars presuppose a year beginning in autumn.

The list of agricultural tasks in the Gezer tablet also begins in autumn: it is not the natural order, which would begin with the sowing, but the text shows that it agrees with a civil year beginning in autumn.[2]

In 2 S 11: 1=1 Ch 20: 1 and in 1 K 20: 22, 26, we find the expression *t'shûbath hashshannah*, literally the 'return' of the year; in the first text and its parallel it is explained as 'the time when kings take the field', and in the other two it is used to date a military expedition. According to repeated indications in the Assyrian annals, this was usually in the spring. This 'return' of the year would be the time when the year was half over, and beginning to return from winter to summer, when the days began to equal the nights, our spring equinox. This again presumes an autumnal year. The expression continued to be attached to this time of the year after the change of the calendar,

1. Cf. p. 498.   2. Cf. p. 184.

and in 2 Ch 36: 10 it again refers to the spring: from other sources we are able to date the event referred to, the capture of Jerusalem, in March 597.

The story of Josias' reform (2 K 22-23) tells of the discovery of the Book of the Law, how it was read before the king, then before the whole people assembled in Jerusalem, how measures of reform were applied in the capital, in Judah and the former kingdom of Israel, and finally of the celebration of the Passover. All these events took place in the eighteenth year of the king: this would be impossible if the year began in the spring, just before the Passover, and postulates a year beginning in autumn.

Finally we may recall that Mesopotamia too originally had an autumnal year: the seventh month of the Babylonian spring year kept its name of *Teshritu*, that is 'beginning'.

But there are other Old Testament texts which presume a different reckoning. When the scroll of the prophecies of Jeremias was read to Joiaqim, the king was in his winter house, warming himself at a brazier, because 'it was the ninth month' (Jr 36: 22), evidently the ninth month of a year beginning in spring, that is, November-December.

According to 2 K 25: 8 = Jr 52: 12, the Temple was destroyed by Nabuchodonosor in the fifth month. Josephus and Jewish tradition say that it was at the same time of the year that the second Temple was burnt by the Romans, and we know that this event took place in August. The tradition is ancient: according to Zacharias, at a time when the spring calendar was certainly in use (cf. the dates of Aggaeus in connection with the years of Darius), the destruction of the Temple was commemorated by a fast in the fifth month (Za 7: 3 and 5). This is confirmed by Jr 40-41, which records the events immediately after the capture of Jerusalem: wine, fruit and oil were gathered in (Jr 40: 10), and after the murder of Godolias, in the seventh month of the same year, wheat, barley, oil and honey were already stored (Jr 41: 8); all this is inexplicable except in a spring year.

Some of the liturgical texts are quite explicit. The law of the Passover begins thus in Ex 12: 2: 'This month comes to you as the head of the months; it is for you the first month of the year.' This insistence is intentional, emphasizing something new. According to Ex 23: 15 and also Dt 16: 1, the Passover must be celebrated in the month of Abib in the autumnal year. Between these texts and the redaction of Ex 12, the date of the feast was not altered, but the calendar was changed: a spring year was being followed. (The same remarks apply to the religious calendars of Lv 23, Nb 28-29 and Ez 45: 18-25.)

All the Old Testament passages in which the months are denoted by ordinal numbers are easily explained if the year begins in the spring. We have already shown that this new nomenclature was introduced after the death of Josias[1]; if we compare the story of Josias' reform (2 K 22-23) with

1. Cf. p. 185.

that of the capture of Jerusalem (2 K 25), we observe that the spring year had also been introduced by this date. Possibly, too, this was the time when they began to reckon the day from evening to evening,[1] and the months from the appearance of the new moon at sunset.[2] All this points to the adoption of the Babylonian calendar and is explained by the historical circumstance that under Joiaqim, son of Josias, the kingdom of Judah became a vassal state of Nabuchodonosor.

These conclusions hold good for the kingdom of Judah, about which we are better informed. It may be presumed that the autumnal calendar was also followed in the kingdom of Israel so long as it remained independent, but that the Babylonian calendar was imposed, at least for official use, in the Assyrian provinces constituted after the conquests of Tiglath-Pileser III in 733 B.C., and then for the rest of the territory after the fall of Samaria. The cuneiform contracts at Gezer, dated in the Assyrian manner, are evidence of this. An earlier date has been suggested for the adoption of the spring calendar in Israel, in order to throw light on the way in which the Books of Kings synchronize the reigns in Israel with those in Judah; but this synchronization raises difficult problems in itself, which the addition of another unknown element is not likely to solve.

The spring year was naturally retained when the Babylonian month-names replaced the ordinal numbers. Only one passage raises a difficulty. According to Ne 1: 1 and 2: 1, the month of Kisleu and the following month of Nisan fell in the same twentieth year of Artaxerxes, which would imply an autumnal year. But it is unlikely that Nehemias, living at the Persian court, where the Babylonian calendar was followed and the Babylonian month-names were used, did not also follow the official reckoning of the year. On the other hand, the Hebrew text of Ne 1: 1 has only 'the twentieth year', without the name of the reigning king, which is strange. The text must be corrupt, and the likeliest explanation is that originally it did not contain, or it accidentally lost, the mention of the year, which was later supplied mechanically from Ne 2: 1; it was really the nineteenth year of Artaxerxes. It has also been suggested that an autumnal year is found in one of the Elephantine papyri, but the date is apparently incorrect.

The Seleucids introduced an autumnal year at Antioch and in the Macedonian colonies, but in Babylonia they conformed to the spring calendar, which the Jews had already adopted. The first Book of Maccabees dates the events of general history by the Syro-Macedonian reckoning, but keeps the Babylonian reckoning for facts directly concerning the Jewish community. The few dates in the second Book are given according to the same calendar, except for the foreign documents of 2 M 11.

These variations in the course of the Old Testament history puzzled the Rabbis, who did not distinguish between the relative ages of the texts. They

1. Cf. pp. 181-182.   2. Cf. p. 183.

reckoned four beginnings to the year: in Nisan, the New Year for kings and for festivals; in Elul, the New Year for the tithe on cattle; in Tishri, the New Year for years, the sabbatical year and the Jubilee year; in Shebat, the New Year for the tithe on trees.

7. The eras

An era is the starting-point of a chronology which in theory continues for ever, such as the Christian era, the Moslem era, etc. Jewish chronologers have calculated an era of Creation, based on Biblical data, which is still followed by Judaism: the year 5718 of Creation began on September 26th, 1957. But the Old Testament knew nothing of the kind. It has been suggested that Nb 13: 22, according to which Hebron was founded seven years before Tanis, and Ex 12: 40, which gives the sojourn in Egypt as 430 years, refer to an 'era of Tanis', going back to the establishment of the Hyksos in Egypt. It is a mere hypothesis, and this chronology is in any case foreign to Israel. Figures like the 300 years of Jg 11: 26 and the 480 years of 1 K 6: 1 are based on calculations of the redactors of the Bible. To fix a date, reference was made to a roughly contemporary event which had made an impression: the prophecy of Amos is dated 'two years before the earthquake' (Am 1: 1). The oracle of Is 20: 1f. is in 'the year that the chief cupbearer came to Ashdod . . . and took it.' Ezechiel reckons the years from the deportation of Joiakin (Ez 1: 2; 8: 1; 20: 1; 24: 1; 26: 1, etc.) and 2 K 25: 27 (= Jr 52: 31) does the same.

This way of reckoning simply carries on the official reckoning of the kingdoms of Israel and Judah, in which events were dated by the years of the reign of each king. This system lasted till the end of the kingdom of Israel (2 K 17: 6), and of the kingdom of Judah (2 K 25: 1-2), and it went back at least to Solomon (1 K 6: 1, 37, 38). Something of the same sort may even be found in the time of the tribal federation, if we suppose that the 'lesser' Judges of Jg 10: 1-5; 12: 8-15 represent a permanent institution[1]: men would have reckoned time by the years of their office, the precise duration of which is noted in the texts.

It has been suggested that in the lists of Solomon's officials (1 K 4: 3) there is an official of the priestly caste 'over the year'; he would be an eponymous magistrate, one whose name served to describe the year: the list of these eponyms would provide a chronology. Israel would then have the equivalent of the eponyms of Assyria (*lîmu*) and of Southern Arabia (*kabîr*). But this interpretation of a word which both the text and the versions represent as a proper name (Elihoreph or Elihaph) is a very fragile theory.

If dates were computed by the year of the reigning king, and if, as seems likely, this year coincided with the civil year, all that remains is to decide how the beginning of the reign was reckoned. The months between the enthronement and the next New Year might be counted as a complete year, the first year of the reign: this is the system of antedating, in which the year of a

1. Cf. pp. 93 and 151.

king's death and his successor's enthronement is counted twice. Alternatively the months before the New Year could go uncounted, the first year of the reign being reckoned from the New Year following the accession. This is the system of postdating.

The reigns of Assyria and Babylon were postdated. This system, it seems, was followed in Judah at the end of the monarchy: Jr 26: 1 gives as a date the 'beginning of the reign', *re'shîth mamleketh*, of Joiaqim, which is the exact equivalent of the Akkadian *rêsh sharruti*, meaning the incomplete year of the accession. On the other hand we cannot take into account Jr 27: 1 and 28: 1, where the same expression is found in passages which are corrupt or glossed. The *re'shîth malkûth* of Sedecias in Jr 49: 34 could be interpreted in the same way and would give a precise date: recently published Babylonian documents have shown us that there was exactly a month between the accession of Sedecias and the next New Year. We have no reliable information on earlier times. Various conjectures have been made, some of which result in a regular criss-cross of antedating and postdating between Israel and Judah. The object of these hypotheses is to support the synchronization given by the Book of Kings, but, as we have already remarked, this raises a special problem of chronology, which is perhaps insoluble. Simply on the basis of the evolution of the calendar, as we have traced it in the preceding pages, one would be inclined to suppose that postdating, a Babylonian custom, began with the adoption of the Babylonian calendar under Joiaqim, and that in earlier reigns the custom was to antedate, as it was in Egypt.

It was only under the Seleucids that a genuine era was inaugurated, the era of the 'kingdom of the Greeks', as it is called in 1 M 1: 10. Its beginning was fixed by Seleucus I in the year in which he conquered Babylon. The difference between the autumnal year observed at Antioch and the spring year observed in Babylon makes this era begin in the autumn of 312 B.C. in the Syro-Macedonian reckoning, but in the spring of 311 B.C. in the Babylonian. The dates in the Books of Maccabees are divided between these two reckonings in the manner already stated with reference to the beginning of the year.[1] When the autonomy of the Jewish nation was recognized in 142 B.C., acts and contracts began to be dated 'in the first year, under Simon the high priest, eminent general and leader of the Jews' (1 M 13: 41-42). This was not the foundation of a new era, but a return to the custom followed under the independent monarchy. All the same, the era of the Greeks continued in use (1 M 14: 1; 15: 10), and even serves to date the death of Simon (1 M 16: 14). The Jews resumed an independent but short-lived reckoning during their two revolts against the Romans in A.D. 66-70 and 132-135.

The special era of the free cities of Syria and Palestine at the end of the Hellenistic and Roman periods, and the more general eras of Pompey and of Arabia, are of no interest for the Old Testament.

1. Cf. p. 192.

CHAPTER THIRTEEN

WEIGHTS AND MEASURES

1. Israelite 'metrology'

METROLOGY is by definition an exact science. It presumes that units of length, volume and weight can be mathematically determined and rigorously classified. In practice, it requires the sanction of an authority to impose a system and to ensure that the measures used by everyone are in conformity with the statutory standards. This is the law in modern states and was, in varying degrees, the practice in the great empires of antiquity, but it is doubtful whether any such regulations existed in Israel. Some have claimed that 2 S 8: 1 contains a mention of a 'standard cubit' captured by David from the Philistines, but the text is corrupt and may conceal a geographical name. We hear of swindlers who gave short measure and overcharged (Am 8: 5), of weights which were 'heavy' or 'light' (Dt 25: 13), of a short bushel and of faked weights (Mi 6: 10-11; cf. Pr 20: 10). By contrast, Lv 19: 35-36 prescribes just weights, a just measure, a just ephah (cf. Ez 45: 10). But all these texts refer to commonly accepted estimates, not to official standards. The Rabbinical tradition that samples of the standard cubit were kept in the Temple is unverifiable and is perhaps based only on 1 Ch 23: 29, where the Levites are placed in charge of the loaves of oblation, the flour of wheat, the wafers and all sorts of measures. From the context, this simply means they were to see that the offerings were of the required quantity (cf., e.g. Ex 29: 40) and that God was not defrauded (cf. Ml 3: 8-10). We must not turn them into inspectors of weights and measures. We may appreciate these texts better if we see what happens to-day in Jerusalem, even after the metric system has been imposed, and all are required to use the authorized measures; certain shopkeepers in the bazaars weigh their wares with a small stone or a horse-shoe, peasants measure out milk or oil in jam-pots, Bedouin measure the rope they buy with outstretched arms. Like the Arabs of to-day, the Israelites of old were satisfied with a measure which conformed to custom. We shall see that in certain cases this measure was guaranteed by a mark or inscription on the receptacle or the measuring instrument, but this was not as accurate as our modern systems, nor, it seems, as those of ancient Mesopotamia or Egypt. It is useful to compare the data of the Bible with these ancient Eastern systems and (by way of filling the gaps) with the Graeco-Roman metrology. But it must be remembered that our estimate of their units is often uncertain and that there is no guarantee that the Israelite measures were exactly equivalent to those used in these foreign countries. In our own day, measures with the same name have had, and sometimes still have, appreciably different values in Syria, in Egypt and in Palestine, and even in different regions of Palestine itself. Moreover, values changed with the passage of time, both in Israel and in the adjacent countries. Finally, when we are confined, as here, to the Old Testament, the data gleaned from the texts and excavations is very inadequate.

These factors should incline us to a degree of prudence which has not always been observed by authors of specialized works on biblical metrology. One may, with a certain degree of probability, arrange the measures of each category in their order, but it is futile and misleading to give their modern equivalents to four or five places of decimals, when we can be sure neither of the ancient standard nor of its relation to our system. Approximations are all that can be given. Biblical 'metrology' will probably never become an exact science.

2. Linear measures

According to the universal practice of antiquity, the commonest measures of length were named from the limbs of the human body, and in Israel, from the arm and the hand which the craftsman employed for his art.

The cubit, 'ammah, is the distance between the point of the elbow and the tip of the middle finger. The span, zereth, is measured from the tip of the thumb to the tip of the little finger, the hand being extended and the fingers apart: the Vulgate, by translating this as palmus, has caused confusion with the following term. The palm or handbreadth, tephah or tophah, is in fact the breadth of the hand at the base of the fingers. The finger or thumb, 'esba', which is frequently mentioned in ancient metrologies and in the Talmud, is found only once in the Old Testament as a unit of measurement (Jr 52: 21).

The rod, qaneh, employed in Ezechiel's description of the Temple, is an instrument for measuring rather than a unit of measurement (cf. Ez 40: 3). This rod of Ezechiel was of six 'great' cubits, like the measure of the same name in Mesopotamia. The flaxen cord of Ez 40: 3 and the measuring cord of Am 7: 17; Za 1: 16; 2: 5, are also measuring instruments, and we do not know whether they were standardized, like the Mesopotamian cord.

Finally, Jg 3: 16 says that Ehud had a sword one gomed in length. The word is a hapaxlegomenon in the Bible, and neither the conjectures of ancient versions ('span' or 'palm') nor those of modern scholars ('short cubit') throw any light on the size of this measure.

The Old Testament nowhere indicates the relation of these units to one another, but they obviously had the same proportional relations as the limbs of the human body from which they took their names. Probably, too, these relations were adjusted in the same way as in Mesopotamia and Egypt, which have an identical subdivision of the common cubit:

Cubit	1			
Span	2	1		
Palm	6	3	1	
Finger	24	12	4	1

According to Herodotus, Mesopotamia had, in addition, a 'royal cubit' which measures 27 fingers. In Egypt, too, there was a royal cubit of 7 palms or 28 fingers. A greater and a smaller cubit seem to have existed in Israel also, though not at one and the same time. Repeating the dimensions of Solomon's Temple as they are given in the books of Kings, 2 Ch 3: 3 states clearly that they are 'cubits of the old measure'. The rod of the heavenly measurer in Ez 40-42 (cf. Ap 21: 15-16) measured six cubits 'of a cubit and a palm' (Ez 40: 5; cf. 43: 13). Probably Ezechiel adopted the ancient measure for the description of the future Temple and gave its equivalent in the measure of his time: the old cubit would then have 6 palms of 24 fingers, but these were bigger. On the other hand we must not forget the Egyptian royal cubit, divided into 7 palms or 28 fingers.

The length of a cubit according to our modern systems of measurement can be found by comparing the neighbouring systems; but these are not all the same. The graduated rules engraved on two statues of Gudea, prince of Lagash about 2000 B.C., show a cubit of 19½ inches (0·495 metres), which is probably the greater cubit of the time. According to graduated rules found in Egypt, the royal cubit measured 20¾ inches (0·525 or 0·53 metres). Excavations in Palestine have so far not yielded any similar standards, and we have only one positive piece of information to use: the inscription engraved in the tunnel of Ezechias says that it is 1,200 cubits long, and it is in fact 583 yards long (533·10 metres); this would make the cubit 17·490 inches (0·44425 metres) long. Such precision, however, is absurd, for 1,200 is evidently a round number, like the 100 cubits in the same line of the inscription indicating how far underground the tunnel is, and secondly, there is the inevitable margin of error in the measurement of its winding course. Next, one would have to decide whether this cubit of Ezechias' time was still the old cubit mentioned in 2 Ch 3: 3, or the longer cubit of Ez 40: 5, or the shorter cubit implied by the same text. There is consequently something rather arbitrary in the estimates given in books, and they vary from about 17·716 inches (0·45 metres) for the common cubit to about 20·472 inches (0·52 metres) for the cubit of Ezechiel.

These calculations are in any case rather pointless because there was no official standard. In practice, the architects, masons and craftsmen measured with their own arms, their extended hands, their palms and their fingers.

Arab metrology mentions a 'black cubit': it was one measured by a tall negro in the service of the Caliph.

Travelling distances are indicated only by empirical methods in the Hebrew books of the Old Testament. The step or pace (*peśa'*) is mentioned only in 1 S 20: 3, and then as a metaphor: 'there is but one step between me and death'. The reckoning by days of marching is equally vague: one day (Nb 11: 31), three days (Gn 30: 36; Ex 3: 18; Jon 3: 3), seven days (Gn 31: 23). In Gn 35: 16=48: 7; 2 K 5: 19, the distance is indicated by the expression *kibrath ha'areṣ*, 'an extent of country': it is anything but an exact measurement, and simply means 'some distance'.

Two Hellenistic measures appear in the books of Maccabees. Bethsur is about five *schoinoi* from Jerusalem (2 M 11: 5). The *schoinos* is an ancient Egyptian measure, which in the Ptolemaic period was equal to approximately 3¾ miles or 6 kilometres: Bethsur is in fact 18 miles (29 kilometres) from Jerusalem. The *stadion* is mentioned several times, all grouped, as it happens, in the same chapter (2 M 12: 9, 10, 16, 17, 29). The *stadion* is a Greek unit which was in use in Palestine during the Hellenistic, and later, during the Roman, period. The Alexandrian *stadion*, which the author of 2 M must have had in mind, for it was almost certainly the one employed by the Jews in Palestine, measured just over 202 yards (a little less than 185 metres). The distance of 600 *stadia* (2 M 12: 29) between Jerusalem and Scythopolis (Beth Shan) corresponds exactly to this measure: the two places are just over 68 miles (110 kilometres) apart. The 248 *stadia* of 2 M 12: 9, however, if calculated at the same length, are definitely too short for the distance between Jerusalem and the port of Jamnia. The 750 *stadia* of 2 M 12: 17 cannot be estimated because the terminal points are unknown.

There are no terms in Hebrew for measures of area, and these are indicated by giving the lengths of the sides of a rectangle or square, the diameter and the circumference of a circular space (1 K 6: 2f.; 7: 23; 2 Ch 4: 1, 2; Ez 40: 47, 49; 41: 2, 4, etc.).

Agricultural measurements were empirical. The acre (*ṣemed*), literally a 'yoke' or 'harnessing', is the area which a team of oxen can work in a day: it is mentioned as a measurement in Is 5: 10 and in the corrupted text of 1 S 14: 14. The area of a piece of ground was also calculated by the amount of grain needed to sow it. This method was also used throughout the ancient East and is attested in Palestine in the Talmudic period, but in the Bible it occurs only in 1 K 18: 32, a passage which is difficult to interpret. Elias digs a ditch round the altar, with a content of two *s°ah* of seed. Whatever the size of the *s°ah* may have been, and however densely we suppose it to be sowed, whether we apply the measure to the surface area of the ditch itself or extend it to the space it enclosed, the estimate is still highly exaggerated.

It is not likely that Lv 27: 16 means that a field is to be valued at fifty shekels per *homer* of barley needed to sow it, for that would mean a vast area could be bought for a ridiculously small price. The text must refer to the grain to be harvested, and is an estimate of the value of the field, not of its area.

3. Measures of capacity

The names used are generally those of the receptacles which contained provisions and which were used to measure them, as in many metrologies, included those of our own country, like the tun, the hogshead, the bushel and so on. When these words are used to translate Hebrew terms, it is only to indicate a measure of roughly the same size, not to give an exact equivalent. To avoid all confusion, we shall here use only transcriptions of Hebrew words.

The *homer* is, by derivation, an 'ass-load'. It is a large measure for cereals (Lv 27: 16; Ez 45: 13; Os 3: 2). In Nb 11: 32, the *homer* is used, by way of exception, as a measure for the quails which fell in the desert: they covered the ground to a depth of 2 cubits for a day's march around the camp, and each man gathered ten *homer*; the figures are deliberately fantastic, to show the people's gluttony and to justify their chastisement. The text of Is 5: 10 is meant to produce astonishment, but for the opposite reason: a *homer* of seed will produce only an *'ephah* of crop: it is a curse.

Similarly, the *kor* is a large measure for flour (1 K 5: 2), for wheat and barley (1 K 5: 25; 2 Ch 2: 9; 27: 5; Esd 7: 22). The mention of *kor* for oil in 1 K 5: 25 is a mistake for *bath* (cf. the Greek word and the parallel in 1 Ch 2: 9), but the confused and overloaded text of Ez 45: 13 makes *kor* a measure for liquids and the equal of the *homer*.

The *letek* is mentioned only in Os 3: 2 as a measure for barley, smaller than the *homer*. The versions interpret it as half a *homer*.

The *'ephah* in the vision of Za 5: 6-10, denotes a large receptacle, closed with a lid and large enough to hold a woman. It is often the name for a measuring instrument: there must be a just, a perfect *'ephah* (Lv 19: 36; Dt 25: 15); the *'ephah* must not be made too small (Am 8: 5; Mi 6: 10); there must not be two kinds of *'ephah*, large and small (Dt 25: 14; Pr 20: 10). Usually the word means the measure itself: an *'ephah* (Jg 6: 19; Rt 2: 17; 1 S 1. 24, etc.), one-sixth of an *'ephah* (Ez 45: 13; 46: 14), one-tenth of an *'ephah* (Lv 5: 11; 6: 13; Nb 5: 15; 28: 5; cf. Ex 16: 36). The articles measured are flour, meal, barley or roasted corn, but never liquids. It is the commonest unit of measure for solids.

For liquids the equivalent is the *bath*. The measure must be just (Ez 45: 10). It is used for water (1 K 7: 26, 38; 2 Ch 4: 5), wine (2 Ch 2: 9; Is 5: 10) and oil (2 Ch 2: 9; Ez 45: 14; 1 K 5: 25, corrected).

The *shalish*, found only in Is 40: 12 and Ps 80: 6, is an instrument for measuring one-third of an indeterminate unit.

The *s'ah* is a measure for flour and cereals in ancient historical texts (Gn 18: 6; 1 S 25: 18; 1 K 18: 32; 2 K 7: 1, 16, 18).

The *hîn* is a measure for liquids. Apart from Ez 4: 11, where one-sixth of a *hîn* represents the minimum a man needs to drink in a day, the *hîn* is only mentioned in rituals, for offerings of wine and oil: the whole *hîn* (Ex 30: 24; Ez 45: 24; 46: 5, 7, 11), the half-*hîn* (Nb 15: 9, 10; 28: 14), one-third of a *hîn* (Nb 15: 6, 7; Ez 46: 14), one-quarter *hîn* (Ex 29: 40; Lv 23: 13; Nb 15: 4, 5; 28: 5, 7, 14).

The *'omer*, a word meaning 'sheaf', is used only in the story of the manna (Ex 16 *passim*): every man gathers an *'omer* a day. The gloss of Ex 16: 36 reckons it as one-tenth of an *'ephah*.

The *'iśśarôn* (one-tenth) is a measure of meal in the liturgical texts (Ex 29: 40; Lv 14: 10, 21, etc.).

The *qab* appears only in 2 K 6: 25: during the siege of Samaria a quarter of a *qab* of wild onions is sold for five shekels of silver.

The *log* is a small unit for liquids, mentioned only in the ritual for the purification of lepers (Lv 14 *passim*).

If we try to arrange these terms in order of size, the gloss of Ex 16: 36 indicates that the *'omer* is one-tenth of an *'ephah*, and probably the 'tenth' (*iśśarôn*) is also one-tenth of an *'ephah*. According to Ez 45: 11, the *'ephah* and the *bath* are of the same capacity and are equal to one-tenth of a *homer*. This gives the following series:

homer	1		
'ephah = bath	10	1	
'omer = 'iśśaron	100	10	1

This is all that can be deduced from the Hebrew text alone. But Mesopotamian metrology enables us to establish another series: in the Neo-Babylonian period the proportions between the three units of measure are: 1 *gur* = 30 *sûtu* = 180 *qa*. The resemblance of the names justifies our drawing up the following table for the exilic and post-exilic period:

gur = kor	1		
sûtu = s'ah	30	1	
qa = qab	180	6	1

These proportions are confirmed by the documents of the Jewish period and the Talmud.

These two series, one of which is founded on the decimal system and the other on the sexagesimal, are apparently independent. Their interrelation is only a hypothesis, founded on the Greek version of Ex 16: 36 and Is 5: 10, which renders an *'ephah* by τρία μέτρα; now μέτρον is the ordinary translation of *s'ah*, which would then be one-third of an *'ephah*. On the other hand, though the text of Ez 45: 14 is obscure, we can deduce that the *homer* and the *kor* are equivalent, and so we can draw up the following table:

homer = *kor*	I				
'ephah = *bath*	10	I			
sᵉ'ah	30	3	I		
'omer = *'iśśarôn*	100	10	–	I	
qab	180	18	6	–	I

The position of the *hîn* and the *log* can only be deduced from sources which are even later: the comparison made by Josephus with the Graeco-Roman metrology, the interpretations of St Jerome and Talmudic data. From them we conclude that I *qab*= 4 *log* and I *bath*= 6 *hîn*. Leaving aside the *lethek* and the *shalîsh*, which are too seldom mentioned to concern us, the complete table would be as follows:

homer = *kor*	I					
'ephah = *bath*	10	I				
sᵉ'ah	30	3	I			
hîn	60	6	2	I		
'omer = *'śśarôn*	100	10	–	–	I	
qab	180	18	6	3	–	I
log	720	72	24	12	–	4	I

This table, we must insist, is hypothetical, and in any case is valid only for a very late date. It depends on identifications which are sometimes uncertain and always late, the oldest being those of Ezechiel. And even of these last, no one can say whether they record measurements which had fallen into disuse, or foretell a reform which was perhaps never put into effect in biblical times.

It must be admitted that we have no means of drawing up a table, however limited in its accuracy, for proportions in use before the Exile. The only useful term of comparison would be the Assyrian system, which preceded the Neo-Babylonian used above. The Assyrian nomenclature was as follows: I *imêru* = 10 *sûtu*= 100 *qa*. As it is generally agreed that the *qa* did not change its value in Mesopotamia, the *imêru* is almost half the Babylonian *sûtu*. The Hebrew *homer* has the same name as the *imêru*, which also means 'an ass-load'. This makes it doubtful, in spite of Ez 45: 14, whether the *homer* was the equivalent of the *kor*, which corresponded to the *gur*. The position of the *sᵉ'ah*= *sûtu* is equally puzzling: according to the Assyrian system, it should be ¹⁄₁₀ of an *imêru*= *homer*, and therefore equal to the *'ephah*= *bath*, as it was later defined in Ez 45: 11. All the same, it would be surprising if the *sᵉ'ah* of the monarchical period had the same value as the *'ephah*= *bath*, also mentioned in ancient texts, though we do not know their relative values.

These gaps in our knowledge make it impossible to give, for the Old Testament period, a table of equivalents with our modern systems. The most one could attempt would be to determine the value of a particular unit at a particular period. We can compare the Hebrew measures *homer*, *kor* and *sᵉ'ah* with the Mesopotamian measures of the same names, which are better known. In the Neo-Babylonian period, according to recent calculations, the *kor* was equal to 53 gallons and $\frac{1}{10}$ pint (241·20 litres), and the *s'ah* to 14·15 pints (8·04 litres): the basic unit, the *qa* was 2·35 pints or 1·34 litres. In the Assyrian system the *imêru*= *homer* would be 29 gallons 3 pints (134 litres), the *sûtu* (= *s'ah? 'ephah?*) 2 gallons 7$\frac{1}{2}$ pints (13·4 litres). Unfortunately, the estimate of the *qa* is uncertain and other authors value it as 1·42 pints (0·81 litres); an inscribed vase recently found at Persepolis would point to a *qa* of 1·62 pints (0·92 litres), or a little more. Egypt had a measure called *'pt*= *'ephah* for solid and *hnw*= *hîn* for liquids, but their values are even more doubtful. Different authors reckon the *hnw* between 4$\frac{2}{5}$ and 8$\frac{4}{5}$ pints (2·5 and 5 litres), and the number of *hnw* in the *'pt* is not certain—perhaps 40; even taking the lowest estimate for the *hnw*, this would demand a higher capacity for the *'ephah* than anything yet proposed.

One might think that a start could be made from the apparently precise data of the Bible: the sea of bronze in Solomon's Temple had a diameter of 10 cubits, a depth of 5 cubits and it contained 2,000 *bath* (1 K 7: 23, 26). But we do not know exactly either the value of the cubit or the form of the receptacle, and the parallel passage in 2 Ch 4: 5 gives a capacity of 3,000 *bath*, with the same measurements in cubits. The facts about the bronze basins (1 K 7: 38) are even less adequate.

Archaeology alone might provide us with more reliable information. At Tell ed-Duweir (Lakish) the upper part of a jar has been found on which has been engraved *bt mlk* (royal *bath*): the same inscription can perhaps be restored on a handle from Tell en-Nasbeh, and a fragment inscribed *bt* comes from Tell Beit-Mirsim (Debir?). Having been engraved before baking, these inscriptions are evidently meant to indicate a recognized official capacity. Unfortunately the largest fragment, that from Tell ed-Duweir, does not allow of our calculating the capacity of these jars with any accuracy. Other vases had only the stamp *lmlk*. It has been possible to reconstruct entirely only one example, also from Tell ed-Duweir, whose capacity is nearly 10 gallons (45·33 litres). But at Tell en-Nasbeh there is an almost complete jar, stamped *lmlk*, which contains only 40·7 litres. If this stamp certified that these jars conformed to an official measure, and if, as used to be thought, the jars stamped *bt* or *bt lmlk* had the same capacity, we could then arrive at the approximate size of the *bath*. But the fragments marked *bt* certainly belong to receptacles smaller than the jars marked *lmlk*. It has therefore been suggested that the latter were of double capacity and represented two *bath*; the size of the *bath* would then be about 4 gallons 7 pints (22 or 23 litres). Such a string of hypotheses hardly leads to a certain conclusion.

The inscriptions *bt lmlk* are of the eighth century B.C. and some of the stamps *lmlk* are rather later. A final piece of evidence comes from the Roman period. In a cave at Qumran an unbroken jar was discovered on which is written in charcoal: '2 *s'ah* 7 *log*'. Its capacity is about 61 pints or 35 litres, which would make the *log* just about one pint (0·64 litres) and the *s°ah* about 27 pints (15·30 litres). This could agree with the 10-gallon (45-litre) estimate of the *lmlk* jars, which contained 1 *bath*= 3 *s°ah*. Unfortunately, this inscription, being traced in charcoal and not inscribed before baking, may not be an indication of capacity at all, but simply the amount of provisions put in the jar, without filling it. This makes it useless for fixing a metrology. Moreover, it would only hold good for the Roman period. Here we need only say that the tables which have been drawn up for this period, after comparison with Graeco-Roman metrology and after consulting the Talmud, vary as much as 100%, and are then, quite wrongly, applied to the Israelite period. If such tables must be given, the probabilities, at least, should be respected: a *homer*, being originally an ass-load, may have been as much as 5 bushels, 6 gallons (209 litres), the lowest figure proposed, but certainly not the 12 bushels, 3 gallons (450 litres) suggested by an alternative reckoning.

4. *Measures of weight*

While foodstuffs were measured by volume, precious materials and metals were weighed. Small things were weighed on a beam-balance with two scales. The weights, usually of hard stone, were called *'eben*, which means both 'stone' and 'weight'; they were kept in a purse (Dt 25: 13; Mi 6: 11; Pr 16: 11).

'To weigh' is *shaqal* and the *sheqel* or shekel was consequently the basic unit of weight. This unit is common to all ancient Semitic metrologies. The original text of 2 S 14: 26 speaks of 200 shekels 'at the king's weight', and a series of post-exilic texts mentions the 'shekel of the sanctuary' (Ex 30: 13, 24; 38: 24-26, Lv 5: 15; 27: 3, 25; Nb 3: 47, 50; 7 *passim*; 18: 16). In all these references it is the weight which conforms to the official standard, or else a unit of the same name but heavier; some of the Ugaritic texts reckon in 'heavy' shekels and in Mesopotamia there was a series of 'royal' weights, double the ordinary weights. In a story from the patriarchal period, before the institution of the State, there is a reference to shekels which were 'current among the merchants' (Gn 23: 16). But it sometimes happened that traders had large and small 'stones' (Dt 25: 13), two kinds of weights (Pr 20: 23), according to whether they were buying or selling.

The multiples of the shekel are the mina and the talent. The mina (*maneh*) appears only rarely and is apparently late (1 K 10: 17, perhaps radactional; Ez 45: 12; Esd 2: 69; Ne 7: 70, 71; cf. Dn 5: 25). The mina is often mentioned in Mesopotamian texts, but we may note that at Ugarit it is attested only in Akkadian texts of foreign origin, or by Ugaritic translations of them; in practice, however, weights of 50 shekels were used, the equivalent of one mina. The talent (*kikkar*) takes its name from the fact that it is a weight of circular shape (root: *krr*). It is a unit for gross reckoning, often used in the historical books but seldom in the Pentateuch (Ex 25: 39; 37: 24; 38: 24-29).

Several fractions of the shekel are mentioned: a half-shekel (Ex 30: 13), one-third of a shekel (Ne 10: 33), a quarter-shekel (1 S 9: 8). But there are also special names for the small units of weight. The *beqa'*, literally a 'fraction', is mentioned only in Gn 24: 22 and Ex 38: 26, and is a half-shekel. The *gerah* (probably 'grain') is the smallest unit of weight (Ex 30: 13; Lv 27: 25; Nb 3: 47; 18: 16; Ez 45: 12). The *payim*, familiar to archaeologists, is mentioned in 1 S 13: 21, a text which was for a long time incomprehensible; it represents two-thirds of a shekel (cf. Za 13: 8). Another term occurring only once in the Bible, but known in Akkadian, is quoted in Dn 5: 25, 28 (Aramaic), along with the mina and the shekel: it is the *p'res*, with the plural or dual *parsin* ('part'), representing half a mina or, more probably, half a shekel.

Finally we must mention the *q'sîṭah*, an otherwise unknown unit of weight, used by Jacob when paying for the field of Shechem (Gn 33: 19; cf. Jos 24: 32, and repeated in Jb 42: 11 by a deliberate archaism).

The basic elements of these units are found among Israel's neighbours. In Mesopotamia they are arranged on a sexagesimal basis: the shekel contains 180 'grains' and is also divided into multiple fractions, from two-thirds to a twenty-fourth of a shekel. The mina is 60 shekels and the talent is 60 minas= 3,600 shekels. At Ugarit the talent is only 3,000 shekels; the value of the mina is not given by the texts where it is mentioned, but it appears from the series of weights that it was only 50 shekels, and so there were 60 minas in the talent.

For Israel, the following values are given by the texts: according to Ex 38: 25-26, the talent is worth 3,000 shekels and the *beqa'* is a half-shekel. From Lv 27: 25; Nb 3: 47; 18: 16; Ez 45: 12, the shekel contains 20 *gerah*, and the first three texts make clear that this is the shekel of the sanctuary. Evaluation of the mina is more difficult: the Hebrew of Ez 45: 12 reads: 'the mina shall be for you 20 shekels and 25 shekels and 15 shekels', which gives a total of 60 shekels, like the Babylonian mina. The manner of counting is odd, but is perhaps explained by the existence of weights of 15, 20 and 25 shekels, the last representing half a mina of 50 shekels, as at Ugarit. Ezechiel seems to try to revalue the mina, as Ez 40: 5 would revalue the cubit and Ez 45: 11 would perhaps revalue the *'ephah* and the *bath*. Reckoning the shekel as 20 *gerah* Ez 45: 12, followed by the later texts, would then be part of the scheme of reform. The best plan is therefore to draw up two tables. One depends on Ex 38: 25-26, and runs as follows:

talent	1			
mina	60	1		
shekel	3,000	50	1	
beqa'	6,000	100	2	1

These values seem to be confirmed by the penalties of 100 shekels (Dt 22: 19) and 50 shekels (Dt 22: 29) and the tax of 50 shekels imposed on the wealthy by Menahem (2 K 15: 20). We must remember that the name of the mina is very rare and that here we have its equivalent in shekels. The system is of a respectable antiquity, and, as we have seen, obtained at Ugarit.

From the data given by Ezechiel, we can produce another table:

talent	. . . .	1			
mina	. . . .	60	1		
shekel	. . . .	3,600	60	1	
gerah	. . . .	72,000	1,200	20	1

This value for the mina seems to be found in an ancient text: according to Ex 21: 32, a fine of 30 shekels is imposed in a case where the Code of Hammurabi imposes half a mina.

To transpose these weights into our modern systems is very difficult. In the system most commonly used in Mesopotamia, the shekel weighed 0·30 ounces (8·4 grams), but there was a series derived from the 'royal' talent in which all the units weighed double. At Ugarit a collection of weights postulates a light shekel of 0·34 ounces (9·5 grams), and the texts speak of a 'heavy' shekel, perhaps its double, which would give a weight of 0·67 ounces (18·7 grams).

For Israel, excavations in Palestine have yielded numerous weights, some of which bear a numerical mark or the name of a unit of weight, or both together. Though their archaeological context is rarely beyond dispute, these inscribed weights can generally be dated, by epigraphic criteria, towards the end of the monarchy. But there are notable differences of weight between specimens belonging to the same type and apparently to the same period, and found in the same site (*e.g.* at Tell ed-Duweir, which has produced a large collection). Only the small units are represented by inscribed weights, and none bears the name 'shekel'; it is replaced by a symbol, followed by a number. Since it was the commonest unit, the word 'shekel' must also be supplied in many reckonings in the Bible.

The longest series of inscribed weights bears the symbol and the numbers 1, 2, 4 or 8. At least twenty-five examples are known, a dozen of them for eight units. The mark is that of the shekel, and they weigh about 0·41 ounces (11·5 grams). A small bronze weight, found at Gezer, is marked *lmlk* with a figure 2; this would be a 'royal' weight. It actually weighs 0·79 ounces (22·28 grams), which would give a shekel of 0·39 ounces (11·14 grams), but the metal may have lost some of its weight through oxidization.

Half a dozen weights connected with this series are inscribed *pym*; the word can be recognized, as we said, in 1 S 13: 21, and stands for two-thirds of a shekel. Judging by what they weigh, a shekel is about 0·42 ounces (12 grams).

The weights inscribed *bq'* evidently represent half-shekels (cf. Ex 38: 26).
The six known specimens weigh roughly 0·21 ounces (6 grams) and suggest
a shekel of at least 0·42 ounces or 12 grams.

Besides these, we possess a dozen weights inscribed *nṣp*. This seems to mean
the 'half' of a unit, but the unit is not the Israelite shekel, for judging by what
they weigh the *nṣp* averages 0·35 ounces (10 grams). It belongs, therefore, to
another system, also represented by a small weight, marked ¼ *nṣp*, weighing
0·09 ounces (2·54 grams), and perhaps by certain uninscribed weights, some
of which weight 0·18 ounces (5 grams) and others 0·72 ounces (20 grams).
Clearly, they represent ½ and 2 *nṣp* respectively. The name is never found in
the Old Testament as that of a weight, but it is found in the Ugaritic texts
together with the shekel, and is perhaps represented by a weight of 0·34
ounces (9·5 grams) in the weight system: in the Ugaritic system, the *nṣp*
would be a 'light' shekel, 'half' of the 'heavy' shekel. Perhaps the *nṣp*
weights found in Palestine were lost there by 'Canaanite' traders.[1]

Uncertainty about the exact value of the shekel and the theoretical nature
of Ezechiel's classification prevent us suggesting more than approximate
values for the mina and the talent. The ancient mina must have weighed
between 1·213 and 1·323 pounds (550 and 600 grams), the talent between 75
and 80 pounds (34 and 36 kilograms). In Ezechiel's system the mina would
have weighed about 1·54 pounds (700 grams). It is useless to be too precise in
what has always been a fluctuating metrology.

5. *The coinage*

Study of weights leads us naturally to that of the coinage. The earliest form
of trade was bartering merchandise, and payment was made, at first, in
goods which could be measured or counted—so many measures of barley or
oil, so many head of cattle, etc. For the sake of convenience, metal was soon
adopted as the means of payment; sometimes it was wrought, sometimes in
ingots, the quality and weight of which determined the value in exchange.
Metal was used in large quantities for the payment of tribute (2 K 15: 19;
18: 14, etc.), in small amounts for individual transactions with foreign
countries (Gn 42: 25, 35; 43: 12f.; 1 S 13: 21; 1 K 10: 29), and always, it
seems, for the purchase of land (Gn 23: 14f.; 2 S 24: 24; 1 K 16: 24; 21: 2;
Jr 32: 9). Solomon paid Hiram in kind (1 K 5: 25) and Mesha used to pay a
tribute of sheep and wool (2 K 3: 4). The two methods of payment might be
combined: Osee acquired his wife for 15 shekels of silver, a *homer* of barley
and a *lethek* of barley (Os 3: 2).

The metals of exchange were copper, gold and, chiefly, silver. The word
keseph, silver, thus came to mean both the metal itself and the medium of
payment, like *kaspu* in Akkadian, *argent* in French and 'silver' in Scottish

1. Cf. pp. 77-78.

usage. At a very early date in the Eastern Mediterranean, at Mycenae, in Cyprus, in Egypt, in Mesopotamia and in Syria, the metal was melted into ingots of different shapes, or into discs, bars, brooches and rings, sometimes bearing signs certifying their weight and purity, but this was not yet coinage. Payments were always made by weight. The weight of the silver or gold is often mentioned on Egyptian monuments and is described in one of the Ras Shamra poems. This remained the only method of payment among the Israelites until the Exile; the *q'sîṭah* of Gn 33: 19 is not 'coinage of the patriarchal period', but a weight of unknown value. The verb *shaqal* means both 'to weigh' and 'to pay', and the shekel became the basic unit in the Jewish monetary system after first being the basic unit of the Israelite weight-system. To pay for the cave of Macpelah Abraham 'weighs' 400 shekels to Ephron (Gn 23: 16); Jeremias 'weighs' 17 shekels to his cousin for the field at Anathoth (Jr 32: 9, etc.). Merchants are called 'weighers of silver' in So 1: 11. The State acted in exactly the same way. To finance the repairing of the Temple, King Joas placed at the entrance to the sanctuary a chest, prototype of our church alms-boxes, in which the faithful deposited silver of every shape. When they saw the chest contained a large amount of silver, the royal secretary came and the silver found in the Temple of Yahweh was melted down and calculated. Then they sent the silver, after checking it, to the master-builders, who paid it out (2 K 12. 10-13). This should be compared with what Herodotus relates about Darius: 'The gold and silver of the tribute are kept by the king in this fashion: he has them melted down and poured into earthenware jars. When the vessel is full, the clay covering is taken off and, when the king needs money, he has so much metal broken into pieces as is required for each occasion' (*Hist.* III, 96).

But between Joas and Darius came the invention of coinage. A coin is a piece of metal stamped with a mark which guarantees its denomination and weight. In theory, then, it can be accepted at sight, without weighing or checking. It was invented in Asia Minor in the seventh century B.C., and the custom spread through the Near East, largely through the influence of the Persians. The earliest coins were made of electrum, a natural alloy of gold and silver, which was collected in the sands of river-beds, especially in the Pactolus. Croesus invented a bimetallic system of gold and silver staters. These 'croesids' were replaced under Darius by 'darics' of gold and shekels of silver. The daric had no rival as a gold coin, but the use of the Median shekel was not widespread and it did not compete with the Greek silver coins.

Naturally, then, the first references to coinage in the Bible appear in the post-exilic books. Gold darics are mentioned in Esd 8: 27 and, by an anachronism, in 1 Ch 29: 7, which refers to the time of David. The reckonings of Esd 2: 69 and Ne 7: 69-71 are made in gold drachmas. The silver drachma was the Greek coin most highly valued, especially the Athenian drachma, the 'owl' of the fifth century B.C. But the gold drachmas were struck only rarely, and were never in wide circulation. It seems certain, then, that the 'drachmas' of Esd and Ne are darics, the confusion being due to the redactor, or to a copyist's fault. We cannot tell whether the silver shekels of Ne 5: 15; 10: 33 refer to a weight or a coin; but they are certainly not Median shekels, for these were never current in Palestine.

The oldest coins discovered in Palestine are Greek Macedonian coins: an electrum coin dated *circa* 500 B.C. comes from the latest excavations at Balata (Shechem), and a silver four-drachma piece struck at Aegaea about 480 has been found in a tomb at Athlith. It is obvious that these coins from remote lands were not current in Palestine, and circulated only for their value as ingots, estimated by their weight.

But Judaea, like other provinces of the Persian Empire, eventually struck its own coinage. The first Jewish coin seems to have been a small silver piece of the fifth century B.C., originating from Hebron and similar to those, of uncertain series, from Arabia and Philistia in the same period. It bears the inscription *bq'* in old Hebrew script, and weighs 0·14 ounces (3·88 grams), which is approximately the weight of the Attic drachma. It has been ascribed to the time when Nehemias was governor of Judaea, but this is only a hypothesis, and it is not even certain that the coin is Jewish: the type is not characteristic, and the Phoenician alphabet was then in use far beyond the boundaries of Judaea. More authentic are two silver pieces with the legend *yhd*, that is, *Y'hud*, the official name of the Persian province of Judah in the Aramaic Esd 5: 1, 8; 7: 14 (cf. Dn 2: 25; 5: 13; 6: 14). A silver coin found at Bethsur also carries the stamp *Y'hûd* and the proper name 'Ezechias'. This is probably the priest Ezechias who, according to Josephus, became in old age the friend of Ptolemy I around 315 B.C.; but it is scarcely probable that the Ptolemies would have authorized silver coinage to be struck locally. The coin must date from the time when Ezechias administered the province of Judaea, immediately after the conquest of Alexander or at the very end of the Persian rule. The other two coins inscribed *Y'hûd* are earlier.

Palestine, and indeed, the entire Near East, then came under the monetary systems of the Seleucids or the Ptolemies. This followed the Phoenician standard, the silver drachma of 0·13 ounces (3·6 grams) and the tetradrachma, or shekel, of approximately 0·51 ounces (14·4 grams). It was only when Simon Maccabaeus was recognized by Antiochus VII Sidetes as priest and ethnarch of the Jews that he received the right to strike a coinage (1 M 15: 6). As in similar concessions made by the Seleucids, this only extended to a bronze coinage for local use. This event took place in 138 B.C. But Simon did not use his privilege, and it must have been revoked by the same Antiochus, who very soon turned against him (1 M 15: 27), and Simon died shortly after, in 134. In any case, no bronze coins of his age have reached us: the silver and bronze coins which were for a long time attributed to him date in fact from the First Revolt, in A.D. 66-70. Jewish coinage began only with Simon's successor, John Hyrcanus, and then only when he considered himself independent, after the conquest of Samaria, around 110 B.C. It was an inferior bronze coinage, which continued under his successors, the Hasmoneans; among silver coins, Tyrian money, which was valued for its alloy, circulated almost to the exclusion of all others. The history of this coinage and its successors under Herod and the Procurators does not concern us here. The Jews began to strike bronze and silver coins again during their two revolts against the Romans, in A.D. 66-70 and 132-135. Their coins have an inscription in Hebrew and are dated from the years of the 'deliverance of Sion' or the 'deliverance of Israel'. But this has taken us far beyond the Old Testament era.

III

MILITARY INSTITUTIONS

CHAPTER ONE

THE ARMIES OF ISRAEL

WE have a fair knowledge of the military organization of the Egyptians, the Assyro-Babylonians and the Hittites. Reliefs, paintings and drawings portray their soldiers, their battles, their camps and their strongholds; inscriptions describe their campaigns; and copies of peace treaties record the titles, functions and careers of particular individuals in the army.

Our information about the military organization of Israel is by no means so complete. Not a single relief or drawing of a military kind has survived; perhaps there never were any. Even the fortifications and weapons brought to light by excavations belong, for the most part, to the Canaanites, whom the Israelites conquered and displaced. There are, of course, numerous texts, and the historical books of the Bible are full of wars. But these narratives are not contemporary records of the events. There are, it is true, some very old traditions in the books of Josue and Judges; but it was nearly six hundred years later, just before the Exile, when the military history of this period received its final literary form in the books as we possess them to-day. The books of Samuel and Kings, on the other hand, do contain passages committed to writing very soon after the events took place, but the vivid and life-like character of these passages does not compensate for their lack of precision about military details. Quite the most detailed information on the military organization under the monarchy is to be found in Chronicles; but these two books were written in an age when there was neither independence nor an army to defend it. Lastly, the Exodus itself and the wanderings in the deserts were described, centuries later, as the movements of a well-disciplined army. Such are the sources of our information, and yet they can be used to good purpose, provided they are carefully tested and dated by literary and historical criticism. The military institutions of a people change more rapidly than any other form of its social organization, for they are subject to many kinds of influence. The army is affected by every change in the type of government, by the varying requirements of policy, by the enemy it may have to face, and, of course, by progress in the development of armaments. The period between the Conquest under Josue and Nabuchodonosor's siege of Jerusalem is longer than that which separates the Hundred Years' War from the second World War, and though the organization of the army and field tactics evolved more slowly in ancient times, those six centuries saw extensive changes in both.

It is obvious, therefore, that the military institutions of Israel must be studied in the order in which they developed. Secondly, the general character of the sources must be taken into account: the texts are religious texts, and as a rule they are not concerned with merely military matters such as the constitution of the army or the technique of war. Moreover, even the texts treating directly of war need careful interpretation, and this is particularly true of the older texts, for war was regarded as a sacral undertaking with a ritual of its own. Indeed, this notion of a holy war persisted to the very end of Old Testament times; but the concept underwent many transformations until it emerged as a kind of holy ideal. The religious character of these military institutions will be treated at the end of this part of the book; we must first concern ourselves with their non-sacred aspects.

1. *A people under arms*

Among nomads[1] there is no distinction between the army and the people: every able-bodied man can join in a raid and must be prepared to defend the tribe's property and rights against an enemy, under his sheikh or another commander. As a rule, each tribe acts on its own, but from time to time several tribes will unite for a common enterprise. There are customs of war and rules for fighting, but there is no stable military organization. This was probably true of Israel also, as long as it was leading a semi-nomadic life, but it is not easy to perceive the true situation which underlies the stories of Exodus and Numbers. Ex 12: 37; 13: 18 and 14: 19-20 picture a people in arms marching out of Egypt; Nb 1: 3, 20, 22, etc.; 2: 1-31 and 10: 11-28 show them marching through the desert in formation; but these pictures are idealizations composed in a later age when the entire people was called to arms in times of national danger. In Josue, too, the Conquest is presented as the achievement of a unified Israelite army, though certain passages, with the parallels in Jg 1, give a more realistic picture of what actually happened. These latter texts show tribes or groups of tribes, such as Judah and Simeon and the house of Joseph, conquering their part of the Holy Land independently of each other; and the very ancient notes preserved in Nb 32: 1, 16, 39-42, which record the settlement of Reuben, Gad and Manasseh (Eastern half), are of a similar character. There was never any question of an organized army.

We are somewhat better informed on the period of the Judges. Each tribe is securing its hold on its own territory and defending this land against the counter-attacks of the Canaanites who formerly held it; neighbouring peoples wage war against them, and nomads make raids. Sometimes the tribes, who

1. Cf. p. 9.

were bound together by the pact of Shechem (Jos 24) join together for military enterprises. Gideon, for example, summons to arms not only his own tribe, Manasseh, but Aser, Zebulon and Nephthali as well (Jg 6: 35); in the end he calls upon Ephraim too (Jg 7: 24) where men were complaining because they had not been called to arms at the beginning (Jg 8: 1). The prose narrative in Jg 4: 6f. tells how Baraq mobilized Zabulon and Nephthali against the Canaanites, but the Song of Deborah (Jg 5: 14f.) includes in its list contingents from Ephraim, Benjamin, Makir and Issachar as well, and takes to task Reuben, Gilead, Dan and Aser for remaining neutral. Similarly, to avenge the outrage committed at Gibeah, all Israel, except the men of Yabesh in Gilead (Jg 21: 8f.) takes up arms (Jg 20).

In the same way Saul called 'all Israel' to arms against the Ammonites (1 S 11: 1-11), and the subsequent victory ensured him the throne. By this, political unity was at last achieved, and the people had a king 'who would lead it forth and fight its battles' (1 S 8: 20). Saul called upon the entire people for the holy war against the Amalekites (1 S 15: 4) and assembled 'all Israel' against the Philistines (1 S 17: 2, 11); this is the reason why David's three brothers went to the war (1 S 17: 13), leaving in Bethlehem only their aged father and David, who was too young to bear arms. According to 1 S 23: 8, the king even called out 'the entire people' to pursue David when he took refuge in Qeilah. For the battle of Gilboa, where he would meet defeat and death at the hands of the Philistines, Saul had gathered 'all Israel' (1 S 28: 4). Certainly things had changed considerably since the period of the Judges, but it was a smooth evolution. The 'Judges' were 'saviours' marked out by God to set his people free, and Saul himself was a leader of the charismatic type, moved by the spirit of Yahweh (1 S 10: 10 and especially 11: 6), smashing the Ammonites in a way which recalls the military successes which marked out the greater Judges.

There were various ways for the leader, Judge or King, to call the people to arms. Sometimes a trumpet was sounded (Jg 3: 27, Ehud; 6: 34, Gideon; 1 S 13: 3, Saul), or messengers were sent around the tribes (Jg 6: 35; 7: 24). Sometimes the message was underlined by a symbolic action, as when Saul cut to pieces a yoke of oxen and sent their quarters to every part of the territory of Israel with the threat: 'Whoever does not follow Saul to battle will have his own oxen treated in the same way' (1 S 11: 7). When the men of Gibeah so maltreated a Levite's concubine that she died, the Levite cut her body into twelve pieces and sent one to each tribe in order to rouse the entire people against the men of that town (Jg 19: 29-30). During the period of the Judges, the response to these appeals depended on each group, which made its own decision. The Song of Deborah twice insists on this freedom to fight or not to fight (Jg 5: 2 and 9), and expresses nothing stronger than reproach or regret about the tribes which chose to stand aside (Jg 5: 15-17). Meroz alone, a town in Nephthali which did not follow its tribe, is cursed (Jg 5: 23), for Nephthali was the first of all the tribes to take up arms. Threats might be uttered against those who refused to do their duty (Jg 21: 5; 1 S 11: 7), but we do not know what sanctions were in fact applied. According to the tradition recorded in Jg 21: 6-12, the expedition against the men of Yabesh was not a punitive expedition because of their abstention; its sole purpose was to find wives for the rest of the tribe of Benjamin without breaking the oath which the other combatants had taken.

In spite of this mass call-up, the number of fighting men was small. Exaggerated numbers have crept into the older narratives; they tell us that 400,000 men marched against Benjamin (Jg 20: 17), that 300,000 Israelites and 30,000 men of Judah answered the call of Saul (1 S 11: 8), that 200,000 infantrymen followed him when he marched on the Amalekites (1 S 15: 4). Other texts are more sober: Jg 4: 10 reckons the joint forces at Zabulon and Nephthali at not more than 10,000, and Jg 5: 8 gives 40,000 as the greatest number which could be mustered from all the tribes; this latter figure, 40,000, is also the size of the entire army of Israel facing Jericho (Jos 4: 13). But these figures, too, are symbolic.

The men assembled in battle dress *halûṣîm* (literally, 'unclothed', 'stripped', *i.e.* in short cloaks). They provided their own arms, of a very simple kind. The usual weapons were swords and slings (the tribe of Benjamin had some expert slingers, Jg 20: 16). In Deborah's day there was 'not a shield or spear among the forty thousand men of Israel' (Jg 5: 8). The Philistines disarmed the Israelites at the beginning of Saul's reign, and at the battle of Mikmas only Saul and Jonathan had a sword and a lance (1 S 13: 19-22). Saul's spear became the symbol of his royal rank (1 S 22: 6; 26: 7, 16, 22; 2 S 1: 6; cf. 1 S 18 : 11; 19: 9), but his shield is mentioned only in David's elegy (2 S 1: 21). Jonathan, on the other hand is shown as an archer (1 S 18: 4; 20: 20f.; 2 S 1: 22). The bronze helmet and the breast-plate which Saul wanted David to wear produce a splendid literary effect, but they are probably an anachronism (1 S 17: 38f.).

The units of the army were based on those of society. The unit was the clan (*mishpaḥah*), which in theory provided a contingent of 1,000 men, though in fact the number was far smaller; compare 1 S 1: 10 (*'eleph*) with verse 21 (*mishpaḥah*), and the use of 'a thousand men' for 'a clan' in Jg 6: 15; 1 S 23: 23. When the people take up arms, they are referred to as the 'thousands of Israel' (Nb 31: 5; Jos 22: 21, 30; Jg 5: 8). These units were commanded by a 'leader of a thousand', *śar 'eleph* (1 S 17: 18; 18: 13). They could be divided into small units of 100 men (1 S 22: 7; cf. Jg 7: 16) and 50 (1 S 8: 12). The term *ḥamushîm*, which (apart from Ex 13: 18 and Nb 32: 17, corrected by the ancient versions) occurs only in Jos 1: 14; 4: 12 and Jg 7: 11, is sometimes explained by the fact that the army was divided into groups of fifty. More probably, however, the word refers to soldiers drawn up in 'five' corps on the march and in camp. Arabic dictionaries give, as one meaning of the

Arabic *hamîsh* ('five'), the formation of an army with a vanguard, main body, two flanks and a rearguard. This brings to mind the arrangement of the camp in the desert, where, according to Nb 2: 2-31, four divisions (*d'gulîm*) surrounded the Tabernacle, which was guarded by the Levites—five units in all; it recalls the *hamushîm* in the Midianite camp (Jg 7: 11) and the marching order described in Nb 10: 11-28: first the divisions of Judah and Reuben, then the Tabernacle with its Levites, lastly the divisions of Ephraim and Dan. (Compare also the *hamushîm* of Ex 13: 18; Jos 1: 14; 4: 12.)

These ill-armed and poorly trained troops were terrified at the fortified cities of Canaan (Nb 13: 28; Dt 1: 28), at iron-clad chariots (Jos 17: 16-18; Jg 1: 19; 4: 13; 1 S 13: 5; 2 S 1: 6) and at the heavily armed Philistine warriors (1 S 17: 4-7). Yet, in the very first stages of the conquest, the Israelites took advantage of the fact that the Canaanite forces were scattered, and that the withdrawal of Egypt had left a void. They infiltrated where victory was theirs, but stopped short at the edge of the plains, where fortified cities and chariots barred their way (Jos 17: 12, 16; Jg 1: 19, 27-35). Whenever the capture of a town is related in any detail, it is always prepared by espionage, and victory itself is secured either by treachery or by guile (cf. Jericho in Jos 6, Ai—which was already in ruins—in Jos 8; Bethel in Jg 1: 23-25). The Canaanite enclaves which survived were only gradually absorbed.

Pitched battles were fatal for the Israelites (1 S 4: 1-11; 31: 1-7). To compensate for their inferior armament and for their lack of military formation they would attack with a small group of picked men (cf., even during their days in the desert, Ex 17: 9; Nb 31: 3-4). The men of Dan who set off to conquer land were a mere 600 (Jg 18: 11); Saul picked 3,000 men out of all Israel to wage war on the Philistines (1 S 13: 2) and he gained his first victory with a force of only 600 (1 S 13: 15; 14: 2). By the skilful use of daring attacks, bold tricks and ambushes, these small groups of troops, under the firm control of good leaders, succeeded in worsting enemy forces which were superior in numbers or in weapons. Jonathan and his armour-bearer went forward unaccompanied to attack the Philistine post at Mikmas and threw the place into panic; then 600 of Saul's men fell upon the enemy, the 'Hebrew' auxiliaries deserted from the Philistine side, the Israelites from the hill country of Ephraim joined in the chase, and the Philistine defeat was turned into a rout (1 S 14: 1-23). Gideon's action against the Midianites is even more typical; of the 32,000 men who answered his call, he sent home all who had no heart to fight, and only 10,000 remained; of these, he chose 300, and divided them into three columns. Reconnaissance showed him that the morale of the enemy was low, and he made careful preparations for a night operation. His troops covered their torches with jars until the signal for attack, when the trumpet-sounds and the war-cries were calculated to throw the enemy camp into confusion by creating the impression of a vast force. The trick succeeded; the Midianites lost their heads and took to flight (Jg 6:

33-7: 22). There follows the exploitation of victory; other Israelite contingents took part in the pursuit (as in 1 S 14: 22), the Ephraimites cut off the enemy's retreat (Jg 7: 23-25), and Gideon's tiny force harassed the survivors right to the edge of the desert (Jg 8: 4-12). Though the story combines a series of distinct episodes, it gives a fair idea of warfare in the period of the Judges.

From time to time, two enemy forces would agree to settle the issue by single combat. There is evidence of this custom as early as the 18th century B.C.; an Egyptian story about a certain Sinuhet says it was practised among the Canaanite semi-nomads. The Philistine's challenge to the Israelites in 1 S 17: 8-10 is quite clearly a proposal that the fate of the two peoples should be settled by a single combat. The individual feats of arms attributed to David's heroes (2 S 21: 15-21) can be explained in the same way. The champions, it seems, were called *'îsh habbenaym*, 'the man-between-two' or 'the man for combat between two' (1 S 17: 4, 23). The term is never found again except in the Qumran work entitled 'The Order of the War' and there its meaning is not the same; in the Qumran scroll it means light infantry.

During the war between Saul's partisans and those of David, Abner proposed to Joab that they should decide the issue by a fight between twelve picked men from each side, but no decision was reached, because all twenty-four were killed and a general fight ensued (2 S 2: 14f.). These customs used to obtain among Arab tribes, and persisted until modern times. At the most critical moment in the conquest of Algeria, when the Duke of Aumale had been sent by his father Louis-Philippe to take over command of the army, the Emir Abd-el-Kader suggested to the Duke that they should end the war either by a single combat between the two of them before both armies, or by engaging an equal number of soldiers picked from either side.

This study of military institutions before the time of David has not taken into account their religious aspect, which will be discussed later.[1] But it must not be forgotten, even now, that the warriors of Israel were upheld by their firm belief that Yahweh fought with them and that he could grant them victory whatever the odds against them (1 S 14: 6; 17: 47).

2. *The professional army*

The enemies of Israel, the Canaanites and the Philistines, had standing armies, including both infantry and charioteers; the soldiers were professional soldiers, some native-born, some foreigners. Such a military organization was incompatible with the spirit and the traditions of the federation of the Twelve Tribes. There were exceptions, of course, but these can be explained. Abimelek recruited mercenaries (Jg 9: 4), but he was only half-Israelite by birth and was scheming to set up a kingdom on the model of the Canaanites.

---

1. Cf. pp. 258-267.

Jephthah, too, collected a band of armed supporters, but this was outside the territory of Israel (Jg 11. 3). Nevertheless, the setbacks encountered in the war against the Philistines proved to the Israelites that wholesale conscription of the nation would not provide a force capable of effective opposition to a professional army; the latter might be the smaller force, but it would be well trained and ready for action at a moment's notice. The creation of a similar army was the work of the first kings of Israel.

(a) *The corps of mercenaries.* Saul began the recruiting of mercenaries: whenever he saw a brave and fearless man, he took him into his service (1 S 14: 52). He preferred, presumably, men from his own tribe, Benjamin (cf. 1 S 22: 7), but he took men from other Israelite tribes also, like David, from Judah (1 S 16: 18f.; 18: 2), and even foreigners, like the Edomite Doeg (1 S 21: 8; 22: 18). They were never very numerous, for they had to be paid (cf. Jg 9: 4), and Saul's kingdom was poor. After breaking with Saul, David recruited mercenaries for himself: he had 400 men at first (1 S 22: 2), and later 600 (1 S 25: 13), with whom he went over into the service of the Philistines (1 S 27: 2). These partisans stayed with him when he became king of Judah and of Israel, and their numbers increased as the victories of David widened his field for recruiting and provided the necessary income to pay them. They came from everywhere: among the Thirty heroes of David (2 S 23: 24-39), whom we shall discuss later,[1] the majority came from Judah and the neighbouring regions, but there was also an Ephraimite, a man from Manasseh, a man from Gad and several foreigners, including an Aramaean from Sobah, an Ammonite, and Uriah the Hittite, the husband of Bathsheba (cf. 2 S 11: 3f.). After conquering the Philistines, David recruited among them and their vassals a corps of K'rethi and P'lethi (2 S 8: 18; 15: 18; 20: 7, 23; 1 K 1: 38, 44). There was also a contingent of 600 men from Gath in Philistia (2 S 15: 18f.). By this policy David was copying an institution of the Canaanite and Philistine principalities. It has recently been suggested that the special term for these mercenaries may have been preserved in the expressions y'lidê ha'anaq (Nb 13: 22, 28; Jos 15: 14) and y'lidê haraphah (2 S 21: 16, 18). The word yalîd would not mean 'descendant', but 'dependent, serf', and would be applied to professional soldiers because they gave up their freedom to enter a military corps, such as the corps of Anaq or of Raphah (the meaning of these words remaining open to investigation).[2] The other uses of the word yalîd, in the expression y'lidê bayth would be a confirmation of this hypothesis: it refers to slaves who have a particular status in the family, and Gn 14: 14 shows they were used for military purposes. The hypothesis is not without interest, but for lack of a sufficient number of clearer texts it cannot be classed as certain.

These mercenaries did not enjoy the rank of free men. They were directly under the king. They were Saul's 'men' (1 S 23: 25-26) or David's 'men'

1. Cf. p. 220.   2. Cf. p. 242.

(1 S 23 *passim*; 24: 3f.; 27: 3, 8, etc.), the servants (*'abadîm*) of Saul (1 S 18: 5, 30; 22: 17) or David (1 S 25: 40; 2 S 2: 17; 3: 22; 11: 9, 11, 13; 18: 7, 9; 20: 6; 1 K 1: 33). The king acknowledged their services by exempting them from taxes or forced labour (1 S 17: 25), by granting them lands, or a claim on tithes (1 S 8: 14-15). When the king died, his mercenaries passed to his heir: thus the 'servants' of Saul became the servants of Ishbaal (2 S 2: 12; 4: 2). They were stationed near the king at Jerusalem under David (2 S 11: 9, 13; 15: 14; 20: 7; 1 K 1: 33).

They formed the royal bodyguard.[1] We cannot say anything precise about its organization, for it seems to have been rather flexible. Apart from the general term ''*abadîm*', and indications of racial origin, the soldiers who composed this bodyguard are referred to by different names, but we do not know the precise relation which these names bear to each other. Saul's (and later David's) personal bodyguard is called, collectively, the *mishma'ath*, meaning, literally, 'those who obey, who answer the call' (1 S 22: 14; 2 S 23: 23). David was its leader under Saul, and Benayahu commanded it under David; but Benayahu was also the leader of *K'rethi* and the *P'lethi* (2 S 8: 18; 20: 23; cf. 1 K 1: 38, 44). The latter seem to constitute the entire bodyguard at the time: they are put alongside the army of the people in 2 S 8: 16; 20: 23, like the *'abadîm* in 2 S 11: 11. On the other hand, the 'champions' (*gibbôrîm*) are mentioned in 2 S 20: 7 alongside the *K'rethi* and the *P'lethi*. But the *gibbôrîm* seem to be the same as the *K'rethi* and the *P'lethi* (2 S 16: 6 compared with 2 S 15: 18, and 1 K 1: 8, 10 compared with 1 K 1: 38, 44), and the *gibbôrîm* alone are mentioned alongside the people's army in 2 S 10: 7.

Among these 'champions' two groups were outstanding for their bravery: the Three, whose leader was Ishbaal (2 S 23: 8-12), and the Thirty, commanded by Abishai (2 S 23: 18 and 24-39). Since the majority of them came from Southern Judah, it is probable that they were the bravest of David's companions in the early days, and that they were formed into a special company of picked men when he was living at Siqlag. (An Egyptian text mentions a 'troop of thirty' among the immediate attendants of Ramses III.)

These soldiers, or a group of them, are sometimes called *n'*arîm*, literally, 'youngsters', but in the military sense of 'cadets'. When David fled for his life, they accompanied him (1 S 21: 3, 5; 25: 5f.) and no one knows precisely what distinguished them from the rest of David's 'men' (1 S 25: 13, 20). Saul too had his cadets (1 S 26: 22). The 'cadets' of David and Ishbaal, Saul's son, faced each other at Gibeon (2 S 2: 14), and they are called the *'abadîm* of David and Ishbaal in the same passage (2 S 2: 12-13). The 'cadets' of 2 S 16: 2 seem to be the same as the soldiers of the guard who accompanied David on his flight, as the mercenaries of 15: 18, and the *gibbôrîm* of 16: 6; cf. also 2 S 4: 12. Later, we meet the 'cadets' of the district commissioners, who were distinct from the national army (1 K 20: 14-19). Although they sometimes acted

1. Cf. p. 123.

as squires or armour-bearers (1 S 20: 21f., 35 f.; 2 S 18: 15), they were not, apparently, young recruits in contrast to veterans, for when the term is to be taken in a strictly military sense, it means simply professional soldiers (cf. also Ne 4: 10). The word had a military sense in Canaanite, and passed into the Egyptian language, where *na'aruna* means an army corps, possibly recruited from Canaan.

Lastly, Saul had *raṣîm*, 'runners' (1 S 22: 17); Doeg the Edomite was probably their commander (21: 8, corrected). They are called *'abadim* and, in this context, figure as men who carry out the king's orders for revenge (like the *n'arîm* in 2 S 4: 12). They were a personal bodyguard, an escort platoon,[1] like the fifty runners who went before Absalom and Adonias when they were affecting a royal retinue (2 S 15: 1; 1 K 1: 5). They are mentioned, perhaps for the same reason, along with the squires (*shalishîm*) in the story of Jehu (2 K 10: 25). They were responsible, together with the Carite mercenaries, for guarding the palace in Jerusalem, which had a room for the 'runners' and a gate called the 'Runners' Gate' (1 K 14: 27-28; 2 K 11: 4, 6, 11, 19). They must therefore have been numerous enough to be divided into companies, or centuries.

Saul used his household troops against the Philistines (1 S 18: 27, 30; cf. 23: 27) and in the pursuit of David (1 S 23: 25f.), but the professional army did not really show its capabilities until the reign of David. He used his mercenaries for the capture of Jerusalem (2 S 5: 6) and to defeat the Philistines (2 S 5: 21; 21: 15) and daring feats of his champions became the subject of a story (2 S 21: 15-22; 23: 8-23). These professional troops formed a special command, and remained distinct from the contingents which Israel and Judah furnished in times of emergency. In the list of David's officials there are two soldiers: Joab is commander of the army, and Benayahu is commander of the Kerethites and Pelethites, that is, of the household troops (2 S 8: 16, 18; 20: 23). The detailed account of the Ammonite War throws light on the relationship between the two forces: both the household troops and all Israel are sent into action (2 S 11: 1), but during the investment of Rabbah of the Ammonites, Israel and Judah camp in huts while the guards sleep in the open country (11: 11); attacks are launched by the guards (11: 14-17; 12: 26) and the contingents of Israel and Judah are held in reserve until the final assault (12: 29). The same tactics are used in the Aramaean wars of Achab: the 'cadets' of the district commissioners, professional soldiers, are sent off first to launch the offensive, and then Israel (*i.e.* the national army) comes up in support and gives chase to the enemy (1 K 20: 15-20).

This last text reminds us that the professional army continued in existence long after the reign of David. We have already referred to the 'runners' of Roboam (1 K 14: 27-28) and of Jehu (2 K 10: 25), and to the 'runners' and the Carites under Athaliah (2 K 11: 4). The forts built by Roboam were

1. Cf. p. 123-124.

undoubtedly manned by professional soldiers (2 Ch 11: 11-12). Again, 2 Ch 25: 6f. states that Amasias, king of Judah, recruited mercenaries in Israel, and the Annals of Sennacherib mention the auxiliaries of Ezechias who deserted during the siege of 701 B.C. This is the last unquestionable reference to these mercenary troops.

(b) *The chariotry*. When the Israelites were still consolidating their position in the Promised Land, they had to contend with the war-chariots of the Canaanites and of the Philistines (Jos 17: 16-18; Jg 1: 19; 4: 13; 1 S 13: 5; 2 S 1: 6), for, from about 1500 B.C., chariotry had become the essential, and sometimes the principal, arm in the military forces of the Near East. It was first introduced by the Indo-Europeans who helped to build the state of Mitanni in Northern Mesopotamia; they were men skilled in breeding horses, and in the art of making light but strong two-wheeled chariots. The new weapon was quickly copied by the Hittites, and was soon adopted throughout Mesopotamia, Egypt and Syria-Palestine. Every little Canaanite state had its chariots and its charioteers, and they were known by the Indo-European name of *maryannu*. The Philistines and the other 'Peoples of the Sea' who lived along the coast of Palestine soon had their charioteers, too, and the new Aramaean states which were just coming into being in Syria could not afford to be without chariots either.

To set up and to maintain a chariot corps was an expensive undertaking, and in the early days the Israelites were poor; hence they were unable to adopt this new and important weapon for some time. After his victory over the Aramaeans at Sobah, David had the captured chariot horses hamstrung (cf. Jos 11: 6-9; 2 S 10: 18); he kept only one hundred of them (2 S 8: 4). He may have acted in the same way when he annexed Canaanite cities, and in this way he may have built up a small chariot force for his own use; but if he did, the chariot force must have been very unimportant compared with his foot-soldiers, for it is never once mentioned in the accounts of his campaigns. On the other hand, we do find that both Absalom and Adonias, when each was plotting for the throne, drove out in a chariot, with runners going before them (2 S 15: 1; 1 K 1: 5).

Solomon's great military innovation was the establishment of a strong chariot force. This force quite overshadowed the mercenary foot-soldiers, who are never once mentioned in his reign. They were not disbanded, but they were relegated to a secondary position, so that the situation was exactly the reverse of what had obtained in David's reign. Since Solomon had not made any conquests himself, he must have raised this chariot force from the money in the exchequer. The text of 1 K 10: 28-29 is far from plain, but it seems that the king bought chariots in Egypt (where they made excellent ones) and horses in Cilicia (which had a reputation for stud-farms). As a result, he had 1,400 chariots and 12,000 horses, according to 1 K 10: 26. The number of chariots is quite feasible: at the battle of Qarqar, in 835 B.C.,

Achab, king of Israel, put into the field 2,000 chariots, and the king of Damascus, 1,200. The number of horses, however, seems too high: reliefs, paintings, and non-biblical texts inform us that each chariot had three horses attached, two in harness and one in reserve. The number 12,000 may have originated in a tradition which estimated that Solomon could put 4,000 chariots into the field (2 Ch 9: 25; cf. the gloss on 1 K 5: 6).

These troops were quartered in Jerusalem, where there was a 'Horses Gate' (2 K 11: 16) and in the 'Chariot towns' (1 K 10: 26). These 'Towns for chariots and horses' or garrison towns, are listed in 1 K 9: 15-19: Hazor, Megiddo, Gezer, Lower Beth-Horon, Baalath, Tamar. Fortified by conscripts of the national labour forces (1 K 9: 15), these places formed a defence network which straddled the main roads leading to the heart of the kingdom, and all lay close to level country where the chariots could manoeuvre. Of these towns, at least the first four were formerly royal cities of the Canaanites, which had once possessed their own chariot force: Solomon was continuing a tradition. Solomon's prefects organized the supplies of corn and fodder for this force (1 K 5: 8). Excavations at Megiddo have shown what these 'chariot towns' looked like: part of the town was given over to enormous stables with a separate stall for each horse. In the middle was an open courtyard with drinking troughs; the courtyard was used to exercise and to train the horses. The stables discovered at Megiddo could hold 450 horses.

In Egyptian chariots, there were two riders, one to hold the reins and one to fight; Hittite chariots had a driver, a combatant and an armour bearer, but in the Neo-Hittite states the number was reduced to two. In Assyria, at the time of the Israelite monarchy, the team had three men; this number was raised to four at some date between Tiglath-Pileser III and Assurbanipal, but afterwards they reverted to a three-man team. The 'third' was called, in Assyrian, shalshu(rakbu) or tashlishu. Israelite chariots also carried three men, the driver (called simply rakkab or 'charioteer' in 1 K 22: 34), the combatant and the 'third' (shalish: 1 K 9: 22; 2 K 10: 25). The king's armour-bearer or squire enjoyed a special rank and was rather like an aide-de-camp.[1]

When the kingdom was split after the death of Solomon, the principal chariot garrisons (Hazor, Megiddo, Gezer and probably Lower Beth-Horon) fell into the hands of the Israelites. Judah had very few chariot troops left, and we do not know whether Roboam posted any in the new towns he fortified. Nevertheless, the horses of Judah fought side by side with those of Israel in the war against Moab (2 K 3: 7), and Joram had chariots which were defeated by the Edomites (2 K 8: 21). The chariot force of Judah seems to have been increased in the eighth century, when Isaias says: 'Its land is full of horses, and of chariots too numerous to count' (Is 2: 7), and curses those who place their trust in horses and a large chariot force (Is 31: 1; cf. 30: 16; Mi 1: 13; 5: 9). These armaments came from Egypt, where Judah had once more

1. Cf. p. 122.

turned in quest of an ally (Is 31: 1-3), and Isaias seems to be condemning this recourse to armaments as something new. The country did not benefit thereby, for in 701 Sennacherib captured every town in Judah except Jerusalem without fighting a single battle in which chariots were engaged. It seems that chariot troops were never again raised after this time. The only witness is the text of 2 Ch 35: 24, more detailed and unquestionably more exact than the parallel in 2 K 23: 30: when Josias was wounded at Megiddo, they took him out of his chariot and carried him to Jerusalem in his 'second chariot'. It shows that the king had two chariots at his disposal, but it does not prove that there was a chariot corps.

The greater part of Solomon's chariotry fell to the kingdom of Israel, where Canaanite traditions still persisted; consequently, mounted troops retained a greater measure of importance. Under Elah, they were divided into two corps, one of which was commanded by Zimri (1 K 16: 9). According to the Annals of Shalmaneser III, 2,000 Israelite chariots took part in the battle of Qarqar, but the reverse suffered in the Aramaean wars weakened this branch of the army very considerably. There were still some chariots at Samaria (2 K 7: 13; 10: 2), though not very many (cf. 2 K 7: 6), and at the most critical moment in these struggles, Joachaz had only ten chariots left (2 K 13: 7). The losses were never made good: Sargon of Assyria, who boasted that he captured 300 chariots at Hamath, gained only 50 by his conquest of Samaria.

About 1000 B.C. mounted cavalry made its first timid appearance in the Near East, though it had long been used among certain Northern peoples and was to remain the principal fighting arm of the Scythians. Warriors on horseback are represented on the bas-reliefs of Tell Halaf at the beginning of the ninth century B.C., and some elements of cavalry were introduced into the Assyrian army about the same time; but troops in chariots still preponderated. The Egyptian army never had any cavalry except for mounted scouts. Nor did the Israelites; Sennacherib's envoy made the ironical proposal to Ezechias that he would give him 2,000 horses if he could find horsemen to ride them (2 K 18:23). In the stories of the monarchical period, the term *parashîm*, often translated 'horsemen' or 'cavalry', means either chariot teams or the men who rode in chariots. Sometimes men did jump on horseback to flee more quickly (1 K 20: 20; Is 30: 16; Am 2: 15). Moreover, horsemen could be used as scouts or despatch riders, as in Egypt (2 K 9: 17f.; cf. Za 1: 8-11). The description of the war-horse given in Jb 39: 19-25 is inspired by foreign customs, and the horsemen referred to in Ez 23: 6, 12 (Assyrians), 38: 4 (the army of Gog), Esd 8: 22 and Ne 2: 9 (Persians) are all foreigners. These texts, moreover, date from after the fall of the monarchy. Much later, in the early Maccabean wars, the Jews could field only infantry against the powerful Greek cavalry and elephant mounts (1 M 1: 17; 6: 30f.; 8: 6; 2 M 11: 4; 13: 2, 15). The accounts of the defeat at Bethzacharia (1 M 6: 29-47) and of

Jonathan's victory over Apollonius (1 M 10: 73–83) are particularly significant. A corps of Jewish cavalry appears for the first time under Simon in 136/135 B.C., but it was still very small (1 M 16: 4, 7). Herod had 30,000 infantrymen in his army, but only 6,000 cavalry.

3. The conscript army

We have seen that, in all probability, the mercenary and mounted troops of the kingdom of Judah were not re-formed after the events of 701 B.C.: they were too costly to maintain. Instead, the territory secured its freedom, and later defended itself, with an army of conscripts. These are the only soldiers mentioned in the accounts of the capture of Jerusalem by Nabuchodonosor. We hear nothing of mercenaries or chariots, but only of 'men of war' ('anshê (ham)milḥamah, in 2 K 25: 4, 19; Jr 38: 4, or 'osê milḥamah, 2 K 24: 16). It is true that officers and their men are spoken of (2 K 25: 23f.; Jr 40: 7f., and also in the ostraka from Lakish), but these soldiers, or 'men of war', are men of Judah who had been called to arms and who would return to their homes and the fields after the war (Jr 40: 10).

According to 2 K 25: 19 Nabuchodonosor took prisoner a high ranking official, a sarîs,[1] 'set over the men of war'; perhaps he was a commander-in-chief, or a civilian in charge of the administration of the army, i.e. a minister of national defence, for the supreme command was exercised by the king himself. Among the prisoners there was also a scribe (sôpher), 'charged to enlist the people of the country'. This text should be compared with 2 Ch 26: 11, where we are told that a register of the army of Ozias was made under the secretary Yeiel and a shôṭer or clerk, named Maaseyahu.

According to Dt 20: 5–9 there were several shôṭrîm, who were responsible for recruiting, obviously in different districts. The same text makes provision for a certain number of men who are to be exempted: those who own a new and as yet unoccupied house, or a vineyard which has not yielded its first harvest, and men who are engaged but have not yet married: according to Dt 24: 5, newly-weds had a deferment for one year. The dismissal of the faint-hearted (Dt 20: 8) is perhaps an addition inspired by Jg 7: 3. (The same rules were applied by Judas Maccabee when he raised the liberation army, 1 M 3: 56.) Mobilization affected everyone aged 20 or over (2 Ch 25: 5; cf. Nb 1: 3; 26: 2). Enrolment was by family groups, and therefore by localities (2 Ch 17: 14; 25: 5), and a distinction was drawn between the contingents from Judah and those from Benjamin (2 Ch 17: 14-17; 25: 5). The recruits did not bring their own arms, as in olden times; they were provided by the king (2 Ch 26: 14).

After enlistment, the men were put under the command of their officers (sarîm: Dt 20: 9). The latter were normally the heads of families or clans, the

1. Cf. p. 121. 2. Cf. p. 155.

rô'shê ha'abôth (2 Ch 26: 12). The structure of the army and its efficiency in the field, however, necessitated a corps of professional officers permanently in the service of the king; they were part of his *'abadîm* or *śarîm* (2 K 24: 12, 14; Jr 52: 10; cf. 2 Ch 26: 11). The king remained, as in the time of Saul and David, the supreme head of the army and took an active part in operations (1 K 22: 29; 2 K 3: 9; 14: 11; 23: 29; 25: 4-5), even though he might (again like David) have a general to command his troops (2 Ch 26: 11; perhaps 2 K 25: 19).

The units were composed of 1,000, 100, 50 and 10 men. This organization dated back to the desert period, according to Ex 18: 21 and Dt 1: 15. Perhaps Ishbaal, who came with ten men to assassinate Godolias just after the fall of Jerusalem, was a leader of a group of ten (Jr 41: 1, 2; cf. 15). Leaders of fifty men are mentioned in the story of Elias (2 K 1: 9, 11, 13). The commanders of one hundred and of a thousand men are listed in the statistics of 2 Ch 25: 5, and the same organization of the conscript army dated back to the period of David, according to 1 Ch 27: 1. The last statement, however, is not wholly arbitrary, for units of one hundred and of a thousand men were already in existence when the entire people used to take up arms (1 S 22: 7; 17: 18) and among the mercenary troops (2 K 11: 4).

Except for these names which indicate numbers, the words used for army units are of uncertain meaning. According to 2 Ch 26: 11, the army was divided into *gᵉdûd*. In other passages the word means a troop of armed men, often brigands (1 S 30: 8f.; 2 K 13: 20, etc.), or sometimes (and the meaning is closely allied), soldiers sent on a raid into enemy territory (2 K 5: 2; 6: 23; 24: 2), and thirdly (and this meaning is not very unlike the others), a troop of mercenaries (2 S 4: 2; 2 Ch 25: 9; cf. 13). The use of the word in 2 Ch 26: 11 to denote the formations of the conscript army is quite exceptional. If it is a legitimate use, then it may be noted that the proportion between officers and soldiers in 2 Ch 26: 12-13 would give each officer roughly 120 men to command: the *gᵉdûd* or 'company' would be roughly equivalent to a hundred men. The *degel* seems to have been a higher unit. This word does not mean a standard or ensign, as so many modern dictionaries and translations interpret it, but a division of the army. This is the right meaning in Nb 1: 52; 2: 2-34; 10: 14-25; it is also the sense given by the ancient versions, and it is used with this meaning in the papyri of Elephantine and in the Order of the War from Qumran. The only questionable point is the size of this unit. In the Qumran text, the *degel* comprises about 1,000 men, but in the Elephantine documents it must be smaller, for there were several *dᵉgalîm* in the colony. On the other hand, according to Nb 2 and 10, the men of the twelve tribes formed only four *dᵉgallîm* and even if we do not accept the colossal figures which are cited in Nb 2, each *degel* must have included several thousand men. Another argument in support of this theory is the use of 'a thousand' for *mishpaḥah*.[1]

1. Cf. p. 216.

If *degel* means a 'division', there is little evidence left for the existence of standards or ensigns in the Israelite army. In one text only, Nb 2: 2, the word *'oth* ('sign, signal, miraculous sign') may mean the emblem or standard around which men of the same clan camped; there are good parallels to this custom among the Bedouin, but there is no certain evidence for the use of the word in the sense of military ensign except in the Dead Sea Scrolls, where it may be a translation of the Latin *signum*. The *nes*, often translated 'banner', is not really an ensign, but a pole or mast, which was raised on a hill to give the signal to take up arms or to rally together (Is 5: 26; 11: 10, 12; 13: 2; 18: 3; Jr 4: 6; 50: 2; 51: 12, 27; cf. Ex 17: 15); but apart from these references in the prophets, the word is never used in texts concerning the army or in accounts of battles. The same custom exists among the Arabs, and only a few years ago, when a surveyor named Schumacher was making topographical surveys in Galilee, he brought about the mobilization of a neighbouring tribe by fixing a sighting picket on the top of a hill. The main argument in favour of ensigns in the army of ancient Israel is that all the Eastern armies had ensigns at the time; but the ensigns of other nations were usually religious emblems, and this may have been the reason which dissuaded the Israelites from copying them. We may note, however, that at the beginning of the monarchic period, the Ark of the Covenant played a similar role; we shall return to this later.[1]

This national army was never called to arms except in time of war. But when the mercenaries had fallen in numbers, or perhaps even ceased to exist, probably a certain number of recruits were kept under arms in peace-time to ensure the security of the territory and to garrison the fortresses. Information however, is lacking, and anyone should be wary of using the text of 1 Ch 27: 1-15, which says that David divided the people into twelve classes of 24,000 men, each of which did service for the king for one month of the year. The figures quoted are too high, and the names of the commanders of these classes are the names of David's champions, who had quite a different function. The information certainly does not date back to the reign of David, but, if we suppress the figures and the names, it may have been true of a later epoch. On the other hand, the idea may have originated with the Chronicler himself, drawing his inspiration from Solomon's twelve prefectures, each of which supported the king, his household and his troops for a month of each year (1 K 5: 7-8).

One recent suggestion is that the conscript army was an innovation of Josias, and that the notes scattered throughout Chronicles, which have been used in the last few pages, should all be referred to this age. This conclusion is unfounded. It is perfectly true that the mercenary troops had lost their importance, that they may even have ceased to exist towards the end of the monarchy, and that the conscript army (alone, it appears) ensured the defence

1. Cf. p. 259.

of the country during these times. But this same conscript army was already in existence, years before, alongside the mercenary troops. During the Aramaean wars, a census was made of the entire 'people' as well as of the 'youngsters' or 'cadets' (1 K 2: 15, cf. 19). The people of Israel and the people of Judah were involved in the alliance between Josaphat and Achab (1 K 22: 4), and in that between Joram and the king of Judah (2 K 3: 7). Thus the tradition of a people under arms persisted, but the mass response to a call from a leader inspired by God had given place to mobilization organized by the royal administration. The first indication of this development can be seen as early as David's reign: his census (2 S 24: 1-9) had a military purpose and was equivalent to drawing up a register for conscription, but this step was condemned as an abandonment of the rules of a holy war, and a profanation (cf. verses 3 and 10). Putting names on a register was seen as a usurpation of a divine prerogative: Yahweh alone keeps the register of those who are to live or to die (Ex 32: 32-33); a census is a move fraught with danger, against which one must take religious precautions. The new texts from Mari throw light on passages from the Bible such as this: 'When you make a census of the Israelites, each one of them must pay Yahweh the ransom-price of his life, so that no plague may break out against them on the occasion of the census' (Ex 30: 12). David, by disregarding this right of God's, brought a plague down on the people (2 S 24: 10-15). War, however, was becoming a non-religious matter, and the system of conscription forced itself upon them in the end. There is no reason to doubt that military registrations took place under Asa (2 Ch 14: 7), Josaphat (2 Ch 17: 14-18), Amasias (2 Ch 25: 5), and Ozias (2 Ch 26: 11-13); certain details show that the Chronicler has made use of ancient sources. Yet no one will deny that he has introduced into his text figures which are improbably high.

Chapter Two

FORTIFIED CITIES AND SIEGE WARFARE

THE ancient cities of Canaan, each of which was the centre of a tiny State, were encircled by ramparts and defended by towers and fortified gates. The Egyptian illustrations of campaigns under the Pharaohs of the New Empire give a picture of what they looked like, and excavations in Palestine allow us to study the plan of these defences and the techniques employed in their construction. It is understandable that these heavily fortified towns struck fear into the Israelite invaders (Nb 13: 28), for their ramparts reached 'to the sky' (Dt 1: 28); they were 'strongholds enclosed by high walls, protected by gates and bars' (Dt 3: 5). After their conquest or occupation of these towns, the Israelites took care to rebuild the defences (though archaeological evidence of this begins only at the reign of Saul); they preserved intact the parts which remained, and repaired them if necessary. Where the destruction had been complete, they rebuilt the ramparts in new ways, and they applied these new methods in the towns they themselves founded. These latter fortifications, replanned or erected by the Israelites, are the only ones which interest us here.

1. Fortified towns

Every town ('ir) was normally encircled by a rampart, which distinguished it from an open village (haser, cf. Lv 25: 31). But a town which was defended by solid constructions was called a 'fortified town' ('ir mibṣar: cf. Jr 34: 7 and many other texts).

The entire population of the neighbourhood would seek protection behind these defences in times of danger (Jr 4: 5; 8: 14). Lists of strongholds and isolated references to them occur in the Old Testament; but though these texts throw some light on the system of protecting the territory, the information is incomplete, and applies only to certain periods.

David's first objective after the capture of Jerusalem was to build a wall around it (2 S 5: 9): we should take it to mean that he merely repaired the Jebusite ramparts. The Bible mentions no similar work outside the capital during his reign, but it is quite certain that he secured the defences of other places as well, and archaeologists attribute to him the building of the ramparts at Tell Beit-Mirsim and at Beth Shemesh. Solomon's chariot garrisons[1] were obviously quartered in fortified towns, and at Megiddo, archaeologists have found a gate and rampart contemporary with the stables.

One passage of Chronicles, which has no parallel in the books of Kings, gives a list of fifteen places fortified by Roboam (2 Ch 11: 6-10). There is no good reason for assigning this text to the age of Josias, as some authors have proposed. It is sound historical information, recording a fact which is relevant in the reign of Roboam: the campaign of the Pharaoh Sheshonq in Palestine (1 K 14: 25) had proved that the country needed to reinforce its defences. A line of fortified towns guarded the ridge road running from the south towards Jerusalem, and dominated the Eastern desert: Jerusalem, Bethlehem, Etham, Teqoa, Bethsur, Hebron, Ziph. From Ziph to the west, the southern front was protected by Adorayim, Lakish and Gath. Northwards from Gath, the principal passes into the hill-country of Judah were closed on the western side by: (1) Gath, Mareshah; (2) Azeqah, Soko, Adullam; (3) Soreah; (4) Ayyalon. These fortresses were not strung out along the frontiers of the kingdom, but built along routes where resistance was practicable, and at the most favourable strategic points; the list is probably incomplete, for it mentions only the new ones built by Roboam, without counting the towns which David and Solomon had fortified and which were still in existence.

The northern front still lay open, for the boundary between the new kingdoms of Israel and Judah was at first undecided. Basha of Israel attempted to fortify Ramah, about six miles north of Jerusalem, but Asa of Judah drove him out and brought his own frontier forward to Geba in Benjamin and to Mispah, which he equipped for defence (1 K 15: 17-22). He restored other strongholds in Judah, too, according to 1 K 15: 23 and 2 Ch 14: 5-6. They were still in commission under Josaphat, who posted troops in them (2 Ch 17: 2, 19; 19: 5). Ozias, in addition to his work at Jerusalem (2 Ch 26: 9), built forts in the desert and improved the methods of defence (2 Ch 26: 10 and 15); we shall return to these last texts further on.

Besides rebuilding its chariot force, Judah 'built many strongholds' (Os 8: 14), in the eighth century[2]; Sennacherib boasted that he had besieged and captured 46 fortified towns in Judah. The biblical account, too, states that Sennacherib attacked the fortresses in Judah and captured them (2 K 18: 13), mentioning Lakish and Libnah by name (2 K 18: 17 and 19: 8); it was only by a miracle that Jerusalem itself was saved. (A most interesting Assyrian bas-relief is extant which does in fact represent the capture of Lakish by Sennacherib.) We do not know to what extent the destruction caused by the Assyrians was ever made good. The defence work undertaken at Jerusalem by Ezechias (2 Ch 32: 5; cf. Is 22: 9-11) was continued by Manasseh (2 Ch 33: 14), and there is no reason to doubt this precise information of the Chronicler. We know for certain that shortly before the

1. Cf. p. 223.   2. Cf. p. 223.

final ruin of the kingdom of Judah, the people placed its trust in strongholds (Jr 5: 17) and that, during the siege of Jerusalem, two cities, Lakish and Azeqah, were still holding out against Nabuchodonosor (Jr 34: 7); these two places are also mentioned in an ostrakon found at Lakish and written at the very time.

After their victory the Chaldeans razed to the ground the fortifications of Jerusalem (2 K 25: 10) and of every town in Judah (Lm 2: 2, 5), and archaeological evidence confirms this. The walls of Jerusalem were not rebuilt until the time of Nehemias, and those of other towns, like Gezer and Bethsur, not until the Hellenistic period.

The Bible gives us very little information about the northern kingdom. Jeroboam I fortified Shechem and Penuel in Transjordan (1 K 12: 25). We have already mentioned the abortive enterprise of Basha at Ramah (1 K 15: 17f.). Under Achab, Jericho was rebuilt and fortified with a gate (1 K 16: 34). In his letter to the leading men of Samaria (2 K 10: 2) Jehu writes that they have on their side a 'strong place'. The Massoretic text is often corrected to the plural 'strong places', but there is no doubt that the singular should be retained; he is referring to Samaria alone. Samaria had powerful defences, as is proved by the long sieges it withstood (1 K 20: 1f.; 2 K 6: 24f.; 17: 5; 18: 9–10), and excavations have confirmed the fact. Outside the Bible, the stele of Mesha speaks of the towns of Ataroth and of Yahas as 'built' (i.e fortified) in Moab by Omri and Achab. The penury of biblical information is due to the Judahite origin of the historical books, and should not mislead us: there is no doubt that the northern kingdom had a defence system just as elaborate as Judah's.

As long as the chariot force and the mercenaries existed, these professional soldiers provided the garrisons of strongholds, but we do not know how the staffing was organized. We know only that Josaphat stationed troops in the fortified towns of Judah and that there were at Jerusalem a garrison and an officers' corps to form the backbone of the conscript army (cf. 2 Ch 17: 2, 13b 19) The numbers quoted are fantastic, but, these apart, the information may stem from an ancient source. According to 2 Ch 33: 14, Manasseh posted officers in the fortified towns of Judah; but there is no mention of troops being sent with them. This, however, is after the destruction of the military power of Judah by Sennacherib, and it is possible that in these last days of the monarchy the garrisons of the strongholds were reduced to token forces; they would employ forced labour (following the very old and extreme example cited in 1 K 15: 22) to keep the defences in good repair, and in times of crisis, they would man them with defenders raised on the spot.

It has been argued from 1 Ch 27: 1-15 that the strongholds were held by contingents of conscripts who served by turns for one month of each year, but the meaning and value of this text are far from certain (cf. p. 227).

2. Ramparts

Archaeology contributes to a better understanding of the biblical evidence by revealing the lay-out and the construction of defences. We have mentioned that the Israelites refitted some of the old Canaanite fortifications: apart from these, two distinct types of Israelite ramparts can be distinguished, casemated ramparts, and ramparts with redans.

A casemated rampart is a wall along which stand blind rooms, which used to be filled with earth or rubble, or which served as stores. The purpose of these rooms is to widen the rampart, and thereby to strengthen it, while economizing in building by furnishing the store-rooms necessary for any garrison town. Splendid examples of this type have been brought to light at Tell Beit-Mirsim (the ancient Debir), and at Beth Shemesh, both dating from the reign of David or Solomon; similar ones have been discovered at Tell Qasileh, near Jaffa (going back to the first Israelite occupation, probably under Solomon), at Hazor and at Gezer (also from the time of Solomon). This type of fortification seems to have originated in Asia Minor: there is evidence of it at Boghazkoi and at Mersin in the 14th-13th century B.C., and, at a slightly later date, in the fortresses of Senjirli and Charchemish. In Palestine, it was generally replaced by the type with redans, but a magnificent specimen of casemated rampart is still to be seen at Samaria in the palace walls, which must have been built by Achab in the ninth century B.C. Another casemated rampart, also from this period, has recently been uncovered at Ramath Rachel, just south of Jerusalem.

In building their ramparts, Canaanite architects were anxious to follow as closely as possible the escarpment of the hill; consequently, they would often follow a curved line, or break the straight line of the walls; they thus obtained a series of redans. This procedure was adopted as a principle in certain Israelite fortifications, even when the configuration of the terrain did not demand it. The most obvious reason was to provide a series of salients which would give more effective defence against an enemy which had come close to the walls. But these salients were sometimes so unimpressive that they hardly increased the range of weapons at all; clearly, the main advantage of the process was to strengthen the rampart without increasing its thickness: several angles well knit together and firmly anchored in the soil offered more resistance to the rams or to the undermining techniques used by assailants. Megiddo is a very fine example, probably later than Solomon: the entire town was encircled by a rampart four yards wide, divided into stretches six yards long, which are placed, alternately, half a yard forward and half a yard back. The rampart of Tell en-Nasbeh= Mispah follows the same design, but it is less regular: it may be dated to the time of Asa, who fortified Mispah (1 K 15: 22). There is a similar plan at Tell ed-Duweir= Lakish. These walls with redans were reinforced here and there by towers: there are a dozen of them at Mispah. At Gezer, along a rampart of the tenth or ninth century, the exterior and interior redans do not correspond, but go in opposite directions, which gives a series of reinforcements, of wide towers, all along the rampart. These flanking constructions, salients or towers, were called 'angles' or 'corners' (pinnah, 2 Ch 26: 15; So 1: 16; 3: 6).

Ramparts of this kind could be protected by a glacis, which would put to good use the slope of the hill (as at Mispah), or by a forward wall built some distance below (as at Lakish). This forward wall is the ḥel spoken of in Is 26: 1; Lm 2: 8; Na 3: 8, in contrast to the ḥômah or rampart. The text of 2 S 20: 15-16 is eloquent, and needs no correcting: during the siege of Abel Beth-Maaka, they heaped up an embankment on the forward wall (ḥel) and began tunnelling to bring down the rampart (ḥômah).

We do not know the shape of the top of these walls. On the basis of a find at Megiddo, it has been suggested that they were surmounted by crenelated battlements—a view which could claim the support of some Assyrian representations; but the connection of the stonework found at Megiddo with the rampart is only a hypothesis. The word shemesh could mean 'crenel' in Is 54: 12; Ps 84: 12, but it can also mean (from its ordinary sense of 'sun'), round shields, rondaches, which were fixed on the top of the walls. They are shown on the top of the rampart in the Assyrian bas-relief of the capture of Lakish. We may compare with this Ez 27: 11: 'They hung their shields all around thy walls', and Ct 4: 4: 'Thy neck is like the tower of David . . . a thousand shields are hung around it.'

All the Israelite fortifications which have so far been uncovered by excavations were built in the first half of the monarchical period, between 1100 and 900 B.C., and it is difficult to lay down any characteristics for ramparts of the following period. In some towns, e.g. in the two capitals and in the garrison towns, as long as there were any, the Israelites kept the defences in good repair, but elsewhere they allowed them to deteriorate. Men were happy enough with the indifferent protection afforded by the half-ruined ramparts or by the line of houses built over their ruins; the houses would be squeezed against each other, with no windows on the outside. Only a few strong points were retained, such as the gates, or a tower or bastion. The majority of the '46 fortified towns' of Judah which Sennacherib captured in 701 must have been just as feebly defended, and archaeology does not justify (no more than history did) the confidence which the men of Judah placed in their 'countless strong places' during the eighth century (Os 8: 14; Jr 5: 17).

3. Fortified gates and citadels

The gate was fortified in a special way. In Canaanite towns, the gate with tenailles was a classical type: two or three pairs of pilasters protruding in the bay made narrows (tenailles) in the entry. The object was to strengthen the walls and to establish successive barriers. The Israelites kept this type of gate in service, with or without modification, at Beth Shemesh, Shechem, Megiddo and Tirsah, and themselves built a few similar ones at the beginning of the monarchical period. Very soon, however, their pilasters began to protrude far more than the Canaanite ones had done, and so formed small rooms at the entry where the guards could lodge. Solomon's gate at Megiddo is a very fine example; it had four pairs of pilasters, though this is exceptional; an identical plan, from the same period, was adopted at Hazor and Gezer also. (Note that Ezechiel foresees the same plan being used in the porches of the Temple, cf. Ez 40: 6-16). The gate of Esyon Geber, also from Solomon's reign, had three pairs of pilasters, and the first Israelite gate at Tell ed-Duweir perhaps had three as well. In the following period, the gate of Megiddo had only two pairs, like that at Tell en-Nasbeh and the oldest gate at Tell Beit-Mirsim. Sometimes, as at Tell en-Nasbeh, in the modified gate at the northern Tell el-Far'ah (= Tirsah), and later at Tell ed-Duweir, benches were fixed against the wall: this at once brings to mind the biblical texts about the Elders 'who sat at the gate' to give judgement in law suits or to settle municipal affairs.[1]

As a rule, the gate was flanked by towers, either at each side or jutting out in front, and sometimes there was yet another bastion before it with a preliminary entry, as at Megiddo. The axis of the gate generally ran at right angles to the rampart, but at Tell en-Nasbeh it runs parallel, and you entered through a wide detour in the line of fortifications.

Towards the end of the monarchy, another type of gate appears, a gate with indirect access: it had been foreshadowed in the Solomonian gate at Megiddo. A good example of this type of gate has been discovered at Tell ed-Duweir: a bastion covered the entry, and you had first to walk along the rampart until you entered a courtyard; from here a simple right turn took you through the ordinary gate which stood open in the town wall. Further development led to a zigzag gate, one example of which is the last gate of Tell Beit-Mirsim; it reappears in far later times in Eastern towns.

In addition to the defences provided by the fortified gates and by the towers on the rampart, the capital cities had a second surrounding wall and bastions which shut off the royal palace and its outbuildings; it was the acropolis of the town. The clearest example is in Samaria, where a casemated wall flanked by a massive tower surrounds the palace with its arsenals and stores. Jerusalem had the equivalent in the City of David, which was the former citadel of Sion (2 S 5: 7 and 9). Rabbah of the Ammonites had its acropolis, too, which David stormed after Joab had captured the lower city (2 S 12: 26-29). Other towns had at least a citadel built on the highest point, and the citizens would gather there for their last resistance. Excavations have uncovered some which date from the Israelite period, but unfortunately they

1. Cf. pp. 152-153.

are badly damaged. The oldest is at Tell el-Ful = Gibeah, Saul's capital; it was a rectangular building, with a casemated wall and towers at the corners. Others can be recognized at Tell Zakariyah = Azeqah, at Tell el-Hesy = Eglon(?), and at Tell Ta'annak = Tanak. The plan is always polygonal, with small towers and buttresses to reinforce the walls.

These fortifications inside a town are called by the name *migdal*. The term is usually translated 'tower', and in fact it does denote towers or bastions raised on or near the ramparts in Jr 31: 38; 2 Ch 14: 6; 26: 9, 15; 32: 5; Ne 3: 1, 11, 25—all late texts. In older texts, however, the word *migdal* is better rendered by 'citadel' or 'castle', in the sense of the Latin *castellum*. This explains the story about Abimelek at Tebes: the town had been captured, but 'inside the town there was a redoubtable *migdal* where all the men and women and the leading figures in the town had taken refuge, etc.' (Jg 9: 50f.). There is no doubt that we should interpret the more difficult story of the destruction of Shechem, which comes immediately before this (Jg 9: 45-49), in the light of this text: the town had been taken, but the inmates of the *migdal* of Shechem took refuge in the crypt of the temple of Baal-berith, where, in the end, they were burned alive; this *migdal* is the citadel of Shechem, with a fortified temple, and it has been cleared by excavations at Tell Balata, the site of ancient Shechem. It has been suggested, however, that Migdal-Shechem is a place-name, and that the place was distinct from Shechem. Similar 'castles' are mentioned at Penuel (Jg 8: 9 and 17) and at Yizreel (2 K 9: 17).

The sense 'castles' (Latin *castella*) would also give a good meaning for the *migdalîm* which Ozias and Yotham built in the desert (2 Ch 26: 10; 2 Ch 27: 4). One of those little forts, perhaps even earlier than Ozias' time, is recognizable at Qedeirat near Qadesh; its plan reminds us of the citadels at Tell Zachariyah and at Tell el-Ful. Another has recently been identified at Khirbet Ghazza, about 20 miles east of Beersheba. This provides an explanation of place-names composed with *migdal*: they would be little places grouped around a small citadel. (One might compare the French place-names compounded with Château, Châtel- or Castel-.) When the second element is a divine name, such as Migdal-El or Migdal-Gad, this 'castle' would be a fortified temple, like that of Baal-berith in Shechem.

Yotham built *migdalîm* and *bîraniyyôth* (2 Ch 27: 4). The two words seem to be almost synonymous, the latter being a more modern word (cf. 2 Ch 17: 12). For example, in later texts the singular *bîrah* takes the place of *migdal* when the reference is to a citadel inside a town: thus it is used of the citadel of Jerusalem under Nehemias (Ne 2: 8; 7: 2) and the same term is used abroad for the citadel or for the whole of the fortified town of Susa (Ne 1: 1; Dn 8: 2 and frequently in Est) and for the fortress of Ecbatane (Esd 6: 2 *bîrta'*, the Aramaic form).

In the palaces at Tirsah and Samaria, there was a more heavily fortified part called the *'armôn* (1 K 16: 18; 2 K 15: 25): it was the keep. In the plural, the word means the fortified dwellings in Jerusalem (Jr 17: 27; Lm 2: 7; Ps 48: 4, 14; 122: 7) or elsewhere (Am 1: 4, 12; 2: 2, 5, etc.).

4. Siege warfare

Ramparts and bastions gave towns effective protection against assailants whose only long-range weapons were bows and slings. The latter had to resort to stratagems or to resign themselves to the prospect of a siege.

Stratagem is the method which figures in the accounts of the conquest. Josue sent spies to reconnoitre the defences of Jericho; the spies made contact with Rahab, and agreed on a sign (Jos 2): this story is apparently all that remains of a tradition which explained the capture of Jericho by an act of treason on the part of Rahab, a tradition which was eclipsed by the other tradition about the miraculous collapse of its walls. The text about Bethel is clear: a traitor tells the spies of a passage-way, where the Israelites gain entry (Jg 1: 23-25). At other times they coaxed the defenders out of the town: at Ai, the Israelites pretend to run away, the whole town gives chase, and a contingent which Josue has concealed then enters the town and sets it on fire (Jos 8: 3-22). It was a classic trick, which was successfully employed on another occasion at Gibeah, in the war against the Benjamites (Jg 20: 29-41); the king of Israel suspected the Aramaeans of the same trick when they raised the siege of Samaria (2 K 7: 12). Lastly, a group of determined men could effect an entry by surprise: this, apparently, was how David conquered Jerusalem (2 S 5: 7-8): Joab climbed up the tunnel which led from the spring to the interior of the town.

A powerful enemy could dispense with such subterfuges: it could intimidate a town into opening its gates or accepting its conditions (cf. Dt 20: 10-11). The inhabitants of Yabesh Gilead would have been prepared to surrender to Nahash the Ammonite if only his demands had not been so cruel (1 S 11: 1f.). When Ben-hadad pitched his camp below the walls of Samaria, Achab accepted the very first demands he made (1 K 20: 1f.). Sennacherib's envoy tried to bring about the surrender of Jerusalem by describing the power of the Assyrians, the futility of resistance and the horrors of a siege (2 K 18: 17f.).

If the town could not be captured by stratagem or surprise, and if negotiations failed, then the assailants had to mount a regular siege. They pitched camp near the city (2 S 11: 1; 1 K 16: 15-16, etc.), blocked the roads, occupied the watering-places (cf. the late text of Jdt 7: 12, 17-18) and waited until hunger and thirst got the better of the inhabitants (2 K 6: 25f.; Jdt 7: 20f.). The assailants would harry the defenders posted on the walls (2 K 3: 25). The besieged might try to break the grip by making sorties (2 S 11: 17; 1 K 20: 15-21), or, if they thought they were beaten, might try to escape (2 K 3: 26; 25: 4).

If resistance was too stiff, or if the defenders showed signs of weakening, the besiegers might hasten a decision by mounting an assault. A mound would be thrown up against the wall to provide a ramp giving access to the town; sappers might try to break through the wall (the operation is described at the siege of Abel Beth-Maakah under David, 2 S 20: 15-16). The technical term for this ramp or embankment is *solalah* (cf. once more 2 K 19: 32, Sennacherib at Jerusalem; Jr 32: 24 and 33: 4, the Chaldeans at Jerusalem, and the texts of Ezechiel which will be cited later). Attempts would be made to set fire to the gates (Jg 9: 52). When the assailants reached the foot of the rampart, they were exposed to the onslaught of the defenders, who would redouble their efforts at this critical moment: at Tebes, Abimelek was killed by a mill-stone thrown by a woman (Jg 9: 53). But the defenders, as a rule, had only these chance weapons or ordinary arms. True, according to 2 Ch 26: 15, Ozias 'built machines designed by engineers, at Jerusalem, to install them on the castles and corners to shoot arrows and big stones'. It has often been thought that this was a kind of artillery, of ballistic machines or catapults; and those who have refused to allow Ozias the honour of possessing machines the Assyrians themselves did not possess have simply denied the historical value of the text. In fact, this text refers to something quite different: these 'engines' were simply frames arranged as corbelling along the curtains of the walls and bastions, so that the archers and slingers could shoot at the foot of the wall without exposing themselves to the enemy missiles. It was the equivalent of the hoardings which were used in military architecture during the Middle Ages. And, in fact, these contrivances do surmount the walls of Lakish in the Assyrian bas-relief of the capture of the city. The Jews never used machines to attack or to defend towns before the Maccabean wars, and then they were copying the Greeks against whom they were fighting (1 M 6: 20, 51-52; 11: 20; 13: 43f.).

The religious rules for siege warfare are given in Dt 20: 10-20. When the town lies in foreign territory, it must first be offered peace terms: if it there-upon opens its gates, the population may be subjected to forced labour, but to nothing else; if it refuses, then it should be invested, its menfolk put to the sword, and everything else, people and property alike, could be taken as spoil of war.

Where the town is a Canaanite town inside the frontiers of the Promised Land, all its inhabitants were to be put to the sword without giving them the choice of surrender. During the siege of a town, fruit trees were to be left standing, but other trees might be felled and used for the siege-works. These commands were not always followed in early times (2 K 3: 19, 25), and when Deuteronomy was promulgated under Josias, there was scarcely any occasion to apply them: there were no Canaanites left to exterminate, and the Israel-ites were no longer likely to besiege foreign towns: they had quite enough to do in defending their own against the Assyrians.

The Assyrians were past masters of siege by encirclement, and their monuments give a vivid picture of their methods of attack. The besieged city was encircled by a mound, ramps were constructed and machines brought up. These machines were mobile redoubts sheltering archers and men who manœuvred a ram, *i.e.* a long wooden beam with a metal-covered head for battering the wall. Those inside the city would throw flaming torches and stones down on these machines, or try to immobilize the rams by means of grappling hooks. The infantry moved up to the assault behind the machines, and were given covering fire by archers: these archers were in turn protected by movable mantelets held by servants. Once the rams had opened a breach in the walls, the assailants could enter there; alternatively, they would scale the walls with ladders. The bas-relief of the capture of Lakish shows these different methods of attack in action, and the Annals of Sennacherib state that the king captured the towns of Judah 'by using earthen ramps, rams taken up to the walls, infantry attack, mines, breaches and tunnels'. The biblical texts provide the corresponding Hebrew words. The collective *maṣôr* is used for siege operations as a whole. We have seen that *solalah* meant a ramp; this ramp could be covered with stones or wooden logs to enable machines to pass (cf. Jr 6: 6). The encircling mound or trench is called *dayeq*, the mantelet or great siege-shield is the *ṣinnah*, and the rams are called *karîm*. When Ezechiel is ordered by God to do a mime of the siege of Jerusalem, he takes a brick to represent the city, and then builds around it a trench, makes a ramp and sets up rams (Ez 4: 2). In another text the same prophet shows Nabuchodonosor drawing lots to march to Jerusalem 'to bring rams against its walls, to pile up a ramp, to dig a trench' (Ez 21: 27). In his prediction of the siege of Tyre (Ez 26: 8-9), there are two obscure terms in addition to these others: 'he will direct against thy walls the blows of his *q'bol*' (clearly a type of ram), 'and will dismantle thy castles with his *ḥarabôth*', where the ordinary meaning (sword) is out of place: *ḥarabôth*, in this context, must mean either rams with pointed heads or sappers' picks (cf. Ex 20: 25, where it means 'chisel').

5. *The water supply*

It was not sufficient for the besieged to lie behind the shelter of a solid rampart; they had to live there, and the water supply was a problem which had to be tackled. It was solved, too, for Samaria held out for over two years against the Assyrians in 723-721, and Jerusalem withstood Nabuchodonosor for a year and a half in 587. Famine eventually raged inside Jerusalem (2 K 25: 3), as it did at Samaria during a siege by the Aramaeans (2 K 6: 25); but in neither instance are we told they were short of water. If such precautions had not been taken, however, disaster was inevitable: in the story of Judith, the army of Holofernes had occupied the springs outside the city, and the inhabitants of Bethulia were fainting from thirst after thirty-four days (Jdt 7: 20-22), though there is no question of a famine.

The Canaanites had already faced the problem and had resolved it in different ways. Here we shall discuss only the hydraulic installations built, or re-used, by the Israelites. Since the towns were built on hills and never had a spring within their walls, there were only three possible solutions, all of which were used: (a) a tunnel from inside the town, running under the ramparts to a water-supply outside the town; alternatively, a canal running from a water-supply outside the town which would bring water into the town; (b) deep wells dug inside the city down to the underground water level; (c) reservoirs and cisterns to collect rain water.

(a) *Water Tunnels*. There is archaeological evidence for these at Jerusalem and at Megiddo from the Canaanite period onwards, at Gibeon during the Israelite period, at Etham and at Yibleam at a date which cannot be fixed for certain. At Jerusalem, there is a tunnel, and a well cut through the rock, down to the spring of Gihon. It has been rediscovered by archaeologists and 2 S 5: 8 probably refers to this. The text would then mean that Joab climbed up it into the city; the word *sinnôr*, which is used here, can mean this type of canal and, in common usage, the name was extended to similar installations. At Megiddo, a very rudimentary Canaanite shaft was replaced by a most elaborate installation, which was modified several times during the period of the Israelite monarchy: a large rectangular well with flights of steps led into a sloping shaft, then into a horizontal tunnel which continued as far as the the water pool; when the water-supply was normal, the water flowed to the end of the horizontal tunnel, which lay within the ramparts. The shaft which has recently been uncovered at Gibeon followed a sloping line to the spring; it was dug out like a tunnel, except for the central part, which was a deep trench covered by flag-stones. The installations at Etham and at Yibleam have so far not been explored; that at Etham may be connected with the fortification of the town by Roboam (2 Ch 11: 6).

At Jerusalem, the configuration of the terrain eventually made a much more practical system possible. When the old Canaanite shaft had been abandoned, the Israelites had dug out a canal along the side of the Kedron Valley, running from the spring of Gihon; this canal, however, lay outside the rampart and would have served the enemy rather than the city during a siege. Faced with the threat of an Assyrian attack, Ezechias had a tunnel dug under the hill of Ophel; it brought the water from the spring at Gihon to a pool in the Tyropoeon valley, inside the ramparts. It was a masterly piece of work, which still survives as a water supply; an inscription was carved in the rock to mark the event, and the story is told with pride in 2 K 20: 20; 2 Ch 32: 30; Si 48: 17.

(b) Elsewhere, attempts were made to reach water-level by digging deep *wells* inside the town. At Beth Shemesh a well ten feet in diameter went down 67 feet; it was dug out by the Canaanites, and remained in use until the end of the Israelite period. On the crest of Tell ed-Duweir, a well protected by a salient part of the rampart reached water level at a depth of 120 feet; it was probably Canaanite to begin with, but it remained in use until the capture of the town by Nabuchodonosor. At Gezer, a series of steps over 40 yards long led down to a cave where a spring flowed, still within the ramparts; the work seems to date from the very early part of the second millennium B.C and may have been in use at the beginning of the Israelite period. At Gibeon, a large circular well has recently been discovered: it was reached by a flight of steps leading into a sloping shaft which ended in a cave where water dripped from the rock: this well at Gibeon seems to have been in use at the same time as the sloping tunnel mentioned above. We do not know how the Israelite engineers found these deep-water supplies without a considerable amount of digging. Perhaps the spring at Gezer originally flowed into the open on the side of the hill. At Gibeon, perhaps the first idea was to install a system like that at Megiddo, but when they came up against the dripping water, they stopped the project; the flow was too small, so they then dug a shaft going straight to the source.

(c) Finally, *reservoirs* and *cisterns* could be provided inside the city. Progress in the art of making waterproof coatings allowed the Israelites to build more cisterns as the number of dwelling-houses or public buildings increased. The excavations at Tell en-Nasbeh and Samaria have shown that they were particularly numerous from the ninth century B.C. onwards. During a siege, these two towns would have had no other water supply at all.

At Lakish, they decided to dig a large ditch in the form of a cube 20 yards square and deep; it was to drain off all the water from a particular quarter, and more especially from the plastered esplanades near the governor's residence; this ambitious project was never finished. It dates from the last days of the monarchy; perhaps it was only begun after the first attack of Nabuchodonosor in 597, when they started to rebuild the fortifications.

CHAPTER THREE

ARMAMENTS

VERY little is known about the equipment of Israelite soldiers. The biblical texts do not describe their weapons; indeed, the very words used for military equipment are far from precise, and their meaning is often uncertain. Archaeology might be expected to help, but only a few weapons have been found in the course of excavations. Illustrations from Egyptian and Mesopotamian monuments are certainly helpful, but one can never be sure that the Israelites were always using the same kind of weapon as their enemies.

1. Offensive weapons

The main offensive weapon was the *hereb*, which became the symbol of war (Is 51: 19; Jr 14: 15; 24: 10; Ez 7: 15; 33: 6, etc.). The word is used for both dagger and sword, since the two weapons have the same shape and are distinguished—quite arbitrarily—merely by their length. The *hereb* of Ehud (Jg 3: 16, 21-22) was obviously a dagger, whatever the precise meaning of *gomed*, which gives its length.[1] In all military texts, the word may be translated as 'sword', but we must remember that it was a short sword, about 20 inches long, or perhaps a little more, like the Assyrian sword. Illustrations in Egyptian monuments portray a long sword, which was used by the Peoples of the Sea; specimens of this type have been discovered in Greece and in the Aegean, but it was never used by the Israelites. The Philistine Goliath, however, may have had one, which was later wrapped up in a cloak and was quite unique (cf. 1 S 21: 9-10). The sword was carried in a sheath (*nadan* or *ta'ar*, 1 S 17: 51; 1 Ch 21: 27; Jr 47: 6; Ez 21: 8-10) attached to the belt (2 S 20: 8).

Goliath also carried 'between his shoulders' a *kîdôn* of bronze (1 S 17: 6, 45). Josue wielded the same weapon at the battle of Ai (Jos 8: 18-26), and Jeremias said the invaders from the north would use it (Jr 6: 23 = 50: 42). It is usually translated 'javelin', but the Order of the War discovered at Qumran[2] seems to describe the *kîdôn* as a sword one and a half cubits long and four finger-breadths wide. It has been suggested that the late text of Qumran drew its inspiration from the Roman *gladius*, but the meaning would fit the biblical texts also: a type of sword longer and broader than the *hereb*, and hung from

1. Cf. p. 196.　　2. Cf. p. 266.

a cross-belt slung 'between the shoulders'. More probably, however, the *kîdôn* was a scimitar, a *harpe*, like those shown on monuments and discovered in excavations. Certain details of the Order of the War seem to refer to precisely such a weapon. In the biblical texts, the *kîdôn* seems to be an unusual weapon which (except in Jos 8) is never found in the hands of an Israelite. A recent writer has suggested that the Philistine name for a scimitar, the *harpe* in Greek, may be preserved in the expression 'the sons of *hrph*' (2 S 21: 16, 18, 20, 22): the phrase would then denote a corps whose emblem was a scimitar, whereas the Massoretic vocalization and the ancient versions have all taken it to mean 'sons of Rapha' (as if it were a proper name with the article).

The word *romaḥ* (pike) is often mentioned, but the weapon is never described in detail. Originally, it was simply a pointed stave, but at a very early date a metal head was fixed on by a pin or socket. It was a weapon for hand-to-hand fighting (cf. Nb 25: 7-8). It is mentioned in the lists of weapons given in 2 Ch 11: 12; 14: 7; 25: 5; 26: 14; Ne 4: 10; Ez 39: 9 and even in the very old Song of Deborah, Jg 5: 8. According to the Order of the War, it was about seven or eight cubits long, but in biblical times it cannot have been much longer than the height of an average man; this was its length in Egypt and Assyria. In the Order of the War, the socket which held the iron in place is called the *seger*; the term is also found, alongside *ḥanîth*, in Ps 35: 3, where it may well stand (*pars pro toto*) for the pike itself.

The *ḥanîth*, which is usually mentioned in old texts, is not the same as the *romaḥ*. It seems to be a shorter and lighter lance, which could also be thrown like a javelin (cf. 1 S 18: 11; 20: 33, where there is no need to correct the Hebrew text). To balance the weight of the head and to make the throw more accurate, the lower end was iron-shod; the lance could then be stuck in the ground (1 S 26: 7) and its butt could be used as a weapon (cf. perhaps 2 S 2: 23). Specimens have been found in excavations. It was Saul's personal weapon (cf. once more 1 S 19: 9; 22: 6; 26: 7f.; 2 S 1: 6). According to 2 Ch 23: 9, the Temple guards were equipped with it (and 2 K 11: 10 depends, no doubt, on this reference), but it is never mentioned among lists of weapons and, in accounts of wars, it is only once mentioned in the hands of an Israelite (2 S 2: 23). On the other hand, an 'Egyptian' was armed with it (2 S 23: 21), and Goliath carried one (1 S 17: 7; 2 S 21: 19). The wood of this giant's lance was 'like a weaver's *manôr*'. Until recently, this was taken to refer to the size of the lance, as if it were as big as a yarn-beam, that part of a weaving-loom around which the threads are wound. A better explanation has recently been put forward: the *manôr* is the heddle-bar, the wooden rod which supports the heddle by a series of kinks or snarls. Goliath's *ḥanîth* also had a leather thong, rolled round the shaft, with a loop at the end; it made it easier to throw, and increased its range. This method of throwing was known at a very early date in Greece and in Egypt, but the other peoples of the Near East did not know of it; the Israelites therefore described this strange weapon by comparing it with an instrument they knew well. This explanation confirms the view that the *hanîth* was used as a projectile.

The *shelah*, by etymology, is also a projectile, and the meaning dart or javelin would suit in 2 S 18: 14 (corrected in the light of the Greek; cf. Jl 2: 8); but in other texts it bears only the general meaning of a weapon carried in the hand (2 Ch 23: 10; 32: 5; Ne 4: 11, 17).

The bow (*qesheth*) is one of the most primitive weapons, both for hunting and for war, but in the Near East it passed through an evolution which we can trace with the help of texts and monuments. To begin with, the bow was simply a piece of pliable wood held bent by a taut string; the wood was later reinforced by ligaments; finally, a bow was invented which was a clever combination of wood and horn, and this had a considerably longer range. It was a splendid weapon, and came into widespread use in the middle of the second millennium B.C., through the influence of the Hyksos; in fact it became the normal weapon in Egypt. Among the Israelites, however, bows were at first used only on a small scale in war. It was Jonathan's weapon (1 S 20: 20; 2 S 1: 22), and it remained the weapon of leaders and kings (2 K 9: 24; 13: 15; Ps 18: 35; 45: 6). Yet neither Saul's army nor David's household guard used bows; at least, there is no mention of it in the Books of Samuel, though 1 Ch 12: 2 mentions some archers of Benjamin among the picked troops of David, and this information should not be lightly disregarded. To keep a balanced view, one should remember that arrow-heads inscribed with the names of their owners and dating from 1300–900 B.C. have been discovered in Phoenicia and in Palestine; this proves that there was a class of professional archers at the time, as there had been two centuries earlier at Ugarit.

The bow probably came into general use in Israel when the chariot force was introduced, for chariot tactics cut out hand-to-hand fighting and demanded the use of long-range weapons (1 S 31: 3 compared with 2 S 1: 6; 1 K 22: 32-34; 2 K 9: 24). The infantry would have been provided with bows as a result of this change, in imitation no doubt of the pattern set by the Assyrian infantry. In the relief of the capture of Lakish by Sennacherib, the ramparts are manned by archers. The statistics of Chronicles record archers on the general strength of the army of Judah only from the time of Ozias (2 Ch 26: 14; cf. Ne 4: 7, 10), but the archers of Benjamin had been famous long before that (1 Ch 8: 40; 12: 2; 2 Ch 14: 7; 17: 17). In a whole series of texts, the sword and bow symbolize every kind of weapon, and, indeed, war itself (Gn 48: 22; Jos 24: 12; 2 K 6: 22; Os 1: 7; 2: 20). David's elegy on Jonathan was used 'to instruct the Judahites in the use of the bow' (2 S 1: 18), *i.e.* for their general military training (cf. the same word in Jg 3: 2 and 2 S 22: 35).

In spite of 2 S 22: 25 = Ps 18: 35 and Jb 20: 24, there was never such a thing as a 'bronze bow': the term refers to the metal coverings of certain bows. The bowstring is called *yether* (Ps 11: 2) or *mêthar* (Ps 21: 13); the same words are also used for tent-ropes, but this does not prove that the same material was used for both purposes, since the primary meaning of the root is simply 'to stretch'. Israel's neighbours used flax cords or plaited hair for bowstrings; they were also made of catgut or, more often, from the nerve-strings of animals. The bow was bent only when action was imminent, by resting the lower part of the wood on the ground, and then pressing it down with the foot: Egyptian illustrations portray the technique, which is called in Hebrew 'stepping on the bow' (darak qesheth, Is 5: 28; 21: 15; Jr 46: 9; 50: 14; Ps 7: 13; 11: 2, etc.).

Arrows (heṣ) were made of wood, or from reed stems, but in Palestine no specimens have survived from pre-Roman periods. Countless arrow-heads, however, have been preserved. The tips were at first made of bronze, but bronze tips later gave way to iron ones. The shape varied: some were shaped like spear-heads and were fastened to the shaft by a cord as far as a protuberance that is sometimes found on the metal head. This was the only type in service at the beginning of the monarchy, and it never went out of use. Secondly, there were shorter arrows, with a diamond-shaped head, fixed to the shaft by a pin or socket; some had a barb at the side, to prevent the arrow from being pulled out of the wound. At the end of the monarchy, heavy arrows came into use, triangular in shape and designed to pierce armour; at the same period, three-bladed arrow-tips were in use, a type which originated in the north and whose use became general during the Hellenistic period. The same years saw the appearance of flat, barbed arrows. Incendiary arrows were also known (Ps 7: 14), and one of them has been found at Shechem: little holes were pierced in the blades, and oil-soaked tow was packed into them. The bow was carried in the left hand, the arrows in the right (Ez 39: 3) or in a quiver ('ashpah: Is 22: 6; 49: 2; Jr 5: 16; Ps 127: 5; Jb 39: 23).

Last of all, the sling (qela‘) was a thong with a wide centre (the 'palm' of the sling, 1 S 25: 29). It was a simple, primitive weapon, used by shepherds (1 S 17: 40), but it was also a weapon of war (2 K 3: 25; 2 Ch 26: 14). The men of Benjamin had crack slingers who would not miss by a hairsbreadth, with the right hand or left (Jg 20: 16; cf. 1 Ch 12: 2). The stones used in the slings were carefully picked pebbles (1 S 17: 40), except when they were specially trimmed for the purpose (2 Ch 26: 14). They were rounded to the shape of large olives; and some have been unearthed by excavations. During the Hellenistic epoch, slingers used lead balls also.

2. Defensive arms

The most common defensive arm was the buckler or shield. It has two names, magen and ṣinnah, and since these two names occur together in several texts, they must denote two different kinds of shields. According to 1 K 10: 16-17 = 2 Ch 9: 15-16, the magen was far smaller than the ṣinnah. This is confirmed by 1 S 17: 7, 41 (the ṣinnah of Goliath was carried by a servant) and by Ez 26: 8 (where the same word is used for a siege mantelet). This no doubt explains why this type of shield is most often associated with the pike (*romaḥ*) as in 1 Ch 12: 9, 25; 2 Ch 11: 12; 14: 7; 25: 5. It must have been like the enormous covering shield of the Assyrians. The *magen* is mentioned rather with swords and bows (Dt 33: 29; 1 Ch 5: 18; 2 Ch 14: 7; 17: 17; Ps 76: 4). The text of 2 Ch 14: 7 is particularly informative: the men of Judah had the *ṣinnah* and the pike, while the men of Benjamin had the *magen* and the bow. In our terms, this would represent the difference between heavy and light infantry. The *magen* was round-shaped, like the shields fixed on the walls in the bas-relief of Lakish (cf. also Ct 4: 4). The Assyrian infantry and cavalry were equipped in the same way. In Jb 15: 26, there may be a reference to a boss reinforcing the centre of the shield, corresponding to the handle on the other side.

For purposes of parade, there were bronze shields (1 K 14: 27), and shields plated with precious metals (1 K 10: 16-17; cf. 2 S 8: 7), but the shields used in battle were made of leather, coated with fat (2 S 1: 21-22; Is 21: 5) and stained red (Na 2: 4). When not in use, they were kept in housing (Is 22: 6).

Sheleṭ is a rare word, very similar in meaning to *magen*: the two terms are parallel in Ct 4: 4, and cf. Ez 27: 11; and in 2 Ch 23: 9 *magen* is a gloss for the *sheleṭ* of 2 K 11: 10. This last text refers to 2 S 8: 7=1 Ch 18: 7, which in its turn is similar to 1 K 10: 17, where *magen* is used. It may therefore be translated 'rondache', *i.e.* a small circular shield or buckler; Jr 51: 11 is the only text which seems to raise any difficulty, and it has even led some people to suggest the meaning 'quiver', but the correct translation of the phrase is 'Prepare the rondaches' (cf. the same verb in Za 9: 13).

The helmet was called *koḥa‘* or *qoba‘* and this inconsistency in pronunciation reveals the foreign, non-Semitic origin of the word and of what it represented. Goliath wore a bronze helmet (1 S 17: 5), but it is questionable whether Saul had one for David to try on (1 S 17: 38). It is recorded as part of the equipment of foreign troops in Jr 46: 4; Ez 23: 24; 27: 10; 38: 5, and is said to be part of the equipment which Ozias issued to his troops (2 Ch 26: 14). This piece of information has been questioned, but the defenders of Lakish are shown with bronze helmets in the Assyrian bas-relief so often referred to. The only question is whether these helmets were of leather or metal. The crest of a bronze helmet was found during the excavations at Lakish, but there is no doubt that it belonged to an Assyrian soldier; in the same bas-relief, some of the assailants are wearing a helmet with a crest.

The breast-plate (*siryôn* or *shiryôn*) was, like the helmet, of foreign origin. It is almost certain that the Hurrites introduced it into the Near East during the first half of the second millennium B.C. It was made of small plates, first of bronze, later of iron, 'scales' which were sewn on to cloth or leather. According to documents from Nuzu, horses and chariots, as well as men, were equipped with them, and this may be the explanation of the 'iron chariots' of the Canaanites in Jos 17: 16; Jg 1: 19; 4: 3 and 13; cf. perhaps Na 2: 4. These breast-plates were adopted by the Egyptians, and later by the Assyrians, and can be recognized on their monuments; to begin with, they were worn only by charioteers, but eventually the infantry too were issued with them. Some of the assailants of Lakish are shown wearing them, but it is impossible to make out whether they are made of small metal plates or of strips of leather. In Israel, the same development took place. In the early days, Goliath wore a 'breast-plate of scales' (*shiryôn qashqashshîm*: 1 S 17: 5) but he was a foreigner and his equipment was quite unusual anyway; we have already mentioned his sword, unique of its kind, his lance with its leather thong for throwing, and v. 6 says he also wore bronze greaves (literally 'leg-fronts'). There is no evidence that greaves were known in the East at this period, though they were used in the Aegean. Saul's breast-plate is as questionable as his helmet (1 S 17: 38), but it would be normal for Achab to wear a breast-plate in his chariot (1 K 22: 34). Under Ozias, helmets and breast-plates were issued to troops under marching orders for action (2 Ch 26: 14), and they were issued to the defenders of Jerusalem under Nehemias (Ne 4: 10). Bronze or iron scales from such breast-plates have been found in Palestinian excavations. The Greeks and Romans were familiar with this armour, but they also had coats of chain-mail: the soldiers of Antiochus Epiphanes wore them (1 M 6: 35), and this is how the Septuagint translates the armour of Goliath.

CHAPTER FOUR

WAR

1. A short military history of Israel

THE first wars in which Israel took part were wars of conquest, and biblical tradition shows the people taking possession of the Promised Land by force of arms and with the help of God. The defeat of Sihon, king of Heshbon, and of Og, king of Bashan (Nb 21: 21-35), and the campaign against Midian (Nb 31: 1-12) secured a territory for Reuben, Gad and half the tribe of Manasseh. The Book of Josue describes the occupation of Palestine west of the Jordan as a military operation in three sweeping actions: first, the people cross the Jordan and cut their way through to the very heart of the land (Jos 1-9); next, a coalition of five Canaanite kings from the south is overthrown and the whole of southern Palestine occupied (Jos 10); finally, the northern kings are defeated at Merom and their cities fall into the hands of the Israelites (Jos 11). It is quite certain that this is an extremely simplified version of what really happened, that the actions of the tribes were less concentrated and far slower and that they did not all meet with equal success (cf. Jos 15: 13-17; Jg 1). It is also true that the Israelites infiltrated in a peaceful manner wherever they could; but they did meet opposition, which they had to overcome by force of arms.

The wars in the period of the Judges, and under Saul, were defensive wars. The Israelites first had to withstand the counter-attacks of the Canaanites and of those other peoples out of whose lands they had carved their territory; later they had to fight against the Philistines, who were making inroads from the coast. The reign of David, on the other hand, was a period of reconquest and, later, of expansion. We are not fully informed of the reasons for David's wars. He declared war on the Ammonites because they had insulted his ambassadors (2 S 10: 1-5), and on the Aramaeans for going to the help of the Ammonites (2 S 10: 6-19; cf. 8: 3-6). We do not know what provoked the wars against Moab (2 S 8: 2) and Edom (2 S 8: 13). The bravado of the Ammonites and the eagerness with which the Aramaeans went to their aid show that the neighbouring States were growing anxious about the increasing power of Israel. But they also show that they underestimated the ability of its new leader, and it could well be that their provocation and the Israelite victories led David to adopt a policy of conquest of which he had never dreamed.

The territory he conquered was badly defended by his successors. The Ammonites declared themselves independent as soon as David was dead, and Solomon took no action when part of Edom and Aram broke away from his empire (1 K 11: 14-25); indeed, Solomon did not fight a single war. On the death of Achab, the king of Moab revolted, and even a punitive expedition by the king of Israel, with assistance from the king of Judah and his Edomite vassal, did not bring Moab back to obedience (2 K 3: 4-27). Shortly afterwards, Edom shook off the domination of Judah, after a disastrous campaign by Joram (2 K 8: 20-22).

After the schism, the artificial frontier between Israel and Judah led to conflict between the brother-kingdoms under Basha and Asa (1 K 15: 16-22), under Joas and Amasias (2 K 14: 8-14), and, for the last time, under Achaz and Peqah (the Syro-Ephraimite War: 2 K 16: 5; 2 Ch 28: 5-8). And yet both kingdoms had quite enough to do defending their own territory against foreign pressure. Roboam avoided a war with the Pharaoh Sheshonq by surrendering the treasures of the Temple and palace (1 K 14: 25-26), but in later ages, until Josias, Egypt was more often a worthless ally than an enemy. On the Philistine frontier, there was fighting under Joram (2 K 8: 22; 2 Ch 21: 16), Ozias (2 Ch 26: 6), Achaz (2 Ch 28: 18), and Ezechias (2 K 18: 8); but we have little information about it, except that Judah was sometimes the victor, sometimes defeated. Judah fought against Edom for the possession of Elath (2 K 14: 7 and 22; 16: 6) in order to keep open the trade route to the Red Sea and Arabia.

The kingdom of Israel, too, had a common frontier with the Philistines in the south-west. Gibbethon, a Philistine stronghold which constituted a threat to Gezer, was besieged by Nadab and by Omri (1 K 15: 27; 16: 15). Later still, Isaias pictures Israel hemmed in by the Philistines and the Aramaeans, both equally rapacious (Is 9: 11). The Aramaeans of Damascus were for generations an enemy to be feared. Israel was at war with them for almost the whole of the ninth century B.C.; sometimes Israel gained the upper hand, but more often victory went to the Aramaeans. The main prize of these wars was the possession of what remained of David's Aramaean possessions in Transjordan (cf. the battles before Ramoth Gilead in 1 K 22: 3, 29; 2 K 8: 28; 9: 1f.) and the districts of northern Galilee (1 K 15: 20; cf. 20: 34). Twice the Aramaeans laid siege to Samaria (1 K 20: 1f.; 2 K 6: 24f.). Hazael of Damascus even tried to gain complete control of Israel and nearly succeeded (2 K 10: 32-33; 12: 18; 13: 3, 7). The situation was stabilized under Joas (2 K 13: 25) and Jeroboam II (2 K 14: 25), but only because the power of Damascus had been crushed by the Assyrians.

The Assyrians, however, were a still more formidable enemy. When Shalmaneser II made his appearance in central Syria, a coalition tried to stop him, and in 853 B.C. Achab took part in the battle of Qarqar, in the valley of the Orontes, with 2,000 chariots and 18,000 infantrymen. The strange thing is that this expedition, the only really distant one undertaken by an Israelite army, is not mentioned in the Bible and is known to us only through cuneiform documents. Only twelve years later, in 841, Jehu agreed, without making any show of resistance, to pay tribute. In the following century, during the second great Assyrian thrust under Tiglath-Pileser III, Menahem declared himself a vassal in 738 (2 K 15: 19-20) but in 734-732 the king of Assyria occupied the greater part of the territory of Israel without meeting any serious opposition (2 K 15: 29). The end came in 724, when Shalmaneser V laid siege to Samaria; though its king had been taken prisoner, the city held out until the beginning of 721.

At the time of Tiglath-Pileser's attack, the kings of Aram and Israel tried to persuade Achaz of Judah to join them in their struggle against Assyria; when Achaz refused, they laid siege to Jerusalem: this was the 'Syro-Ephraimite' War. Achaz then appealed for help to Assyria, and Judah became, without a fight, the vassal of Assyria (2 K 16: 5-9; Is 7-8). Ezechias tried to throw off the yoke, by taking advantage of a general revolt against Assyria. He allied himself with the coastal states and with the still more distant states of Egypt and Babylon. Sennacherib's reply was terrible: in 701, every town in Judah was captured, in spite of their resistance (which Assyrian documents record); they were handed over to the king of Philistia, who had remained true to Sennacherib. Jerusalem alone was saved (2 K 18: 13-19: 37; Is 36-37). We do not know how Ezechias and his son Manasseh made good these losses, but we do know that Judah remained a vassal-state of Assyria. When the power of Assyria had declined, Josias threw off the yoke and freed not only the territory of Judah but even part of the former territory of Israel as well (cf. 2 K 23: 15-20). At that time the supremacy of Assyria was crumbling everywhere, and perhaps he did not need to resort to force to achieve this reconquest. The Bible, preoccupied with his religious policy only, does not mention any military action in this context. On the other hand, when the Pharaoh Nechao went to the help of the last king of Assyria, who had been cornered by the Babylonians and Medes, Josias tried to stop him at the pass of Megiddo, in 609: he did not want to see Assyria reprieved, or Palestine falling into the clutches of Egypt. The battle was a short one, and Josias was mortally wounded (2 Ch 35: 20-25; which is more detailed than 2 K 23: 29-30). Nechao annexed Palestine and installed a vassal king, Joiaqim. But the overlordship of Egypt did not last for long. After the defeat of the Egyptians at Charchemish in 605, all Syria-Palestine fell into the hands of the Babylonians, and Judah became one of their vassals. Joiaqim tried to break away, and thereby stung Nabuchodonosor into reprisals. The pace of events quickened: first siege of Jerusalem in 597, the installation of Sedecias as king, his revolt, second siege (interrupted for a moment as a result of Egyptian intervention), and the final ruin of Jerusalem in 587 (cf. 2 K 24: 1-25: 21, and scattered references in Jr). The biblical narratives describe only what took place in Jerusalem, but we know that operations went on elsewhere. According to Jr 34: 1 and 7, Lakish and Azeqah were still holding out during the siege of Jerusalem. Excavations at Tell ed-Duweir (Lakish) provide evidence of the destruction of the town suffered during the two Chaldean invasions, and of the rebuilding of the defences in the meantime. The ostraka found there give some idea of the activity just before the second siege: arranging liaison with Jerusalem, exchange of signals between towns, sending a mission to Egypt.

Seen as a whole, the military history of Israel under the monarchy clearly shows that the era of wars of conquest begins and ends under David. After David, all the wars were defensive wars, rarely and by way of exception to bring a vassal back to obedience or to keep a trade route open, more often to protect or to establish a frontier; in the end they were all attempts to resist expansionist policies of the great powers. Even Achab at Qarqar and Josias at Megiddo wanted only to safeguard the integrity of their country.

For several centuries the Jews were subject to foreign masters, but in the end they revolted. The rebellion broke out under Antiochus Epiphanes, who wanted to lend unity to his empire by imposing Greek culture everywhere; in contrast with all his predecessors, he refused to allow the Jews to live according to their own law. The War of Independence under the Maccabees was therefore a religious war, and we shall have to consider it later under this aspect.[1] Here we are concerned only with its peculiar military characteristics. To begin with, it was conducted as guerilla warfare, with small groups harassing the Seleucid garrisons and the reinforcements sent to them, but Judas Maccabee very soon appealed to all the people of Israel and organized the army on the old traditional lines (1 M 3: 55-56). It was a war of mobile forces, with operations extending, sometimes at one and the same time, from south of Hebron to Galilee, and from the Mediterranean coast to Transjordan. The strongholds which held out were soon reduced, thanks to the new techniques of investment which the Jews learnt from their enemies. Religious freedom was once more achieved (1 M 6: 57-60), but Judas knew it would never be secure unless the nation became independent, and he went on with the fight. Under his brother Simon, the Jews finally achieved national independence, and 'the yoke of the nations was lifted off Israel' (1 M 13: 41).

2. The conduct of war

We said above that, before the time of David, war was conducted by the people's taking up arms.[2] Our present task is to see (as far as the documents will allow us) what strategy and tactics were followed by the organized army of monarchical times.

There was no declaration of war. The nearest approach to one is the challenge flung down by Amasias of Judah to Joas of Israel: 'Come and let us

1. Cf. p. 265.   2. Cf. pp. 215-218.

test our strength!' (2 K 14: 8), but it is unusual. The customs of those ages were different from ours: only when a commander had pitched his camp in enemy country and shown his power would he lay down conditions, the refusal of which would unleash hostilities (1 S 11: 1f.; 1 K 20: 1f.; cf. Dt 20: 10-12)[1]; but the war had already begun.

The accounts of wars provide no details about mobilization. They merely state that the king 'collected' the army or the people (1 K 20: 1; 2 K 6: 24), that he 'made a census' of them or 'reviewed' them (1 K 20: 27; 2 K 3: 6). This was simple enough with the professional army, but not so easy with the conscripts. In the days when the whole people took up arms, they used to send round messengers or to blow a trumpet.[2] In the next period certain texts presume that a trumpet was blown and a signal (the *nes*[3]) set up. In Jr 51: 27, the mobilization of the nations against Babylon is described thus:

> Raise a signal throughout the world,
> blow the trumpet among the nations!
> Consecrate nations against her,
> Gather kingdoms against her . . .
> Appoint a recruiting sergeant against her!

Most of Israel's wars, however, were defensive, not aggressive, and so when the prophets speak of the trumpet-sound or the setting up of a signal, they are predicting an invasion, and warning their countrymen of imminent danger: it is an alarm signal in the strict sense, a call to arms or to flight (Jr 4: 5-6; 6: 1; Os 5: 8; Am 3: 6; cf. Jl 2: 1). In the quotation from Jr 51: 27 'recruiting sergeant' is a translation of the word *ṭipsar*, which is simply a Hebrew naturalization of the Akkadian *ṭupsharru*, meaning 'scribe'. In this text it refers to the official in charge of conscription, usually called in Hebrew the *sôpher*, 'the secretary who enlists the people of the country (2 K 25: 19) or the *shôṭer*, the 'clerk' who, according to Dt 20: 5-8, gave public notice of exemptions from service.[4]

According to 2 S 11: 1 and its parallel (1 Ch 20: 1), 'the time when kings begin their campaigns' is 'the turn of the year', that is, spring.[5] In fact, almost all the Assyrian campaigns whose dates are known with precision began between April and June; in the Neo-Babylonian period, the dates stretch on to autumn and sometimes even into the winter, according to the needs of the operations. It was natural enough to choose the beginning of the good weather, whenever possible, for the roads were then in good condition; hence there were no complications over transport or camping. Supplies, too, were easily arranged, for the army would arrive in enemy territory just after the cereal harvests. All this, of course, is true of a professional army, but it must have been much harder to mobilize peasants just at the heaviest period of work in the fields, from the harvest to seed-time.

1. Cf. p. 236.   2. Cf. p. 215.   3. Cf. p. 227.   4. Cf. p. 225.   5. Cf. p. 190.

We have little information on strategy. The Hittites and the Canaanites, it seems, generally tried to draw the enemy far away from his bases and to come to grips near a strong position where their chariots could launch a surprise attack; the bulk of the army was held in reserve to exploit the success or to retreat in good order. This was how the battles of Megiddo (against Thutmoses III) and of Qadesh (against Ramses II) developed. Perhaps Josias was trying to put this old strategy into practice when he allowed Nechao to advance as far as Megiddo; when the first attack, led by the king in person, was repulsed, the Israelite army withdrew (2 K 23: 29-30; 2 Ch 35 20-24).

2 S 11: 11 tells us that during David's war against the Ammonites, the national army was *bassukkôth* with the Ark, while the professional army was encamped before Rabbah. According to 1 K 20: 12, 16, Ben-hadad and the kings allied with him got drunk *bassukkôth* while the envoys were negotiating with Achab in Samaria and the young cadets making their successful sortie. The usual translation is 'in the huts', *i.e.* in the camp pitched before Rabbah or Samaria. One writer has recently suggested the translation 'at Sukkoth', on the supposition that Ben-hadad or David had established a 'strategic advanced base' in the Jordan valley, where the bulk of the army was held in reserve. It is an interesting hypothesis, but it seems unlikely that these old stories reflect such a modern concept of strategy. The text of 1 K 20: 1, 12-13, 20 takes it for granted that Ben-hadad and his army are camped very near Samaria. And the immediate context of 2 S 11: 11 favours the ordinary translation: Uriah refuses to go home as long as the Ark and the people are living in huts, and while his comrades in the household guard are camping in the open air.

The war against Moab (2 K 3: 4-27) gives a fine example of an indirect attack: the king of Israel, instead of attacking Mesha on their common frontier north of the Arnon, persuades the king of Judah to make an alliance with him. Then by a long turning movement across Judah and Edom, he invades the territory of Moab from the south and marches on to the capital, systematically destroying everything in his path. David had used the same strategy against the Philistines, though on a smaller scale (2 S 5: 23).

Our information about combat tactics is equally incomplete. Clearly, tactics would vary with the arms and the troops employed: it depended on whether chariots were used or not, whether the professional troops were engaged alone, or the conscripts alone, or both together. If both were used together, the professional soldiers fought in the front line and led the attack, while the conscripts were held as uncommitted reserves: these tactics were employed in the Ammonite war under David and in the Aramaean wars under Achab.[1] In mobile warfare, or when a surprise attack was to be made on a camp, the commander divided his force into three assault corps (Jg 7: 16; 9: 43; 1 S 11: 11; 2 S 18: 2; cf. the Philistines also in 1 S 13: 17). Alternatively,

1. Cf. p. 221.

instead of this encircling manœuvre, a detachment might be despatched to attack the enemy from the rear (2 Ch 13: 13-15). If a good general were thus attacked from behind, he would continue to fight on both fronts while keeping his two combat forces in close liaison to give each other support (2 S 10: 8-11).

The baggage was left with guards or reserves behind the fighting line or at the departure point (1 S 17: 22; 25: 13; 30: 24; cf. vv. 9-10). According to the Hebrew text of 1 K 20: 27 (missing in the Greek and often suppressed by critics), the army was equipped with supplies before its departure; the supplies were taken from depots (misk*nôth), which are mentioned alongside chariot garrisons under Solomon (1 K 9: 19) and alongside citadels under Josaphat (2 Ch 17: 12). We do not know how the army in the field received its supplies. David, as a young boy, brought parched corn and loaves to his brothers at the battle front (1 S 17: 17), but as a rule the troops had to live off the land as they went. Sometimes the inhabitants would bring victuals (2 S 16: 1f.; 17: 27-29; 19: 33), and sometimes the army would requisition them (Jg 8: 4f.; 1 S 25: 7-18). An Egyptian papyrus gives a vivid description of these same methods, which the Egyptian army used in Canaan; but it would be rash to use this text, combined with 1 S 25: 18, to estimate the daily ration of an Israelite soldier.

Liaison was maintained by orderlies, on foot (Jg 9. 31; 2 S 11. 19; 18: 19) or mounted (2 K 9: 17f.). But they also used signals: the mas*'eth was a fire kindled on a height, whose smoke or light could be seen far away and which gave a signal agreed on beforehand (Jg 20: 38) or a simple warning (Jr 6: 1). An ostrakon found at Lakish is most explicit: 'We are watching the signals (ms't) of Lakish according to my Lord's orders, for we cannot see Azeqah': there must have been a code, then, to interpret these signals. In the tradition about the Exodus and the stay in the desert, the cloud of light which revealed the presence of Yahweh gave the people the signals for marching and camping, and they are represented as an army in the field (Ex 13: 21-22; Nb 9: 15-23). 'They camped on Yahweh's orders and struck camp on Yahweh's orders' (Nb 9: 20, 23).

Trumpets were also used for signalling. Immediately after the passage about the cloud of light, Nb 10: 1-10 mentions the two silver trumpets (haṣoṣ*rah), which were used to call the assembly together and to accompany worship; but they were also used to give the order to break camp, and they were to be used for departure for battle. They were in fact carried by the priest Phinehas when Israel opened its campaign against Midian (Nb 31: 6). Similarly, according to 2 Ch 13: 12-15, the priests sounded the trumpet in the war between Abiyyah and Jeroboam. In Os 5: 8, the trumpet stands in a parallel with the horn (shôpar, strictly, a ram's horn); in another ancient text, the shôpar alone is mentioned, playing the part which the late passages just cited ascribe to the trumpet. The horn was a signal for mobilization or rallying (Jg 3: 27; 6: 34; 1 S 13: 3; 2 S 20: 1). Not to hear the sound of the horn is a synonym for being threatened with war no longer (Jr 42: 14). But the horn was also used to order the cessation of hostilities (2 S 18: 16; 20: 22).

When the battle was about to commence, the *shôpar* gave the signal to shout the battle-cry (Jos 6: 5f.; Jg 7: 16f.); the *haṣoṣ'rah* also is said to be used for this (Nb 10: 9; 2 Ch 13: 12-15). This battle-cry (*t'rû'ah*: cf. also the corresponding noun and verb in 1 S 17: 20, 52; Jr 4: 19; 20: 16; 49: 2; Ez 21: 27; Os 5: 8; Am 1: 14; 2: 2) was originally a savage shout meant to inspire the ranks and to strike fear into the enemy. But it was also a religious cry, closely bound up with the rôle of the Ark in fighting (cf. 1 S 4: 5f.[1]); it then became part of the ritual surrounding the Ark (2 S 6: 15), and finally passed into the Temple liturgy (Lv 23: 24; Nb 29: 1) and certain Psalms.

3. The consequences of war

There is 'a time for war and a time for peace' (Qo 3: 8). The word *shalôm*, peace, used in a political sense, means not only the absence of war, in a purely negative sense, but includes the idea of friendly relations between two peoples, just as, in other contexts, it means friendly relations between two individuals (Jg 4: 17; 1 S 7: 14; 1 K 5: 4, 26; 22: 45; cf. Gn 34: 21; 1 Ch 12: 18). These relations would be guaranteed by a pact or treaty (*b'rîth*: 1 K 5: 26), and breaking the treaty is the equivalent of going to war (1 K 15: 19-20; cf. Is 33: 7-8).

Conversely, war ends by the establishment of peace, and this peace is the fruit of victory; to return 'in peace' from a campaign is a synonym for 'to return victorious' (Jg 8: 9; 2 S 19: 25, 31; 1 K 22: 27-28; Jr 43: 12). The peace was sealed by the conclusion, or the renewal of a treaty. For example, when Ben-hadad had been defeated at Apheq, he sued for peace, offering to return to Achab the Israelite towns occupied by his forces, and to allow the Israelites to open bazaars at Damascus like those the Aramaeans had at Samaria: Achab then signed a treaty with him (1 K 20: 34). Ben-hadad had first sent messengers (1 K 20: 32); they are the 'messengers of peace' (Is 33: 7). The victor too could propose peace (Jg 21: 13). These offers of, or requests for, peace could be made even before the commencement of hostilities, if the superior power of one party made the issue virtually certain: thus the Gibeonites sought to make a treaty with Josue, and the latter granted them peace and a treaty (Jos 9: 6, 15). The inhabitants of Yabesh asked Nahash for a treaty when he pitched camp before their town (1 S 11: 1); and Deuteronomy lays down that peace terms must be offered to a foreign city before it is attacked (Dt 20: 10).

In these three instances, the weaker party, if it accepted the peace-terms, was reduced to slavery. The outcome of a victorious war was always conquest by one side and vassaldom for the other: *e.g.* David against Aram,

1. Cf. p. 259.

Edom, Moab and Ammon, or the Assyrians against Israel, or Sennacherib, Nechao and Nabuchodonosor against Judah. In their accounts of these wars, the historical books of the Bible never mention a treaty imposed by the victor, but Ez 17: 13-21 states it clearly of Sedecias: Nabuchodonosor had made a treaty (*b'rîth*) with him, which Sedecias had confirmed with an imprecatory oath; later, Sedecias had broken the treaty, and his oath (cf. 2 K 24: 17, 20b). Similarly, Os 12: 2: 'They have made a *b'rîth* with Assyria, but they are taking oil to Egypt', refers to the policy of the last king of Samaria, a vassal of Shalmaneser, who turned to Egypt for help (cf. 2 K 17: 3-4). Lastly, Is 33: 8: 'They broke the *b'rîth*', refers, according to some exegetes, to the pact between Sennacherib and Ezechias. Such treaties existed even when victory was not overwhelming, *e.g.* those between Hittite and Assyrian kings and their vassals in Syria, copies of which have survived. The obligations of a defeated enemy who accepted vassaldom had to be fixed, and among these was the tribute he had to pay. The usual term for tribute is *minḥah*, a 'present', but the amount was fixed by the suzerain (2 K 18: 14; 23: 33; 2 Ch 27: 5), and withholding payment was equivalent to revolt (2 K 3: 4-5; 17: 4).

The laws of war were crude. The Annals of the kings of Assyria have a constant refrain of towns destroyed, dismantled or burnt, levelled as if by a hurricane, or reduced to a heap of rubble. It was the usual custom also in biblical wars, from a period of the Judges to the time of the Maccabees; it made no difference whether the Israelites were attacking other towns or Israelite towns were being captured by invaders (Jg 9: 45; 20: 48; 2 S 17: 13; 1 K 20: 10; 2 K 3: 25; 8: 12; 25: 9-10; 1 M 5: 35; 11: 48; 16: 10). At the very least, the fortifications were dismantled (2 K 14: 13).

Yet war had to bring profit to someone. Before being burnt, conquered towns were pillaged (2 S 8: 8; 12: 30; 2 K 14. 14; 25: 13f.; 1 M 5: 28, 35, etc.); a camp abandoned by the enemy would be pillaged (2 K 7: 16; 1 M 4: 23); flocks were carried off as booty (1 S 14: 32; 27: 9; 30: 20); even the dead were stripped of everything worth while on the very field of battle (1 S 31: 8); the victors took away everything they could carry (2 Ch 20: 25; cf. Dt 20: 14). The appetite for plunder and for the joy it brought (1 S 30: 16) was a spur to the combatants (2 K 3: 23), but there was a danger that the soldiers might take to plundering instead of exploiting their victory (1 S 14: 24; 1 M 4: 17-18). Few pleasures were accounted comparable to that of sharing in the distribution of booty (Is 9: 2; Ps 119: 162). This was how the fighting men made themselves rich, for they had no other way: Yahweh promised Nabuchodonosor the riches of Egypt as wages for his army (Ez 29: 19).

The story of 1 K 20: 39-40 could mean that every man had a right to what he himself laid hands on: a man had captured a prisoner whom he had left a comrade to guard: if the latter let him escape, he had either to take his place or to pay a large fine (cf. Jos 7: 21; 2 K 7: 8, though in these two texts, for different reasons, such behaviour is frowned on). From very ancient times, the custom was to collect and then to share out the booty (Jg 5: 30; cf. Is 9: 2; Pr 16: 19). A law is ascribed to Moses according to which the booty had to be divided equally, one half for the fighting men and the other half for the rest of the community, after both parts had been subjected to a tax for the Levites (Nb 31: 26-47). David introduced the rule that the men left behind to guard the baggage should share the spoil along with the fighting men (1 S 30: 24-25). In the early wars of Israel, the leader had a special portion which his men left him of their own free will (Jg 8: 24-25; perhaps 1 S 30: 20). Later on the king reserved the most valuable articles for himself or for the treasury of the sanctuary (2 S 8: 7-8, 11; 12: 30). In a confederate army, the allies had a right to share the booty (cf. Gn 14: 24), the amount of which was probably agreed upon beforehand, as it was among other ancient peoples.

People, as well as things, fell into the hands of the victor. The historical books of the Bible record instances of barbarous treatment meted out to defeated enemies: under Josue, five Canaanite kings were trampled underfoot and put to death (Jos 10: 24-26); Adoni-Sedeq had his thumbs and big toes cut off (Jg 1: 6); under Gideon, the Midianite leaders were beheaded (Jg 7: 25). When David went raiding in the Negeb, he killed every single man and woman (1 S 27: 9, 11); he massacred all the Amalekites who fell into his hands (1 S 30: 17), and put to death two-thirds of the population of Moab (2 S 8: 2). Amasias executed 10,000 Edomite prisoners of war (2 Ch 25: 12), and the law of Dt 20: 12-13 lays down that if a city refuses to surrender, every male in it shall be put to death. But these instances are exceptional, and the law of Dt was purely theoretical.[1] Apart from the *herem* in a holy war which involved all living beings,[2] the massacre of prisoners was never a general rule, nor were the tortures of which Assyrian texts and monuments offer only too many examples. Even Gideon, in his day, would have spared Zebah and Salmunna if he had not been bound by the law of blood-vengeance (Jg 8: 18-21), and the kings of Israel had a reputation for mercy (1 K 20: 31): they did not kill their prisoners of war (2 K 6: 22—which need not be corrected).

The reasons for this conduct were not purely humanitarian. The last two texts do not clearly state that this was the motive, and Dt 20: 19 seems to exclude the idea, when it says that trees should be spared because they are not men. Self-interest would counsel moderation, for both the community and the individual stood to gain by keeping enemy prisoners alive. They would pay tribute, could be used for forced labour, or as public slaves, or as Temple slaves; they could even be sold as slaves to private individuals. We said above that in Israel, as among other ancient peoples, war was one of the sources of the slave-supply,[3] and that, in all probability, prisoners of war became public slaves in the service of the king or the sanctuary.[4]

1. Cf. p. 81.   2. It will be studied in the next chapter, cf. pp. 260-261
3. Cf. pp. 80-81.   4. Cf. pp. 88-90.

The short story in 1 K 20: 39 states that the soldier really meant to keep the prisoner as his own slave. According to Jl 4: 3, the nations drew lots for the people of Yahweh and sold the boys and girls. We are better informed about women captured in war. The soldiers of Sisera, if they had won the battle, could have had 'a young girl, or two young girls, for each warrior' (Jg 5: 30). According to Nb 31: 18, 27 after the campaign against Midian the women who were virgins were divided between the fighting men and the rest of the people. The law of Dt 21: 10-14 authorizes an Israelite to marry a woman captured in war,[1] but she thereby ceases to be a slave, 'puts off her captive's robes' and (though she may be divorced) may never be sold. This presumes that if a female prisoner is not taken to wife by her master, she remains a slave.

Lastly, political reasons led first the Assyrians and then the Babylonians to substitute deportation for enslavement, and whole populations were deported, as they had previously been enslaved. The Israelites never had an opportunity to copy this practice, but they suffered from it: the inhabitants of the northern kingdom were deported *en masse* after the conquests of Tiglath-Pilesar (2 K 15: 29) and after the fall of Samaria (2 K 17: 6). Part of the population of Judah was deported after each of the two sieges of Jerusalem by Nabuchodonosor (2 K 24: 14f.; 25: 11; Jr 52: 27-30). At the beginning of the Exile, their lot was an unenviable one, but at least they were not slaves.

1. Cf. p. 81.

THE HOLY WAR

AMONG all the peoples of antiquity, war was linked with religion. It was begun at the command of the gods, or at least with their approval, manifested by omens; it was accompanied by sacrifices, and conducted with the help of the gods who ensured victory, for which they were thanked by an offering of part of the booty. In antiquity, then, every war was a holy war, in a broad sense. More strictly, the Greeks gave the name of 'holy wars' (ἱεροὶ πόλεμοι) to those which the amphictyony of Delphi conducted against any of its members who had violated the sacred rights of Apollo. More strictly still, the holy war of Islam, the *jihad*, is the duty incumbent upon every Moslem to spread his faith by force of arms.

This last notion of a holy war is utterly foreign to Israel. It is incompatible with the idea of Yahwism as the particular religion and the peculiar possession of the chosen people. But, precisely because of this essential relation between the people and its God, all the institutions of Israel were invested with a sacred character, war just as much as kingship or legislation. This does not mean that every war was a religious war—a concept which does not appear until very late, under the Maccabees: Israel did not fight for its faith, but for its existence. This means that war is a sacred action, with its own particular ideology and rites; this ideology, these rites, give it a specific character of its own, and single it out among the other wars of antiquity, where the religious aspect was something accessory. Such was the primitive concept of war in Israel but (as with kingship), this sacral character faded into the background and war became a 'profane' thing. Nevertheless, it did retain a religious character for a long time; the old ideal survived, sometimes modified, sometimes taking on a new lease of life in particular surroundings or at particular times. We shall attempt to trace the evolution of this process.

1. *The concept of the holy war, and its rites*

When the people took up arms they were called the people of Yahweh or the people of God (Jg 5: 13; 20: 2), the troops of God (1 S 17: 26), or the armies of Yahweh (Ex 12: 41; cf. 7: 4). The combatants had to be in a state of ritual cleanliness, *i.e.* 'made holy' (Jos 3: 5; cf. Jr 6: 4; 22: 7; Jl 4: 9). They were bound to remain continent (1 S 21: 6; 2 S 11: 11), and this obligation of cleanliness extended to the camp, which had to be kept 'holy' if Yahweh was to encamp with his troops (Dt 23: 10-15).

The reason is that the wars of Israel were the wars of Yahweh (1 S 18: 17; 25: 28), and the national epic was sung of in the 'Book of the Wars of Yahweh' (Nb 21: 14), a book no longer extant. The enemies of Israel were the enemies of Yahweh (Jg 5: 31; 1 S 30: 26; cf. Ex 17: 16). Before marching out to battle a sacrifice was offered to Yahweh (1 S 7: 9; 13: 9, 12); most important of all, Yahweh was consulted (Jg 20: 23, 28; 1 S 14: 37; 23: 2, 4) by means of the ephod and sacred lots (1 S 23: 9f.; 30: 7f.) and he decided when to go to war. He himself marched in the van of the army (Jg 4: 14; 2 S 5: 24; cf. Dt 20: 4).

The visible sign of this presence of Yahweh was the Ark. Tradition told how it had been with the people during their many wanderings in the desert, wanderings which are represented as the marches of an army on the move, and Nb 10: 35-36 has preserved some ancient battle-cries. When the Ark was leaving, they shouted: 'Arise, Yahweh, and let thy enemies be scattered . . .', and when it came to rest: 'Return, Yahweh, to the countless thousands of Israel.' It had led the Israelites across the Jordan, when they themselves had been 'sanctified' for the war of conquest (Jos 3: 6), and had been carried in solemn procession around the walls of Jericho (Jos 6: 6f.). Even under David, the Ark was in the camp with all Israel in front of Rabbath Ammon (2 S 11: 11). The history of the battle of Apheq is particularly instructive (1 S 4). The success of the Philistines is attributed to the absence of the Ark; so it is brought from Shiloh and the Philistines deduce that 'God has come into the camp'. This time, however, the Ark does not bring victory; worse, it is itself captured by the enemy, and this capture is felt as an inexplicable disaster, more painful than the massacre of the army itself.

When the Ark arrived at Apheq, the Israelites had raised the battle-cry, the t'rû'ah (1 S 4: 5f.), which was the signal for battle,[1] but this cry was also part of the ritual surrounding the Ark (2 S 6: 15) and was a religious cry. It is not quite so certain that the title Yahweh Sabaoth should be connected with the Ark and its rôle as a *palladium* in the wars of Israel, though the assertion is often made. This title seems to stem originally from the sanctuary of Shiloh,[2] but not strictly with reference to the Ark which was kept there; besides, it is not certain that Yhwh S'ba'ôth means 'Yahweh of the armies' (of Israel), or that the title had any connection whatever with the military institutions of Israel or with their religious aspect.

The combatants in a holy war left home with the certainty of victory, for 'Yahweh had' already 'given the enemy into their hands' (Jos 6: 2; 8: 1, 18; Jg 3: 28; 4: 7; 7: 9, 15; 1 S 23: 4; 24: 5, etc.). Faith was an indispensable condition: they had to have faith and to be without fear (Jos 8: 1; 10: 8, 25). Those who were afraid did not have the necessary religious dispositions and were to be sent away (Jg 7: 3; cf. Dt 20: 8, where the dismissal of such men is explained by a psychological reason, which was not the original reason for the custom).

During battle, it was Yahweh who fought for Israel (Jos 10: 14, 42; Jg 20: 35). He called into service the elements of nature (Jos 10: 11; 24: 7; Jg 5: 20; 1 S 7: 10) and threw the enemy into confusion (Jg 4: 15; 7: 22; 1 S 7: 10; 14: 20), striking a 'divine terror' into them (1 S 14: 15).

But victory was neither the last act of the holy war nor its culmination. This occurs in the *ḥerem*, the anathema carried out on the vanquished enemy and his goods. The meaning of the root and the usage of the cognate verb show that the word *ḥerem* denotes the fact of 'separating' something, of taking it out of profane use and reserving it for a sacred use; alternatively, it may stand for the thing which is 'separated' in this way, forbidden to man and consecretated to God. The term found its way into the general vocabulary of worship (Nb 18: 14; Lv 27: 21, 28; Ez 44: 29), but originally it belonged to the ritual of the holy war: it meant leaving to God the fruits of Victory. The precise form of this varies in different texts. As a general rule, the *ḥerem* originates from an order of Yahweh (Dt 7: 2; 20: 17; Jos 8: 2; 1 S 15: 3); by way of exception, it may be the result of a vow by the people (Nb 21: 2). In theory, it admits of no exception whatsoever: at Jericho, all living things, men and beasts, had to be put to death, the town and all its movables were burnt, the metal objects consecrated to Yahweh (Jos 6: 18-24). Akan, by transgressing the *ḥerem*, brought down a curse upon the people; he was therefore punished and the goods he had stolen were destroyed (Jos 7). In Saul's war against the Amalekites (1 S 15), too, the anathema was to admit of no exception and Saul was condemned for not having interpreted it strictly. The destruction of cultic objects in the towns of Canaan is explicitly prescribed in Dt 7: 5, 25. The *ḥerem* was to be applied with the utmost rigour against any Israelite town which had denied Yahweh (Dt 13: 13-18). Elsewhere, however, the *ḥerem* was more or less restricted: it applied to all human beings, but the cattle and movable goods could be kept as booty (Dt 2: 34-35; 3: 6-7 and probably 20: 16; Jos 8: 2, 27; 11:14 and probably 10: 28f.); sometimes women who were virgins might be excepted (Nb 31: 14-18; Jg 21: 11, though in these two references a special reason is given). When a foreign town was captured, only the male population was put to death (Dt 20: 14, but here the word *ḥerem* is not found and the text does not refer to a holy war, in contrast with the reference to towns in the Holy Land, Dt 20: 16-17).

It is hard to say to what extent these prescriptions were in fact applied. It is remarkable that they should be laid down in Deuteronomy, published at a period when the holy war was little more than a memory, and that the concrete examples should be found in the Book of Josue, the final redaction of which is equally late. On the other hand, neither the word nor the custom is found in the stories of the Judges, who really did conduct holy wars. Yet there is no doubt that both the notion and the practice of the *herem* are of great antiquity. They are found in the old story of the war of the tribes against Benjamin (Jg 21: 11), and in the prophetical tradition about Saul's war against the Amalekites (1 S 15). In addition, we have one parallel from outside the Bible: Mesha, king of Moab in the ninth century B.C., boasts in his inscription that he had massacred the entire Israelite population of Nebo, which he had vowed to anathema (verb: *hrm*) in honour of his god Ashtar-Kemosh.

2. *The holy wars at the beginning of Israel's history*

What we have just said about the *herem* applies also, in a more general way, to the whole picture of the holy war sketched out in the preceding paragraph. The features which go to its making are borrowed from various books, and among all the accounts of the early wars of Israel, there is not one where all the several elements are found. Yet the way in which some of the stories are grouped, the recurrence of the same formulas, and the common spirit which pervades these texts all stamp these wars as genuine holy wars. Let us take a few examples.

The character is clearly seen in the war of Deborah and Baraq against Sisera, both in the prose account (Jg 4) and in the Song of Deborah (Jg 5). Yahweh gave Baraq the order to march and promised to deliver Sisera into his hands (4: 6-7); even before the fighting starts, Yahweh has already handed over Sisera, is marching ahead of Baraq, striking panic into the enemy, so that not a man will escape (4: 14-16). The poem sings the praises of those who freely answered the call, *i.e.* of those who had faith in their victory (5: 2, 9): the fighting men were, then, God's champions (5: 8), the people of Yahweh (5: 13) come to Yahweh's aid (5: 23). It was Yahweh himself who went forward in the earthquake and in the rending of the skies (5: 4); the stars themselves fought on his side (5: 20) and the enemies of Yahweh were annihilated (5: 31). Both the prose account and the song are close enough to the events to have given us a faithful version of what the participants thought of this war: for them, it was a sacred action.

We discussed above[1] the strategy of Gideon against the Midianites, but that examination did not take into account the religious element, which is an essential factor in Jg 6-8. Gideon had received the spirit of Yahweh (6: 34), who had intervened twice to assure him of success (6: 36-40; 7: 9f.). It was Yahweh who delivered Midian into the hands of Israel (7: 2, 7, 14-15; 8: 3, 7). It was Yahweh and not Israel who emerged victorious (7: 2); the timid, who had no faith to support them, had been sent away (7: 3), and the army itself had then been reduced to a tiny group, in order to make the divine intervention even more striking (7: 7). The battle-cry (*t'rûah*) was: "The

1. Cf. pp. 217-218.

sword for Yahweh and for Gideon!' (7: 20). Yahweh threw the enemy camp into confusion (7: 21). This too was a war of Yahweh.

The wars against the Philistines will provide a last example. Jonathan and his armour-bearer went unescorted to attack the Philistine post at Mikmas, for Yahweh would give them victory, whether they were many or few (1 S 14: 6f.); a sign assures Jonathan that Yahweh had delivered the enemy into his hands (14: 10, 12); the earth quaked, and a panic sent by God fell upon the camp (14: 15). Saul consulted the oracles (14: 18), and the panic among the Philistines increased until they took to flight: 'that day, Yahweh gave the victory to Israel' (14: 18-23). A fast had been ordered for all combatants.

During the period of the Judges and under the reign of Saul, the Israelites fought only defensive wars, and it has recently been suggested that the holy wars of Israel were always defensive wars. But the conquest of the Promised Land is certainly described as a holy war, as *the* holy war, in the Book of Josue, and whatever the date of its redaction or the part to be attributed to its redactors, they certainly did not invent this tradition. It is represented also by the quite independent account in Jg 1: Judah and Simeon undertake the conquest of their territory after consulting Yahweh, who gives them the land (Jg 1: 1-2, 4). In addition, we must admit that arms played at least some part in the settlement in Canaan, and that this conquest created a climate of opinion particularly favourable to the idea of the holy war: then above all Yahweh the Warrior (Ex 15: 3), the Master of War (1 S 17: 47), had to fight for his people.

This is the principal fact: it was Yahweh who fought for Israel, not Israel which fought for its God. The holy war, in Israel, was not a war of religion. According to the ancient texts, the wars in the time of Josue and the Judges were not undertaken in order to spread belief in Yahweh, as the *jihad* is undertaken to spread the Moslem faith; nor was their object to defend a faith against a foreign religion. It is worthy of note that, in the Book of Josue, the accounts of the conquest do not contain a single allusion to the gods or the worship of Canaanites. Similarly, in the Book of Judges, Israel is not fighting (directly) for its religious freedom, but for its existence as a people. The Song of Deborah contrasts Yahweh and his champions with Sisera and his chariots, but not with Sisera and his gods; Gideon destroys an altar to Baal, but the episode has no connection whatever with his holy war against the Midianites. Religious preoccupations appear only in texts which are of late redaction, in the prescriptions of Deuteronomy on the *herem* (Dt 7: 2-5, 25; 20: 17-18), in the Deuteronomic framework of the Book of Judges (Jg 2: 2-3), and in the still later redaction of the war of Moses against Midian (Nb 25: 17-18; 31: 15-16). But everything we have so far said shows that, even if these holy wars were not wars of religion, they were essentially religious: in these wars, Yahweh was fighting for the life of his people, and the people associated themselves with this action by an act of faith and by conforming to a definite ritual.

3. Religion and the wars under the monarchy

One could say that this strictly sacred character of war disappeared with the advent of the monarchy and the establishment of a professional army. It is no longer Yahweh who marches ahead of his people to fight the Wars of Yahweh, but the king who leads his people out and fights its wars (1 S 8: 20). The combatants are no longer warriors who volunteer to fight, but professionals in the pay of the king, or conscripts recruited by his officials. This transformation was obviously going to precipitate a crisis: the ground was prepared for it under Saul, who transgressed the ritual laid down for a holy war (1 S 15), and it happened under David, who engaged a large number of foreign mercenaries, and ordered a census of the people for military purposes (2 S 24: 1-9). War became, of necessity, the state's concern; it was 'profaned'.

To begin with, however, certain rites of the holy war were retained. In the Ammonite war, the Ark accompanied the troops, and Uriah (a Hittite mercenary!) kept strict continence (2 S 11: 11). David 'consecrated' to Yahweh the silver and gold of his conquests (2 S 8: 11). But these rites became accessory things, mere trappings, and even if the saying 'Yahweh gives the victory' (2 S 8: 6, 14) was still heard, it was certainly David who secured it by human means and who received the glory which ensued (2 S 12: 28).

Yahweh was no longer consulted, by drawing lots, about the opportuneness of war or about the manner in which it should be waged, but prophets did intervene with the king (1 K 20: 13-14, 22, 28); sometimes the king would even ask them for an oracle (1 K 22: 5-12). Eliseus accompanied the kings of Israel and of Judah in their expedition against Moab and passed on to them the word of Yahweh (2 K 3: 11-19; cf. also 2 K 13: 15f.). These prophets still used the time-honoured vocabulary of the holy war: Yahweh would deliver the enemy into the hands of Israel (1 K 20: 13, 28; 22: 6, 12; 2 K 3: 18), but whereas in olden times it had been the leader in war who was inspired by God, the prophets were no longer anything more than the religious auxiliaries of the king. In the first prophetical schools the idea of the holy war lived on, but precisely because the wars were no longer holy, the prophets often stood opposed to the king. In opposition to a false prophet who foretells that Yahweh will deliver Ramoth of Gilead into the hands of Achab, a true prophet predicts disaster (1 K 22: 19-28), and Eliseus refused to consult Yahweh on behalf of the king of Israel, who is nevertheless leader of an expedition against Moab (2 K 3: 13-14).

In the following century, Isaias stood out as the defender of the ancient concept of the holy war, against those who would appeal to political motives. When Aram and Ephraim launched their attack on Judah, he foretold disaster for them; if only Achaz would have faith in Yahweh (Is 7: 4-9), and when Sennacherib was threatening Jerusalem, Isaias assured the people that God would save the city (37: 33-35). He condemned military preparations (22: 9-11) and the seeking of help from abroad (31: 1-3), for 'Yahweh Sabaoth would come down to fight on mount Sion and on its hill' (31: 4). Against Assur, Yahweh would come from afar 'in the heat of his anger, in the heart of a consuming fire, in a storm of rain and hail' (30: 27-30). Against Egypt, he would come on a cloud, and the Egyptians would lose heart and turn against one another (19: 1-2). Characteristics of the holy war recur in these passages: there is a certitude of victory, faith in Yahweh, a warrior action on the part of God, who unleashes the elements and strikes his enemies with terror: we can still hear an echo of the Song of Deborah, of the conquest stories and of the period of the Judges. Isaias and other prophets probably borrowed their concept of the 'day of Yahweh' from this ancient ideology; it would be a day when Yahweh would come for a victorious battle. But these new 'wars of Yahweh' take place only in the visions of the prophets and are no longer the wars of Israel: the latter have become utterly profane. Isaias tells his contemporaries: you counted on human means 'but you have not looked at their Author nor seen him who made all things long ago' (22: 11), or: 'Salvation lay in conversion and calm, your power lay in perfect confidence, and you did not want them' (30: 15).

What is even more remarkable is that the rules of the holy war should have received their clearest and most complete expression at the end of the monarchy in the redaction of Deuteronomy. The book contains many very ancient elements, and this justifies the use made of it above to describe the practices of the holy war. But our particular interest at present is to study the new spirit which animates these laws, and which dominates the speeches at the beginning and end of the book. The entire history of Israel is presented as a holy war. And the past is a pledge against the future: 'Yahweh your God, who marches in front of you, will fight for you, just as you have seen him do in Egypt' (Dt 1: 30). Again, 'Remember what Yahweh your God did to Pharaoh and to all Egypt . . . so Yahweh your God will deal with all the peoples you are afraid to face' (7: 18-19). 'It is not the uprightness of your behaviour nor the rightness of your heart which will win you possession of their country; it is because of their perversity that Yahweh your God will dispossess these nations to your advantage' (9: 5). 'No one will hold his ground before you; Yahweh your God will make you feared and formidable throughout the length of the land your feet shall tread' (11: 25). 'Be strong and hold fast, do not be afraid, for it is Yahweh your God who is marching with you' (31: 6). And the book closes with the Blessings of Moses, an old song breathing a warlike spirit, which ends (Dt 33: 29):

Happy art thou, O Israel—who is like thee?
People victorious through Yahweh,

whose shield is thy help,
whose sword is thy victory.
Thy enemies will stoop low to worst thee,
but thou shalt trample on their backs.

When Deuteronomy was edited, under Josias, the age of conquests and military triumphs was long past, and there was no longer any occasion to apply its prescriptions about the siege of foreign towns (Dt 20: 10-20) or the execution of an anathema (Dt 2: 34-35; 3: 6-7; 7: 2, 5). Yet this new reflection on the idea of the holy war, though transformed by the progress in theology, does fit in with a concrete historical situation. Under Josias, the revival of the national spirit and the overthrow of the Assyrian yoke gave new and lively hope to the people, and it is by no means impossible that these texts of Deuteronomy inspired the king when he tried to halt the march of Nechao (2 K 23: 29; 2 Ch 35: 20f.). But it was only a momentary blaze, which the disaster of Megiddo quenched utterly. Jeremias lived through these events, and he has no place for the holy war in his preaching: the contrast with Isaias is striking. The last wars of Judah and the desperate resistance against the Chaldeans, recorded in the books of Jeremias and Kings, had no religious character. The reason was that Yahweh had deserted the camp of Israel, and decided, in anger, to chastise his people (2 K 23: 27; 24: 3, 20); he even fought against them (Jr 21: 5) and issued orders to the Chaldeans 'to attack, to capture and burn Jerusalem' (Jr 34: 22). It is impossible to imagine anything more opposed to the ancient ideology of the holy war.

4. The religious wars of the Maccabees

During the Jewish period, in the books of Maccabees, we meet once more some of the characteristics of the holy war. Judas and his brothers conduct 'the fight of Israel' (1 M 3: 2). The raising of the liberation army recalls many ancient memories (1 M 3: 46-60): the assembly met at Mispah, as it had once done for the holy war against Benjamin (Jg 20: 1); they fasted, and sought to know the will of God by opening the book of the law, since there was no longer any ephod or prophet; they sounded the trumpet, shouted the battle-cry (cf. Nb 10: 9 and the t'rûah), and mobilized the army according to the rules set down in Dt 20: 5-8. Before the battle of Emmaus, Judas exhorted the people not to fear and to call upon God: 'All the nations shall acknowledge that there is someone who saves Israel' (1 M 4: 8-11; cf. 1 S 17: 46), and after the victory they blessed God for the 'great salvation' he had wrought in Israel (1 M 4: 24-25; cf. 1 S 14: 45). Judas overthrew altars in Philistine territory, burnt their idols and sacked the towns (1 M 5: 68; cf. Dt 7: 5, 25). In the second book, the echo of ancient texts rings fainter, but the same ideas are found: they prepare for battle by prayer and fasting (2 M 13: 10-12), and Iudas' exhortation to the troops runs: 'The enemy trusts his arms and his boldness, but we—we have placed our trust in God, master of all things' (2 M 8: 18). 'Help from God' (2 M 8: 23) or 'Victory from God' (2 M 13: 15) are the passwords. Judas asks the Lord 'to send a good angel before us to sow fear and fright' among the enemy (2 M 15: 23).

But in spite of these resemblances, the spirit is no longer that of the holy war. The Maccabees and their men are not inspired by God; God did not order the war and he does not intervene directly in it. The most one dare ask is that he should send an angel (2 M 15: 23), and God answers this prayer when an armed rider appears on the road to Bethsur (2 M 11: 6-8). But this heavenly envoy plays only a symbolic part: this fight, like all the others, is undertaken and won by merely human means. It is significant that the allusions to the help God gave his people in ancient times refer to the crossing of the Red Sea (1 M 4: 9), and to the deliverance of Jerusalem from Sennacherib (1 M 7: 40-42; 2 M 8: 19; 15: 22), but never to the holy wars of the conquest and the period of the Judges.

All this prevents us from taking the Maccabean war as a holy war. But it is a war of religion. Mattathias calls upon 'everyone who is zealous for the law and who observes the Covenant' to follow him (1 M 2: 27); Judas fights for the people and the holy place (1 M 3: 43, 59), for 'the town, religion and the Temple' (2 M 15: 17). The combatants fight for religious freedom, not only against foreign masters who proscribe the observance of the law, but also against their perjured brethren 'who abandon the holy Covenant' (Dn 11: 30), and 'who have abandoned the law' (1 M 10: 14; cf. 1: 52). The rebellion began when Mattathias cut the throat of a Jew who had agreed to offer sacrifice on the altar at Modin (1 M 2: 24). Always and everywhere, the Maccabees vow to fight against the 'wicked', the 'miscreants', the 'sinners' (1 M 2: 44, 48; 3: 5-6; 6: 21; 7: 23-24), who were allying themselves with pagans (1 M 3: 15; 4: 2; 7: 5; 9: 25; 11: 21-25). It was a war of religion which set the faithful Jews fighting against their fellow-Jews who had rallied to the cause of Hellenism and against their foreign protectors. It was inevitable that both sides should soon introduce into it political interests, as happened in the French wars of religion during the sixteenth century, and in Holland during the seventeenth century.

5. The 'Order of the War' from Qumran

An astonishing document has recently been found which shows that the ideas of the holy war gained a new lease of life among a group of Jews: it is the 'Order of the War' found in the caves of Qumran. The book dates, in all probability, from the first century B.C., and gives rules for the war which will take place at the end of time between the 'Sons of Light' and the 'Sons of Darkness', i.e. between the faithful Jews, those of the Qumran community, on the one hand, and all the pagan nations on the other. One can, of course, point to external similarities with the Books of Maccabees, but in the Qumran writing the struggle is evidently regarded as a holy war. It is worthy of note that of the five explicit citations of the Old Testament, three refer to texts used above (Nb 10: 9; Dt 7: 21-22; 20: 2-5), and there are in addition many expressions which recall the ancient ideology. This 'war', like the holy war of bygone ages, had its own rites; it even turns into a ceremony in which priests and Levites have an essential part to play. The army is 'the people of God', and the soldiers are volunteers called to fight the battles of God. In battle the standards are inscribed 'Right hand of God', 'God's moment', 'God's slaughter', and God himself, who is called 'The Hero of the Fight', marches along with his faithful, accompanied by the army of angels. It is the Hand of God which is raised against Belial and his empire. Victory is certain: there may be moments of distress, but the enemies of God and Israel will finally be annihilated, and the eternal reign of Light will begin.

The vision is not of a religious conquest of the world, of a conversion imposed by force of arms; there is nothing resembling the Moslem *jihad*. The world is at the moment divided between Light and Darkness, between Good and Evil, and order can only be established by the total destruction of the forces of Darkness and of Evil, by the total victory of God and the Sons of Light. Against the background of this dualist thought, the old notion of the holy war takes on a particularly violent character, expands to cosmic dimensions, and yet is referred to the end of the present era of time: it is an apocalyptic war.

In this curious text, visionary dreams are mingled with practical arrangements that could be taken straight from a Roman military text-book; yet the authors of the work were apparently convinced that this war was certainly coming, and were waiting for it. The text was copied time and time again, and fragments of many copies have been found. In its pages, the readers could feed their hatred for the Sons of Belial, whom they recognized in the pagan occupants of the Holy Land. Possibly it was inspired by the fanaticism of those Zealots who took part in the revolts against the Romans, and who may have thought that the time was come for the final struggle between the Sons of Darkness and the Sons of Light.

IV

RELIGIOUS INSTITUTIONS

INTRODUCTORY

THOUGH this section has been entitled 'Religious Institutions', to keep the parallel with the three previous sections, the title is not meant to indicate a rigid distinction, for religion penetrated the entire social life of the nation. Circumcision had a religious significance; in the sense defined above, the monarchy was a religious institution; war itself, at least at the beginning of Israel's history, was a religious act; and Israelite law, even where it concerned profane matters, remained a religious law, and allowed for the possibility of an appeal to the judgment of God. In this section, however, we shall discuss those institutions which are directly concerned with the external worship of God.

By 'cult' we mean all those acts by which communities or individuals give outward expression to their religious life, by which they seek and achieve contact with God. But since God, as Creator, necessarily takes precedence of every creature, man's action in cultic worship is basically the response of a creature to his Creator. Lastly, cultic worship is essentially a social phenomenon: even when an individual offers such worship, he does so in accordance with fixed rules, as far as possible in fixed places, and generally at fixed times. If we take cult in this, its strict sense, it cannot exist without ritual.

The usual Hebrew word for the cult is 'abodah: it is a 'service', like the service given to the king (1 Ch 26: 30). The primary meaning of 'serving' God is giving him outward worship (Ex 3: 12; 9: 1, 13, etc.). The Bible speaks of the 'service' of Yahweh (Jos 22: 27), of the 'service' of the Tent (Ex 30: 16, etc.), of the Dwelling (Ex 27: 19, etc.) and of the Temple (Ez 44: 14, etc.). The same word is used for a particular act of cultic worship (Ex 12: 25-26; 13: 5).

By 'rites' we mean the outward forms which this service takes. Israelite ritual may be similar to the rituals of other religions, or even borrowed from them; but its important feature lies in the new meaning which these rites received, a meaning which was determined by the religious ideas of Israel's faith. Without trespassing into the domain of biblical theology, we must underline the characteristics of the Israelite cult, and see what distinguishes it from other Oriental cults, even when the rites are the same.

(1) The Israelites worshipped a God who was the only God. From the first settlement in Canaan almost to the end of the monarchy, this did not prevent them from worshipping in several sanctuaries, but it did mean that in all these sanctuaries the same God was adored, and that any worship offered to gods

other than Yahweh was condemned, as in the first of the Ten Commandments (Ex 20: 3; Dt 5: 7) and in Dt 6: 13: 'Thou shalt fear Yahweh thy God,
and shalt "serve" none but Him'. In particular, this faith precluded belief in
any female deity as consort of Yahweh, and thereby excluded all those sensual
rites which stemmed from belief in wedded divinities. For Israel there was
only one God, a holy God, before whom man became conscious of his
uncleanness and his sins: hence one of the purposes of Israelite cult was purification and expiation, though the precise degree to which this idea was
present depended on the particular act of worship and the stage of religious
development at the time.

(2) The Israelites worshipped a personal God who intervened in history:
Yahweh was the God of the Covenant. Their cult was not the re-enacting of
myths about the origin of the world, as in Mesopotamia, nor of nature-
myths, as in Canaan. It commemorated, strengthened or restored that Covenant which Yahweh had made with his people at a certain moment in history.
Israel was the first nation to reject extra-temporal myths and to replace them
by a history of salvation, and all the echoes of ancient myths which can be
perceived in certain passages of the Old Testament do not lessen the originality of this idea. To-day, when some writers would hold that even in Israel,
ritual was the expression of myth, it is important to stress that the Israelite
cult was connected with history, not with myth.

(3) The Israelites had no images in their cult. Both versions of the Decalogue
contain the prohibition of images (Ex 20: 4 and Dt 5: 8), and the prohibition
certainly dates back to the age of Moses. This prohibition was a primitive
and characteristic feature of Yahwism, and the reason for it was that Yahweh
was a God who could not be seen, and who therefore could not be represented. Yahweh spoke from the height of heaven (Ex 20: 22-23), and the
Israelites saw nothing when Yahweh spoke to them out of the fire on Sinai
(Dt 4: 15-18): the two texts draw the same conclusion, that men must not
fashion cultic images. This does not mean that Yahweh was thought of, from
the very beginning, as a purely spiritual being, for such words would have
meant nothing to the Hebrew mind; but it does mean that any image of God
would be inadequate. In other words, the prohibition of images is an implicit
recognition that God is transcendent; it was left to later ages to define him as
a spiritual being. From the very beginning, the prohibition of images safeguarded the religion of Israel from copying foreign systems of worship,
where gods were represented like men, with bodily and sensual needs
demanding satisfaction. The consequences of this were important. In spite of
modern arguments to the contrary, there was never any image of Yahweh
in the Ark. There was never any such image at Shiloh or in the Temple of
Solomon, and Jeroboam's 'golden calves' were originally only the supports
of the invisible godhead. The Holy of Holies, where Yahweh made himself
present, was not open to the faithful; and the altar of Yahweh, unlike other

altars, had no statue or divine symbol connected with it. Rather, Israelite sacrifices rose in smoke to the heaven where Yahweh dwelt.

The study of cultic institutions is therefore bound up with biblical theology. But it is connected also with the history of religions, where it looks for analogies, for the explanation and perhaps even the origin of rites. In the present work, however, we are not concerned to describe how in fact the Israelites practised their religion, for they were, especially at certain periods, allured to a syncretist, or even to a purely pagan, cult. Such deviations will be touched on only indirectly in the following chapters. Our aim is rather to describe those cultic institutions which the Old Testament presents as legitimate institutions of true Yahwism. We shall describe first, the places of cultic worship, secondly, the persons involved in it, then the acts prescribed (especially sacrifice, the main act), and lastly, the religious calendar and its feasts.

CHAPTER ONE

SEMITIC SANCTUARIES

CULT is the outward homage paid to a god. Since the god is thought of as receiving this homage and listening to the prayer of his suppliant in the place where this worship is offered, the god is considered to be present there in some way or other, at least while the act of worship is being performed. This notion is common to all religions, and our present purpose is to see how it was expressed among the Semites, and, more particularly, among the Canaanites and Israelites.

1. *Sacred territory*

It seems to be a characteristic of Semitic religion that the holy place is not merely the precise spot, an altar of sanctuary, where worship is performed; it includes also a certain space around the temple or altar. Of course, this is not something exclusively Semitic: the larger Greek Temples were surrounded by a *temenos*, enclosed by a *peribole*: the area inside was the sacred precinct. Among the Semites, however, this sacred precinct seems to have had a special importance.

At Khafajeh in central Mesopotamia, there was from 3000 B.C. onwards a temple which had a large forecourt and which was surrounded by an oval precinct of 100 by 70 yards. There may have been a similar sanctuary at the same epoch in northern Mesopotamia, at El-'Obeid. At Uqair the temple stood on a broad esplanade, but occupied less than half of it. Though this type of temple did not survive, the great Babylonian temples generally had a large forecourt; the strictly Assyrian temples, however, did not, but their plans show evidence of non-Semitic influence. Inside big towns, the temples with their courts were grouped together in a sacred quarter. Under the Third Dynasty of Ur, the ziggurat and the buildings connected with the cult were enclosed in a precinct measuring 200 yards square; it was repaired time and time again, and even enlarged in the neo-Babylonian period. At Babylon, the ziggurat of Etemenanki stood inside an enclosure 400 yards square, with religious buildings along its sides. At Mareb in Arabia, in the first millennium B.C., there was a sanctuary of the moon-god Ilumqah, to which later tradition gave the name *Maḥram Bilqis*, the 'sacred territory of Bilqis', the Arabic name for the queen of Sheba: its shape was oval, its size 100 by 70 yards, and it was flanked by a large peristyle entry.

In Phoenicia and in Syria, the oldest temples which have been well preserved date back only to the Hellenistic period, but they certainly carry on the tradition of a more ancient style. The most impressive is the sanctuary of Bel at Palmyra, which stands in the centre of an esplanade 225 yards square. Similarly, the sanctuary of Betotece, near Tartus, is a little Ionic temple in a courtyard of 140 by 90 yards; Amrit and Umm el-'Amed could also be mentioned.

Solomon's temple in Jerusalem followed this tradition: it too was surrounded by a courtyard. This court was enlarged by Herod until it became an esplanade 300 yards broad and nearly 500 yards long. Indeed, even in the desert sanctuary, according to Ex 27: 9–19, the Tent stood in an enclosure of 100 by 50 cubits, and Ezechiel visualized the future temple as standing in a court 500 cubits square 'to separate the sacred from the profane' (Ez 42: 20).

Where public worship was conducted in the open air outside the cities, the sacred space could be marked off by a line of stones, like those which nowadays surround certain Moslem *welis* or which mark a place of prayer in the desert. If any of these crude installations have survived from antiquity, it is impossible to distinguish them from enclosures of a much later period. But one biblical text throws light on them. The first halt of the Israelites after crossing the Jordan was *ha-Gilgal*, 'the Gilgal'. Here they camped (Jos 4: 19; 5: 10; 9: 6; 10: 6, etc.), were circumcised (Jos 5: 9), and celebrated the Passover (Jos 5: 10). Under Saul, sacrifices were offered there 'before Yahweh' (1 S 10: 8; 11: 15; 13: 7f.; 15: 21, 33). Later, however, the prophets condemned the sacrifices at Gilgal, along with those offered at Bethel (Os 12: 12; Am 4: 4). Gilgal, then, was a place of public worship, which retained its importance for several centuries, but there is no mention of a temple built there. (The Beth-ha-Gilgal of Ne 12: 29 refers to another place.) Now the word *gilgal* means a 'circle' (of stones)—cf. *galgal*, 'a wheel'—and Jos 4: 20 says that Josue there set up twelve stones taken from the bed of the river Jordan. These stones, then, probably marked the boundaries of the sacred enclosure: they may have been placed there by the Israelites when they selected their first place of worship in the Promised Land; or it may be that they marked the site of an older Canaanite sanctuary, and that their presence was explained later by a reference to the history of Israel.

The 'holy place' might be a vast stretch of land or even an entire mountain. Mecca is surrounded by sacred territory, the *haram*: it takes several hours to walk through it, and, in days gone by, its boundaries were only vaguely indicated by a number of stones (*anṣab*). The whole of mount Hermon was sacred, as its name (a cognate of *haram*) implies. Indeed, just before the great theophany of Sinai, Moses was commanded by Yahweh to mark out the circumference of the mountain: no one was to climb it, or even to touch its base (Ex 19: 12).

2. The sacred character of places of cultic worship

A place of worship was sacred, *i.e.* withdrawn from profane use: this is the ultimate meaning of 'sacred'. The 500 cubits around the temple of Ezechiel were there 'to separate the sacred from the profane' (Ez 42: 20). There were two possible reasons for setting apart a space which was held to be sacred: men may have decided to cut off a definite portion of land from their own territory in order to consecrate it to God, as a kind of tithe on the earth; by paying this tithe, they could then make free use of the rest; alternatively, they may have put a stop to profane activity because the mysterious and fearful presence of a divinity in his sanctuary radiated around the place of worship, and this second reason is more in conformity with the texts, the rites and the spirit of Semitic religion. But whichever view be correct, the consequences are the same: the sacred territory was reserved, and characterized by certain prohibitions and privileges. Throughout the whole of Mecca's *ḥaram*, hunting, cutting down trees and even cutting grass are forbidden, apart from a few exceptions which the skill of casuists has devised. Before entering it, everyone must perform certain sacral rites, and put on special clothes; at least one part of this territory is a place of asylum.

It was exactly the same in Israel. The interdict concerning Sinai has already been mentioned (Ex 19: 12). After his dream at Bethel, Jacob cried out: 'How fearsome is this place!' (Gn 28: 17). God said to Moses at the burning bush: 'Do not come near this place. Take off thy sandals from thy feet, for the place where thou art standing is holy ground' (Ex 3: 5). The Israelites were forbidden to go near the Tent (Nb 18: 22). In the Temple at Jerusalem, notices protecting the sanctuary were posted up, and the admonitions became more and more severe as one approached the sanctuary itself. Gentiles were not allowed into the court of Israel, and notices reminded them that the penalty for infringing this precept was death. The liturgy itself did not take place in the Holy of Holies; the high priest alone could enter there, and then but once a year, and alone, on the great Day of Atonement (Lv 16: 15; He 9: 7). The Temple was also a place of asylum (1 K 1: 50-53; 2: 28-31). The six cities of refuge, which also enjoyed this privilege of asylum (Jos 20: 1-6), had inherited it from ancient sanctuaries in the same place.[1]

3. The choice of places of cultic worship

The choice of places where the cult might be practised was not left to man's discretion. In such a place, the worshipper could meet his god: the place had to be indicated, therefore, by a manifestation of the god's presence or by his activity. This could happen in two ways: by an explicit manifestation, *e.g.* when the deity appeared, or gave a command, or a sign; or by an

1. Cf. p. 163.

implicit manifestation, when natural effects were ascribed to the power of a god.

(a) *Theophanies*. We shall see later[1] how divine apparitions determined the places where the patriarchs worshipped. Under the Judges, the sanctuary of Ophra was founded by Gideon on the spot where, according to one tradition (Jg 6: 24), the Angel of Yahweh appeared to him or, according to another tradition (Jg 6: 25-26), where he received the command of Yahweh in a dream. The Temple of Jerusalem was built on the spot where the Angel of Yahweh had stood and where David had set up an altar (2 S 24: 16-25). In Ex 20: 24 (the text needs no correction), God promises to accept the sacrifices offered in any place where he may 'call to mind his Name', *i.e.* wherever he may manifest his presence.

There is nothing quite like this anywhere else in the Semitic world, presumably because we do not happen to have sufficiently explicit texts about the first foundation of sanctuaries. In Mesopotamia, however, the deity intervenes when his temple has to be restored. Akkadian ritual prescribes that when a temple is in danger of falling down, it may be demolished and rebuilt only if favourable omens can be obtained. Marduk gave Nabopolassar the order to restore the ziggurat of Babylon, the Etemenanki. Under Nabonidus, Marduk is said to have stirred up the winds which uncovered the foundations of the temple which the king was to restore. Again, Nabonidus saw Marduk and Sin in a dream, ordering him to restore the temple of Sin at Haran. But the most explicit example of all is the dream of Gudea at Lagash, about 2000 B.C.: the god Ningirsu appeared to him and commanded him to restore his temple, the Eninnu, according to a plan which he showed him. If the gods intervened in this way to have their sanctuaries restored, they must have done the same when they were first built and when the site itself was selected.

(b) *Sacred waters*. The nature-religion of Canaan saw a manifestation of divine presence or action in the springs which made the earth fruitful, in the wells which provided water for flocks, in the trees which bore witness to this fertility, and in the high places where the clouds gathered to give their longed-for rain. The Israelites and their ancestors were shepherds and peasants, and they too shared this mentality.

If, however, we set aside all ideas and myths concerning the sacredness of waters, rivers and the sea, and fix our attention on places of worship connected with water, we are struck by the relative scarcity of such places. In Syria, there is a spring at Palmyra and the pool of Hierapolis; in Phoenicia, there is the spring of Afqa and a few others. Monuments and texts provide no evidence of any public worship in these places before the Hellenistic epoch, but the cult practised at that time was a Syrian or Phoenician cult in a Greek disguise, and the cult had probably been in vogue in earlier ages.

1. Cf. p. 288 ff.

In Palestine, during the Graeco-Roman epoch, there was a sanctuary dedicated to Pan near one of the sources of the Jordan: it must have taken the place of an earlier sanctuary of a Canaanite divinity. A few place-names in the Bible, taken in their immediate context, probably point to the existence of sanctuaries near a spring or well: Qadesh, whose name marks it out as a 'holy' place, is also called (Gn 14: 7) the Spring of Judgment or of the Oracle—En-Mishpat. On the road from Jerusalem to Jericho, there was a Spring of the Sun—En-Shemesh (Jos 15: 7; 18: 17); in Jerusalem there was a Dragon's Spring—En-ha-Tannin (Ne 2: 13); a village in the Negeb was called Baalath-Beer, which may mean 'Lady of the Well' (Jos 19: 8); all these names are evidence of a cult, or at least of a religious legend. The well of Lahai-Roi, 'of the Living One who sees', preserved the memory of the divine apparition to Hagar (Gn 16: 13-14), and Isaac lived there (Gn 24: 62; 25: 11). According to 1 K 1: 33-40, Solomon was consecrated king at the spring of Gihon in Jerusalem, and there seems to have been a sanctuary there (perhaps for the Ark) before the Temple was built.[1] Best known of all are the wells of Beer-sheba, where Abraham called upon Yahweh (Gn 21: 31), and where Isaac set up an altar to Yahweh who had appeared to him there (Gn 26: 23-25).

(c) *Sacred trees*. Throughout the ancient Near East, certain trees were acknowledged to have a religious character. Sacred trees are especially frequent in Mesopotamian iconography. They are shown as a symbol of fertility or as closely associated with the fertility gods, but it is questionable whether the tree itself ever represented the gods: the tree was incidental to the cult, and, strictly speaking, was not itself worshipped. All our information from Phoenicia is of late date, and affected by Greek influence, but the association of trees with the cult of female divinities must not be forgotten. The cypress in particular was consecrated to Astarte.

In modern Palestine, an isolated tree or a group of trees often marks the site of a Moslem *wely*. The tradition is age-old. The prophets condemned those Israelites who went to sacrifice on the tops of hills in the shade of trees (Os 4: 13-14), or near terebinths (Is 1: 29; 57: 5). Deuteronomy, and the texts which stem from it, condemn the places of worship set up 'on the hills, under every verdant tree' (Dt 12: 2; 1 K 14: 23; 2 K 16: 4; 17: 10; cf. Jr 2: 20; 3: 6; 17: 2; Ez 6: 13; 20: 28 and also Is 57: 5). But here too it must be noted that not one of these texts speaks of any worship paid to these trees: they merely mark the place of worship.

In ancient Israel, legitimate places of cultic worship could also be marked by a tree but one must beware of applying this principle to all the trees mentioned in the Old Testament. There is no sign whatever of a sanctuary in the Valley of the Terebinth (1 S 17: 2), and the Oak of Thabor (1 S 10: 3) may be nothing more than a topographical reference. The Palm-tree of Deborah, on the other hand, between Ramah and Bethel, where the prophetess used to

1. Cf. p. 102.

settle disputes between Israelites, probably did have a religious significance (Jg 4: 5): and it is clearly a different tree from the Oak of Tears, which stood below Bethel and marked the grave of a different Deborah, who was Rachel's nurse (Gn 35: 8). It is still more certain that the Oak near Shechem, where Jacob buried his family's idols (Gn 35: 4), belonged to a place of worship. This is apparently the tree which stood 'in the sanctuary of Yahweh' at Shechem, beneath which Josue set up a big stone (Jos 24: 26); hence we may identify it with the 'Terebinth of the stele which stands at Shechem' (Jg 9: 6, correcting the text), which marked a place of worship where Abimelek was proclaimed king. The same tree is also called the Oak of Moreh, *i.e.* the 'Oak of the Teacher' or 'of the Soothsayer': it is called the *maqôm*, *i.e.* the holy place, of Shechem in Gn 12: 6, and must be the same as the Oak of the Soothsayers near Shechem (Jg 9: 37). Near Hebron, there stood the Oak of Mambre, where Abraham set up an altar (Gn 13: 18), and under which he received the three mysterious visitors (Gn 18: 4, 8); it was venerated until the Byzantine epoch.[1] In describing the foundation of the place of worship at Beersheba, Gn 21: 33 says that Abraham 'planted a terebinth'.

The translations 'oak' and 'terebinth' are inspired by the ancient versions of the Bible, and are only approximate. The two Hebrew words seem to be synonymous and to mean simply any large tree.

(d) *Heights*. Since the mountains reached up to heaven, they were considered as the dwelling-place of the gods. Babylonian mythology placed the birth of the great gods on the Mountain of the World. East of this mountain, they believed there was a Mountain of the East where the sun arose, and where the gods assembled on New Year's day, to fix the destinies of the universe. In the Epic of Gilgamesh, too, the Mountain of Cedars was a dwelling-place of the gods.

The poems of Ras Shamra mention a holy mountain called Saphon. On the crests, or peaks, or slopes of Saphon, the gods met together; there Anath built a temple for Baal, and Baal had his throne. Because of his connection with this mountain, Baal was called Baal Saphon, and Phoenician sailors carried his worship, under this name, to Pelusium and probably as far as Corfu. Traces of this mythology can be found in the Bible. The fallen tyrant of Is 14: 13-15 who wanted to be equal to God had said: 'I shall take my seat on the mountain of the assembly, on the slopes of Saphon, I shall climb to the very top of the black clouds, and I shall be like Elyon'. In Ez 28: 14-16, the king of Tyre, identified with Melqart, the god-king of his city, stood on the 'holy mountain of God' before being cast down from it.

Devotion and cult alike demanded that this holy mountain should be fixed in a definite spot on earth. Concrete reality and the pure ideal, cult and myth were inseparable: Olympus was both the home of the gods and a mountain in Greece. In the same way, Saphon was both the home of Baal and Jebel

1. Cf. pp. 292-293.

al-Aqra', lying on the northern horizon from Ras Shamra: in Graeco-Roman times it was called Mount Casios, and Zeus Casios was venerated there: he was the heir of Baal.

There were other holy mountains in the land of Canaan. Lebanon and Siryon (another name for Hermon, Dt 3: 9) are mentioned in lists of gods given in Hittite treaties of the second millennium B.C. Several centuries later, an inscription from Cyprus records that a Phoenician invoked the Baal of Lebanon. It has already been stated that the very name of Hermon indicates that it was a holy mountain,[1] and the slopes and peaks of this massif are even to-day covered with the ruins of several sanctuaries, which were still in use in the fourth century A.D. There was a place in the neighbourhood called Baal Hermon, according to 1 Ch 5: 23, and the apocalyptic Book of Henoch states that the angels who sought to have relations with women came down on to Hermon.

Thabor, too, was a place of worship. In the blessings of Zabulon (Dt 33: 19), the mountain where the peoples come to offer sacrifices is very probably Thabor, which stood on the frontier of this tribe: the lawfulness of this worship is not questioned in this text, but Os 5: 1 accuses the priests, the king and the leaders of Israel of having been 'a snare set on Thabor', *i.e.* of having paved the way for the ruin of the people through an unholy cult. On the other hand, quite a plausible case can be made out for a slight textual correction which would include Thabor among the sacred mountains of the Phoenicians listed by Philo of Byblos: it would then stand together with Saphon, the Lebanon and Hermon. In the text of Osee just quoted, the Greek version translated Thabor by Itabyrion, which, together with Atabyrion, is its name in Greek authors. Now Rhodes had a sanctuary dedicated to Zeus Atabyrios; in all likelihood, the cult was brought to Rhodes from abroad, and did in fact represent a Baal of Thabor. Christian tradition eventually fixed upon Thabor as the site of the unnamed mountain where the Transfiguration took place (cf. Mt 17: 1).

Carmel, too, had a long history as a place of worship. The Sacred Cape, *rôsh qadôsh*, mentioned in Egyptian geographical lists from Thutmoses III onwards, is probably Carmel. In the fourth century B.C., the Periplus of Scylax calls Carmel a holy mountain of Zeus. Tacitus says it is the name both of a mountain and of a god: there was an altar on the top, where Vespasian offered sacrifice, but no temple or statue. The god was the Baal of the mountain, the manifestation of a great Oriental god, now identified as Baalshamem or, more probably, as Melqart, the patron of Tyre. Just as the Phoenicians and the Israelites disputed over the possession of the mountain, so the cult of the Tyrian Baal was a rival to that of Yahweh: Yahweh's exclusive rights were finally established by the miraculous triumph of Elias over the prophets of Baal (1 K 18: 20-48).

1. Cf. p. 275.

This is but one example of how Yahweh appropriated the mountains formerly consecrated to the old gods. He made the Lebanon and Siryon leap like young calves (Ps 29: 6); he created Saphon and the 'South' (the word must have replaced the name of another mountain); Thabor and Hermon sing for joy to his name (Ps 89: 13). And yet the Old Testament expressly teaches that Yahweh had only two holy mountains, Sinai where he had revealed himself, and Sion where he lived. Sinai-Horeb is called the 'mountain of God' in the stories of the Exodus (Ex 3: 1; 4: 27; 18: 5; 24: 13), and of Elias' pilgrimage (1 K 19: 8). Yahweh came from Sinai (Dt 33: 2, and the obscure text in Ps 68: 18), and made his home in the Temple of Jerusalem (1 K 8: 10-13). The mountain of Bashan (does this mean the massif of Hauran? or Hermon, which overlooks that region from the north?) was a 'mountain of God'; why, then, did it despise Sion, the little mountain Yahweh had chosen for his home (Ps 68: 16-17)? Mount Sion is the 'holy mountain' of the Psalms (Ps 2: 6; 3: 5; 15: 1; 43: 3; 99: 9) and of the later prophetical texts (Is 27 :13; 56: 7; 57: 13; 65: 11; 66: 20; Jr 31: 23; Ez 20: 40; Dn 9: 16, 20; Ab 16; Jl 2: 1; 4: 17; So 3: 11). The true 'slope of Saphon' was mount Sion, the dwelling place of Yahweh, the great king (Ps 48: 2-3). In days yet to come, mount Sion would be raised still higher, 'set upon the peak of the mountains, raised high above the hills, and peoples would come to the "mountain of Yahweh"' (Is 2. 2-3 = Mi 4 · 1-2). The future temple of Ez 40: 2 stood 'on a very high mountain', where an ideal Jerusalem was built (cf. Za 14: 10).

4. Ziggurats

The feeling that divinity revealed itself on the mountains led men to build high sanctuaries not only where there was already a mountain, but even in the low-lying plains. Some of the oldest temples of Mesopotamia are built on top of a high terrace (e.g. Uruk, Khafajeh, El-'Obeid, Uqair, etc.). The artificial base upon which the temple stood was built as a series of terraces, and was shaped like a pyramid; and eventually it became the principal element in the structure, giving birth to a type of religious architecture which is characteristic of Babylonia and of the regions which came under its influence: the many-storeyed tower, or ziggurat.

The thickest concentration of ziggurats is in Lower Mesopotamia, but they are found in Assyria too, on the Syrian side of the Euphrates at Mari, and at Susa in Persia. At Tchoga-Zanbil in Persia an enormous ziggurat has recently been discovered, 114 yards square at its base, and over 165 feet high. These vast constructions were merely sub-structures: texts and monuments alike make it clear that there was a sanctuary on top, and excavations have proved that there was another sanctuary at the base. There are two possible explanations for this fact: either the god was held to live in the sanctuary at the top, and to come down to make his presence known in the lower sanctuary, or the upper sanctuary was thought of as a kind of rest-house for the god on his way down to earth, as if he stopped there on his way to the lower sanctuary, which was his permanent residence on earth. Whichever explanation is right, it certainly seems to be true that the ziggurat was built as a kind of 'mountain' where the god could meet his devotees, a giant stairway which the god could go down, and the devotee go up, to meet each other.

The ziggurat in Babylon was called *E-temen-an-ki*, the 'temple of the foundation of heaven and earth'. Its base was 100 yards square, and we learn from a cuneiform tablet and from Herodotus that it was at least as high. The earliest references to it are in the 7th century B.C., but it must have been in existence long before this date: it was several times destroyed and restored. The biblical tradition about the Tower of Babel (Gn 11: 1-9) must refer to this, or to some other ruined tower of Babylon. The idea in building it was to bring their god closer to them, but the Tower fell down, and the theological mind of the biblical author interpreted this disaster as a divine chastisement of men whose pride had sought to climb into heaven.

5. Temples

A temple may be defined as a building in which public worship is performed, erected on a 'holy place'. The older Semitic languages have no special word for a temple. In Akkadian, it is called simply the 'house' (*bitu*) or the 'palace' (*ekallu*: from the Sumerian E-KAL, meaning 'Big House') of the god; another Akkadian word is *ekurru*, which is also borrowed from the Sumerian E-KUR, meaning 'House of the Mountain'. In Phoenician, the Ras Shamra texts give us the words *bt* (house) and *hkl* (palace: from the Akkadian *ekallu*): both are equally common. In Hebrew too, the temple is a 'house' (*beth*) or a 'palace' (*hekal*, from the Akkadian, via the Phoenician). In the later books of the Bible, especially Ezechiel, the Temple is often called *miqdash*, which, strictly speaking, means a 'holy place or sanctuary', and not a building which is used as a temple. In older texts, the word stands parallel with 'high places' (Is 16: 12; Am 7: 9), and it is used for the open-air sanctuary under the Oak of Shechem (Jos 24: 26).

In Akkadian, Phoenician and Hebrew, then, the same words are used for the 'house' or 'palace' of a god and for the 'house' or 'palace' of a king. And in fact, every temple was built as a home for a divinity. Mesopotamian temples usually followed the same plan as a large house or palace; and the god, represented by his statue, was held to dwell there. But the plans of Assyrian temples are not the same as those in Babylonia, except where Babylonian influence was felt; and the reason is that the two nations built their houses in different ways. In Babylonia, the worshippers entered a courtyard flanked by buildings to pray in front of the rooms where the service was conducted: they were not allowed into these rooms, but a door in the middle gave them a straight view of the divine image which stood in the *cella* at the back. Those Assyrian temples which were untouched by Babylonian influence had no courtyard; instead, an open door led into one of the longer sides of the temple, and you had to turn to see the statue, which stood at the back of the room where the services were held: the statue stood where the fireplace was in ordinary houses. Thus the approach to the divinity was both closer and more mysterious than in Babylonia, and this fact corresponds to a difference of religious feeling between the two peoples.

It has also been debated whether some of the buildings in Syria-Palestine were religious buildings or not (*e.g.* the 'palace' or 'temple' at Ai); this is in itself sufficient proof that the house of a god was built on the plan of the king's palace. In the third millennium B.C. the temples discovered at Jericho, Megiddo and the (northern) Tell el-Farah, and the building at Ai, all have an indirect entry on the longer side, like the old Assyrian temples. In the second millennium, the plan was modified (as were presumably, the plans of the royal residences): the buildings became much more elaborate. A *cella* (sometimes raised), and a portico or a vestibule were added; these stood one behind the other, and worshippers entered on the shorter side of the building. This plan is followed in a sanctuary built about 1400 B.C. which has recently been discovered at Hazor, and in the little temple at Tell Tainat in Syria, *ca.* 1000 B.C. It is also the plan which Solomon adopted for his Temple in Jerusalem.

We have more information about Mesopotamian temples than any others, and in them the daily routine of the god was the same as the king's: the statue was first dressed, then had meals served to it, and was taken for walks with a sumptuous escort. This daily ritual meant that the temple had to be surrounded with a great many dependent buildings, such as lodgings for the priests and the servants, stores, kitchens and stables, all of which emphasized still more the similarity between the god's temple and the king's palace.

Even in Mesopotamia, however, the god did not live only in the temple, in the sense that his presence and his activity were restricted to this building. Some of his devotees may have thought so, but this was not the real meaning of their religion. The statue or sacred symbol was not the god himself, but only a visible sign and tangible embodiment of his presence. The temple was, of course, his dwelling-place, but he could have several temples in the same country, or even in the same town, and the great gods, whether their name was Marduk or Assur or Baal, could act throughout the length and breadth of the universe. The purpose of ziggurats was, as we have seen, to meet the god half-way when he was coming down from heaven to his temple.

When we come to discuss the Temple at Jerusalem, we shall see how these same ideas are found, in a purified form, in the religion of Israel. Though the lawful worship of Yahweh forbade images, the Temple was still referred to as the 'house of Yahweh' and the place of which he had said: 'My Name shall be there' (1 K 8: 29).

6. 'High places'

(a) *The name*. The Bible often refers to Canaanite sanctuaries, and to those Israelite sanctuaries which were imitations of them, as *bamôth*, which the Vulgate translates as *excelsa*, and modern versions as 'high places'. This rendering is not exact, and calls at least for clarification.

We do not know the verbal root from which the noun *bamah* is derived, and the noun itself may be pre-Semitic. The cognate word in Ugaritic means the 'back' or 'trunk' of an animal, and the corresponding word in Akkadian has this meaning too, though it can also denote any elevated ground, such as the crest of a hill or a height. In the Bible, apart from the cultic references and some obscure texts, *bamah* can mean the 'back' of one's enemies (Dt 33: 29), 'heights' (used of ground, without further precision, Dt 32: 13; Is 58: 14; Mi 1: 3; Am 4: 13; Ha 3: 19; Ps 18: 34), the 'back' of clouds (Is 14: 14) or the 'waves' of the sea (Jb 9: 8). The idea which the word expresses, therefore, is something which stands out in relief from its background, but the idea of a mountain or hill is not contained in the word itself.

(b) *The situation of the 'high places'*. The last statement is confirmed by the information given in the Bible about the place of the *bamôth*. It is quite true that some, perhaps many, of them, stood on the heights of Palestine: men 'went up' to the neighbouring *bamah* from Samuel's home-town (1 S 9: 13, 14, 19), and 'came down' from it (1 S 9: 25). In Ez 20: 28-29, the word *bamah* is interpreted, by a play on words, as the name of the lofty hill where men went to offer sacrifice, and the worship conducted in the *bamôth* is set along-side worship on the hills (in 2 K 16: 4; 17: 9-10). Solomon built a *bamah* for Kemosh and Milkom on the mountain east of Jerusalem (1 K 11: 7). The fact that high hills seemed to be places destined for worship is a sufficient explana-tion of these texts. But not all the *bamôth* were on uninhabited hills: there were *bamôth* in the towns (1 K 13: 32; 2 K 17: 29; 23: 5), and even at the gate of Jerusalem (2 K 23: 8). In Ez 6: 3, Yahweh, tells not only the mountains and hills, but even the ravines and valleys, that he is going to destroy their *bamôth*. The *bamah* of Topheth stood in the valley of Ben-Hinnom at Jerusalem (Jr 7: 31; 32: 35). Clearly, the rendering 'high places' will not fit these last texts. The one and only meaning which suits all the references is 'a mound or knoll' for purposes of cultic worship. They may have used, sometimes, a prominent rock, but it would seem that this mound was usually artificial: this would make sense of the texts which speak of *bamôth* being 'built' (1 K 11: 7; 14: 23; 2 K 17: 9; 21: 3; Jr 19: 5), 'torn down' and 'destroyed' (2 K 23: 8; Ez 6: 3).

(c) *The evidence of archaeology*. Recent discoveries throw light on this explanation of *bamôth*. A large oval platform, 8 by 10 yards across, has been uncovered at Megiddo: it stood approximately 6 feet above the surrounding ground. It was built of big stones, had a flight of steps leading up to the platform, and had a rectangular wall around it. It was built about the middle of the third millennium B.C., and remained in use for several centuries. It is quite certain that sacrifice was offered there, and temples were later built beside it. At Nahariyah, near Haifa, there is a little sanctuary whose foundation is dated in the eighteenth or seventeenth century B.C., and beside it a heap of stones, roughly circular in form, which was originally 6 yards in diameter, and later widened to 14 yards. A similar platform has been unearthed at Hazor in a thirteenth century sanctuary. South-east of Jerusalem, on the crest of a hill near Malhah, there is a series of artificial mounds, two of which have been excavated. The one which is better preserved is 25 yards in diameter, and is made of earth and stones held in position by a polygonal wall: a flight of man-made steps led to the top. The pottery associated with this level belongs to the seventh and sixth centuries B.C.

There is no need for hesitation: these installations were *hamôth*. Their dates range from the old Canaanite epoch to the end of the monarchy in Judah, *i.e.* the first ones were places of worship for the Canaanites, and the last ones for the Israelites. Sometimes they stand in a town (as at Megiddo), sometimes near a town (as at Nahariyah, where the site of the ancient town has been discovered close by), and sometimes in the open country, on a natural height (as at Malhah): here, then, are three examples from the Bible of the different places in which *bamôth* were found.

(d) *Cultic installations.* Since the 'high place' was a place of worship, each one had to have its altar. The knoll itself, from which the name *bamah* comes, could serve as an altar, but an altar could also be built on it, and some biblical texts do in fact mention an altar as part of the 'high place' (2 K 21: 3; 2 Ch 14: 2, 4; Ez 6: 6).

The most characteristic adornments of a *bamah*, however, were the *maṣṣebah* and the *'asherah*, mentioned in connection with 'high places' in 1 K 14: 23; 2 K 18: 4; 23: 13-14; 2 Ch 14: 2, 4. To these must be added texts which, though not expressly mentioning any *bamah*, certainly have the same type of worship in mind: Ex 34: 13; Dt 7: 5; 12: 3; 16: 21-22; Mi 5: 12-13. On the other hand, such furnishings are not found only in *bamôth*: Achab installed an *'asherah* according to 1 K 16: 33, and a *maṣṣebah* according to 2 K 3: 2, in the temple of Baal at Samaria.

A *maṣṣebah* is a stone standing upright, a commemorative stele. It stood as the sign of an alliance or an undertaking (Gn 31: 45, 51-52; Ex 24: 4; Is 19: 19-20): compare with these texts the 'stone' set up by Josue in the sanctuary at Shechem (Jos 24: 26-27); alternatively it might be a monument in honour of the dead (Gn 35: 20; 2 S 18: 18). As an object of cult, it recalled a manifestation of a god, and was the sign of the divine presence. Jacob, after his vision at Bethel, set up the stone he had used for a pillow as a *maṣṣebah*, and declared that this was a *beth El*, a 'house of God' (Gn 28: 18; cf. Gn 31: 13 and the parallel tradition in 35: 14). It was a short step from this reasoning to accepting the stone itself as a representation of the divinity, and there was no need for the stone to be hewn into the form of a statue: even in its crude, natural shape, it was a symbol of the divinity. This explains why the *maṣṣebôth*, which older texts regard as legitimate signs of the divine presence, are, in later texts, condemned, along with all the other panoply of Canaanite worship. (Note that in some of these texts, *maṣṣebah* stands close beside *pesel*, 'a sculptured idol': Lv 26: 1; Dt 7: 5; 12: 3; Mi 5: 12.)

A *maṣṣebah* was the symbol of a male deity (2 K 3: 2 mentions the *maṣṣebah* of Baal: and cf. 2 K 10: 26-27, though the text is here uncertain). The female divinities were represented by an *'asherah*, a name which stands both for the goddess and for her cultic symbol. The Ras Shamra texts mention the goddess Asherah as the consort of the god El, and in the Bible she is the consort of Baal (Jg 3: 7; 2 K 23: 4). The *'asherah* itself was made of wood (Jg 6: 26), cut into shape by man (Ex 34: 13; Jg 6: 25), and could be burned (Dt 12: 3; 2 K 23: 6, 15). Apparently, it could also be a living tree planted by man (Dt 16: 21) and uprooted by him (Mi 5: 13; 2 K 23: 14); but, far more commonly, it was a wooden object made by man (1 K 14: 15; 16: 33; 2 K 17: 16; 21: 3; Is 17: 8), erected like the *maṣṣebôth* (2 K 17: 10), and standing upright (2 K 13: 6; Is 27: 9)—which means it must have been a kind of post or stake. It is impossible to be more precise about its appearance, and there is no proof that the post was carved to look like a goddess.

Some texts include among the appurtenances of the *bamôth* the *ḥammanîm* (Lv 26: 30; 2 Ch 14: 4; 34: 4, 7; Ez 6: 4, 6). The word is never found outside *bamôth* except when it is with an *'asherah* (Is 17: 8), or with an altar and an *'asherah* (Is 27: 9). These *ḥammanîm* could not have been very large, for, according to 2 Ch 34: 4, they could be placed on an altar. For a long time, they were thought to be 'pillars of the sun', but Nabatean and Palmyra inscriptions leave no doubt that the correct translation is 'altars for incense'. None of the texts which contain the word is earlier than the Exile, and Ez 6: 4, 6 appears to be the oldest. (Is 17: 7-8 is commonly considered as an addition.) Now some excavations in Palestine, especially those at Lakish, have yielded small stone objects, cubic or elongated in shape, which date from post-Exilic times: the upper part is hollowed out like a cup, and bears traces of fire; it is a reasonable theory to identify them as *ḥammanîm*. Possibly the name and this particular type of perfume-brazier were introduced into Palestine at a rather late date, but incense-offerings (with no mention of *ḥammanîm*) are connected with the cult of *bamôth* in the Deuteronomic redaction of the Books of Kings (1 K 3: 3; 22: 44; 2 K 12: 4, etc.); Jr 19: 13 and 32: 29 tells us that incense was offered on the roof-tops, and Os 4: 13 records these offerings as an element of the cult practised on the heights. Perhaps in those earlier days, the incense-offerings were offered on something larger than the *ḥammanîm* of Lakish: excavations have yielded perfume-braziers of baked clay from the Canaanite period, and little stone altars from the period of the Israelite monarchy have been discovered at Megiddo and at Shechem: all of these may be called 'altars for incense'.[1]

The Bible speaks time and time again of the 'high places' set in the shade, 'under every verdant tree',[2] which proves that they were open-air sanctuaries: but buildings were sometimes attached to them. When it simply says that a 'high place' was 'built', it may mean, as we have seen, merely that the artificial mound, the bamah, was constructed. But other texts presuppose that roofed buildings also existed there. According to 1 S 9: 22, in the town where Samuel lived the high place had a 'room' which could hold thirty guests. At the great high place of Gibeon where Solomon spent the night and had a vision of Yahweh in a dream (1 K 3: 5), there was probably a building for him to sleep in. Several texts refer to the 'houses', the temples in the bamôth, like the one Jeroboam built at Bethel (1 K 12: 31) or those in which the Samaritan colonists installed their idols (2 K 17: 29) and conducted their services (2 K 17: 32), which were demolished by Josias (2 K 23: 19).

(e) 'High places' and funeral services. Apparently, the bamôth were also used for funeral services. It has already been stated that a stele, a maṣṣebah, could mark the place of a grave (Gn 35: 20) or stand as a monument to the dead (2 S 18: 18). On the other hand, a heap of stones was sometimes piled over a tomb, e.g. Akan's (Jos 7: 26), the king of Ai's (Jos 8: 29), and Absalom's (2 S 18: 17). These funeral mounds looked exactly the same as the mounds used for worship, the bamôth, in the sense defined at the beginning of this section. This throws light on a number of texts. The Qumran manuscript of Isaias allows us to translate Is 53: 9 as: 'They set his grave among the wicked, and his bamah with the rich (or, the wicked, or, demons)'. A simple change of the vowels makes the meaningless text of Jb 27: 15 read: 'those who survive them will be buried in bamôth, and their widows will shed no tears for them'. Ez 43: 7 needs no correction, and reads: 'They shall no longer defile my holy name by their prostitution, and by the funeral pillars of their kings in their bamôth' (cf. v. 9). The word translated 'funeral pillar' is peger, which in the Bible usually means 'a corpse': but in the Ras Shamra texts it means 'monument, stele'. It is therefore a synonym for maṣṣebah, and it recurs in connection with the 'high places' in Lv 26: 30: this verse can therefore be translated: 'I shall destroy your high places (bamôth), reduce your altars of incense (ḥammanîm) to dust, and heap your steles (peger) on the steles (peger) of your false gods'. Archaeology confirms these statements: there was a line of steles on what has been rightly called the 'high place' of Gezer, and a Canaanite sanctuary with several upright steles has recently been discovered at Hazor: both of these must have been memorials to deceased of some rank. These conclusions are very reasonable, but they must not be pressed too far: the 'high places' were destined for general purposes of worship, and funeral rites were merely one element in this worship.

---

1. On the altar of perfumes in the Temple, cf. p. 411.   2. Cf. pp. 278–279.

(f) *The lawfulness of 'high places'*. These places of worship were not at first condemned by Israel's religion. Samuel offered a sacrifice in the high place of his home-town (1 S 9: 12f.); Gibeon had 'the biggest high place' where Solomon offered sacrifice and was favoured with a divine message (1 K 3: 4f.). The Israelites flocked to these sanctuaries right to the end of the monarchical period. Ezechias, of course, wanted to destroy them in the first attempt to centralize worship (2 K 18: 4), but Manasseh brought them back into service (2 K 21: 3), and they stayed in use until Josias' reform (2 K 23, which makes it quite clear that they were sanctuaries of Yahweh[1]).

They did, however, keep alive Canaanite traditions, often on the very same spot; and there was a strong temptation to practise a syncretist cult, to place beside the altar of Yahweh the stele of Baal and the sacred stake of Ashera, and to introduce the immoral practices of the Canaanites, and their funeral rites. This is what the prophets so often reacted against, and when they explicitly attack the *bamôth* by name (Os 10: 8; Am 7: 9; Jr 7: 31; cf. 19: 5; 32: 35), it is precisely because of the sins against true worship which were being committed there. The abuses continued, and the movement to centralize worship led to the condemnation of all 'high places' without discrimination: so the word *bamôth* became a synonym for pagan sanctuaries, or, at the very least, for unlawful sanctuaries. The Deuteronomic editor of the Books of Kings takes the word *bamôth* in this sense of 'illegitimate sanctuaries' and condemns all the kings of Israel and of Judah, except Ezechias and Josias, for not suppressing them: and the same censure is found in the later texts of the Pentateuch.

1. Cf. p. 337.

CHAPTER TWO

THE FIRST ISRAELITE SANCTUARIES

1. *The places where the Patriarchs worshipped*

THE Israelites attributed the foundation of certain sanctuaries to the Patriarchs. Obviously, the historian of to-day cannot verify this assertion, but he must acknowledge that the tradition is in perfect agreement with two proven facts: first, the places in question all stand along the line of demarcation between arable land and the zone where shepherds and goat-herds pastured their flocks; and this corresponds perfectly with the social position of the Patriarchs, who were semi-nomads. Secondly, these sanctuaries were not the most popular ones in the period of the Judges and under the monarchy, as they would have been if the tradition had been invented at a later date to provide an illustrious origin for certain places of worship. (Bethel is an exception, but it owed its importance under the king of Israel to political reasons.) From the time of the monarchy all these patriarchal sanctuaries became, apparently, suspect to orthodox Yahwists: they were certainly very old even in those days.

The last chapter described the rules which governed the choice of a place for worship, and the patriarchal sanctuaries were founded in accordance with these principles. Sanctuaries were erected where nature manifested the presence of the God of Abraham, Isaac and Jacob—near a tree, for example, or on a natural height, or by a water-source: but they were erected principally in places where God had shown himself in a theophany. Sanctuaries of this kind are found all along the route the patriarchs travelled.

(a) *Shechem.* According to Gn 12: 6-7 (Yahwistic tradition), Abraham's first stop in Canaan was at Shechem. He stopped at the *maqôm, i.e.* at the holy place where the Oak of Moreh stood: it was also called the 'Oak of the Teacher' or 'of the Soothsayer', and must therefore have been a tree where oracles were sought. It was in fact a Canaanite sanctuary, as the text itself recognizes by adding the explanation: 'the Canaanites were living in the country at the time'. But Yahweh appeared there to Abraham and promised the country to his descendants. So Abraham built him an altar there. Here, in skeleton form, is a typical story about the foundation of a sanctuary: theophany, divine message, beginning of the cult.

The origins of this sanctuary, however, have deeper roots in the Elohistic tradition, in its stories about Jacob and his sons. When Jacob was returning from Mesopotamia, he camped just outside Shechem, bought the piece of land where his tent stood from the sons of Hamor and set up an altar there (some critics prefer to read: a *maṣṣebah*), which he called 'El, God of Israel' (Gn 33: 18-20). After the agreement with the Shechemites had been broken by the treacherous attack of Simeon and Levi, Jacob left Shechem for Bethel (Gn 35: 1-4): it was a pilgrimage from one sanctuary to the other, for which he and his followers purified themselves and changed their clothes. The idols belonging to Jacob's family were buried 'under the Oak near Shechem', *i.e.* the Oak which is called, in the story of Abraham, the Oak of Moreh. Several theories have been advanced about the original significance of this ritual act of burying the idols: and yet there is no doubt what the Bible takes it to mean. It was an abandoning of pagan practices, parallel to the rejection of foreign gods which Josue demanded of the Israelites at Shechem because they had chosen to serve Yahweh (Jos 24: 21-24). One last memory of patriarchal times was connected with Shechem: Joseph's bones were said to have been taken there from Egypt, and in later ages his tomb was shown to visitors (Jos 24: 32). We have already discussed, under 'high places',[1] how tombs and funeral monuments were connected in this way with places of worship.

The pact which bound the tribes together and bound them all to Yahweh was concluded at Shechem, and Josue erected 'under the oak in the sanctuary at Yahweh' (*i.e.* the tree mentioned in the stories about Abraham and Jacob), a 'large stone', *i.e.* a *maṣṣebah* (Jos 24: 25-28). It was under this tree (called the tree of the *maṣṣebah*, if we accept a commonly received correction of the text) that Abimelek was proclaimed king (Jg 9: 6). This, too, was evidently the sanctuary where Roboam met the northern tribes when they were going to recognize him as king, and where his own clumsy behaviour destroyed all prospects of ending the political schism (1 K 12: 1-19).

Shechem was eclipsed by Shiloh during the period of the Judges, and by Bethel after the schism. It is possible, however, that the Deuteronomic redactors of the canonical books drew a veil over the survival of a sanctuary where the worship, to them, seemed stained by pagan practices. We have mentioned that they did not dare to call the 'great stone' of Jos 24: 26 a *maṣṣebah*, and probably they or their copyists suppressed the *maṣṣebah* of Jg 9: 6. In the book of Deuteronomy itself, the name of Shechem is not even mentioned, but the book does order large stones, with the Law written on them, to be set up on mount Ebal, and commands that an altar be built there: curses and blessings for the breaking and keeping of the Law are then to be pronounced on the two mountains, Ebal and Garizim (Dt 27). The same command is given more briefly in Dt 11: 26-32, with a mention of the Oak of Moreh in a retouched context. The Deuteronomic redaction of Jos 8: 30-35 relates, with important nuances, how this command was executed. Now Shechem stands between Ebal and Garizim, and there is certainly some con-

1. Cf. p. 287.

nection between these texts and that of Jos 24: 25-28, which relates how the inter-tribal pact was sealed at Shechem.[1] Lastly, Dt 31: 10-13 prescribes that the Law should be read periodically, during a feast. It is a tenable hypothesis, therefore, that the texts just mentioned may preserve the memory of a ritual for the renovation of the Covenant, celebrated at Shechem.

(b) *Bethel*. The Yahwistic tradition says that Abraham erected a second altar in Canaan, at his second camping station, between Bethel and Ai (cf. the short note in Gn 12: 8). Yet Gn 28: 10-22, which is much more detailed, and which combines both Yahwistic and Elohistic traditions, attributes the founding of this sanctuary to Jacob (cf. the analogous stories about Shechem). According to this text, when Jacob was on his way to Haran, he stopped for the night in a holy place, a *maqôm*. He had a dream in which he saw a 'ladder' (better, a stairway or a ramp) between heaven and earth. Thereupon he recognized that this was a *beth-El*, a 'house of God', and the gate of heaven: here we meet the same religious thought which gave rise to the building of ziggurats in Mesopotamia.[2] Jacob set up the stone he had used for a pillow as a *maṣṣebah*, and anointed it with oil. He made a vow that if he returned safe and sound, he would build a sanctuary there to which he would pay a tithe of all his possessions: so far the Elohistic narrative. The Yahwistic tradition adds an account of an apparition of Yahweh, who reaffirmed in Jacob's favour the promises made to Abraham. On his return from Mesopotamia, Jacob went on pilgrimage from Shechem to Bethel and set up there an altar and a stele (Gn 35: 1-9, 14-15: Elohistic tradition): this is presented as the fulfilment of his vow in Gn 28: 20-22, but it is also a doublet, for the erection of the stele and the explanation of the name Bethel in 35: 14-15 are a repetition of Gn 28: 18-19.

The actions of the founder constituted a ritual which was perpetuated by the faithful: there was, then, at Bethel a sanctuary which was said to have been founded by the patriarchs: the faithful went on pilgrimage there, poured oil on a stele and paid tithes. The pilgrimage is attested by 1 S 10: 3, the tithe by Am 4: 4. The tradition enshrined in Jg 20: 18, 26-28; 21: 2 told how men gathered before Yahweh at Bethel, offered him sacrifices, and consulted him: even the Ark was kept there for a time.

After the political schism, Jeroboam chose Bethel as the site for a place of worship to rival Jerusalem. We shall treat of the later history of the sanctuary elsewhere,[3] and content ourselves here with the story of its origin. It seems that at Bethel the cult of Yahweh had ousted that of a Canaanite divinity as it had done at Shechem. Jacob stopped in 'the *maqôm*', took one of the stones of the *maqôm* for his pillow, and slept in 'this *maqôm*' (Gn 28: 11): when he awoke after his dream, he cried out: 'How fearful is this *maqôm*!' (Gn 28: 17). The repetition of the word suggests that in the context it means—as it can— more than just 'place' or 'spot', and denotes rather a 'place of worship'.

1. Cf. pp. 143, 147, 148.   2. Cf. pp. 281-282.   3. Cf. pp. 333-335.

According to Gn 28: 19; 35: 7, Jacob gave the place the name Bethel or El-Bethel. Now El was the principal god in the Canaanite pantheon, and Bethel was for many centuries a divine name in the popular religion of Israel (cf. the documents from the Jewish colony at Elephantine and also two biblical references, Am 5: 4 and, clearer still, Jr 48: 13). The revelation which Jacob received was that it was his own God who was showing himself in this place.

(c) *Mambre*. Gn 13: 18 says that Abraham erected an altar under the Oak of Mambre. This is the only text in Genesis which refers to Mambre as a place of worship: elsewhere it is mentioned as the residence of Abraham, Isaac and Jacob (Gn 14: 13; 18: 1; 35: 27), or to help locate the cave of Macpelah 'facing Mambre', where the Patriarchs and their wives were buried (Gn 23: 17 and 19; 25: 9; 49: 30; 50: 13). Yet Abraham was sitting by the Oak of Mambre when he welcomed the three mysterious guests among whom Yahweh concealed himself (Gn 18), and Mambre is the best site for the scene of the Covenant in Gn 15, if we retain that scene in its present context. These two theophanies, and the presence of an altar and a tree, indicate that there was a sanctuary there.

Mambre is never mentioned in the Bible outside Genesis, but later texts prove that it continued to be a place of worship, and many legends grew up about the sacred tree. According to Josephus (*B.J.*, IV, ix, 7 and *Ant.*, I, x, 4), Abraham's Oak had existed from the creation of the world and was called Ogyges: in Greek mythology, Ogyges was the founder of Eleusis and was connected, therefore, with mystery-religion. The Book of Jubilees (XIV, 11) explicitly locates the nocturnal scene of Gn 15 in Mambre, and other apocryphal books interpret it as a revelation of mysteries: Abraham, it is said, there saw the future Jerusalem and learnt the secrets of the end of time. In the first centuries A.D., Mambre was a pilgrimage centre, and the tree of Abraham was greatly venerated: every year a big fair was held where, according to Sozomenus (*Hist. Eccl.*, II, iv), Jews, Christians and pagans transacted business and performed their devotions, each in his own way. This was the final chapter in a long history: the Roman and Byzantine ruins of Mambre are still to be found at Ramath el-Khalil, 2 miles north of Hebron, and beneath these later sanctuaries traces of Israelite occupation have been found.

In all probability, a syncretist cult was practised there, and was regarded with disfavour by orthodox Yahwism. This would explain why Mambre was ostracized, and why it is never mentioned in the Bible outside Genesis; in Genesis itself, the text seems to have been deliberately obscured whenever Mambre is mentioned. In Gn 13: 18; 14: 13; 18: 1, the Hebrew text speaks of the Oaks of Mambre in the plural, while the better ancient versions read the singular (which is in fact demanded by the story of Gn 18: 4 and 8): the idea was to water down the superstitious veneration of a particular tree, and the Jewish commentators went a step further by substituting the word 'plain of'

Mambre. Again, the editors of Genesis try to do away with the independence of the sanctuary by misleading the reader about its position: 'the Oaks of Mambre which are at Hebron' (Gn 13: 18), and 'Macpelah, facing Mambre' in the five texts cited above, when in fact the tomb of the Patriarchs faced ancient Hebron. In the end, Mambre was simply identified with Hebron in Gn 23: 19: 'Macpelah, facing Mambre, *i.e.* Hebron', and Gn 35: 27: 'at Mambre, Qiryath-Arba, *i.e.* Hebron'. All these texts were edited at a later period. It is no doubt possible that the sole aim of the redactors was to put side by side a tomb and a sanctuary which were both venerated, as when the nearby tomb of Rachel is mentioned in connection with Bethel (Gn 35: 8), but it seems far more probable that they were trying to minimize the religious importance of Mambre.

(d) *Beersheba*. Beersheba stands at the southern extremity of the Holy Land: its name was interpreted as meaning the Well of the Oath or the Well of the Seven (Gn 21: 22–31; cf. 26: 33). The memory of Isaac was particularly cherished there. Yahweh had there appeared to him one night and confirmed the promise made to Abraham: there Isaac had set up an altar and had called on the name of Yahweh (Gn 26: 23–25). There Jacob offered a sacrifice to the God of his father Isaac, and was favoured with a vision (Gn 46: 1-4). In the end, however, the foundation of the sanctuary was attributed to Abraham: Gn 21: 33, which has all the marks of an addition, says that Abraham planted a tamarisk at Beersheba and there called on the name of Yahweh El-'Olam, Yahweh El of Eternity. This divine name, which is never mentioned elsewhere, must be the name of the Canaanite divinity whom Yahweh replaced. There is a good parallel to this divine title in the Phoenician inscription of Karatepe, where we find a Shamash 'Olam, and perhaps, too, in the Elath-'Olam inscribed on an amulet originating from Arslan-Tash.

According to 1 S 8: 1-2, Samuel made his sons judges at Beersheba; this presupposes there was a sanctuary there, as at Bethel, Gilgal, Mispah and Ramah, where Samuel himself had judged Israel (1 S 7: 16-17). Under the monarchy, the northern Israelites went there on pilgrimage (Am 5: 5), and took oaths by the Dod, the Darling, of Beersheba (Am 8: 14: corrected, but perhaps the Hebrew text should be retained: 'by the Way of Beersheba'). These lasting links between Beersheba and the northern tribes are interesting precisely because they confirm the antiquity of the sanctuary. In the context, the prophet is condemning this place of worship along with Gilgal, Bethel, Dan and Samaria.

(e) *Conclusion*. The study of the patriarchal sanctuaries leads to a paradoxical conclusion: on the one hand, the links which connected Shechem, Bethel, Mambre and Beersheba with Abraham, Isaac and Jacob were multiplied as time went on: on the other hand, all these sanctuaries were condemned by the spokesmen of Yahwism—Bethel and Beersheba explicitly, Shechem and Mambre implicitly. This odd conclusion cannot be explained by a centralization of worship, for Amos was not aiming at that. It must mean that Yahwism eventually rejected the very cult which was celebrated there. What probably happened was that these places were Canaanite sanctuaries adopted by the Israelites when they settled in Palestine: the new immigrants continued the kind of cult which was celebrated when they arrived, without anyone's taking offence at it. Twice the divinity to whom these sanctuaries belonged is named: El-Bethel at Bethel, and El-'Olam at Beersheba. It is tempting to attach El-Shaddai to Mambre, for the name occurs for the first time in Gn 17: 1 (Priestly tradition, and a doublet both of the account of the Covenant in Gn 15, which probably took place at Mambre, and of the story in Gn 18, which is explicitly placed at Mambre). We may reasonably suggest that at Shechem, where covenants were concluded and renewed, there was an El-Berith (cf. also Jg 9: 46), an El of the Covenant, parallel to the Baal-Berith who had, and who retained, a temple at Shechem (Jg 9: 4): in later times, the Deuteronomic redactor condemned the Israelites for 'taking Baal-Berith as god' (Jg 8: 33).

El-Bethel, El-'Olam, El-Shaddai and El-Berith, were not, however, different local deities: they were all manifestations of the supreme god El, whose exalted and universal aspect is better known to us now through the the texts of Ras Shamra. For this stage in revelation, it was sufficient for the ancestors of the Israelites to recognize the El venerated in these ancient sanctuaries as their one and only God, author and guarantor of the promises made to their race. The altar set up by Jacob at Shechem was called 'El, God of Israel' (Gn 33: 20): it was 'El, the God of thy father' who appeared to Jacob at Beersheba (Gn 46: 3), and Ex 6: 3 says that God first revealed himself to Abraham, Isaac and Jacob under the name of El-Shaddai. In the following period, Yahwistic revelation became more exigent. Yahweh assumed the place and the most exalted attributes of El; the new centres of the Yahwistic cult eclipsed the old sanctuaries, though the populace still remained attached to them. The transition, however, was peaceful, without any of the struggles which ensued where the worship of Yahweh came face to face with that of Baal.

2. The desert sanctuary: the Tent

Before passing on to Israel's own sanctuaries in the Promised Land, we must study another set of traditions about the first beginnings of the cult of Yahweh. The Bible tells us that in the desert, the Israelites had a tent as a sanctuary, which has become known in Christian literature, through the influence of the Vulgate, as the Tabernacle. This Tent is called in Hebrew the 'ohel mô'ed, the Tent of Re-union, or, of Meeting, or, of Rendezvous. In fact, it was the place where Yahweh talked with Moses 'face to face' (Ex 33: 11), or 'mouth to mouth' (Nb 12: 8). These texts belong to the oldest tradition, which stresses the rôle of the Tent in oracles: everyone who wanted 'to consult Yahweh' went to the Tent, where Moses acted as his spokesman before God (Ex 33: 7). The Priestly tradition kept the name, with the same meaning: the Tent of Re-union was the place where Yahweh 'met' Moses and the people of Israel (Ex 29: 42-43; 30: 36). This tradition, however, prefers to call it the Dwelling, or Abode, *mishkan*, which seems to be a term originally used for the temporary dwelling of a nomad (cf. the very old text in Nb 24: 5, and the corresponding verb in Jg 8: 11; cf. also 2 S 7: 6), *i.e.* a tent. The Priestly tradition chose this archaic word to express the way in which the God who resides in heaven dwells on earth. By doing so, they were preparing the ground for the Jewish doctrine about the Shekinah, and St John too remembered how 'the Word . . . pitched a tent among us' (Jn 1: 14).

Nevertheless, in the Priestly tradition, the divine presence in the Tent appears to be more stable than it was in the old Elohistic tradition. The latter tells how the presence of Yahweh revealed itself by the descent of a cloud which covered the entrance of the Tent, and Moses spoke with God inside the cloud (Ex 33: 9): again (Nb 12: 4-10), it says that the cloud came down over the Tent when Yahweh was arriving, and left it when he was departing: both of these accounts suggest visits rather than a permanent abode. According to the Priestly tradition, the cloud covered the Dwelling as soon as it was erected, for Yahweh was taking possession of his sanctuary (Ex 40: 34-35); afterwards, it apparently stayed over the Dwelling all the time, doing duty for the pillar of cloud and the pillar of fire which had guided the Israelites during the Exodus: it indicated where and for how long they were to set up camp, and when the moment had come to strike camp (Nb 9: 15-23; cf. Ex 40: 36-38). The two traditions do not agree about the position of the Tent: according to Ex 33. 7-11 and Nb 11: 24-30 (Elohistic), it stood outside the camp, while Nb 2:2, 17 says it stood in the middle of the camp. Ex 25:8 adds that Yahweh lives there in the middle of his people, and Nb 5: 3 gives this as the reason why the Israelites must keep careful watch over the purity of their camp (Priestly texts).

The most ancient texts give no indication what this Tent looked like, how it was set up, or what its furnishings were. The Priestly tradition, on the other hand, gives a lengthy description of the Dwelling when Yahweh orders it to be built (Ex 26) and when Moses carries out the order (Ex 36: 8-38). This description is very difficult to understand, and it is hard to see how the various elements it mentions can be combined. The Dwelling was made of wooden frames which were put together and made a rectangular building of 30 by 10 cubits, and 10 cubits high: it stood open on the eastern side. The building seems then to have been covered with bands of fine-woven material, sewn together to make two big pieces, which were then fastened together with hooks and clips: they were embroidered with figures of cherubim. Next, goat-skin bands were stretched 'like a tent over the Dwelling': they were a little wider and a little longer than the first material, and fell down over the sides of the Dwelling. Lastly, the whole construction was covered with the skins of rams, dyed red, and then by very light leather hides. There was a curtain over the entry to the Dwelling, and a costly veil drawn across the innermost ten cubits marked the division between the Holy Place and the Holy of Holies. Behind the veil, in the Holy of Holies, stood the Ark: in the Holy Place, there stood the candle-stick and the table of shewbread. The altar, with the basin for washing, stood outside the entrance of the Tent (Ex 40: 30). Around the Dwelling there was an open court of 100 by 50 cubits, the edge of which was indicated by a barrier of bronze posts and silver curtain-rods from which linen curtains fell down to the ground (Ex 27: 9-19).

It is only too obvious that much of this description is merely an idealization: the desert sanctuary is conceived as a collapsible temple, exactly half as big as the Temple of Jerusalem, which served as the model for this reconstruction. However, not everything in the description is made up, and the notion of a 'prefabricated' sanctuary clashes with the idea—so firmly rooted in tradition that the authors of this description could not wholly remove it—that the dwelling was a Tent.

This tradition fits in excellently with Arab usage, ancient and modern. Bedouin tribes have a little tent, a sort of palanquin or litter, which they call 'utfa, merkab, or abu-Dhur. When the tribe is moving camp, they always take it with them and it is the last object they pick up when leaving. It is carried on a camel. In combat, the sheikh's daughter or another beautiful young girl used to ride in it to spur on the fighting men. It is considered to be blessed with supernatural power, and sometimes a sacrifice is offered to the 'utfa or to the divinity who is thought to dwell in it. There is an evident analogy with the Ark of the Covenant and its rôle in the early wars of Israel,[1] and also with the Tent, the travelling sanctuary of the desert years. From the thirteenth century onwards, caravans making the pilgrimage to Mecca from Damascus or Cairo were led by a camel carrying a maḥmal, a little cubic tent containing a copy of the Koran. In spite of the apparent resemblances, however, it is not altogether certain that the maḥmal was related to the 'utfa of Bedouin tribes: and on the other hand, it is quite certain that the modern 'utfa is a continuation of a pre-Islamite institution, the qubba. This was a little sacred tent of red leather in which the stone idols belonging to the tribe were carried. It was carried on camel-back in religious processions and in combat, and young women looked after it. In camp, it was set up beside the sheikh's tent, and men came there to seek oracles. Here we perceive the rôle of the desert Tent in the giving of oracles (Ex 33: 7), and even the colour, red, of the ram-skins which covered it (Ex 26: 14). Indeed, the very women who looked after the qubba recall the women who 'were in service' at the entrance to the Tent of Re-union, according to the somewhat enigmatical text of Ex 38: 8.

1. Cf. p. 259.

This *qubba* of the pre-Islamic Arabs itself had Semitic antecedents. Diodorus (XX, 65, 1) tells us that in a Carthaginian camp a sacred tent was set up near the chief's tent. Little statues of baked earth originating from Syria represent women (*i.e.* goddesses or assistants in the cult) riding on camel-back in a litter covered by a pavilion. A bas-relief from Palmyra, of the first century A.D., shows a religious procession in which a camel is carrying a little tent still bearing traces of red paint, and there are other Palmyra texts which contain the word *qubba*. In the Bible, the word *qubbah* occurs once only, in Nb 25: 8, and it may mean a tent, or part of a tent: the Tent of Re-union is mentioned in the same passage (verse 6), but it is not clear what connection if any, it has with this *qubbah*.

It is reasonable then to suggest an hypothesis which fits the evidence of the texts and to assert that the ancestors of the Israelites, during their nomad life, had a portable sanctuary, and that this sanctuary was a tent, like their own dwelling-places. It would be quite in order for this sanctuary to disappear when they settled in Canaan. The Tent of Re-union was set up in the Plains of Moab, the last station before the entry into the Promised Land (Nb 25: 6), and this is the last indisputable mention of it. The tradition which speaks of the Tent's being at Shiloh under Josue (Jos 18: 1; 19: 51) is late, and in Ps 78: 60 (a late psalm) the *mishkan* and the Tent of Shiloh are poetic expressions. Moreover, the sanctuary which housed the Ark at Shiloh towards the end of the period of the Judges was a building (1 S 1: 7, 9; 3: 15). The tent under which David is said to have put the Ark in Jerusalem (2 S 6: 17) is evidently meant to recall the desert sanctuary, but it is no longer the Tent of Re-union, though it is so called by a glossator in 1 K 8: 4. The same anxiety to connect the new worship with the old inspired the Chronicler when he pretended that the Tent of Re-union stood on the high place of Gibeon under David and Solomon (1 Ch 16: 39; 21: 29; 2 Ch 1: 3-6).

3. *The Ark of the Covenant*

Ex 26: 33 and 40: 21 state that the Tent was designed to house the Ark of the Testimony (*'arôn ha-'edûth*) This 'Testimony' or 'Solemn Law' means the two 'tablets of the Testimony', *i.e.* the stone tablets on which the Law was inscribed: God had given them to Moses (Ex 31: 18) and he put them inside the Ark (Ex 25: 16; 40: 20). That is why the Tent containing the Ark was called the Tent of the Testimony (Nb 9: 15; 17: 22; 18: 2). The Ark is described in Ex 25: 10-22; 37: 1-9. It was a chest made of acacia wood, about 4 feet long, $2\frac{1}{2}$ feet wide and $2\frac{1}{2}$ feet high: it was covered with gold plates and had rings attached, through which the poles used for carrying it could be passed. Over the Ark was a plate of gold, of the same size as the Ark, and called the *kapporeth*, which is sometimes translated 'propitiatory' or 'mercy-seat', in accordance with the meaning of the verbal root and the rôle the *kapporeth* played on the Day of Atonement (*Yôm ha-kippurim*: Lv 16). Two cherubim stood at the end of the *kapporeth* and covered it with their wings.

According to Dt 10: 1-5, Moses built an Ark of acacia wood at Yahweh's command, and put inside it the two stone tablets on which Yahweh had written the Ten Commandments. Dt 10: 8 says that the honour of carrying this chest was entrusted to the Levites, and that it was called the Ark of the Covenant (*'arôn habb'rith*) because it contained the 'tablets of the Covenant' which Yahweh had made with his people (Dt 9: 9). The 'second Law' of Deuteronomy was eventually itself placed 'beside the Ark of the Covenant of Yahweh' (Dt 31: 9, 26).

Nb 10: 33-36 says that when the Israelites left Sinai, the Ark of the Covenant went before them, and signalled the halts. When it was leaving, they cried: 'Arise, Yahweh, and let thy enemies be scattered . . .', and when it came to rest: 'Return, Yahweh, to the countless thousands of Israel'. And Nb 14: 44 adds that when the Israelites, disobeying Moses' orders, attacked the Canaanites and were defeated, the Ark of the Covenant did not leave the camp.

These are the only explicit details about the Ark of the Covenant mentioned in the Pentateuch, and it is obvious that they stem from different traditions. The texts from Exodus belong to the Priestly tradition, and, like the description of the Tent, they are influenced by the memory of the Temple of Solomon, where the Ark stood in the Holy of Holies, overshadowed by the Cherubim (1 K 8: 6). The Deuteronomic tradition gives no description of the Ark, and does not connect it with the Tent. It has therefore been suggested that it was a cultic object adopted by the Israelites (from the Canaanites!) only after the settlement in Palestine, and later attributed to the years in the desert by the authors of the Priestly traditions. Two considerations are fatal to this theory: first, the passage in Nb 10: 33-36 (except verse 34, an interpolation) is quite certainly a very old text and it too connects the Ark with the journeying through the desert; secondly, the Ark plays the same rôle of guide in the traditions about the entry into the Promised Land (Jos 3-6), where its part in the story cannot be suppressed.

The Ark, then, like the Tent, was part and parcel of the worship in the desert, but it had a longer history than the Tent. The Ark, without the Tent, stood in the camp at Gilgal (Jos 7: 6), and when Jg 2: 1-5 says that the Angel of Yahweh went up from Gilgal to Bokim, near Bethel, we should of course take it to mean that the Ark was transferred. In fact, it is next mentioned at Bethel (Jg 20: 27). (True, Jos 8: 33 notes that it was at Shechem, but the passage is part of the Deuteronomic redaction of the book.) We are on much firmer ground when the Ark is said to be kept at Shiloh, during Samuel's young days (1 S 3: 3). From Shiloh it was taken to the battle of Apheq (1 S 4: 3f.), where it was captured by the Philistines (1 S 4: 11). After its travels from Ashdod to Gath, and from Gath to Eqron, it was given back to the Israelites at Beth-Shemesh and housed for a while at Qiryath-Yearim (1 S 5: 5-7: 1), until David brought it to Jerusalem and installed it in a tent (2 S 6). Solomon built his Temple to house the Ark in its holiest place (1 K 6: 19; 8: 1-9). From this time onwards, the historical books do not mention it again, but it probably shared the fate of the Temple, and disappeared only when the Temple itself was destroyed in 587 B.C. (cf. Jr 3: 16, which is later than 587). An apocryphal tradition used in 2 M 2: 4f. says that before the final ruin of Jerusalem, Jeremias had hidden the Ark, along with the Tent (!) and the altar of incense in a cave on mount Nebo.

What, then, was the religious significance of the Ark? The texts concerning it allow us to glimpse two notions which, according to many critics, are irreconcilable: the Ark is presented as the throne of God and as a receptacle for the Law.

In the very detailed passages of 1 S 4-6; 2 S 6 and 1 K 8, the Ark is the visible sign of the presence of God. When it arrives in the Israelite camp, the Philistines say: 'God has come into their camp!' (1 S 4: 7), and the capture of the Ark is taken as the loss of God's presence: the 'glory' has been taken away from Israel (1 S 4: 22). Similarly, in the very old text of Nb 10: 35, when the Ark leaves, it is Yahweh who is arising. Psalm 132: 8 sings of the transfer of the Ark by David (2 S 6) in similar terms: 'Arise, Yahweh, into thy rest, thou and the Ark of thy strength!' When the Ark is brought into the Temple of Jerusalem, the 'glory of Yahweh' takes possession of the sanctuary (1 K 8: 11), as it had once filled the Tent in the desert when the Ark was put there (cf. Ex 40: 34-35). In the desert wanderings (Nb 10: 33-36) and in the holy wars (1 S 4; 2 S 11: 11), the Ark was the palladium of Israel.[1] Since it was the symbol of Yahweh's presence, its power was formidable: the Philistines felt its effect (1 S 5), and seventy men from Beth-Shemesh were struck down for not rejoicing when the Ark appeared (1 S 6: 19); Uzzah was struck dead for touching it (2 S 6: 7), and according to the Priestly Code, the Levites approached it only when it had been veiled by the priests (Nb 4: 5, 15), and carried it by poles which were never taken off it (Ex 25: 15; cf. 1 K 8: 8).

In the account of the Philistine war, the Ark is called 'the Ark of Yahweh Sabaoth who sits above the cherubim' (1 S 4: 4), and this epithet, which was presumably applied to the Ark from the time of its stay at Shiloh, continued to be used in later days (2 S 6: 2; 2 K 19: 15=Is 37. 16). In 1 Ch 28: 2, the Ark is the 'foot-stool' of God, and it is clearly the Ark which is meant by the same expression in Ps 99: 5; 132: 7; Lm 2: 1. When Is 66: 1 says: 'Heaven is my throne, and the earth my foot-stool! What kind of a house could you build for me?', the protest is certainly directed against the Temple, which the Jews wished to rebuild when they returned from the Exile, but it refers directly to the sacred furniture of the old Temple, i.e. to the Ark, which was considered as the 'throne' or the 'foot-stool' of God: the text is, as it were,

1. Cf. p. 259.

an echo of Jr 3: 16-17. Ez 43: 7 should be taken in the same way: Yahweh, returning to his Temple, says: 'Here is the place of my throne, the place where I put the sole of my feet'. It has been suggested that we should make a distinction between the foot-stool and the throne, *i.e.* between the Ark, and a throne which was attached to it during its stay at Shiloh, and which was later transferred, along with the Ark, to the Debir of the Temple. There seems little foundation for this theory: in the prose texts, the throne is never mentioned as an object distinct from the Ark, and there is no evidence that there was anything other than the Ark and the Cherubim inside the Debir. When Jr 3: 16-17 offers some consolation for the disappearance of the Ark by foretelling that in a future age all Jerusalem will be called 'the throne of Yahweh', it assumes that the Ark could be considered either as the throne or as the foot-stool of God. More precisely, the Ark, with the Cherubim, could be said to represent both the foot-stool and the throne of Yahweh. Since the religion of Israel forbade all images, the throne was empty, but even this is not without parallels. Oriental and Greek religions had among their sacred furniture empty thrones, or thrones on which only a symbol of the god was set: some of them, originating from Syria, are flanked by winged sphinxes which remind one of the Cherubim. It is pointless to ask how the Cherubim and the Ark could be both a throne and a foot-stool: it is like asking how Yahweh could actually sit down there, and the question would have seemed as absurd to the Israelites as it does to us: both Cherubim and Ark were the all-too-inadequate symbol of the divine presence, the 'seat' of this presence. When the idea became an image, in the minds of visionaries, it took on various shapes which had nothing to do with the Ark: it is called a throne by Isaias (Is 6: 1), and a chariot by Ezechiel (Ez 10; cf. Ez 1).

According to the Priestly tradition about the desert cult, Yahweh 'met' Moses and spoke to him from above the *kapporeth*, from between the Cherubim (Ex 25: 22; cf. 30: 6; Nb 7: 89). This *kapporeth* stood on top of the Ark but was distinct from it (Ex 35: 12); it is described at length and seems to have been more important than the Ark itself (cf. Ex 25: 17-22; 37: 6-9). In the ritual for the Day of Atonement, which stems from the same tradition, the high priest sprinkled blood on the mercy-seat, and in front of it (Lv 16: 14-15); this makes us suspect that the mercy-seat was something more than the simple gold plate which, in the description given of the desert worship by the same tradition, covered the Ark; moreover, there is no suggestion of any rôle for the Ark or for the Cherubim in this ritual of Lv 16. It is justifiable to conclude that the *kapporeth* was a substitute for the Ark in the post-Exilic tradition, for no new Ark was ever made (cf. Jr 3: 16); this would be confirmed by 1 Ch 28: 11, where the 'room of the *kapporeth*' stands for the Holy of Holies. This *kapporeth* fulfilled the rôle formerly ascribed to the Ark: it was the seat of the divine presence (Lv 16: 2, 13 and the texts cited at the beginning of this paragraph). In the end, it too disappeared: Josephus (*Bell.*, V, v, 5) tells us that in Herod's Temple there was nothing in the Holy of Holies at all.

Leaving aside the *kapporeth* then, it seems probable that the Ark and the Cherubim represented the throne of God in the sanctuaries of Shiloh and Jerusalem. But can we say the same of the simple Ark of the desert period, in which there were neither Cherubim nor *kapporeth* below them? It is possible to do so, for the oldest tradition of the Pentateuch, in Nb 10: 35-36, which links the Ark with the movements of Yahweh, seems to look upon the Ark as the support of the invisible godhead, a pedestal rather than throne—if the distinction is of importance: but the religious idea was the same.

Yet there is a second interpretation of the Ark's significance to be considered. According to Dt 10: 1-5 (cf. 1 K 8: 9), the Ark appears to be nothing more than a small chest containing the tablets on which the Ten Commandments were written: from this it takes its name as 'the Ark of the Covenant' (*b'rith*). The idea is not limited to the schools of Deuteronomy, for the Priestly tradition uses a synonymous expression, 'the Ark of the Testimony' (*'eduth*), and in this tradition *'eduth* is the name used for the Law which was kept in the Ark (Ex 25: 16; 40: 20). However, as extra-biblical documents show, there is no contradiction involved in the vivid contrast presented by the notions of the Ark as a pedestal or throne and of the Ark as a receptacle. A rubric of the Egyptian Book of the Dead (ch. LXIV) reads: 'This chapter was found at Khmun on an alabaster brick, under the feet of the Majesty of this venerable place (the god Thot), and it was written by the god himself': the comparison with the tablets of the Law, written by God's own finger and placed in the Ark which was his foot-stool, is obvious. The finding of the Book of the Dead under the feet of Thot is no doubt a legendary detail, but it fits in with a custom attested by historical documents. Hittite treaties stipulate that the text shall be placed in a temple at the foot of an image of a god. A letter from Ramses II about his treaty with Hattusil is most explicit: 'The writing of the oath (pact) which I have made to the Great King, the king of Hattu, lies beneath the feet of the god Teshup: the great gods are witnesses of it. The writing of the oath which the Great King, the king of Hattu, has made to me, lies beneath the feet of the god Ra: the great gods are witnesses of it'. In the same way, the Decalogue was the official instrument of the pact between Yahweh and his people, and was put into the Ark, under the feet of Yahweh.

We still have to clarify the connection between the Ark and the Tent. If we look at the Pentateuchal traditions in the probable order in which they were committed to writing, it is noticeable that the oldest tradition speaks of the Tent (Ex 33: 7-11) and of the Ark (Nb 10: 33-36; 14: 44) but never connects the two. Again, Deuteronomy knows of the Ark (Dt 10: 1-5; 31: 25-26) and mentions the Tent (Dt 31: 14-15) apart from the Ark. Later the Priestly tradition describes both the Ark and the Tent as things connected with worship in the desert: the Tent houses the Ark which contains the Testimony, and the

Tent is the Dwelling of Yahweh who reveals himself above the Ark (Ex 25-26; 36-40).

We have tried to prove above that both the Ark and the Tent existed in the desert; if this is admitted, how can one explain that the oldest traditions never connect the two? Perhaps this is an indication that the two objects belonged to different groups among the ancestors of Israel. The Priestly tradition, taking its inspiration from the Temple of Solomon, combined the two objects of worship in its literature, just as the two groups who had each possessed one of the objects had combined together in history. But it is more probable that the Ark and the Tent were in fact originally connected with each other. If the oldest tradition does not mention this connection explicitly, that is because the final redactors of the Pentateuch have preserved only fragments of this tradition, and have omitted what was described well enough in a later tradition. And in fact the old texts referring to the Ark and the Tent seem rather out of place in the middle of a Priestly tradition. There is one text about the Tent (Ex 33 : 7) which may even contain the proof that it has been torn from a context which also mentioned the Ark: 'Moses took the Tent and set it up for him (or, for it) outside the camp'. The pronoun *him* may refer to Moses or to Yahweh, but it can also be translated *it*, and might then refer to the Ark, which is masculine in Hebrew and which, originally, might have been mentioned immediately before. This interpretation is accepted by some distinguished exegetes, and it would mean that in the oldest traditions the Ark and the Tent were related in exactly the same way as in the Priestly description. But even without relying on this text, we may call on one argument of a general nature: the Ark needed to be sheltered, and the normal shelter in the desert is a tent. Conversely, the Tent itself must have covered something: we have compared it with the *qubba* of the pre-Islamic Arabs, which contained divine symbols. It would appear, then, that we ought not to separate the Ark and the Tent, and that the Priestly description of the desert sanctuary—however deeply influenced by Solomon's Temple and even (for the *kapporeth*) by the post-Exilic temple—did preserve an authentic tradition.

4. The sanctuaries in the land of Israel before the building of the Temple

We have seen[1] that the places of worship whose foundation was attributed to the Patriarchs are scarcely mentioned in the Bible once Israel is settled in Canaan. But from this time onwards other sanctuaries are brought to the fore.

(a) *Gilgal*. There are in the Old Testament various scattered references to Gilgal, a place whose precise location once occasioned some dispute among critics. Modern scholars, however, claim that all the texts refer to a site in the neighbourhood of Jericho, which raises a difficulty over the Gilgal mentioned in the story of Elias (2 K 2: 1; 4: 38): this one seems rather to lie in the hill-

1. Cf. p. 289.

country of Ephraim. But in Jos 4: 19 the sanctuary called Gilgal in the early days of Israel is situated east of Jericho, *i.e.* between Jericho and the Jordan, in a spot which cannot be located more precisely. The place of worship was marked by a circle of stones (Jos 4: 20), from which it took its name.[1] This name, which is here mentioned for the first time and without comment, seems to be pre-Israelite and to indicate a sanctuary which was already in existence; the explanation of the name in Jos 5: 9 is evidently secondary. In Jos 5: 13-15, the 'leader of the army of Yahweh' appears to Josue and orders him to take off his shoes, for 'the place is holy': if this episode is to be placed at Gilgal itself, we should here have the usual theophany for the foundation of a sanctuary. It may be so, but this episode is only a fragment of an independent tradition, and is connected with Jericho, not Gilgal. But it is quite certain that Gilgal was an important sanctuary immediately after the conquest, for tradition recorded that the Ark had come to rest there after the crossing of the Jordan (Jos 4: 19; 7: 6); there the people had circumcised themselves (Jos 5: 2-9), and there they celebrated the first Passover in Canaan: there the manna had ceased to fall (Jos 5: 10-12). It was the place, then, where they kept alive the memory of the entry into the Promised Land, of the end of desert wanderings, and of the first stages of the conquest (Jos 2-10). The Gibeonites came to Gilgal to seek an alliance with the Israelites (Jos 9: 6), and the oath by Yahweh's name which confirmed this pact must have been made at this sanctuary (Jos 9: 19).

Samuel came to Gilgal to judge Israel because there was a sanctuary there, as at Bethel and Mispah (1 S 7: 16), and the story of Saul's life underlines its importance: one of the traditions about the institution of the monarchy (1 S 11: 15) says that Saul was proclaimed king 'before Yahweh' at Gilgal, and that sacrifices were offered there. Both traditions agree in placing the rejection of Saul by Samuel at Gilgal (1 S 13: 7-15; cf. 10: 8 and 1 S 15: 12-33), and both of them place this rejection in a cultic context: Saul offered sacrifice, and Samuel cut the throat of Agag 'before Yahweh'. Lastly, Judah came out to Gilgal to meet David on his return from Transjordan, and Israel and Judah quarrelled whose king he was near the sanctuary where Saul had been proclaimed the first king of Israel (2 S 19: 16, 41).

Although Gilgal is not mentioned after this in the historical narratives, people continued to attend the sanctuary. We have no details about the kind of cult which was conducted at the time, but the prophets condemn Gilgal along with Bethel (Os 4: 15; Am 4: 4; 5: 5; cf. Os 12: 12). In Os 9: 15, the 'wickedness' of Gilgal seems to lie in the fact that Saul was there proclaimed king, and the reason seems to lie in Osee's hostility to the monarchy (cf. Os 8: 4). Perhaps there is a veiled censure of Gilgal as early as Jg 3: 19, 26: the 'idols near Gilgal' might mean the *maṣṣebôth* of the sanctuary, which had been the focus of a suspect cult.

1. Cf. p. 275.

(b) *Shiloh*. During the period of the Judges Gilgal was eclipsed by Shiloh, which became the central sanctuary of the tribal federation at that time. Its origins are obscure. The book of Josue makes Shiloh a meeting-place for the tribes (Jos 18: 1; 21: 2; 22:. 9, 12), and says that the territory of seven tribes was there apportioned by lot (Jos 18: 8), and even adds that the Tent of Re-union was set up there (Jos 18: 1; 19: 51). It is very questionable whether the Tent was ever at Shiloh,[1] but there was certainly a sanctuary there from very early times. Every year there was a pilgrimage to Shiloh, a *ḥag*, during which groups of young girls used to dance in the vineyards (Jg 21: 19-21). Elqanah, the father of Samuel, went there every year to offer a sacrifice to Yahweh Sabaoth (1 S 1: 3). During these years the cult centred round a building, a 'house of Yahweh' (1 S 1: 7, 24; 3: 15), a *hêkal* or 'palace' of Yahweh (1 S 3: 3), a 'house of God' (Jg 18: 31): in a word, it was the first temple of Yahweh, and the Ark was kept there (1 S 3: 3).

It was at Shiloh, apparently, that Yahweh was first called 'Sabaoth, who sits above the Cherubim'. The first mention of Yahweh Sabaoth is in 1 S 1: 3, and the first mention of 'who sits above the Cherubim' is in the story of how, during the Philistine war, the Ark was taken from Shiloh to the battle-front (1 S 4: 4). Could there have been, in pre-Israelite times, a deity called Sabaoth who was represented as carried by Cherubim? It is not impossible, but it cannot be proved. In any case, the application of this title to Yahweh underlined his majesty and his supreme dominion, for whatever be the exact meaning of Sabaoth, the word certainly includes the idea of power.

We have only scattered allusions to the sanctuary at Shiloh until the time of Samuel, and just when we are beginning to know more about it, its end is near: the Philistines captured the Ark at Apheq (1 S 4: 1-11), and their victory probably opened up the road to Shiloh, and the town was sacked. Excavations at Seilun, the modern name of the site, show that the town was destroyed in the middle of the eleventh century, and that it was unoccupied, or at least in decline, for a long period afterwards. Jeremias sees in the ruins a lesson for the people of Jerusalem, who are rather too confident that God will not abandon their Temple (Jr 7: 12-14; 26: 6, 9), and the echo of his words can be heard in Ps 78: 60. The destruction of Shiloh must have taken place around 1050 B.C., but half a century later David recovered the Ark and Jerusalem became the successor of Shiloh.

(c) *Mispah in Benjamin*. In the story of the crime of Gibeah, the Israelites assemble before Yahweh at Mispah and there take a solemn oath (Jg 20: 1, 3; 21: 1, 5, 8). Mispah was clearly a sanctuary. It is next mentiôned in the stories of Samuel and Saul: the Israelites meet together at Mispah, call on the name of Yahweh there, pour out water in supplication and offer sacrifice to Yahweh (1 S 7: 5-12). Samuel judged Israel at Mispah (1 S 7: 16), as he did in the sanctuaries of Bethel and Gilgal. Lastly, the tradition of 1 S 10: 17-24 tells

1. Cf. p. 297.

how Saul was chosen king when the sacred lots were drawn 'before Yahweh' at Mispah. After that, Mispah is not mentioned as a religious centre until the time of the Maccabees: the Jews gathered there, fasted, prayed and consulted the Law 'for in former times there was a place of prayer for Israel at Mispah' (1 M 3: 46-54).

This last text is evidently inspired by the passages in Jg and 1 S cited in the last paragraph: hence it is not an independent witness to what actually happened in ancient times. But even the value of the texts from Jg and 1 S has been questioned: in Jg 20-21, Bethel, where the Ark was kept at the time, seems to be a serious rival to Mispah (Jg 20: 18, 26-28; 21: 2); the portrait of Samuel as judge and liberator in 1 S 7 is not based on an ancient document and is an introduction to the anti-monarchist account of the institution of kingship; 1 S 10: 17-24 also belongs to this tradition, but the monarchist version places the proclamation of Saul as king (1 S 11: 15) at Gilgal. Some authors, however, have rushed to the conclusion that these texts are trying to heighten the importance of Mispah because immediately after the fall of Jerusalem, under the aegis of Godolias, it became the centre of the Jewish community (Jr 40-41). To this we may reply that the texts in question belong to the Deuteronomic redaction of the historical books, and must therefore represent an older tradition, memories concerning an old sanctuary, like those about Bethel and Gilgal. If we could use Os 5: 1 without qualms, we should be on surer ground, for it accuses the priests and leaders of Israel of having been 'a snare' for the people 'at Mispah'. Unfortunately, it may refer to a Mispah in Gilead, and even if it does refer to Mispah in Benjamin, Osee is probably thinking only of the choice of Saul as king in this sanctuary (cf. 1 S 10). But this would at least confirm the antiquity of this tradition.

Once we admit that there was a sanctuary at Mispah, another problem arises. The Mispah of Godolias, which is also the Mispah of 1 K 15: 22, is generally identified as Tell-en-Nasbeh north of Jerusalem. Extensive excavations on this site have shown that it was not densely populated until after the time of Solomon: this tempts us to look elsewhere (though still, of course, in Benjamin) for the site of the Mispah which is mentioned under the Judges and Samuel. The name was originally a common noun, meaning 'The Watch-post', and the Bible mentions several Mispah or Mispeh. Yet it would be unwise to over-estimate the negative argument from excavations: a sanctuary can be an important religious centre without necessarily being connected with a large town, and Tell-en-Nasbeh may have been a place of worship before the town developed.

(d) *Gibeon*. If we take it that the Mispah of the Judges was not the same place as the Mispah of the monarchical period, the former may be the same place as the high place of Gibeon which, under Solomon, was 'the greatest high place'.[1]

1. Cf. p. 288.

The popularity of Gibeon implied in this title cannot be explained unless the sanctuary had a long history behind it, even though it is never mentioned earlier in the Bible. Now if this 'high place' of Gibeon stood, as is probable, on the height nowadays called Nabi-Samwil, the site would well deserve the name of 'The Watch-post' (Mispah), and the connection with Samuel which the Arabic name records would fit in well with the traditions of 1 S 7 and 10.

The story about the descendants of Saul whom David handed over to the Gibeonites for vengeance (2 S 21: 1-14) is clearly connected with this sanctuary. According to the Hebrew text (verse 6), the victims were dismembered before Yahweh 'at Gibeah of Saul, the chosen one of Yahweh', but the text should certainly be corrected to read, with the Greek, 'at Gibeon, on the mountain of Yahweh' (cf. verse 9). The ritual brings to mind the Canaanite practices and presupposes that the cult of Yahweh had there replaced an older form of worship. Lastly, that clause of the pact with the Gibeonites which obliged them to cut wood and to carry water for the house of God and to do service for the altar of Yahweh would presumably first be put into practice in this sanctuary (Jos 9: 23, 27).

(e) *Ophra*. While the origins of Mispah and Gibeon are unknown, we have information about the foundation of two other sanctuaries in the period of the Judges, Ophra and Dan.

There are two accounts of the foundation of Ophra. In the first (Jg 6: 11-24), the Angel of Yahweh appeared under a tree which belongs to Yoash, the father of Gideon, near a rock where Gideon was treading corn. Gideon was then charged to save Israel from the Midianite oppressors. Gideon had prepared a meal before he knew who was speaking to him, and Yahweh accepted it as a sacrifice upon the rock. Gideon thereupon built an altar which he called Yahweh-Shalom, 'Yahweh-Peace'. This story is close akin to the tales of the patriarchal period and contains all the elements of a *hieros logos*, *i.e.* of a narrative which sets the seal on the authenticity of a sanctuary: it mentions a sacred tree, a theophany, a message of salvation, the inauguration of worship on an altar of rock, and finally the building of an altar.

A second account follows immediately (Jg 6: 25-32): Yahweh spoke to Gideon in a dream, and ordered him to destroy the altar of Baal which belonged to his father Yoash, to cut in pieces the *'asherah*, to build an altar to Yahweh on the hill and there to offer sacrifice with the wood of the *'asherah*. When Gideon carried out this command, the townspeople were angry, but Yoash stood by his son: 'Let Baal defend his own rights if he is god' (a tendentious explanation of the name Yerubbaal, a second name of Gideon). This second account brings to mind the story of Elias on Carmel: the theme of it is that the worship of Yahweh replaced the worship of Baal because the latter was powerless to defend his rights.

It is not suggested that there were two different sanctuaries at Ophra: the big tree of the first account means that it was already a place of worship, and the tree belongs to Yoash, as does the altar in the second account. It was a private sanctuary, if the term may be used, but a private sanctuary such as the Patriarchs had: it was the sanctuary of the clan which Yoash represented. But there were two traditions about the origin of the worship of Yahweh in Ophra: one told how it had replaced a previous worship without any trouble, and the other told how it had forcibly ousted the cult of Baal. The first tradition seems to be the older, and would show how the people did not at once realize that the cult of Yahweh was incompatible with worship of Baal. (Note that Yoash, the patron of Baal's altar, has a Yahwistic name, and that Gideon's second name, Yerubbaal, means 'May Baal defend (the bearer of his name)'.) The second tradition reflects the struggle which eventually took place against the worship of Baal.

These two aspects are found also in the one and only episode which can be related to the sanctuary at Ophrah: after his victory over the Midianites, Gideon used part of the booty to make an ephod.[1] Here the ephod is a cultic object which formed part of the furnishings of a sanctuary, as it did with the Canaanites (cf. Jg 17: 5). Gideon, who had just refused supreme power because Yahweh alone ought to reign over Israel, meant this ephod for the cult of Yahweh, but the redactor condemns it as an idolatrous object: 'All Israel prostituted itself there' (Jg 8: 22-27). This local sanctuary is never again mentioned in the Old Testament.

(f) *Dan*. The sanctuary of Dan had a longer history. Its foundation is connected with the migration of the tribe of Dan described in Jg 17-18. We shall return to this account later, when we study the priesthood in Israel[2]; here we shall concern ourselves only with the facts about the sanctuary, or, rather, about the two successive sanctuaries at Dan: the domestic chapel of Mikah and the tribal sanctuary of Dan.

Its origin was, you could say, just about as unlawful as possible: Mikah had stolen some silver from his mother, and given it back to her; with some of this silver she had an idol made. Mikah put it in a sanctuary, a 'house of God', with an ephod and some teraphim. He installed his son as priest, and later hired a wandering Levite. Then a passing clan of Danites stole all the sacred furniture during their migration northwards, and easily talked the Levite into going with them: the Levite found it far more advantageous to be priest to a group than to a private individual. Mikah bewailed the fact that he had at one blow lost both his god and his priest. When the Danites reach Laish, they massacred a peaceful population, changed the name of the place to Dan and set up Mikah's idol there.

There is nothing here in the least like any of the accounts of the foundation of patriarchal sanctuaries or of Ophrah. It is not God, but men, who take the initiative, and the men are not very likeable. There is an accumulation of faults which the Law and the Prophets will condemn: an image they call a

1. Cf. p. 350, 351.   2. Cf. pp. 361, 362.

'god', a highly-suspect ephod, teraphim and a priest who is not a Levite. This tale is certainly not the account of a foundation, a *hieros logos* destined to show the legitimacy of a sanctuary. A Jewish reader of the book would draw quite the contrary conclusion: it is a false sanctuary served by a false priest—which is exactly the impression the redactor wanted to produce by telling this story. His plea is that the first sanctuary of Dan was worthless, and was a fitting predecessor of the sanctuary into which Jeroboam brought the second golden calf (1 K 12: 29-30): it was to be condemned along with Bethel (2 K 10: 29).

Yet the account is really concerned with a sanctuary of Yahweh: Mikah's mother consecrated the stolen silver to Yahweh, and Mikah was blessed by Yahweh for returning it to its owner. Mikah was at first content to have his son as priest, but he was glad to replace him by a Levite because that would bring Yahweh's blessing upon him: the spies from the tribe of Dan consulted God through Mikah's ephod, and received a reply: and the sanctuary where the idol stood was served by Jonathan, a grandson of Moses.

Neither the hypothesis of two literary sources for Jg 17-18 nor the suggestion that the document is full of long interpolations explains away the fact that here we have a sanctuary of Yahweh set up in defiance of all the rules of Yahwism.

The account does reproduce an old tradition of which the Danites must have been proud, but the story contains many elements which astonish us in the same way as they shocked the redactor of the book: it is a story from the time when 'there was no king in Israel and everyone did as he pleased' (Jg 17: 6, cf. 18: 1). This story shows us, even better than the story about Ophra, the great danger which Yahwism encountered when Israel first came into contact with the settled population of Canaan.

According to Jg 18: 30, Jonathan's descendants continued as the priests of the sanctuary of Dan until the Assyrian conquest. The following verse (Jg 18: 31) adds that Mikah's idol stayed there 'all the time that the house of God in Shiloh stood', which may mean that it disappeared when Shiloh was destroyed by the Philistines or that this idolatrous cult continued all the time that the true 'house of God', *i.e.* Shiloh, lasted. The second period of the history of the sanctuary at Dan, from the schism of Jeroboam, will be discussed when we deal with the sanctuaries which were rivals to Jerusalem.[1]

(g) *Jerusalem.* Jerusalem was the last of all the sanctuaries founded in the first period of Israel's history. Its foundation under David comprised two stages: the installation of the Ark, and the erection of an altar on the site of the future Temple.

After his conquest of Jerusalem and his first victories over the Philistines, David had deprived the Philistines of the control they could still exercise over the Ark at Qiryath-Yearim: he then went to bring it back (2 S 6). It was brought back in a religious procession, with shouts of joy, and the noise of

1. Cf. pp. 334-336.

trumpets, with David himself offering sacrifice and dancing before the Ark. Its transference was marked with incidents which revealed the holiness, beneficent and yet awesome, of the sacred object: the death of Uzzah, its stay with Obed-Edom and the subsequent blessing of his house, the punishment of Mikal. At length the Ark was laid at rest in its *maqôm*, its 'holy place', under the tent which had been specially prepared for it. Ps 24: 7-10 and 132 should be compared with this account: they were sung on the anniversary of this entry of Yahweh Sabaoth into Sion where he had chosen to dwell, and this feast probably influenced the cultic aspect of the account in 2 S 6. The most questionable conclusions have been deduced from these texts. It has been suggested that this liturgy of the Ark coincided with the crowning of David as king of Jerusalem in the Canaanite fashion, that it was repeated at the crowning or on the coronation anniversaries of the kings of Judah, or even that it formed part of a feast for the enthronement of Yahweh. This seems to be reading far too much into the texts.

Nevertheless, it is quite certain that David's action had important consequences. From the political point of view, the capital was his own personal conquest, and did not belong to the territory of any of the Twelve Tribes: in it he had installed the Ark, which all the tribes venerated and which had formerly been the focal point of their common worship; he thereby increased his power over the various parts of the nation and ensured national unity around his own throne. But the religious aspect was even more important: the restoration of a sanctuary for the Ark meant that Jerusalem was the heir to the sanctuary of Shiloh and to the Tent in the desert. The installation of the Ark in Jerusalem meant that the religious traditions of the Twelve Tribes were centred there, and Jerusalem became the focal point of that history of salvation which stretched from the Exodus from Egypt to the conquest of the Holy Land: the continuity of Yahwism was assured. By the transfer of the Ark, Jerusalem became the Holy City, and its religious significance was destined to eclipse its political importance: as a religious centre it would survive the break-up of David's empire, and even the total destruction of national independence.

The second step was taken when David set up an altar in the place where Solomon's Temple would stand. The story in 2 S 24: 16-25 may perhaps combine two traditions which the parallel passage in 1 Ch 21: 15-22: 1 harmonizes and explains. It is a foundation-story, with all the essential elements we have met so often before: a theophany—the appearance of the Angel of Yahweh to David near the threshing-floor of Araunah the Jebusite; a message of salvation—the arresting of the plague; the inauguration of worship—the setting up of an altar on the site of the apparition, and the first sacrifices.

We have seen how the patriarchal sanctuaries and some of those which date from the period of the Judges had perpetuated or replaced previous places of worship. The texts so far examined do not justify similar conclusions about Jerusalem, but there are some others which should be taken into consideration. In Ps 110: 4, the king of Israel is called a priest after the manner of Melchisedech.[1] The only other text which mentions Melchisedech is Gn 14: 18-20, which tells the story of his meeting Abraham. Melchisedech was king of Shalem, *i.e.* Jerusalem (Ps 76: 3), and also a priest of El-'Elyon. He blessed Abraham by his god and Abraham paid him a tithe. By linking Abraham with the future capital of David, the text is trying to justify Israel's very ancient connections with Jerusalem, and the rights which the king and the priesthood of Jerusalem held over Israel; but at the same time we learn from this text the name of the pre-Israelite god who was venerated there. El-'Elyon was a Canaanite god. According to Philo of Byblos, the Phoenician pantheon included an 'Eliun called the Most High', who was the father of Ouranos (heaven) and of Gé (earth); now, in Gen 14: 19, the name El-'Elyon is followed by the epithet 'Creator of heaven and earth'. We may also compare the Phoenician inscription from Karatepe and a Neo-Punic inscription from Leptis Magna where the 'Creator of the earth' is invoked: the same epithet is attached to the name El in an inscription and on potsherds from Palmyra, and in the Hittite translation of a Canaanite myth the name and epithet are transcribed El-Kunirsha. An Aramaic treaty from Sfire includes among the gods who guarantee it 'El *and* 'Elyon', which some writers have interpreted as two distinct divinities. But El *and* 'Elyon may mean, as in Gn 14, 'El who is 'Elyon'. Thus the title represents another form in which the supreme god reveals himself, like the El-Bethel, El-'Olam and El-Shaddai we met when discussing the sanctuaries of the Patriarchs. And, as in the previous instances, Yahweh replaced the former divinity and assumed his titles: he is 'the God of heaven and the God of earth' in Gn 24: 3. 'Elyon became an epithet of Yahweh (Ps 47: 3), and is employed as a parallel for Yahweh (Ps 18: 14), for he alone is "'Elyon over all the earth, most high above all the gods' (Ps 97: 9).

Some writers have tried to go further, but the ground becomes very unsure. It has been said that just as Yahweh replaced 'Elyon, so he usurped his sanctuary. But the text does not say so, and in fact suggests the contrary: in Gn 14 there is no mention of a sanctuary of El-'Elyon, though of course there must have been one, because his priest was present and Abraham gave a tithe. The narratives in the books of Samuel stress that David put up a special tent to house the Ark (2 S 6: 17; cf. 7: 2) and that he set up his altar in a place which had previously been profane ground: it was a barn for threshing corn which belonged to a private individual (2 S 24: 18-10). Yet it could be objected that the silence of Gn 14 and the insistence of 2 S were deliberately meant to conceal the fact that the Temple of Jerusalem had been built on the site of a pagan sanctuary. It is easier to put the objection than to answer it; but any answer must recognize the fact that there was a genuine tradition of a tent

1. Cf. pp. 109, 114.

over the Ark, and that this Tent remained the centre of Yahwistic worship until the Temple was built, for it is almost certainly the 'tent' where Solomon was anointed (1 K 1: 39), and the 'tent of Yahweh' where Joab sought refuge (1 K 2: 28f.). This question, moreover, is tied up with another one: did Yahweh inherit the priesthood of El-'Elyon? Under David, another line of priests, that of Sadoq, makes its appearance in Jerusalem itself. Its origins are obscure, and some authors have maintained Sadoq was the priest of 'Elyon at the time of the conquest, and that he was subsequently engaged by David for the service of Yahweh. This problem will be treated when we discuss the priesthood,[1] but it is already obvious that unless some link can be established between the sanctuary of Yahweh and that of 'Elyon, the principal argument in favour of a Canaanite origin for the priesthood of Sadoq falls to the ground, for Sadoq is never mentioned except in connection with the Ark and the tent of Yahweh (2 S 15: 25; 1 K 1: 39).

Whatever be the answer to these questions, it was under David that the Ark, the symbol of the divine presence, was brought to Jerusalem, and that the city acquired a site for worship which was chosen by Yahweh himself. Everything was set for the work of Solomon.

1. Cf. pp. 373-374.

CHAPTER THREE

THE TEMPLE AT JERUSALEM

DAVID'S purpose in transferring the Ark to his new capital was to make Jerusalem the religious centre of Israel, but the Ark had to be kept in a tent, for there was no building to house it. According to 2 S 7: 1-7, David thought of building a 'house' for Yahweh, but was dissuaded by a divine command which Nathan brought him. The text of this prophecy, however, contains an addition (2 S 7: 13), according to which Yahweh was reserving the honour of building such a sanctuary for the son and successor of David. The Deuteronomic redaction of the book of Kings tells us that Solomon recalled this promise and presented himself as the executor of a plan which his father had conceived but had failed to carry out because he was too preoccupied by his wars (1 K 5: 17-19; 8: 15-21). The Chronicler, however, assigns a far more important rôle to David: David did not build the Temple because he was a man of war and had shed blood, whereas Solomon was predestined for this task by his name, which means the 'peaceful' king (1 Ch 22: 8-10; 28: 3). David, however, had prepared everything; he was responsible for the plans of the Temple and the inventory of its furnishings; he collected the materials for the building and the gold ingots which were to be used for the sacred objects; he assembled the teams of workmen, and fixed the classes and functions of the clergy (1 Ch 22-28). The theological ideas expressed in these different traditions will be discussed at the end of the chapter: for the moment, we are concerned only with what they have in common, namely, that David first thought of having a Temple, and that Solomon actually built it.

1. *Solomon's Temple*

The building of the Temple occupied Solomon from the fourth to the eleventh year of his reign (1 K 6: 37-38; cf. 6: 1). He made a contract with Hiram, king of Tyre, for the timber to be brought from the Lebanon (1 K 5: 15-26), while the stone was quarried near Jerusalem (1 K 5: 29, 31). The Israelites were conscripted to provide the bulk of the labour force (1 K 5: 20, 23, 27-30), but the skilled workmen (*i.e.* the lumbermen in the Lebanon, the sailors who transported the wood, the carpenters and the stonemasons in Jerusalem) were Phoenicians (1 K 5: 20, 32). Hiram, who cast the two pillars and the other bronzes in the Jordan valley, was also a Phoenician, though his mother was an Israelite (1 K 7: 13-47).

There is a description of the Temple and its furnishings in 1 K 6-7, of which 2 Ch 3-4 is a summary, with some variations. This description certainly goes back to a document which was almost contemporary with the building, and the final editor had seen the Temple still standing; but the description is very hard to interpret. The editor did not have the interests of an architect or an archaeologist and he has omitted details which would be essential for a reconstruction (*e.g.* the thickness of the walls, the layout of the façade, the way in which it was roofed). Moreover, the text is full of technical terms, and has been disfigured by scribes who understood it no better than we do; and it has been loaded with glosses meant to enhance the splendour of the building. Lastly, not a stone of this glorious building is to be seen to-day. Our only guides are the texts, where the exegesis is often uncertain, and the comparisons which can be drawn from the archaeology of Palestine and of the neighbouring countries. It is not surprising that the reconstructions which have been attempted differ considerably from each other, and the interpretation presented here makes no claim to be definitive.

(a) *The buildings.* The Temple was a long building, open on one of its shorter sides. The interior was divided into three parts: a vestibule, called the Ulam (from a root meaning 'to be in front of'), a room for worship called the Hekal (which has the double meaning of 'palace' and 'temple' in both Hebrew and Phoenician),[1] and which was later called the 'Holy Place', and lastly the Debir (roughly, the 'back room') which was later called the 'Holy of Holies': this was the part reserved to Yahweh, and the Ark of the Covenant stood there.

The measurements given in the Bible do not include the thickness of the walls. The Temple was 20 cubits wide: the Ulam was 10 cubits long, the Hekal 40 cubits and the Debir 20 cubits. There is no mention of walls which partitioned it inside, and yet there certainly was one between the Ulam and the Hekal, though we do not know whether there was one between the Hekal and the Debir. The Hekal and the Debir are in fact treated as one whole (1 K 6: 2): properly speaking they formed the 'house', the Temple, and together they were 60 cubits long: it is only later in the description that we are told the Debir was 20 cubits long, and the Hekal 40 cubits (1 K 6: 16-17). If there had been a real wall separating them, the total length would have been 60 cubits plus the thickness of the wall. Moreover, the details given about the Debir seem to confirm this conclusion: though the text has been tampered with, a very slight correction gives an excellent sense (1 K 6: 16): Solomon 'used cedar planks to build the twenty cubits from the back of the Temple, from the ground to the rafters, and (these twenty cubits) "were set apart" from the Temple for the Debir'. These planks are not the wooden

1. Cf. p. 282.

panelling on the main walls, which was mentioned in the preceding verse and which was found both in the Hekal and in the Debir: they seem to be a partition-wall in front of the Debir. Later texts lend support to this hypothesis: in the Tent of desert days, the description of which is inspired by the Temple at Jerusalem,[1] the Holy of Holies was separated from the Holy Place by nothing more than a veil (Ex 26: 33): Ezechiel's Temple has only a comparatively thin wall at this point (Ez 41: 3); the Mishnah, treating of Herod's Temple, records only curtains between the Holy Place and the Holy of Holies, and Josephus, whose description is more trustworthy, speaks only of a veil (*B.J.*, V, v, 5).

In ancient Oriental temples, the *cella* stood somewhat higher than the level of the room, or, failing this, the symbol of worship itself stood on a raised platform or podium. Though the Bible does not mention it, at Jerusalem too the Debir seems to have been on a higher level than the Hekal. The measurements given in 1 K 6: 20 make the Debir a perfect cube with a 20-cubit side, but the Hekal was 30 cubits high according to the Hebrew, 25 according to the ancient Greek version and the Lucianic recension (1 K 6: 2). To explain this difference of 10 or 5 cubits in height, it has been suggested that the roof of the Debir was lower than that of the Hekal, as was the *cella* of some Egyptian temples, or that there was a room over the Debir. Both these solutions are improbable, and it is better to say that the floor of the Debir stood higher than the floor of the Hekal, and that it was approached by a flight of stairs. The Hebrew text makes this podium 10 cubits high, which is higher than any other examples we know of, but according to the Greek text it would be only 5 cubits higher, which is quite reasonable.

Two bronze pillars stood before the vestibule (1 K 7: 15-22; 41-42). They were 18 cubits high, and were crowned by capitals, also in bronze, 5 cubits high. They were not, apparently, supports for the lintel of the vestibule; on the contrary, they stood upright in front of it, on each side of the entrance. It has recently been suggested that they were enormous cressets or pillars on top of which lights could be burnt, but it is far more probable that they were traditional steles or *maṣṣebôth*, which had always had their place in the old Canaanite sanctuaries. There is no lack of Phoenician analogies, and one may compare also the two pillars of Heliopolis mentioned by Lucian, *De Dea Syria* § 28, the two steles of Heracles' Temple at Tyre mentioned by Herodotus II 44, and the two pillars which decorate a relief from the neighbourhood of Tyre; for a period nearer to that of Solomon's Temple, one can point to a model, in baked clay, of a sanctuary (from Idalion in Cyprus), and to two similar models recently discovered in Transjordan and at Tell el-Farah near Nablus. The names of the two columns, *Yakîn* and *Bo'az*, are still a riddle: they have been explained as meaning 'he will establish with strength', or as the opening words of royal oracles, with the following phrase understood

1. Cf. p. 296.

('Yahweh will establish . . .; In the strength of Yahweh . . .'), or as dynastic names (*Bo'az* would represent the husband of Ruth, David's forefather, and *Yakîn*, it has been suggested, might be an ancestor of Bathsheba). The two words are never found again, and there is no guarantee that they were engraved on the pillars. It has been suggested that they were so named by the Tyrian artist who made and erected them, and perhaps they merely express his satisfaction on seeing his masterpieces completed: *Yakîn* (or, better, *Yakûn*, the Phoenician form preserved in the Greek version) meaning 'It is solid!', and *Bo'az* (perhaps with a Phoenician vocalization) 'With strength!'

1 K 6: 5-10 describes a construction which surrounded the Temple on three sides. It seems to have been a building in three very slight storeys, erected against the walls of the Debir and the Hekal, but leaving the surrounds of the Ulam quite clear. It is sometimes called *yaṣia'*, in the singular, and sometimes *ṣ'la'ôth*, a plural, the singular of which denotes one of three storeys. The two words are not synonyms, and seem to indicate that our present text is combining information about two successive stages in the form of this building. The *yaṣia'*, to judge by etymology, was a low construction, a bottom storey which surrounded the Temple on three sides. It was only 5 cubits high, and was like the low rooms which flanked certain temples in Egypt and Mesopotamia: like the latter, it was an adjunct to the sanctuary and was used as a store-place for offerings. It was built at the same time as the Temple, and was closely connected with it (1 K 6: 10). Later on, this building proved too small for its purpose, so it was raised by storeys, either at the same or at different times. The name *yaṣia'*, which meant a low building, was no longer appropriate, and so the whole structure was then called *ṣ'laôth*, the singular of which means primarily a man's rib, and then the side of an object or of a building: here it means each of the storeys which flanked the Temple. Since the upper two storeys of this building were added later, they were not part of the plan of the Temple like the *yaṣia'*; but their joists rested on the already existing recesses in the wall: consequently, each storey was a cubit wider than the lower one (1 K 6: 6). The entrance to the *yaṣia'* was at the right corner of the Temple, obviously from outside. When the upper storeys were added, *lûlim* were put in. The ancient versions and many modern translations take this term to mean spiral staircases; but the meaning of the word in Rabbinical Hebrew makes it more likely that they were merely trap-doors connecting the different storeys, for they all had low ceilings and were used as store-places.

The description of the side-building shows that the wall of the Temple receded one cubit at three points. There was a technical reason for these recesses: the higher parts of the wall were not so heavy, and the wall was thus more stable. The upper parts of buildings excavated in Syria and Palestine have all been destroyed, so that we cannot point to archaeological confirmation, but clay models of sanctuaries, found at Beisan, clearly indicate the same kind of recess. The Egyptians obtained the same result by giving a pronounced batter to the surface of high walls.

How was it built? There is one piece of information about the walls of the Temple courts and of the Palace (1 K 6: 36; 7: 12) which is most useful: they had three courses of dressed stones, and one course of cedar-timber. The Temple walls were probably built in the same way, for when it was to be rebuilt after the Exile, Cyrus' edict gave orders for it to have three courses of stones and one of timber (Esd 6: 4). Excavations in the Near East have unearthed many parallels which show that these timbers formed a series of wooden ties to hold the wall together. Sometimes these wooden joists are found in a wall built entirely of stones; alternatively, the joist-framing sometimes begins above a stone footing and locks together a brick superstructure. There is good evidence of this at Troy, and it seems to have been followed in the Solomonian buildings at Megiddo: we shall see later that it is also found in the sanctuaries which are most similar to Solomon's Temple. It may be, then, that the Temple had stone foundations, on top of which was a brick superstructure: the walls would have been panelled with cedar (1 K 6: 15) to hide the brickwork: and there are several parallels for this, too.

A text about the Palace may perhaps give the technical name for this framework of wooden ties which held the bricks locked together. 1 K 7: 9 says that all the royal buildings were built of magnificent stones 'from the foundation to the ṭ'paḥôth'. The ancient versions translated the word anyhow, and modern commentators have guessed at its meaning, suggesting a crenellated balcony or wall-brackets for the ceiling joists. But it is quite certain that the word is only a metaphorical use of ṭepaḥ, meaning 'the palm of the hand'. Now the Assyrian equivalent, ṭappu, means both 'the sole of the foot' and 'plank' or 'joist'. Three letters from El-Amarna contain this phrase: 'The brick may slip from under its ṭappati, but I shall never slip from under the feet of the king, my master'. Ṭappati has been translated 'companions', but its sense seems clear: the puppet kings of Canaan are protesting that they will never stir under the feet of Pharaoh, not even as much as the bricks of a wall may move under the wood which locks them together. Ṭappati then, in these letters, stands for the whole framework, like the ṭ'paḥôth of 1 K 7: 9, and this text would mean that the walls were of splendid stonework up to the wooden framework which held together the brick superstructure: it would be the equivalent of the three courses of stones crowned by one of cedar timber in 1 K 6: 36; 7: 12; Esd 6: 4.

The Temple, like other Semitic sanctuaries,[1] stood in the middle of a courtyard called the inner court (1 K 6: 36), by contrast with the great court (1 K 7: 12), which included both the Temple and the Palace. The Palace, too, had an inner court (1 K 7: 8), the northern wall of which was common to the inner court of the Temple. You passed straight from the king's domain into

1. Cf. pp. 274-275.

the domain of God, and this close proximity later aroused the indignation of Ezechiel: 'The house of Israel, they and their kings, shall no longer defile my sanctuary . . . by building a wall common to them and to me' says God (Ez 43: 7–8).

The inner court of the Temple was later divided, or extended, at the expense of the great court. 2 Ch 20: 5 speaks of a 'new court' under Josaphat, and we are told that Manasseh set up altars 'in the two courts of the house of Yahweh' (2 K 21: 5); Jr 36: 10 mentions an 'upper court', apparently the top of the esplanade on which the Temple stood, by contrast with a lower court. Thus the divisions of Herod's sanctuary are already beginning to appear: the court of Israel, the court of the women, and the court of the Gentiles.

(b) *Analogies and influences*. It was once customary to see Egyptian influence in Solomon's Temple. But its architectural concept was entirely different from that of Egyptian temples. The latter were spreadeagled over a large area, behind a broad façade, with a network of buildings surrounding the *cella* of the god, while Solomon's Temple consisted of three rooms one behind the other, with a narrow front. Other writers have thought of Assyrian influence, and the plans of certain sanctuaries are in fact quite similar; but differences still remain, and above all, Palestine and Assyria were too far from each other, and had no contacts at this period. We must look for comparisons closer to Jerusalem.

The threefold division into Ulam, Hekal and Debir, found in Solomon's Temple, is very common. It is found, for example, in the Ditch temple at Tell ed-Duweir, which belongs to the pre-Israelite period, and again in the little sanctuaries of Beisan, which are not quite so old. On the other hand, this division is quite natural: what is characteristic of the Jerusalem Temple is rather that the three rooms stand one behind the other in a straight line, and that the building is the same width all along its length. Several recently dis-covered sanctuaries follow the same plan: at Alalakh (Tell Atchana) in nor-thern Syria, a badly preserved temple of the thirteenth century B.C.; at Hazor in Palestine, a temple, somewhat better preserved, from the same period; at Tell Tainat, not far from Tell Atchana, a temple of the ninth century B.C. The similarity extends even to methods of building. The method we described for the building of the Temple in Jerusalem was followed in these temples: they had brick walls locked together by a framework of wooden ties, which, at least at Alalakh and at Hazor, stood on a stone footing; at Alalakh and perhaps at Hazor too, the brick walls were faced with woodwork.

These parallels fall within the same chronological framework as the Temple of Solomon, and all come from the Syro-Phoenician region where we must certainly look for the model Solomon copied. We have already stated that the skilled workmen he employed on the Temple were Phoenici-ans, and that the bronze-work was cast by a Tyrian artist. It is quite likely that the architect responsible for the plan and for its building was also a

Phoenician, and it is tempting to identify him with the superintendent of the king's major works, the master of conscripted labour, Adoram, who has a Phoenician name (1 K 5: 28).

(c) *The site of the Temple.* David set up an altar on the threshing-floor of Arauna (2 S 24: 18-25), and according to 1 Ch 22: 1 he destined the place to be the 'house of Yahweh', and the altar to be 'the altar of holocausts for Israel'. Solomon built his Temple on this 'place prepared by David' (2 Ch 3: 1). The general position is unquestionable: it is the rocky ridge which overlooks Ophel, the site of the original town, from the north. The temple of Zorobabel and that of Herod were later built in the same place, and the Herodian enclosure is to-day the esplanade of the Mosque of Omar, the Haram esh-Sherif. Similarly, there is no doubt about the orientation of Solomon's Temple: like Ezechiel's (Ez 47: 1) and Herod's, its entrance faced east (cf. also 1 K 7: 39).

To place it exactly is more difficult. Towards the centre of the Haram esh-Sherif, at its highest point, the dome of Omar to-day rises above a rocky protuberance called the 'Sakhra' or the 'Rock', beneath which there is a cave. The Temple must certainly be closely connected with this rock which has remained the object of such great veneration. But two hypotheses here confront each other. The more common opinion to-day is that the rock which is still visible was the foundation-mass of the altar of holocausts, which stood in front of the Temple: the Temple would therefore lie to the west of the sacred rock. It is claimed that traces of the altar's supports can be distinguished in the rock, that the cave underneath was the place where the ashes and the refuse of sacrifices were thrown, and that a canal running north was used to get rid of the blood and the water used for cleansing. Following the tradition of 1 Ch 22: 1, it is claimed that the altar of holocausts was erected on the very site of David's altar, and it is assumed that David's altar stood on the highest point of the rock. None of the arguments brought forward is self-evident, and if the Temple stood to the west of the rock, then it stood where the hill slopes away very rapidly: the Debir would then have been supported by enormous substructures, and this seems rather odd. There is another objection to this location if we look at it from the east: in Herod's Temple, the steps leading from the court of Israel to the court of the women would not correspond to any irregularity in the rock, while a sharp difference of level would have cut across the court of the women.

These reasons have led a number of authors to come back to an old theory which held that the sacred rock was the foundation of the Debir, of the Holy of Holies. The area of the rock is larger than that covered by the Debir, but this is no difficulty, for the Debir was built on the rock, not around it, and it would be quite in order for the rock to be somewhat higher than the rest of the ground if, as we have said, the Debir was higher than the Hekal. If this hypothesis is accepted, then there is no longer any need for substructures supporting the Debir, the steps of Herod's Temple would be found where one would expect them, at the edge of the upper terrace, and there would be no shelf cutting across the court of the women. This theory, too, has its disadvantages: it is hard to see how the walls of the Debir could have been built on top of the rock; it gives no explanation of the cave and the canal; lastly, in Herod's Temple, that part of the court of the Gentiles which stood directly in front of the Temple would be reduced almost to nothing, whereas the area to the north and the south would have been very large.

Both theories present good arguments, and both run up against serious difficulties. All things considered, the second seems the more acceptable. There is a kind of confirmation of it in the rabbinical tradition that the surface of a rock broke through in the Holy of Holies: it was called *'eben sh'tiyyah*, the 'foundation stone', and was considered as the foundation stone of heaven and earth. Could it perhaps be that when Jesus told Peter: 'Thou art Peter, and upon this rock I shall build my church' (Mt 16: 18), he was alluding to this rock upon which the sanctuary of the Old Covenant was built?

(d) *Furnishings of the Temple.* The Ark of the Covenant, which has already been studied,[1] stood in the Debir. Above it were two great wooden figures of cherubim, plated with gold, which stretched right across the width of the Debir and reached half-way to the ceiling (1 K 6: 23-28; 2 Ch 3: 10-13; cf. 1 K 8: 6-7; 2 Ch 5: 7-8). The cherubim were winged animals with human heads, like the winged sphinxes of Syro-Phoenician iconography. Their name, however, *K'rûb*, comes from the Akkadian, in which the word *karibu* or *kuribu* means a genie who was the adviser to the great gods and an advocate for the faithful. In the Temple, the cherubim, together with the Ark, represented the throne of Yahweh,[2] just as, in 2 S 22: 11 = Ps 18: 11, they served as his steeds, and according to the visions of Ez 1 and 10, drew his chariot.

In the Hekal there stood the altar of incense (also called the altar of cedar in 1 K 6: 20-21, and the altar of gold in 1 K 7: 48), the table of shewbread and ten candlesticks (1 K 7: 48-49). The altar of sacrifices is not mentioned, but this is merely an oversight, for it is spoken of later on: it is the altar of bronze (1 K 8: 64), which Solomon set up (1 K 9: 25). It was a metal structure, which according to 2 K 16: 14, stood in front of the Temple, outside the building, like the altar in Herod's Temple.

In the court, south-east of the temple, there stood also the 'Sea' of bronze, an enormous basin supported by twelve statues of bulls (1 K 7: 23-26). The best parallel is the stone basin from Amathonte in Cyprus, but one could also compare the reservoir (?) called *apsû* which is found in some Mesopotamian temples. There were also ten wheeled pedestals, each supporting a bronze basin, five to the right and five to the left of the entrance (1 K 7: 27-29). There are parallels, though much smaller models, in Cyprus and at Megiddo. We

1. Cf. pp. 297-302.   2. Cf. p. 299-300.

shall discuss the symbolism of all this material later, but its practical use is clear: 2 Ch 4: 6 says that the Sea was used for the priests to purify themselves (cf. Ex 30: 18-21), and that the basins were used to wash the victims.

(e) *The Temple as a national sanctuary*. The Temple was only one of a group of buildings which included the Palace and its dependencies. Elsewhere in the East, temple and palace are often connected, but not always in the same way. In Egypt, the temple occupied more space and the palace annexed to it was not the usual residence of the Pharaoh: he merely stayed there when he came to visit the temple and to perform ceremonies: clearly, it was not so in Jerusalem. In Syria and Mesopotamia, on the other hand, the temple was a mere annexe to the palace, a royal chapel, more or less, where the king and his court could perform their devotions. This is particularly true of the temple of Tainat, which has already been compared with that of Jerusalem.

Consequently, many exegetes hold that Solomon's Temple was a palace chapel, the private temple of the king and his household. It stood side by side with the Palace, which occupied much more ground; it was built by Solomon on ground bought by David, at the public expense; it was endowed by the king and dedicated by him. His successors, too, made gifts to the Temple (1 K 15: 15; 2 K 12: 19), but withdrew funds from its treasury just as freely as they did from the Palace treasury (1 K 15: 18; 2 K 12: 19; 16: 8; 18: 15). They undertook work on it, repairing and modifying the Temple buildings and its furnishings (2 K 15: 35; 16: 10-18; 18: 16; 23: 4f.). They had their own dais set up in the court (2 K 11: 14; 16: 18; 23: 3).[1] Joas ordered his civil servants to look after the collection and distribution of the offerings of the faithful (2 K 12: 5-17; 22: 3-7). In short, the Temple at Jerusalem, was, like that at Bethel, a 'royal sanctuary' (Am 10: 13).

This is all perfectly true, but it does not mean that the Temple was nothing more than a chapel attached to the Palace. The intervention of the king was quite justified by his right of patronage, to which he was entitled as founder or benefactor, and by the privileges he inherited by reason of his sacral character and his lawful rôle in worship.[2] But the Temple was not a private chapel; like the sanctuary at Bethel (Am 10: 13), it was a 'temple of the kingdom', a national sanctuary where both king and people offered public worship to the national God. Nor did the Temple at Jerusalem gradually acquire this character over the years: it had it from the time of its foundation. When Jeroboam began the worship at Bethel, immediately after Solomon's death, he was openly trying to prevent his subjects from going to the Temple at Jerusalem (1 K 12: 26-33), and he wanted to have a sanctuary for his people inside his own domains; Jerusalem had been precisely such a sanctuary for the United Kingdom, and, in Jeroboam's mind, was obviously going to continue as a national sanctuary for the kingdom of Judah. When David brought the Ark to Jerusalem, his intention was not to confiscate it for his own private

1. Cf. pp. 102-103.   2. Cf. pp. 113-114.

chapel, but to make it the centre of worship for all the tribes, and when he first thought of building a temple, it was to give Yahweh a 'house' where he could be at home (2 S 7: 1-2). This was the 'house' which Solomon built and consecrated with 'all Israel' (1 K 8: 1-5, 13, 62-66). There were, of course, political, as well as religious, advantages in the idea: the Temple and the Palace stood next door to each other, as if Yahweh and the king chosen by him to rule his people lived next door to each other, and this fact expressed the theocratic ideal of Israel.

2. *The history of Solomon's Temple*

Since the Temple of Jerusalem was the national sanctuary in the capital city, and the religious centre of the nation, its destiny was of course closely bound up with the political and religious history of the nation. It remained standing for four centuries after its foundation, until the kingdom itself ceased to exist. Throughout this long period its structure was never altered, and its buildings were only slightly modified. We argued above[1] that the upper two storeys of the side building were not part of the original structure; if this is true, then Asa may have been responsible for this additional construction when he wanted somewhere to put the offerings he made to the Temple (1 K 15: 15). According to 2 Ch 20: 5, a new court was laid out under Josaphat, lower than the original court, which then became the upper court of Jr 36: 10. The two courtyards were connected by a gate built by Yotham (according to 2 K 15: 35), which would be the Upper Gate of Jr 26: 10; 36: 10.

The rising against Athaliah, the proclamation and sacring of Joas, which are recounted in detail in 2 K 11, took place in the Temple court: there too, all the kings of Judah after Solomon were anointed. The maintenance of the buildings was a permanent source of anxiety, and the biblical account of Joas' reign gives some details about it. The king had at first ordered the priests to take from the Temple income the amount necessary for repairs (2 K 12: 5-6). Since they did not do so, Joas issued a new order transferring the matter to the civil power: a chest would be placed near the entrance to the Temple for the offerings of the faithful, and would be emptied by the royal secretary, who would give the money to the foremen attached to the Temple (2 K 12: 7-17). This arrangement was still in force in the reign of Josias, for his secretary learnt of the discovery of the Book of the Law when he went to empty the money-chest (2 K 22: 3-10).

On the other hand, the kings always kept a tight control over the Temple, and their own religious attitude or political considerations guided their conduct towards the building. Achaz removed the bronze altar erected by Solomon and had a new altar built like the one he had seen at Damascus (2 K 16: 10-16). He dismantled the wheeled pedestals and took away the

1. Cf. p. 315.

bulls underneath the Sea: in all probability, he had no intention of changing the form of worship, but merely wanted some ready cash to pay the tribute he owed to Tiglath-Pileser (2 K 16: 17): similarly, when he had the royal dais and entrance removed from the Temple, he was only trying to please his suzerain by doing away with the symbols of independence. The irreligious king Manasseh erected altars to false gods and an idol of Ashera in the Temple (2 K 21: 4-5, 7).

The pious kings, on the other hand, made away with these defilements of the sanctuary. Ezechias removed the Nehushtan, an idolatrous object venerated by the Israelites as the bronze serpent of desert days (2 K 18: 4). But it was above all Josias who, after the discovery of the Law, swept out of the Temple 'all the cultic objects which had been made for Baal, for Asherah and for all the hosts of heaven' and the very detail is astounding: the sacred post, the house of male prostitutes where women wove veils for Asherah, the horses and the chariot of the sun dedicated by the kings of Judah, the altars which the kings of Judah had set up on the terrace, and those which Manasseh had built in the two courtyards (2 K 23: 4-12). His reform, however, was short-lived: Ez 8 describes the rites practised, with official approval, in the Temple on the eve of its ruin. The Temple mirrored the religious life of the nation, and these deviations in worship, which were accepted, or at least tolerated, in the official sanctuary of Yahwism, show how permanent a danger syncretism was. They also provide a partial explanation of why some genuinely faithful Israelites looked unfavourably on the Temple: we shall return to this subject later.[1]

The king had control of the Temple treasury,[2] but conquerors too turned covetous eyes on it: immediately after Solomon's death, Shesonq emptied it (1 K 14: 26), and even a king of Israel, Joas, was not afraid to pillage the house of Yahweh after his victory over Amasias (2 K 14: 14). Pillaging sanctuaries was just another custom of war in ancient times: the post-exilic Temple was sacked by Antiochus Epiphanes, and Herod's Temple by the soldiers of Titus.

This, too, was how Solomon's Temple came to an end. After the first invasion of Nabuchodonosor, in 597, the Temple treasury was pillaged along with the royal exchequer (2 K 24: 13). After the second attack, in 587, the Temple shared the fate of the city of David and Solomon. Everything was carried away, even the two great pillars and the Sea of Bronze, which were broken up so that the metal could be sent to Babylon (2 K 25: 13-17; Jr 52: 17-23). Such was the end of the Temple which had been the pride of Israel.

3. The post-exilic Temple

Ezechiel, in the land of Exile, had a vision of a new Temple in a restored and idealized Jerusalem. His long description of the buildings (Ez 40: 1-44: 9)

1. Cf. pp. 329-330.   2. Cf. pp. 139 and 320.

is only of indirect interest to us, for this Temple was never built. The prophet however, had himself seen Solomon's Temple while it was still standing, and he arranged his idealized sanctuary in essentially the same way: moreover, these chapters seem to have inspired the later reconstructions of the Temple: this is perhaps true of Zorobabel's reconstruction, and can be affirmed with greater certainty of the Temple of Herod.

More important, however, was the mentality which gave birth to this vision: a reformer was there planning how to give concrete expression to those ideas of holiness, purity and spirituality which were the soul of his preaching. The stains which had defiled the former sanctuary were to disappear (cf. especially Ez 43: 1-12; 44: 4-9). The Temple would stand in a sacred square, cut off from profane land, and encircled by two walls, the gates of which would be guarded to prevent any foreigner from entering. Ezechiel does not mention any cultic installations except the altar of holocausts in front of the Temple: this altar is like a miniature ziggurat with three storeys whose names, interpreted in the light of cognate Akkadian words, have a cosmic symbolism (Ez 43: 13-17). Otherwise the only cultic object he mentions is a 'kind of altar' in the Hekal: it was to be made of wood, and is called 'the table before Yahweh' (Ez 41: 21-22), *i.e.* the former table of shewbread. In the Debir, which he calls explicitly the Holy of Holies (Ez 41: 3-4), there would no longer be any Ark of the Covenant, but the glory of Yahweh would fill the sanctuary (Ez 44: 4), where he would make his dwelling among the children of Israel (Ez 43: 7) as he had once done in the desert days (Ex 25: 8). The Temple would be the centre of a restored theocracy (Ez 37: 23-28). These theological ideas had a deeper influence on the thought of Judaism than his description had on the buildings of after-time.

In 538 B.C. Cyrus authorized the Jews to return to Jerusalem and to rebuild their Temple there at the expense of the royal exchequer; he also returned to them the gold and silver furnishings which Nabuchodonosor had carried off as booty. This decree of Cyrus has been preserved in two forms: one is in Aramaic, as cited in the decree of Darius of which we shall speak soon (Esd 6: 3-5), and one in Hebrew (Esd 1: 2-4). The authenticity of the Aramaic decree is well founded, but many writers will not allow that the Hebrew text is authentic: this latter is probably a free composition of the Chronicler, who knew that there had been such a document and reconstructed its text. Other scholars, however, have argued in favour of its authenticity, suggesting that there were in fact two official acts: an Aramaic memorandum destined for the royal exchequer (which was afterwards kept in the archives), and a proclamation in Hebrew addressed to the Jews.

The first exiles to return to Palestine erected an altar on the site of the old one (Esd 3: 2-6), and, under the direction of Sheshbassar, began work on the Temple (Esd 5: 16). Apparently, they merely cleared the rubble away from the line of the old walls and did some levelling: work was then interrupted, because of Samaritan obstruction, according to Esd 4: 1-5, because of the lack of interest among the Jews, according to Ag 1: 2. In the second year of Darius, 520 B.C., the task was again taken in hand, under the direction of Zorobabel and of Josue, and with the encouragement of the two prophets, Aggaeus and Zacharias (Esd 4: 24—5: 2; Ag 1: 1-2, 9; Za 4: 7-10). Tattenai, the satrap of Transeuphrates, was worried by this activity, and asked Darius for instructions: the emperor, when he had read the memorandum left by Cyrus, ordered him to honour its terms and to allow the Jews to continue their work. It was finished in 515 B.C.

We know very little about this Temple. Cyrus' decree laid down its measurements (Esd 6: 3: unfortunately, the text is corrupt) and the way in which it was to be built: three courses of stone and one course of wood (Esd 6: 4; cf. 5: 8), as in Solomon's buildings.[1] It is quite certain that it followed the plan of the former Temple, and it is highly probable that it was exactly the same size. The books of Esdras and Nehemias show that some dependent buildings were attached to it: the rooms for the offerings Esdras brought (Esd 8: 29) remind us of the side-building of Solomon's Temple (1 K 6: 5-10), and of the side-cells or rooms of Ez 41: 5-11; 42: 1-14. Tobiyyah was given a lodging in these rooms, until he was evicted by Nehemias (Ne 13: 4-9).

Esd 3: 12-13 and Ag 2:3 say that the older generation, which had seen the former Temple, wept at the sight of this new one, which was 'like nothing' in comparison. It had been deduced, all too hastily, that the Second Temple was a poverty-stricken building, but the two texts cited refer to the very beginning of the work and not to the completed building; and Esdras' text is inspired by that of Aggaeus. It is quite possible that the payments Cyrus had allowed from the royal exchequer, and Darius from the taxes of Transeuphrates (Esd 6: 4 and 8), were not paid in full, and that the Jews had to revert to raising the money locally, among men of no great means; but Tattenai's report implies that the work was solid and carefully executed (Esd 5: 8), and even if the result did not achieve the legendary splendour of Solomon's Temple, it must have been quite suitable for worship. Aggaeus, to encourage the builders, had promised that the treasures of the Gentiles would flow there, and that the glory of the new sanctuary would surpass that of the old one (Ag 2: 7-9).

At the turn of the fourth century B.C., Hecataeus of Abdera, cited by Josephus in c. Apionem, I, xxii, wrote that the Temple was a large building encircled by a wall: near it stood an altar of stones, which was the same size as the altar of Solomon, according to 2 Ch 4: 1, and as the altar of Ezechiel (Ez 43: 13-17). Inside the building was an altar and a golden chandelier, the flame of which was kept continually alight. A century later, the Letter of Aristeas, a piece of Jewish propaganda writing, stresses, in its description, the splendour of the sanctuary, the three walls marking off the courts, the curtain hanging

1. Cf. p. 316.

before its door, the altar and the ramp which led up to it. Josephus, in *Ant.*, XII, iii, 4, has preserved an order of Antiochus III from the same epoch: its authenticity has been defended recently by strong arguments. Like the inscriptions which later stood on the barrier separating the court of the Gentiles in Herod's Temple, it forbade any foreigner to enter the precincts of the sanctuary. Antiochus' order may have been hung or engraved at a similar place in the Temple of Zorobabel, perhaps on that 'wall of the inner court of the sanctuary' which Alkimus, who had forced his way to the high priesthood, wanted demolished, to please the Greeks (1 M 9: 54).

The books of Maccabees give us some details about the Temple when relating how Antiochus Epiphanes pillaged it in 169 B.C.: he took away the golden altar, the chandelier, the table of offerings, the veil, the gold plating, the precious vessels and the treasures (1 M 1: 21-24; 2 M 5: 15-16). Like the story of Heliodorus (2 M 3), this presupposes that the Temple was rich. In 167, the Temple, already pillaged, was profaned, when the lawful sacrifices were suppressed and the worship of Zeus Olympios was introduced there (1 M 1:44-49; 2 M 6:1-6): this indeed was the 'abomination of desolation' (Dn 9: 27; 11: 31). Three years later, in 164, Judas Maccabee purified and repaired the Temple, built a new altar, and put back in the sanctuary the candelabra, the altar of perfumes, the table and the curtains: worship was restored and this feast of the new dedication was thereafter celebrated every year (1 M 4: 36-59).

A hundred years later, when Pompey took Jerusalem, he entered the Temple, but respected the sanctuary and did not touch the treasury, which was then estimated at 2,000 talents. In 20-19 B.C. Herod began to rebuild the entire Temple, and all the essential work was finished in ten years. But Herod's Temple is not one of the institutions of the Old Testament.

4. *The theology of the Temple*

Solomon's Temple was the religious centre of Israel, and it remained so even after the separation of the two kingdoms, and this in spite of Jeroboam's building a rival sanctuary at Bethel. When Ahiyyah, a prophet from Shiloh in Israel, foretold the political schism, he still spoke of Jerusalem as the city which Yahweh had chosen (1 K 11: 32), and the faithful in the Northern Kingdom never ceased to look towards Jerusalem: even after the fall of the city, pilgrims from Shechem, from Shiloh and from Samaria brought their offerings to the ruined Temple (Jr 41: 5). If Jerusalem was regarded as the Holy City, the reason lay in its possession of the Temple. We must therefore try to define the religious significance of the Temple.

(a) *The Temple as the seat of the divine presence.* The Temple was the 'house of God'.[1] When the Ark was taken there, God took possession of his house,

1. Cf. pp. 282-283.

and the Temple was filled by a cloud (1 K 8: 10), that cloud which, in the stories of the desert, was the sign of Yahweh's presence in the Tent of Re-union (Ex 33: 9; 40: 34-35; Nb 12: 4-10).[1] In the short poem which he read aloud on the occasion of the dedication, Solomon says he has built Yahweh 'a dwelling-place, a home where he will live for ever' (1 K 8: 13), and the darkness of the Debir, where Yahweh was enthroned above the Ark and the cherubim, recalled the cloud (1 K 8: 12). This belief in Yahweh's presence in his Temple was the whole reason for the worship celebrated there and for the pious customs of the faithful. Ezechias' action provides a most striking example: when he received Sennacherib's threatening letter, 'he went up to the Temple of Yahweh and spread it out before Yahweh' (2 K 19: 14). The connection of the Psalms with worship and the Temple is evident: they often speak of devotion to the 'house of Yahweh' or to the 'courts of Yahweh', and they do so because of the writers' confidence that God lived in the Temple (*e.g.* Ps 27: 4; 42: 5; 76: 3; 84; 122: 1-4; 132: 13-14; 134, etc.).

The Prophets share the same belief, in spite of their reservations about the worship practised there. 'Yahweh roars from Sion, and from Jerusalem he makes his voice heard' (Am 1: 2). Isaias was called to take up the office of a prophet when he was in the Temple; he had a vision of Yahweh seated on his throne, and of a cloud filling the sanctuary as on the day of its dedication (Is 6: 1-4). The Temple was built on the 'mountain of Yahweh' (Is 2: 2-3) and especially from the time of Isaias onwards the name Sion takes on a religious meaning.[2] For Jeremias, too, the throne of Yahweh's glory is in Sion (Jr 14: 21). This presence of God amid his people, however, was a grace, and would be withdrawn if the people were unfaithful. It was in the Temple itself that Jeremias preached against the Temple, and against that blind confidence in the building which was unaccompanied by the desire to reform one's life (Jr 7: 1-15; 26: 1-15). Ezechiel, too, saw the glory of Yahweh leave the Temple, which had been defiled by Israel's sins (Ez 8-10); but God would come back to the new Temple, which would be the place of his throne, where he would live forever among the children of Israel (Ez 43: 1-12). The name of Jerusalem would then be 'Yahweh-is-there!' (Ez 48: 35). Again, after the Return, the Prophets encourage the rebuilding of the Temple: and the reason is that God must come back to live in Jerusalem (Ag 1: 9; Za 2: 14; 8: 3). The Temple, the holy Dwelling-place, still remained the very centre of Jewish piety.

This same period saw an evolution in the notion of the divine presence in the Temple. If God dwelt in this 'house', if he made his voice heard from Sion (Am 1: 2; Is 2: 3; Mi 4: 2), if he acted from his sanctuary (Ps 20: 3; 134: 3), was there not a risk of limiting, or at least of binding, his presence to the material temple? Theological thought was conscious of the tension between the transcendence of Yahweh, who from the beginning had been

1. Cf. pp. 294-295.   2. Cf. the texts cited on p. 281.

recognized as master of the universe, and his historical and human proximity to Israel. The Deuteronomic redactor of the books of Kings asks and answers the question in the prayer he ascribes to Solomon for the dedication of the Temple: 'But is God really to dwell with men on earth? The heavens, even the highest heavens, cannot contain him, much less this house which I have built' (1 K 8: 27). The solution is given in the following verses: the faithful pray at the Temple, and Yahweh hears their prayer from heaven, where he dwells (1 K 8: 30–40). To avoid too crude a concept of the divine presence, they said it was the Name of Yahweh which dwelt there (1 K 8: 17, 29), following the usage of Deuteronomy (Dt 12: 5, 11, etc.). To the Semitic mind, the name expressed and represented the person: God was present in a special way wherever the 'Name of Yahweh' was. The last development of this theology came when Judaism evolved the notion of the Shekinah, 'the dwelling', which is an attempt to express the gracious presence of God amid Israel without taking anything away from his transcendence.

(b) *The Temple as the sign of election.* This presence, we have just asserted, was a grace. God himself chose to live among his own, and he chose to live in *this* city and in *this* Temple. Before ever it was built, the site was marked out by a theophany (2 S 24: 16; 2 Ch 3: 1). Yahweh chose Sion as his home (Ps 132: 13); Sion was the mountain God chose for his residence (Ps 68: 17; cf. 76: 3; 78: 68). Deuteronomy stresses, even more than it stresses the choice of the people, the fact that Yahweh selected this place among all the tribes, that his Name might be there, and might dwell there (Dt 12: 5): the formula occurs, complete or in shortened forms, no less than twenty times in the book. The 'place' itself is never identified by name, but later ages recognized it as Jerusalem and the Temple there, where Josias would centralize the nation's worship.[1] The idea itself, however, dates back to the time before Josias. It was a consequence of Yahweh's choice of David, and of the promise that his dynasty would endure in Jerusalem (cf. 1 K 8: 16 (Greek) and 2 Ch 6: 5–6; 1 K 11: 13, 32). In the end, the people became utterly convinced of this as a result of an historical event, namely, the deliverance of Jerusalem, under Ezechias, from Sennacherib's siege. Yahweh had kept his promise: 'I shall protect this city and save it, for my own sake, and for the sake of my servant David' (2 K 19: 34; Is 37: 35). The formula of Deuteronomy was perhaps coined at this time, and there is an echo of it in 1 K 8: 44, 48; 11: 13, 32, 36; 14: 21; 2 K 21: 7; 23: 27, and their parallels in Chronicles.

The saving of the Temple in 701 was the visible sign of divine election, and the memory of this miraculous deliverance gave rise to a confidence that the Temple would always afford unfailing protection. The Israelites went on repeating 'This is the sanctuary of Yahweh, the sanctuary of Yahweh, the sanctuary of Yahweh!' and thought they were safe against the world (Jr 7: 4). The destruction of the same Temple in 587 was an agonizing trial for

1. Cf. pp. 336–339.

Israel's faith, but all was not lost, for the election would be renewed: after the return from the exile, Zacharias proclaimed that Yahweh would once more make Jerusalem his choice (Za 1: 17; 2: 16; 3: 2), and Nehemias, taking up the formula of Deuteronomy, reminded God that he had promised to re-assemble the exiles in the place which he had chosen as the home for his Name (Ne 1: 9).

(c) *Symbolism of the Temple?* Jewish thought, especially in certain apocry-phal works, and Hellenistic thought also, in Josephus and Philo, endeavoured to find in the Temple a cosmic symbolism; the Temple hill was for them the centre of the world. Similar speculations can be found in the Fathers of the Church and in medieval theologians, and some modern writers have tried to justify a symbolic interpretation by seeking analogies among the religious concepts of the Ancient East.

In the Bible there is very feeble support for these theories. The idea of the Temple hill as the centre of the world is nowhere explicitly affirmed, and the most one can say is that the ground is prepared for the theory when Mount Sion is exalted as the 'holy mountain', or when in poetry, it is identified with Saphon, the home of the gods.[1] But there is not a single text which suggests that the Temple itself ever had a cosmic significance. A late psalm reads: 'He built his sanctuary like the heights of heaven, like the earth which he made firm for ever' (Ps 78: 69), but all this verse means is that God's choice of Sion as his dwelling-place, and of David as his servant (cf. vv. 68 and 70), is definitive, and as enduring as the heavens and the earth. This statement adds nothing to what we have already said about the Temple as the sign of God's election. Only one point seems to have been established: the cosmic symbol-ism of Ezechiel's altar can be deduced from the names which he gives to its various parts. But Ezechiel was a visionary, borrowing his images from the foreign background in which he lived, and describing the ideal altar of a Temple which was never built.

If we keep to the real Temple, that of Solomon, the reader will remember that its plan and decoration were of foreign inspiration and that they were executed by foreign craftsmen. We do not know what symbolism these foreigners gave to this plan or decoration, nor do we know whether the Israelites accepted this symbolism. It is quite arbitrary to suppose that the three parts of the Temple represented the three parts of the world: the Debir certainly was symbolic, but what it signified is explained in the text and it is not a cosmic symbolism: it stands for the cloud in which God concealed him-self (1 K 8: 12). It is most improbable—to cite a few examples current to-day—that the two bronze pillars represented the sun and the moon, or summer and winter, or that the ten candelabra represented the five planets twice over, or that the wheeled pedestals stood for clouds charged with rain. There is less certainty, however, in saying that the 'Sea' of bronze does not represent the

1. Cf. pp. 279-280 and 281.

primordial waters. It has been said that this 'Sea' is the equivalent of the *apsû* in Mesopotamian temples, a name which also denotes the ocean under the earth. But we are ill informed as to what precisely this *apsû* in the temples was, and we have no information whatever about its symbolic value. And the 'Sea' of Solomon's Temple is called in Hebrew *yam*, a word which stands for the sea, or a lake, or a large river (*e.g.* the Euphrates or the Nile), but which in later Hebrew also means a 'basin' or 'vat'.

If the Temple and its furnishings had had a cosmic significance, the theological problem of how God dwelt there, which we examined above, would have presented itself in quite a different way. Moreover, the solution of the problem would have emerged: God, the master of the universe, would have dwelt in the Temple which was an image of the universe. But Israelite thought did not move in these patterns: right to the end of the monarchy, the Israelites were confronted with the paradox that here was a man-made house in which there dwelt that God whom the heavens could not contain (1 K 8: 27); consequently, they distinguished between the Temple, where men prayed, and heaven, where God dwelt (1 K 8: 30, etc.). They did not think of the Temple as representing the universe, and ideas of cosmic symbolism emerged only long afterwards.

If the Temple did not have a symbolic value, then we ought to look for the key to it not in myths nor in cosmology, but in Israel's history, for the religion of Israel is not a religion of myths nor a nature religion, but an historical one. Just as the great liturgical feasts recalled the different events of the Exodus, and the Ark of the Covenant recalled God's pact with his chosen people, so the Temple recalled and signified Yahweh's choice of Jerusalem and of David's dynasty, and then the subsequent protection afforded to this city and this dynasty.

(d) *Opposition to the Temple*. We have stressed the importance of the Temple in the religious life of Israel, and the positive attitude which the Prophets themselves adopted towards it, even when they condemned the abuses which had crept in there. Yet there was opposition to the Temple itself. When David wanted to build a Temple, Nathan took him a message from Yahweh: David will not build a 'house' for Yahweh, rather Yahweh will make a 'house' (a dynasty) for David. Yahweh had never had a house since he had brought the Israelites out of Egypt, and had never asked for one (2 S 7: 5-7). This does not mean that Yahweh was refusing to accept David's temple but would accept Solomon's when the time comes, as the glossator of 2 S 7: 13 understood it (also the redactor of 1 K 5: 19 and the Chronicler, 1 Ch 17: 12; 22: 10; 28: 6; 2 Ch 6: 8-9). What it does mean is that Yahweh did not want a temple built at all, but that he wanted the desert customs maintained. Nathan's prophecy deliberately omits all mention of the fact that there had previously been a temple built at Shiloh. It would seem then, that certain Israelites viewed the building of a 'house' for Yahweh as an act of infidelity, as a concession to the influence of Baal's religion, the 'established' religion of Canaan, and we know for certain that the institution of the Temple brought with it the danger of syncretism, and that this danger was not always avoided, as we have seen.

This school of thought which disliked the Temple continued in existence, though it is rarely mentioned. The Rekabites, that group of Yahwistic reactionaries who lived in tents and never built a house for themselves (Jr 35), saw no need to have a house for their God, and when they fled to Jerusalem to seek refuge, they did not attend the Temple services until Jeremias persuaded them to after he had 'talked with them' (Jr 35: 2). When the Temple was rebuilt after the Exile, a prophet protested: 'Thus says Yahweh: Heaven is my throne, and the earth is my foot-stool! What kind of a house would you build for me, and where is the spot that would be the place of my rest?' (Is 66: 1). The question asked in 1 K 8: 27 here receives a different answer from the one in Deuteronomy: Yahweh has no need of any Temple.

Stephen the deacon, referring to Nathan's prophecy and citing explicitly Is 66: 1, will later affirm in front of the Jews that 'the Most High does not dwell in buildings made by human hands' (Ac 7: 48). Jesus himself is accused of having said: 'Destroy this temple, and within three days I shall build another not made by human hands' (Mk 14: 58), and in fact, according to Jn 2: 19, he did say: 'Destroy this sanctuary; within three days I shall raise it up again'. But the Evangelist explains that 'he was speaking of the sanctuary which was his body'. The old economy came to an end because it was superseded: the privileges of the material Temple, seat of the divine presence and sign of election, were transferred to the body of the Word made flesh, who from that time onward becomes the 'place' where we encounter the Presence and the Salvation of God.

CHAPTER FOUR

THE CENTRALIZATION OF THE CULT

IN the course of time, the Temple of Jerusalem became the only place where sacrificial worship could legally be performed; it was destroyed in 70 A.D., and since then Judaism has been deprived of both altar and sacrifice. But the Temple did not attain this unique position in a day; first came long years of hard struggle against rival sanctuaries, and against a trend which favoured decentralization.

1. Central sanctuary or sole sanctuary?

In the period of the Judges and in the early days of the monarchy, there were numerous sanctuaries in Palestine,[1] and even the 'high places' were recognized as lawful institutions[2]; but this does not mean that these various places of worship were all of equal importance. The federation of tribes was held together by a religious bond, and when all the tribes took part in a common cult at a central sanctuary, their presence was a witness to, and a confirmation of, this religious bond. In early days these meetings were almost certainly held at Shechem, for that was where the tribes had made their pact of confederation.[3] But the place of worship was changed when the Ark was moved, for the Ark was the symbol of God's presence among his people. The Deuteronomic redactor of Jos 8: 33 mentions the presence of the ark at Shechem, but in the time of the Judges it was certainly kept at Shiloh, in a building; indeed, by then it must have been at Shiloh for some time, because the tribes met there and went on pilgrimage there from very early times.[4] Since the place where the Ark was kept was the central sanctuary for the tribes, a serious religious problem had to be faced when the Philistines captured the Ark and dismantled the temple at Shiloh: where should Israel go to pray in common 'before Yahweh'? During these troubled years, Gibeon seems to have taken the place of Shiloh. According to 2 S 21: 6 (corrected in accordance with the Greek version), the sanctuary of Gibeon stood on the 'mountain of Yahweh', and it is significant that at the beginning of his reign Solomon first went to Gibeon to offer sacrifice there; there he was favoured with a divine message and in the same text

1. Cf. pp. 289-294 and 302-310.   2. Cf. p. 288.   3. Cf. pp. 289-291.
4. Cf. the texts cited on p. 304.

Gibeon is referred to as 'the greatest high place' (1 K 3: 4-15). And if, as has been suggested, the high place of Gibeon is identified with the sanctuary of Mispah in Benjamin,[1] then we may note that it was an important place under Samuel and Saul (1 S 7: 5f. and 10: 17), *i.e.* after the ruin of Shiloh. Lastly, 1 Ch 16: 39; 21: 29; 2 Ch 1: 3 all assert that the Tent of Reunion was kept at Gibeon; is this perhaps a distorted tradition of the years when Gibeon was for a short time the central sanctuary of Israel?

The central sanctuary of the tribes was not, however, the only sanctuary. There is evidence in the historical books that the cult of Yahweh was practised at one and the same time in various places. In Chapter II we discussed only the more important of these sanctuaries, or those about which we have the most information, but if all the evidence available in the Old Testament had been used, a far longer list, still not complete, could have been drawn up. After the conquest the Israelites installed their national God in several Canaanite sanctuaries; and though the number of these old sanctuaries may have contributed to the multiplication of sanctuaries in Israel, it does not provide the ultimate explanation. This is to be found in the progressive development of society. After the settlement, tribal bonds were weakened, the clan became more important, and small autonomous groups fixed themselves permanently on the land they cultivated; this process affected the cult also, which became a concern of the village or the city. Provincialism in politics led to provincialism in religion, and the latter proved a counter-balance to the movement which sought to gather the tribes around a common centre of cultic worship.

The Book of the Covenant, which was the law of the tribal federation, recognized that it was quite lawful to have several sanctuaries. This collection opens with a law about altars (Ex 20: 24-26) which allows that sacrifice may be offered, and the divine blessing thus obtained 'in every place, says Yahweh, where I shall remind men of my Name'. This does not authorize anarchy in public worship; the altars, and therefore the sanctuaries too, are not to be erected in places chosen arbitrarily, but only where God makes his presence known in some way; thus we return to the foundation-stories discussed above. Yet the fact remains that there could be as many sanctuaries as there were places where the divine presence was recognized.

2. Solomon's Temple and rival sanctuaries

(a) *The attraction of Jerusalem.* David's altar in Jerusalem is in harmony with this law; it was erected on the spot where the Angel of Yahweh appeared (2 S 24: 16-25). But David had also transferred to Jerusalem the Ark of the Covenant, the sacred cultic object which was venerated by all the tribes. He thus restored the tradition which had been broken while the Ark

1. Cf. p. 305.

was in the hands of the Philistines, and in his mind Jerusalem was to succeed Shiloh as the central sanctuary of Israel.[1] This objective, however, was not attained during David's lifetime; even after his death Gibeon remained the 'greatest high place', and Solomon visited it even before he offered sacrifices beside the Ark of Covenant (1 K 3: 4-15).

Jerusalem did not become an Israelite city until long after Israel had settled in Canaan. David's conquest and David's personality made it the political capital, and the presence of the Ark made it, in the eyes of the tribes, the lawful capital. Yet it remained the king's private domain, and only when Solomon built his Temple for the Ark did Jerusalem become the centre of the nation's public worship. Solomon summoned the elders of Israel for the dedication of the new sanctuary (1 K 8: 1) and visitors came from the furthest parts of his kingdom 'from the Pass of Hamath to the Brook of Egypt' (1 K 8: 65); from that time onwards crowds of pilgrims made their way to Jerusalem, drawn there by the splendour of the cult in that magnificent building which was the pride of the nation.

(b) *The religious schism of Jeroboam.* The attraction of Jerusalem as a religious centre meant that in practice there was some centralization of the cult, but it had another consequence also: it strengthened the political unity of the kingdom. Hence the political division which took place when the Northern tribes seceded after the death of Solomon was followed and perpetuated by a religious schism. The motive which led to this schism is given in the words ascribed to Jeroboam: 'If this people continues to go up to the Temple of Yahweh in Jerusalem to offer sacrifices, the people's heart will turn back to their lord Roboam, king of Judah' (1 K 12: 27). It was to arrest this trend that 'he made two golden calves and told the people: "You have gone up to Jerusalem for long enough! Here is thy God, Israel, who led thee up from the land of Egypt." He set up one of them at Bethel . . . and the people went in procession before the other as far as Dan' (1 K 12: 28-30).

Yet this was not a change of religion: the God Jeroboam asked his subjects to adore was Yahweh who had brought Israel out of Egypt. The novelty lies in the cultic symbol, the 'golden calves'. But the word '*egel*, which certainly can mean 'calf', can also mean a young bull, and this is its sense here. They were wooden statues covered with gold plate. It seems certain that these statues were not thought of, originally, as representations of Yahweh. In the primitive religions of Asia Minor, Mesopotamia and Egypt, the sacred animal is not the god and is not confused with the god; it merely embodies his attributes, is an ornament of his throne or a support for it, or a footstool for his use. There are several examples extant of gods riding on the animal which is their symbol. The Temple of Jerusalem had the Ark, and the Cherubim above it formed the throne of Yahweh;

1. Cf. pp. 308-309.

Jeroboam needed something similar for the sanctuaries he founded and he made the 'golden calves' as the throne for the invisible godhead. Perhaps, too, he was giving a new lease of life to an old tradition of the Northern tribes: there is clearly some connection between the step taken by Jeroboam and the story of the golden calf at Sinai (Ex 32). It has often been presumed that the story in Exodus was made up to support attacks on the cult of the Northern kingdom by ascribing to Moses and to God himself a condemnation of such worship; but it is possible that the story in Exodus preserves an ancient tradition which was later distorted by hostile elements in Judah. Perhaps certain groups which claimed descent from Aaron[1] had with them a bull which was a sign of the divine presence, to guide them in their wanderings (Ex 32: 1, 4; 1 K 12: 28), just as the groups which belonged to Moses had the Ark to go before them and to indicate the stages of their journey (Nb 10: 33-36).

That Jeroboam's measures did not imply any abandonment of Yahwism is proved by the fact that the oldest texts are not at all hostile to them; Elias and Jehu fought strenuously against paganism in Israel, yet neither of them ever spoke a word against the golden calves (cf. 2 K 10: 29). Amos, too, who preached in the temple of Bethel, does not say a word against the statue which was there in front of him, though he condemns the religious moral faults of Israel. And yet the choice of the bull, even if it were understood as a mere pedestal for the invisible presence of Yahweh, had its dangers. The bull was the animal which symbolized the great Canaanite god Baal, and the discoveries at Ras Shamra are most instructive on this point. Whatever may be true of the more educated classes, the mass of the people were bound to confuse the bull of Yahweh and the bull of Baal; they would also confuse Yahweh with the cultic statue which symbolized his presence; the door was thus opened to syncretism and idolatry. Hence the reaction of the loyal Yahwists: tradition tells how Ahiyyah, a prophet in Shiloh contemporary with Jeroboam, condemned these 'molten idols' (1 K 14: 9). Osee, living at the same time as Amos, says that the 'calf of Samaria' is not a god but a man-made idol (Os 8: 5-6; cf. 10: 5), that men blow kisses to calves as tokens of adoration (Os 13: 2), as others do to the statues of Baal (cf. 1 K 19: 18). The Deuteronomic redactor of the Book of Kings makes the same judgment; he says that the Israelites offered sacrifices to the bulls of Dan and Bethel as if they were gods (1 K 12: 32), and Jeroboam's great sin, shared by all his successors (cf. especially 2 K 10: 29) and by all the people (2 K 17: 22), consisted in setting up these statues.

(c) *Dan and Bethel*. Jeroboam merely wanted to set up two rival sanctuaries to Jerusalem, and his choice of Dan and Bethel was shrewd. The two towns stood at the northern and southern extremities of his kingdom. Dan, near one of the sources of the Jordan, would cater for the most northerly

1. Cf. p. 395.

tribes, who were always tempted to keep to themselves, and Bethel, close to the southern frontier, would draw off the pilgrims who were on the road to Jerusalem. Moreover, both Dan and Bethel had, in Israelite tradition, older titles to respect than Jerusalem. Dan was a sanctuary dating back to the period of the Judges, and was still served by the descendants of Moses[1]; as a place of cult, Bethel could trace its origins back to Abraham,[2] and Aaron's grandson had there kept watch over the Ark of the Covenant (Jg 20: 28).

Although we know that one of the golden calves was put in the sanctuary, we have no further details about the organization of the cult at Dan under Jeroboam, nor about the later history of the sanctuary. Amos condemns Dan along with Samaria and Beersheba, and the redactor of Jg 18: 30 says that a priesthood of Mosaic origin continued there 'up to the deportation of the country'; the inhabitants of Dan were exiled after the conquest of Galilee by Tiglath-Pileser III in 733–732 (cf. 2 K 15: 29), but by that time Dan, apparently, had long lost its importance as an official sanctuary of the kingdom.

We are somewhat better informed about Bethel. The site was hallowed by the memory of Abraham and Jacob,[3] before ever Jeroboam established a sanctuary, a *beth bamôth*, there. (*Beth bamôth* means literally a 'temple of the high places', the plural form being no more extraordinary than in the place-name Beth-Bamoth which is mentioned in the stele of Mesha.) It is tempting to look for the site of the temple some distance outside the town, at Borj Beitin, where a Byzantine church was built on the ruins of a pagan *temenos* of the second century A.D. There was, of course, an altar in the sanctuary (1 K 13: 1f.; 2 K 23: 15f.) and the oracle in Am 9: 1, first delivered at Bethel, suggests that this altar stood in front of a door or a portico with columns. Like Solomon's temple at Jerusalem, Jeroboam's sanctuary was built by the king; he staffed it with priests and he controlled the cult (1 K 12: 31–32)[4]; it was a state temple, a 'royal sanctuary', in which Amos preached (Am 7: 10f.). This building survived the destruction of the Northern kingdom, for, according to 2 K 17: 28, one of the deported priests was sent home by the king of Assyria to instruct the new immigrants in the worship of Yahweh, and he settled at Bethel. The altar of Bethel and the 'high place' built by Jeroboam were dismantled by Josias during his great reform (2 K 23: 15).

(d) *Other sanctuaries.* Neither Dan nor Bethel, the official sanctuaries of the kingdom of Israel, nor Jerusalem, the official sanctuary of the king of Judah, ever replaced the other centres of worship. Everyone continued to attend the 'high place' of his own town, and the ancient sanctuaries of the pre-monarchic period continued to attract pilgrims. This we know not only from the Deuteronomic redaction of the Book of Kings, where the introductory notes to each reign in Israel and Judah repeat the refrain that

---

1. Cf. p. 308.   2. Cf. pp. 291–292.   3. Cf. pp. 291–292.   4. Cf. p. 320.

'the high places did not disappear', but also from the Prophets who accuse the Israelites of still going to Beersheba (Am 5: 5; 8: 14) and to Gilgal (Os 4: 15; Am 4: 4; 5: 5). From Am 7: 9 to Ez 7: 24 the Prophets raise their voices against 'the sanctuaries' of Israel.

3. *Reforms aiming at centralization*

Nevertheless, even when confronted with these many places of worship, the Temple at Jerusalem always retained a place of pre-eminence. As the official state sanctuary in the capital, it was always the religious centre of the kingdom of Judah, and in spite of the rivalry of an official temple at Bethel, it continued to attract the faithful from the kingdom of Israel; even when it lay in ruins, pilgrims came from the North to make offerings on the site (Jr 41: 5).

Two kings of Judah tried to make Jerusalem's Temple not merely the central sanctuary of the nation but the one and only sanctuary in which public cult could be performed. The Books of Kings praises Ezechias for having suppressed the high places (2 K 18: 4), and in the speech which they place on the lips of Sennacherib's Lord Chamberlain, they say that Ezechias 'has done away with the high places and the altars, and told the people of Judah and Jerusalem: "You must worship before this altar, at Jerusalem"' (2 K 18: 22; Is. 36: 7). There is no reason to doubt this information: Ezechias had learnt a lesson from the destruction of the Northern Kingdom, and wanted to strengthen and to unite the nation by a return to traditional ways; the centralization of the cult at Jerusalem, under his own eyes, was one element in this policy. The Chronicler develops the history of this reform in three chapters (2 Ch 29-31), and gives more space to it than to the reform of Josias, though his narrative is inspired by the latter. According to him, Ezechias cleansed the Temple, celebrated a solemn Passover and reorganized the clergy; the historical information afforded by the Books of Kings, that he did away with the high places, is almost lost in the length of this description (2 Ch 31: 1). The work of Ezechias, however, died with him, and his immediate successor, Manasseh, re-established the high places (2 K 21: 3).

The second attempt to centralize the cult at Jerusalem came under Josias, and it too formed part of a great movement of religious reform (2 K 23); historically there is more evidence for this reform than for that attributed to Ezechias by the Chronicler. When the empire of Assurbanipal was in the process of disintegration, Josias shook off the yoke of Assyria and tried to make Judah independent once again. The nationalist movement brought with it the rejection of religious customs borrowed from Assyria, and indeed the rejection of all those foreign cults, of Baal and Astarte and the rest, which were contaminating the cult of the national God, Yahweh. To secure the centralization of Yahwistic cult, Josias recalled to Jerusalem all the Priests in Judah 'from Geba to Beersheba' and suppressed the local sanctuaries, *i.e.* the 'high places' (2 K 23: 5, 8-9: the text shows quite clearly that it refers to sanctuaries and to priests of Yahweh, for they are called to join their 'brothers' in Jerusalem).[1] The reform covered the territory of the former Northern kingdom, too: the sanctuary at Bethel was certainly dismantled, but the details given in 2 K 23: 15-20 are clearly inspired by the prophetical midrash which was inserted in the story of Jeroboam in 1 K 13. The conclusion of the reform was celebrated by a solemn Passover, attended by the entire nation, at Jerusalem; it was a natural consequence of the centralization of worship (2 K 23: 21-23). This was the Passover of the year 621. Unfortunately, the reform was quickly compromised: after the death of Josias at Megiddo in 609, the country once again fell under foreign domination, first Egyptian, then Babylonian. The old errors returned—syncretism in the Temple, foreign cults, and a new lease of life for the country sanctuaries (Jr 7: 1-20; 13: 27 and elsewhere). In the interval between the two sieges of Jerusalem, Ezechiel foretold the chastisement of the mountains of Israel and the destruction of their high places (Ez 6: 1-6, 13). The situation in Judah, it seems, scarcely changed during the Exile: shortly after the return, a prophet of the school of Isaias condemned his contemporaries along with those ancestors of theirs who had burnt perfume on the mountains (Is 65: 7). From 586 onwards, the Temple lay in ruins, and although pilgrims still paid visits to the site (cf. Jr 41: 4-5) and presumably offered sacrifices there, historical circumstances seemed to have put an end to the reforms of Josias. But his ideas triumphed in the end, for the community which returned from exile never had any sanctuary in Judah except the rebuilt Temple in Jerusalem. The reason was that the reform was based on a written law which survived longer than the men who opposed it: it was the Book of Deuteronomy.

4. *Deuteronomy*

According to the Books of Kings, Josias' reform was the result of the discovery in the Temple of a 'Book of the Law', the prescriptions of which were put into practice by the king (2 K 22: 1—23: 3; cf. 23: 21). According to Chronicles (2 Ch 34-35) the reform had begun in the twelfth year of Josias' reign, and the discovery of the Law in the eighteenth year marked only the second stage. This additional precision given by Chronicles deserves credence; the obvious time for Josias to begin his attack on foreign cults was when he threw off the Assyrian domination, and it is probable that he rose in revolt just before, or just after, the death of Assurbanipal in 627-626 B.C. But the suppression of the high places where Yahweh was

1. For further details on this episode see the history of the priesthood, p. 363.

worshipped and the centralization of the clergy and of the cult at Jerusalem were evidently inspired by Deuteronomy which is, basically, that 'Book of the Law' found in the Temple in 621.

For a long time critics favoured the idea that this 'discovery' was a pious fraud and that Deuteronomy was written to show the lawfulness of Josias' reform; to-day this opinion has long been abandoned. It is quite certain that the work belongs to an older age, and recent studies seem to have proved that it is a collection of Levitical traditions which originated in the Northern kingdom and which were brought to Judah after the fall of Samaria; this assertion, however, is not necessarily true of each and every one of its prescriptions, and the law insisting on one sanctuary needs to be examined on its own. It is given in chapter 12, where a change in style enables us to recognize two parts. The first part (12: 1-12) is in the plural and states a general law: the Israelites must suppress all the places of cult in Canaan and must perform their own strictly cultic acts only 'in the place chosen by Yahweh, your God, for his Name to dwell there'. The second part (12: 13-31) is in the singular, and gives a series of particular injunctions: 'Beware of offering holocausts in every sacred place thou shalt see; only in the chosen place of Yahweh in one of thy tribes shalt thou offer holocausts' (vv. 13-14); similar injunctions are then given for tithes and offerings.

The second section, which is in the singular, debars the Israelites from attending Canaanite sanctuaries, but the first part, in the plural, adds to this the obligation of destroying such places of worship; this first section seems to have been edited at a later date. Apart from this distinction, the law expressed in the two sections is basically the same: Israel has only one God, and it is to have only one sanctuary and one altar. This is a new idea, as can be seen by comparing v. 8 with the Book of the Covenant, which authorized the erection of an altar wherever the divine presence made itself known (Ex 20: 24), or with the ancient custom that regarded slaughtering an animal as always equivalent to sacrifice (and therefore needing an altar, cf. 1 S 14: 32-35). Since there was to be henceforth only one altar, the same law of Deuteronomy authorized the slaughtering of beasts for food without any religious rites, retaining only the prohibition against eating the blood (Dt 12: 15-16, 20-25).

The sole sanctuary was to stand 'in the place which Yahweh has chosen for his Name to dwell there', and, apart from Dt. 12, the formula recurs frequently throughout the rest of Deuteronomy. At the time of Josias' reform and in those later writings which stem from Deuteronomy, this 'place' was evidently Jerusalem. But the place is never explicitly named: the reason may be that since the book was presented as spoken by Moses. Jerusalem could not be mentioned by name. But there is another possibility: perhaps the formula referred originally to a central sanctuary in the Northern kingdom (where Deuteronomy originated), such as Shechem or Bethel, whose servants wanted to make it the only sanctuary in Israel. It is hard to decide, and both solutions are attractive. There are two alternatives: either the reform of Ezechias (2 K 18: 4) derived some stimulus from this law, already formulated in the North by Levites and brought by them to Jerusalem after 721; if so, then Dt 12: 1-12, which insists on the abolition of other places of worship, must have been added after this reform. Alternatively, the law prescribing that there should be only one sanctuary is, in general, a reflection of the reform of Ezechias, and was added, during his reign, to the traditions originating in the North and compiled by the King's command (like certain collection of proverbs, cf. Pr 25: 1); if this be so, then the 'place chosen by Yahweh' always referred to Jerusalem, and the section which is in the plural (Dt 12: 1-12) would point only to a later redaction, possibly connected with the reform of Josias. In support of the second solution, three arguments may be noted. First, the story of Ezechias' reform makes no reference to any previous law, whereas the account of Josias' reform does; secondly, if this hypothesis is accepted, there is no need to postulate, for Ezechias' reform, anything more than a royal policy of establishing a strong and united kingdom; thirdly, the formula 'the place chosen by Yahweh for his Name shall dwell here' seems to be connected with the theology of the Temple in Jerusalem.[1]

The Book of Deuteronomy was put together in some form or other under Ezechias, but was forgotten, lost or hidden during the syncretist reaction of Manasseh, and re-discovered under Josias; and this discovery either set in motion (Kings) or gave the support of tradition to (Chronicles) the great reform.

5. Later sanctuaries outside Jerusalem

The influence of Deuteronomy lasted longer than the reform it inspired, and its precepts dictated the religious attitude of the deportees in Babylon. The exiles never built a sanctuary in that foreign land, and their thoughts and their hopes were still turned towards Jerusalem (Ps 137). The episode recorded in Esd 8: 15-20 has sometimes been interpreted as indicating the existence of a place of cult in Babylonia, and the argument runs as follows: when Esdras assembled his caravan he found he had both priests and layfolk, but no Levites; he asked Iddo, who lived with his brothers at Kesiphya, for some Levites, and was given a whole contingent. From this some authors conclude that this region, peopled by Levites, was a place of cult. But the mere fact that Kesiphya is called a *maqôm* is not enough to prove that it was a 'holy place',[2] and the great number of Levites there may be explained by the fact that the exiles lived in family groups, and according to their place of origin; we are not told that priests came from Kesiphya.

1. Cf. p. 327.   2. Cf. p. 291.

Similarly, the post-exilic community of Palestine had no sanctuary except Jerusalem, but we do know that during this period there were two sanctuaries of Yahweh outside Palestine, one at Elephantine and the other at Leontopolis; in addition, there was, in Palestine itself, outside the district of Judaea, the temple of the dissident Samaritans.

(a) *The Temple at Elephantine*. At Elephantine, on the southern frontier of Egypt, there was a military colony in which Jewish mercenaries were stationed at some unknown date, probably in the sixth century B.C. Our information about them comes from certain papyri, dating over the whole of the fifth century, from which we know that they spoke Aramaic, not Hebrew, and that they practised a syncretist religion which the Prophets had condemned. The only point of interest to us at the moment is their sanctuary. They had a temple of Yaho (Yahweh), which was in existence before the invasion of Cambyses in 525 B.C. The precise spot in Elephantine where it stood is not known for certain, and we hardly know anything about its design. It was called in Aramaic *egora* a word borrowed from the Akkadian *ekurru*, meaning 'temple'. In 410 B.C. an Egyptian priest of the god Khnum, the ram-god who was patron of Elephantine, took advantage of the absence of the satrap on a visit to the court of Persia to persuade the local governor to destroy the temple of Yaho. The Jews asked Bagoas, the govenor of Judaea, and Yohanan, the high priest in Jerusalem (cf. Ne 12:22-23), to intervene in their favour, but received no answer to their request. Three years later, they again approached Bagoas and wrote also to the two sons of Sanballat, who was governor of Samaria while Nehemias was governor of Judaea. This time they received an answer, which took the form of a memorandum entrusted to a messenger: the messenger was to request the satrap of Egypt for permission to rebuild the temple and to present offerings and incense there. This document, however, makes no reference to holocausts, which the Jews had specifically mentioned in their request. The temple was in fact restored, and is mentioned in a document dated 402 B.C. Some years later, and shortly after the end of Persian rule over Egypt, the Jewish colonists at Elephantine were scattered, and the temple disappeared.

It is clear that these Jews were either unaware of, or paid no attention to, the law of Deuteronomy forbidding sanctuaries outside Jerusalem. Various explanations have been put forward. Some say that the community originated from the Northern kingdom, before the reform of Josias: this date seems, for other reasons, far too early, and it does not explain why they called themselves Jews, that is, 'Judaeans', or why they sent their first appeal to the governor of Judaea and to the high priest in Jerusalem. One recent suggestion is that they came from a Judaean enclave in the North of Syria—to be precise, near Ya'udi = Senjirli—where Solomon established an outpost of his empire; the existence of this outpost is known from cuneiform inscriptions. In spite of certain historical difficulties, this hypothesis could, at a pinch, explain the name 'Judaeans', but it does not explain why they should have appealed to the governor of Judaea. The only solution left is that the group came from Judaea itself; they must have left when the recently promulgated prescriptions of Deuteronomy had once more become a dead letter after the failure of Josias' reform. These Jews practised the popular religion as described and denounced by Jeremias and Ezechiel at the time of the fall of Jerusalem, and during the Exile. They were unaware of the changes which had taken place since the return from Babylon and so sent the high priest a request which they considered quite in order, but which the clergy of Jerusalem, applying the Law of Deuteronomy, could not countenance.

(b) *The temple at Leontopolis.* From texts in Josephus and from a passage in the Mishnah, we learn of another temple of Yahweh in Egypt, at a later date. Josephus' information is sometimes self-contradictory, but he states that after the murder of the high priest Onias III (cf. 2 M 4: 33–34), his son Onias sought refuge in Egypt and commanded a Jewish contingent in the service of Ptolemy VI Philometor and of Cleopatra. This Onias was commander of the Jewish military colony stationed at Leontopolis, probably Tell el-Yahudiyeh, and he obtained permission from the monarchs to build a temple for the Jews on the site of an abandoned Egyptian temple; there he could exercise the functions of high priest which were his by birth (Josephus, *Ant.* XIII iii 1–2[1]). The temple, built on the model of the Temple at Jerusalem, was smaller and less magnificent than its original, according to *Ant.*, XIII, iii, 3, and was different in its plan and its furnishings, according to *Bell.*, VII, x, 3. It was served by a lawful priesthood, and Onias, to justify his action, had invoked the prophecy of Is 19: 19 which foretold that there would be an altar in the centre of Egypt as a witness to Yahweh Sabaoth. Though this prophecy is post-exilic, it was not made up in Maccabean times to justify the step Onias had taken. This temple was founded about 160 B.C. and remained standing until 73 A.D., when it was pulled down by the Romans because Leontopolis, which was still called 'the region named after Onias', had become a centre of Jewish nationalism (*Bell.*, VII, x, 2–4).

This temple was regarded with disfavour by the Jews. Josephus accuses Onias of bad faith, and the Mishnah (*Menahoth*, XIII, 10) questions the validity of the sacrifices offered and of vows fulfilled in the temple of Onias. Nevertheless, it is strange that the rabbis did not condemn it more severely, by virtue of the law prohibiting sanctuaries other than the one at Jerusalem. Perhaps they were restrained by the undoubted legitimacy of its priesthood, or impressed by the text of Isaias and by the memory of the altar of the Transjordanian tribes which, according to Jos 22: 26-28, 34, had been authorized to remain as a 'witness' of Yahweh; perhaps they even considered that the law of Deuteronomy did not apply so strictly outside

1. Cf. p. 401.

Palestine, for it was only in the Holy Land that Dt 12: 14 spoke of 'the place chosen by Yahweh in one of the tribes' (note that this would excuse the Jews of Elephantine also). But the simplest solution of all is that the temple on Leontopolis owed its existence solely to the vanity of Onias and the political schemes of Ptolemy, and that it never had any real attraction, even for the Egyptian Diaspora; it was not considered of any great importance, and the rabbis merely took it as a rather curious phenomenon on which they could exercise their casuistic ingenuity.

(c) *The Temple at Garizim.* The Samaritans claimed that they possessed the 'place chosen by Yahweh' in Palestine itself; it was, they said, mount Garizim, where they built a temple. No one knows the precise date at which it was built. Samaritan tradition says that it was founded by Josue, destroyed by Nabuchodonosor and restored by Sanballat after the return from the Exile; its history, then, is modelled on that of the Temple in Jerusalem, but Sanballat lived long after the return, for he was a contemporary of Nehemias. Josephus, curiously enough, assigns the construction of the temple on Garizim to the period of a certain Sanballat, but this one is said to have lived a century later than Nehemias. He says (*Ant.*, XI, vii, 2 to viii, 4) that Sanballat's daughter married Manasses, whose brother was high priest in Jerusalem, and that Manasses fled to his father-in-law to get away from the criticisms of his brother and the elders in Jerusalem. Sanballat promised to build him a temple on Garizim if he could obtain the consent of the king, Darius. During these negotiations, however, Darius was defeated by Alexander the Great; Sanballat abandoned the cause of the Persians and rushed to make his submission to Alexander, who was then besieging Tyre. He returned thence armed with the authorization of the conqueror, and quickly built his temple and appointed Manasses as its priest. Thus we should be able to date its foundation exactly, in 332 B.C.

In spite of the efforts of certain historians to justify this claim, there is nothing in this story which is worthy of credence: in placing the foundation during the lifetime of Alexander, it contradicts what Ne 13: 28 tells us about one of the sons of Yoyada, the high priest, who became the son-in-law of Sanballat and was expelled by Nehemias. On the other hand, if we reject the story of Josephus, it is arbitrary to retain, as some authors do, the date presupposed by this story for the foundation of the temple on Garizim. It may have existed before Alexander, or only after his days, and there is no need to connect its foundation with the definitive break between the Samaritans and the Jews, the date of which is itself disputed. All one can say for certain is that the temple was in existence in 167-166 B.C. when Antiochus Epiphanes dedicated it to Zeus Xenios (according to 2 M 6: 2), or to Zeus Hellenios (according to Josephus, *Ant.*, XIII, v, 5). It was destroyed by John Hyrcanus after the death of Antiochus VII Sidetes in 129 B.C. (again according to Josephus, *Ant.*, XIII, ix, 1). There is no mention in any later text of its having been rebuilt, or even of its existence, but the conversation of Jesus with the Samaritan woman (Jn 4: 20-21) implies that the sanctuary remained in existence at least until the first century A.D.

6. The origin of synagogues

Synagogues were buildings erected not for sacrifice, but for prayer, reading of the Law and instruction: they first came into existence when Judaism was finally organized, and they were soon found throughout Palestine, in the Diaspora and even in Jerusalem itself, alongside the Temple. The origin of the synagogues (and it is only with their origin that we are here concerned) is shrouded in mystery. The predominant opinion to-day is that they originated in Babylonia during the Exile as a substitute for the Temple services, and that they were introduced into Palestine by Esdras. Others, however, think they first came into existence in Palestine itself after the time of Esdras and Nehemias, or even after the end of the Persian period. A few scholars consider them an institution of Palestinian origin, and pre-exilic; they would then be a result of the reform of Josias. Their idea is that when the country people were deprived of their local sanctuaries, and of their sacrifices, too (apart from those rare occasions on which they could go off to Jerusalem for the big feasts), they began to meet on certain days for public worship, but without offering sacrifice.

The reason for this variety of hypotheses is that there is nothing really explicit in ancient texts. Inscriptions and papyri show that there were 'places of prayer' (προσευχή) in Egypt from the middle of the third century B.C., and Josephus (Bell., VIII, iii, 3) says that there was a synagogue at Antioch under the successors of Antiochus Epiphanes; this is the earliest evidence we possess. None of the biblical texts (not even Ez 11: 16 or Esd 8: 15-20) which are usually cited prove the existence of common places of prayer in Babylonia during the Exile, and Ps 137 seems to prove the contrary. The mention of 'meeting houses' in the apocryphal Book of Henoch (46: 8) is usually brought forward to support the theory that there were synagogues in Palestine, but its testimony refers, at the earliest, to the time of Maccabees. There remains Ps 74: 7-8: 'They have burnt thy sanctuary . . . they have burnt every meeting-place of God throughout the land'. Many critics assign this psalm to the Maccabean period, but this seems too late, and the passage cited is much easier to explain if we take it to refer to the destruction of the Temple in 587; the other meeting-places could have been the predecessors of the synagogues. Nevertheless, it is not easy to connect these institutions with the reform of Josias, for we have seen that the local sanctuaries were closed only for a short period. Could not these 'meeting-places' be the same local sanctuaries which were once more functioning at the time of the fall of Jerusalem? The hortatory character of certain passages in the Book of Jeremias does not necessarily mean that these texts were written to be read in synagogues.

There is, then, no way of deciding for certain when synagogues came into existence. The institution probably came into being gradually, under the pressure of two factors, which played a great part in post-exilic Judaism. The first was the application of the law insisting on one sole sanctuary; once this was admitted, it seemed not merely lawful but necessary to have places of prayer (without sacrificial worship) outside Jerusalem. Secondly— and perhaps this was the more important factor—the Law became more prominent, and this meant that it had to be read and taught in the communities; and in the synagogues teaching was at least as important as prayer. These factors were at work in Palestine as well as in Diaspora, and it is mere chance that the first synagogue we know of happens to be in Egypt. 2 Ch 17: 7-9, in its account of the reign of Josaphat, tells how layfolk, Levites and priests were sent out with the book of the Law to teach the people throughout the towns of Judah. This information seems to be modelled on the reform of the judiciary by the same king (2 Ch 19: 4-7), and though it is certainly not true of the reign of Josaphat, it may reflect a practice in vogue at the time of the Chronicler; and there must have been buildings in which they could give this teaching. But wherever we turn, we are still in the realm of hypothesis, and it is not until the beginning of the Christian era that we are fully informed about synagogues; these synagogues, however, are no longer institutions of the Old Testament.

CHAPTER FIVE

THE PRIESTLY OFFICE

THERE was no official priesthood in the time of the Patriarchs; acts of public worship (especially sacrifice, the central act) were performed by the head of the family (Gn 22; 31: 54; 46: 1). The Patriarchs themselves, who were nomads, offered their sacrifices in the sanctuaries they visited, and the Book of Genesis never mentions priests except in reference to foreign nations, which were not nomadic (e.g. the Egyptian priests referred to in Gn 41: 45; 47: 22, and Melchisedech, the king-priest of Salem in Gn 14: 18). There are only two texts which imply the existence of a sanctuary served by regular attendants. Gn 25: 22 says that Rebecca went 'to consult Yahweh' about the twins, Esau and Jacob, whom she was soon to bear: the normal meaning of this expression is that she went to a holy place to ask for an oracle from a man of God. Secondly, in Gn 28: 22, Jacob promises to pay tithes to the sanctuary he had founded at Bethel—which implies that it was a sanctuary administered by a group of clergy (cf. Gn 14: 20); but this, too, is an act attributed to the founder of a sanctuary to justify a later custom (cf. Am 4: 4). The priesthood properly so called did not appear until the social organization of the community had developed considerably; then certain members of the community were entrusted with the special tasks of looking after the sanctuaries and of performing rites which were becoming ever more and more complicated.

1. *The Name*

The only name by which the Old Testament ever refers to priests of Yahweh is *kohen*; the same word is used for priests of foreign gods, whether Egyptian (Gn 41: 45; 47: 22), Phoenician (2 K 10: 19; 11: 18), Philistine (1 S 5: 5; 6: 2), Moabite (Jr 48: 7) or Ammonite (Jr 49: 3). The word has the same form in both Hebrew and Phoenician, and is frequently found in Nabatean also. There is another noun, however, derived from the root *kmr*, which was used from about 2000 B.C. in the Assyrian colonies of Cappadocia, then in ancient Aramaic, and later on in the dialect of Palmyra and in Syriac. The corresponding Hebrew word, always in the plural *k'marîm*, occurs only three times in the Bible and always refers to priests of false gods (2 K 23: 5; Os 10: 5; So 1: 4).

The etymology of *kohen* is not known. It has been suggested that it is related to the Akkadian verb *kanu*, from the root *k'n*, which, in the Shaphel, means 'to bend down, to do homage'. It is more common, though, to connect it with the root *kwn* meaning 'to stand upright'; the priest would then be a man who stands before God (cf. Dt 10: 8) like a servant. But all this is still uncertain.

2. *The installation of priests*

In Israel, the priesthood was not a vocation but an office. The texts speak of a man being called or chosen by God to be a king or a prophet, but they never use the term of a priest. True, in 2 Ch 24: 20, the Spirit of God descends on Zachary, a priest's son, but it is to make him a prophet, not to raise him to priesthood. Again, tradition told how Yahweh had chosen the tribe of Levi for the service of his sanctuary, but this did not involve any particular charisma for the individual members of the tribe. In fact, according to the older documents, priests were appointed by men without any divine intervention: Mikah chose first one of his sons (Jg 17: 5) and then a Levite (Jg 17: 10) for his private sanctuary; the men of Qiryath-Yearim chose Eleazar to keep watch over the Ark (1 S 7: 1), and the kings nominated and dismissed the servants in their official sanctuaries (1 K 2: 27; 12: 31). Later on, a man was sufficiently qualified for the priesthood if he was of priestly descent, unless he suffered from some physical disability which constituted an impediment (Lv 21: 16-24).

The oldest and most explicit text about a priest's assuming office is Jg 17: 5-12, which uses the term 'filling his hand' for 'appointing him'. The phrase is found again in Ex 32: 29; 1 K 13: 33 and then in a number of texts belonging to the Priestly tradition (Ex 28: 41; 29 *passim*; Lv 8: 33; Nb 3: 3); in the end the literal meaning of the word was forgotten and it came to mean, in Ez 43: 26, inaugurating an altar. As a result, the cognate noun *millu'îm*, literally 'a filling' (of the hand), means 'investing' a priest in Ex 29: 22-34; Lv 8: 22-33. The original meaning of the expression is debated. One explanation is found in Lv 8: 27-28 and Ex 29: 24-25; Moses puts into the hands of Aaron and his sons parts of the victims which are to be placed on the altar, makes the gesture of presentation along with them, and then takes the offerings from their hands and burns them on the altar: 'it was the sacrifice of *millu'îm*'. By so performing, for the first time, the ritual gesture of a minister of the altar, the man was invested with priestly power. Unfortunately, these are late texts which are trying to give an explanation of a phrase whose original meaning had been forgotten. Alternatives have been suggested: some authors hold that the phrase originally referred to the salary the priest received, and that he was given a first instalment at the beginning of his ministry; the hypothesis can claim support from Jg 17: 10; 18: 4, in which the Levite whom Mikah engages 'had his hand filled' and 'was engaged' for ten silver shekels per annum, plus food and clothing. Another suggestion is that the phrase is connected with the Akkadian expression 'to fill someone's hand', which means 'to put a man in charge of something', to give him a task to perform. Lastly, the archives of Mari have yielded texts from the time of Hammurabi concerning the distribution of booty, part of which, was assigned, as of right, to certain types of officers; it is called 'filling the hand'; perhaps this is the closest parallel, and then the Hebrew phrase would mean that the priest was given the right to a part of the revenues accruing to the sanctuary and to a share of the offerings made there. This would be 'the priest's right' mentioned in 1 S 2: 13, and later defined in greater detail by the Priestly laws. But whatever be the truth of the matter, the precise meaning of this ancient phrase had been lost by the time the Israelites began to use it; it does not describe a rite of ordination.

Similarly, in Nb 8: 10, the Israelites lay hands upon the Levites, but this is not a rite of investiture either: it is a gesture of offering[1] whereby the Levites are offered to Yahweh as substitutes for the first-born.[2] The s*mikah* or imposition of hands is not mentioned in the post-exilic ritual for the investiture of priests (Ex 29; Lv 8), and in post-biblical times it was never practised by the Jews except for the installation of Doctors. These later Jews based their practice on the text which states that Moses laid his hands on Josue (Nb 27: 15-23), and they presumed that he had done the same for the seventy elders of Israel (Nb 11: 16-17).

According to the post-exilic ritual, the high priest was anointed (Ex 29: 7; Lv 8: 12, etc.) and the last redaction of the Pentateuch added that in fact all priests were anointed (Ex 40: 12-15, etc.).[3] But it seems quite certain that this rite did not exist before the Exile and that it was in fact the transference of a royal prerogative to the high priest insomuch as he was head of the new community.[4]

Consequently, priests in ancient Israel were not 'ordained': they began their work without any religious rite conferring on them grace, or special powers. And yet a priest was made holy and sacred by virtue of his work. 1 S 7: 1 does not use the technical phrase 'to fill the hands' but says instead that Eleazar was 'sanctified' (*qiddesh*) for the services of the Ark. Priests were 'sanctified' (Lv 21: 6), and the high priest had to wear on his forehead a golden flower on which was engraved 'sanctified for Yahweh' (Ex 28: 36). This means that the priest no longer belonged to the profane world, but, like the territory around the sanctuary and the offerings presented there, he was 'set apart'; according to Nb 8: 14; Dt 10: 8, the Levites were 'set apart' for the service of God, and according to 1 Ch 23: 13, Aaron was

1. Cf. p. 416.
2. Cf. p. 360.
3. The texts were quoted and discussed on p. 105.
4. Cf. *ibid.* and also below, pp. 399-400.

'set apart' to consecrate the most holy things. The priest, therefore, had quitted the profane world, and entered into a sacred realm. He could therefore move around on sacred ground without sacrilege, enter into the sanctuary, handle sacred objects, eat gifts offered in sacrifice, and so forth. But he had to remain detached from profane things, and was subject to certain prohibitions and special rules concerning purity. In their daily life, priests were forbidden to take part in funerals; an exception was made for the funeral of a close blood-relative, but even then, they were bound to abstain from certain practices (Lv 21: 1-6). They were forbidden to marry a woman who had been a prostitute, or a woman who had been divorced by her husband (Lv 21: 7). When they were performing their duties, every care was taken to avoid any confusion between the sacred and the profane: they had to put on special vestments to enter the sanctuary (Ex 28: 43), to wash their clothes (Nb 8: 7), to purify themselves in special ways (Ex 30: 17-21; 40: 31-32; Lv 8: 6) and to abstain from wine and alcohol (Lv 10: 8-11).

This transference into the order of things sacred conferred a real dignity on the priest. When Mikah engaged the Levite he said 'Be a father and a priest to me' (Jg 17: 10), even though the Levite was only a young man (cf, vv. 7 and 10) the significance of this remark is that the priest had inherited those religious prerogatives which, in the patriarchal period, had belonged to the head of the family.

3. The priest and the sanctuary

Every priest was chosen and installed to serve in a sanctuary. The ruling was universally acknowledged particularly by the Arabs in the days before Islam. The priest was for them essentially a *sadin*, a 'guardian' of the temple; he looked after the sanctuary, received visitors and took charge of their gifts. Indeed, the bond tying him to the sanctuary was so strong that when a tribe emigrated, the *sadin* stayed behind and continued to exercise his office among strangers. His sons would then take his place, so that the various sanctuaries were always administered by priestly families. The same was true of Israel. In the stories about the wanderings in the desert, the Levites camped around the Tent (Nb 1: 53); each clan had its appointed place (Nb 3: 23, 29, 35), and Aaron's sons were posted in front of the Tent to prevent layfolk entering it (Nb 3: 38). The word used for this office is 'the guard' (Nb 1: 53; 3: 28, 32, etc.). In Israel, however, the Tent was a movable sanctuary; the priests moved with it and carried it (Nb 4: 5f.; Dt 10: 8). Ezechiel, when he was describing the partition of the Holy Land, drew his inspiration from this ideal of the desert and assigned to the priests the sacred ground around the Temple (Ez 45: 4).

Consequently, it is impossible to imagine a sanctuary without any priest to look after it. In the time of the Judges, Mikah built a private domestic sanctuary, but he appointed a priest at once; at first he installed his own son, but later replaced him when a Levite happened to pass by (Jg 17). This same Levite joined the men of Dan when they were migrating to the North, and took charge of the new sanctuary at Laish-Dan (Jg 18: 30). The temple where the Ark was kept at Shiloh was entrusted to the family of Eli (1 S 1-2). And when the Ark was laid at rest in Qiryath-Yearim, on its way home from Philistia, a priest was at once consecrated (*i.e.* set apart) to look after it (1 S 7: 1).

The destinies of the priesthood in Israel were therefore bound up with the fate of the sanctuaries. Under David, Sadoq and Ebyathar were in charge of the Ark (2 S 15: 24-29), but under Solomon, Ebyathar was dismissed (1 K 2: 26-27) and Sadoq alone was left in charge of the Temple; later, he was succeeded by his son (1 K 2: 35; 4: 1). When Jeroboam founded the sanctuary at Bethel, he at once installed priests there (1 K 12: 31). But just as the Temple in Jerusalem far outshone all the other places of public worship, so the priesthood of Jerusalem was far more important than the priests who looked after the smaller sanctuaries in the provinces; and, naturally enough, the attempts made to centralize cultic worship were accompanied by a regrouping of the clergy (2 K 23: 8). However, we have detailed information only about the priests of the Temple, and we shall have occasion to discuss them in later chapters.[1]

4. Priests and divine oracles

In ancient Israel men went to a sanctuary 'to consult Yahweh', and the priest gave oracles. It is noteworthy that in Dt 33: 8-10 the rôle played by the sons of Levi in giving oracles is mentioned even before the teaching of the Torah and their service of the altar. In the desert, the Israelites turned to Moses 'to consult God' (Ex 18: 15), and although, on Jethro's advice, Moses accepted help from others in the administration of justice, he kept for himself the task of taking the people's quarrels before God (Ex 18: 19). Anyone who wanted 'to consult Yahweh' went to the Tent; Moses then went inside, alone, and conversed face to face with Yahweh (Ex 33: 7-11). This last action, however, was a personal privilege of Moses (Nb 12: 6-8) which the priests did not share (cf. Nb 27: 21). They used to consult God by means of the ephod and of the Urim and Thummin. What exactly is meant by these procedures is a most intricate and obscure question.

(a) *The ephod.* The texts in which the Bible mentions the ephod ('*ephôd*) can be classified under three headings:

(1) Some texts refer to a linen ephod ('*ephôd bad*), which in the oldest historical texts is one of the priest's vestments. Samuel wore one as a boy in the temple of Shiloh (1 S 2: 18); the priests of Nob wore it (1 S 22: 18)

and so did David when he danced in front of the Ark (2 S 6: 14). It was worn around the waist (1 S 2: 18; 2 S 6: 14) but did not cover much of the body (cf. 2 S 6: 20); hence it must have been a kind of loin-cloth such as Egyptian priests wore, which may originally have been the only clothing worn by the priests in performing their offices.

(2) Other texts refer to an ephod which was a special part of the clothing of the high priest; it was part of his outer clothing, worn over the tunic and the cloak (Ex 29: 5; Lv 8: 7). It is described in Ex 28: 6-14; 39: 2-7, but the description is overburdened with later additions reflecting the changes in the high priest's robes during the post-exilic period. The earliest edition of the text, dating from the Exile, may well preserve information dating from the end of the monarchy. The ephod is there presented as a wide band of material woven out of golden and linen thread, and of variously coloured wools; this strip of material was lined with a belt, with which it was fastened around the body. (The mention of braces in conjunction with the ephod seems to be a later addition.)

The *ḥoshen* or 'breast-plate' was distinct from the ephod, but attached to it (Ex 28: 15-30; 39: 8-21). It was woven out of the same material as the ephod, and was shaped like a small (?) square bag in which were kept the Urim and Thummim; in Ex 28: 15, 30 it is called *ḥoshen hammishpaṭ*, 'the breast-plate of the (oracular) decision'.

(3) Yet other texts refer to an ephod which was an object of cultic worship. Mikah had one made for his sanctuary (Jg 17: 5; 18: 14, 17, 20); Gideon too made one with the gold he captured from the Midianites and kept it in his home-town (Jg 8: 27). It was a portable object (1 S 2: 28; 14: 3), and could even be held in the hand (1 S 23: 6); it could be 'brought out' or 'put away' (1 S 23: 9; 30: 7). In the sanctuary at Nob, Goliath's sword was kept behind the ephod (1 S 21: 10). Lastly, the ephod was left in the care of the priests and was used for consulting Yahweh (1 S 23: 10; 30: 8).

The original meaning of the word—a subject of long dispute in the past—is no longer in doubt: *'epd* is the word used for the robe of the goddess Anath in a poem of Ras Shamra, and *epattu* (plural: *epadatu*) means 'rich vestment' in the ancient Assyrian tablets from Cappadocia. Now priestly vestments easily come to perpetuate archaic customs, and the *'ephôd bad* would be a traditional garment still worn by the priests, of which the high priest's ephod was a later and more luxurious form; in the intervening years, however, what had once been the sole vestment of a priest had become a large piece of material worn on top of all the other priestly vestments.

At first sight, this meaning does not seem to suit the third series of texts mentioned above, in which the ephod is spoken of as a cultic object used for consulting Yahweh: the texts do not give us to understand that it was anything like an article of clothing, but rather that it was something solid which could be carried, brought out, put away or put down. As a result, many scholars have refused to see any connection between this ephod and that worn by the priests and the high priest. Some of them prefer to correct the text and to read instead of 'ephôd the word 'arôn (ark) or, in other passages, 'abbir (bull). Others, less radical in their views, presume that the word 'ephôd stands sometimes for a statue of a god; and there are some who understand it as a small-scale model of the desert Tent where oracles were delivered, or a little box in which the sacred lots were kept.

Yet the difficulty remains: why should one and the same word, in the same cultic context, at the same period, be used both for a priestly vestment and for a box? The use of these words in biblical and other Semitic texts makes it quite certain that the ephod worn by the priests and the high priest was a garment; it is only reasonable to try to find some similar meaning for the ephod used in delivering oracles. Various suggestions have been made. First, we know that statues of gods were sometimes clothed in a richly decorated garment; the ephod, it is suggested, was at first a vestment used to decorate the statute of a god; later it became the distinguishing mark of a priest who gave oracles in the name of a god, and finally it became the official dress of the high priest.

In contrast to this, a very recent opinion maintains that the primary meaning of the ephod as one of the high priest's vestments lies behind its use in connection with the oracles. This apron or loincloth, it is said, was very stiff by reason of the thread of gold in it, and kept its shape when put down; hence the sword of Goliath could be hidden behind it, it could be carried by hand and brought out when needed: and the ḥoshen, the pocket containing the Urim and Thummim, was attached to it, so that the ephod itself was brought out when oracles were needed. A third opinion suggests that the ephod for oracles was different from the ordinary ephod worn by the priests and from that worn by the high priest, too, but was still a vestment or outer covering for a statue of a god (cf. the cognate word 'apuddah in Is 30: 22); it is suggested that, though Israel did not have any statues of its god, it kept an ephod for some time as an instrument for giving oracles. This would explain why the priests carried it or brought it out, but never put it on, and why Gideon's ephod weighed 1,700 shekels and was condemned by the redactor of Jg 8: 26-27; it would also explain why Os 3: 4 groups the ephod with the teraphim, domestic idols from which men sought oracles (Ez 21: 26; Za 10: 2).

None of these hypotheses is absolutely convincing. The last interpretation seems the least improbable, but it could go further. Since the Israelites refused to have statues of their God, they could not use the ephod except for oracles; in some way or other, the ephod was a receptacle for sacred lots. There is an old proverb which may not refer directly to the ephod but which does at least indicate how a vestment could be used for drawing lots:

'From the pocket (*i.e.* the fold of the vestment: *ḥeq*) men draw lots, but the decision (*mishpaṭ*) always comes from Yahweh' (Pr 16: 33). This reminds us of the *ḥosen hammishpaṭ*, the pocket of the oracle's reply; this pocket contained Urim and Thummim, and it was attached to the ephod of the high priest (Ex 28: 30).

(b) *Urim and Thummim.* These were the sacred lots. The etymology and the meaning of the words is unknown, and modern attempts to explain them are not much better than the arbitrary translations of the ancient versions. The names must have been borrowed, like the things, from the pre-Israelite civilization of Canaan, and the plural form is just a singular which has retained its primitive mimation.

Nor have we any idea what they looked like. Small pebbles or dice have been suggested, and, more often, little sticks (cf. Os 4: 12?); they were picked out of the pocket of the ephod. Some authors see a parallel in the ancient Arab custom called *istiqsam, i.e.* divining by means of small sticks or arrows, similar to that practised by the king of Babylon in Ez 21: 26-27; but according to the term used by Ezechiel, this was a practice of diviners (the *q'samîm*), and may well have nothing to do with the Urim and Thummim used by the priests.

According to Nb 27: 21, these lots were entrusted to the priest Eleazar: Dt 33: 8 says they were entrusted to the tribe of Levi. The way in which the oracle worked is shown in 1 S 14: 41-42 (corrected in accordance with the Greek). 'Saul then said: "If I or my son Jonathan should be to blame, Yahweh, God of Israel, give *urim*; if thy people Israel is to blame, give *tummim*." Saul and Jonathan were picked out and the people escaped. Saul said: "Cast lots between me and my son Jonathan", and Jonathan was picked out'. Verse 36 presumes that the priest had a rôle to play. Now this text does not prove that Thummim was the favourable object, and Urim the unfavourable one; on the contrary, it implies that, like our 'heads or tails', the two objects had a purely conventional meaning, which was fixed each time by the parties; this is itself a warning against trying to find a meaning for the words. The answer of the oracle lies in producing one rather than the other. Its answer, then, was always 'Yes' or 'No', and it proceeded by elimination or by becoming more precise (cf. also 1 S 23: 9-12). Hence the procedure could go on for a long time; in 1 S 14: 18-19 (corrected in accordance with the Greek) Saul wants to know whether he should attack the Philistine camp, but as the questioning of the oracle takes longer and longer, Saul, seeing the excitement in the enemy camp increasing, tells the priest to 'withdraw his hand'. Thus he interrupts the consultation of Yahweh and goes into action. Sometimes, too, the oracle refused to give an answer (1 S 14: 37; 28: 6), presumably because nothing came out of the pocket, or because both came out together.

(c) *The decreasing importance of oracles given by priests.* After the reign of

David, there is no evidence that the ephod, with the Urim and Thummim, was ever used for oracles. If Pr 16: 33, cited above, does in fact refer to the ephod, this would give us a slightly later date, and Os 3: 4 seems to say that the ephod was used in the Northern kingdom down to the fall of Samaria; but Osee groups the ephod with teraphim and *maṣṣebôth*, which are forbidden by the law of Yahwism. Whatever be the truth on this matter, Achab and Joram of Israel and the kings of Judah contemporary with them (1 K 20: 13-14; 22: 6; 2 K 3: 11) consult Yahweh through prophets, in circumstances where Saul and David used to consult him by the ephod. Under Josias, the head of the priesthood in Jerusalem goes in person to ask guidance from the prophetess Huldah (2 K 22: 14; cf. also Jr 21: 1-2, under Sedecias). If the description of the ephod and of the 'breast-plate' of the high priest in Ex 28: 6-30 comes (basically) from the last years of the monarchy, it was no longer an instrument for giving oracles; it is significant that the Urim and Thummim are mentioned there, but not described in minute detail, as all the other ornaments of the high priest are; they are probably mentioned to give an archaic touch, and the writer himself probably did not know exactly what they were. There is a perceptible development in the last edition of the text: stones engraved with the names of the tribes of Israel were fixed on the ephod and on the breast-plate, and their purpose is merely to remind Yahweh of his people (Ex 28: 12 and 29).

Esd 2: 63 = Ne 7: 65 says that after the Exile there was no priest to handle the Urim and Thummim; this is confirmed by the Jewish tradition which often repeats that there was neither Urim nor Thummim in the second Temple. One text of the Talmud (*Sota* 48a) even asserts that there had been no Urim and Thummim since the death of the 'first prophets', *i.e.* Samuel, David and Solomon. It is possible, however, that down to the ruin of the Temple, the priests continued to give answers in God's name (though without using means of divination) to those pilgrims who came to offer sacrifice and to pray for favours there: certain psalms and a number of passages in second Isaias can be explained in this way. But this procedure was utterly different from using the ephod with its Urim and Thummim.

5. *The priest as a teacher*

In the Blessing of Levi (Dt 33: 10), a twofold duty is assigned to the Levites; they are to take charge of the Urim and Thummim, and to instruct the people: 'They shall teach thy decisions (*mishpaṭîm*) to Jacob, and thy instructions (*tôrôth*: read the plural) to Israel'. The *tôrah* belongs to the priest, as the virtue of judgment belongs to the king, or wisdom to the wise man, or vision and message to the prophet. Three texts state this clearly: 'Its princes give judgment in return for presents, its priests teach for reward, its prophets speak out in return for money' (Mi 3: 11) 'The priest shall not be found lacking in the *tôrah*, nor the wise man in counsel, nor the prophet in words' (Jr 18: 18). 'They shall ask the prophet for a vision, and the priest will be found wanting in the *tôrah*, and the elders in counsel' (Ez 7: 26).

It has been suggested that *tôrah* comes from the verb *yarah*, meaning 'to throw', and occasionally 'to cast lots' (Jos 18: 6); consequently, this rôle of the priest has been linked with his rôle as a man who gives oracles, and a comparison has been drawn with the Assyrian *tertu*, which means 'an oracle'. But the way in which the word is used and the verbs which are used with it indicate that its root is rather *yrh*, which is frequently employed in the factitive form with the meaning 'to show', to 'teach'. The *tôrah* is, therefore, in the strict sense 'instruction' and the usual translation of this word as 'law' is not quite accurate.

This 'law' came from God, but he entrusted it to the priests (Dt 31: 9, 26). According to Dt 33: 10, the priests are to teach the *tôrôth* of Yahweh to Israel (cf. Os 4: 6) and the priest as a teacher is a 'messenger of Yahweh Sabaoth' (Ml 2: 7). Naturally enough, this instruction was delivered in the sanctuary to which the priest belonged and where men came on pilgrimage, or to offer sacrifice, or simply to consult the man in charge of the sanctuary; as a result, the teaching of the *tôrah* was, in pre-exilic days, confined to the Temple, and texts like Is 2: 3 = Mi 4: 2; Dt 31: 10-11 reflect a most ancient custom.

The *tôrah* was originally a short instruction on a particular topic, a rule of practical conduct, more especially about how to perform cultic worship, in which the priest was a specialist; he had to decide what was sacred and what was profane, what was clean or unclean, and to instruct the faithful on the point (Lv 10: 10-11; Ez 22: 26; 44: 23). After the return from the Exile, the prophet Aggaeus asked the priests for a *tôrah* about the effects of touching clean and unclean things (Ag 2: 11-13), and on other occasions the priests were asked whether it would be opportune to hold a fast (Za 7: 3).

But it would be a grave error to restrict the teaching rôle of priests to casuistry of this kind. Whatever may have been true in very early days, texts like Os 4: 6 and Jr 2: 8 shows that the priests' competence extended far beyond strictly cultic precepts. The priestly *tôrah* became the Torah, the Law, a collection of precepts governing the relations of man with God, and the priests were recognized as its interpreters; at the same time, men became ever more anxious to have the right interior dispositions which would make their worship agreeable to God; and as these two changes made themselves more widely and more deeply felt, the priests became teachers of morality and of religion. The prophets played the same part, but in a different way. A prophet was a man of the *dabar*, of the word, a spokesman of God, therefore, who was directly inspired by God to give a particular message in definite circumstances; he was an instrument through whom God actually revealed himself. The priest, on the other hand, was the man of the *tôrah*; knowledge (*da'ath*) was entrusted to him for interpretation, and though this knowledge certainly came from God long ago, it was handed down to men century after century by teaching and practice.

From the time of the Exile onwards, the priests ceased to have the monopoly of teaching the Torah. The Levites, who by then had been taken away from strictly priestly functions, became preachers and catechists. In the end, teaching was given quite apart from worship, in the synagogues, and a new class arose, of scribes and teachers of the Law. This class was open to all, priests and Levites and layfolk alike, and eventually it displaced the priestly caste in the work of teaching.

6. *The priest and sacrifice*

In the Blessing of Levi, those functions which are strictly connected with worship are mentioned last of all: 'They shall put incense in thy nostrils, and the sacrifice upon thy altar' (Dt 33: 10). The low position assigned to sacrifice in this hierarchy of functions may astonish anyone who thinks of later theology in which the offering of sacrifice is seen as the principal function of a priest. Philo (*De Vita Moysi*, II (III), 29) says that at the Passover all are priests because everyone offers the lamb, and the Epistle to the Hebrews says that 'every high priest is appointed to offer gifts and sacrifices' (He 5: 1; 8: 3). But these texts come at the end of a long development, of which Dt 33: 10 is merely one stage. We may pass over in silence the period of the Patriarchs, when there was no official priesthood. In the time of the Judges, God ordered Gideon to construct an altar and to offer a holocaust (Jg 6: 25-26), and the Angel of Yahweh invited Manoah, Samson's father, to offer a holocaust, which was accepted (Jg 13: 16-23). In the old account of Samuel's childhood, his father Elqanah himself ordered a sacrifice at Shiloh (1 S 1: 3, 4, 21; 2, 19), and the priest Eli seems to be the guardian of the sanctuary (1 S 1: 9); the 'priest's right', against which his sons offended, refers only to the right the priests had to a part of the victims (1 S 2: 12-17), and that part of the story which states that only priests might go up to the altar and set fire to the holocaust is an addition to the primitive text (1 S 2: 27-36).

Saul, David and Solomon all offered sacrifice, and we have explained elsewhere[1] that this does not mean that the kings of Israel were priests; but neither does it mean that priests did not offer sacrifice at that time. Achaz himself offered the first sacrifice on the new altar he had built, but the priest Uriyyah was entrusted with the care of it afterwards (2 K 16: 12-16). Shortly before this time, presumably between 800 and 750 B.C., the Blessings of Moses (Dt 33) were given their final form in the Northern kingdom; in this chapter, verses 8-11 are about Levi, and they recognize that the offering

1. Cf. pp. 113-114.

of sacrifice is a privilege of the priests. Before the Exile, in Jerusalem, the men who compiled the Law of Holiness based the special rules of cleanliness for priests on the holiness of their functions: they must be clean because they place on the altar the holocausts and the parts of other sacrifices (Lv 21: 6).

For (and this is important) the priest in the Old Testament is not strictly a 'sacrificer' in the sense of an 'immolator'. He may at times have taken care of the slaughtering of a victim, but this was always an accessory function and was never his exclusive privilege. According to Ex 24: 3-8 (generally regarded as Elohistic tradition) Moses ordered some young men (and there is no indication that they were priests) to immolate holocausts and communion-sacrifices, but it was Moses himself who took the blood and sprinkled it on the altar and on the people. The law on sacrifice expressly stipulated that the victim was to be killed by the man making the offering (Lv 1: 5; 3: 2, 8, 13; 4: 24, 29, 33). If the man making the offering was not ritually clean himself, or if it were one of the great public sacrifices (2 Ch 30: 17; Ez 44: 11), then the animal was killed by someone from the lower ranks of the clergy. The priest's rôle began when they had to use the blood, partly because this was the holiest part of the victim (Lv 17: 11, 14), but mainly because the blood had to be brought into immediate contact with the altar; similarly, it was always a priest who presented and who placed upon the altar that part of the sacrifice which belonged to God. Indeed, this ruling was so absolute that when the victim was a bird and had to be killed on the altar itself, the person bringing it lost his right to put it to death (Lv 1: 14-15; 5: 8). Similarly, when the writer wants to say, in 2 K 23: 9, that the priests of the high places were deposed after the reform of Josias, he simply says that they could not 'go up to the altar'. A text written about the same time says that priests were chosen to 'go up to the altar' (1 S 2: 28). Again, incensing was a privilege of the sons of Levi because the incense had to be burnt upon the altar (according to Dt 33: 10); according to Nb 17: 5; 1 Ch 23: 13 it was a privilege reserved to the descendants of Aaron, and 2 Ch 26: 16-18 says that king Ozias was punished for usurping this right. The priest was, then, in a very real sense, the 'minister of the altar' and this Christian expression can trace its ancestry far back into the Old Testament.

If we understand it in this very precise way, then the rôle of the priest in sacrifice is certainly very ancient, but as time went on, this part of their work came more to the fore, for people ceased to ask them for oracles, and others came to share with them the rôle of teaching. Conversely, the offering of sacrifice was reserved to them more and more as time went on; it became an essential function of the priesthood, and as a result the ruin of the Temple marked the end of their influence. The religion of the Torah replaced the ritual of the Temple, and the priests were replaced by rabbis.

7. *The priest as mediator*

All these various functions have a common basis. When the priest delivered an oracle, he was passing on an answer from God; when he gave an instruction, a *tôrah*, and later when he explained the Law, the Torah, he was passing on and interpreting teaching that came from God; when he took the blood and flesh of victims to the altar, or burned incense upon the altar, he was presenting to God the prayers and petitions of the faithful. In the first two rôles he represented God before men, and in the third he represented men before God; but he is always an intermediary. What the Epistle to the Hebrews says of the high priest is true of every priest: 'Every high priest who is taken from among men is appointed to intervene on behalf of men with God' (He 5: 1). The priest was a mediator, like the king and the prophet. But kings and prophets were mediators by reason of a personal charisma, because they were individually chosen by God; the priest was *ipso facto* a mediator, for the priesthood is an institution for mediation. This essential feature will reappear in the priesthood of the New Law, as a sharing in the priesthood of Christ the Mediator, Man and God, perfect victim and unique Priest.

CHAPTER SIX

THE LEVITES

THERE are many texts in the Bible which refer to the clergy as 'Levites' or 'sons of Levi', and which state or imply that only those men who were descended from Levi could undertake sacred functions. These texts raise a number of difficult problems which must be examined, though we shall not be able to give a satisfactory solution to all of them.

1. Etymology

The etymology of the word *lewy* is not known for certain. In Hebrew, the root *lwh* has three meanings, each of which has been attributed to the noun, *lewy*:

(1) *lwh* can mean 'to turn around, to whirl around', and one suggestion is that the Levites were men who performed ecstatic dances, rather like the whirling dervishes and prophets;

(2) another meaning of *lwh* is 'to accompany someone, to be attached to someone', and this is the etymology put forward in the Bible itself. Leah called her new-born child Levi because, she said, 'This time my husband will cling to me' (Gn 29: 34); similarly, the members of the tribe of Levi were 'attached' to Aaron (Nb 18: 2 and 4). The corresponding root in Arabic is *wly* (with inversion), from which is derived the noun *wely*, meaning, 'one who is attached to God, a holy person';

(3) *lwh* can also mean 'to lend, to give as pledge or surety'. Although the Bible never uses the verb *lwh* in this sense when it is referring to the Levites, it does contain some very similar expressions: the Levites were 'given' to Yahweh instead of the first-born (Nb 3: 12; 8: 16), and Samuel was 'given over' to Yahweh as a boy (1 S 1: 28). Again, several Minaean inscriptions in Arabia use the word *lw'* 'of things and persons consecrated or vowed to a divinity'.

The first derivation can be rejected as quite arbitrary. The second can claim the support of biblical texts, but we know that the etymologies advanced in the Bible do not always give the true meaning of a word. The third raises the whole problem of how the Levites originated, which we shall examine at the end of the chapter. All three hypotheses try to explain *lewy* as if it denoted a function, but according to the Bible the word originated as the proper name of one of Jacob's sons. This proper name could be a shortened form of Levi-El, which has been discovered in texts from Mari (*La-wi-ili*), and was previously known in an Egyptian form (*Rw'r*). The name seems to mean 'attached to God, a client of God' or something similar.

2. *The hereditary priesthood*

In the ancient East, professions were generally hereditary, and crafts were handed down from father to son.[1] This was particularly true of Egypt, where, at one time, no one was allowed to practise any trade other than that practised by his father. Long genealogies show how highly this system of succession was esteemed, and under Darius I, one architect even pretended that he could trace his ancestry back through twenty-four generations to Imhotep, the builder of the pyramid at Zaqqara.

Such a system was particularly suitable for the priesthood; it ensured that sanctuaries were well looked after and kept in good repair, and that religious rites were left unchanged: the father would initiate his son into the skills required of him. We know that the priesthood was hereditary in Egypt at least from the XIXth Dynasty onwards, and anyone who could prove his priestly ancestry was assured of entry into the priestly caste. In Assyria, at least among certain categories of priests, the succession passed from father to son. There is evidence of priestly houses in Phoenician and Punic inscriptions, too; at Palmyra, the priesthood seems to have been restricted to certain families; among the pre-Islamic Arabs, every sanctuary belonged to a particular family which owned it from generation to generation; and finally, we may recall, as an example from another civilization, the great priestly families attached to the sanctuaries of Greece.

It is not surprising, then, that the priesthood was hereditary in Israel, too. A few examples from the texts which everyone recognizes as ancient will suffice to illustrate this remark. The Levite whose services Mikah had engaged became custodian of the sanctuary at Dan, and his descendants continued to serve there (Jg 18: 30). Eli was the priest at Shiloh, and two of his sons were also priests there (1 S 1-2). When the Ark was at Qiryath-Yearim, the priesthood remained in the line descended from Abinadab (1 S 7: 1; 2 S 6: 3). At Nob, Ahimelek had around him 'all the house of his father, the priests of Nob' (1 S 22: 11), eighty-five of whom were put to death by Saul (1 S 22: 18); another, Ebyathar, escaped and lived to become David's priest (1 S 22: 20-23).

On the other hand, these same ancient texts depict the Levites as strangers to the places where they exercise their functions. The Levite mentioned in Jg 17-18 was first a resident alien, a *ger*, in Bethlehem of Judah; later he tendered his services to Mikah in the hill-country of Ephraim, and in the

1. Cf. pp. 49 and 77.

end he migrated, with the men of Dan, to the North. The Levite in Jg 19 was a resident alien in the hill-country of Ephraim, but he had a woman from Bethlehem in Judah as his concubine; and when he wished to avenge the crime of Gibeah, he appealed not to his kinsfolk, as the law of blood-vengeance required, but to all the tribes of Israel. From the texts listed in this and the preceding paragraph, three conclusions may be drawn: first, that the priesthood was hereditary in certain families; secondly, that these families could stay in one sanctuary for generations; thirdly, that they were not bound to stay in the same place, for they were not tied to a particular region. All this suggests that these families formed a group which was bound together not because it lived in one region, but because all its members performed the same functions; they formed a priestly tribe.

3. *The priestly tribe of Levi*

This, in fact, is how the Israelite priesthood is presented in the Bible as we have it to-day. The descendants of Levi, Jacob's son, were set apart to perform sacred functions by a positive intervention of God (Nb 1: 50; 3: 6f.). They were taken by God, or given to God, instead of the first-born of Israel (Nb 3: 12; 8: 16). According to Nb 3: 6, they were to assist Aaron, but according to Ex 32: 25-29, they were chosen in opposition to Aaron since he had encouraged idolatry among the people; lastly, according to our present text of Dt 10: 6-9, it was only after the death of Aaron that they were chosen by Moses.

They held, in consequence, a special place among the people: they were not counted in the census of the other tribes (Nb 1: 47-49; all chapter 4; 26: 62). They had no share in Israel (Nb 18: 20; Dt 18: 1), and were not allotted any territory in the division of Canaan, for 'Yahweh is their inheritance' (Jos 13: 14, 33; 14: 3-4; 18: 7). Instead, they were provided with revenues or tithes (Nb 18: 21-24), and with real estate in the territories of the other tribes, *i.e.* the Levitical towns (Nb 35: 1-8; Jos 21: 1-42; 1 Ch 6: 39-66). Hence the members of the priestly tribe are commonly referred to as sons of Levi or Levites.

One branch within this tribe received the promise of a perpetual priesthood, as a result of which the other Levites were relegated to a subordinate position and restricted to the less important functions of the cult: this branch was the family of Aaron, Moses' brother (Ex 29: 9, 44; 40: 15). The priesthood was handed on to the sons of Aaron, Eleazar and Ithamar (Nb 3: 4), and the promise was later renewed in favour of Phinehas, the son of Eleazar (Nb 25: 11-13). According to 1 Ch 24: 3, the priesthood of Shiloh, of Nob and of Jerusalem itself, until the dismissal of Ebyathar, was descended from Ithamar. Sadoq, who replaced Ebyathar (1 K 2: 35) traced his ancestry back to Aaron through Eleazar, and his family retained the priesthood until the ruin of the Temple (1 Ch 5: 30-41; 6: 35-38; Esd 7: 1-5).

The Bible contains several examples of Levitical genealogies (Gn 46: 11; Ex 6: 16-25; Nb 26: 57-60 and especially 1 Ch 5: 27 to 6: 38, which goes down to the Exile). One incident which took place after the return from the Exile underlines the importance of these genealogies: those who could not bring evidence of their ancestry were excluded from the priesthood (Esd 2: 62; Ne 7: 64).

4. Historical development

Nevertheless, if we compare these various texts with one another, the differences between them become evident. We have already mentioned that it is not certain when, or why, the Levites were chosen for the service of the sanctuary. Even the genealogy in Ex 6: 16-25 is composed of different elements, and that in Nb 26: 57-58 gives two different divisions of the clans of Levi. The genealogies in 1 Ch 5-6 combine and harmonize information of various kinds. In addition, some of the texts were not 'edited until a fairly late period, and the data they contain are by no means in perfect harmony with what the older texts say. The editors of these later texts knew that the tribe of Levi alone had the right to perform liturgical functions, and saw the pre-eminence of the priesthood of Jerusalem; they must have regarded these two privileges as dating back to the earliest period of the people's history, though in fact they emerged only after a long development.

(a) *Non-Levitical priests.* In the period of the Judges and at the beginning of the monarchy, not all priests were 'Levites'. Mikah, a man of Ephraim, appointed his own son a priest (Jg 17: 5). Samuel, too, was an Ephraimite (1 S 1: 1), but he was attached to the sanctuary at Shiloh, wore the priest's loincloth (1 S 2: 18), and offered sacrifices (1 S 7: 9; 9: 13; 10: 8); it was only centuries later that he and his ancestors were given a place in a Levitical genealogy (1 Ch 6: 18-23). Abinadab was a man of Qiryath-Yearim, but his son Eleazar was appointed to be the priest in charge of the Ark (1 S 7: 1). In the lists of David's chief ministers, the sons of David are mentioned as priests, and they must have belonged to the tribe of Judah (2 S 8: 18). Ira the Yairite, who belonged to a clan of Manasseh (2 S 20: 26) is also called a priest, and in spite of 1 Ch 18: 17, there is no reason to think that the word *kohen* has any other meaning in this context.

The action of Jeroboam I must be given separate consideration: according to 1 K 12: 31; 13: 33 (cf. 2 K 17: 32); 2 Ch 13: 9, he appointed to the royal sanctuary at Bethel priests who were not of Levi's line. It is, of course, possible that Jeroboam appointed non-Levitical priests, like those just mentioned; later we shall consider the same possibility with reference to the priests who served the Temple in Jerusalem.[1] But the texts which record this action of Jeroboam were edited by men in the school of Deuteronomy, whose home lay in Judah, and who were anxious to condemn a hated rival to the Temple; is it not possible that they were trying to blacken Jeroboam, Bethel and its priests? After all, there were Levites in other sanctuaries of the Northern kingdom (cf. Dt 18: 6 and 2 K 23: 9), even in the other royal sanctuary set up by Jeroboam at Dan (Jg 18: 30).

This latter sanctuary traced its origin back to the migration of the men of Dan, and the story of their migration throws light on the history of the priesthood (Jg 17-18). Mikah had installed his son as priest when a Levite passed by. He engaged the Levite immediately and exclaimed: 'Now I know that Yahweh will grant me prosperity, because I have this Levite as priest' (Jg 17: 13). The Levite was Yehonathan, son of Gershom, Moses' son (Jg 18: 30). There is no reason to doubt the truth of this detail in such an ancient story, though it scandalized the Massoretes so much that they added a letter to make the text read 'Manasses' instead of 'Moses'. Nor is there any reason to deny the Levitical ancestry of Moses himself, which is asserted by Ex 2: 1 (Elohistic tradition) and traced in detail both by the Priestly tradition (Ex 6: 20; Nb 26: 59) and by the Chronicler (1 Ch 5: 29; 23: 13).

Therefore we can say that even from the period of the Judges, the Israelites preferred to have a Levite as priest, and the only Levite of the period whose genealogy we can trace is a descendant of Moses, and, through Moses, of Levi. In the first half of the eighth century, at the very latest, the priestly tribe of Levi was quite certainly in existence, and alone exercised the priesthood (Dt 33: 8-11). Like the other tribes of Israel,[2] this tribe must have incorporated into itself other stock, but these newcomers were received into an already existing line.

(b) *Levite-priests*. The Books of Kings are interested only in the priesthood of Jerusalem, which we shall study later.[3] Apart from the accusation against Jeroboam (which, we said, may be without foundation), they never once mention the Levites, and to find any record of them under the monarchy, one must open Deuteronomy. It is still the common opinion that this book equates priests and Levites, and attributes to both the same functions. The entire tribe of Levi was set apart to carry the Ark, to serve God and to bless the people (Dt 10: 8), and members of this tribe are called 'the priests, the Levites' (Dt 17: 9, 18; 18: 1; 21: 5; 24: 8; 31: 9). The text of Dt 18: 1 should be translated: 'the Levite priests, all the tribe of Levi', with the two phrases in apposition, and not 'the Levite priests and all the tribe of Levi'. The text could scarcely bear the latter meaning, for this would make a distinction between Levites who were priests and others who were not. There are, of course, texts which use the word 'priest' alone, or 'Levite'

1. Cf. pp. 372 ff.   2. Cf. p. 6.   3. Cf. p. 372.

alone, but a comparison of these texts proves that the terms are employed as synonyms. Thus, in Dt 31: 9, it is 'the priests, the Levites' who carry the Ark, whereas in Dt 31: 25 it is the Levites; again, Dt 18: 6-7 makes provision for a Levite, when he comes to the central sanctuary, to perform the functions of a priest together with all his brother Levites.

Nevertheless, within the book of Deuteronomy itself, a certain distinction can be perceived. It has recently been argued that the 'Levite-priests' were the servants of the central sanctuary; in general, this is true, but it does not apply to Dt 21: 5, where the Levite-priests are those in any town near which a murder has been committed. Conversely, in Dt 18: 7, we read of 'Levites', not 'Levite-priests', although the text refers to the central sanctuary. The terminology of Deuteronomy then, is not hard and fast, and the book implies that all the Levites could perform priestly functions. In practice, however, the great number of Levites made it impossible for everyone of them to find employment at the central sanctuary in Jerusalem. Those Levites who were not employed in the service of the altar did not, of course, share its emoluments (Dt 18: 1-4), and since their tribe had no territory assigned to it, they had no source of income. Hence the writer of Deuteronomy commends to the charity of the Israelites 'the Levite who dwells in thy gates' along with the stranger, the fatherless and the widow, *i.e.* all those who had no assured means of livelihood (Dt 12: 12, 18, 19; 14: 27, 29; 16: 11, 14; 26: 11-13). But every Levite retained his priestly rights, and when he came to the central sanctuary, he not only officiated there but received a stipend equal to that of his brother Levites who were attached to the sanctuary (Dt 18: 6-7).

These prescriptions are not a codification of the reform of Josias. They date from before it, and could not be applied in their entirety even at the moment of reform, cf. 2 K 23: 9: 'Nevertheless, the priests of the high places could not go up to the altar of Yahweh in Jerusalem, though they ate unleavened bread among their brothers'. These 'priests of the high places' were Levites, and the clergy of Jerusalem, jealous of their own privileges, did not allow them to take part in the liturgy; the mention of unleavened bread is no doubt a reference to the great Passover which closed the reform (2 K 23: 21-23); *i.e.* instead of applying the rules of Dt 18: 6-7, the priests of Jerusalem followed the line of conduct indicated in Dt 12: 11-12.

The position of the Levites, then, as described in Deuteronomy, was not the result of Josias' reform, but it must have been connected with some movement which sought to centralize worship; here we meet once more the problem already discussed when we were speaking about the Deuteronomic law allowing only one sanctuary.[1] The inequality in position between those Levites who were ministers of the sanctuaries and those who were scattered among the tribes was either a result of some attempted reform in

1. Cf. pp. 338-339.

the Northern kingdom, or a reflection of the reform attempted by Ezechias. The question of the priesthood is, however, more complicated, and a third solution is possible. Before there was any reform or any project of reform seeking to restrict legitimate worship to one place, there was both in Israel and in Judah a movement to draw the faithful to the great national sanctuaries of Jerusalem and Bethel. The local sanctuaries continued in existence, but their guardians had suffered from the competition, their revenues had decreased and many of their members had lost their positions; they could still have offered their services as priests, but in the meantime they were reduced to the position of resident aliens, *gerîm*, as Deuteronomy describes them. Thus a distinction already existed, *de facto* though not *de jure*, between the priests of the large sanctuaries (or, during the attempts at reform, of the sole sanctuary) and the priests in the provinces.

(c) *Priests and Levites*. In Deuteronomy, the distinction between priests and Levites lies under the surface; in Ezechiel it is explicit. The main text is Ez 44: 6-31. The Israelites sinned by introducing uncircumcised men into the service of the Temple: this is a reference to the public slaves employed in the Temple, the descendants of those slaves employed by Solomon (cf. Esd 2: 55-58), the '*n'thînîm*' ('given')[1] whose origin went back to David, according to Esd 8: 20. These men, says the prophet, will be replaced by the Levites who helped Israel to commit idolatry; but as a punishment, the Levites will be forbidden to perform strictly priestly functions and will be relegated to lower offices: they will slaughter the victims and be at the service of the people (Ez 44: 6-14). Clearly, Ezechiel is not referring to priests who worshipped idols; he could never assign to them a place in the future Temple. He is referring to Levites who had served the small sanctuaries where worship was not always pure; they are the Levites in the provinces mentioned in Deuteronomy, those whom 2 K 23: 9 calls the 'priests of the high places', those whose worship was suppressed in Josias' reform. In Ezechiel, we can perceive a distinct echo of this reform, and of the incidents which it provoked; the violence of Ezechiel's protest shows that these struggles did not happen in the distant past. And yet the prophet is anxious to give these Levites a recognized standing; they are to be accepted among the clergy, but in an inferior rank.

Ezechiel contrasts them with the Levite priests, and this term too reminds us of Deuteronomy. Priestly functions are to be reserved to this class: these alone may approach Yahweh, offer up fat and blood, and go into the sanctuary. This close contact with holy things binds them to observe special rules of purity (Ez 44: 15-31). They are called sons of Sadoq in Ez 44: 15, and also in Ez 40: 46; 43: 19; 48: 11: in short, this class represents the priesthood belonging to the Temple of Jerusalem. Here again, Ezechiel gives his approval to the reform of Josias.

1. Cf. p. 89.

There are still other texts which tell of a distinction within the ranks of the clergy. There was one room for the 'priests who serve the Temple' and another for the 'priests who serve the altar, *i.e.* the sons of Sadoq' (Ez 40: 45-46). Some land was reserved for priests who served the sanctuary, and some other land for the Levites who served the Temple (Ez 45: 4-5). There were kitchens for the 'priests' to cook the sacrifices offered for sin, and other kitchens for 'those who serve the Temple' to cook the sacrifices for the people (Ez 46: 20-24). The territory around the Temple was allotted to the priests, the sons of Sadoq, who had not gone astray, and a different area was allotted to the Levites, who had gone astray (Ez 48: 11-14). All these distinctions repeat, and are in conformity with, the distinction drawn in Ez 44: 6-31, where the Levites are 'those who serve the Temple' (v. 11), and the priests are 'those who serve the sanctuary' (v. 15). But it is interesting to note that in Ez 40: 45-46, both categories are called 'priests'. The passage must have been written soon after Deuteronomy.

Ezechiel, then, is not a radical innovator; he is merely trying to regularize a situation which had long existed and which had deteriorated as a result of Josias' reform. We must now compare this project with the legislation of the priestly writings. The supposed background to this legislation is the sojourn in the desert. According to Nb 3: 6-9, the Levites were placed at the service of Aaron and his sons, were 'given' to them, and served the Dwelling; according to Nb 8: 19, they were 'given' to Aaron and his sons for the service of the Tent; according to Nb 18: 1-7, which is the principal text, they were to serve Aaron and the Tent and they were 'given', but Aaron and his sons performed the strictly priestly functions, such as the service of the altar and the sanctuary, and of 'everything which stands behind the veil'. Here there is an evident parallel with Ezechiel: the Dwelling, the Tent of desert days, is here equated with the Temple of Ezechiel; the Levites are 'given' and, as in Ezechiel, they take the place of those 'given' men who had formerly been attached to the Temple. Thus far there is harmony, and the differences are by comparison of secondary importance: the main one is that Numbers ascribes the priesthood to Aaron, whereas Ezechiel called the priests 'sons of Sadoq'; we shall see later what this difference of names implies.[1] Clearly, the text of Numbers was edited after Ezechiel: it is more precise, more calm, and devoid of any polemical note; the Levites were not identified with the 'given' servants until after the return from the Exile (cf. the lists in Esd 2 and Esd 8: 20), and the Aaronitic ancestry of the priests is stressed only in secondary passages in the books of Esdras and Nehemias (Esd 7: 1-5; Ne 10: 39; 12: 47). On the other hand, it is hard to admit that legislative arrangements like those in Numbers can have been inspired by an idealistic description like that in Ezechiel. It is more probable that both texts, Numbers and Ezechiel, represent two parallel

1. Cf. pp. 394-397.

trends originating from a common source, *i.e.* the situation created in Jerusalem by the reform of Josias. Indeed, it is not impossible that the laws in Numbers are a development of rules issued towards the end of the monarchy by the priests in the Temple.

Whatever solution be preferred, the Levites were distinguished from the priests and relegated to an inferior position, and this explains why they were not over-anxious to return from exile. In the list of Esd 2: 40= Ne 7: 43, there were only 74 Levites as against 4,289 priests, and in his own caravan, Esdras had difficulty in mustering a mere 38 Levites (Esd 8: 18-19). When we discuss the priesthood of the Second Temple, we shall see how the Levites tried to improve their status.[1]

5. *Levitical towns*

Deuteronomy describes the Levites as scattered throughout the land, living as resident aliens, and deserving of charity from those who possess the land; Ezechiel planned to group them together in a region near Jerusalem; but the book of Josue allots them 48 towns, including the environs, and these towns are divided equally among the twelve tribes; Josue's list is repeated, with some variations, in 1 Ch 6: 39-66. According to Jos 21: 2, God himself had ordered Moses to grant cities of this kind to the Levites, and this is explicitly asserted in Nb 35: 1-8 also. Lastly, the law of Jubilees contains a special clause concerning these towns (Lv 25: 33-34). The essential text is Jos 21, on which the others depend.

The problem raised by these texts is far from simple. At first sight, the institution of Levitical towns seems to be a Utopia thought out in later days. Many of the 48 towns, theoretically four in each tribe, were important centres, and it is impossible to imagine their being left exclusively to the Levites. And, we should add, the Levites were to possess also the land around these cities, to a greater or lesser extent (Nb 35: 5). Next, the list includes the six cities of refuge (Nb 35: 6; Jos 21: 13, 21, 27, etc.), which were, basically, a very ancient institution[2]; but the connection between the cities of refuge and Levitical towns was introduced at a later date, and those texts which give independent witness to cities of refuge do not consider them as Levitical towns. Lastly, the list presumes that there is a clear distinction between priests and Levites, that the Levites are divided into three classes, and that the priests are known as 'the sons of Aaron'; none of these things is ever mentioned in a pre-exilic text.

In its present form, then, Jos 21, like Jos 20 on the cities of refuge, belongs to the latest edition of the book of Josue; for our present purposes, it matters little whether we ascribe this edition to someone of the priestly school or to a later Deuteronomic editor. But the chapter on cities of refuge has a kernel of ancient tradition within it, and the list of Levitical towns might

---

1. Cf. pp. 393-394.   2. Cf. pp. 160-163.

also be based on a pre-exilic tradition. Two hypotheses have recently been put forward. The first states one important fact: the cities in the list were in existence and ruled by the Israelites only towards the end of David's reign and under that of Solomon; therefore the original list and the institutions of Levitical towns must date from this period, from the first half of Solomon's reign. The second hypothesis brings forward an objection to this view which is rather shrewd: if we plot these towns on a map, there are only two zones not occupied by the Levites, the centre of the kingdom of Judah to the south of Jerusalem and the centre of the kingdom of Israel (Shechem is an insertion). The explanation of this fact may be sought in the reform of Josias: the king brought all the priests in Judah to Jerusalem (2 K 23: 8), and put to death all the priests of the high places in the towns of Samaria (2 K 23: 19-20). The list therefore belongs to the time of Josias, or to some period after him, but was written before the return from the Exile. This interpretation is not convincing. The historicity of 2 K 23: 19-20 is not above suspicion, and 2 K 23: 8 expressly states that the towns of Judah from which the priests came stretched 'from Geba to Beersheba', i.e. from the entire kingdom of Judah, in which there were a dozen Levitical towns outside the centre. The only remaining possibility is that the list represents a partial execution of the measures taken by Josias. The first hypothesis does not explain the lacunae, but the second explains only the lacunae and gives no reason for the rest.

In the end, we must confess that this list is a riddle. Its systematization is certainly Utopian, but otherwise it must be based upon an ancient document, and must at some time have reflected a real situation. Several of the towns mentioned are referred to elsewhere in the Bible as the home-towns of priestly families. On the other hand, it does not represent a list of sanctuaries served by Levites; in fact, it seems rather to represent the home-towns of Levites who were not employed at the big sanctuaries, i.e. Levites who had no assured source of income and who were therefore in the position of the Levites described in Deuteronomy. Let us propose a slight modification of the first of the hypotheses just mentioned, and take the risk of stating our own view: the list originally represented the dispersal of the Levite population after the foundation of the Temple and after the organization of the official cult at Bethel. The foundation of the Temple would explain why no other Levites are mentioned in the immediate environs of Jerusalem, and the foundation at Bethel would explain why there were no Levitical cities in the centre of Israel either.

6. Was there ever a non-priestly tribe called Levi?

According to the Bible, this priestly tribe originated from Levi, one of twelve sons of Jacob. We have already stated that in the blessings of Moses

(Dt 33: 8-11) this same Levi, considered as representing his descendants, received as his inheritance the functions of the priesthood. But two other texts present the man in a very different light. In the blessings of Jacob (Gn 49: 5-7), Levi and Simeon are condemned together for their violence; they have killed men and mutilated bulls and will therefore be scattered throughout Israel. This text is evidently connected with the same tradition as Gn 34: in order to avenge the honour of their sister Dinah, Simeon and Levi made a treacherous attack on the inhabitants of Shechem, killed the men and made off with the cattle, and for this crime they were condemned by Jacob. Other texts show that Simeon was a non-priestly group which very soon lost its autonomy and whose members were scattered throughout the territory of Judah. It is reasonable to conclude that there was also a non-priestly tribe called Levi which suffered the same fate.

Some critics, however, reject this conclusion. They hold that the story in Gn 34 is mere legend, and that the oracle in Gn 49 is an artificial explanation of the unusual situation in which the priestly tribe of Levi found itself: they hold, then, that the tribe of Levi had always been priests, that it had never had any part in politics, and that its members lived scattered among the other tribes. Against this, we know that Levi formed part of the old system of the Twelve Tribes; it is improbable that at some later date, when tribal divisions corresponded to territorial divisions, a tribe which had no territory was introduced into the Twelve Tribes. The blessings of Jacob, in their present form, go back to the reign of David, and some oracles among them are even older. And Gn 34 has none of the characteristics of an aetiological narrative; nor does it contain any allusion to the dispersal of Simeon and Levi; yet, according to the thesis we are opposing, it was written to explain this dispersal! Gn 34 relates a fact, and Gn 49: 5-7 gives the consequences of that fact. The fact itself is an episode from the pre-history of Israel. The groups which belonged to Simeon and Levi had a serious quarrel with the indigenous population near Shechem; the quarrel may have occurred when they were passing through the area with their flocks, or perhaps when they had settled in the region before Ephraim and Manasseh arrived and drove the remaining members of these tribes further south. We can only make up hypotheses, but we should not reject this very ancient tradition which takes us back before the time of Moses; there was a non-priestly tribe of Levi, and its ancestor's name is found, in its unabbreviated form, both in cuneiform and in Egyptian inscriptions.

And yet the problem with which we are concerned is not thereby resolved. One could suppose (and some have done so) that the connection of this profane tribe of Levi with the priestly tribe of Levites was purely accidental: the latter would have been called Levites because the word expressed their function. Eventually the function became hereditary, and the similarity between the name given to the priests and the name of Jacob's son would then have led people to connect these men, now a priestly tribe, with the old, profane tribe which had disappeared. This leads us to our last question: what was the origin of the Levites?

7. The origin of the Levites

In Hebrew, the same word is used for 'Levi' and 'Levite': *lewy*. Even those texts which refer to the tribe of Levi use the same word, but with the article, to make it a common noun: *hallewy* (Ex 6: 19; Nb 3: 20; Dt 10: 8, etc.). All the many texts which speak of the Levites employ the plural of this word, *l'wiyyim*, as if it were the name of men performing a function.

On the other hand, among the inscriptions discovered in the Minaean script and dialect at El-Ela, the ancient Dedan, in Northern Arabia, there are several which contain the word *lw'* or, in the feminine, *lw't*. This word has sometimes been translated 'priest' or even 'Levite', by reason of its resemblance with the Hebrew *lewy*; and some writers have concluded that the Israelites adopted the institution of Levites from those early Arabs with whom they had been in contact at Sinai. Consequently, the connection of the Levites with a profane tribe of Levi (whether the latter existed or not) is quite artificial.

Close study of these inscriptions, combined with more accurate research into the epigraphy and history of ancient Arabia, has led to a very different solution. The words *lw'* and *lw't* do not mean 'priest' or 'priestess', but denote an object given to a god, a pledge. This object may be a person, man or woman, or a thing; but it is never a person engaged in performing the cult. Since this meaning is quite different from that of the Hebrew *lewy*, it is quite possible that there is no connection between the terms. Even if we admit that the primary meaning is 'consecrated, given', and that the word evolved differently in the two languages, this does not mean that the Hebrew borrowed from the Minaean. In fact, the Minaeans were a people from the South of Arabia, and their kings did not rule the region around Dedan in Northern Arabia until the 4th century B.C., at the earliest. Now the words *lw'* and *lw't* are found only in Minaean inscriptions from Northern Arabia, at Dedan, and never in those from the South, nor in any other South Arabian dialect. It is quite possible then, that they were borrowed from a population of Dedan which was neither Minaean nor even proto-Arab in the widest sense. Again, we should not forget that, according to Arabic authors writing in the early days of Islam, the oasis of Dedan was then occupied by Jews, who seemed to have been there a very long time. A recently discovered inscription of Nabonidus states that this king installed a colony of soldiers in Northern Arabia, at Dedan itself, and that these soldiers were recruited, for the most part, from the West of his empire. There probably were Jews among them, and if so, then Jews, including Levites, would have been living at Dedan two centuries before it came under the control of the Minaeans. If anyone borrowed the word *lewy*, it was the Minaeans, who modified the sense of the term and gave it a feminine which did not exist in Hebrew.

Furthermore, it is not so evident as is sometimes claimed that 'Levite' in Hebrew is primarily the name of a function. It is significant that in the Bible this word occurs only once in the construct state, as a common noun (Ne 10: 1), whereas *kohen* is often used in this way ('the priests of Yahweh, of the high places', etc., 'my priests, your priests, their priests', etc.). In its form and usage, 'Levite' is first and foremost a *nomen gentilitium*: it means 'a descendant of Levi' and there is no reason to reject the biblical tradition which constantly connects the Levites with their ancestor Levi.

After the very ancient episode recorded in Gn 34, we find the remainder of the tribe of Simeon associated with Judah in the South. The survivors of the tribe of Levi probably accompanied them. But, whereas the Simeonites integrated themselves into the surrounding population, the descendants of Levi specialized in cultic functions. Ethnology and history provide other examples of the way in which an ethnic minority has specialized in a particular profession or trade, not excluding professions associated with worship. The ancient accounts of relations between the Levites and Judah and the South are clear enough. According to the patriarchal traditions, Levi was a son of Leah, like Simeon and Judah; and according to the traditions about the wanderings in the desert, the Levites were set apart for the cult during this period; they are closely associated with Moses, and he is one of them. Moses had certainly been in Egypt, and the Levites with him; this would explain the surprisingly high proportion of Egyptian names found among them. The text of Nb 26 : 58 has preserved a division of Levites into clans which does not harmonize with the canonical division into three classes, representing three families, the Gershonites, Qehathites and Merarites. The text in Nb 26 however, lists five clans: Libnite, Hebronite, Mehlite, Mushite, Qorahite. The Greek version omits the Mahlite clan: of the other four names, Mushite is generally interpreted as a *nomen gentilitium* derived from Moses, and Qorahite is connected with the Qorah of 1 Ch 2: 43 (a list of the 'sons' of Caleb, most of which are place-names: Qorah is listed between Hebron and Tappuah). The Libnites and Hebronites were obviously the inhabitants of Libnah and Hebron. This list is very ancient, certainly pre-monarchic; it tells us where the Levites lived, and seems to place them all in the territory of Judah. From the time of the Judges they began to spread further afield. The Levite who figures in the story of the crime of Gibeah lived in the hill-country of Ephraim, but he still had contacts with Judah, where he had taken a concubine (Jg 19: 1). The Levite engaged by Mikah was connected with a clan of Judah (Jg 17: 7) and was recognized by the men of Dan (and therefore must have lived among them, Jg 18: 3); he was engaged by Mikah in the hill-country of Ephraim (Jg 17: 1), and later followed the men of Dan north to the sources of the Jordan (Jg 18: 30); yet there is nothing whatever to make his Levitical ancestry suspect; indeed, it is expressly affirmed by the last text, and he would evidently belong to the Mushite clan. This is just one example of the way in which men of this tribe spread over the country away from Judah, and when the document which forms the basis of the list of Levitical towns in Jos 21 was first edited, the Levites were already scattered through all the tribes of Israel.

This geographical expansion was accompanied by a corresponding expansion in the original nucleus of the tribe. Levi, like the other tribes, presumably adopted into its ranks individuals and even groups; entire families which had officiated as priests in the various sanctuaries would thus be integrated into the tribe of Levi, whatever their ancestry.

We are very ready to admit that this reconstruction of the early history of the Levites is still a hypothesis, but it seems to take into account those rare ancient texts which are certainly trustworthy; it also explains how the profane tribe of Levi (which certainly existed) was transformed into the priestly tribe of Levites, and how this latter became one of the great institutions of Israel. But there is certainly no need to look for the origin of this institution outside Israel.

CHAPTER SEVEN

THE PRIESTHOOD IN JERUSALEM UNDER
THE MONARCHY

THOUGH there were many sanctuaries in Palestine from the early days of the monarchy down to the reform of Josias, we have no detailed information about the priests who served in these sanctuaries. Jerusalem is the only exception, and this is not surprising. The Temple at Jerusalem was the richest and the most frequented centre of worship; it was the official sanctuary of the kingdom of Judah, and its priests were the only priests who played any part at all in the political life of the nation. Furthermore, the only sources we can use are the Books of Samuel and Kings, all four of which were written in Judah under the influence of Deuteronomy, and edited, therefore, by men who refused to acknowledge the legitimacy of any sanctuary other than the Temple. Yet even the information which these books provide is scanty, and often difficult to interpret. We should be able to present a more complete picture if we could feel safe in using everything which the Books of Chronicles relate about the organization of the clergy by David (1 Ch 23-26); unfortunately, the clergy (whose divisions and tasks are described in minute detail) are there spoken of as serving in the Temple, and the Temple, in David's time, had not yet been built. The only possible conclusion is that this picture reflects the ideal of the Chronicler, and that it was inspired by the situation in his own day; we shall use these chapters, therefore, for the history of the priesthood after the Exile.

1. Ebyathar and Sadoq

1 S 22: 20-23 says that the sole survivor after Saul's massacre of the priests in Nob was called Ebyathar, the son of Ahimelek and grandson of Ahitub, through whom he could trace his ancestry to Eli, the priest of Shiloh (1 S 14: 3, cf. 1 K 2: 27). It is impossible to trace his ancestry any further in pre-exilic texts, but the names of Eli's two sons, Ophni and Phinehas, show that the family was of Levitical origin (cf. also 1 S 2: 27, which is the work of a later editor). Ebyathar took refuge with David and followed him in his wanderings, acting as his priest (1 S 23: 6, 9; 30: 7).

The next time Ebyathar is mentioned is after the conquest of Jerusalem, and he is then in the service of the Ark, along with another priest, Sadoq

(2 S 15: 24–29). These two priests are always mentioned together right to the end of David's reign (2 S 17: 15; 19: 12), and are named next to each other in both lists of David's chief officials (2 S 8: 17 and 20: 25). In every text Sadoq is mentioned before Ebyathar; Ebyathar seems, therefore, to have been relegated to a secondary position after the king had moved his capital to Jerusalem. In the intrigues over the succession to David, Sadoq supported Solomon; but Ebyathar (who had always remained faithful to David himself, cf. 1 K 2: 26) supported Adonias against Solomon (1 K 1: 7, 19, 25; 2: 22), and consequently, when David died, he soon found himself banished by Solomon to his family estate at Anathoth (1 K 2: 26–27). This was a Levitical town (Jos 21: 18) and the nearest one to the disused sanctuary at Nob where Ebyathar had begun his career.

Sadoq became the sole holder of the priestly office (1 K 2: 35). He must have died shortly afterwards, for he is never again mentioned in the history of Solomon's reign; and in the list of the main officials which was compiled in the middle of the reign, it is his son Azaryahu who holds the title of priest (1 K 4: 2). (The mention of Sadoq and Ebyathar in verse 4 of this list is obviously an interpolation.)

Sadoq, then, appears in history only after the conquest of Jerusalem; at first he shares the priesthood with Ebyathar and in the end ousts his partner. What was his origin? The question is extremely obscure, because the Bible has provided him with two genealogies. The first makes him a descendant of Eleazar (1 Ch 24: 3), and 1 Ch 5: 29–34 and 6: 35–38 give his complete genealogy from Aaron through Eleazar. The second (cf. the Hebrew text of 2 S 8: 17) calls Sadoq the son of Ahitub, and seems to connect him with the family of Eli. The genealogies on Chronicles, however, are artificial, and Sadoq cannot possibly have been a descendant of Eli since his appointment is presented as the fulfilment of the curse pronounced against the house of Eli (1 K 2: 27; cf. 1 S 2: 27–36; 3: 11–14). Furthermore, there is, in 2 S 8: 17, an indication that the verse is in disorder: it reads 'Sadoq, son of Ahitub, and Ahimelek, son of Ebyathar, were priests'; now Ebyathar was the son of Ahimelek, not his father (1 S 22: 20). The Syriac version has made this correction, but we must go further: in 1 S 22: 20, Ebyathar is called 'son of Ahimelek, the son of Ahitub', and it may be that in 1 S 8: 17 Ahitub has been transferred to make him father of Sadoq, perhaps by accident, or perhaps on purpose. The original reading would then be: 'Sadoq and Ebyathar, son of Ahimelek, son of Ahitub'. Thus Sadoq is left without any genealogy.

Several hypotheses have been advanced about his origin. Some suggest that he may have been the high priest of Gibeon. It is an idea of the Chronicler (1 Ch 16: 39) which has been adopted by some modern scholars: under David, Ebyathar would then have been in the service of the Ark, and Sadoq in the service of the Tent, which, at the time, was kept at Gibeon (cf. 2 Ch 1: 3). In the early texts, however, Sadoq is never mentioned except, like Ebyathar, in connection with the Ark. A second suggestion is that Sadoq was one of the priests at Qiryath-Yearim (1 S 7: 1), and that he took part in the transfer of the Ark to Jerusalem; according to 2 S 6: 3-4, the cart was driven by Uzzah and 'Ahyo'; it is suggested that instead of 'Ahyo', we should read "*ahiw*', meaning 'his brother'. This brother would in fact be Sadoq, who afterwards remained at Jerusalem as one of the two men who carried the Ark: and Uzzah would have been replaced by Ebyathar (2 S 15: 29). There is no text which formally contradicts this theory, but neither is there one which gives it positive support; it is certainly possible, but it is not proven.

A third, and last, hypothesis enjoys great favour at the moment. Since Sadoq does not appear until after the capture of Jerusalem and since his genealogy is not given, may he not have belonged to the city of Jerusalem itself? His name reminds us of the ancient names connected with Jerusalem, such as Melchisedech in the time of Abraham, and Adoni-Sedeq at the time of the conquest. The suggestion is that he was the priest of the Jebusite sanctuary, and therefore the heir of Melchisedech (Gn 14: 18-20; Ps 110: 4).[1] David would have placed the Ark in the old sanctuary, and retained the services of its priest in order to win over those Jebusites who remained in the town. Certainly, there is nothing impossible in this idea of utilizing an old sanctuary, and of employing the priests who served that sanctuary; we have seen several examples of the way in which the early Israelites took over the sanctuaries of Canaan. Indeed, the character of the god who was worshipped in Jerusalem could have facilitated the change; it was not Baal, but El-'Elyon, one of the forms of El under which the Patriarchs had worshipped the true God,[2] and one of the titles Yahweh had appropriated.[3] The meeting between Abraham and Melchisedech (Gn 14: 18-20) could have been cited to justify the rights of Jerusalem's priesthood and to prove its ancient origin. If we hesitate to adopt this solution, it is for lack of positive evidence. First, it implies that a sanctuary of El-'Elyon was later used for the cult of Yahweh, and the texts never once mention any such sanctuary; the Ark was kept in a Tent until the end of David's reign. Secondly, Sadoq is never mentioned in the Bible except in connection with the Ark and the Tent of Yahweh.[4]

It is safer to admit that we do not know where Sadoq came from. Possibly he really was of Levitical origin, though not from the same branch as the house of Eli, and the later tradition in Chronicles may rest on a firm basis. We do know, however, that his descendants kept their position in Jerusalem until the Exile, and that the legitimacy of their priesthood was never called in question, though a feud continued between the house of Sadoq and the family of Ebyathar, which they had ousted.

1. Cf. p. 114.   2. Cf. p. 294.
3. Cf. p. 310.   4. Cf. p. 311.

2. The descendants of Sadoq

1 Ch 5: 34-41 gives a list of the men who succeeded Sadoq as head of the clergy in Jerusalem. It contains eleven names from Ahimaas (Sadoq's son) to Yehosadaq (the father of Josue, who was the first high priest after the Restoration, Ag 1: 1). This gives exactly twelve generations of priests from the building of the Temple under Solomon to its reconstruction after the Exile. Now the list of Sadoq's ancestors is given immediately before (1 Ch 5: 29-34), and this too has exactly twelve generations from the making of the Tent in the desert to the building of the Temple; and 12 generations of 40 years make exactly 480 years, as given in 1 K 6: 1. Thus the foundation of Solomon's Temple would mark the middle year in the history of Israel's sanctuary. This symmetry is deliberate, and other facts underline the artificial character of these lists. Ahimaas was undoubtedly Sadoq's son (2 S 15: 36), but Azaryahu, who was priest under Solomon, was another son of Sadoq, not his grandson (as 1 Ch 5: 35 has). Moreover, the list is incomplete; though it contains some names which are found elsewhere in the Bible (Azaryahu, 1 K 4: 2; Hilqiyyahu, 2 K 22: 4; Serayah, 2 K 25: 18; Yehosadaq, Ag 1: 1), it omits Yehoyada, the priest under Joas (2 K 12: 8), Uriyyah, the priest under Achaz (2 K 16: 10), and at least two others who are mentioned in the narrative part of Chronicles itself (an Azaryahu under Ozias, 2 Ch 26: 20, and an Azarya under Ezechias, 2 Ch 31: 10). Another difficulty is that the series Amarya-Ahitub-Sadoq recurs in identical form among the immediate ancestors of Sadoq (vv. 33-34) and among his descendants (vv. 37-38). The list, then, expresses a real fact, namely, the continuity of Sadoq's line, but it cannot be used to write a detailed history of his house.

The Books of Kings tell us very little about this history, apart from what they say about the relations between the priests and the kings, which will be studied later. It seems that the descendants of Sadoq were a conservative-minded family, with little liking for innovations which might change their way of life. We know, for example, that the religious reforms were initiated by the kings, not by the priests: cf. the reforms of Asa (1 K 15: 12-13; cf. 2 Ch 14: 2-4; 15: 1-15), of Ezechias (2 K 18: 3-4) and of Josias (2 K 23). The only exception to this is the revolution against Athaliah, directed by the priest Yehoyada, which culminated in the destruction of the temple of Baal (2 K 11: 18); but this revolt was primarily a reaction against the foreign queen and her entourage. The same Yehoyada is blamed for having neglected the upkeep of the Temple, and the integrity of the lay craftsmen is contrasted with the mean behaviour of the priests (2 K 12: 8 and 16). Here, as on other occasions, the kings and the priests were in opposition to each other; yet Sadoq's descendants never lost their standing and they even won a victory against Josias' reform when the Temple clergy succeeded in preventing the application of the law of Deuteronomy to the provincial priests who came to Jerusalem (2 K 23: 9).

The principal opponents of this Sadoqite monopoly were the descendants of Ebyathar. A trace of this struggle can be seen in the verses added to the history of Eli by someone from the Sadoqite camp; in 1 S 2: 27-36, Yahweh is made to say to Eli: 'I shall keep one of thy line near my altar to wear out his eyes with weeping and to break his spirit . . . I shall raise unto myself a faithful priest (*i.e.* Sadoq) . . . I shall ensure that his house endures . . . Every survivor of thy family will come and bow before him to have a little bit of money and a piece of bread'. The Sadoqites certainly rejoiced at the humiliation of their rivals, but the party of Ebyathar had one voice to speak in reply—that of Jeremias. This prophet came from a priestly family at Anathoth, the village to which Ebyathar had been banished, and he aroused the fury of the priests when he began to preach, in the Temple itself, against the Temple and its cult (Jr 7 and 26). In two texts, Jr 7: 14 and 26: 6, he predicts that the Temple at Jerusalem will meet the same fate as the sanctuary at Shiloh; we have just seen how the Sadoqites used to taunt their luckless rivals with the curse pronounced at Shiloh against the house of Eli, and it is hard not to see in these words of Jeremias a retort that their own Temple and priesthood will suffer the same fate.

It is unlikely that the Sadoqites, in their resistance to religious reform, confined themselves to polemic of the kind just mentioned, and it is probable that they tried to put forward a code of law which would be a rival to that of Deuteronomy. The basic laws which underlie the Law of Holiness in Lv 17-27 seems to stem from the priests of Jerusalem in the last years of the monarchy. In the next chapter we shall see how a compromise between these two conflicting parties and their tendencies was worked out in the post-exilic period.

3. *The priests and the kings*

The Temple in Jerusalem was a state sanctuary, and its priests were civil servants appointed by the king. The head of the clergy is mentioned among the king's officials (1 K 4: 2) and he was appointed and dismissed by the king (1 K 2: 27 and 35). The king issued all orders concerning the upkeep of the sanctuary and the furnishings to be used in worship. Even Yehoyada, who had placed Joas on the throne, had to bow to two orders of this same king, the second of which revoked one of the priests' privileges and placed them under the control of a lay official (2 K 12: 5-17); even the successors of Yehoyada could not emancipate themselves from this control (2 K 22: 3-7). Or, to take another example, when Achaz ordered Uriyyah to build a new altar, the priest obeyed without a word of protest (2 K 16: 10-16).

This last text is a reminder that the power of the king included more than the administration of the Temple; Achaz 'went up' to the altar he had ordered the priest to make, and there offered sacrifice. We discussed the intervention of the kings in public worship when we were treating royal institutions,[1] and we concluded that it was based on the sacral character of the king. He was not a priest in the strict sense, nor even the head of the clergy; but he was the patron of the priesthood.

Conflicts between the priests and kings were not unknown. The priest Yehoyada led the revolt which overthrew the regime of Athaliah (2 K 11). According to 2 Ch 24: 17-26, king Joas fell into evil ways after the death of Yehoyada, and ordered Zacharias, the son of Yehoyada, to be stoned to death; 2 K 12: 21-22 records without comment the subsequent assassination of the king, but the Chronicler presents it as the revenge of the priest's party. This story was not made up by the Chronicler; he must have taken it from the midrash on the Book of Kings to which he refers in 2 Ch 24: 27. Again, the conspiracy against Amasias was hatched in Jerusalem (2 K 14: 19; 2 Ch 25: 27), and it is often said that it was inspired by the priests. The Bible does not say so explicitly, but the revolts against Joas and against Amasias both followed a plundering of the Temple treasury, necessitated by the bad policies of these two kings (2 K 12: 19; 14: 14). Understandably, the priests would have been annoyed, but their annoyance was only one element amid the general dissatisfaction of the population. On the whole, the priests probably did try to prevent the king from intervening in the Temple and in affairs concerning the cult, and this opposition is described in a late narrative in Chronicles (2 Ch 26: 16-20): it tells how the priests dragged Ozias from the altar of incense when he was on the point of offering incense there. There certainly was friction, though the texts which record it are mainly post-exilic: the 'perfect peace' which Za 6: 13; cf. 4: 14 and the late passage in Jr 33: 17-26 foretold for the Messianic age did not always reign. Yet at least the alliance between the descendants of David and the line of Sadoq was never broken up; as a text of Sadoqite inspiration puts it, a 'faithful priest' always walked before Yahweh's Anointed (1 S 2: 35).

4. The hierarchy

There was in Jerusalem, as in all the great ancient sanctuaries, a large number of priests. Lucian (De Dea Syra, 42-43) says that there were at least three hundred priests at Hierapolis, not counting the singers and the Galli. Strabo (XII, ii, 3) says that the temple of Comana in Cappadocia had a staff of six thousand priests. The accounts from Citium show that there must have been many there also, and examples of this kind could be multiplied. Under Saul, the sanctuary at Nob was looked after by Ahimelek and eighty-five priests descended from Eli (1 S 22: 16, 18). Certainly, there

1. Cf. pp. 113-114.

must have been still more in the Temple at Jerusalem, but it is impossible to give any precise number.

These priests must have been organized in some way; who, then, was their head? The term 'high priest' (*hakkohen haggadôl*) is found only four times in pre-exilic texts (2 K 12: 11; 22: 4, 8; 23: 4); but in the parallels to these texts, 2 Ch 24: 11 (=2 K 12: 11) has *kohen harôsh* ('the head priest'), 2 Ch 34: 14, 18 (=2 K 22: 4, 8) has merely *kohen* and the Greek version of 2 K 23: 4 also presumes the reading *kohen*. Thus all four references to the 'high priest' before the Exile seem to be later modifications. Since the title 'high priest' did not exist before the Exile, some writers have argued that the king performed the functions attached to the office, just as the high priest after the Exile took the place of the king. In fact, the question is more complicated. We shall see in the next chapter how Josue, the first priest of the new Temple, was also the first to be called 'the high priest'; but beside Josue stood Zorobabel, the supreme civil authority, and the 'royal' character of the high priest was asserted only little by little. Nevertheless, it is quite true that before the Exile the king had supreme control over the Temple and its clergy; and that in certain circumstances, he officiated himself; yet the king was never a member of the hierarchy of priests.

The head of the clergy is usually referred to in the Bible as 'the priest', without any qualification; he was *the* priest (cf. the list of Solomon's ministers, 1 K 4: 2; Yehoyada 2 K 11: 9f.; 12: 8f.; Uriyyah, 2 K 16: 10f.; Is 8: 2; Hilqiyyahu, 2 K 22: 12, 14: all these were quite evidently heads of the clergy). The title 'head priest' (*kohen harôsh*) is found once in Kings (2 K 25: 18 and its parallel in Jr 52: 24) and several times in Chronicles (2 Ch 19: 11; 24:6 (?) and 11; 26:20); the formula is expanded in 2 Ch 31: 10 to 'the priest, the head of the house of Sadoq'.

But even if we leave aside the question of his title, it is quite evident that the clergy had someone at their head. (Similarly, we read of a 'head of the priests' in the texts from Ras Shamra and in several Phoenician inscriptions.) But one should not imagine that this head of the priesthood had the importance or the rank which the high priests had after the Exile. Before 587, the principal priest had control over the clergy of Jerusalem only, and he was himself responsible to the king (cf. 2 K 12: 8; 16: 10), whereas the high priest after the Exile was the religious and civil head of the community. Indeed, during that brief period when the Jews gained their independence under the Hasmoneans, the high priest acted as their king, and he even took the title of king from 104 onwards (Aristobulus I).

Immediately under the head priest was the 'second priest' (*kohen mishnê*, 2 K 23: 4 and 25: 18=Jr 52: 24, where the name is given, Sephanyahu). Sephanyahu is mentioned several times in the Book of Jeremias (Jr 21: 1; 37: 3); in Jr 29: 24-29 he is called 'the superintendent of the Temple' and he seems to have been responsible for policing the sanctuary; his predecessor in this office was called Yehoyada (Jr 29: 26), who had succeeded a man called Pashehur (Jr 20: 1-2).

After the head priest and the second priest, 2 K 23: 4 and 25: 18=Jr 52: 24 mention the 'keepers of the threshold'. These men are therefore the senior officials of the Temple, not mere door-keepers (2 Ch 34: 9 [cf. also 1 Ch 9: 22] seems to have confused them with the Levites who looked after the entrances). These officials were only three in number, according to 2 K 25: 18, and Joas placed them in charge of the collections from the people (2 K 12: 10; 22: 4).

As well as the five principal officers of the Temple, the 'elders of the priests' held an important position among the clergy. Ezechias sent them, along with the master of the palace and the royal secretary, to consult Isaias (2 K 19: 2; Is 37: 2). Jeremias took as witnesses some elders of the people and some elders of the priests (Jr 19: 1, in the Hebrew: the Greek text reads 'some priests'). If the analogy with the 'elders of the people' holds good,[1] the 'elders of the priests' must have been the heads of the priestly families; thus they would be forerunners of those men who headed the various divisions of the clergy after the Exile, the origins of which are attributed to the time of David by 1 Ch 24: 1-18.

5. The revenues of the clergy

Unlike the temples of Mesopotamia and of Egypt, the Temple in Jerusalem did not possess vast tracts of real estate; it was, however, a state sanctuary, and one must conclude that the king paid the normal expenses of public worship and the cost of repairs to the building. At least, he must have done so until the time of Joas, who, as we shall see, gave particular instructions about the cost of repairs. Yet there is no indication that the king contributed to the upkeep of the clergy. There is little information available for the period of the monarchy, and it is sometimes difficult to interpret what there is.

There was a universal ruling that the priest should gain a livelihood from the altar; he was entitled to a part of the sacrifices offered there, except for the holocaust, which was completely burnt. The story of Eli's sons (1 S 2: 12-17) records how this right of the priests was interpreted at Shiloh: after every sacrifice, one of the priest's servants took some of the meat out of the pot in which it was cooking. The fault of Eli's sons lay, not in taking their portion of meat, but in demanding the meat raw, *i.e.* before the fat had been offered upon the altar; they were thus serving themselves before they had served Yahweh. Osee accuses the priests of feeding on the 'sin' of the people (Os 4: 8). Now in sacrifices for sin, the priest kept

1. Cf. p. 69.

everything which was not offered on the altar (according to Lv 6: 19); it is possible, however, that Osee is referring not to this custom, but to sacrifices in general which are offered with bad dispositions and are therefore considered by him as a 'sin' (cf. Os 8: 11); in either case, the priest was taking his food from sacrifices. The same principle was certainly applied in the Temple at Jerusalem, with some modifications of the ritual.

The priest was also entitled to a part of the collections given to the Temple, as we learn from the two edicts of Joas (2 K 12: 5-17; cf. 22: 3-7). The first edict left the priests all the money the faithful gave, compulsory taxes and voluntary offerings alike, with the condition that the priests should undertake the repairs which were then needed in the Temple. But, as the following verses show, the novelty of this lay not in giving the priests a right to the revenue, but in imposing on them a charge which diminished their revenue. When the priests failed to carry out the repairs, the king issued a second order taking away from them the greater part of this revenue, and leaving them only the money given as satisfaction for a crime or a sin; it does not matter, for our present purposes, whether this refers to a fine for faults similar to those which were expiated by sin-offerings, or to a contribution which was made along with sin-offerings, or to a contribution made instead of them.[1]

The rights of the priests are contained in Dt 18: 1-5: Levite priests shall live on the meat offered to Yahweh because they have been chosen for the service of God; they are to be given the shoulder, the jaw and the stomach of all victims sacrificed, and also the best (*rêshîth*) of the wheat, of the wine or oil, and of the wool from shearing. This text is most precise, but it seems difficult to reconcile with other prescriptions in the same book of Deuteronomy. The Israelites are commanded to bring to the central sanctuary their sacrifices and all their offerings, tithes (*ma'aser*), first-born (*b'kôr*), etc., and to eat them in the presence of Yahweh along with their family, their servants and the Levite who dwells with them (Dt 12: 6-7, 11-12, 17-19). The same command is repeated in the law about the first-born (*bikkûrîm*, Dt 26: 1-11), but elsewhere a further directive is given about tithes and the first-born: if the central sanctuary is too far away, then they may sell their offerings and bring the money to the sanctuary to buy on the spot what they need to make a feast before Yahweh; and they are not to forget 'the Levite who is in thy towns' (Dt 14: 22-27). Lastly, Dt 14: 28-29 and 26: 12-15 prescribe that every three years the tithes are to be kept at home and there distributed to the Levites, the stranger, the fatherless and the widow; instead of presenting this tithe at the sanctuary, the pilgrim shall make a declaration that he has used it according to the law (Dt 26: 13). The Levites to whom these texts refer lived scattered throughout the land of Israel; they could accompany pilgrims to the sanctuary, and they were

1. Cf. p. 430.

commended to the charity of the Israelites; there is no reference here to the Levite priests who officiated in the sanctuary. From this some scholars have argued that Dt 18: 1-5, which describes the rights of Levite priests, is a later text, and that Deuteronomy originally made no provision for the priests who served the sanctuary.

Such a conclusion fails to take into account the character of Deuteronomy, which is a code of reform (cf. Dt 12: 8 for the subject under discussion). Sacrifices, dues and tithes existed before Deuteronomy, and so did the rights of those priests who served the various sanctuaries. Deuteronomy is promulgating a new law insisting on one sole sanctuary; this law naturally entailed new measures, and all the texts about the Levites can be explained against this background. The suppression of the local sanctuaries would deprive their guardians of their revenues, and the Israelites are therefore ordered to maintain them out of the things owed to Yahweh, exactly as they had done before: those Levites who might take part in pilgrimages were to be invited to the religious meals, and all Levites were to share in the tithe every third year. Yet no one can possibly imagine that the Israelites and their guests ate everything they brought to the sanctuary, for the offering would then be almost meaningless; they must, therefore, have given part of that offering to the servants of the sanctuary, even though no text mentions it. Thus we can harmonize all the other references with Dt 18: 1-5; this text refers to the priests of the sole, central sanctuary, not to the priests and Levites from the provinces. The latter, however, are affected by the statute which follows immediately afterwards: if Levites from the provinces come to live at the central sanctuary, they may exercise their priestly office and share the revenues attached to it (Dt 18: 6-8).

It is impossible to say how far these prescriptions were followed, and we know that the last one, at least, could not be enforced by Josias (2 K 23: 9). But, far from showing that the priests had no means of livelihood, these texts all presuppose that they lived on the revenues from public worship.

Nor is this conclusion weakened by the silence of the oldest laws: the Elohistic code of the Covenant (Ex 23: 19) and the Yahwistic Code (Ex 34: 26) both command that the best of the first-fruits of the earth should be brought to the house of Yahweh. There is no mention of any part of these first-fruits being allotted to the priests, but then these two codes of law never mention priests at all; we know that the priests shared in the sacrifices, from the very beginning, and it would seem normal enough for them to have shared in the first-fruits, too. The same principle would seem to apply to tithes, which are not mentioned in either of these two codes; but the tithe was certainly a very ancient institution, attested, for the sanctuary at Bethel, by Am 4: 4 and by the foundation-story contained in Gn 28: 22. In a word, the situation which Ezechiel describes in his plan of the future Jerusalem (Ez 44: 29-30) is the situation which obtained under the monarchy; there is no need to eliminate part, or all, of these verses, as some recent authors have done. On this matter of the revenues accruing to the clergy, there is not such a pronounced contrast between the first and the second Temple as most writers claim. But there certainly was a development, and more precise rulings, about which we shall speak in the next chapter.[1]

6. *The lower-ranking personnel*

The Chronicler attributes to David not only the division of priests into classes, but also the institution of twenty-four classes of singers (1 Ch 25), and of several classes of door-keepers who were to keep watch for twenty-four hours a day (1 Ch 26: 1-19). In these chapters he is describing a later situation in which door-keepers and singers had been incorporated into the Levites; but he is not inventing everything. Though the pre-exilic texts never mention the singers or the door-keepers, every large sanctuary in ancient times had them, and the liturgical services of the Temple always needed such men. Our present Psalter contains psalms which were sung in the Temple by professionals, sometimes accompanied by musical instruments. Amos refers to the religious music in the sanctuary at Bethel (Am 5: 23), and Yahweh had to have his singers, exactly as the king had his.[2] The names of the three heads of the families of singers in Ch 6: 18-32; 25: 1 (Asaph, Heman and Ethan or Yeduthun) are also a proof of the antiquity of the institution. We cannot, of course, set much store by the Psalm titles which ascribe twelve psalms to Asaph, one to Heman, one to Ethan and three to Yeduthun. But 1 K 5: 11 mentions Heman and Ethan along with Kalkol and Darda as famous wise men in order to stress how much wiser Solomon was, and we know that in ancient times singers also gave lessons in wisdom; moreover, in this same text, Heman, Kalkol and Darda are called 'sons of *maḥôl*', which is not a proper name, but a common noun; they were 'sons of the choir', *i.e.* choristers. The names are not Israelites, and Kalkol is found, in an Egyptian inscription from Megiddo, as the name of a woman singer from Ascalon. Ethan, on the other hand, is called the Ezrahite, literally, an indigenous person, and therefore, in this context, a Canaanite. It is not too bold to think that the first choir of singers for the Temple at Jerusalem was recruited from among non-Israelites. Lastly, since singers and door-keepers returned from the Exile (Esd 2: 41-42=Ne 7: 44-45), their offices must have existed before the Exile, though in those days they would not have been Levites. The 'keeper of the vestments' who is mentioned in 2 K 22: 14 was also, very probably, an employee of the Temple; there is a similar reference in 2 K 10: 22 to a keeper of the vestments in the temple of Baal at Samaria.

The door-keepers and the singers were presumably free men, but slaves

1. Cf. pp. 403-405.   2. Cf. pp. 121-122.

also were attached to the Temple. The list of the caravans returning from exile mentions, after the singers and the door-keepers, the '*n'thînîm*' or 'given' persons, and 'the descendants of the slaves of Solomon', and the two groups are counted together (Esd 2: 43-58=Ne 7: 46-60). There were 'given' men in the group led by Esdras also (Esd 8: 20). Some of their names are of foreign origin: these would be the descendants of the public slaves in the time of the monarchy,[1] when a number of such slaves were directed to work in the Temple. Esd 8: 20 says that David put them under the control of the Levites; Jos 9: 23 says they originated in the days of Josue, and the editor of the book knew that in his own day Gibeonites were still employed in the Temple as wood-cutters and water-carriers (Jos 9: 27; cf. Dt 29: 10). Ezechiel condemned this custom of using uncircumcised foreigners for the service of the Temple (Ez 44: 7-9).

Were there any women employed in the Temple? Ex 38: 8 speaks of the 'women who served at the entrance of the Tent of Reunion' and who gave their mirrors to make the bronze basin; the text is repeated in a gloss of 1 S 2: 22, which is not found in the Greek version. No one really knows how to interpret this information. The women who served at the Tent remind us of the young girls who used to guard the sacred pavilion among the pre-Islamic Arabs,[2] but there is no indication that they had any office to perform in public worship. Perhaps the late text in Ex is based on 2 K 23: 7, stripped of its syncretism: the verse in Kings tells how, as part of his reform, Josias dismantled the house of the sacred prostitutes which stood inside the Temple enclosure, and in which women used to weave veils for Ashera. This house, however, was one of those Canaanite intrusions into Yahwism of which we shall speak later. Another text cited as referring to women is the title of Ps 46: '*al 'ălāmôth*, which is sometimes translated 'for the young girls'; the theory is that there were women in the Temple choir, and in support of this, our attention is called to Esd 2: 65, which lists male and female singers in the caravan returning from Babylonia. In Esdras, however, the musicians are not listed with the staff of the Temple; they were layfolk, the servants of rich families in exile. And though the meaning of the title of the psalm is not certain, it is definitely not 'for young girls'; the same phrase is found in 1 Ch 15: 20, in connection with male singers, and must mean either a musical instrument or a key. It is even more daring to make the '*almah* of Is 7: 14 and the '*ălāmôth* of Ct 1: 3; 6: 8 persons connected with the liturgy. Though it is quite true that women are represented as singing and dancing at religious festivals (Ex 15: 20; Jg 21: 21; Ps 68: 26), this does not mean that they formed part of the staff regularly appointed for the cult. And the suggestion that there were women among the clergy of the Temple clashes with an important linguistic fact: there were priestesses in Assyria, priestesses and high priestesses in Phoenicia, where

1. Cf. p. 89.   2. Cf. p. 296.

they are known by the feminine of *kohen*; in the Minaean inscriptions, there was a feminine form of *lw'* which some scholars would link with the Hebrew *lewy*[1]; but Hebrew has no feminine noun corresponding to *kohen* or *lewy*[1]; no women ever held a place among the Israelite clergy.

There were, nevertheless, periods in which religious syncretism defiled the cult in the Temple, when men and women were brought there to practise something which Yahwism rejected with horror. The women who wove veils for Ashera lived in the 'house of the sacred prostitutes' (2 K 23: 7). Prostitutes of both sexes (*q'deshîm* and *q'deshôth*) were attached to Canaanite sanctuaries, and Israel had followed this practice (Os 4: 14; 1 K 14: 24; 15: 12; 22: 47). And in spite of the condemnation in Dt 23: 18-19, they had made their way even into the Temple at Jerusalem (2 K 23: 7; perhaps also Ez 8: 14).

7. Were there prophets attached to the Temple?

There is an inaccurate but widespread theory which asserts, without nuances, that the priests were the ministers of public worship, and the prophets its enemies. Some recent studies, reversing this judgment, have tried to show that there were some prophets attached to the Temple in an official capacity, 'cultic prophets'. In fact, the Bible often does mention the priests and the prophets together (2 K 23: 2; Jr 23: 11; Lm 2: 20; Os 4: 4-5 and especially Jr 26, where Jeremias is preaching against the Temple, in the Temple itself, in the presence of the priests, of the prophets and of all the people; he arouses opposition among the priests and the prophets, but he is defended by the people and by the magistrates). On the other hand, the Psalter contains certain prophetical compositions which were written to be recited or sung in the Temple, and these have been attributed to the cultic prophets. Furthermore, 1 Ch 25: 1 describes Asaph, Heman and Yeduthun, the ancestors of the singers, as 'prophets' (*n'bi'îm*); the passage goes on to say that they 'used to prophesy' and that Heman was the 'seer' of the king (1 Ch 25: 2, 3, 5). From this, some modern scholars have concluded that the singers in the post-exilic Temple were the successors of the prophetical guilds in the first Temple, and that the latter were themselves a continuation of those brotherhoods of prophets (*n'bi'îm*) which are mentioned so often in the stories of Samuel, of Saul and of Eliseus, sometimes in connection with a particular sanctuary. The supporters of this theory also appeal to analogies in neighbouring countries: Mesopotamian temples had their seers and ecstatics, and Canaan had its prophets. Since Jehu assembled the prophets and the priests of Baal in the temple of this god (2 K 10: 19), it is probable, they argue, that the Temple of Yahweh had its prophets too.

The more moderate among these writers admit that, apart from the anonymous compositions in the Psalter, these cultic prophets have left no

1. Cf. p. 369.

trace of their existence; some will even admit that they should be identified with the false prophets, the 'professionals' who are condemned by the Bible. Others, however, go much further. They hold that our prophetical books are to a large extent the works of cultic prophets: Isaias had his inaugural vision in the Temple, Jeremias and Ezechiel were both priests, and the Books of Joel, Habaquq, Nahum and Sophonias are, they claim, liturgical compositions.

This extreme position is quite untenable. We may grant that the Books of Nahum and of Habaquq are imitations of liturgical works, that the prophecy of Joel may have been delivered in some rather extraordinary cultic ceremony, and that the Lamentations attributed to Jeremias may have been used for religious services on the site of the ruined Temple during the Exile; but this does not make the prophets officials of the Temple. As far as the great Prophets are concerned, the question ought never to have been raised: Ezechiel is a priest, but all his prophetical activity took place after the ruin of the Temple; Jeremias was a priest, but since he belonged to the line of Ebyathar, he was debarred from any official service by the Sadoqites, and his behaviour in the Temple proves that he did not belong to the regular staff there; and the fact that Isaias received his vocation in the Temple does not imply that he held an office there.

The more moderate position, which does not count the literary prophets among the Temple staff, is itself far from certain. It is unscientific to apply indiscriminately to Israel everything which happened in neighbouring religions, especially where biblical evidence is lacking. As for 1 Ch 25: 1f., we have endeavoured to show above that the post-exilic singers traced their ancestry from the singers of the first Temple. The Chronicler is the only one who calls them *n'bi'îm*, and this term, it must be remembered, has various meanings: the Chronicler considers them as 'inspired' and he may have done so merely because the writing and singing of psalms required a kind of inspiration; in the very same passage, 'to prophesy' alternates with 'to sing' (1 Ch 25: 6). When the Chronicler wants to speak of true prophetical inspiration, he uses other words: Josaphat panicked during an invasion, and assembled the people in the Temple: then 'the Spirit of Yahweh came upon Yahaziel' and he spoke out like a great prophet. Yahaziel was one of the sons of Asaph, and the text is used by the champions of cultic prophets to prove that the singers were in fact cultic prophets. There is, however, a close parallel in 2 Ch 24: 20 where, in the Temple, 'the Spirit of God enveloped Zacharias', who then spoke like a second Jeremias; but Zacharias was the son of the priest Yehoyada, not one of the singers. In spite of the terms used in 1 Ch 25: 1f., there never was a class of prophets in the second Temple, and apparently the Chronicler himself did not think there had been such a class of men in the Temple before the Exile. Finally, the old brotherhoods of *n'bi'îm* are never mentioned in connection with the Temple in Jerusalem, and though they had connections with other sanctuaries, they did not, apparently, form part of the regular staff of those holy places.

The only point to be retained is that we should not pretend that the priests and the prophets were in complete opposition to each other. Prophets, whether true or false, had connections with the cult and with the Temple where it was celebrated. Conversely, the priests had something in common with the prophets, not so much because they gave oracles, for that function had died out,[1] but rather because they taught the people religion.[2] But it is impossible to prove that prophets were once attached to the Temple at Jerusalem, or that they formed a particular section of its clergy.

1. Cf. pp. 352-353.   2. Cf. pp. 353-355.

CHAPTER EIGHT

THE PRIESTHOOD AFTER THE EXILE

THE fall of Jerusalem brought disaster to the clergy of the Temple. The head priest, the second priest and the three keepers of the threshold, *i.e.* all the leading Temple officials, were taken prisoner and executed by Nabuchodonosor at Riblah (2 K 25: 18-21=Jr 52: 24-27; 39: 6). The two deportations affected first and foremost the population of Jerusalem (2 K 24: 14; 25: 11=Jr 52: 15; 39: 9). Most of the Sadoqite clergy and of the other persons in the service of the Temple were taken away into exile. Those members of the tribe of Levi who were not employed at the Temple (*e.g.* the family of Ebyathar) were deported with the rank and file of the population. We have shown above[1] how the *de facto* distinction between priests and Levites which resulted from Josias' reform became more clear-cut in Babylonia. On the other hand, the superiority of priests over Levites had no practical consequences during the Exile, because there was no sanctuary where priests could exercise their office.

The deportations did not, however, empty Palestine of all its inhabitants. Part of the tribe of Levi stayed on in Judah: the members of the line of Ebyathar or the Levites who lived up and down the country were counted among the common people whom the Chaldeans left to work the land (2 K 24: 14; 25: 12=Jr 52: 16; 39: 10). Moreover, the community in Judah still kept up its religious and liturgical life in some way; the people continued to frequent the provincial sanctuaries which had been reopened after the failure of Josias' reform, and the same syncretist cult was practised there as in the days before the reform. Some of the people, however, remained faithful to the legitimate forms of Yahwism: at least some of the Lamentations ascribed to Jeremias were probably used for liturgical assemblies in Judah: men fasted on the anniversary of the destruction of the Temple (Za 7: 1-3) and some even came to offer sacrifices amid its ruins (Jr 41: 4-5). Thus the Levite priests who stayed in Palestine found work once again, now that the monopoly of the Sadoqites no longer existed.

Such was the situation, in Babylonia and in Judah, and it must be kept in mind in order to understand how the priesthood was reconstituted in Jerusalem after the Return.

1. Cf. pp. 364-366.

1. *Priests and Levites down to the period of Esdras and Nehemias*

In the first caravans to return to Jerusalem after the Exile (according to the statistics in Esd 2: 36–39 and Ne 7: 39–42), there were 4,289 priests divided into four families, called after Yedayah, Immer, Pashehur and Harim. The family of Yedayah was the smallest in number, but it is named first because Josue, the first high priest after the Exile, belonged to it; the second family is named after the Immer mentioned in Jr 20: 1. The heads of the other two families are not referred to elsewhere in the Bible. By contrast, these first caravans brought with them only 74 Levites (Esd 2: 40; Ne 7: 43).

The same disproportion between priests and Levites is found in the caravan led by Esdras. He assembled a group containing two families of priests (no number is given, Esd 8: 2), but not a single Levite, and it was only after an urgent appeal that he mustered 38 (Esd 8: 15–19). Two reasons explain the small numbers of Levites in these caravans: first, far more priests than Levites had been deported to Babylonia, and secondly, those Levites who had gone into exile had little inclination to return to Judaea, where discrimination would be practised in favour of the priests, and where they would become mere 'servants of the Temple' (Esd 8: 17).

Though the biblical texts give no precise information about the origin of the four priestly families which returned, all four of them very probably claimed Sadoqite ancestry. Jr 20: 1 proves that this was true of the family of Immer; again, Josue, who belonged to the family of Yedayah, was the son of Yehosadaq (Ag 1: 1), and therefore, according to 1 Ch 5: 40, the grandson of Serayah, the last Sadoqite high priest before the Exile (2 K 25: 18); and there is no reason to doubt the value of this text in Chronicles. Besides, it was principally the Sadoqite priests who had been deported. When Esdras arrived in Jerusalem, the entire priesthood there was drawn from these four great families still (Esd 10: 18–22), and it is presumably by a mere accident of textual tradition that only three of them (Yedayah, Immer and Pashehur) are mentioned in the list of Jerusalem's population compiled under Nehemias (Ne 11: 10–14; note that the family of Yedayah is here expressly related to Sadoq).

By contrast, the priests in Esdras' caravan were of mixed origin: one group was descended from Phinehas and another one from Ithamar (Esd 8: 2). Phinehas was the son of Eleazar, the ancestor of Sadoq, according to the genealogies in 1 Ch 5: 30–34; 6: 35–38. The descendants of Ebyathar had claimed Ithamar as ancestor (1 Ch 24: 3; cf. 1 S 22: 20). Thus, when this caravan reached Jerusalem, that branch which was rival to the Sadoqites at last recovered its right to exercise the priesthood. Eleazar and Ithamar were both sons of Aaron, and we shall see[1] shortly how, after the time of Esdras

1. Cf. pp. 394-397.

the expression 'sons of Aaron' replaced the terms 'sons of Sadoq': both phrases mean simply 'priests'.

In the early caravans, there were only three families of Levites (Esd 2: 40; Ne 7: 43). Two other families returned with Esdras. In the meantime, the number of Levites increased by the integration into these families of others who had not gone into exile; other names appear in the account of the rebuilding of the city walls under Nehemias, and the entire district of Qeilah seems to have been occupied by Levites (Ne 3: 17-18); the famous pledge taken by the whole community (Ne 10: 10-14) was signed by the heads of the three families mentioned in Esd 2: 40, but it bore the signature of fourteen other Levites as well. The list of the population of Jerusalem compiled under Nehemias gives 284 Levites resident in the city (Ne 11: 18), apart from others who lived in the province (Ne 11: 20). One writer has recently suggested that the list in Ne 11: 25b-35, cf. 36, represents the places where these Levites lived, but all one can say for certain is that the list mentions three towns (Hebron, Geba and Anathoth) which also occur in the list of Levitical towns in Jos 21.

In the caravans, the singers are all called sons of Asaph; they are listed separately from the Levites, and are more numerous than them (Esd 2: 41; Ne 7: 44). The priests and the Levites settled in Jerusalem, but the singers and the door-keepers and the 'given' men went to live in their own home towns (Esd 2: 70; Ne 7: 72). This distinction between singers and Levites is maintained in the authentic parts of Esdras' account (Esd 7: 7, 24; 10: 23-24), and also, it would seem, in Nehemias' memoir about his second mission (Ne 13: 5). The other passages in the Books of Esdras and Nehemias, in which the singers are included among the Levites, were either edited by the Chronicler, or inserted by a later glossator. There is only one text which causes any difficulty: in the list of the population of Jerusalem, the singers are mentioned among the Levites (Ne 11: 17), and though this list is not part of Nehemias' memoir, it is a trustworthy document from some archives, contemporaneous with the events it describes. Perhaps it was retouched on this point, or perhaps singers and Levites were then beginning to amalgamate. This solution would also explain why, in Ne 13: 10, the word 'Levites' is explained as 'the Levites and the singers who did the work'.

The integration of the door-keepers into the body of Levites took place even more slowly. The door-keepers who returned with the first caravans (Esd 2: 42; Ne 7: 45) are listed separately from the Levites and from the singers; there were six families of door-keepers, all small in number, and this denotes that they did not have the social standing of the singers, who together formed one large family. These door-keepers have nothing in common with the three 'keepers of the threshold' in the monarchic period; in fact, we never hear of these three officials after the Exile. No door-keepers are mentioned in the caravan of Esdras, but they are mentioned, along with the Levites and the singers, in the memoirs of Esdras and of Nehemias, in the passages cited in the last paragraph; but even in those texts where the singers are included among the Levites (e.g. Ne 11: 19), the door-keepers are listed apart. They are, however, named along with the Levite-singers in the editorial passage in Ne 12: 25; this is the Chronicler's point of view, for in his day the door-keepers definitely belonged to the Levitical class.

We have already spoken of the 'given' men and of 'the descendants of the slaves of Solomon' in reference to the staff of the Temple in the monarchic period.[1] The number of these who joined the caravans returning from exile was relatively large (392 in the first caravans, Esd 2: 58; Ne 7: 60, and 220 in the caravan led by Esdras, Esd 8: 20); yet the number of persons in each family was relatively small; these two facts would indicate that they were not well-off in Babylonia and that they hoped to better their fortunes by returning to Palestine. They must certainly have been integrated into the people of Israel, or Esdras would never have accepted them for the service of the Temple (cf. Ez 44: 7-9). They were housed on the hill of Ophel (Ne 11: 21), and near the Temple there stood a house which the 'given' men shared with the Temple merchants (Ne 3: 31). They are never again mentioned but it is doubtful whether more than a few individuals were ever absorbed into the Levites.

More probably, the institution itself went out of existence, and the work was done by the Levites: hence later ages considered the Levites as having been 'given' to the priests for the service of the sanctuary (Nb 3: 9; 8: 19).

2. The Levites in the work of the Chronicler

After Esdras and Nehemias, more than a century passes before we have any further information about the status of the clergy in Jerusalem. Our next source is the work of the Chronicler, the author of 1 and 2 Ch, Esd and Ne; he probably composed his work about the year 300 B.C., but it was retouched at a later date. The longest additions to his work are 1 Ch 1-9 and 23-27, all of which chapters are particularly important for a study of the priesthood. All the information we can gather must be picked out of this great work which traces the history of Israel down to the restoration after the Exile; what makes it difficult is that the author ascribes to ancient times situations and ideas which were unheard of until much later. Indeed, he includes ideas from his own day, and ascribes them to ancient times; to make it worse, the annotators of his work have added ideas and customs from their day, too, and backdated them as well. In the period which separates the memoirs of Esdras and Nehemias from the work of the Chronicler, several changes took place which are of interest to us here. The Priestly laws of the Pentateuch were put into practice, with modifica-

1. Cf. p. 383.

tions as the occasion demanded, and certain changes were made in the rules governing the clergy; the changes took place gradually, but the different stages of development have not been recorded. All these factors explain why it is so difficult to reconstruct a coherent picture out of the work of the Chronicler, and we shall restrict ourselves to the broad outlines. Since the distinction between Levites and priests at this period is an undisputed fact, we shall treat of the priests in the next section, and begin with the Levites.

Anyone who reads Chronicles alongside the Books of Samuel and Kings (which cover the same period) will be struck at once by the importance which the Chronicler gives to the Levites. They have the principal rôle in looking after the Ark of the Covenant (1 Ch 15-16); their duties in the Temple are laid down even before it is built, and there too they play the principal part (1 Ch 23-26). They are the predominant figures in the religious reforms of Ezechias (2 Ch 29-31) and of Josias (2 Ch 34-35). But even apart from these long texts, they are found intervening everywhere, whether their action is relevant or not. The attention paid to genealogies, which was already showing itself in the days of Esdras, develops even further. The ancestry of all the Levites is traced to the three sons of Levi, Gershom, Qehath and Merari (1 Ch 6: 1-32; 23: 6-24), in perfect harmony with the Priestly tradition recorded in Nb 3-4; even people like Samuel, who, in the pre-exilic books, had no Levitical ancestry, are given a place in these genealogies.

(a) *The Levites and the Ark*. The theory of the original Chronicler was that the Levites were primarily meant for the service of the Ark: 'the Ark of God may be carried by Levites only' (1 Ch 15: 2). They looked after it at Jerusalem until the Temple was built (1 Ch 16: 4f.) while the priests remained at Gibeon with the Tent (1 Ch 16: 39). The Levites (not the priests, as in 1 K 8: 3) carried the Ark into Solomon's Temple (2 Ch 5: 4; and cf. also 2 Ch 35: 3). This idea does not originate from the Priestly tradition, for in this the Levites are connected with the Tent (Nb 1: 50; 3: 8); its source is Deuteronomy (Dt 10: 8), to which 1 Ch 15: 2 certainly refers. It is a way of giving the support of tradition to Levitical claims: since the Levites carried the Ark into the Temple, their presence in the Temple is in accordance with the Law, and therefore they have rights there. In the additions made to the Chronicler's work, this claim has been obscured by the Priestly tradition; the Priestly editors say that the Levites carried the Tent and that they were under the authority of the sons of Aaron (1 Ch 23: 26-28).

(b) *The singers*. Once the Ark had been laid to rest in the Tent which David made for it, and later in the Temple which Solomon built, the Levites had no more work to do as porters (1 Ch 23: 25-26; cf. 2 Ch 35: 3). David set some of them apart for choral service (1 Ch 16: 4). Thus the singers in the second Temple, who were definitely counted among the Levites, traced their foundation back to David, the first singer of Israel. Indeed, one of the dominant features of the Chronicler is this interest in sacred music. Singing had come to occupy an important place in the liturgy, and the status of the singers had risen as a result. The body of singers had grown larger, too. Only one group, that of Asaph, had returned from exile (Esd 2: 41; Ne 7: 44), but the Chronicler mentions three families of singers in the time of David: Asaph's family was connected with the Ark, and the two families of Heman and Yeduthun (or Ethan) were employed at the sanctuary of Gibeon (1 Ch 16: 37, 41). This would seem to imply that the guilds of Heman and Yeduthun were descended from Temple singers of monarchic times[1] who had not gone into exile; in the Chronicler's day, all three families were counted as Levites.

The later additions to the book are meant to show the legitimacy of the institution of singers, and to give a more exact definition of their rights. The three head singers under David have their ancestry traced to the three sons of Levi: Heman is the descendant of Qehath, Asaph of Gershom, Ethan (Yeduthun) of Merari (1 Ch 6: 18-32). In 1 Ch 25, the sons of Asaph, Heman and Yeduthun (v. 1) or, as verse 6 has it, the sons of Asaph, Yeduthun and Heman, are divided into twenty-four classes, each composed of twelve members. The artificial character of this list, referring to the time of David, is too obvious for words, and the most curious feature in it is that the names of Heman's nine last sons (v. 4) when put together, form a little poem, a fragment of a psalm. Note, too, that the names of the ancestors are not always in the same order; this variation reflects rivalry between the different groups. The sons of Asaph, who had been in exile, were given seniority, but the sons of Heman also claimed it (cf. 1 Ch 6: 18; 15: 17, 19) on the grounds that they were descended from Qehath, from whom Aaron and the priests were also descended, and that they formed the largest group.

(c) *The door-keepers.* Eventually, the door-keepers too were shown to be Levites. The six families which returned from the Exile were not Levites (Esd 2: 42; Ne 7: 45; cf. Ne 11: 19), but when Chronicles is repeating the list given in Ne 11, it gives the door-keepers a Levitical ancestor, Qorah (cf. 1 Ch 6: 7): from the days in the desert, says 1 Ch 9: 19, the door-keepers kept watch over the Tent and the camp. Apart from the Qorahites (1 Ch 26: 1f.), there was another class of door-keepers, also Levites, called the Merarites (1 Ch 26: 10 f., 19). Between these two classes, 1 Ch 26: 4-8 lists the sons of Obed-Edom. Though this man was not an Israelite, the Ark had been left in his house (2 S 6: 11), and 1 Ch 15: 24 says that David appointed him a door-keeper in the service of the Ark; 1 Ch 16: 38 adds that he was a son of Yeduthun, and therefore a Levite. A group of door-keepers in the second temple claimed to be descended from him.

But the claims of these door-keepers did not stop there; they aspired to

1. Cf. p. 382.

the position of singers. Now, since Yeduthun had been a singer, it was natural that his son too, should have been a singer; at least, this is what 1 Ch 15: 21 and 16: 5 suppose. The Qorahites disregarded the ill-defined border between the two classes, and promoted themselves: they are listed as singers in 2 Ch 20: 19, and in the titles of the Psalms, no less than twelve are attributed to the sons of Qorah.

(d) *Other Levitical functions.* The reader will have noticed that much of our information about the singers, and almost all our information about the door-keepers, comes from passages inserted into the Books of Chronicles after the original work was completed. These passages describe the very end of a long development, and the number of references cited may mislead a person into thinking that the Levites were merely singers or door-keepers.

According to 1 Ch 23: 3-5, the Levites mentioned in David's census were employed as follows: 24,000 looked after the Temple's affairs, 4,000 were employed as clerks and judges, 4,000 were door-keepers, and 4,000 'praised Yahweh on musical instruments'. What interests us here is not the figures (which are fantastic), but the proportion between the figures: the great majority of Levites were engaged in the service of the Temple, and only a relatively small proportion of them were musicians; it would be quite arbitrary to say that the first class were singers and the second the accompanists. This conclusion is confirmed by 1 Ch 23: 25-32 (though the text belongs to another tradition, since the age at which Levites begin service is here fixed at twenty years, not thirty, as in verse 3): the Levites will no longer have to carry the Ark, since Yahweh will henceforth dwell in Jerusalem, but they are to do all the work in the Temple, and their choral duties are mentioned only at the end.

The Levites, therefore, were placed at the service of the sons of Aaron (1 Ch 23: 28), or at the service of the faithful, according to 2 Ch 35: 3-6 (a parallel text, but it refers to the unusual circumstances at the celebration of the great Passover under Josias). They are responsible for the administration of the Temple (1 Ch 9: 26; 26: 20f.; 2 Ch 24: 6, 11; 31: 11-15), but they have duties in connection with worship also: they are to purify the holy things, to prepare the shew-bread and vegetable offerings (1 Ch 23: 28-29); they are to take charge of the slaughtering and of the carving up of victims (2 Ch 29: 34; 35: 11). Thus their work touches on the domain reserved to the priests, and there must have been conflicts, though they are not mentioned explicitly in Chronicles. The story of Qorah and his followers in Nb 16 clearly reflects this tension (cf. especially Nb 16: 8-11): Qorahites were always the same, full of intrigue, battling their way forward, first as door-keepers, then as singers,[1] and finally even usurping Priestly functions!

David's census of the Levites included clerks and judges also, according to 1 Ch 23: 4. These clerks could have been secretaries, for the Temple

1. *V. supra.*

would certainly have needed secretaries for its administration (cf. 2 Ch 34: 13), and a letter of Antiochus III cited by Josephus (*Ant.* XII, iii, 3) lists the categories of the clergy in Jerusalem as 'the priests, the Temple scribes and the sacred singers'. But the *shôṭrîm* whom Chronicles lists alongside the judges were clerks of the courts, assistant officials,[1] and they were appointed for 'outside' duties in Israel (1 Ch 26: 29). This last phrase does not mean Temple affairs unconnected with worship (as it does in Ne 11: 16), but affairs which have nothing to do with the Temple. We may compare them with the Levites whom Josaphat appointed to judge cases along with the priests and the elders (2 Ch 19: 8); indeed, Josephus presumes, in *Ant.* IV, viii, 14, that every town had a tribunal consisting of seven judges and fourteen Levite assistants.

Lastly, the Levites were also teachers. The Chronicler first refers to this privilege in the report of Esdras (Ne 8: 7, 9). He attributes the same rôle to them under Josaphat, saying that the king sent them out 'armed with the Law of Yahweh, to teach Judah'; the group he sent comprised eight Levites and only two priests (2 Ch 17: 8-9). In 2 Ch 35: 3, the Levites are called 'men who have understanding', *i.e.* knowledge of the things of God.

The Chronicler's work, then, gives wide testimony to the ever-increasing influence of the Levites in the second Temple. It seems, too, that their struggle for emancipation continued in the last centuries before the Christian era. In the Apocrypha, *e.g.* in the Book of Jubilees or in the Testament of Levi, the figure of their great ancestor is exalted: in these books, it is no longer Aaron but Levi himself who was appointed priest by God, and all his sons after him hold this rank. From the historical point of view, this new attitude may have been connected in some way with the eviction of the Sadoqites by John Hyrcanus, who himself came from a Priestly family of secondary importance; there is no way of knowing, however, whether the general body of Levites ever really profited from his action. Nevertheless, they continued their intrigues to the end: some years before the ruin of the Temple, the singers persuaded Agrippa II to let them wear linen vestments, as the priests did, and the other Levites who served in the Temple were all promoted to the rank of singers (*Ant.* XX, ix, 6).

3. '*Sons of Sadoq*' and '*Sons of Aaron*'

From Solomon to the Exile, the descendants of Sadoq provided the priesthood of the first Temple, and in Ezechiel, the priests are always called 'sons of Sadoq'. Yet in the priestly documents of the Pentateuch, in Chronicles and in some post-exilic Psalms, they are called 'sons of Aaron'. In the present section we shall try to explain what this change of name signified, and how it came about.

In the oldest traditions of the Pentateuch, Aaron is a rather hazy figure at

1. Cf. p. 155.

first, but little by little his character becomes more defined; unfortunately, it is impossible to make a clear distinction between the earlier and later sources, and to assign the precise order in which the texts should follow one another. Aaron was Moses' brother, and he was called 'the Levite'; he was Moses' spokesman before the people (Ex 4: 14-16) and before Pharaoh (Ex 7: 1f.); he even worked miracles (Ex 7: 9, 19; 8: 1, etc.). He stands at Moses' side during the battle against the Amelekites (Ex 17: 8, 10), at the meeting with Jethro (Ex 18: 12) and at Sinai (Ex 19: 24; 24: 1, 9). In these traditions, however, he is never once mentioned as a priest or as an ancestor of priests. On the contrary, he opposes Moses on religious questions, by making a golden calf (Ex 32; cf. Dt 9: 20), and by leading a revolt in company with his sister Miriam (Nb 12).

In the Priestly tradition of the Pentateuch, Aaron is quite a different character: here he is the first high priest of Israel, his sons are the only lawful priests, and the other members of the tribe of Levi are given to them as servants (Ex 28-29; 39; Lv 8-10; Nb 16-18). This new picture of Aaron was built around the old tradition of Aaron 'the Levite', and it marks the triumph of a trend which had to overcome considerable opposition: the stories in Ex 32 and Nb 12, with their unfavourable account of his actions, are an echo of this opposition.

The differing accounts of Aaron's rôle during the Exodus reflect a struggle between different groups of priests; unfortunately, we cannot trace this development in detail, so we must fall back on hypotheses. One suggestion, which has recently been put forward in an extreme form, is that 'sons of Aaron', is a name for the priests who served the sanctuary at Bethel, where men worshipped a golden calf, as the Israelites had done at Sinai. The sanctuary at Bethel, it continues, was spared destruction after the fall of Jerusalem, and its priests stayed on there; they continued to exercise their ministry, and so became the dominant religious force in Palestine during the Exile. Those priests who returned from Babylonia had to reckon with the group at Bethel, and the latter would have instigated all kinds of obstacles to the rebuilding of the Temple; finally, Za 7: 1-3 means that men were sent from Jerusalem to consult the priests of Bethel, who were in the end recognized by the Sadoqites, on condition that the Sadoqites should retain their precedence. The foundations on which this theory rests are far from solid: the text of Za 7: 1-3 is undoubtedly obscure, but it certainly does not bear the meaning given to it here; there is not a single fact to prove that the sanctuary of Bethel took on a new lease of life after the reform of Josias, or that it was active during the Exile; and the connection between the cult practised at Bethel and the episode of Aaron's golden calf can be interpreted in a number of ways.[1]

A more moderate and more widespread theory is that the priests who

1. Cf. p. 334.

returned from Babylonia had to amalgamate with a non-Sadoqite group which had maintained continuity of worship in Jerusalem during the Exile; this latter group claimed descent from Aaron. Against this, the only evidence in our texts would seem to indicate that the Aaronite group was formed in Babylonia, not in Jerusalem. We have seen[1] that the first caravans to return included priests who were probably Sadoqites, and the evidence given in the Books of Esdras, Aggaeus and Zacharias about the restoration of worship in Jerusalem contains no trace of any opposition from a non-Sadoqite group which was already in possession of the Temple. The first time two different groups of priests returned from Babylonia was when Esdras brought with him the families of Phinehas and of Ithamar (Esd 8: 2). This was the period when everyone was preoccupied with genealogies: the Sadoqites priests traced their ancestry back to Phinehas (cf. 1 Ch 5: 30-34), to whom God had promised an everlasting priesthood among his descendants (Nb 25: 10-13), and Phinehas was the son of Eleazar, to whom Aaron's priesthood had been transferred by God himself (Nb 20: 24-26). The only explanation for the references to Phinehas in Esd 8: 2 is that at some date between Zorobabel and Esdras, the Sadoqites had begun to claim Aaron as their ancestor. They probably did so in order to counteract the claims of another group of priests who were tracing their ancestry back to a far more ancient and far more noble figure than David's priest, Sadoq, i.e. to a near relative of Aaron 'the Levite', Moses' brother. This group of rivals can be identified as the family of Ebyathar, who represented the house of Eli and who boasted (rightly, it seems) of their Levitical origin. The verses inserted in 1 S 2: 27-36 were certainly written before Esdras, and may date from shortly after the reform of Josias; and this text states that the house of Eli had been chosen as priests when the Israelites were still in Egypt. Only the name of their ancestor was lacking, and once Aaron had been acknowledged as the first high priest of Israel, they claimed descent from him. Eventually an agreement was reached between the descendants of Sadoq and those of Ebyathar; the former traced their ancestry to Eleazar (or to his son Phinehas), and the latter to Ithamar.

They reached this agreement in Babylonia, and Esdras gave it his blessing by taking with him representatives of both the great Priestly families. But this does not mean that there was no parallel movement in Palestine, where descendants of Ebyathar had stayed on through the Exile, and to which descendants of Sadoq had returned after the Exile; similarly, there may have been a combined movement both in Palestine and in the land of Exile; but the agreement was actually concluded in Babylonia. When Esdras reached Jerusalem, he found the Priestly offices held by the same families as had held them in the first days after the return (Esd 10: 18-22 and Esd 2: 36-39). The sons of Aaron did not occupy any positions at that time.

1. Cf. p. 388.

After Esdras' reform, the situation was straightened out, and from that time onwards the two families shared the priesthood, which thus became the privilege of all the sons of Aaron. Their titles to this office are given in the work of the Chronicler in his genealogies of Levi and of Aaron (1 Ch 5: 27-29; 6: 34-38, and above all in the organization he ascribes to David, 1 Ch 24: 1-6): this last text states that all Aaron's sons were priests, though the two eldest, Nadab and Abihu, died childless in punishment for a crime against the cult: hence the two youngest, Eleazar and Ithamar, inherited the priesthood (cf. Lv 10: 1-3; Nb 3: 1-4). Sadoq was a descendant of Eleazar, and Ebyathar a descendant of Ithamar. David divided the work between the two families by instituting twenty-four classes of priests; sixteen belonged to the family of Eleazar, which was the more numerous, and eight to the family of Ithamar. The following passage (1 Ch 24: 7-18) gives a list of these twenty-four classes, but the text was retouched in the Maccabean period, for the first class is that of Yehoyarib, the ancestor of the Maccabees (1 M 2: 1), who is never previously mentioned in an authentic text.

Thenceforward all the priests could be called 'sons of Aaron', but the Sadoqites still retained a certain distinction: their ancestor Eleazar is presented as more noble than Ithamar, since he is the only priest mentioned in the stories about the end of the desert wanderings (Nb 25: 11; 26: 1; 31 passim). According to the Chronicler (Esd 7: 1-5), Esdras himself was a Sadoqite, and the family filled twice as many classes as the sons of Ithamar. Finally, they continued to provide the high priest down to the time of Antiochus Epiphanes.

4. The high priest

(a) *His titles.* We said above that the title 'high priest' (*hakkohen haggadôl*) was not used to indicate the head of the priesthood before the Exile. We must now emphasize that even after the Exile it was used only rarely, and that it did not become the regular title until very long afterwards.

In the Law of Holiness, which is the oldest part of Leviticus, the head of the priesthood is called *hakkohen haggadôl me'ehaw*, i.e. 'the greatest priest among his brothers' (Lv 21: 10); the rest of the phrase is an addition (see below), but this formula is a description, not a title. The formula is never once found in Ezechiel, and only three times in the entire Pentateuch, in a passage belonging to its last redaction (the ruling on cities of refuge: Nb 35: 25, 28 and 32? cf. the Greek). The 'high priests' in the desert, Aaron, Eleazar and Phinehas, are never called by any name other than 'the priest'. In the Chronicler, the title is found only four times: 2 Ch 34: 9 uses it of Hilqiyyah before the Exile, Ne 3: 1, 20 and 13: 28 use it of Elyashib. In contrast to this, 'high priest' is found eight times in Aggaeus and in Zacharias, and it refers on every occasion to Josue, the son of Yehosadaq, and the contemporary of Zorobabel (Ag 1: 1, 12, 14; 2: 2, 4; Za 3: 1, 8;

6: 11). Lastly, the Hebrew text of Si 50: 1 eulogizes Simon 'the high priest', who lived about 200 B.C. That is the complete list of references in the Hebrew Bible. The title, therefore, certainly existed from the moment of the return from exile. A papyrus from Elephantine, dated 408 B.C., refers to the high priest of Jerusalem, Yehohanan, as *kahna rabba*, which is the Aramaic equivalent of *kohen gadôl*. On the other hand, the term was rarely used, and people usually said simply 'the priest', as they had done before the Exile, and as the Priestly texts of the Pentateuch have it. It is only in the Mishnah and in the Talmudic treatise that the title is commonly used, either in Hebrew (*kohen gadôl*) or in Aramaic (*kahna rabba*).

It is interesting to compare with this the usage of the Greek Bible: the older books of the Septuagint always translate *hakkohen haggadol* by ὁ ἱερεὺς ὁ μέγας. But in the Books of Maccabees, this literal rendering is replaced by a technical term, ἀρχιερεύς, which is regularly applied to all the high priests; the New Testament and Philo follow the same practice. Now, the word ἀρχιερεύς is a term from the Seleucid chancery, and denotes a man whom the king appointed as head of the state religion in a particular district or town. The Hellenistic Jews used the word in this official sense: the first instance of it, in 1 M 10: 20, occurs in a letter of Alexander Balas to Jonathan: 'This day we appoint thee high priest (ἀρχιερεύς) of thy nation'. Greek-speaking Jews continued to use this pagan title when referring to the high priest, and this practice brought the terms *kohen gadôl* and *kahna rabba* into common usage, as the Hebrew and Aramaic equivalents of the Greek word.

The post-exilic books contain a few rare examples of other terms denoting the high priest. In 1 Ch 9: 11; 2 Ch 31: 13; Ne 11: 11, he is the *nagîd* of the Temple. In the language of the period, this word is used of officials and of men of high rank, but in these three texts it may preserve its loftier meaning of a prince or a leader appointed by God.[1] It certainly does have this latter meaning in Dn 9: 25; 11: 22, where the expressions 'Anointed Prince' and 'Prince of the Covenant' refer to the high priest.

The phrase 'Anointed Prince' corresponds with another title of the high priest: in Lv 4: 3, 5, 16 he is called *hakkohen hammashiah*, 'the anointed priest' (cf. Lv 6: 13, 15; 16: 32); an addition to the primitive text of Lv 21: 10 speaks of the priest 'upon whose head anointing oil is poured'. This title brings us to the ritual of investiture.

(b) *The investiture of the high priest*. In the priestly documents of the Pentateuch (Ex 29: 4-7 and Lv 8: 6-12), the consecration of Aaron is described in three stages: purification, clothing and anointing. First he washes himself, then they clothe him with the tunic, with the cloak, with the ephod and with the breast-plate or pectoral: next they place upon his head a turban (*misnepheth*), on the front of which the holy *nezer* is fixed. (We shall discuss

1. Cf. p. 70.

the meaning of *nezer* in a moment.) Finally, anointing oil is poured over his head.

Ex 28 and 39 give a detailed description of the high priest's vestments. We shall confine ourselves to what they say about the turban. In Ex 28: 36, the decoration on the turban is called *ṣiṣ*, not *nezer*, whereas in Ex 39: 30, *ṣiṣ* and *nezer* are used together, as in Lv 8: 9. The basic meaning of *nezer* is 'consecration', and here 'a sign of consecration'. The usual translation 'diadem' is inaccurate, for the shape of this 'sign of consecration' is indicated by the other noun *ṣiṣ*, which means 'a flower'. Thus the high priest wore above his forehead, on his turban, a golden flower, as a symbol of life and of salvation. This flower had on it the inscription 'consecrated to Yahweh' (Ex 28: 36; 39: 30); it was, as it were, the seal of his consecration.

It is most interesting to compare these texts with Za 3: 1-9, which describes the consecration of Josue, the first high priest after the Exile. Here, too, a ceremony of purification precedes the ceremony of clothing: when Josue is stripped of his dirty clothes, his 'impiety' is taken away; thereupon he is clothed in rich vestments, and they place a turban (*ṣaniph*) upon his head; finally, a stone is placed in front of him, upon which Yahweh himself is going to engrave an inscription. Though the interpretation of this last detail is debated, the most probable meaning is that the stone was a precious stone which had to be engraved before the high priest began to wear it. The parallelism with the priestly documents is striking: *miṣnepheth* and *ṣaniph* mean respectively a flower engraved like a seal, and a precious stone inscribed in some way.

Josue's consecration, however, stops at his clothing: similarly, in Nb 20: 26-28, Eleazar is installed as Aaron's successor once he has been clothed in the vestments which the first high priest had worn. In both instances, there is no anointing. Some authors would see a reference to anointing in the subsequent vision of Zacharias (Za 4: 1-14), where Zorobabel and Josue are represented by two olive trees; the angel explains that they are 'the two sons of oil'. This is sometimes translated as 'the two anointed ones', on the grounds that Josue had been anointed priest, and that the writer hoped Zorobabel would be anointed king; but such a translation presupposes that a rather difficult problem of exegesis has been solved in a particular way. In fact, it is unlikely that the text refers to anointing at all; the expression 'sons of oil' is never used anywhere else for 'anointed one', and the word used for oil is not the one used for anointing-oil. Moreover, Zorobabel was an official appointed by the king of Persia, and he was never anointed as king; nor is there any other text to indicate that Josue was anointed as high priest. Indeed, the vision in Za 3 would seem to indicate, by its silence, that he was not.

It is hard to say when the rite of anointing was introduced. Ex 29: 7 and the passages of Leviticus cited above presuppose it, but we cannot say for certain when these passages were edited: they do not belong to the very last redaction of the Pentateuch, in which all priests are said to be anointed[1] (though this prescription, it would seem, was never put into practice). In all probability, the custom of anointing the high priest was already practised from the end of the Persian period, though the first written evidence we can date with certainty comes much later. The texts are Si 45: 15, in its eulogy of Aaron, Dn 9: 25-26, which calls Onias III the 'Anointed Prince' and 'The Anointed', and 2 M 1: 10, where the dynasty of high priests is called the race of anointed priests. Nor do we know when the practice died out; it may have lasted until the end of the dynasty of the Hasmonean king-priests. Certainly it was not practised any more in the Herodian and Roman period, for in those days the sole rite used at the installation was the clothing. The rabbis no longer remembered the time when the high priests were anointed; according to some of them, the practice was suppressed under Josias.

(c) *The high priest and the idea of kingship.* These rites of investiture (accompanied by anointing) made the high priests of post-exilic times rather like the kings before the Exile. Anointing was the principal ceremony in the coronation, for it made the king the Anointed of Yahweh.[2] The clothing worn by the high priest is equally significant: the turban (*saniph*) which Josue receives is a royal head-dress in Is 62: 3; Si (Hebrew text) 11: 5; 40: 4; 46: 16, and the *misnepheth* mentioned in the Priestly texts is worn by the prince in Ez 21: 31. In addition, Si 40: 4 says that the king's *saniph* had on it a *sis, i.e.* a flower as worn in front of the turban by the high priest. *Nezer,* the equivalent of *sis,* is a sign of royal rank in 2 S 1: 10; 2 K 11: 12; Ps 89: 40, and the meaning we ascribed to *nezer* is confirmed by a royal psalm (Ps 132: 18): 'his *nezer* shall blossom'. Last of all, the breast-plate covered in precious stones (Ex 28: 15f.) recalls the rich breast-plate worn by the Pharaohs, and by the kings of Syria in imitation of them, as the finds at Byblos show; it is quite likely that the kings of Israel also wore a similar breast-plate.

Once the monarchy had disappeared, all this royal paraphernalia was appropriated to the high priest. This does not mean merely, or mainly, that the high priest inherited the cultic privileges of the king, for we have proved that the king's rights in the exercise of worship were far from unrestricted. What it does mean is that the high priest became the head of the nation, and its representative before God, as the king had been in days gone by. But it was only gradually that this idea of the high priest as head of the nation took shape. We have seen that at first he was not anointed, and in the original text of Za 6: 9-14, the crown ('*atarah*)—a royal ornament, cf. 2 S 12: 30; Jr 13: 18; Ez 21: 31—was destined for Zorobabel; he was to be clothed with royal majesty and he was to be enthroned with the priest

---

1. The texts are cited on p. 105.   2. Cf. pp. 103-106.

standing at his right hand. Later on, these royal prerogatives were transferred to Josue, and his name was substituted in the text for that of Zorobabel.

Under the Hasmoneans, this ideal became a reality: the eight heads of this dynasty, from Jonathan to Antigonus, were both high priests and heads of the Jewish nation. They also took the title of king, probably from the time of Aristobulus I (104-103 B.C.).

(d) *The succession of high priests*. The advent of the Hasmoneans marked a turning-point in the history of the priesthood from other points of view also. The Chronicler has inserted into the Book of Nehemias (Ne 12: 10-11) a list of the high priests from Josue to Yaddua, *i.e.* down to the time of Darius II (cf. Ne 12: 22), *viz.* until about 400 B.C. (Darius died in 405 B.C.). This list may be incomplete, and it presumes, too, that the succession always passed from father to son; yet it does collect together the information given in Nehemias' memoir, and the last name but one (Yohanan) is given in the papyrus of Elephantine as the name of the high priest in 411 and again in 408.

There is no information extant about the following century and a half. After this, Josephus and the Book of Maccabees allow us to trace the line of Onias' descendants, from Onias I in the middle of the 3rd century B.C. to Simon the Just, eulogized in Si 50: 1f., and to Onias III, who held the office of high priest when Antiochus Epiphanes succeeded to the throne in 175 B.C. He was deposed by the new king and replaced by his brother Jason, and three years later, treacherously assassinated (2 M 3-4).

There is no reason to doubt that the high priesthood remained in the Sadoqite family until the death of Onias III, its last legitimate representative. His brother Jason obtained the post by bribing Antiochus and by introducing Greek customs into Jerusalem (2 M 4: 7-20). Thereafter, the office became a prize in the troubled politics of the period. Jason was dismissed when Menelaus made a higher bid (2 M 4: 23-26): this Menelaus was of the tribe of Benjamin, according to the Greek text of 2 M 3: 4; cf. 4: 23, and therefore not a priest at all; more probably, he belonged to the class of Bilga, as the Vetus Latina reads, *i.e.* he was a priest belonging to a family of secondary importance (Ne 12: 5, 18). It was the intruder Menelaus who arranged the murder of Onias III (2 M 4: 30-38); once he had sold his services to Antiochus, he upheld the king's policy of Hellenization and retained his position even after the first victories of the Maccabees, though his rank was, from this time onwards, merely nominal. He spent most of his time in Antioch, where he continued to intrigue and to pose as the spokesman of the Jews (2 M 11: 27-33) until he was put to death on the orders of Antiochus V, according to 2 M 13: 3-8. His successor was called Alkimus, one of the sons of Aaron (1 M 7: 14), but not of the Sadoqite branch. After the fall of Antiochus V, Alkimus secured confirmation of his position from Demetrius I (1 M 7: 9; 2 M 14: 3, 13). In Jerusalem itself, he began to knock down the wall separating the two courts of the

Temple,[1] but he died of a thrombosis in 159 B.C. (1 M 9: 54-56); the office of high priest then remained vacant for seven years.

In the end, Jonathan, the brother of Judas Maccabaeus and his successor in the struggle for independence, was named high priest (ἀρχιερεύς) by Alexander Balas, the pretender to the throne, who shortly afterwards defeated Demetrius I (1 M 10: 17-20). Jonathan was clothed in the sacred vestments at the Feast of the Tents in the year 152 B.C. He was both the high priest and the leader of the nation, for Alexander quickly promoted him *strategos* and *meridarches*, i.e. military and civil governor of Judaea (1 M 10: 65). Jonathan was certainly of priestly descent, for his father Mattathias, who had started the Jewish revolt against Antiochus Epiphanes, was a priest of the line of Yehoyarib (1 M 2: 1). This was, however, an obscure family which was placed at the head of the Priestly classes in 1 Ch 24: 7 only after the triumph of the Hasmoneans; it was a late date for such a correction, and since the family was not Sadoqite, those who were partisans of traditionalism could consider the Hasmonean high priests as illegitimate usurpers. On the other hand, the office became less and less a purely religious one: the high priest held an official rank in the Seleucid Empire and he was appointed by the sovereign; his rôle as civil and military governor also involved him in purely political affairs. The century following Jonathan's appointment saw a development of this political rôle: Simon, his brother, became high priest, *strategos* and *hegoumenos* of the Jews (1 M 13: 42); when the people decreed that he should be styled *ethnarches* (1 M 14: 47), a title higher than *strategos* but lower than that of king, Antiochus VII acquiesced (1 M 15: 2). John Hyrcanus, Simon's son, broke away from his Seleucid protectors and secured national independence; he even began to strike coins, which bore the inscription: 'Yehohanan the high priest, head of the Jewish community'. He decided that the time was not yet come to take the title of king; it was Aristobulus I who took this step, according to Josephus, and the title of king was quite certainly used by Alexander Jannaeus, according to Strabo and the inscriptions on coins. The new title certainly underlined the kingly rôle of the high priest, but it was a blow to religion, and the traditionalists among the Jews no longer recognized in these political high priests the spirit which had made the Maccabees national heroes. Opposition movements began to form: the Pharisees were hostile, and the group which founded the community at Qumran seceded from the regular worship of Judaism.

The final turning point came with the end of the Hasmonean dynasty: Antigonus Mattathias, the last king and high priest of this line (40-37 B.C.) was displaced by Herod the Great. From then onwards the office of high priest was at the disposal of the sovereign, who could appoint and dismiss nominees at his own caprice. There were no less than twenty-eight high

1. Cf. p. 325.

priests, chosen from several different priestly families, between 37 B.C. and
A.D. 70. The members of these families thus formed a Priestly aristocracy,
that group of 'high priests' (in the plural) which is referred to so often in
the New Testament. Their history, however, is outside the scope of this
book.

5. The revenues of the Temple and of the clergy

(a) *The Temple*. Before the Exile, the Temple was a state sanctuary, and
the king provided for the expense of public worship.[1] Ideally, according to
Ezechiel, the prince would receive the contributions of the people, but he
would be responsible for the offerings and for all the sacrifices offered on
behalf of the house of Israel (Ez 45: 13-17). After the return from exile,
however, there was neither king nor prince. Darius, of course, issued an
edict that in addition to the cost of reconstructing the Temple, which Cyrus
had already authorized (Esd 6: 4), everything necessary for sacrifice and for
offerings should be furnished to the priests out of the provincial treasury
(Esd 6: 9-10); but these orders were not obeyed for long. The letter of
credentials which Artaxerxes gave to Esdras contained important provisos
about finance: Esdras was to take with him contributions from the king
and from his counsellors, from the rich men of Babylon and from the
Jews, and he was to spend this money on victims, offerings and libations to
be used for sacrifice in the Temple (Esd 7: 15-18). This letter implies that the
edict of Darius had not been applied, and that the Temple was desperately
poor. Help such as this, however, was exceptional, and the Temple needed
a regular income.

Ne 10: 33-35 tells how a regular source of income was arranged. Each
man was to give one-third of a shekel per annum for the purposes of public
worship and for all the service of the Temple (*i.e.* for its general maintenance),
and there was to be an annual delivery of wood (cf. also Ne 13: 31). There
is an allusion to this measure in the Priestly redaction of the Pentateuch
(Ex 30: 11-16): everyone of twenty years and over is to contribute half a
shekel for the service of the Tent of Reunion. This Temple tax was still
collected in New Testament times (Mt 17: 24).

However, the generosity of the Persian kings was copied on several
occasions by the Seleucids, according to documents cited by Josephus and
by the Books of Maccabees; the authenticity of these documents has recently
been questioned, but it seems well-founded. There is a vague allusion in
2 M 3: 3 which says that the founder of the Seleucid dynasty paid for all
the sacrifices out of his personal income; but, more important, a letter of
Antiochus III is quoted by Josephus in *Ant.* XII, iii, 3; the king has decided
to contribute twenty thousand drachmas for victims to be offered in
sacrifice, and also a large quantity of flour, of corn and of salt. Demetrius I,

---

1. Cf. pp. 320 and 379.

in his struggle for power, offered Jonathan all the revenues from Ptolemais and from its environs, and an annual subsidy from the royal list to cover the expenses of worship; he even promised to pay for all the work necessary in repairing the Temple (1 M 10: 39-45). And yet verse 47 tells us that the Jews decided in favour of Demetrius' rival, Alexander Balas, 'because, in their opinion, he offered them more help'.

Such were the sources of income, some of them permanent, others ephemeral; in addition, the Temple received voluntary donations and probably part of the votive offerings, the other part being reserved for the priests. In the course of time, the wealth of the Temple continued to increase, and many covetous eyes were turned on it: cf. the history of Heliodorus (2 M 3), the plundering by Antiochus Epiphanes (1 M 1: 21-24), the tribute of 10,000 talents demanded by Pompey (Josephus, *Ant*. XIV, iv, 5), the confiscation by Crassus of 2,000 silver talents left by Pompey and of 8,000 gold talents as well (Josephus, *Ant*. XIV, vii, 1), and the final sacking of the burnt-out Temple by the soldiers of Titus (Josephus, *Bell*. VI, v, 2, vi, 1).

(b) *The clergy*. Ezechiel drew his inspiration, presumably, from the situation which obtained in the last years of the monarchy, when he assigned to the priests part of the sacrifices, everything which was vowed to the Temple, the best of the first-fruits and of the dues, and the best of the flour which was offered to the sanctuary (Ez 44: 29-30).

The dispositions made in Nb 18: 8-32 are far more detailed and even more favourable to the clergy. Different arrangements are there made for the priests and for the Levites. The priests are to take their food from the sacrifices and from the offerings brought by the people. Lv 6-7 expressly states the part which falls to the priests in every instance, and he is better off than in the parallel ruling given in Dt 18: 3: instead of the shoulder, the jaw and the stomach, the priest is now to receive the breast and the right leg the finest pieces (Lv 7: 30-34); Dt 18 does not mention the sacrifices for sin and the sacrifices of reparation, but Lv 7: 7-10 entitles the priest to everything from these sacrifices which is not burnt upon the altar—in short, almost everything; he is to keep also the skin of the victims offered as holocausts, and all vegetable offerings. The priests are also to have (as in Ezechiel) the best (*rêshîth*) of the produce of the land, the first-fruits (*bikkûrîm*) and everything which is vowed by an anathema (*ḥerem*), according to Nb 18: 12-14; Nb 18: 15-18 adds to this the first-born (*b'kôr*), which must be offered in the sanctuary or else, if it is a man or an unclean animal, redeemed.

The Levites were to be supported by the tithes (*ma'aser*) on corn and new wine. Yet one-tenth of this tithe was to be considered as a levy for Yahweh, and the Levites had to pay this to the priests, who thus had a further increase in their income (Nb 18: 20-32). The obligation of paying a tithe was extended to cattle by Lv 27: 30-33, though the cattle, like the farm-produce, could be redeemed, there is an allusion to this tithe on cattle in 2 Ch 31: 6, but it is impossible to say whether it was ever paid.

Certainly, the tithe on cattle is not mentioned in the parallel texts in the Book of Nehemias. When Nehemias arrived on his second mission, he was informed that the Levites had left the Temple because the tithes, their only source of income, were not being paid. Nehemias placed the blame on the upper classes, brought back the Levites, and set up a committee to administer the stores (cf. Ne 13: 5) and to distribute them (Ne 13: 10-14). To prevent the recurrence of the abuses he had found, Nehemias then made the community undertake a number of solemn promises, in which the income due to the clergy was not forgotten: the first-fruits of the land and of fruit-trees, the first-born, the best of the wheat flour, of the fruits, of new wine and of oil were to be given to the priests, and the tithes were to be given to the Levites (Ne 10: 36-38a). He was putting into practice the laws of Nb 18. Yet it appears that the obligation was not always well honoured: Malachi probably preached about this time, and he accuses the people of not paying tithes and of not making offerings to the Temple treasury (Ml 3: 7-10). An insertion in Nehemias (Ne 10: 38b-39) probably belongs to these same years; it allows the Levites to go themselves to collect the tithes in the towns, under the direction of a priest.

The system was functioning smoothly at the time when the Chronicler was writing, and he, forgetting the difficulties of bygone days, paints the period of the Return as a golden age for the clergy: 'Judah rejoiced in the priests and in the Levites who served there. . . . In the time of Zorobabel and in the time of Nehemias, all Israel paid the singers and the door-keepers their dues, in accordance with their daily needs. They gave the Levites the sacred dues, and the Levites gave part of them to the sons of Aaron' (Ne 12: 44-47).

This prescription remained in force (cf. Si 7: 31; Jdt 11: 13), and the cost to the faithful grew heavier when old obligations, which these new measures had replaced, were also re-enforced; the tithe of Dt 14: 22-26 was understood as a 'second tithe' which was changed into money and spent at the sanctuary, and the three-yearly tithe of Dt 14: 28-29 became 'a third tithe'. Yet all these tithes were paid by the pious Tobias, as a man who faithfully observed the Law (Tb 1: 6-8).

Chapter Nine

ALTARS

THE altar is an essential element in a sanctuary; and in the stories about the Patriarchs, the phrase 'setting up an altar' means, in effect, founding a sanctuary (Gn 12: 7, 8; 13: 18; 26: 25; 33: 20). From the beginning, the priest's office consisted in the ministry of the altar, and as time went on, his work became more and more restricted to this ministry; sacrifice, the principal rite in public worship, means the offering of a gift upon an altar. Before passing, then, from the study of the priesthood to the study of sacrifice and ritual, we must say something about altars.

The Hebrew word for an altar is *mizbeaḥ*, from a verbal root meaning 'to slaughter', and therefore 'to slaughter with a view to sacrifice'. The word took on a broader meaning when the ritual became more developed: in the Temple, victims other than birds were killed at some distance from the altar and then placed upon it; vegetable offerings were also placed on the altar; and the same word was used for the altar of incense. An altar, then, was a place where men offered sacrifices, whatever their nature.

1. *Pre-Israelite altars in Palestine*

In Palestine, sacrifice was offered on various types of altars: the altar might be just the natural surface of the rock, or a rock which had been hewn into a certain shape, or a piece of rock jutting up on its own; and there were, of course, man-made altars.

Excavations in Palestine have revealed many rocky surfaces which have been artificially hollowed out. It would be an exaggeration to say that every-one had some connection with worship. The majority of them could have served a profane purpose: for example, those which stand near a well or a cistern or a spring may have been used as watering-troughs for animals, and the largest of them may have been used to do the laundry; those which are near a press are obviously connected with the making of wine or of oil. And when they are found near tombs, they are to be explained by funeral rites, but not necessarily by sacrifices: the dead could be hungry and thirsty.[1]

There are, however, examples in which other evidence proves that some of these hollowed rocks were used in connection with sacrifice. We shall

1. Cf. p. 60.

speak in a moment of the rock altar at Sar'a; at Gezer, the hollows in the surface of the rock lead down to a cave where the bones of pigs offered in sacrifice were found. But where evidence of this kind is wanting, it is impossible to decide whether a surface of rock, with or without such hollows, was used as an altar. At least two passages in the Bible, Jg 6: 19–23 and 13: 19–20, indicate that the custom of using such rocks existed.

Everyone quotes, as examples of altars hewn out of the natural rock, those found at Petra and in the district around; the altars there are cut out of the surrounding rock, and steps are even hewn in front of them. Petra became an important Nabatean centre in Hellenistic times, but there is no reason why these installations should not be even older; on the other hand, it must not be forgotten that tombs and houses carved out of the rock are also a characteristic feature of Petra; it would be imprudent, then, to make generalizations about altars from observations which may not be valid outside this region.

A large stone or a detached piece of rock could serve as an altar. We shall cite only two examples: near Sar'a, a large, cubic piece of stone stands in a field; it is rough-shapen, about four feet three inches high, with steps near the top, and hollowed out on top in several places. It is called, without any proof, the altar of Manoah (Jg 13: 19–20). Recent excavations at Hazor have unearthed an enormous rectangular block weighing about five tons, with a basin hollowed out on one of its surfaces; the site in which it was found was a Canaanite temple of the 13th century B.C.

Lastly, we have man-made altars. Here we must recall what was said about the 'high places'.[1] The *bamah* was a knoll or a mound upon which sacrifice was offered, but not every *bamah* had an altar erected upon it; the knoll itself could take the place of an altar. Platforms of large stones have been uncovered in the excavations at Megiddo, at Nahariyah near Haifa and at Hazor in Galilee.

In other pre-Israelite sanctuaries, altars have been discovered standing against the back wall, built of large stones and earthen mortar, or built in plain brick. Recent excavations have provided examples for all periods: at Megiddo, for the periods around 3000 B.C. and around 2000 B.C., at Et-Tell (Ai) for a period between 3000 and 2000 B.C., and at Tell ed-Duweir (Lakish) for the 14th–13th centuries B.C.

2. *Israelite altars outside the main sanctuary*

Examples of the different types of altars are found in the most ancient biblical texts. In Jg 6: 19–23, Gideon wanted to offer a goat and some unleavened bread to the Angel of Yahweh; the Angel ordered him to put the meat and the bread on a rock, where they were burnt up by a fire which shot

1. Cf. pp. 284-285.

out of the rock: it was a sacrifice. In Jg 13: 19-20, Manoah, the father of Samson, offered up a goat as a whole-burnt offering to Yahweh; he offered it upon a rock, and in the following verse the rock is called an 'altar'.

Other examples show that large stones were used as altars. When the Ark was being brought back from Beth-Shemesh, the wooden chariot and the cows which had drawn it were used for a whole-burnt offering on a 'large stone' which stood nearby (1 S 6: 14). In Saul's war against the Philistines, the people began to slaughter the captured sheep on the ground itself; thereupon Saul intervened with the command 'Roll a big stone over here towards me!' and he insisted that the beasts should be slaughtered on the stone: the implication is that this was an altar, for all slaughtering of animals had a sacrificial character until the time of Deuteronomy (Dt 12: 20-25).

As a general rule, however, all the altars mentioned in the Bible (with the exception of those in the Temple) were altars built out of stone: e.g. those which the Patriarchs set up, those in the period of Josue (Jos 22: 10) and of the Judges (Jg 6: 24: the altar built on the rock where the meal prepared for the guests had been burnt up by fire from Yahweh, and 6: 26: a parallel tradition); this is true of all the altars down to the time when David built an altar on the site of the future Temple (2 S 24: 25). Elias restored the altar of Yahweh which had stood on Carmel and which had been demolished; then he laid on it the wood and the quarters of the victims which were to be sacrificed (1 K 18: 30 and 33). A gloss inspired by Ex 24: 4; Jos 4: 1-9 states (vv. 31-32a) that this altar was made of twelve stones to symbolize the twelve tribes of Israel.

Apart from this gloss, we are never told whether the altars were made of (plain) bricks or of stones. As we have seen, both kinds of material were used for pre-Israelite altars in Canaan, and both kinds are authorized by the law of Ex 20: 24-26: the altar must be of earth (i.e. plain bricks); if it is made of stone, the stone must not be trimmed with a chisel. Dt. 27: 5 repeats this command: an altar of stones untouched by any iron is to be erected on Ebal; the order was carried out by Josue, according to the Deuteronomic passage in Jos 8: 30-31. The rabbis found some very subtle explanations of this precept forbidding trimmed stones to be used for an altar: 'The altar is for forgiving, and iron is for punishing', or 'The altar prolongs life, but iron cuts it short'. Ex 20 merely says that iron 'desecrates' stone; the meaning is that things should be used for the service of God only in their natural condition, before they have been interfered with in any way by man (cf. Nb 19: 2; Dt 21: 3-4; 1 S 6: 7, etc.); the principle reminds us of altars erected on rocks or upon a large unhewn stone. The law of Ex 20: 26 also forbids steps leading up to the altar. Some Canaanite altars had them, and later Israelite altars were approached by a series of steps or by a ramp. Ex 20: 26 gives modesty as the reason for this prohibition: a priest wearing only a loincloth might expose himself as he was stepping up to the altar; consequently, when, in later ages, the high altar was approached by a series of steps, another law was introduced by which the priests were obliged to wear a pair of drawers (Ex 28: 42-43). The explanation advanced in Ex 20: 26 does not seem to be the original one; the prohibition was originally based, it would appear, rather on the sacred character of the altar, which was to be as far removed as possible from anything profane: steps which touched the altar and upon which the priest trod would bring the altar into contact with the profane.

We shall discuss later the little movable altars which were used for offerings of incense.[1]

3. The altars used in the desert

According to the description of the desert sanctuary, the Tent or the Dwelling had two altars: one was the altar of holocausts which stood immediately in front of the entrance to the Dwelling (Ex 40: 6, 29; cf. Lv 4: 18), and the other was the altar of incense which stood inside the Dwelling, in front of the veil which cut off the rear part where the Ark was kept (Ex 30: 6; 40: 5, 26).

The altar of holocausts is described in Ex 27: 1-8 and 38: 1-7. It was constructed of planks of acacia-wood, five cubits long, five cubits wide and three cubits high. Bronze plates were fitted over these planks, and the altar is sometimes called 'the bronze altar'. It had a bronze grating (i.e. some kind of trellis work), a cornice or rim, and four rings for the bars by which it was carried. Also, it was hollow. This description is obscure; in particular, it is hard to see how the trellis work fits in with the rest, and very difficult indeed to see how victims could have been burnt on this wooden chest, even if it was covered in bronze. Some exegetes have suggested that the structure was filled with earth and with stones each time the people pitched camp, but this is not stated in the text and the grating would make it impossible. Finally, its height is given as four and a half feet; this means a step would have been needed, but the text does not mention one.

The altar of perfumes is described in Ex 30: 1-5 and 37: 25-28: its surface was one cubit square, its height two cubits. It was made of acacia wood, and the upper part was plated with gold; it had golden horns, and four golden rings by which it could be carried (hence it is sometimes called simply 'the golden altar'). The description is clear, but it seems that the mention of this altar as among the appurtenances of the desert sanctuary is a later insertion into the text. The altar is not mentioned among the furnishings of the Dwelling in Ex 25; nor is its siting indicated where one would expect it, in Ex 26: 33-37; instead, the altar itself, its site and its use are described in Ex 30: 1-10, which looks very like a passage out of context. Lastly, this altar is never mentioned in the stories about the desert: in the desert, offerings of perfume were made with a little incense-shovel (Nb 16: 6-7, 17-18; 17: 11-12).

1. Cf. p. 411.

Israelite tradition, then, was not certain that there had been an altar of perfumes in the desert sanctuary, and only included it among the furnishings of the Tent in order to make the Tent a copy of the Temple of Jerusalem. Indeed, the altar of holocausts itself is a movable replica of the altar in the Temple. Thus we reach the same conclusion from studying the furnishing of the Tent as we reached from examining the priestly description of it.[1]

4. *The altars in Solomon's Temple*

Like the Tent, Solomon's Temple had two altars, standing in the same position to each other as the two altars in the Tent: the altar of holocausts stood in front of the Temple (2 K 16: 14), and the altar of perfumes stood in the Hekal, in front of the Debir (1 K 6: 20-21). (The exact position of the altar of holocausts on the modern Haram esh-Sherif depends on the view one takes about the general site of the Temple.[2])

(a) *The altar of holocausts.* One curious fact to be noticed is that the altar of holocausts is never once mentioned in the long description of the Temple and its furniture (1 K: 6-7). There are allusions to it in 1 K 8: 22 and 54 (which are part of the Deuteronomic redaction) and also in 1 K 8: 64 and 9: 25 (which are older texts). Several explanations have been given for this strange silence. It is not likely that Solomon simply transferred into his Temple the altar which David had built (2 S 24: 25), for he had a habit of ordering new and costly things. It is more likely that he installed a new altar, which (according to 1 K 8: 64 and 2 K 16: 15) was called a bronze altar and which (according to 2 K 16: 14) was movable: it would then be a large grille upon which sacrifices could be burnt. Possibly the editor of 1 K 6-7 suppressed the description of this altar because it was not the kind of altar demanded by the customs and laws of Israel (Ex 20: 24-26); it was, in fact, a type used by the Phoenicians, as two inscriptions tell us. The Chronicler has made good this omission by attributing to Solomon the construction of a bronze altar ten cubits square and five cubits high (2 Ch 4: 1): the measurements he gives, however, seem to be more in accord with the altar built by Achaz, or with the one which must have existed in the Chronicler's own day.

In the time of Achaz, Solomon's altar was replaced by a new one modelled on an altar the king had seen at Damascus when he went there to take an oath of fealty to Tiglath-Pileser (2 K 16: 10-16). In all probability, the model Achaz copied was Syrian, not Assyrian (though many writers defend the latter view): the new altar was of imposing dimensions (v. 15) and it was approached either by steps or by a ramp (v. 12); it was a copy of the large altar in the temple of Hadad-Rimmon at Damascus (cf. 2 K 5: 18). The old bronze altar was moved a little to the north, and Achaz kept it so that he could use it in examining victims for omens: this interpretation of the final

1. Cf. p. 296.   2. Cf. pp. 318-319.

phrase in v. 15 is quite possible, for the verb *biqqer* could have this meaning. In spite of its origin, which was not above suspicion, the new altar remained in use until the Exile, and the altar in the second Temple was apparently of the same shape, though perhaps larger.

(b) *The altar of perfumes*. Some authors have denied, though without convincing arguments, that there ever was an altar of perfumes in Solomon's Temple. There is a reference to it in the overloaded and confused text of I K 6: 20-21, which may be reconstructed thus with the help of Greek texts: 'He made an altar of cedar ⟨ ⟩ in front of the Debir, and covered it with gold'. It is referred to as the 'golden altar' in I K 7: 48. Moreover, in the inaugural vision of Isaias (where the Temple either is, or is imagined to be, the place where Yahweh speaks to him) one of the Seraphim takes a piece of burning coal from an altar: and since the altar is inside the Temple, it can only be the altar of perfumes. The last reference occurs in 2 Ch 26: 16: Ozias tried to offer incense on the altar of perfumes, inside the Hekal.

In I K 7: 48, this altar is called simply 'the golden' one (*zahab*), and the same term is sometimes used for the corresponding altar in the desert Tent. A new explanation of this name has recently been put forward: in Southern Arabia *dhb* was used both for 'gold' and for 'perfume', and the word has been discovered in an engraving on a small perfume-brazier, along with the names of other aromatic perfumes. It is suggested, therefore, that the 'golden altar' (*mizbeaḥ hazzahab*) of I K 7: 48 should be translated 'altar of perfumes'. The rendering is certainly possible, but if it is accepted, one must admit that the original meaning was very soon lost: both I K 6: 20-21 (describing the altar in Solomon's Temple) and Ex 30: 1-5 (describing the altar in the Tent) lay great stress on its covering of precious metal in order to justify its name (*mizbeaḥ hazzahab*); and all the Greek texts, biblical or non-biblical, in referring to it speak of it as 'golden' altar.

Palestinian archaeology enables us to trace the development of this kind of altar. The Canaanites used cylindrical or rectangular objects made out of baked earth in order to burn perfumes. From the beginning of the Israelite monarchy, limestone altars are found, shaped like square pillars; usually, they have four horns on the top corners. (Examples of this type have been unearthed at Shechem and at Megiddo.) This is the shape of the altar of perfumes described in Ex 30: 1-5, but the specimens found in excavations are not as big as that described in this text. One specimen of a very tiny altar of the same type, dating from the eleventh century, was found at Tell Beit Mirsim, and a large group of similar small ones, dating from the Persian period, was found at Lakish. The use of these altars outside the central sanctuary was eventually condemned,[1] but an altar of the same type, only more imposing, must have stood in the Temple from the time of Solomon.

1. Cf. pp. 286-287.

5. The altar of Ezechiel

Yet we should note that when Ezechiel is describing the future temple, he makes no mention of the altar of perfumes. Ez 41: 21-22, which is often cited in this connection, refers to the table of shewbread. By contrast, the altar of holocausts is described in minute detail (Ez 43: 13-17), but this description (with the later insertion about the consecration of the altar, Ez 43: 18-27) seems to have been added at a later date; it certainly does not stand in its original context. The altar described by Ezechiel had three tiers, and seems to be a small-scale model of the many-storied tower (the ziggurat)[1]; the terms used for its different parts are evidently taken from a Babylonian background. The base is called *ḥeq ha'areṣ*, i.e. 'bosom of the earth', which is a translation of the Akkadian *irat erṣiti*, the name given to foundations of a temple or ziggurat. The upper part is called *'ari'el*; or *har'el*; the word *har'el* means 'mountain of God', and is a Hebrew interpretation of the Akkadian term *arallu*, which stands both for the world underneath the earth and for the mountain of the gods. The top platform had horns at the four corners, and was approached by a flight of steps on its eastern side.

Ezechiel planned that this new altar should be ten cubits high, and from eighteen to twenty cubits square at the base: this is more or less the size of the altar in Solomon's Temple, according to 2 Ch 4: 1. Ezechiel may have been thinking of the altar in the first Temple, for he had himself seen it, but the shape of the new altar and the names given to its parts are of Babylonian inspiration, as is the symbolism which results. There is no evidence whatever that the altar built after the Return was modelled on the description given by the prophet.

6. The altars in the second Temple

We have already stated that Chronicles refers to Solomon's altar (2 Ch 4: 1) and to the altar of perfumes (2 Ch 26: 16): these two references may preserve information about the first Temple, or they may have been inspired by what the Chronicler saw in the second Temple, but otherwise we have no information in the Hebrew Bible about the altars in the post-exilic Temple. Two non-biblical texts are extant, both dating from the Hellenistic period. According to the Pseudo-Hecataeus (cited by Josephus, *C. Apionem* I 198), there stood in the Temple enclosure a square altar, twenty cubits wide and ten cubits high, built of untrimmed stones. Beside it there was a building containing a golden altar and a golden chandelier. This text confirms the existence of two altars, one for whole-burnt offerings and one for perfumes; the dimensions of the altar of holocausts are those given by 2 Ch 4: 1, and it is presented as if it had been built in accordance with the law of Ex 20: 25. This perfect harmony with the biblical texts is, however, disconcerting

1. Cf. pp. 281-282.

rather than probative, for the Pseudo-Hecataeus is a work of Jewish propaganda written at Alexandria shortly after 200 B.C. The second text, in the Letter of Aristeas, comes from the same place, and from almost the same period: it says, quite simply, that 'the size of the altar's structure was in proportion to the place where it stood, and to the victims burnt upon it: it was approached by a ramp of similar proportions. The place had a slope, for the sake of propriety'. All these facts, too, are an echo of biblical texts.

Shortly after these propaganda works were written, Antiochus Epiphanes launched his persecution, and the altars in the Temple did not escape. In 169 B.C., Antiochus plundered the Temple and took away the golden altar, *i.e.* the altar of perfumes (1 M 1: 21); in December, 167, he erected an altar to Zeus Olympios over the altar of holocausts, and had sacrifices to Zeus offered there (1 M 1: 54, 59; 2 M 6: 2, 5). The pagan altar is 'the abomination of desolation' referred to in 1 M 1: 54 and Dn 9: 27.

As soon as the Maccabees had regained freedom for the Jews to practise their religion, they made away with this scandal: a new altar was built, and the stones of the old one, which had been desecrated by the pagan worship performed over it, were put away in a side-building of the Temple (1 M 4: 44-47; 2 M 10: 3). A new altar of perfumes was also put in the Temple (1 M 4: 49).

7. The religious significance of altars

In Israel, the altar had the same significance as in other ancient religions, but with appreciable nuances. The altar is only rarely referred to as the table of Yahweh (Ez 44: 16; Ml 1: 7, 12), and never in ancient texts: conversely, the table of shewbread is said to be 'like an altar' in Ez 41: 21-22. This distrust of the word 'table' is based on a reaction against the idea that a sacrifice provided the god with a banquet (cf. Is 65: 11 and the satire in Dn 14: 1-22).

Since the Temple was the house of God, it had to have a hearth, and the altar was this hearth. The idea is not expressed in explicit terms, for the *'ari'el* of Ez 43: 13-17 does not mean (as we have seen above) a 'hearth', though many writers have thought so. The idea is expressed in another way: a fire must always be burning upon the altar (Lv 6: 5-6; cf. 2 M 1: 18-36), just as the lamp must always be kept alight in the Temple (Ex 27: 20-21; Lv 24: 2-4).

The altar was the sign of God's presence. In the earliest period of Israel's history, it commemorated a theophany (Gn 12: 7; 26: 24-25) or was called by some name which reminded men of God: Jacob called the altar he erected at Shechem 'El, God of Israel', and Moses called the altar he erected after the defeat of the Amalekites 'Yahweh-Nissi', 'Yahweh is my rallying-standard'. Later on, the altar was specially consecrated, and purified each year on the Day of Atonement: it thus acquired an altogether exceptional holiness (Ex 29: 36-37; 30: 10; Lv 8: 15; 16: 18-19).

This holiness was connected in a particular way with the 'horns' of the altar, those four parts which stuck out at the top corners of the altar of holocausts and of the altar of perfumes. The blood of victims was rubbed on them to consecrate the altar, or in rites of expiation to make atonement (Ex 29: 12; 30: 10; Lv 4 *passim*; 8: 15; 9: 9; 16: 18; Ez 43: 20). A fugitive claiming asylum would grasp the horns of the altar (1 K 2: 28). It is not quite clear what these horns stand for: in the Bible, a horn is a symbol for power, but this interpretation is inadequate in the present context; nor is it likely that these horns represent the horns of the victims slaughtered, like the bucrane often found on Roman altars. Possibly they took the place of little steles, *i.e.* of small *maṣṣebôth*, which had once been placed on the altar as emblems of the divinity; possibly they are just visible symbols emphasizing the special importance and holiness of the extremities of the altar. The extremities of a priest's body (the lobe of his ear, his thumb and his big toe) were rubbed with blood in the late ritual for investing a priest in his office (Ex 29: 20), and the same parts were rubbed with blood and anointed with oil in the rite for the purification of a leper (Lv 14: 14-17).

Lastly, the altar was used as an instrument of mediation. The offerings of men were placed upon it and there burnt: by this ceremony, the offerings were taken out of man's domain and given to God, and God replied by bestowing blessings (Ex 20: 24). Thus the Covenant itself between God and his people was maintained in force, or re-established, upon the altar of sacrifice.

CHAPTER TEN

THE RITUAL OF SACRIFICE

THE altar was the place of sacrifice, and sacrifice was the principal act in Israel's cult. We shall endeavour to define the meaning of sacrifice in the religion of Israel, but before we can do so, we must first make a study of the rites connected with sacrifice, and trace their development. For the moment, we may give the following provisory definition: sacrifice is any offering, animal or vegetable, which is wholly or partially destroyed upon an altar as a token of homage to God. The study of the ritual is complicated by the fact that several terms are used for sacrifice, and they are not always clearly distinguished: one and the same word can denote several kinds of sacrifice, and one kind of sacrifice can be described by a variety of terms. The vocabulary reflects an historical development and the fusion of various practices, similar to one another, but originating from different backgrounds.

We shall start with the latest and most complete ritual, and we shall then endeavour to retrace the history of sacrifice to its origin. The code of sacrifices followed in the second Temple is contained in Lv 1-7. These chapters belong to the last redaction of the Pentateuch: they are legislative in character, and break the story of the institution of worship in the desert which ought to continue straight on from the erection of the sanctuary (Ex 40) to the installation of the priests (Lv 8-10).

1. *Holocausts*

The English word 'holocaust' comes, through the Vulgate, from the Septuagint, and in the Septuagint it is a translation of the Hebrew *'olah*, from a root meaning 'to go up': a holocaust, then, is a sacrifice which is 'taken up' on to the altar, or, more probably, whose smoke 'goes up' to God when it is burnt. The characteristic feature of this sacrifice is that the entire victim is burnt and that nothing is given back to the man who offers it or to the priest (except the skin). This is why the Greek translates it 'holocaust' (meaning, 'wholly burnt'), and why the term *'olah* has sometimes been replaced by the word *kalil*, meaning a 'total' sacrifice (1 S 7: 9; Dt 33: 10; cf. Ps 51: 21, where *'olah* is used alongside *kalil*).

In the ritual of Lv 1, the victim must be a male animal without any blemish (cf. the older Law of Holiness, Lv 22: 17-25); it may be a small or a large beast, or a bird (though only a turtle-dove or a pigeon). The victim is presented by the man making the offering and he must be in a state of ritual purity. He lays his hand upon the head of the victim. This action is not a magic gesture to establish contact between God and man, nor is it a symbolic action implying that the victim is a substitute for the man, whose sins are thereby transferred to the victim for expiation. (It is true that in the ceremony of the scapegoat, Lv 16: 21,[1] the sins of the people are transferred to the goat by the same gesture, but precisely because the scapegoat is thereby loaded with the sins of the people, it is regarded as defiled, and unworthy to be sacrificed.) Nor is this laying of hands on the victim a simple *manumissio* or abandoning of the victim to God: rather, it is a solemn attestation that this victim comes from this particular individual who is laying his hands on it, that the sacrifice which is going to be presented to God by the priest is offered in his name, and that the fruits of this sacrifice shall be his.

The man making the sacrifice would himself cut the throat of the victim at some distance from the altar. The priests and the Levites slaughtered only the animals offered in public sacrifices (2 Ch 29: 22, 24, 34; Ez 44: 11). The priest's rôle, properly speaking, did not begin until the victim was brought into contact with the altar, and it consisted in pouring the blood around the altar. The blood contained the life; indeed, in the Hebrew mind, the blood was life: 'the life of all flesh is its blood' (Lv 17: 14; cf. Gn 9: 4; Dt 12: 23; Lv 7: 26-27), and therefore the blood belonged to God alone.

Afterwards, the victim was skinned and cut up, and its four quarters were put on the altar by the priests, there to be burnt by the fire which was always kept alight (Lv 6: 5-6). (The reference to the lighting of the fire in Lv 1: 7 applies only to the first sacrifice ever offered, which is represented as taking place after the promulgation of the Law.) Everything, including the head, the intestines and the hooves or feet, was first washed, then placed on the altar, and then burnt.

When the victim was a bird, the ritual was modified: the man bringing the offering did not lay hands on it, nor did he cut its throat; instead, everything was done on the altar, and therefore done by the priest. Lv 5: 7 and 12: 8 show that these sacrifices of birds were offered by the poor as a substitute for sacrifices of beasts, which only the rich could afford. For the same reason, sheep and goats were more common offerings than cattle.

The latest rituals in Israel's history lay down that, along with the holocaust, there must be an offering (*minḥah*) of flour kneaded with oil, and a libation of wine; this ruling applied to the feast of Weeks (according to Lv 23: 18), to the daily holocausts (according to Ex 29: 38-42) and to all sacrifices of 'olah and zebaḥ (according to Nb 15: 1-16). The flour was burnt, and the wine was poured out at the foot of the altar, like the blood of the victim (cf. Si 50: 15).

1. Cf. pp. 508-509.

This first chapter of Leviticus presents us with the whole problem of the fluidity of the terms used in sacrificial language. The holocaust is called a *qorban* in Lv 1: 2, 10, 14, *i.e.* that which a man 'brings near' God or the altar: the same term is used by Leviticus, Numbers and Ezechiel for all sacrifices, and even for non-sacrificial offerings, such as the material destined for use in the sanctuary (Nb 7 *passim*); and in later Judaism, it acquired the meaning of 'consecration'. In the same chapter, the holocaust is also called an *'ishsheh* (Lv 1: 9, 13, 17). The etymology of this word is still a subject of debate, but whatever it is, there is no doubt that the editors of the Bible thought the word applied to any offering which was wholly or partially destroyed by fire (*'esh*). The word, which is frequently found in the Priestly writings and which occurs also in the Hebrew version of Si (45: 20; 50: 13), is used only three times elsewhere, *viz.* in Dt 18: 1; Jos 13: 14 (Hebrew) and in 1 S 2: 28: all three texts are the work of the Deuteronomists, and all of them refer to the rights a priest has over sacrifices. In the Pentateuch, the word is often accompanied by the expression 'a fragrance pleasing to Yahweh'. This anthropomorphism means that God accepts the sacrifice (cf. Gn 8: 21, where it corresponds to a similar, but cruder, expression in the Babylonian account of the Flood).[1] The formula, without any materialistic overtones, remained in use in liturgical language.

2. Communion sacrifices

We are adopting the translation 'communion sacrifice' for want of a better rendering of what is called in Hebrew *zebah sh lamîm*, or *zebah* (without qualification) or simply *sh'lamîm* (always in the plural except once, *shelem*, in Am 5: 22). All these terms are equivalent to one another, as is proved by the way in which they are interchanged inside certain passages or in parallel passages, and by the fact that the motives and the rites of this sacrifice are always the same: *zebah sh'lamîm* is the official name in the Priestly rituals which we are studying here, and it is rarely found elsewhere. The renderings 'peace-offering' and 'welcome offering' are inspired by the Greek version, but the ritual and the practice of Israel present it rather as a sacrifice of thanksgiving to God which brings about union with him.

The ritual divides communion-sacrifices into three types: the sacrifice of praise (*tôdah*), Lv 7: 12-15; 22: 29-30, the voluntary sacrifice (*n'dabah*), *i.e.* one offered out of devotion, not because of any precept or promise, Lv 7: 16-17; 22: 18-23, and the votive sacrifice (*neder*), *i.e.* one to which a person has bound himself by a vow, Lv 7: 16-17; 22: 18-23. The distinction between the three types is, however, not very precise.

The principal ritual is described in Lv 3, and its characteristic feature lies in the fact that the victim is shared between God, the priest and the person

1. Cf. p. 433.

offering the sacrifice, who eats it as a holy thing. The victims prescribed are the same as those for a holocaust (though birds are not allowed), but they may be male or female, and minor blemishes are tolerated in a victim offered as a voluntary sacrifice (*n'dabah*), according to Lv 22: 23. The laying on of hands, the cutting of the throat and the sprinkling of blood are carried out exactly as for a holocaust.

The part which is given to Yahweh is burnt upon the altar: this comprised all the fat around the intestines, the kidneys, the liver, and the fat of a sheep's tail, and only the fat. The reason is that fat, like blood, was considered a life-giving part: 'All fat belongs to Yahweh . . . You shall eat neither fat nor blood' (Lv 3: 16-17; cf. 7: 22-24).

Two parts are assigned to the priest: the breast, which was 'weighed' before Yahweh (according to the common explanation of the word *t'nûphah*) but not burnt upon the altar, and the right leg, which was a 'sample' (*t'rûmah*) due to the priest by right (Lv 7: 28-34; 10: 14-15). The two words, however, are often used without distinction, and perhaps they both mean a 'contribution'; both of them may have been borrowed from the terminology of Babylonian contracts.

The remainder of the animal belongs to the person who offers the sacrifice: he eats it with his family and with any guests he may invite, but they must be in a state of ritual purity. The victim of a sacrifice of praise (*tôdah*) must be eaten on the day it is offered (Lv 7: 15), but a victim of a voluntary or votive sacrifice (*n'dabah* or *neder*) can be eaten on the following day, though anything left over must be burned on the third day (Lv 7: 16-17). The *tôdah* sacrifice is to be accompanied by an offering (*minḥah*) of unleavened cakes and of leavened bread. One of the cakes is a 'sample' for Yahweh, and reverts to the priest.

3. *Expiatory sacrifices*

Almost half of the sacrificial code of the second Temple concerns those sacrifices which we call expiatory sacrifices, though the ritual itself does not have one name which is applicable to them all; it treats, sometimes consecutively and sometimes simultaneously, of two kinds of sacrifice whose purpose is to re-establish the covenant with God when it has been broken by the sin of man. They are called respectively, the sacrifice for sin (*ḥaṭṭa'th*) and the sacrifice of reparation (*'asham*). In spite of the length of the passages devoted to them, it is difficult to determine the exact significance of each sacrifice or to say why they are distinguished from each other.

(a) *Sacrifice for sin*. In Hebrew, the word *ḥaṭṭa'th* means both sin and the rite which does away with sin (Lv 4: 1—5: 13; 6: 17-23). The type of victim depended on the rank of the person who had sinned. A bull was to be offered for a sin of the high priest, the 'anointed priest',[1] for his guilt defiled

1. Cf. p. 398.

the entire people; a bull was also prescribed when the people itself had sinned; a he-goat was to be offered for the sin of the 'prince' (*nasi'*), *i.e.* the lay head of the community, in Ezechiel's mind; a she-goat or a sheep was the offering for the sin of a private individual. The poor could offer two turtledoves or two pigeons instead of these expensive victims: one of the birds was used as a sacrifice for sin (*ḥaṭṭa'th*), and the other was offered a holocaust. The poor could make an offering of flour instead of any of these animals.

The ritual for these sacrifices is distinguished from that used in other sacrifices by two things, the use to which the blood is put, and the way in which the victim's flesh is disposed of. The blood played a more important part in this sacrifice than in any other. When the sacrifice was offered for the high priest or for the entire people, there were three successive rites: the priest who is performing the sacrifice first collected the blood, entered into the Holy Place and there sprinkled the blood seven times against the veil which curtains off the Holy of Holies; next, he rubbed blood upon the corners of the altar of incense, which stood before the veil; thirdly, he poured out the rest of the blood at the foot of the altar of holocausts. These were the only animal sacrifices in which part of the victim was carried inside the Temple building. When sacrifice was offered for the sin of the lay head of the community, or for the sin of a private individual, the blood was put on the horns of the altar of holocausts, and the rest poured out at its base; in these two sacrifices, nothing was taken within the Holy Place.

These rites underline the value which blood has in expiating sin; it can be used to expiate sin because it is the means of life: 'the life of flesh is in its blood. This blood I have given to you, in order that you may perform the rite of expiation upon the altar, for your lives; for blood makes expiation for a life' (or: 'for blood makes expiation, by reason of the life that is in it,' Lv 17: 11). We may compare the parallel text in He 9: 22: 'Without the shedding of blood, there is no forgiveness at all'.

All the fat was burnt upon the altar, as in communion-sacrifices, but the meat was put to a different use: since the person offering the sacrifice admitted his guilt, he received no part of the victim, and everything reverted to the priests. And when the sacrifice of *ḥaṭṭa'th* was offered for the sin of the community, or for the sin of the high priest as head of the community, the priests themselves were not allowed to eat any part of the victim: all the remains were carried outside the sanctuary and placed on the ash-heap. The fact that the fat was burnt on the altar, and that the meat of sacrifices offered for the sins of private individuals was eaten by the priests 'as a most holy thing' (Lv 6: 22) contradicts the theory according to which the victim was loaded with the sin of the person offering the sacrifice and thus itself became 'sin'. On the contrary, it was a victim pleasing to God, and he, in consideration of this offering, took away the sin. It is evidently in this ritual sense that

St. Paul uses the word: 'Christ, who had not known sin, God made "sin" (*ḥaṭṭa'th*: a victim for sin), in order that we might become, in him, God's justice' (2 Co 5: 21).

The rites which are prescribed in Lv 1-7 for the sacrifice of *ḥaṭṭa'th* are not the same as those prescribed in Nb 15: 22-29. In the text of Numbers, there is no mention of a sin committed by the high priest or by the prince, but only of sins committed by the community or by a private individual. Faults which the community has committed inadvertently are effaced by offering a bull as holocaust and a he-goat as a sacrifice of *ḥaṭṭa'th*; faults which a private individual has committed inadvertently are effaced by offering a kid as a sacrifice of *ḥaṭṭa'th*. No details are given about the rites to be followed. If the sin is deliberate, sacrifice cannot atone for the guilt and no forgiveness is possible (Nb 15: 30-31). Perhaps this law is even later than the law in Leviticus.

These sacrifices for sin took on a particular solemnity on the Day of Atonement, which we shall discuss in the chapter about the later religious feasts.[1]

(b) *The sacrifice of reparation.* The other kind of expiatory sacrifice is called an *'asham*. The word means an offence, and then the means by which the offence is righted, and, finally, a sacrifice of reparation. The sacrificial code deals with this kind of offering more briefly (Lv 5: 14-26; 7: 1-6), and states that the rites to be followed are the same as in the sacrifice for sin (Lv 7: 7). This sacrifice, however, was offered only on behalf of private individuals, and as a result, the blood was never taken into Holy Place, and the victim was never burned away from the sanctuary; secondly, the only victim referred to is a ram; thirdly, in certain cases the sacrifice was to be accompanied by the payment of a fine (cf. Lv 5: 14-16, 21-26; Nb 5: 5-8): if the rights of God or of a man had been infringed in a way which could be estimated in terms of money, then the guilty person had to offer a ram for reparation, and to restore to the priests (as representatives of Yahweh) or to the person whom he had wronged the monetary equivalent of the damage, plus one-fifth. It should be stressed, however, that this restitution did not form part of the sacrifice.

(c) *The distinction between sacrifice for sin and the sacrifice of reparation.* It is very difficult to say exactly what distinguishes these two kinds of sacrifice from each other. The ancient writers themselves are not in agreement. Philo (*De Victimis*, 11) thought the *ḥaṭṭa'th* was offered for involuntary faults against another man, and the *'asham* for involuntary faults against God and for all deliberate faults. Josephus (*Ant.* II ix 3) thought the distinction was between sins committed without witnesses, and sins committed in front of witnesses; and the rabbis too had theories of their own. The opinions of modern scholars are generally better founded, but they are just as varied.

1. Cf. pp. 507-510.

The examples cited in Lv 4-5 give the impression that the *ḥaṭṭa'th* covers a wider field, and that the *'asham* relates to faults by which God (or his priests) or a fellow-man has been cheated of his rights; this would explain why the *'asham* is essentially a sacrifice of reparation. And yet, even within the sacrificial code, there are inconsistencies: the *ḥaṭṭa'th* is also called *'asham* in Lv 5: 6, 7; the *ḥaṭṭa'th* is offered when a man sins inadvertently against any commandment of Yahweh (Lv 4: 2), but the *'asham* is offered if a man has unwittingly done something forbidden by the commandments of Yahweh (Lv 5: 17); in general, then, the two sacrifices cover the same offences. The two sacrifices are prescribed for very similar cases: anyone who does not come forward as a witness in court when he ought to, or anyone who makes a declaration in court without consideration, must offer a *ḥaṭṭa'th* (Lv 5: 1, 4), and anyone who commits perjury must offer an *'asham* (Lv 5: 22, 24). The confusion grows worse when we compare certain particular laws with the sacrificial code: for the purification of a leper, three sacrifices must be offered, an *'asham*, a *ḥaṭṭa'th* and a holocaust (Lv 14: 10-32). Similarly, a Nazirite who has been defiled by touching a dead body must offer two turtle-doves or pigeons, one as a *ḥaṭṭa'th*, the other as a holocaust, and, in addition, a lamb as an *'asham* (Nb 6: 9-12). Nor is it possible to state clearly the moral aspect of the sin which is expiated by these sacrifices: the *ḥaṭṭa'th* and the *'asham* are offered when a person has sinned inadvertently (Lv 4: 13, 22, 27; 5: 15, 17 and cf. Nb 15: 22-31). On the other hand, examples are given where there can be no question of mere inadvertence: *e.g.* for the *ḥaṭṭa'th*, the refusal to appear in court as a witness (Lv 5: 1), and for the *'asham*, fraud connected with sureties or with an object which has been found (Lv 5: 21-22).

This confusion and uncertainty can, of course, be partially clarified by literary criticism which can show how the texts have been adapted and re-cast. But the fact remains that the last redactors who drew up these confused rulings had no clear idea of what exactly was meant by a *ḥaṭṭa'th* and an *'asham*: either they were trying to draw a distinction between two terms which had originally been synonymous or they confused terms whose precise meaning they did not understand. We shall return to the point when we are discussing the history of sacrifice,[1] but enough has already been said to show that the ritual of the second Temple was not written without any reference to older documents or traditions: if it had been, the exposition would have been clearer.

4. *Vegetable offerings*

Vegetable offerings are called a *minḥah* (a word which most probably means 'a gift'). The ritual in Lv 2 distinguishes various kinds of offerings. One was of pure wheaten flour, unbaked, mixed with oil, which was accompanied by an offering of incense: a handful of the flour and all the

1. Cf. p. 429.

incense were burnt upon the altar, and the rest of the flour was given to the priests (Lv 2: 1-2; 6: 7-11; 7: 10). A second kind of offering was of the same mixture of flour, but baked on a tray or in a mould; part of it was burned, and the rest was given to the priests (Lv 2: 4-10; 7: 9). These offerings had to be unleavened and seasoned with salt (Lv 2: 11-13). A third and similar kind of offering is prescribed in Lv 2: 14-16: the offering of first-fruits, parched corn or baked bread, together with an offering of oil and of incense, was treated like the *minḥah*; part of this offering, too, was burnt upon the altar.

In all these offerings, that part which is burnt upon the altar is called *'azkarah*. The precise meaning of this term is not known: it may mean a 'memorial', because the sacrifice reminded God of the person who offered it, or a 'pledge', because the little part which was given to God reminded him of the whole offering and represented the whole.

In special instances, the *minḥah* was offered alone; *e.g.* in the daily offering of the high priest (all of which was burnt, because the priest could not give and receive one and the same offering, Lv 6: 13-16). Similarly, only the *minḥah* was offered on behalf of a poor man, and it then took the place of the sacrifice for sin (Lv 5: 11-13); and only the *minḥah* was offered as the 'sacrifice for jealousy' (Nb 5: 15); in all these instances, no oil or incense was used. More frequently, however, the *minḥah* was offered along with a sacrifice in which blood was shed, *i.e.* along with a holocaust or with a communion-sacrifice, and the *minḥah* was then accompanied by a libation of wine (cf. Ex 29: 40; Lv 23: 13, and especially Nb 15: 1-12).

5. *The shewbread*

Rather similar to the offerings just described is the shewbread, called in Hebrew *leḥem happanîm* ('the bread of the face' (of God), or 'the bread of the Presence') or *leḥem hamma'areketh* ('the shewbread'). According to Lv 24: 5-9, twelve cakes of pure wheaten flour were laid out in two lines on a table which stood in front of the Holy of Holies; they were renewed every sabbath day. They were a pledge of the Covenant between the twelve tribes and Yahweh. These cakes, or loaves, were eaten at the end of the week by the priests, but they were not placed on the altar; incense, however, was placed alongside each line of loaves as an *'azkarah*, and was burnt (on the altar of perfumes) when the loaves were changed. The fact that incense was placed there justifies us in regarding the loaves as something like a sacrificial offering, and Ezechiel himself likens the table on which they were put to an altar (Ez 41: 21-22). This table is described as part of the furniture of the desert Tent (Ex 25: 23-30).

6. Offerings of incense

In the last chapter we spoke of the altar of perfumes[1]; and in the present chapter we have frequently referred to the offering of incense along with vegetable offerings. The Hebrew word q'toreth means 'that which goes up in smoke', and may be used of any sacrifice which is burnt upon an altar (thus, probably, in 1 S 2: 28; Is 1: 13); in liturgical language, it is applied to offerings of perfumes, the full expression being q'toreth sammîm, which occurs frequently in the Priestly texts. Incense (l'bonah) is only one constituent of the offering, and Ex 30: 34-38 gives the recipe for the perfume to be used in worship: it contained equal parts of storax, onyx (obtained from certain shell-fish), galbanum and incense. Rabbinical writings contain a recipe for a much more elaborate mixture in which no less than sixteen ingredients were used; perhaps this formula was used in the last centuries of the second Temple. It is not surprising to find such mixtures of perfumes, for they are often mentioned in inscriptions from Southern Arabia. They were imported into Palestine from abroad, and were used in cultic worship as an added refinement. Indeed, they were used in all Oriental religions, as we shall see later on.

In incense-offerings, pieces of coal were taken from the altar of holocausts on a shovel or a scoop, the powder was sprinkled on the glowing embers and the shovelful was placed on the altar of perfumes, in front of the Holy of Holies. This offering was to be made each morning and each evening (Ex 30: 7-8), and could be made only by a priest (2 Ch 26: 16-18; Lk 1: 9). The rite was also performed on the Day of Atonement, and on this day the censer itself was taken inside the Holy of Holies (Lv 16: 12-13). Apart from these instances, in which the offering of perfumes was a special rite in the cult, incense was used in the second Temple only along with a minḥah, and in connection with the shewbread; and in these two instances, it was used on its own, not mixed with other substances.

1. Cf. p. 411.

CHAPTER ELEVEN

THE HISTORY OF SACRIFICE IN ISRAEL

THE sacrificial rites described in the preceding chapter were those followed in the second Temple, after the Exile. The final redaction of the Pentateuch assumes that the liturgy had always been practised in this way, from the time when Moses instituted the liturgy of Israel in the desert. Literary critics, however, divided the Pentateuch into several different documents, and by dating these documents, they have reconstructed a history of sacrifice which is very different from that which the last editors of the Pentateuch took for granted. We shall now examine this reconstruction.

1. *The critical theory*

Wellhausen's powerful synthesis, which has had, and still has, so much influence on exegesis, divided the history of sacrifice in Israel into three periods:

In the first period, down to the reform of Josias in 621 B.C., men were not much concerned about rites: their main anxiety was to know to whom they were offering sacrifice, not how to offer it. The rites used in sacrifice did not matter, if the offering was made to Yahweh and was accepted by him. In this period, there were only two types of sacrifice, the holocaust and the communion-sacrifice, and the latter was the more common. This is the situation we find in the ancient parts of the historical books, in the prophets of the eighth and seventh centuries, and in the Yahwistic and Elohistic passages of the Pentateuch.

With the reform of Josias a new period opened. The ritual for sacrifices was not altered, except on one essential point: all sacrifices had to be offered in the Temple at Jerusalem. This new law evidently entailed a unification of the ritual. It was a decisive step towards the systematization of the different usages which had previously obtained in the high places and in the various sanctuaries throughout the provinces. This is the state of affairs which is reflected in Deuteronomy.

From the beginning of the Exile, new trends appeared, and among them was a passionate concern for ritual. It can already be seen in Ezechiel's description of the rites to be followed when the cult was restored, and in his insistence on the idea of expiation. Ezechiel introduced two sacrifices which are not mentioned in earlier texts, namely, the sacrifice for sin and the sacrifice of reparation. These trends underwent several developments and eventually led to the final redaction of the Priestly Code, which contains all the texts referring to sacrificial worship. The ritual was given its definitive form in the days of Esdras, and this code of rites was then followed until the ruin of the Temple.

2. General considerations

We have presented the theory in its broad outlines, and without qualifications, but Wellhausen himself made certain reservations, and his followers have stressed them still more. In the years since the theory was put forward, critics have become more and more ready to admit that the late ritual code contains some ancient elements, but these elements, they say, have been integrated into a new system. This change, they hold, took place during the Exile, and it consisted in a fusion of the ideas contained in Deuteronomy with those contained in Ezechiel and the Priestly Code. And it is here that the fundamental weakness of the evolutionary scheme lies. The centralization of worship certainly did precipitate the unification of the ritual, but Deuteronomy cannot be used to reconstitute the ritual followed in the Temple during the years after Josias' reform, because Deuteronomy contains no code of law about sacrifices. It mentions sacrifices only incidentally, and only in connection with two related subjects which it has at heart: the law insisting upon one sanctuary (Dt 12), and the law about rights of priests (Dt 18). Of the cultic terms discussed in the preceding chapter, Deuteronomy mentions only *zebah*, *'olah*, *n'dabah* and *neder*, and makes no reference to *hatta'th* or *'asham* (this is the principal argument for calling these two sacrifices an invention of Ezechiel); but Deuteronomy never mentions offerings, perfumes, incense or the shewbread either, and these things were certainly used in the pre-exilic liturgy. The picture given in Deuteronomy, therefore, is not complete. Moreover, in the story of the reform, everything indicates that when the Temple became the sole legitimate sanctuary, the ritual which had previously been practised there continued in force, for the same priests, and they alone (cf. 2 K 23 : 9), held office there. The code of ritual used in the pre-exilic Temple should be sought, not in Deuteronomy, but in the Law of Holiness (Lv 17-26), the basic prescriptions of which probably date from the last years of the monarchy. Now this ritual in Leviticus is quite evidently connected with the thought of Ezechiel, and it bridges the gap between this prophet and the pre-exilic period, *i.e.* it comes from those years in which, according to Wellhausen's school, the great break occurred in the history of sacrifice. And yet the Law of Holiness does not contain a true code of sacrificial law, no more than Deuteronomy does; but it does contain prescriptions about holocausts and about the different kinds of communion-sacrifices (Lv 17: 1-12; 19: 5-8; 22: 18-25, 29-30) which fit in well enough with the sacrificial code of the second Temple. On the disputed issue of expiatory sacrifices, it is the Law of Holiness which contains the most explicit text (Lv 17: 11), and the sacrifice of *'asham* is mentioned in Lv 19: 20-22. We are quite ready to admit that a new edition of the Law of Holiness was written during the Exile, and that additions were made to it even later, but surely it is unsound scholarship to dismiss the passages just cited as the work of a redactor merely because they have no parallels in Deuteronomy and because they are in agreement with Ezechiel? One can only do so if one already accepts a particular theory about the history of sacrifice, and this theory must first be proved.

The fact remains, however, that the evidence contained in the Law of Holiness is not accepted by everyone, and we must therefore try to see how much truth there is in the theory of Wellhausen's school. We shall therefore examine two questions: first, we shall ask to what extent the forms of sacrifice used in the second Temple are mentioned in the historical books, in the pre-exilic prophets and in those traditions of the Pentateuch which are admitted to be ancient: this question will form the subject-matter of the present chapter. We shall then ask whether the neighbours of Israel practised these same kinds of sacrifice in ancient times; and if we find that this is so, we shall then inquire whether the Israelites borrowed their ritual from these neighbouring peoples, and if so, at what period, or whether the similarities can be sufficiently explained by the common racial origin and the common history of Israel and its neighbours: this second question will be studied in the next chapter.

3. *Holocausts and communion-sacrifices*

From the first historical texts to the book of Deuteronomy, there is a continuous line of evidence to show that these two kinds of sacrifice were practised in Israel. We shall mention only the most ancient witnesses.

In the days of the Judges, Gideon offered a holocaust (*'olah* Jg 6: 26, 28). The second tradition about Gideon's sacrifice (Jg 6: 18-22) is not so clear, but the obvious explanation is that at first Gideon does not recognize the Angel of Yahweh, and that he therefore prepares a meal for him as a guest: this meal is then transformed into a holocaust by the fire which shoots out of the rock. There is a similar, but more explicit, story about the holocaust offered by Manoah, the father of Samson (Jg 13: 15-20). Afterwards the Bible mentions the holocaust offered when the Ark is brought back from the land of the Philistines (1 S 6: 14), the holocausts of Samuel (1 S 7: 9; 10: 8), of Saul (1 S 13: 9f.), of David (2 S 6: 17f.) of Solomon, both before and after the building of the Temple (1 K 3: 4; 9: 25), and later, away from Jerusalem, the sacrifice of Elias on Carmel (1 K 18: 38). The victims offered on these occasions are, as in Leviticus, cattle and small livestock. And the characteristic feature of the holocaust, as described in Leviticus, is found in every instance: everything is burnt upon the altar. The sacrifices of Gideon and of Manoah are rather exceptional, but apart from these two, the Bible gives no details about the ritual which was followed, for the rubrics of sacrifice were of no interest to the authors of the historical books. It seems, however, that there was one point on which ancient custom and Leviticus differed: in ancient times, it would appear that the victim was slaughtered upon the altar (cf. the sacrifice of Abraham, Gn 22: 9-10, and the story of the war against the Philistines, 1 S 14: 33-34). In the sacrifice on Carmel, however, the bull was cut into pieces before being placed upon the wood which had been set upon the altar (1 K 18: 23, 33).

The communion-sacrifice is mentioned in ancient texts even more frequently than the holocaust. It is called simply *zebah* in several passages of the historical books (Jos 22: 26f.; 1 S 1: 21; 2: 13, 19; 3: 14; 6: 15, etc.; 2 S 15: 12; 1 K 8: 62; 12: 27; 2 K 5: 17; 10: 24, etc.), in the prophets (Is 1: 11; 19: 21; Jr 7: 22; Os 3: 4; 4: 19; Am 4: 4; So 1: 7, 8, etc.) and in the ancient collections of laws in the Pentateuch (Ex 23: 18; 34: 15, 25). It is also referred to, very frequently, simply as *sh'lamîm* in the historical books (Jg 20: 26; 21: 4; 1 S 13: 9; 2 S 6: 17, 18; 24: 25; 1 K 3: 15; 9: 25; 2 K 16: 13, etc.), in the ancient parts of the Pentateuch (Ex 20: 24; 32: 6, etc.) and in Ezechiel (Ez 43: 27; 45: 15, 17; 46: 12). The singular (*shelem*) occurs once only, in Am 5: 22. By contrast, the expression *zebah sh'lamîm*, which is constantly found in the Priestly writings, is rarely found outside them, and in Ex 24: 5; 1 S 11: 15, cf. Jos 22: 27 we have the phrase *z'bahîm sh'lamîm*, with the two words in apposition or, perhaps, with one as a gloss to explain the other.

These two names, then, are both very ancient, and they do not seem to denote two different ways of offering sacrifice. One of the words describes the sacrifice by reference to its outward ritual: it is a 'slaughtering' or 'immolation' (*zebah*). The other describes it by a reference to the intention with which it is offered: opinions here vary, but the most probable is that *sh'lamîm* implies the idea of a tribute offered to God to maintain or to re-establish good relations between him and his worshipper (cf. the words *shillem* and *shillum*, meaning 'retribution', and the Ugaritic word *shlmm*, which is used of gifts sent as pledges of peace).[1]

Like the sacrifice described in Leviticus, the communion-sacrifice of ancient times was a joyous sacrifice, in which the priest and the man (or the people) who offered it ate a part afterwards: but the blood was poured out and the fat was burnt upon the altar (1 S 2: 15-16). There is very little information about the ritual which was followed, but we do know that the details of the ritual varied somewhat until after the Exile. If the generally accepted correction of 1 S 9: 24 is the true original reading (and this is not certain), then the fat of a sheep's tail was eaten by the faithful, whereas this part is offered to God in the ritual of Lv 3: 9; 7: 3. The rights of priests

1. Compare the meaning of *shalôm*, p. 254.

developed, too: in ancient times, at least at Shiloh, the priest stuck a fork into the meat as it was boiling in the pot and so took a part at random (1 S 2: 13-14); according to Deuteronomy, he was given the shoulder, the jaws and the stomach (Dt 18: 3); according to Leviticus, he had a right to the breast and the right leg before they were cooked (Lv 7: 34).

The stories and the laws in the Pentateuch presuppose that the Israelites used to offer holocausts and communion-sacrifices before ever they settled in Canaan, while they were still in the desert. Am 5: 25 seems to contradict this: 'O house of Israel, did you make sacrifices and offerings to me during the forty years in the desert?' Jeremias, too, seems to agree with Amos: 'I said nothing, and I gave no commands to your fathers about holocausts or sacrifices when I brought them out of the land of Egypt' (7: 22). These two texts are quite explicit, but precisely because they are so unconditional, they should not be taken literally. The Pentateuch contains ancient traditions about sacrifices in the desert (*e.g.* Ex 3: 18; 5: 3, 8, 17; 10: 25; 18: 12; 32: 6, 8); both Amos and Jeremias must have known of these traditions, Yahwistic or Elohistic, and they did not formally repudiate them. They were familiar, too, with the Yahwistic and the Elohistic codes of the Covenant, both of which speak of sacrifices (Ex 20: 24; 23: 18; 34: 25), and they, like their contemporaries, must have regarded these laws as commandments handed down from the days of Moses; lastly, Jeremias knew of Dt 12: 6-14, and regarded it as a law of Moses. And both these prophets thought of the Passover as an institution dating from the Exodus. There must, then, be some explanation for the two texts cited at the beginning of this paragraph. The words of Amos and of Jeremias quoted there must not be torn out of their immediate context: they form part of oracles directed, not against the cult itself, but against the external and material cult which was practised by their contemporaries. God demands first and foremost an interior religion: he demands that men should 'listen to his voice' (Jr 7: 23), and that they should practise 'right and justice' (Am 5: 24). This ideal had been realized in the desert, according to these same prophets (Jr 2: 2; Am 2: 10), and they are harking back to this ideal here: in the desert, they claim, men did not act as they do nowadays, and to make their argument more striking, they express it without any qualification: in the desert, Israel did not offer sacrifices, and God did not ask them to do so. They ought to have added 'sacrifices like the ones you offer', but they were preachers, not twentieth-century scholars writing a history of Israelite sacrifice. (It is the same principle as that which everyone accepts when speaking of the Priestly authors: they saw the liturgical organization of the Temple in their own day, and ascribed it all to the desert days: yet no one pretends that they were trying to write a critical history of Israelite sacrifice.)

So much, then, for the position adopted by Amos and Jeremias. If we now look at the evidence from the standpoint of modern literary criticism and set aside as late texts all the passages in the Priestly documents, and date the Yahwistic and Elohistic codes of the Covenant to the period when Israel was settling in Canaan, and Deuteronomy to the end of the monarchic period, then one must admit that there is scarcely any information left about sacrificial worship in the desert. Of the very ancient texts quoted above, Ex 1-10 speaks of sacrifices which are to be offered, not of those which actually were offered, and it is a pretext to persuade the Pharaoh to let the Israelites leave Egypt; in Ex 18: 12, it is Jethro who offers the sacrifice, and he is not an Israelite; and in Nb 22: 40; 23: 1f. 14f. 29f. it is Balaq, another foreigner, who offers sacrifice. The sacrifices referred to in Ex 32: 6, 8 were offered to the golden calf, and they are condemned in the present edition of the text. This leaves the Passover, but this is an altogether exceptional kind of sacrifice in which everything takes place away from any altar. Certainly, one must admit that when the Israelites were semi-nomads, they slaughtered beasts as sacrifices: it is a shepherd custom, and there is evidence of such sacrifices in Arabia in far distant times. But we shall never know exactly what rites the Israelites followed in those early days.

4. Expiatory sacrifices

The critical school acknowledged that at least holocausts and communion-sacrifices were offered from the time of the settlement in Canaan; but it claimed that sacrifice for sin (*hatta'th*) and the sacrifice of reparation (*'asham*) were unknown before the Exile. They are first mentioned, it is claimed, in Ezechiel, who refers to both of them several times (Ez 40: 39; 42: 13; 44: 29; 46: 20) and gives some details about the sacrifice called *hatta'th* (Ez 45: 19-20, 23).

Nevertheless, it would be rather odd to find new types of sacrifice, for which there was no precedent, invented during the Exile, when there was no external cult at all. Secondly, it is noteworthy that Ezechiel does not explain what he means by *hatta'th* and *'asham*; in other words, he presumes that the terms are known. Thirdly, the ritual in Leviticus is full of obscurities when it is describing these sacrifices and the way in which they are distinguished from each other: the best explanation of this confusion is that the authors of this ritual piece together ancient elements whose precise meaning they did not understand.[1] Fourthly, if the Law of Holiness in Leviticus is, as was claimed above,[2] older than the book of Ezechiel, then Lv 19: 20-22 implies that at least the sacrifice of *'asham* was known in the last years of the monarchy. We can also appeal to two more ancient documents, but their value is contested.

In the passage containing Joas' commands about the Temple, 2 K 12: 17 says that 'the money from the *'asham* and the money from the *hatta'th*

1. Cf. p. 421.   2. Cf. pp. 144 and 425-426.

(reading the singular, with the Greek) were not given to the Temple of Yahweh, but were given to the priests'. It is difficult to say whether this text refers to faults similar to those which were expiated by sacrifices of *'asham* and *ḥaṭṭa'th*, or to taxes which had to be paid on the occasion of these sacrifices, or to payments of money which might be made instead of the sacrifices. Nevertheless, it is significant that this money reverts to the priest, like the meat of victims offered in these sacrifices for sin, according to the ritual in Leviticus: and the terms used here in the Book of Kings are certainly technical terms in liturgical language. Now, in the evolution of worship, it is not normal for a custom of paying money to be replaced at a later date by the offering of a victim; in fact, it is quite the contrary process which takes place. Thus this text in the Book of Kings implies that the sacrifices themselves are of ancient origin. (If the text refers to payments in addition to the sacrifices, as in the laws of Lv 5: 14-16; Nb 5: 8, then it evidently presupposes that the sacrifices themselves were offered.)

The text in Os 4: 8 is equally difficult: 'They feed on the sin (*ḥaṭṭa'th*) of my people, and are greedy for its wickedness (*'awon*)'. It is tempting to take this as meaning that the priests feed on the *ḥaṭṭa'th* of the people because they receive all the meat offered in a sacrifice of *ḥaṭṭa'th*. But the parallel term, 'wickedness' (*'awon*), is not a word used for sacrifice, and this justifies a different interpretation: the priests and the people are practising a cult which God does not accept (cf. the immediate context, Os 4: 4-7, 12-13), and all the sacrifices, which are eaten by the priests, are a 'sin' and a 'wicked thing'. All the same, it is possible that the word *'awon* ('wickedness') is used here only to make a kind of parallel, and that *ḥaṭṭa'th* is a technical term meaning a sacrifice for sin.

There are, then, a certain number of converging arguments in virtue of which one may admit that expiatory sacrifices existed under the monarchy; but it must be granted that they were less common than the holocaust or the communion-sacrifice.

5. Vegetable offerings and incense-offerings

In the liturgical language of Ezechiel and the Pentateuch, the word *minḥah* always refers to offerings of vegetable produce as distinct from sacrifices in which blood is shed. It is commonly held that in pre-exilic texts the term is used indifferently of all kinds of sacrifice, including sacrifices in which blood is shed. This does not seem precise enough: when *minḥah* is mentioned alongside *zebaḥ* in I S 2: 29; 3: 14; Is 19: 21, alongside *'olah* in Jr 14: 12; Ps 20: 4, and alongside *shelem* in Am 5: 22, it must bear the more precise meaning of a vegetable offering. There are other texts in which it is impossible to decide whether it refers to an animal or a vegetable offering. And, finally, there are some texts where it must refer to a sacrifice of animals (thus I S 2: 17; 26: 19), but the reason is that *minḥah* is then used in its general sense of a 'gift' (or, a 'tribute'),[1] which is true of every sacrifice.

We have already pointed out that the shewbread was rather similar to vegetable offerings, and these loaves are mentioned in the ancient story preserved in 1 S 21: 3-7. They are contrasted with 'profane' bread, and are called the 'holy bread of the face' (of Yahweh); they were regularly replaced 'before Yahweh'. The word *q'toreth*, meaning 'that which goes up in smoke', could also be used in a general sense for any sacrifice which was burnt upon the altar: this is probably the meaning of 1 S 2: 28 and Is 1: 13, and the cognate verb certainly means 'to sacrifice animals' in 2 K 16: 13, 15. The special sense of 'perfume-offerings', which is the meaning of *q'toreth* and of *q'toreth sammîm* in the Priestly writings,[2] is not found in any pre-exilic text, and it has therefore been argued that the custom did not exist before the Exile.

Nevertheless, there is evidence of an equivalent rite in some ancient texts: it is the offering of incense (*l'bonah*) mentioned in Jr 6: 20; 17: 26 (the authenticity is questioned); 41: 5. We have shown above that there was in Solomon's Temple an altar which was used for these offerings.[3] In 1 K 3: 3, the Deuteronomic redactor condemns a certain cult as illegitimate simply because it is practised outside the Temple: he describes this cult by using the verbs 'to make to smoke' and 'to slaughter'; it is quite probable that the first verb refers to offerings of incense, and that the second refers to sacrifices of beasts (cf. 1 K 11: 8).

A recent discovery may confirm this: at Bethel, a seal from South Arabia has been discovered, and this seal may have been used to mark the bags of incense which were imported for the use of the sanctuary there. Again, the papyri from Elephantine state that in the temple there (built before 525 B.C.),[4] the Jews offered sacrifices of animals, of vegetable produce and of incense: and these men followed the customs which obtained in the last years of the monarchy.

The custom of offering incense certainly existed in Israel from ancient times: it was a custom of other nations, too, and especially of the Egyptians, but the rites changed as time went on. Perhaps to begin with, portable censers were used, and there may be some record of them in certain stories about the desert (Lv 10: 1f.; Nb 16: 1f.) and in the instruments, the shovel (*maḥtah*) and the scoop (*kaph*), which were later used to carry the burning coals and the perfume on to the altar. This altar is mentioned for the first time, we said, in Solomon's Temple, and altars dating from the same period have been found in excavations.[5] It seems that for a long time pure incense was used, without any other additional perfumes, and this custom : laid down in the ritual for the *minḥah* (Lv 2: 1f.), for first-fruits (Lv 2: 15) and for the

1. Cf. p. 255.   2. Cf. p. 301.   3. Cf. p. 411.
4. Cf. p. 340.   5. Cf. p. 411.

shewbread (Lv 24: 7): all three are ancient rites. For the special offerings of incense which were instituted after the Exile, the mixture prescribed by Ex 30: 34-38 was used, and the rite was called *q'toreth sammîm*, an 'offering of aromatics', in the plural.

6. Conclusion

In offerings of perfume and of vegetable produce, and for the different types of animal sacrifice, there is, then, a real continuity between the cult practised in the monarchic period and that followed after the Exile: the essential forms of the post-exilic cult are found also in the days before the Exile. But there was a development: before the Exile, communion-sacrifices were more frequent than holocausts, but after the Exile holocausts became the more important kind of sacrifice. After the Exile, the special sacrifices for the expiation of sin developed further and in the end an expiatory value was ascribed to the holocaust itself (Lv 1: 4); the relation of vegetable offerings to communion-sacrifices was more clearly defined; and for the offering of perfumes, a new mixture was prescribed, a new name was given to the rite, and a new ritual for the offering came into force. This is not to be wondered at, and it would have been astonishing if the ritual had not changed throughout the many centuries in which we have followed its history. But these changes should not lead us to forget the antiquity and the fundamental unity of the ritual followed in the sacrifices of Israel.

CHAPTER TWELVE

THE ORIGIN OF ISRAELITE RITUAL

THE last chapter argued from the evidence of biblical texts to the conclusion that the rites used in Israelite sacrifices were of ancient origin. This conclusion can be confirmed by comparing Israelite ritual with the rituals of other Oriental religions, in which there are similar practices. But this similarity raises another question: did Israel borrow its rites from the cultural background of the neighbouring Semitic peoples; for the connections with other nations, belonging to more distant races or lands, are either accidental or of secondary importance.

1. Mesopotamian sacrifice

The normal term for sacrifice in Akkadian is *nequ*, the Akkadian equivalent of the Hebrew *zebaḥ* is *zîbu*, but it is rarely used and may be borrowed from West Semitic. The literal meaning of *nequ* is a 'libation' of water, of wine or of beer and so on, which is made along with a sacrifice. The sacrifice was first and foremost a meal offered to a god. The altar was the table of the god, and every kind of food which men eat was laid upon it: meat (especially mutton, but also beef and gazelle), poultry, fish, vegetables, fruit, sweets, and, of course, drink and bread. In rituals or in descriptions of sacrifices, we sometimes find mention of twelve, twenty-four or thirty-six loaves (the figures are bound up with the sexagesimal system of counting used by the Mesopotamians). The god's table was laid twice a day (four times in the latest ritual), and the priest arranged the feast. Alongside the altar table stood a perfume-brazier upon which fragrant wood and aromatic substances burned in order to delight the gods and to attract them to the feast. In the Babylonian story of the Flood, Utnapishtim, the Babylonian Noah, offered a sacrifice: 'I set up seven and seven incense-burners, and laid upon them reeds, cedar-wood and myrtle; the gods scented the fragrance, the gods scented the lovely fragrance, the gods collected like flies around the sacrificer.'

In Mesopotamia, the blood of victims was used only in a very minor way: it is doubtful whether it was ever used in the ritual, for there is no explicit reference to libations of blood in normal sacrifices. There was an official called 'the sword-bearer', but he merely cut the throat of the animal which was destined to be the food of the god. The food was shared between the gods, the priest-king, the clergy and the staff of the temple, and the part due to each one was prescribed in liturgical texts. It would be inaccurate, however, to call these sacrifices 'communion-sacrifices', for the man who offered the sacrifice received nothing back: those who conducted the cult took it all as their share. The liturgical texts do not say what became of the food set out on the table of the god, but Dn 14: 1-22 gives a satirical explanation of how it disappeared.

In ordinary sacrifices, no part of the victim was burnt upon the altar, and the essential forms of Israelite sacrifice, *viz.* the holocaust and the communion-sacrifice, did not exist in Mesopotamia. Similar customs are mentioned only for particular occasions: an animal was wholly or partly burnt in certain ceremonies of purification, of consecration and of conjuration, and these ceremonies sometimes included an anointing with blood. These two rites, burning an animal and anointing with its blood, are foreign to normal Mesopotamian ritual, and they may have been adopted from West Semitic peoples, among whom there is ample evidence of their use.

There were no expiatory sacrifices either. The nearest parallel to them is what has been called, rather inaccurately, the 'substitution-sacrifice'. Gods might seek revenge, and demons sought to hurt men; and how was man to avert an evil destiny which had fallen to him by lot? The peoples of Mesopotamia took an animal (often a different type of animal from those offered to the gods as food), or made a model of an animal out of reeds, mud and paste: this animal or model was the *puḫu* or the *dinânu*, *i.e.* the 'substitute' of the man offering it. A priest who acted as an exorcist then killed the victim, destroyed or mutilated the model with appropriate formulas, and the anger of the gods or demons was thus turned against the 'substitute'. The sick man was cured, the danger was averted. One text is extremely clear: 'He gave a lamb for his life, he gave a lamb's head for a man's head, he gave a lamb's neck for a man's neck, he gave a lamb's breast for a man's breast!' The same rite could be used to ward off evil. In one Assyrian treaty, the agreement is confirmed by the immolation of a ram, during which the following words were recited: 'This head is not a ram's head, it is the head of Mati'ilu, the head of his sons, of his nobles, of his people and of his country. If the undermentioned person sins against the clauses (of this treaty), may the undermentioned person's head be wrenched off . . . just as this head is wrenched off. This leg is not a ram's leg, it is the leg of the undermentioned person . . . etc.'

Lastly, we must mention a custom known as the 'substitute king' or the 'royal substitute', for several rather adventurous theories have been based upon it. Often enough, these theories are based upon wrong translations of certain texts, and the way in which the texts are then combined leaves much to be desired. It is suggested, then, that each year, at the New Year feast, a man was chosen to take the place of the king and was put to death: the purpose of the ceremony was to ensure a renewal of life for the king and of prosperity for the country. In fact, however, a more sober interpretation of the texts leads to a different conclusion: when particularly dangerous omens were seen, such as an eclipse of the moon or sun, a substitute exercised the royal power for all outward purposes, in order to ward off the danger from the real king and to draw the dangers upon himself. The critical period was held to last one hundred days, and at the expiration of this period the real king began to rule again in the normal way. Most scholars admit that the substitute was put to death at the end of his 'reign', but the texts do not say so explicitly: only once is the death of a substitute king mentioned, and it may have been due to natural causes.

Whether or not the substitute was put to death after his task was over, this custom of replacing the king by a substitute does not prove that human sacrifice was offered in Mesopotamia. Similarly, the magic rites for transferring the vengeance of the gods to an animal or to a model of an animal cannot be called 'substitution-sacrifices' except by a misuse of language. There is no place in them for that religious sentiment which seeks to make reparation to the deity, and they cannot be compared with the expiatory sacrifices practised in Israel.

In the last generation, some scholars thought that the late Jewish ritual which was composed during the Exile had been influenced by Babylonian ritual. It is quite possible that certain secondary terms (*t'nûphah* and *t'rûmah*) were borrowed from the juridical (but not from the liturgical) language of Babylon, and that the occasional references to the altar as a 'table' (Ez 44: 16; Ml 1: 7, 12; Is 65: 11 refers to the table of false gods), and the very common references to the 'table' of the shewbread reflect the language used in Babylonian worship (cf. Dn 14: 12, 18), but the shewbread itself is mentioned in the old, pre-exilic text of 1 S 21: 4-7, at a time when it is most unlikely that Israel was adopting customs from Mesopotamia. In short, there may be some tenuous and secondary contacts between the sacrificial system followed in Israel and that followed in Babylonia, but, these apart, the two systems are very different from each other and certainly independent of each other.

2. Sacrifice among the ancient Arabs

Our information about sacrifice among the ancient Arabs comes from various sources: the relics of pagan practices which survive in Islam, allusions in the Koran, information contained in the rare pre-Islamic writings which have survived, pre-Islamic inscriptions, and above all, old traditions which have been collected by later Arab authors. But all these sources together do not enable us to construct a complete and satisfactory picture: the most modern texts have to be approached in a severely critical way, and the oldest texts (the inscriptions) are very laconic.

One text, which is very often quoted as a description of an Arab sacrifice, must be definitely rejected, though it is frequently cited to prove or to confirm a particular theory about Semitic sacrifice. It is a story written by a monk of Sinai about 400 A.D., and published under the name of St. Nilus. It tells how St. Nilus' son was made prisoner by the Saracens, who decided to offer him as a sacrifice to the Morning Star, as was their practice when they captured handsome young men. Everything was prepared—the altar, the sword, the libation and the incense—but the barbarians woke up too late, for the planet (which had to be visible) was no longer to be seen, and so the young man was saved. The author adds that when the Arabs had no men to offer in sacrifice, they used to kill a camel instead; the man performing the sacrifice first stabbed it and tasted its blood, and then all the others fell upon the beast to tear off a piece of the flesh, which they ate raw: everything, including the intestines, the bones and the marrow, had to disappear before sun-rise. Almost everything in this fantastic story is false, and almost every detail is contradicted by other documents.

A further difficulty is that, before the coming of Islam, the Arabs had not one religion but several: the religions varied from place to place, and we have little information about the ritual practised by any of them. We must restrict our statements to what seems most probable.

The most direct contact the Israelites had was with Northern Arabia, and this is the very region in which information is most scanty. We know that the inhabitants of this area made offerings to the gods, and one Liḥyanite inscription may refer to a human sacrifice, though its meaning is not certain. The Safaites certainly killed animals for sacrifice, but none of the sacrifices mentioned in inscriptions were offered at a sanctuary: they were all offered at a camping-spot, on the occasion of an event in which all the family was concerned.

We have no inscriptions from Central Arabia, and are therefore dependent upon what Arab authors tell us. Offerings of flour and libations of milk were known, but they were rare. In certain ceremonies a man's hair was cut off and offered up; this offering, however, was not a sacrifice, but a rite of de-consecration, like the rite used in Israel for the *nazir* (Nb 6: 18).[1] An extra share of booty and the first-fruits of the harvest were normally offered to the gods. These poor nomadic tribes did not make offerings of incense or perfumes, but they did sacrifice animals. No part of the victim was ever burnt upon an altar; the sacrifices, therefore, were not the equivalent of the *'olah* and *zebaḥ* sacrifices of the Israelites.

Indeed, there was not even an altar in the sense of the Hebrew *mizbeaḥ*: what corresponded to it was the *nuṣub* or *manṣab*, which is the *maṣṣebah* of the Bible, *i.e.* an upright stone which could have a roughly human form. It stood for the deity, and the sacrificial rite consisted in cutting the throat of the

1. Cf. p. 466.

victim in front of this stone, and in rubbing the stone with the blood, which flowed into a ditch out near the stele. The victims were domestic animals, sheep, cattle and camels: to offer a gazelle instead of a sheep was considered to be defrauding the deity. The throat was cut by the man offering the sacrifice, and then, he, along with his family and any guests he had invited, ate the meat. Human sacrifices are mentioned only by Christian writers, and there is no means of checking their testimony.

In Southern Arabia, civilization was far more advanced, and the kingdoms of Ma'an, Saba, Qataban and Hadramut all had both sanctuaries and rituals. Dues and all kinds of offerings were presented to the temples, and sacrifices properly so called were offered upon altars. There were altars for libations and altars for perfumes: they are referred to in inscriptions, and many of them have been found by archaeologists. Both in public and in private worship, the use of aromatics was widespread. Animals were everywhere offered in sacrifice, and the victims chosen were usually sheep or bulls, though wild animals, such as gazelles and leopards, were also used. There is not a single text which certainly refers to human sacrifice. The immolation took place on the altar itself, which is called *mdbht*, the equivalent of the Hebrew *mizbeah*. It is commonly claimed that the holocaust was one form of sacrifice in Southern Arabia, but this not at all certain. There is a word *msrb* which refers to an object used in worship, and which comes from a root meaning 'to burn', but the only inscription in which details are given about this *msrb* refers to a *msrb* of myrrh and a *msrb* of fragrant wood; it may mean, then, an altar for perfumes. There is also a verb *hnr*, meaning 'to burn, to offer a burnt sacrifice', but the contexts in which it is found never mention an animal as victim, and every one of them can be taken as referring to an altar of incense.

To the extent to which it is known, the sacrificial system of Arabia has more in common with Israel than the system followed in Mesopotamia: we may cite, for example, the importance of animal sacrifices, the use of the same kind of animal (usually tame) for sacrifice, the way in which those offering it share in the meat of the victims, the use to which blood is put in Central Arabia, the name of the altar in Southern Arabia, and the widespread use of perfume-offerings in the South. These common features confirm the view that Israelite rites were of ancient origin; the similarities are explained by the common origin of the two peoples, by the pastoral life which the ancestors of Israel led and which the Arab nomads still lead (shepherds normally offer sacrifice from their flocks), and lastly, by the contacts between the two peoples in their culture and their commerce (the perfumes of Arabia). But we cannot conclude that Israel adopted any of these rites from the ancient Arabs, for essential features of the Israelite system are lacking in Arabia: the total or partial burning of the victim upon an altar was a rite followed in every kind of Israelite sacrifice, but there was no such rite in Northern or

Central Arabia, and the assertion that it took place in Southern Arabia is based on a questionable proof.

3. Canaanite sacrifices

Our knowledge of Canaanite sacrifices comes from three different sources: the allusions in the Bible, or the condemnations which it utters against the cult of the Baals and the Astartes when the Israelites took part in them, inscriptions from the Phoenician homeland and from its colonies, and the texts of Ras Shamra.

Among the biblical references, we must first set aside all that is not strictly Canaanite, such as the late Assyrian cults, like the cult of stars (2 K 21: 3*b*; 23: 5*b*; Jr 44: 15-25), and the syncretist or mystery-rites mentioned in the late texts (Ez 8: 7-13; Is 65: 2-5; 66: 3). If we set aside sacrifices of babies also (we shall discuss them later to show that human sacrifice was never lawful in Israel),[1] then, according to the biblical evidence, Canaanite sacrifices do not seem to be materially different from those which were offered to Yahweh. Solomon had in his harem Moabites, Ammonites, and Sidonians, who offered incense and sacrifices to their gods (1 K 11: 8). Naaman offered holocausts (*'olah*) and communion-sacrifices (*zebah*) to other gods, and vowed that he would in future offer them only to Yahweh (2 K 5: 17). The description of the sacrifice on Carmel (1 K 18) tells how the prophets of Baal and Elias himself prepared their holocausts in the same way, and the point of the story is lost if this was not the normal way of offering sacrifice to Baal. Jehu is supposed to be following the Canaanite ritual in the story about the temple of Baal (2 K 10: 18-27), and both *zebah* and *'olah* are mentioned there. For the Deuteronomic redactor of the Books of Kings, the words sacrifice and perfume-offerings sum up that cult of the 'high places' which he condemns in the reign of almost every king of Judah (1 K 22: 44; 2 K 12: 4; 14: 4 etc.), and even in the reign of Solomon during the years before the Temple was built (1 K 3: 3). These were offerings meant for Yahweh, but Jeremias speaks in the same terms of the sacrifices and incense offered to Baal (Jr 7: 9; 11: 12, 13, 17; 32: 29). In all these texts, the verbal form used is the Pi'el (*qitter*), not the Hiph'il (*hiqtir*), for the latter form is normally kept for the cult of Yahweh (but cf. 1 K 11: 8; Jr 48: 35; Os 2: 15); this nicety of writing, however, does not mean that the rite was different. The Bible does not condemn this cult because of the rites it entailed, but because it was offered in illegitimate sanctuaries or to deities other than Yahweh. According to the Bible, then, there was a fundamental similarity between Canaanite sacrifice and Israelite sacrifice; but biblical texts cannot prove that the technical terms used in connection with sacrifice were the same among the Israelites and among the Canaanites.

Canaanite terminology must be sought in Phoenician and Punic inscrip-

---

1. Cf. pp. 443-446.

tions. Among the Punic inscriptions, the most important for our purpose are two price-lists, called respectively the Carthage price-list, and the price-list of Marseilles (where the stone was taken from North Africa). The lists fix the amount of money to be paid for each kind of sacrifice, the part to be given to the priest and the part to be given to the man offering the sacrifice (the 'master of the sacrifice'); they do not, however, give a description of the rites, nor do they tell us the motives for which the various sacrifices are offered. In addition to the offering of vegetable produce (called *minḥah*, and in Hebrew), the price-list from Marseilles mentions three kinds of sacrifice, the *kalil*, the *ṣewa'at* and the *shelem kalil*. In the *kalil*, a very small part of the meat is given to the priest, and nothing to the man offering the sacrifice; in the *ṣewa'at*, the breast and the leg are given to the priest, and the rest to the man making the offering; no indication is given as to how the meat is to be divided in a *shelem kalil*, except when a fowl is offered in an exorcism or in taking auspices: the meat then belongs to the man bringing the sacrifice. By comparing these rules with Leviticus, some scholars identify the *kalil* with expiatory sacrifice, the *ṣewa'at* with communion-sacrifice, and the *shelem kalil* with the holocaust. We cannot be certain of these identifications: the clearest is the similarity between the *ṣewa'at* and the *zebaḥ* or *zebaḥ shelamîm* used in Israel, but it should be noted that the names are not the same. The question becomes more complicated still if we compare also the price-list from Carthage: this gives slightly different regulations for the *kalil* and the *ṣewa'at*, and never mentions the *shelem kalil*. There were, then, certain variations even within the Carthaginian system itself. We find yet other names used throughout the rest of the Punic world: in a Neo–Punic inscription of the Roman period, *'lt* is used alongside *mnḥt*, and these two words correspond to the Hebrew *'olah* and *minḥah*, *'zr* (a 'votive offering'?) is found in several inscriptions. The use of perfumes is attested by a fragment of a ritual which speaks of *qṭrt* and *lbnt*, *i.e.* the equivalent of the Hebrew *q'toreth* and *l'bonah*. The inscriptions date from different periods, but they are all later than Leviticus. In Phoenicia itself, there are inscriptions going back to the era before Israel went into Exile, but unfortunately they contain no information about sacrifices: for this period, we have to rely on the biblical texts cited above. By comparing these texts with the information given in later inscriptions, we can conclude only that the Canaanite system of sacrifice was similar to the Israelite system: they offered at least holocausts and communion-sacrifices, vegetable produce and perfumes, but the two systems developed independently of each other, and their terminology was not altogether the same.

At Ras Shamra, the ancient Ugarit, archaeologists have discovered some texts dating from the fourteenth century B.C., *i.e.* before the Israelites settled in Palestine. Scholars have compiled lists of Ugaritic sacrificial terms and tried to find the corresponding Hebrew terms. Many of these identifications are uncertain, because the meaning of the Ugaritic terms is not beyond dispute. The most significant are those terms which appear in ritual texts: *dbḥ* (sacrifice)—*zebaḥ*; *shlmm* (peace-offering)—*shʿlamîm*; *shrph* (burnt-offering) may correspond to those sacrifices which were wholly or partially burnt upon the altar. The word *'ṭm* has also been cited as the equivalent of the Hebrew *'asham*, but the meaning of the word is not at all certain, and we are not even sure that it belongs to the Semitic language of Ugarit. Perhaps the descriptions of certain actions in the great poems of Ras Shamra are of greater value than this handful of terms from brief and mutilated texts. We read in the story of the sacrifice offered by the hero Keret. 'He rose and painted his face (not: 'put blood on his face'), 'washed his hands to the elbow, his fingers to the shoulder; he entered into the shadow of the tent and took a lamb of sacrifice into his hand, a young beast into his two hands, all his best food, he took . . . ? a bird of sacrifice; he poured wine into a silver cup, honey into a golden cup; he went to the top of the tower, he climbed up on to the shoulder of the wall, he raised his hands to heaven, he sacrificed to the Bull El, his father, he honoured Baal with his sacrifice, the son of Dragon with his offering'. Keret then came down again and got food ready for the town: this food was, it appears, unconnected with the sacrifice, so that the sacrifice would have been a holocaust. It would, however, be imprudent to regard this poetic description as a ritual. We may note, too, that the Ras Shamra texts, like the Phoenician and Punic inscriptions, do not seem to attach any ritual importance to the blood of the victim.

The information gathered here comes from several places and from many different periods. In our opinion, it does not justify the conclusion that Israel took all its ritual for sacrifices from Canaan, but it does indicate that Israelite ritual is far closer to the ritual of Canaan than to that of Mesopotamia or Arabia. The relationship between Israelite and Canaanite ritual is probably more complex than is usually admitted, and we shall attempt to define it.

4. *The origin of the sacrificial ritual of Israel*

The feature which distinguishes Israelite and Canaanite rituals from those of other Semitic peoples is that, when an animal is sacrificed, the victim, or at least a part of it, is burnt upon an altar. This rite did not exist in Mesopotamia or in Arabia, but it did exist among the Moabites and the Ammonites, according to the allusions in the Bible. The rite is thus peculiar to the West Semitic peoples, but it is also a Greek rite. The typical sacrifice (θυσία) is closely connected with the *zebaḥ*: part of the victim is burnt upon the altar, part is given to the priests, and the rest is eaten in a sacred meal. The sacrifice *'olah*, in which the whole victim is burnt upon the altar, corresponds to the Greek holocaust, which was much rarer than the θυσία (as the *'olah* was at first rarer than the *zebaḥ*), and which was confined to the worship of the gods of the underworld, and of dead heroes. One could extend this range of contacts to include other facts in the cult and point out, for example, that βωμός, meaning both a 'platform' and 'altar', may correspond to *bamah* the 'high place' which served as an altar.[1] These kindred customs must have originated in a civilization which preceded both the Hellenes and the Canaanites along the shores of the Eastern Mediterranean. The custom of burning either the whole or part of the victim upon an altar obtained in Canaan before the Israelites came to Palestine. On the other hand, there is no certain proof that the Israelites practised the custom when they were semi-nomads, and perhaps the oldest form of sacrifice they practised is the type which survived in the offering of the Paschal lamb. This sacrifice was closely linked with the history of their sojourn in the desert: no part of the victim was burnt, blood played an important rôle and the meat was eaten by the faithful: we have seen how all these characteristics are found in the sacrifices of the ancient nomadic Arabs. When they settled in Canaan, they adopted from the Canaanites the sacrifices called '*olah* and *zebaḥ*, which were burnt upon the altar; they then combined these sacrifices with the ancient rites about the use of blood—rites, then, which retained their efficacy and which were not found among the Canaanites—and the two rituals, Israelite and Canaanite, afterwards developed independently of each other. We suggest this explanation of the origin of Israelite ritual only as a hypothesis which attempts to take into consideration all the information at present available.

5. *Human sacrifice in Israel*

One theory which is put forward by historians of comparative religion is that animals were sacrificed as substitutes for men, and from this many writers conclude that originally men were put to death in sacrifice. We have already stated that the 'substitution-sacrifices' in Mesopotamia were connected with magic rather than with religion, and that the Israelite custom of laying one's hands on the victim did not mean that the victim was a substitute for the person offering the sacrifice. We shall return to these issues in the next chapter, where we shall put forward a theory of sacrifice.

In fact, however, human sacrifice was known in the ancient Oriental religions, but such sacrifices were so exceptional that one hesitates to call them true sacrifices. At the dawn of Egyptian history, prisoners or foreigners were sometimes put to death, but very soon the practice gave way to a symbolic execution carried out on little clay models. In Mesopotamia, there is the instance of the substitute-king which we have already mentioned[2]; and we know from the large numbers of skeletons found in the royal tombs of Ur that in this distant epoch wives and servants of the kings were buried with them; but this does not mean that these people were put to death as a sacrifice. In Arabia, there is only the evidence, itself suspect, of a few late authors.

The clearest texts comes from the Phoenician world, and they concern the sacrifice of babies: we shall discuss this point in a special paragraph. There are also the so-called 'foundation-sacrifices', which are often mentioned in the reports of Palestinian archaeologists about the excavations of Canaanite towns: as a general rule, these skeletons merely show that the normal practice was to bury children who died in infancy under the ground in the house, but there are some examples which are more decisive (like the one referred to in 1 K 16: 34). We have already stated that the theory of human sacrifice is scarcely tenable for Oriental cultures other than of Israel, but it has been asserted that even Israel practised it. Some writers hold that apostate Israelites offered human sacrifice to foreign deities, that some of them even offered such sacrifices to Yahweh (whom they identified with these foreign deities), and even that at some distant era Yahwism gave official recognition to, and actually prescribed, human sacrifice. Stated in this form, the thesis is, from a critical point of view, quite untenable.

(a) *Human sacrifices in historical texts.* Certain stories in the historical books of the Bible are claimed as evidence in favour of this thesis. We have just cited 1 K 16: 34: in the reign of Achab, Hiel of Bethel rebuilt Jericho: 'at the price of his first-born, Abiram, he laid the foundations, and at the price of his last-born, Segub, he set up its gates' (cf. Jos 6: 26). The meaning of the text is disputed, but even if it does refer to foundation-sacrifices, this could easily be explained, in Achab's reign, by the religious influence of Phoenicia. The execution of prisoners of war, even when it took place 'before Yahweh', was not a sacrifice, but the fulfilment of the *ḥerem*[1] (1 S 15: 33, cf. v. 3). The story of how Saul's descendants were handed over to the men of Gibeon and cut in pieces by them on the high place of Gibeon (2 S 21: 1-14) is presented, from the Israelite side, as the acquittal of a blood-debt; the Gibeonites gave their revenge the form of a fertility-rite (the poems of Ras Shamra throw light on this), but since the Gibeonites were not Israelites, this story teaches us nothing about the religion of Israel. This leaves only the story of Jephthah (Jg 11: 30-40): the obvious meaning of the text (and it should not be toned down) is that Jephthah had promised that, should he return victorious, he would offer as a holocaust the first person who came out of his house: it was his only daughter, and he offered her in sacrifice. But the story is told as a quite extraordinary and shocking incident: so, too, was the action of the king of Moab, when he immolated his only son upon the rampart of his capital while it was being invested by the Israelites (2 K 3: 27). The story of Jephthah cannot be used as evidence in the study of Israelite ritual.

Some authors cite the story of Abraham's sacrifice (Gn 22: 1-19). God asked Abraham to offer his only son as a holocaust, but stayed his hand when

1. Cf. pp. 260-261.

it was already raised to stab Isaac, and a ram was offered instead of the child. This, it is claimed, is an aetiological story, meant to explain and to justify the replacement of human sacrifice by the sacrifice of animals. Yet the meaning of the story in the mind of the editor of Genesis, and in its context of patriarchal history, seems to be quite different: when God commanded Abraham to sacrifice the son in whom the divine promises were centred, he was subjecting Abraham's faith to an extraordinary test, and Abraham's obedience was rewarded by a solemn renewal of the promise made to his posterity. Any Israelite who heard this story would take it to mean that his race owed its existence to the mercy of God, and its prosperity to the obedience of their great ancestor. There is also a liturgical intention, but it is secondary in the story: the Israelites do not offer children to Yahweh as the Canaanites do to their gods. Possibly there is behind the story an old account of the foundation of a sanctuary in which, from the very beginning, animals were sacrificed: the point would then be to contrast this sanctuary with other sanctuaries, Canaanite sanctuaries, in which human victims were killed. But this would only confirm the conclusion which the story is meant to assert, namely, that the religion of Israel rejected human sacrifice.

(b) *Prophetical texts.* Proofs drawn from the prophets are no more convincing either. The text of Os 13: 2 is most obscure and is translated in a number of ways; not everyone will admit that it refers to human sacrifice, but even if it does, it is speaking of sacrifices offered to idols, and it condemns the cult. Mi 6: 1-8 must be taken as one pericope, and there the people answer Yahweh by asking: 'Will Yahweh be pleased with thousands of rams, or with torrents of libations of oil? Must I offer my eldest son as the price of my forfeit, the fruit of my loins for my own personal sin?' (v. 7), but God replies (v. 8) that he asks them only 'to do justice'. The meaning is clear: in the eyes of the prophet, sacrificing one's children would be as absurd and as useless as sacrificing thousands of rams and torrents of oil. This does not mean that the Israelites had a custom of sacrificing their children to Yahweh, any more than that they poured out for him 'torrents of oil'. There is a disputed and late text in Is 66: 3 which does refer to the execution of a man as a ritual, but it contrasts it with the normal sacrifice, a bullock. This leaves only the text in Ez 20: 25-26, which we shall discuss in a moment.

(c) *The law concerning the first-born.* For some critics, certain texts about the first-born are decisive: 'Thou shalt give me the first-born of thy sons. Thou shalt do the same for thy livestock, big and small. The first-born shall be left seven days with its mother, and then, on the eighth day, thou shalt hand it over to me' (Ex 22: 28-29). The command is unqualified, and the texts which state that the first-born of men are to be ransomed, whereas the first-born of beasts are to be sacrificed (Ex 13: 11-15; 34: 19-20) are, it is claimed, of later origin, enacted to mitigate an ancient and cruel custom. Against this view, it should be noted that the last two texts are attributed by literary critics to the ancient sources of the Pentateuch, and are regarded as almost contemporary with Ex 22: 28-29. Conversely, Ex 13: 1-2, which is the work of the later Priestly redactors, is just as unqualified as Ex 22: 28-29: 'Consecrate to me every first-born, the first-fruits of the mother's womb among the children of Israel. Man or tame animal, it belongs to me.' Both texts simply take for granted that the first-born of men are not treated in the same way as the first-born of beasts: all the first-born belong to Yahweh, but men are redeemed and beasts are sacrificed. It seems certain that no Israelite ritual ever prescribed the sacrifice of the first-born.

The critics in reply bring forward the text of Ez 20: 25-26: 'I went so far as to give them laws which were not good, and customs by which they could not live, and I defiled them by their offerings, making them sacrifice all their first-born, to punish them, that they might know that I am Yahweh'. This text seems to say that the custom was normal in Israel, and that it was sanctioned by a command of God. But it is absurd to say that Israel ever sacrificed 'all its first-born' at any period in its history, and it is equally absurd to say that Ezechiel, who in other places condemns the sacrifice of infants (Ez 16: 20; 20: 31), could ever have thought that this custom had been positively enjoined by God. Consequently, the words of the prophet cannot be taken literally. He is attributing to divine causality all the actions, good and bad, of men; he is referring to the permissive will of God, as is the writer of Ex 4: 21; 7: 3, etc. and especially of Is 6: 9-10 (a text cited with reference to the parables of Jesus, Mt 13: 13-15, and by Paul to the Jews of Rome, Ac 28: 26-27). Yahweh had ordered the Israelites to consecrate to him all the first-born: the Israelites, led astray by the example of the Canaanites, killed their children for sacrifice. God let them do so, let them defile themselves 'to punish them, that they might know that I am Yahweh'. The sin was foreseen by God and punished by God, and thus entered into the mysterious plan of salvation. Ezechiel states the fact without nuances, but we have an explicit statement of Jeremias on the same point: 'They built the *bamah* of Tophet in the valley of Ben-Hinnom to burn their sons and their daughters; this I had never prescribed, this I had never dreamt of' (Jr 7: 31; cf. 19: 5).

(d) *Sacrifices to Moloch*. The ground is thus cleared for another question, on which much ink has flowed in the last few years. The word *molek* (Moloch in the Greek and Latin versions) is found five times in the Law of Holiness (Lv 18: 21; 20: 2-5) and then in 2 K 23: 10 and Jr 32: 35; it should be corrected in 1 K 11: 7 and (probably) restored in Is 30: 33. The word is always used in connection with the sacrifice of a child, male or female, who was said to 'pass through the fire': according to 2 K 23: 10 and Jr 32: 35, this took place in the 'roaster' (*topheth*) of the valley of Ben-Hinnom near Jerusalem. Though the word *molek* is not used, the same rite is mentioned in 2 K 16: 3; 17: 31; 21: 6; Jr 3: 24 (?); 7: 31; 19: 5; Dt 12: 31 and presumably Ez 23: 39.

Note that these sacrifices are not related to the ordinary worship practised on the high places, and that the high places are often mentioned without reference to this cult; the use of the word *bamah*, therefore, to describe the 'roaster' in the valley of Ben-Hinnom is somewhat surprising. It should be noted, too, that among the texts cited, those which are in any way detailed appear to restrict the practice to the region around Jerusalem; the nearness of the Temple presumably accounts for the insistence of the Law of Holiness, and this law, as we have said, reflects the teaching of the priests in Jerusalem towards the end of the monarchy. These sacrifices were practised, too, only during a certain period: they are first mentioned under Achaz (2 K 16: 3), when foreign influences were encroaching upon the cult, and 2 K 17: 31; Dt 12: 31 condemns them as a pagan custom. All the texts lead to the same conclusion: the practice was introduced late in the history of Israel and from outside, and it was condemned by all the spokesmen of Yahwism, by the Deuteronomist, the Prophets and the Priestly editors. It never formed part of the Israelite ritual for sacrifices.

Its origin must be sought, evidently, in Canaanite culture (in the broad sense). Punic and Neo-Punic inscriptions contain the expressions *mlk 'mr* (transcribed *molchomor* in Latin) and *mlk 'dm*. Very probably, these phrases mean respectively 'offerings of lamb' and 'offering of man', and refer to the sacrifice of an infant, or of a lamb as substitute. This interpretation is supported by a find in the sanctuary of Tanit at Carthage, where archaeologists have discovered urns containing burnt bones of lambs and goats, and, more often, of children. There is, too, a famous text of Diodorus Siculus (*Biblioth. Hist.* XX 14): in 310 B.C., when a disaster was threatening Carthage, the inhabitants of the town decided it was due to the anger of Kronos, to whom they had formerly sacrificed their finest children: instead, they had begun to offer sickly children, or children they had bought. Thereupon, they sacrificed two hundred children from the noblest families. There was a bronze statue of Kronos with outstretched arms, and the child was placed on its hands and rolled into the furnace. Whether the details be true or false, the story is evidence of a custom to which other classical authors also allude.

These inscriptions and texts are of late date, but the *molk* offering is mentioned in two steles from Malta belong to the seventh or the sixth century B.C. The sacrificial term has not so far been found in inscriptions from Phoenicia proper, but child-sacrifice was practised there: a fragment of Philo of Byblos cited in Eusebius (*Praep. Evang.* I 10) says that the Phoenicians had an ancient custom—'they offered their dearest children in a way full of mystery' when danger threatened the nation. Porphyry (*De abstin.* II 56) says that the Phoenician History written by Sanchuniaton and translated by Philo of Byblos was full of stories about child-sacrifices offered to Kronos in times of calamity. These texts furnish the connecting-link with the story told by Diodorus Siculus, and we may mention also the reference to the king of

Moab's offering his son as a holocaust when his capital was under siege (2 K 3: 27).

The sacrifice of children, then, by burning them to death probably made its way into Israel from Phoenicia during a period of religious syncretism. The Bible mentions only two specific instances, and they are motivated by the same exceptional circumstances as the Phoenician sacrifices: Achaz 'made his son pass through the fire' (2 K 16: 3) during the Syro-Ephraimite War, and Manasseh did the same (2 K 21: 6) when confronted with some Assyrian threat which is not mentioned in the Books of Kings but which may be alluded to in 2 Ch 33: 11f. Yet the custom must have been fairly widespread to have deserved the condemnations uttered by Deuteronomy, Leviticus and the Prophets. Though Phoenician texts properly so called do not mention the word, it is possible (we say no more) that the sacrifice was called *molk* in Phoenicia, as in Carthage, and that it came into Israel under this name.

But even if this is true, the sacrificial meaning of the word was soon forgotten in Israel; perhaps it was never taken in this sense at all. There was a god called Malik ('king') in the pantheons of Assyria and of Ras Shamra, and the god of the Ammonites was called Milkom (2 S 12: 30; 1 K 11: 5, 33; 2 K 23: 13), which is merely another form of the same word. More often, the word *melek* ('king') is an appellative of a god, used instead of the god's proper name. This appellative use is found in the Bible itself in Is 57: 9 (*Melek*) and in the Massoretic text of Is 30: 33 (in connection with the 'roaster' in the valley of Ben-Hinnom); it is also found in composition with divine names (Adrammelek and Anammelek, 2 K 17: 31, again in connection with the burning of infants for sacrifice). These offerings, then, were held to be offerings to a king-god, a Melek, who was an idol (Ez 23: 39), a Baal (Jr 19: 5; 32: 35), a Disgrace (perhaps Jr 3: 24). The form *molek*, which predominated in these texts, is to be explained by a change of vocalization telling the reader to say *bosheth* (disgrace, shame); this is in fact the reading of the consonants too in Jr 3: 24. (Compare the substitution of *bosheth* for Baal in Jr 11: 13; Os 9: 10 and in certain proper names.)

The question is clearly most complicated, and no final solution has yet been proposed. But whether these sacrifices were offered to a god Moloch or offered as *molk*, one thing is certain: the sacrifice of infants in fire was something foreign to the ritual of Israel.

CHAPTER THIRTEEN

THE RELIGIOUS SIGNIFICANCE OF SACRIFICE

S O we come to our last question: what was the purpose of sacrifice? What was its religious significance in the minds of the Israelites? What place did it occupy in their conception of man's relations with God? In seeking to answer these questions, we ought to beware of two dangers. Historians of comparative religion are tempted to misuse the comparative method, and to bring forward, as an explanation of Israelite sacrifice, the practices or the ideas of peoples with different religious concepts; in particular, they look for analogies between Israelite ritual and the customs of so-called 'primitive' peoples, for among these primitive peoples, they claim, we find the fundamental significance of ritual. Theologians, on the other hand, tend to use the sacrifice of the New Testament (and subsequent Christian doctrinal interpretations of it) in order to explain the true meaning of Old Testament sacrifice. Both parties tend to neglect or to underrate elements which may be proper to Israelite sacrifice. It is true, of course, that one must take into consideration the world in which Israel lived, and also inquire how the sacrifices of the Old Law are prolonged and fulfilled in the sacrifice of the New Covenant; but surely the first task is to examine the notion of sacrifice as presented in the Old Testament itself? We shall begin by setting aside a number of theories which are unsatisfactory.

1. *Was sacrifice a gift to a malevolent or a selfish deity?*

This theory was expressed in a particularly brutal way by Renan in his *Histoire d'Israel*: 'That state of madness through which humanity passed in the first ages of its existence has bequeathed to us many errors, but of them all, sacrifice is the oldest, the worst and the most difficult to uproot. Primitive man, whatever his race, thought that the way to quieten the unknown forces around him was to win their favour as one wins the favour of men, by offering them something. This was logical enough, for the gods whose favour he sought were malevolent and selfish. This appalling absurdity (which the first appearance of religious common sense ought to have swept away) had become an act of subjection, with man, as it were, the liege of the Deity. Patriarchal religion could not emancipate itself from this notion. The prophets of the eighth century B.C. were the first to protest against this error,

and even they could not suppress it!' It is doubtful whether so materialistic
an explanation is valid of any people, however 'primitive' or degraded they
are presumed to be, and modern studies in religious ethnology come to very
different conclusions. And it is quite certain that Renan's description does
not apply to any period of Israel's religion: not a single biblical text can be
cited, or even stretched, to justify it.

A less extreme view is that sacrifice is a gift given with the purpose of
profiting both God and man, a kind of contract *do ut des*. It is certainly true
that one of the reasons why man offers sacrifice is to receive some benefit
(material or spiritual) from God; it is an offering made to God, but it is a
gift of a particular kind. True, in every popular religion, including Israel's,
man's desire to receive something from God may become the predominant
motive for sacrifice; it is also true that in certain religions, the deity seems to
be in equal need of something from man (we shall return to this when we
discuss sacrifice considered as a meal for the god), but this cannot have been
the notion of sacrifice in Israel. In the Bible, God is the sovereign lord of all
things, of man and of all his possessions: God does not need to be given
anything by men, for he can take everything.

2. Did sacrifice achieve union with the deity by magic?

This explanation of sacrifice is put forward under two forms: in the first,
God and man are brought together by man's eating a divine victim; in the
second, they are united by the immolation of a victim representing man.

(a) *Union with a god by man's eating a divine victim.* The presupposition of
this theory is totemism: members of the tribe were related by kinship to the
tribal god, who was the ancestor of the entire tribe, and whose life circulated
in the animal (the *totem*) consecrated to him. The object of sacrifice was to
strengthen this relationship, and to share in the god's life by eating his sacred
animal. This idea—so it is claimed—was at the root of the sacrifice of the
ancient Arabs, who attached particular importance to blood-ties, and
Israelite sacrifice was a more highly developed form of the same idea. The
faithful worshipper was the subject of the king-god, he farmed the land
belonging to the god, and sat at his table: basically, it was the same outlook
as prevailed in ancient Arabia. Now this is simply not proven. Totemism,
however, is no longer a fashionable theory: everyone now recognizes that it
is not a regular religious phenomenon. Moreover, it is quite exceptional for
men to eat the totem animal, and even when they do so, their purpose is not
to unite themselves with their god. The only evidence that the ancient
Arabs practised totemism comes from the spurious story of St. Nilus,[1] and it
is impossible to discern any traces of totemism among the early Israelites.

(b) *Union with a god by the immolation of a victim representing man.* The
sacrificer substituted the victim for himself. By placing his hands upon it,

1. Cf. p. 436.

he transferred to the animal his sins and his life-principle. (The life-principle was in the blood.) When the animal was killed, the sins were carried away, and the life-principle was released. The blood which was shed incorporated the life-principle of the victim (and consequently of the sacrificer); when, therefore, this blood was poured out at the foot of the altar or sprinkled on something which represented the deity, it brought the life of the sacrificer into contact with the deity, and thus established, or re-established, the bond between God and his servant. In the previous hypothesis, eating the victim was the essential element; in this second hypothesis, it is immolation and the use of the blood, and the sacred meal is only a complementary rite. In both hypotheses, true sacrifice always demands the shedding of blood.

It is quite true that this use of blood in ritual was meant to bring about the closest possible contact between God and that part of the victim which, because it was held to contain the life-principle, belonged to him alone. But this does not mean that the life of the person offering sacrifice was brought into contact with the life of God. We have already shown[1] that the rite of laying hands on the victim does not symbolize the transference of the life or the sins of man to the victim: it merely testifies that this victim comes from this particular individual, and that it is being presented on his behalf.

3. Was sacrifice a meal taken by the god?

In answer to these theories, some writers assert that the whole problem is much simpler: sacrifice was a meal offered to God, for God was thought to be like men, needing food and enjoying the flavour of meat. Hence the altar is termed 'God's table', and the shewbread is called 'God's loaves'. Hence, too, the need to prepare a sacrifice as one prepares a meal: salt, cakes and wine had to be offered along with it. The supporters of this theory admit that in the texts of Leviticus and in the post-exilic worship, these terms are to be taken in a metaphorical sense, but, it is claimed, the terms bear witness to an older concept of sacrifice, materialist and anthromorphic.

In fact, the neighbours of Israel, especially the Mesopotamians, did strongly emphasize that sacrifice was a meal provided for the god,[2] and the banquets to which the gods invite each other in the poems of Ras Shamra show that the Canaanites, even if they did not have the same concept of sacrifice, at least believed that the gods needed food.

Our concern, however, is with Israel. Apart from a few exceptions (which we shall discuss later), the terms which seem to equate sacrifice with a meal provided for God are found only in late texts, and everyone admits that in these late texts they are not to be taken in the literal sense. What about the ancient texts? In Gn 8: 21, 'Yahweh inhaled the pleasant fragrance' of Noah's sacrifice; later on, this expression became a technical term and in the

1. Cf. p. 416.   2. Cf. p. 433.

late rituals it has lost all its literal meaning. In the text of Genesis, however, it is an echo of the Babylonian story of the Flood, with which the biblical story has so many contacts. We have already cited the text: 'The gods scented the fragrance, the gods scented the lovely fragrance, the gods collected like flies around the sacrificer'.[1] The biblical phrase is borrowed, but it is most discreetly re-phrased. A second text occurs in Yotham's fable, where the trees are trying to choose a king: mention is made of oil 'which brings honour to gods and men', and of must 'which brings joy to gods and men' (Jg 9: 9, 13). This is an old fable, but it may have been composed outside Israel; Ps 104: 15 (which is inspired by it) omits all mention of the gods, and refers only to men, whose hearts find joy in wine, whose faces shine with oil. Two other ancient stories about the sacrifices of Gideon (Jg 6: 18-22) and of Manoah (13: 15-20) reject the notion that Yahweh lives on the food of sacrifices: both Gideon and Manoah invite the Angel of Yahweh (whom they have not recognized) to a meal, and on both occasions, the sacrifice is transformed into a holocaust (cf. Jg 13: 16: 'Even if thou shouldst insist, I would not eat of thy meal'). In only one instance is the anthropomorphism taken to extremes: Abraham welcomed three mysterious visitors, among whom Yahweh was concealed: Abraham prepared a meal for these three 'men' and 'they ate it' (Gn 18: 8). But this meal was not a sacrifice.

One must, however, admit that certain features in Israelite ritual did tend to make sacrifice look like a meal in which Yahweh took part, and it may have been understood as such at the popular level. (We may cite, as examples of these features, the sacrificial meal which accompanied the *zebah*, and the offerings of cakes, of oil and of wine upon the altar: the custom of making these offerings may have been borrowed from Canaanite ritual.) We read in Ps 50: 12-13 a protest against this idea:

> 'If I am hungry, I shall not tell thee,
>   for the world is mine, and all that it contains.
> Am I to eat the flesh of bulls,
>   am I to drink the blood of goats?'

The Canticle of Moses asks where are the gods 'who used to eat the fat of their sacrifices, who used to drink the wine of their libations' (Dt 32: 38). In spite of these foreign influences and these deviations from orthodox Yahwism, we must insist that one cannot satisfactorily explain Israelite sacrifice by calling it a meal offered to a god.

The fault common to all the three theories which we have so far discussed is that they neglect the strictly religious significance of Israelite sacrifice, and that they all presuppose a cruder concept of the divinity, and of man's relations with God, than ever obtained in Israel.

1. Cf. p. 433.

4. Outline of a theory of sacrifice

Sacrifice is the essential act of external worship. It is a prayer which is acted, a symbolic action which expresses both the interior feelings of the person offering it, and God's response to this prayer. It is rather like the symbolic actions of the prophets. By sacrificial rites, the gift made to God *is* accepted, union with God *is* achieved, and the guilt of man *is* taken away. But these effects are not achieved by magic: it is essential that the external action should express the true inward feelings of man, and that it should be favourably received by God. Failing this, sacrifice is no longer a religious act.

On the other hand, sacrifice is one act with many aspects, and we must beware of simple explanations. Sacrifice is not merely a gift, nor merely a means of union with God, nor merely a means of expiating sin: there are several motives for it, which apply at one and the same time, and it satisfies several imperative instincts of the religious conscience.

Some of the rites, and some of the terms which describe these rites, date back to the pre-history of Israel, but we should not admit without proof that the meaning of these rites remained unchanged. Other rites, and other terms, were adopted by Israel from neighbouring peoples, especially from the Canaanites; but again, we should not admit without proof that these rites had the same meaning in Israel as they had among its neighbours. Israel's religion gave a new significance to the forms of worship which it inherited, or which it adopted from abroad. If we wish to discover what value Yahwism placed upon sacrifice, we must look for the answer in the Old Testament itself.

(a) *The gift.* God is the sovereign lord: everything belongs to him, and all man's possessions come from him. This is the theme of Ps 50: 9-12 (on sacrifices), and of the beautiful prayer which 1 Ch 29: 14 ascribes to David: 'Everything comes from thee, and even what we have given thee comes from thy hand'. Man owes everything to God, and it is therefore right that he should render tribute to God, as a subject pays tribute to his king, or a tenant to his land-owner. It is a kind of desecration: by giving a part to God, to whom all belongs, man 'desecrates' things and may use the rest as his own. This intention can be clearly seen in the offering of the first-fruits of the harvest and in the law about the first-born.

Yet sacrifice is something more than tribute. It is a gift, but a gift of a particular kind. More accurately, it is something which every gift ought to be in order to have ethical value: the victims (or the offerings) are domesticated animals (or vegetable produce) which man needs to support his life, and which are, as it were, part of his life and of himself. He deprives himself of them in order to give them away: by doing so he loses the gift, but he also gains something, for the acceptance of the gift involves God in an obligation.

God does not, of course, need the gift, but by accepting it, he binds himself in some way.

In this sense, every sacrifice is a gift, and it is not without significance that the term *minḥah* (meaning, literally a 'gift') is used not only for vegetable offerings, but also in the general sense of 'a sacrifice'.[1] Sacrifice is the means whereby men make gifts to God, and the offering is made in a way of its own: the gifts are wholly or partially destroyed; flour, bread and incense are burnt, liquids are poured out, and animals are slaughtered and burnt.

The purpose of this destruction is not merely to destroy. In opposition to the theory that sacrifice consists in annihilation, and in opposition to a certain modern school of spirituality, we must maintain that God, who is Lord of life and of all being, cannot be honoured by the destruction either of being or of life. In this context we may recall that animals were normally killed by the man offering the sacrifice, not by the priest; the essence of sacrifice, then, does not lie in the immolation. Immolation is only a preparation for the sacrifice, like the laying-on of hands.

Two reasons may be given for the destruction of the victim's carcase or of the vegetable offerings upon the altar, and they are complementary to each other. The first is that such destruction makes the offering useless, and makes it, therefore, an irrevocable gift. This idea harmonizes with a wider concept, that everything which is consecrated to God must be withdrawn from profane use; there are many analogies in other rites and in other religions, such as the custom of breaking vases which have been used for libations, or of throwing votive offerings into a spring, a well, or the sea.

The second reason is that destruction is the only way to give the offering to God, by transferring it into the realm of the invisible. This reason can be perceived first in the vocabulary used: 'to offer' a sacrifice is, in Hebrew, 'to bring near' or 'to make to rise up', and the sacrificial term *'olah* means 'that which goes up'. The rites themselves make this even clearer: sacrifice is essentially connected with the altar, for the altar is the symbol, or the reminder, of God's presence, an instrument of mediation between God and man.[2] That part of the offering which reverts to God is placed upon the altar. Blood, as the life-giving element, is particularly important: in every sacrifice it is poured out around the altar. In sacrifices of expiation it is rubbed upon the horns of the altar; in sacrifices offered for the sin of the high priest or of the people, it is sprinkled upon the veil which hides the Holy of Holies, the Dwelling of Yahweh; and on the great Day of Atonement it is taken inside the Holy of Holies itself, and there sprinkled over the mercy-seat, the throne of the divine Presence. All the other parts which are given back to God are destroyed upon the altar, and they take a spiritual form as they rise in smoke from the altar towards him. The offering is thus brought into contact with the symbols of God's presence, and brought as close as possible to him.

1. Cf. pp. 430-431.   2. Cf. pp. 413-414.

From this point of view, the holocaust may be considered the most perfect sacrifice, for man receives nothing of it, and all is burnt. But making a gift to God is only one aspect of sacrifice.

(b) *Communion*. Religion does not consist merely in expressing our dependence upon God: it includes also (as a consequence of this dependence) a quest for union with God. The Israelites never thought that they could be physically united with God by eating a divine victim, or by transferring into the realm of things divine a victim with which the man offering sacrifice had been identified. But there is another kind of union, which results from sharing the same possessions, from sharing a common life, and from the practice of hospitality. When Yahweh had accepted the victim and had received his part (upon the altar), the men who had offered the sacrifice then ate the rest in a religious meal, and so shared the sacrifice. St Paul is referring to the sacrifices of Israel when he writes 'Are not they who eat the victims in communion with the altar?' (1 Co 10: 18). Just as a contract between men was sealed by their taking a meal together (cf. Gn 26: 28-30; 31: 44-54), so the covenant between the worshipper and his God was established or strengthened by this sacrificial meal. Hence it is called the *zebah sh'lamîm*, the sacrifice of communion, the sacrifice of covenant. It was a joyful sacrifice in which the two ideas of a gift and of communion were both included; the offering was made by man, and it achieved its effect in maintaining friendship with God. Hence it was regarded as the most complete kind of sacrifice, and at the beginning of Israel's history, it was the most frequent kind offered.

(c) *Expiation*. Since in every sacrifice man deprived himself of something useful in order to present it to God, and since all sacrifice tended to establish good relations between God and man, every sacrifice had some expiatory value. When the writer wished to underline the gravity of Eli's offence in 1 S 3: 14, he wrote that 'neither sacrifice (*zebah*) nor offering (*minhah*) will ever efface the fault of Eli'. The sacrificial code in Leviticus ascribes an expiatory value to the holocaust. Blood played an important part in all animal sacrifices, and, according to Lv 17: 11, the blood was given to men 'to perform the rite of expiation upon the altar'.

But there were circumstances in which the need for expiation was more acutely felt. When a man had sinned, he needed to find grace again, and he had to ask God to re-establish the covenant whose terms he had broken. This was the purpose of sacrifices for sin and of sacrifices of expiation: the ritual use of blood was of special importance, and there was no sacrificial meal, for the sinner could not share the company of God until the covenant had already been re-established. We tried to show above [1] that expiatory sacrifice was of ancient origin in Israel, but this kind of sacrifice was developed from the other kinds, and it became much more important when great national

1. Cf. pp. 429-430.

calamities brought home to the people the sense of its own guilt, and when the nation developed a more acute sense of sin and of Yahweh's demands.

5. Polemic against sacrifices

The pre-exilic Prophets uttered some violent attacks on sacrifices: Is 1: 11-17; Jr 6: 20; 7: 21-22; Os 6: 6; Am 5: 21-27; Mi 6: 6-8. They contrast the futility of sacrifices with obedience to Yahweh, and with the doing of right and of justice (Is 1: 16-17; Jr 7: 23; Am 5: 24; Mi 6: 8). Some authors have therefore drawn the conclusion that the Prophets condemned sacrifices of every kind. Since several of these passages mention sacrifices along with pilgrimages and feasts, the same authors admit that the Prophets condemned all exterior worship. But these Prophets do not condemn the Temple itself[1]; hence they are regarded as advocates of a Temple without altar and without sacrifices; they would thus be the Protestants of the Old Testament. If this attitude is adopted, then one should go further, for Is 1: 15 mentions, along with sacrifices and feasts, prayer itself: 'No matter how many prayers you say, I shall not listen.' Now since no one holds that the Prophets condemned prayer, the whole argument leads to an absurd conclusion and simply falls to pieces. These biblical texts, therefore, cannot mean that the Prophets uttered condemnations of sacrifice itself.

Yet the texts must be explained. It is not enough to say that the Prophets are condemning the cult because, in their day, it had been contaminated with pagan practices or ideas. They do, of course, condemn such worship, but in other texts (Os 2: 13-15; 4: 11-13; 13: 2; Am 4: 4-5; Jr 7: 17-18, etc.); in the preceding paragraph we have retained only those texts which appear to be directed against external worship offered to Yahweh in accordance with the rites prescribed. We have already attempted to give an explanation of Am 5: 21-27 and of Jr 7: 21-22 when we were treating of the cult in the desert,[2] and the same principle should be applied to the other texts also. Though the expression of condemnation is unconditional it should be taken in a relative sense: it is a 'dialectical negation', of which several other examples can be cited in Hebrew and in New Testament Greek. 'Not this but that' is a way of saying 'Not so much this as that'. The literal rendering of Os 6: 6, for example, is: 'It is love that I want, not (lo') sacrifices, and the knowledge of God rather than (min) holocausts', and the parallelism demands that the first formula should be comparative, like the second (cf. Pr 8: 10). This is clearer still in the words of Samuel, who was a prophet and who nonetheless offered sacrifices: 'Does Yahweh take pleasure in holocausts and in sacrifices, as in obedience to the word of Yahweh? Yes, obedience is more than the best sacrifice, and docility more than the fat of rams' (1 S 15: 22). The Prophets are opposed to the formalism of exterior worship when it

1. Cf. p. 326.   2. Cf. p. 428.

has no corresponding interior dispositions (Is 29: 13): in these texts they are speaking as preachers. The priestly texts, which are rituals, do not have occasion to say this, but they obviously presuppose that the religious act of sacrifice is of no avail unless the man offering it has sincere dispositions.

The Wisdom books repeat the same lesson: 'The sacrifice of the wicked is an abomination to Yahweh, but the prayer of upright men is his delight' (Pr 15: 8; cf. 21: 27), and 'To put into practice justice and right is, in Yahweh's eyes, of more value than sacrifices' (Pr 21: 3). There are certain Psalms which seem to reject the principle of sacrifice (Ps 40: 7-8; 50: 8-15; 51: 18-19), but these texts should be interpreted in the same way as the texts of the Prophets.

There is another factor also which explains why the Prophets rejected sacrifices: they mention it in their oracles of condemnation. The judgment of God is imminent and will not be averted by outward acts of worship, because the people's sins are too grave (cf. Jr 6: 19-20; 14: 12; Mi 3: 4 and also 1 S 3: 14).

The Prophets, the Wisdom Books and the Law all speak of sacrifice from different angles, but they do not contradict each other, as is sometimes claimed. Nor is there any break between the period before the Exile and the period after the Exile. There is continuity, and Ezechiel is the link. He was a prophet and a priest; he certainly did not reject as illegitimate the whole liturgy of the monarchic period, and he outlined a programme for the future liturgy with all its exterior acts. The post-exilic prophets preached this idea in a restored Israel. During the same years, the ritual became more precise, and it was accepted by everyone as an institution coming from God. After this, there was no further polemic against sacrifices.

But, it will be said, what about the Essenes? According to Philo (*Quod omnis probus liber sit*, 75), they did not offer animals in sacrifice, and according to Josephus (*Ant.* XVIII i, 5), they offered sacrifice only in private, away from the Temple. New light has been thrown on this evidence by the discoveries and the texts which have emerged from Qumran: these texts certainly come from a community which must be called, in some way or other, an 'Essenian' society. These sectaries broke off relations with the priests of Jerusalem and took no part in the official worship, but they still claimed to be scrupulous observers of the Law. Consequently, they did not offer sacrifice, for, outside the Temple, sacrifice would have been unlawful. Excavations at Qumran have brought to light heaps of animal bones which were buried in a ritual way, and some authors have therefore claimed that these bones are the remains of sacrifices: these finds would therefore confirm the statement of Josephus that the Essenes offered private sacrifices. It is more likely, however, that these bones are the remains of religious meals which did not have a strictly sacrificial character. Yet our uncertainty about the text of Josephus and about the finds at Qumran makes no difference to the essential point:

the Essenes did not reject the cult itself which was practised in the Temple. They merely cut themselves off from the priesthood which presided in the Temple at the time, for they considered the men unworthy of that office. The Qumran texts extol the value of sacrifice, and give it a place in the ideal regulations which they lay down for the Community.

The Prophets condemned formalism in worship; Jeremias preached a religion of the heart; Ezechiel demanded sublime holiness; and all the most authentic spokesmen of Judaism repeat the message down to the age when the community of Qumran set before its members an ideal of piety, of penance and of moral purity. All these witnesses contributed to make the cult more interior and more spiritual; the cult was more and more considered as the outward expression of interior dispositions, and it was the inward spirit which gave it all its value. The way was thus prepared for the New Testament. Jesus did not condemn sacrifice; indeed, he offered himself as a sacrifice (Mk 10: 45; Eph 5: 2); he is the Paschal victim (1 Co 5: 7) and his sacrifice is the sacrifice of the New Covenant (Lk 22: 20; 1 Co 11: 25). This is the perfect sacrifice, by reason of the nature and of the dispositions of the victim: he offered himself of his own free will, in an act of obedience. It is perfect also by reason of the manner in which it was performed: it was a total gift, in which the victim returned wholly to God; a communion-sacrifice more intimate than man could ever have suspected; an expiation-sacrifice sufficient to atone for all the sins of the world. And precisely because it was a perfect sacrifice which at one stroke exhausted all the possible aspects of sacrifice, it is unique. The Temple could disappear, and animal sacrifices had to end, for they were merely the imperfect figure, indefinitely repeated, of the sacrifice of Christ who offered himself 'once for all' in a 'unique offering' for our redemption and our sanctification, as the Epistle to the Hebrews repeatedly insists (He 7: 27; 9: 12, 26, 28; 10: 10, 12, 14). And the Church which Jesus has founded will continue, until the end of time, to commemorate this perfect sacrifice and to live by its fruits.

CHAPTER FOURTEEN

SECONDARY ACTS OF THE CULT

1. *Liturgical prayer*

PRAYING means 'speaking to God'; prayer, therefore, establishes a personal relationship between man and God, and it is the basic act of religion. The reason why we are treating it here among the secondary acts of worship is because our theme is the institutions of Israel, and prayer is relevant only in so far as it forms part of exterior worship. In the Old Testament, liturgical prayer was not an institution independent of other cultic acts, as it has come to be in synagogue services. There are, it seems, only two references in the Old Testament to liturgies which consisted entirely in singing or reciting prayers, and they were both penitential services (Ne 9 and Jl 1-2).

(a) *Prayer and the cult.* It is quite certain, however, that in Israel cultic actions were accompanied by words; this was so in all Oriental religions, and indeed, it is true of every religion in the world. The Bible contains some formulas for blessings (Nb 6: 22-27) and for cursing (Dt 27: 14-26: the people joined in these curses); it also gives the formula to be used in the ritual of the 'bitter water' (Nb 5: 21-22), the words to be pronounced when the person responsible for a murder could not be discovered (Dt 21: 7-8), the formulas for the offering of the first-fruits (Dt 26: 1-10) and of the three-yearly tithe (Dt 26: 13-15), and the 'lesson' for the feast of the Passover (Dt 6: 20-25, cf. Ex 12: 26-27).

Sacrifice was the central act of the cult, and the very action of sacrifice was itself a prayer; but it was accompanied by vocal prayer. The code in Lv 1-7 does not mention vocal prayer in connection with sacrifice, because it is concerned only with the actual rites to be followed, but Am 5: 23 says that hymns were sung to the accompaniment of instruments while sacrifice was being offered. And in fact, public prayer naturally tends to become rhythmic hymn-singing. Liturgical singing made its appearance once the cult and the priesthood were organized in a public sanctuary, and Solomon's Temple had a group of singers attached to it from its earliest days.[1] After the Exile, the members of this Temple choir became more important and more highly esteemed, and the Chronicler's interest in sacred music is well-known.[2]

The hymn-book, or the prayer-book, of the second Temple is the Psalter,

1. Cf. p. 382.   2. Cf. pp. 391-392.

and it contains some liturgical hymns dating from the time of the monarchy. The text of the Psalter makes it clear that the psalms were used in connection with worship: some of them make reference to a rite (usually sacrifice) which is to be performed as they are sung (Ps 20: 4; 26: 5; 27: 6; 66: 13-15; 81: 4; 107: 22; 116: 17), and others speak of the Temple in which they were sung (Ps 48; 65; 95; 96; 118; 134; 135). The 'Gradual Psalms' (Ps 120-134) and Ps 84 were songs for pilgrimages. On the other hand, it is often hard to distinguish between individual and collective prayers, or between private and liturgical prayers: psalms which are placed in the mouth of an individual were sometimes written to be used in the Temple services, and others were adapted for liturgical use by the addition of doxologies. In general, we do not have sufficient information to decide at which ceremonies or feasts psalms of this kind were sung. We can, of course, work out hypotheses from the general content of the psalms, but this is still guess-work; and we can use the information given in the titles of psalms, but this information is valid only for a very late period. The Hebrew title of Ps 92 says it is a psalm for the Sabbath, and the Greek titles of Ps 24, 48, 93, 94 say they are to be sung on other days of the week. Ps 30 was a psalm for the feast of the Dedication (according to the Hebrew text), and Ps 29 was sung at the feast of Tents (according to the Greek).

Any discussion about people's motives for praying or the themes of their prayer is part of biblical theology, but a study of Old Testament institutions must discuss the rules which governed the place, the time and the posture to be adopted in prayer.

(b) *The place and time of prayer, etc.* The Israelites normally prayed in the Temple, *i.e.* in the Temple courts, facing the sanctuary (Ps 5: 8; 28: 2; 138: 2). After the Exile, the Jews outside Jerusalem turned towards the Holy City and towards the Temple (1 K 8: 44, 48). Daniel prayed in his high room from a window facing Jerusalem (Dn 6: 11). The custom was sanctioned by later Judaism, and it governed the orientation of synagogues.

Ps 4 is an evening prayer, and Ps 5 a morning prayer; Judith prayed at the hour when the evening sacrifice of incense was being offered in the Temple (Jdt 9: 1). Daniel prayed three times a day (Dn 6: 11), and Ps 55: 18 tells us that the Israelites prayed 'in the evening in the morning and at noon'. These texts, however, are late texts, and concern private prayer. Now, in this later age, only two services were held each day in the Temple, in the morning and in the evening; the rules for private prayer, therefore, had ceased to be connected with the cult in the Temple.

Certain texts seem to indicate that the Israelites prayed standing upright: *e.g.* 1 S 1: 26; 1 K 8: 22; Jr 18: 20 all use the verb *'amad*, the ordinary meaning of which is 'to stand erect'. There are many texts to show that this was the custom in New Testament times. The verb *'amad* can, however, mean simply 'to be' in front of God, without implying that one is actually standing. In

2 Ch 6: 13, we read that Solomon built a platform, 'went up onto it, stopped (*'amad*) and knelt down'. Perhaps, too, the Israelites changed their attitude during prayer, according to the different intentions for which they were praying. The penitential liturgy of Ne 9: 3-5 (re-edited by the Chronicler) began with a reading from the book of the Law, during which the people stood (*wayyaqûmu*); then they knelt down (*mishtaḥawîm*) to confess their sins, until the Levites gave the order to rise ('Stand up!'—*qûmu*); thereupon they sang a psalm (cf. also 1 K 8: 54-55). But the ordinary attitude of prayer was meant to express humility and submission before God; 'Bow down, prostrate yourselves, kneel down before Yahweh' (Ps 95: 6). Men prayed on their knees (1 K 8: 54; Is 45: 23; Dn 6: 11), with their hands raised to heaven (1 K 8: 22, 54; Ps 28: 2; Is 1: 15; Lm 2: 19). Sometimes they prostrated themselves, kneeling and bowing their foreheads to the ground (Ps 5: 8; 99: 5, 9, etc.). The pagans adopted the same attitudes when praying to their gods (Ex 20: 5; Dt 4: 19; 1 K 19: 18; 2 K 5: 18, etc.), and the gestures were part of the normal courtesies towards the king or towards a person whom one wished to honour (1 S 24: 9; 2 S 9: 8; 1 K 2: 19; 2 K 1: 13; 4: 37; Est 3: 2, etc.).

The terms most commonly used for prayer are the verb *hithpallel* and the noun *t'pillah*. The same root in Arabic means 'to make a hole in', 'to cut', and it has therefore been suggested that the Hebrew terms are the relics of an ancient custom: in other words, that the Israelites used to make gashes on their bodies (as the prophets of Baal did on Carmel, 1 K 18: 28) in order to make their prayer more urgent and more effective. Against this, we may point out that the text in Kings uses a different verb, and that the meaning of the root, even in Arabic, is far wider. In Hebrew, the root seems to mean 'to decide, to arbitrate, to intercede' (cf. especially Gn 20: 7; 1 S 2: 25). Prayer, then means making intercession, and the person who pronounces a prayer on behalf of the people or of an individual is a mediator: he may be a holy person, or a consecrated person, such as a king, a prophet or a priest. But whatever be the basic meaning of the root, *hithpallel* and *t'pillah* came to mean respectively 'to pray' and 'prayer'. In the Old Testament, prayer was addressed directly to God, without reference to any heavenly mediator. The notion of angelic intercession for men appeared only after the Exile, when the doctrine of angels began to develop: at first the idea is expressed only timidly (Jb 5: 1; 33: 23-24; Za 1: 12), but it is clearer in Tobias (Tb 12: 12), where Raphael says: 'When you were at prayer, you and Sarra, it was I who presented your requests before the Glory of the Lord, and it was I who read them out' (cf. also 12: 15, according to one of the Greek recensions). This doctrine was stressed in the apocryphal books of Judaism, and was repeated in the New Testament (Ap 8: 3). There is only one mention of intercession by a saint, in 2 M 15: 14, where we read that Jeremias 'prays much for the people and for all the holy city'.

2. *Rites of purification and of de-consecration*

In the minds of the ancients there was a close connection between the notion of ritual impurity and the notion of being consecrated to God. There was a mysterious and frightening force inherent in things which were impure and in things which were sacred, and these two forces acted on everything with which they came into contact, placing the objects or persons which touched them under a kind of interdict. Both what was impure and what was consecrated were alike 'untouchable', and any person who touched them became himself 'untouchable'. These primitive notions are found in the Old Testament: one law forbade men to touch the Ark of the Covenant, and another law forbade men to touch a corpse; a mother had to purify herself after childbirth, because it made her impure, and a priest had to change his clothes after a sacrifice, because it had made him a consecrated person. Yet this impurity is not to be understood as a physical or moral defilement, and this kind of holiness is not to be understood as a moral virtue: they are rather 'states' or 'conditions' from which men must emerge in order to re-enter normal life.

The Bible described the extent of these interdicts, and the rituals for purification and de-consecration; here, perhaps more than anywhere else, the religion of Israel preserved some very archaic customs. It is strange that these customs were integrated into the Priestly legislation, the very latest part of the Pentateuch; yet, though the rites were retained, they were given a new meaning. They served to separate Israel from the pagan world around it, and to inculcate the idea of Yahweh's transcendent holiness and of the holiness which his chosen people ought to preserve. Hence, in the final synthesis of Leviticus, the Law of Purity (Lv 11-16) was put beside the Law of Holiness (Lv 17-26): they are the two aspects, negative and positive, of that holiness which is demanded by God.

(a) *Sacrifices and ablutions.* Sacrifices held an important place in rituals of purification and of de-consecration: after childbirth, women had to offer a holocaust and a sacrifice for sin (Lv 12: 1-8); lepers, on the occasion of their purification, had to offer a sacrifice of reparation (or a sacrifice for sin) and a holocaust (Lv 14: 10-32); men and women had to offer a holocaust and a sacrifice for sin whenever they contracted sexual impurity (Lv 15: 14-15, 29-30). A Nazirite who had become impure through contact with a corpse was obliged to offer a sacrifice for sin, a holocaust and a sacrifice of reparation (Nb 6: 9-12), and, when the period covered by his vow was ended, a holocaust, a sacrifice for sin and a sacrifice of reparation (Nb 6: 13-20).

But there were other rites, too, for purification or de-consecration: some of them were combined with sacrifices, others were not. We have already stated that both what was impure and what was consecrated affected every-one who came into physical contact with it: it was natural to 'wash' themselves clean from the effects of this contact. Thus, for example, the priest who was to conduct worship might have contracted some impurity: consequently, he had to wash himself before beginning the service so that he might safely enter the realm of things sacred (Ex 29: 4; 30: 17-21; Lv 8: 6; 16: 4). The laws about purity prescribed that vessels, clothes or persons which had been defiled by contact with something unclean should be washed in water (Lv 11: 24-15, 28, 32, 40; 15 *passim*; 22: 6). But water was also used to wash things which had been in contact with something sacred: meat which had been offered in sacrifice was a most holy thing, and therefore the metal vessel in which it had been boiled had to be scoured and rinsed in water; if it was an earthenware vessel, it was to be broken (Lv 6: 21). On the Day of Atonement, the high priest had to change his clothes and to wash his entire body after he had come out of the Holy of Holies; similarly, the man who led the scapegoat out into the desert, and the man who burnt the victims offered in sacrifice for sin, both had to change their clothes and to wash themselves (Lv 16: 23-28). Those who took part in the ritual of the red heifer were obliged to follow these rules too (Nb 19: 7-10, 21). Those who took part in a holy war[1] were 'sanctified' by taking up arms in such a cause, and even the booty which they captured was holy; before they could return to normal life, the fighting men and the booty alike had to be de-consecrated, and the period prescribed for this rite was seven days. The fighting men and the prisoners stayed outside the camp for seven days; they washed their clothes and purified themselves. They washed, too, all the leather materials, all the textile and wooden objects, but metal objects were first passed through fire before being washed (Nb 31: 16-24).

(b) *The ashes of the red heifer*. In the text just cited (Nb 31: 16-24), the metal had to be washed in 'lustral water' (*mê middah*, meaning literally 'water to take away defilement'); there was a special ritual for preparing it (Nb 19: 1-10). A red heifer, without blemish and one which had never borne the yoke, was slaughtered outside the town ('outside the camp', the text says, because it is attributing the institution to the desert period); it was slaughtered by a lay person in the presence of a priest. The whole carcase was then burnt, and as it was burning, the priest threw into the fire cedar-wood, hyssop and red cochineal; the ashes were then collected and kept in a ritually pure place. Lustral water was prepared by putting some of these ashes into a vessel and pouring upon them running water, *i.e.* water coming directly from a spring or from a stream. This rite certainly originated in pagan practices, and it must have been originally a magic rite: many peoples regard red as a protective colour to avert evil and to put demons to flight, and the ashes of animals are often used for lustrations, as running water is used to take away defilement. The rite, then, must be of ancient origin; it was accepted by Yahwism, and the rôle of the priest made it a

1. Cf. pp. 258-259.

legitimate ceremony; originally, it had nothing to do with sacrifice, but it was likened to a sacrifice for sin (the very term is used in Nb 19: 17, cf. v. 13, and compare Nb 19: 4 and 8 with Lv 16: 27-28).

This water was used for purification: it was sprinkled on anyone who touched a corpse, or bones, or a tomb; it was also used to purify the house of a dead man and its furniture (Nb 19: 11-22). Outside this text, this kind of water is mentioned only once, in the text previously cited (Nb 31: 23), where it is prescribed for the purification of plunder taken in a holy war: but here it seems to be an addition, which adds nothing significant to the context. Curiously enough, this lustral water is not mentioned in other texts which refer to impurity contracted by contact with a dead body: the Law of Holiness prescribes washing, but with ordinary water (Lv 22: 4-6) and the law about Nazirites lays down a complicated ritual but makes no mention of lustral water (Nb 6: 9-12). On the other hand, the ancient texts which describe funeral rites do not remotely suggest that contact with a corpse brings on defilement (cf. especially Gn 46: 4; 50: 1). Thus the rite concerning the ashes of the red heifer and the use of lustral water is rather paradoxical; it appears to have been an archaic rite which lived on side by side with the official religion; it was not even part of the ordinary life of the people, and yet, in the end, it was incorporated, at a very late date, into the Priestly legislation.

(c) *The ritual for leprosy.* The ritual for leprosy (which takes up two long chapters of the Law of Purity, Lv 13-14) raises a similar problem. The Hebrew word which modern translations render as 'leprosy' is ṣara'ath, but the disease it specifies is not—or not merely—what we nowadays term leprosy. Ṣara'ath is applied to different skin diseases, the symptoms of which are described in Lv 13: 1-44: the symptoms are not those of what we call leprosy (*Elephantiasis Graecorum*), and the diseases described can be cured. Though the priest had to decide whether a particular man was infected with this 'leprosy', he made his decision not as a physician, but as an interpreter of the Law: the 'leper' was declared impure, cut off from the community and compelled to live at a distance from the town (cf. the relatively early text of 2 K 7: 3) until he was cured.

The priest also decided when a man was cured (Lv 14: 3; cf. Mt 8: 4 and parallels; Lk 17: 14). But before the 'leper' could return to ordinary life, he had to undergo a ceremony of purification. A vessel was filled with water from a spring or from a stream, and a bird was then slaughtered over this vessel, so that its blood dripped into the water. Next, another bird was thrust into the water alive; cedar-wood, red cochineal and hyssop were put into the water; then the live bird was released in the open country, the leper was sprinkled with water and he was pronounced clean. Seven days later, he shaved all the hair off his body, washed his clothes and took a bath; and then he was clean (Lv 14: 2-9).

But the text continues: on the eighth day, he is to offer a sacrifice of reparation, a sacrifice for sin and a holocaust. The priest took the blood from the sacrifice of reparation and smeared it on the right ear, the right thumb and the right big toe of the man who had been cured; next, he anointed the same parts with oil and poured the remainder of the oil on the head of the ex-leper (Lv 14: 10-32). Similar rites are prescribed for the investiture of the high priest (Ex 29: 20-21; Lv 8: 12),[1] but in Lv 14 the purpose of the cere-monies is purification, not consecration. Blood was used in the same way as in expiatory sacrifices,[2] and the rites of anointing may be compared with the rite for the 'purification of the forehead' which is mentioned in Mesopo-tamian contracts for the liberation of slaves: there is also a particularly striking parallel in a text from Ras Shamra which records the emancipation of a female slave: 'I have poured oil upon her head, and I have declared her pure'.

Chapter 14 of Leviticus is a combination of two rituals. One of them (vv. 2-9) is of archaic origin: skin diseases, which are so loathsome and so contagious, are caused by a demon, and this demon must therefore be chased away. Here we meet again certain features of the ritual for the red heifer: since red is a colour which frightens evil ones away, reddened water and red cochineal are used; cedar-wood, hyssop and running water have a cleansing power; as the bird flies away in the open country, it carries the evil away with it; and all hair must be shaved off because it bears signs of the disease (Lv 13: 2-44 passim). The second ritual (Lv 14: 10-32) applies to lepers the levitical rules about expiatory sacrifices; it contains, however, one element which does not come from the ritual of expiation, namely, the anointing with oil, but we have seen that this rite was practised in parallel circumstances among the neighbours of Israel.

Not only human beings were subject to 'leprosy': mildew on clothes, on textile or leather-work was called 'leprosy', and the objects became thereby impure. Again, it was the priest's duty to make the decision and to isolate the object. If the corruption showed signs of spreading, or did not disappear after washing, then the thing had to be burnt; if the marks disappeared after a washing, then the object was washed a second time and declared 'pure' (Lv 13: 47-59). Houses, too, could be infected with 'leprosy': if the walls became covered in saltpetre or moss they might well seem to have 'leprosy' (Lv 14: 33-53); if the priest decided that this was so, the affected stones were taken out and the walls were scraped; if the signs of leprosy continued to spread, the house was demolished, but if they disappeared, the house was declared pure. In either case, however, the 'sin of the house' had to be expiated, and the ritual was the same as for the purification of a leper (Lv 14: 2-9).

All these various prescriptions are evidence of very primitive ideas; they are the remains of old superstitious rites. And yet there is no reference to

1. Cf. p. 414.   2. Cf. p. 419.

them in the pre-exilic texts, just as there is no reference to the ashes of the red heifer or to the use of lustral water in the years before the Exile. There is only one possible conclusion, and it must apply to all the laws about purity in Lv 11-16: after the Exile, the Jews became increasingly conscious of the need for purity, and the fear of impurity eventually became an obsession with them; hence the writers of the Priests' Code multiplied the instances of impurity and prescribed all the correct remedies for it; they borrowed material on every side, integrated popular superstitions into the Levitical system and imposed so many prescriptions that the law became too complicated to be practical. Post-biblical Judaism travelled even further in the same direction. The ritual had at first served to give expression to the holiness of God and of his people, but it changed into a narrow system of formal observance, a yoke too heavy to be borne; what had once been a protection became an iron collar. Jesus condemned the scribes and the Pharisees for putting heavy loads upon the necks of other men (Mt 23: 4) and thereby preventing them from entering the Kingdom of Heaven (Mt 23: 13). He proclaimed that the only uncleanness which brings defilement is moral uncleanness (Mt 15: 10-20), and St Paul laid down that 'nothing is of itself unclean or impure' (Ro 14: 14).

3. Rites of consecration

(a) *General remarks.* In the minds of the Israelites, the notion of purification was closely connected with the idea of sanctification, and the words which express the two ideas can be used as synonyms. Yet there is a difference: purification meant removing the obstacle which hindered a man from coming near to God, whereas sanctification either prepared a man to meet God or resulted from close contact with God. Purification expressed the negative, sanctification the positive, aspect. Everything which was related to God was holy, and therefore nothing could penetrate within the realm of the divine unless it had first been 'sanctified', *i.e.* unless it had been withdrawn from the realm of things profane. Hence the verb *qiddesh*, meaning literally 'to sanctify, to hallow', can often be translated 'to consecrate'.

This consecration did not necessarily entail the performance of a special rite: any action which brought a person or a thing into close relationship with God or with divine worship automatically consecrated that person or thing. Those who took part in a holy war were 'sanctified', and the plunder they captured was consecrated to God[1]; priests were sanctified simply by beginning to exercise their office[2]; the desert Tent and the Temple were holy, merely because God dwelt inside them; their furnishings were holy because they served for divine worship; the victims and the offerings were holy because they had been presented to God. Certain interdicts, however,

1. Cf. pp. 257-261.   2. Cf. pp. 347-348.

resulted from this consecration: but these interdicts did not bring about consecration—they were the result, not the cause, of consecration. Things and persons which had been consecrated to God might not be profaned. Fighting men were bound to observe continence (1 S 21: 6; 2 S 11: 11); no one could profit from plunder taken in a holy war (Jos 6: 18f.; 1 S 15: 18-19); the priests were subject to strict rules concerning purity (Lv 21: 1-8); sacrificial victims, offerings and tithes were 'holy things', or even 'most holy things', which had to be destroyed or eaten under special conditions and by particular persons (Lv 2: 3, 10, etc.; Nb 18: 8-9; Ez 42: 13).

In the instances just mentioned, consecration resulted from some contact with the realm of the divine; but late in Israel's history, particular rites were prescribed for certain occasions, with the object of bringing about consecration. We have already studied the post-exilic rite for the consecration of the high priest, and shown how it included purification, clothing and anointing with a specially prepared chrism.[1] The same late texts prescribe that the sanctuary, the altar and all the sacred furniture are to be anointed with this holy oil (Ex 30: 26-29; 40: 9-11; Lv 8: 10).

Under the monarchy, this anointing was the essential feature in the coronation ritual; it was the anointing which made the king a sacred person.[2] The sign of this consecration was the *nezer* which the king wore (2 S 1: 10; 2 K 11: 12; Ps 89: 40); it was also an ornament of the high priest's headdress, an ornament which was identical with the *sis*, the golden flower he wore above his forehead (Ex 39: 30; Lv 8: 9).[3] We may also recall that the correct translation of *nezer* is not 'diadem' but 'sign of consecration'.

The basic meaning of the root *nzr* is 'to separate' or 'to keep separated' from profane use; it means also 'to place under interdict' in the sense of 'to consecrate'. From this verb comes the noun *nazir*, meaning a person consecrated to God. And there is a synonym of *nzr* which is written *ndr*, from which comes the noun *neder*, meaning a 'vow', *i.e.* the consecration of a thing or of a person to God. Since these terms are so closely related, we shall treat here of vows and of the Nazirites.

(b) *Vows*. A vow (*neder*) is a promise to give or to consecrate to God a person or thing, *e.g.* a tithe (Gn 28: 20-22), a sacrifice (2 S 15: 8), plunder taken in war (Nb 21: 2), a person (Jg 11: 30-31; 1 S 1: 11). In all the instances cited, the vow was a conditional promise to give something to God, if God first granted a favour: Jacob promised to pay a tithe if Yahweh brought him home safe and sound; Jephthah promised to sacrifice someone if he won a victory; Anna promised to consecrate her child to God if he would grant her a son and so forth. The purpose of these vows was to add force to a prayer by making a kind of contract with God. All the vows in the Old Testament seem to have been of this kind, even when the condition was not openly expressed, and this justifies the distinction we made above between

1. Cf. pp. 398-400.   2. Cf. pp. 103-106.   3. Cf. p. 399.

'votive' sacrifices and 'voluntary' sacrifices.[1] Some texts of Leviticus, how-ever (Lv 7: 16-17; 22: 18-23), and even of Deuteronomy (Dt 12: 6, 11, 17) are not too clear about this distinction; there are, too, some general expres-sions in the Psalms (Ps 50: 14; 61: 9; 65: 2) which indicate that, as time went on, vows were becoming more like simple promises, and that they were not dependent on the granting of a favour of God. We are going to discuss, in a moment, the vow of the Nazirite, and this, in its final form, was certainly an unconditional promise.

Once a vow had been taken, man was bound to stand by it (Nb 30: 3; Dt 23: 22-24); it was better not to take vows at all if one could not fulfil them (Qo 5: 3-5). Yet certain vows were unlawful: the first-born of cattle could not be consecrated to Yahweh because they belonged to him by right (Lv 27: 26); because God was holy, any vow to consecrate to him the revenues from sacred prostitution was null and void (Dt 23: 19). The Law contained certain special provisions for vows taken by women: any vow taken by an unmarried woman could be annulled by her father; any vow taken by a married woman could be annulled by her husband, but a widow or a woman who had been divorced could take vows validly (Nb 30: 4-17). A vow imposed a grave obligation, but eventually this obligation was not so rigidly enforced, and men were allowed to commute the obligation into a payment of money: the tariffs were fixed down to the smallest details by the late law of Lv 27: 1-25.

(c) *The Nazirites.* Any person, man or woman, could consecrate himself or herself to God for a limited period: this was called taking the vow of a Nazirite, and the rules for it are given in Nb 6: 1-21. During this period of consecration, the *nazir* was to abstain from wine and all fermented drinks, to allow his hair to grow and to avoid all contact with any dead body. Should anyone die unexpectedly in his presence, he became impure: he had to shave himself, to offer one pigeon as a sacrifice for sin, another as a holo-caust, and a lamb as a sacrifice of reparation; then he had to begin once more to live as a Nazirite, and to complete the whole period anew, without counting the time that had already passed. At the end of the period, he had to offer a holocaust, a sacrifice for sin and a communion-sacrifice; he shaved his head and burnt the hair along with the communion-sacrifice; after this ceremony the Nazirite was 'desecrated'. He could then return to normal life and was once more allowed to drink wine.

The practice was certainly known in New Testament times. St. Paul completed a vow of this kind at Cenchreae (Ac 18: 18), and again, along with four other Nazirites, at the Temple in Jerusalem (Ac 21: 23-24). Under the Maccabees, one of the problems was that the Nazirites could not observe the rites which were prescribed for the ending of their vow, since the Temple was profaned (1 M 3: 49-51).

1. Cf. p. 417.

The law in Numbers, however, merely codifies a very ancient custom and adapts it to the Levitical ritual. It also reduces to a temporary vow something which had originally been a consecration for life. According to Am 2:11-12, God raised up prophets and Nazirites in Israel, but the people made the Nazirites drink wine, and forbade the prophets to speak. In this text, the Nazirite is not a person who has taken a vow, but a man possessed of a God-given charisma: it is a life-long state resulting from a call by God. The Nazirite is a man whom God has consecrated to himself, *i.e.* (according to the basic meaning of the word) a man whom God has separated from the realm of things profane. The external symbols of this separation lie in the various things forbidden to the Nazirite; here in Amos, only abstaining from wine is mentioned, but Nb 6: 3-4 extends the prohibition to everything produced from the vine.

The only ancient story which speaks of a Nazirite is the story of Samson, and here, too, the consecration is life-long, and results from a divine call. Even before he was born, his mother had to abstain from wine and fermented drink, because the child she was to bear would be a '*nazir* of God'; Samson himself was to follow the same rule, no razor was ever to 'pass over his head', but he was to be 'a *nazir* of God from his mother's womb to the day of his death' (Jg 13: 4-5, 7, 13-14). His long hair was the sign of his consecration (cf. Nb 6: 9, 18) and the source of his miraculous strength (Jg 16: 17); God had chosen Samson and given him this extraordinary strength to make him his champion. This, too, is the meaning we should give to the adjective *nazir* when it is applied to Joseph in the Blessings of Jacob (Gn 49: 26) and in the Blessings of Moses (Dt 33: 16). The first text implies, and the second expressly states, that uncut hair is the characteristic mark of the Nazirite, and this remained true down to the last examples mentioned in the Bible (Ac 18: 18; 21: 23-24). An extension of this usage can be seen in the application of the word *nazir* to vineyards which were not pruned in sabbatical or jubilee years, *i.e.* in which the seeds were allowed to grow without hindrance (cf. Lv 25: 5, 11).

Possibly we ought to combine with this story of Samson the old rituals concerning the holy war: the combatants were consecrated to God, and from Jg 5: 2 (cf. Dt 32: 42) we are justified in asserting that they wore their hair long. If this was the origin of the institution, it quickly evolved into something different. Samuel was given to God for the whole of his life, and the razor would never pass over his head (1 S 1: 11); though the word *nazir* is not used, this is evidently what is meant. Samuel, however, was consecrated for the service of God, not for war (unless one chooses to link this feature with the description of Samuel as Judge and as the conqueror of the Philistines, 1 S 7: 2-14). Moreover, Samuel's consecration resulted from a vow made by his mother, not from a choice made by God; thus we can already glimpse the first appearance of the idea of a vow, which later became the characteristic feature of Naziritism.

CHAPTER FIFTEEN

THE LITURGICAL CALENDAR

IN Israel, as among all nations, there was a host of feasts which, though they did not celebrate a religious event, had a religious character. The Bible mentions some of them, though usually it gives no details about the way in which these feasts were observed. The family or the clan held a feast to celebrate the various events of human life: *e.g.* the weaning of a child (Gn 21: 8),[1] a marriage (Gn 29: 22f.; Jg 14: 10f.),[2] a funeral (Gn 23: 2; 2 S 1: 11-12, 17f.; 3: 31f.)[3] and so forth. Life in the country provided other occasions for rejoicing (*e.g.* sheep-shearing, 1 S 25: 2-38; 2 S 13: 23-29; cf. Gn 38: 12), and we shall see in a moment how the three great feasts of the year were connected with events of pastoral or agricultural life. Public events were also occasion for feasts: *e.g.* the coronation of the king,[4] or a victory in war, which would be celebrated with singing and dancing (Ex 15: 1-21; 1 S 18: 6-7); and on the occasion of national calamities the people would fast (Za 7: 1f.; 8: 19) and sing lamentations (Jl 1-2 and the Book of Lamentations). Many feasts of which we have now no record must have been observed in the sanctuaries of Israel (cf. Os 4: 15; 12: 12; Am 4: 4-5), for it is only rarely that a really ancient story alludes to one, *e.g.* there was a pilgrimage from Shechem to Bethel (Gn 35: 1-4), and a feast of Yahweh at Shiloh (Jg 21: 19-21; cf. 1 S 1: 3f.). In this book we shall discuss only those feasts which were of importance for a considerable period; we are better informed about these, because they were incorporated into the Temple worship in Jerusalem. We shall begin by describing the ordinary services which were conducted in the Temple, and then pass on to discuss the religious calendars which give the order of the great annual feasts.

1. *The ordinary services of the Temple*

(a) *The daily services.* The laws in Ex 29: 38-42 and in Nb 28: 2-8 lay down that two lambs should be offered daily as holocausts, one in the morning and one in the evening 'between the two evenings', *i.e.* at twilight.[5] An offering of flour kneaded with oil, and a libation of wine were made along with this sacrifice. Lv 6: 2-6 also assumes that two holocausts were offered daily, one in the morning and one in the evening (cf. Si 45: 14).

1. Cf. p. 43.　　　2. Cf. p. 34.　　　3. Cf. pp. 59-61.
4. Cf. pp. 102-107.　　　5. Cf. p. 182.

Ex 30: 7-8 adds that these sacrifices must be accompanied by an offering of incense upon the altar of perfumes, and Judith is said to have prayed at the hour when the evening offering of incense was rising from the Temple (Jdt 9: 1). This daily service was termed the 'perpetual' (tamîd) sacrifice (Ex 29: 42; Nb 28 and 29 passim; Esd 3: 5; Ne 10: 34); when Daniel says it was interrupted, the writer is referring to the persecution of Antiochus Epiphanes (Dn 8: 11, 13; 11: 31; 12: 11), and the Books of Maccabees tell how it was re-established by Judas Maccabee. The ritual is ascribed by the Chronicler to the monarchic period (1 Ch 16: 40; 2 Ch 13: 11; 31: 3), but it is certainly of post-exilic origin. Ezechiel makes no provision for a holocaust in the evening (Ez 46: 13-15), and this ruling is in accordance with pre-exilic usage: 2 K 16: 15 (under Achaz) distinguishes the morning holocaust ('olah) from the evening offering (minḥah). This evening offering (still called minḥah) is an indication of time in Esd 9: 4-5 and Dn 9: 21. These texts prompt us to take minḥah in its strict sense, i.e. as a vegetable offering, when it is used to denote a time in the afternoon: this must be its meaning in 1 K 18: 29, 36, but the time must have been well before dusk because the story (1 K 18: 40-46) places the massacre of the prophets of Baal, the prayer of Elias, the rainstorm, and the return of Achab to Yizreel, on the same day. We have already noted that in the post-exilic ritual, the time for the evening sacrifice was fixed at twilight, but in New Testament times, the lamb was sacrificed in the middle of the afternoon, about three o'clock (according to Josephus and the Mishnah), the hour at which Jesus died on the cross (Mt 27: 46-50 and parallels).

(b) The sabbath. We shall devote a special chapter to the study of the sabbath.[1] Here we are concerned only with the changes it involved in the daily services of the Temple. According to Nb 28: 9 10, every Sabbath day two other lambs were to be offered, with a minḥah and a libation, in addition to the daily holocausts. Since the victims, the offerings and the libations are exactly the same as in the daily sacrifices, it seems that the daily holocaust was simply doubled in quantity on the sabbath; presumably the offerings were made at the same hours. Ezechiel had looked forward to a more costly ritual: the prince would enter by a porch which would remain closed for the rest of the week, and the sabbath holocausts would consist of ten lambs and a ram (Ez 46: 1-5). We do not know what was the practice in the days of the monarchy, but the story of Athaliah shows that on the sabbath the Temple guard was doubled: this would imply that more people came to worship (2 K 11: 5-8; cf. Ez 46: 3).

(c) The new moon. The ritual in Nb 28: 11-15 prescribes that on the first day of each new lunar month a holocaust should be offered which consisted of two bulls, a ram and seven lambs; offerings and libations were to be made along with it, and a goat was to be offered also, as a sacrifice for sin.

1. Cf. pp. 475-483.

Ezechiel had hoped that on this day the prince would offer a bull, a lamb and a ram (Ez 46: 6-7).

This feast, to celebrate the first day of the new moon, was a very ancient one. It is mentioned, along with the sabbath and other feasts, in Is 1: 13-14; Os 2: 13. Like the sabbath, it was a day of rest (Am 8: 5)—a good day, therefore, to visit a 'man of God' (2 K 4: 23). King Saul invited guests to dine with him at the new moon, and the meal had a certain religious character, for the guests had to be 'pure' to take part (1 S 20: 5, 18, 26); the same text may imply that the feast lasted two days (1 S 20: 19, 27). Possibly, too, the first day of a month was chosen for the annual sacrifice on behalf of the clan (cf. 1 S 20: 6, 29). New moons continued to be festal days down to the end of Old Testament times (cf. Esd 3: 5; Ne 10: 34; 1 Ch 23: 31; 2 Ch 2: 3; 8: 13; 31: 3), and even in New Testament days (Col 2: 16); but all except that of the seventh month lost much of their importance (Lv 23: 24-25; Nb 29: 1-6).[1]

2. The religious calendars

Against this background of daily, weekly and monthly worship, the great annual feasts stood out in relief. The general word for a 'feast' is *mô'ed*: the term means a fixed place or a fixed time—a rendezvous—and the desert Tent was called *'ohel mô'ed* or 'The Tent of Meeting'. Thus the word came to mean a meeting or an assembly, and finally an assembly or meeting to celebrate a feast. The term *mô'ed* is mentioned alongside sabbath-days or new moons in Nb 10: 10; 1 Ch 23: 31; Is 1: 14; Lm 2: 6; Os 2: 13, etc., as if it were expressly reserved for annual feasts (cf. Lv 23: 37-38). But it is also found (Os 2: 13; Ez 46: 11) alongside *ḥag*, which is applied particularly to the three great annual feasts, as we shall see. In Nb 29: 39, *mô'ed* occurs at the end of a ritual which begins by speaking of daily sacrifices, of sabbath-days and of new moons, and which then goes on to speak of the annual feasts. The word must therefore have had a rather wide meaning, and it seems to have been used for all kinds of religious assemblies.

The word *ḥag*, on the other hand, was reserved for the three great feasts of pilgrimage: the root means 'to dance, to turn around' (cf. Ps 107: 27), and the noun alludes to the processions and the dances which, in olden times, were part of the ritual of a pilgrimage. Even to-day, the Moslems call the pilgrimage to Mecca the *ḥaj*.

The Old Testament contains several lists of feasts which are spread out over the year: these lists are religious calendars, and it is interesting to compare them with one another, taking them in the probable order in which they were composed. This general review is necessary before we can begin to study each feast on its own: here we take for granted only a general acquaintance with the Israelite calendar.[2]

1. Cf. p. 503.   2. Cf. pp. 188-193.

(a) *The Elohistic Code of the Covenant.* The shortest calendar is that in Ex 23: 14-17: 'Three times a year thou shalt make the *ḥag* for me', *i.e.* the *ḥag* of the *maṣṣôth* (unleavened bread), which lasted seven days in the month of Abib; the *ḥag* of the *qaṣîr* (harvest); the *ḥag* of the '*asîph* (ingathering). The 'harvest' (*qasir*) represented the harvesting of the first cereal crops, whereas the '*asîph* represented the collecting of fruits from the fields and orchards and the storing in barns; the '*asîph* took place *b⁶ṣe'th hashshanah*, 'at the turn of the year', *i.e.* at the beginning of the year, which, at this period fell in the autumn.[1] The text concludes: 'Three times a year, all thy menfolk shall present themselves before the Lord Yahweh'. It has recently been suggested that this text lays upon each individual the obligation of making a pilgrimage three times a year, at dates of his own choosing; he would not have been bound to attend at the three great annual feasts, and these feasts would not have been occasions of pilgrimages. But this does not follow from the text: v. 17 merely repeats v. 14, in which *r⁶galîm* means 'times' and is a synonym of the word *p⁶'anîm* in v. 17 (cf. Nb 22: 28, 32, 33).

(b) *The Yahwistic Code of the Covenant.* Ex 34: 18-23 gives the same prescriptions under a slightly different form: it mentions the *ḥag* of the *maṣṣôth*, which lasts seven days in the month of Abib, the *ḥag* of the *shabu'ôth* ('weeks') for the 'first-fruits of the harvest' (*qasir*) of the corn, and the *ḥag* of the '*asîph* ('ingathering'), which takes place at the *t⁶qûphath hashshanah, i e* at the end of the year.[2] This text contains the same conclusion as Ex 23: 17: 'Three times a year all thy menfolk shall present themselves before the Lord Yahweh, God of Israel.' But this calendar includes also the law about the first-born (vv. 19-20) and the law concerning the Sabbath (v. 21): both these laws are given separately in the Elohistic Code (Ex 22: 28-29 and 23: 12).

It is noteworthy that both these calendars speak of the *maṣṣôth* and yet make no reference to the Passover: it is only mentioned afterwards, and then only incidentally, in Ex 34: 25; it is never mentioned at all in Ex 23 (unless there is a reference to it in Ex 23: 18, though this is not part of the calendar). The feasts are obviously agricultural feasts, and they are not fixed for a certain day; the date depends on the work in the fields, and will vary a little from year to year according to the weather. The 'beginning of the year' mentioned in Ex 23: 16 and the 'end of the year' mentioned in Ex 34: 22 are, in spite of the apparent contradiction, synonymous terms: they stand for the transition-period from one year to the next, and in these early days the year began in autumn, when the fruit was gathered from the trees. No precise date was fixed, but, since both calendars date back long before the centralization of worship, the feasts would be kept in local sanctuaries; it would therefore be easy enough for a community to fix dates for the feasts,

1. Cf. p. 190.
2. Cf. *ibid.*

while taking into consideration the state of work in the district. When the texts of the historical books mention a feast for which 'all Israel' ought to assemble at a particular sanctuary, they expressly state that royal messengers were sent round to make this known (1 K 8: 1-2, under Solomon; 2 K 23: 1, 21, under Josias; 2 Ch 30: 1-6 presumes that it happened under Ezechias too).

(c) *Deuteronomy*. The law in Dt 16: 1-17 retains the same calendar, and the same conclusion as in Ex 23: 17 and 34: 23: 'Three times a year all thy menfolk shall present themselves before Yahweh thy God'. The only difference is that it immediately adds 'in the place which he will choose' (v. 16), and this addition is inserted after each of the three feasts (vv. 2, 11, 15): it is an assertion of the centralization of the cult which Deuteronomy wishes to impose. The three feasts are: the Passover, which is henceforth linked with the *maṣṣôth* in the month of Abib (vv. 1-8 and 16); the *ḥag* of the *shabu'ôth* (of 'weeks'), and the meaning of this name is here explained: it is to be held seven weeks after the cutting of the first ears of corn (vv. 9-12); thirdly, the *ḥag* of the *sukkôth* ('tents'), which is to take place when the produce of the threshing-floor and of the presses is gathered in (vv. 13-15).

The word *sukkôth* is first mentioned at the feast of Ingathering, but its meaning is not explained. This calendar still assumes that the year begins in autumn (cf. its reference to the month Abib, a Canaanite name). The dates were still only vaguely fixed.

(d) *The Law of Holiness*. The first text which mentions precise dates is Lv 23, and these dates are given according to a calendar which begins in spring: the months, too, are called by an ordinal number, because at some period between Dt 16 and Lv 23 the Babylonian calendar was adopted.[1] Lv 23, however, raises a difficult problem of literary criticism. It certainly stems from more than one source: there are two titles (vv. 2 and 4), two conclusions (vv. 37 and 44), two rulings for the feast of Tents (vv. 34-36 and 39-43) and the latter ruling is not homogeneous. We must therefore distinguish at least two strata in the chapter, one of which represents the first Law of Holiness, which (in our opinion) dates from the last years of the monarchy, and another which represents the exilic and post-exilic additions. We cannot say for certain to which of the two editions each verse belongs, but we may propose (with due reservations) that the following verses should be ascribed to the ancient form of the Law of Holiness: Lv 23: 4-8, which treats of the Passover, to be held on the 14th day of the first month, and to be followed by the Feast of Unleavened Bread, which lasts seven days; Lv 23: 16-21*a*, which treats of the feast of Weeks, fifty days after the feast of Unleavened Bread; Lv 23: 34*b*-36, which treats of the feast of Tents, to be held on the 15th day of the seventh month, to last seven days, and to be

1. Cf. pp. 191-192.

followed by a solemn day of rest; Lv 23: 37-38, the conclusion. The additions (which may perhaps contain some ancient elements) concern: the Sabbath (v. 3—which is excluded by the original conclusion, v. 38); the feast of the first sheaf (vv. 10-15); the feast held on the 1st day of the seventh month (vv. 24-25); the Day of Atonement, to be held on the 10th of the same month (vv. 27-32); a different ritual for the feast of Tents (vv. 39-43); a new conclusion (v. 44).

(e) *Ezechiel.* A religious calendar can be drawn up from the prescriptions laid down in Ez 45: 18-25 for feast-days: on the 1st day of the first month (of a year beginning in spring) a sacrifice is to be offered for the sin of the sanctuary; on the 7th of the same month, the sacrifice is to be repeated, for the sins committed inadvertently by individuals. The Greek version gives the 1st of the seventh month as the date of this second sacrifice; this would harmonize with the text of Nb 29: 1, and would assign one sacrifice to each half of the year. The Hebrew reading is to be preferred, however: the second sacrifice marks the 'octave' and the two sacrifices taken together constitute 'the expiation for the sanctuary' (Ez 45: 18-20). The Passover (here called a *ḥag*) is to be kept on the 14th of the first month; it is to last seven days, during which holocausts and sacrifices for sin are to be offered (vv. 21-24). A sacrifice for sin and a holocaust were also to be offered for the 'feast' of the seventh month, and for the seven following days.

This insistence on sacrifices of expiation is characteristic of Ezechiel; and we may note also that he does not mention the feast of Weeks, and that he does mention ceremonies of purification at the beginning of the year. This latter ritual is not mentioned anywhere else, and it would seem that it was never put into practice: Ezechiel's prescriptions were replaced by those of the Priests' Code (Lv 23, in its final edition, and Nb 28-29).

(f) *The rules for sacrifices given in Numbers.* In fact, Nb 28-29 is a commentary on the liturgical cycle of Lv 23 (with the additions to that chapter). It neglects entirely Ez 45: 18-25, and stipulates what sacrifices are to be offered in particular circumstances: for the daily ritual (Nb 28: 3-8); the Sabbath (Nb 28: 9-10); the new moon (Nb 28: 11-15); the Passover and the Feast of Unleavened Bread (Nb 28: 16-25); the Feast of Weeks (Nb 28: 26-31); the 1st of the seventh month, called the 'Day of Acclamation' (Nb 29: 1-6); the Day of Atonement (Nb 29: 7-11); the feast of Tents (Nb 29: 12-38).

This text gives the complete list of the sacrifices offered in the second Temple after the time of Esdras.

(g) *Later feasts.* Later still, other feasts were inserted into the liturgical calendar. The months to which these feasts are assigned are called by their Babylonian names, and this only serves to stress that they were instituted at a late date. Some of them were observed only for a short period: *e.g.* the feast which celebrated Simon Maccabee's capture of the citadel of Jerusalem on the 23rd Iyyar; the feast of the wood destined for the altar, on the 14th

Ab; the feast of Nicanor, on the 13th Adar. Others, however, have been observed down to modern times, namely, the feast of Purim, on the 14th and 15th Adar, and the feast of the Dedication, on the 25th Kisleu. These feasts will be studied along with the post-exilic feasts.[1]

1. Cf. p. 507ff.

CHAPTER SIXTEEN

THE SABBATH DAY

WE have already studied the week, in the chapter on divisions of time[1]; here we are concerned with the religious institution which marked the seventh day of the week, the sabbath day.

1. *The name: its etymology*

The English word 'sabbath' is a transcription of the Hebrew *shabbath*. This noun is used only in religious contexts: it is used for the seventh day of the week (frequently), for the entire week (once, in Lv 23: 15, though this instance is itself doubtful) and for the sabbatical year which occurred every seven years (Lv 25: 2, 8, 34, 35, 43). A longer form (*shabbathôn*) is used for certain feast days and days of rest, but these days did not necessarily fall on a sabbath.

Some ancient writers (Theophilus of Antioch and Lactantius) say that the Hebrew word is derived from *sheba'*, meaning seven; but *'ayin* is a strong consonant, and this etymology is therefore impossible. A number of modern writers have put forward a corrected version of this hypothesis: they, too, maintain that *shabbath* is derived from 'seven', but via the Akkadian. In Akkadian, *'ayin* was not pronounced; *shibittu* means 'sevenfold, seven', and *shapattu* (which means, as we shall see, the day of the full moon) is said to be a dual form, meaning 'twice seven'. The latest suggestion is that a hypothetical Akkadian form *shab'atâni* ('twice seven') gave rise to the Hebrew *shabbathôn*, and that this Hebrew word was afterwards shortened to *shabbath*. But, as we shall show, it is most unlikely that the Hebrew institution was adopted from Mesopotamia, and the form *shabbathôn* is derived from *shabbath*, not vice versa.

The simplest etymology is from the Hebrew verb *shabath*, which often means 'to cease working, to rest', and which may therefore be rendered 'to keep a sabbath'. The basic meaning of this verb is, however, quite independent of the institution of the sabbath, and is simply 'to stop (*intransitive*), to cease' (Gn 8: 22; Jos 5: 12, etc.); in the active form, it means 'to make to cease, to stop (*transitive*)' (Ex 5: 5; Is 13: 11; Jr 7: 34, etc.). This is the etymology which the Bible itself puts forward in Gn 2: 2-3. Nevertheless, if the

1. Cf. pp. 186-188.

noun is derived from the verb *shabath*, and if it is a stative word, meaning 'a day on which men cease to work', then the formation of the noun (*shabbath*) is irregular: the regular form would be *shebeth*. The form *shabbath* ought to have an active meaning, signifying 'the day which stops (*transitive*), which marks a limit or a division', and we shall have to ask whether this was not its first meaning.

2. Was the sabbath of Babylonian origin?

If the etymology of the word is debated, the origin of the institution is even more so. Some writers have argued that the sabbath came from Mesopotamia. Certain Babylonian texts prescribe as 'evil' days the 7th, 14th, (19th), 21st and 28th days of a month, and say that on these days 'the shepherd of the peoples (*i.e.* the king) must not eat cooked meat or baked bread, must not change his clothes or put on clean clothes, must not offer sacrifice, must not go out in his chariot or exercise his sovereign power. The priest must not deliver oracles, and the physician must not touch the sick. It is an unsuitable day for any desirable action.' (There are slight variations among the texts.) On the other hand, the Akkadian word *shapattu* stands for the middle day of the month, *i.e.* the day of the full moon, which was a 'day when the gods' heart was appeased', and therefore a day of good omen.

Now certain texts of the Old Testament draw a parallel between the sabbath day and the day of the new moon, because both of them are days of rest (2 K 4: 23; Is 1: 13; 66: 23; Os 2: 13; Am 8: 5). In these texts, therefore, *shabbath* could mean the full moon, and Ps 81: 4 does actually use the rare word *kese'* ('full moon') in the same way: 'Sound the trumpet at the new moon, at the full moon, on the day of our feast.' Furthermore, the two principal Israelite feasts, the Passover and the feast of Tents, were kept at the full moon of the first and seventh months respectively, and in later times the feast of Purim was fixed for the full moon of the twelfth month.

From this, these writers argue that in ancient times, Israel kept only one sabbath day each month, at the full moon, and that this day was a joyful feast. Ezechiel, it is said, was the first to introduce the idea of a day of rest after six days of work (Ez 46: 1), and he made the weekly sabbath day the sign of the Covenant with Yahweh (Ez 20: 12, 20). He was inspired by the Babylonian custom of regarding the 7th, 14th, 21st, and 28th days of the month as 'evil' days, and this Babylonian influence changed the Israelite sabbath from a joyful feast into a day surrounded by prohibitions. The Israelites, however, were anxious to avoid any contamination with the cult of the sun, moon and stars; the Jewish sabbath was therefore held every seven days irrespective of the phases of the moon, and it thus introduced a continuous series of weeks which were independent of the lunar months.

There are serious objections to this theory. The days specified in Babylonian calendars (7th, 14th, etc.) were 'evil' days, of ill omen; the Israelites never looked upon their sabbath in this way, not even when later legislation forbade them to perform so many actions on this day; any resemblances with the Babylonian text cited above are quite superficial. The Akkadian *shapattu* was simply the day of the full moon, the middle day of the month, and there is no evidence whatever that this was a day of rest on which no work was done; it was even used for closing the accounts in financial transactions. The days of 'evil omen' are never called *shapattu* and the calendars and almanacks are themselves far from clear as to how the 'evil days' should be fixed. It is hard to imagine that the *shapattu*, a day of good omen, could have lost this meaning and have come to signify the days of evil omen; and it is equally difficult to see how these days of evil omen could have lost their connection with the phases of the moon, and have become the weekly sabbath of the Jews. One of the supporters of this theory is forced to admit that 'the Hebrews seem to have borrowed this word because of their utter failure to understand the Babylonian calendar'. This statement is itself an admission that the solution proposed rests on very feeble arguments.

Some biblical texts mention the sabbath along with the new moon; but this does not necessarily mean that the sabbath marked the full moon. In Is 66: 23 (a post-exilic text), the reference is certainly to a weekly sabbath; this, and all the other texts where the sabbath and the new moon are mentioned together, can be sufficiently explained by the fact that both were feast-days which recurred regularly and frequently. Nor can Ps 81: 4 be cited to confirm the theory: the reference there is to the feast of Tents, 'our feast': the horn was blown on the new moon of the seventh month (Lv 23: 24), and on the full moon, the 15th, the feast began (Lv 23: 34).

Yet it is obvious that there is some similarity between the Hebrew word *shabbath* and the Akkadian word *shapattu*. And perhaps they are related, but this connection need not be explained by saying that the Israelites borrowed their word from the Akkadian. If we take the basic meaning of the root *shbth* or *shpth* in Akkadian and Hebrew, then the Akkadian *shapattu* can mean that day in the middle of the month which marked a definite boundary, for it divided the month in two; and the Hebrew *shabbath* may have meant, originally, the day which marked a definite boundary, because it separated the weeks from one another; the two words would then be close to each other in meaning because of their common etymology. But everyone must allow that the Israelite sabbath was not dependent on the Babylonian calendar, or on any lunar calendar at all.

Lastly, the biblical texts themselves contradict the history which this theory presupposes. Ezechiel did not invent the sabbath, for he does not present it as something novel; on the contrary, he accuses the Israelites of having been unfaithful to it (Ez 20: 13; 22: 26; 23: 38). We shall show further on that the Israelite sabbath was of very ancient origin; it existed long before the Babylonian calendar was adopted in the period immediately preceding the Exile.

3. *Was the sabbath of Canaanite origin?*

Other writers recognize that the sabbath was of ancient origin, and that it is most unlikely that the Israelites adopted it directly from the Babylonians; but they are impressed by the similarity of the names, and by the Babylonian calendars (which, they believe, are themselves the product of a very old tradition). Consequently, they assert that the sabbath must have reached Israel via the Canaanites, from whom the Israelites would have copied it when they settled in Palestine.

This hypothesis does not provide a satisfactory answer to the objections raised against the first theory: *i.e.* it does not explain the difference between the sabbath and the *shapattu*, or between the sabbath and the days of evil omen in Babylonia; nor does it explain how a system which was bound up with a lunar month became disconnected from it. And even if we admit that these most unlikely changes were made by the Canaanites, we should still have to prove that the Canaanites knew of the week and of the sabbath. Now there is no evidence whatsoever to prove this, either in Phoenician inscriptions or in the older texts (from Ras Shamra). It is true that some of the poems from Ras Shamra mention periods of seven days and of seven years, but these periods do not form part of a continuous cycle, and the seventh day has none of the characteristic features of the sabbath. All the evidence which we so far possess indicates that the Canaanites were not familiar with the division of time into weeks, and under Nehemias, the Phoenician merchants did not observe the sabbath (Ne 13: 16). Moreover, how could the sabbath have been a characteristic sign of the Covenant between Yahweh and Israel (Ez 20: 12, 20; Ex 31: 12-17), if it was also observed by the Babylonians in the land of Exile, or by the Canaanites in the Palestinian home-land?

4. *Was the sabbath of Qenite origin?*

We must, then, look for the origin of the sabbath at some period before the Israelites settled in Canaan. The Bible does not record the institution of the sabbath: the story of the quails (Ex 16: 22-30) implies that it was in existence before the legislation at Sinai, and the story of creation (Gn 2: 2-3) says that it came into existence at the beginning of the world. The Israelites believed, therefore, that the institution was known before they accepted the Yahwistic religion; since, however, the sabbath was inseparably linked with Yahwism, we should conclude that the Israelites adopted the sabbath when they accepted this religion.

Here we encounter the Qenite hypothesis, which some writers use to explain the origins of Yahwism itself. Yahweh's revelation came to Moses in a land where the Qenites lived; the Qenites were related to the Midianites (Nb 10: 29 and Jg 1: 16), and they afterwards kept up their connections with Israel (Jg 1: 16; 4: 11, 17; 1 S 15: 6). Even the Rekabites, those uncompromising Yahwists, were said to be of Qenite stock (1 Ch 2: 55 and 4: 12).[1] Now, 'Qenite' can mean 'a blacksmith', and the fact that Sinai was in ancient times a mining area would be sufficient to justify their presence in the region, and their contacts with the Israelites in the desert. If we now ask what particular work was forbidden on the sabbath, there is only one hint in an ancient text: 'You shall not light a fire on the sabbath day in any of your dwellings' (Ex. 35: 3). We may recall, too, the story in Nb 15: 32-36, where a man is stoned to death for having collected wood for a fire on the sabbath day. For blacksmiths, the command not to light a fire would mean that they were not to do their ordinary work. Lastly, in much later times, and outside Israel, the seventh day of the week was the day of Saturn, the dark planet: it was, then, a day when the fire in forges could appear to be of ill omen. Now, a difficult and corrupt text in Amos (Am 5: 26) seems to allude to the Israelites' having worshipped in the desert a certain Kevan: and Kevan is one of the Assyrian names of Saturn.

The hypothesis is both ingenious and fragile. We should beware of attributing too many things to the Qenites, of whom we know almost nothing; in particular, we do not know whether they really were blacksmiths, or whether they knew of the week, or whether they venerated Saturn. It is certainly true that the sabbath goes back to the very origins of Yahwism, and perhaps to even earlier times; but, whatever its origin, in Israel it took on a religious significance which it did not possess before. This is what we are now going to show.

5. The antiquity of the sabbath

In Israel, the weekly sabbath was certainly of great antiquity. It is mentioned in the Elohistic Code of the Covenant (Ex 23: 12), in the Yahwistic Code (Ex 34: 21) in the two redactions of the Ten Commandments (Dt 5: 12-14 and Ex 20: 8-10), and in the Priests' Code (Ex 31: 12-17), i.e. in all the traditions of the Pentateuch. And everywhere it is described in the same way, as a seventh day on which men rest after six days of work. The two Codes of the Covenant take us back to the early days of the settlement in Canaan, and the Ten Commandments, in their original form, go back to the time of Moses. The law about the sabbath is given in both redactions of the Decalogue, and there is no reason for saying that in both cases it is a later addition, inserted into the primitive texts. True, the motives for observing it are not

1. But cf. p. 15.

the same in the two forms of the Ten Commandments, but we shall return to this point later. For the present, it is enough to have shown that the weekly sabbath goes back to the first origins of Yahwism.

Should we go further back still? None of the theories we have examined has brought forward sufficient evidence to prove that the sabbath originally came from Mesopotamia, or from Canaan, or from the Qenites; if the Qenite hypothesis looks the least unlikely, this may be merely because we have no documents at all which contradict it. Obviously, the sabbath day may have originated outside Israel, but we cannot prove this.

One thing, however, is certain: it is useless to try to find the origin of the sabbath by connecting it in some way with the phases of the moon: a lunar month of 29 days, 12 hours and a fraction cannot be divided into periods of seven full days. A far more satisfactory explanation is to be found in the almost universal custom of keeping days of rest, or feast days, or market days, at regular intervals: *e.g.* the Romans held their *nundinae* every ninth day, and the Lolo women of South West China refrain from sewing and washing every sixth day. The reasons for picking particular days vary considerably, but they are generally religious, and there are usually laws commanding certain things to be done, and others not to be done, on these 'reserved' days.

6. *The religious significance of the sabbath*

Whatever its origin was, the sabbath took on a particular meaning which made it an institution peculiar to Israel. Its characteristic feature lies not in the regularity with which it recurs, nor in the cessation of work, nor in the various prohibitions which the cessation of work implies: all this is found, more or less, in other civilizations. Its distinctive trait lies in the fact that it is a day made holy because of its relation to the God of the Covenant; more, it is an element in that Covenant. Other religions had a day which was *tabu*; in Israel, this became a day 'consecrated to Yahweh', a tithe on time, just as the first-born of the flock and the first-fruits of the harvest were a tithe on the work of the other days. This is why a clause about the sabbath appears in the various pacts inaugurating the Covenant,[1] in the original pact at Sinai, *viz.* the Ten Commandments, and in the pact of the tribal federation, *viz.* the Code of the Covenant (Ex 23: 12, and its parallel, Ex 34: 21). Neither the sabbath nor the new moon is mentioned in the Code of Deuteronomy (Dt 12-26), but the reason is probably that this Code is concerned only with those feasts for which the people had to come to the one central sanctuary. The sabbath is mentioned, however, in the Law of Holiness (Lv 19: 3, 30; 23: 3; 26: 2) and in the Priests' Code (Ex 31: 12-17; Nb 28: 9-10).

In the original form of the Decalogue, the commandment about the sabbath was given without commentary. At some later dates, motives were

1. Cf. pp. 147-148.

inserted, but these motives reflect two different backgrounds of thought, and they can be perceived in the two longer forms of the Commandments:

(1) In Dt 5: 14b-15, the human and the social aspects stand out: a man, and his servants too, male or female, must have an opportunity to rest. (This attitude is found in Ex. 23: 12 also.) All the same, the sabbath is connected with the history of salvation: 'You shall remember that you were a slave in the land of Egypt, and that Yahweh your God brought you out with a strong hand and an outstretched arm; *that is why* Yahweh your God has commanded you to observe the sabbath day' (Dt 5: 15). This mention of the Israelites' sufferings in Egypt is found in Dt 6: 20 25; cf. 10: 19 also; it is mentioned, too, in connection with the social laws in Dt 24: 18, 22, in the Code of the Covenant (Ex 22: 20; 23: 9) and in the Law of Holiness (Lv 19: 34). But there is more than this in Deuteronomy: God's great actions delivered Israel (Dt 5: 15) and brought it into the Promised Land (Dt 6: 23); there the people found their *m'nûḥah*, *i.e.* their 'place of rest' after the trials they had suffered in Egypt and in the desert (Dt 12: 9; cf. Ps. 95: 11). In memory of this, the Israelites were commanded to rest on the sabbath day.

(2) Ex 20: 11 adds to the original form of the commandment these words: 'For Yahweh took six days to make the sky, the earth, the sea and all that they contain, but on the seventh day he rested; *that is why* Yahweh blessed the sabbath day and consecrated it.' This is the remark of an editor who drew his inspiration from the Priestly account of creation: the work of creation was spread over the six days of the week, and on the seventh day, God 'rested after all the work he had done. God blessed the seventh day, and sanctified it' (Gn 2: 2-3). The connection between creation and the sabbath is developed in the law in Ex 31: 12-17, which also comes from the Priests' tradition; the sabbath is an 'everlasting sign' between Yahweh and his people, an 'unbreakable covenant'. It is a day of rest after six days of work; it is a day consecrated to Yahweh 'because Yahweh took six days making the sky and the earth, but on the seventh day he rested, and paused for breath'. This idea of God's resting is not an anthropomorphism, but the expression of a theological idea: creation is the first action in the history of salvation; once it was over, God stopped work, and he was then able to make a covenant with his creature. (Similarly, the end of the Flood makes possible the covenant with Noah, and the rainbow is the sign of the covenant: Gn 9: 8-17.) The 'sign' of the Covenant made at the dawn of creation is the observance of the sabbath by man (cf. Ez 20: 12, 20): it is a reminder of the first sabbath when God himself rested after creating the world.

Both motives, therefore, are connected with the Covenant. the only difference is that whereas Deuteronomy has in view the people of the Covenant, the Priestly texts place the emphasis on the God of the Covenant. This latter position is more theological, and consequently the Priests' tradition underlines the religious character of the sabbath: it is 'for Yahweh'

(Lv 23: 3), it is the 'sabbath of Yahweh' (Lv 23: 38), the day 'consecrated to Yahweh' (Ex 31: 15), consecrated, in fact, by Yahweh himself (Ex 20: 11). Since, then, the sabbath was a sacred sign of the Covenant, to observe it was a guarantee of salvation (Is 58: 13-14, cf. 56, 2; Jr 17: 19-27 [post-exilic]); if an individual failed to observe it, he ceased to belong to the community (Ex 31: 14; 35: 2; Nb 15: 32-36), and if the people failed to observe it, they would bring upon themselves the punishment of God (Ez 20: 13; Ne 13: 17-18).

7. The history of the sabbath

This theological interpretation was only gradually developed. The old historical and prophetical texts present the sabbath as a day of rest, a joyful feast-day (Is 1: 13; Os 2: 13) on which men visited sanctuaries (same texts) or went to consult a 'man of God' (2 K 4: 23). Normal heavy work was interrupted (Ex 20: 9-10 and Dt 5: 13-14, Ex 23: 12 and 34: 21), and so were commercial transactions (Am 8: 5); but short journeys were allowed (2 K 4: 23), and it was the day for the changing of the guard at the Palace and in the Temple (2 K 11: 5-8).

After the destruction of the Temple, and during the Exile, the other feasts could no longer be observed; hence the sabbath acquired a new importance, for it then became the distinctive sign of the Covenant (cf. Ezechiel, and the Priestly texts cited above). After the Return, the Jews looked upon the sabbath as a 'pleasant and venerable' day (Is 58: 13): special sacrifices were offered in the Temple,[1] but rigid prohibitions were also introduced: no one was to do business or to travel on the sabbath day (Is 58: 13); no one was to carry a load on that day, or to bring loaded beasts into Jerusalem; nothing was to be taken out of the house, and no work was to be done (Jr 17: 21-22, which is an addition to the collection of Jeremias' prophecies). When Nehemias returned for his second mission, he found that these laws were not being observed: men were treading the presses on the sabbath day, and bringing farm produce into Jerusalem; and Phoenician traders were selling their wares (Ne 13: 15-16). To prevent these infringements of the Law, Nehemias had the gates of Jerusalem closed (Ne 13: 19-22), and the community solemnly promised that they would, in future, respect the sabbath law (Ne 10: 32).

The rules became stricter and stricter. Under the Maccabees, a group of Jews let themselves be slaughtered by the Syrians rather than violate the sabbath rest by active resistance (1 M 2: 32-38, cf. 2 M 6: 11, 15: 1-3). Mattathias decided that the Jews could defend themselves if they were attacked on a sabbath day (1 M 2: 39-41; cf. 9: 43-49), but according to 2 M 8: 25-28, the Jews who had defeated Nicanor halted the pursuit when the sabbath began, and did not begin to share the booty until the day after

1. Cf. p. 469.

the sabbath. The Jewish group which adopted a calendar based on the week [1] laid particular stress on the sabbath: the Book of Jubilees (50: 8-12) forbids the use of marriage, the lighting of a fire or the preparation of food on this day; the Document of Damascus, which comes from the Qumran sect, lists a dozen prohibitions, and, according to Josephus (*Bell*. II, viii, 9) the Essenes 'refrain from working on the sabbath more strictly than any Jew: not only do they prepare their food the day before, so that they will not have to light a fire, but they do not dare to move any household object whatsoever, or even to relieve nature'.

In New Testament times, the Pharisees forbade men to carry a bed (Jn 5: 10), to nurse a sick person (Mk 3: 2; Lk 13: 14), to pick a few ears of corn (Mt 12: 2) or to walk further than a 'sabbath day's journey' (cf. Ac 1: 12), which was about two thousand paces or cubits. Jesus did not condemn the sabbath itself (Lk 4: 16; Mt 24: 20) but he did reject narrow-minded interpretations of the laws about it. He preached that the sabbath obligation yielded before the precept of love of one's neighbour (Mk 3: 4; Lk 13: 15-16) that the 'sabbath was made for man, not man for the sabbath' (Mk 2: 27). The Rabbis of the second century after Christ have left behind a similar formula in their gloss of Ex 31: 14: 'The sabbath was given to you; you were not given to the sabbath'; but they did not allow any derogation from the law except in danger of death, or in cases of very special urgency. In the end, the Mishnah codified thirty-nine kinds of work which were forbidden on the sabbath day, and the list became even longer and more complicated in succeeding centuries.

Jesus claimed that 'the Son of Man is lord of the sabbath' (Mk 2: 28); he could therefore abolish the sabbath, and he did in fact do so, for the New Covenant which he brought abrogated the Old Covenant, of which the sabbath was the sign. The Christian Sunday is not in any sense a continuation of the Jewish sabbath. The latter closed the week, but the Christian Sunday opens the week in the new era by commemorating the Resurrection of our Lord, and the appearances of the risen Christ, and by directing our attention to the future, when he will come again. And yet Sunday does symbolize the fulfilment of those promises which the sabbath foreshadowed. Like all the other promises of the Old Testament, these promises too are realized not in an institution, but in the person of Christ: it is he who fulfils the entire Law. Sunday is the 'Lord's Day', the day of him who lightens our burdens (Mt 11: 28), through whom, with whom and in whom we enter into God's own rest (He 4: 1-11).

[1] Cf. p. 188.

CHAPTER SEVENTEEN

THE ANCIENT FEASTS OF ISRAEL

IN ancient Israel, the great annual feasts were the three feasts of pilgrimage (*ḥag*), *i.e.* the feasts of Unleavened Bread, of Weeks and of Tents, and the feast of the Passover, which was eventually combined with the feast of Unleavened Bread.

1. *The feasts of the Passover and of Unleavened Bread*

In New Testament times, the Passover was the principal feast in the Jewish year, and it has remained so ever since; but it was not always the main feast, and several points in its long history are still obscure. It is not our intention to discuss here the form which the feast has taken in post-biblical Judaism (this is the subject of the treatise in the Mishnah entitled *Pesaḥim*), nor the feast which the Samaritans still keep to-day, in accordance with their own ancient rites; we shall restrict ourselves to what we learn from the Old Testament. The information it contains is not very plentiful, and it is sometimes difficult to interpret. First we have liturgical texts: the ritual for the Passover contained in the story of the Exodus from Egypt (Ex 12); the religious calendars in Ex 23: 15; 34: 18 and 25; Dt 16: 1-8; Lv 23: 5-8; the rituals in Nb 28: 16-25 and Ez 45: 21-24; and the story in Nb 9: 1-14, which provides a justification for keeping the Passover in the second month. Secondly, certain historical texts mention or describe the celebration of a particular Passover: the first Passover, at the Exodus (Ex 12); the first Passover in Canaan (Jos 5: 10-12); the one celebrated by Josias (2 K 23: 21-23= 2 Ch 35: 1-18); that celebrated after the Return from the Exile (Esd 6: 19-22); to these we should add the Passover under Ezechias, which is described at length in 2 Ch 30, though it has no parallel in the Books of Kings. Lastly, we must take into account three important non-biblical documents, a papyrus and two ostraka, from the Jewish colony at Elephantine.

(a) *The historical development.* The legislative texts (apart from the one in Ezechiel) all come from the Pentateuch, and they belong to different traditions. Hence they enable us to trace the historical development of the feast; this development is confirmed by the more laconic information in the historical books and in the documents from Elephantine. Since the latest texts are the most detailed and the clearest, the best approach is to start with them and then to trace the history of the feast further back, to see if we can decide anything about its origin.

1. *The Priestly tradition*. This tradition is contained in Lv 23: 5-8; Nb 28: 16-25, cf. Nb 9: 1-14 and, in Ex 12, by vv. 1-20 and 40-51. In fact, these texts speak of two successive feasts, the feast of the Passover and the feast of the Unleavened Bread. The Passover was to be celebrated at the full moon in the first month of a year beginning in spring. According to this account, on the 10th day of the month, every family chose a one-year old lamb, a male and one without blemish; this lamb was killed at twilight on the 14th, and its blood was sprinkled over the lintel and the stiles of the door of the house. This was a *zebaḥ* sacrifice,[1] the meat of which had to be roasted and eaten on this same night of the full moon; not a bone of the victim was to be broken, and the remains of this religious meal were to be burnt. Unleavened bread and bitter herbs were eaten at the meal, and all who took part in the ceremony were in travelling dress. If the family was too small to eat a whole lamb, it joined with some neighbouring family. Slaves and *gerîm* (resident aliens) could share in the meal, provided they were circumcised.

On the following day, the 15th, the feast of Unleavened Bread (*maṣṣôth*) began. All the old, leavened, bread was destroyed, and for seven days, from the 15th to the 21st, only unleavened bread was eaten; the first and the seventh day were days of rest from work, and a religious meeting was held.

This ritual is in harmony with the brief injunction in Ez 45: 21, with the description of the Passover celebrated upon the Return (Esd 6: 19-22), and with the information supplied by the 'Passover Papyrus' from Elephantine. This last document, dating from 419 B.C., lays great stress on the dates to be followed for the Passover and the feast of Unleavened Bread; and the reason for this insistence is that the prescription was new to this Jewish colony.

2. *Deuteronomy*. At first reading, the passage in Dt 16: 1-8 seems to combine the Passover and the feast of Unleavened Bread even more closely than the Priestly texts do. The passage, however, is not a literary unity. Verses 1, 2, 4*b*-7 refer to the Passover: it was to be celebrated in the month of Abib, but the day was not fixed. (In the ancient calendar, where the year began in autumn, the month of Abib corresponded to what was, in the later calendar, the first month of the year, in the spring.) The text then says that the victim could be a head of cattle or a sheep or a goat; it was to be killed at sundown, not wherever a man lived, but 'in the place chosen by Yahweh for his name to dwell there', *i.e.* in Jerusalem. The victim was to be cooked, and eaten during the night, at this sanctuary; in the morning everyone was to return home.

Verses 3, 4*a*, and 8, however, refer to the feast of Unleavened Bread: for seven days, the Israelites were to eat *maṣṣôth*, *i.e.* 'bread of misery'. On the seventh day, no work was to be done, but a religious meeting was to be held.

1. Cf. p. 427.

The connection of the two feasts is clearly artificial, for if the people went home on the morning after the Passover, they did not stay until the final meeting on the seventh day to eat unleavened bread.

The Passover under Josias (2 K 23: 21-23) was celebrated according to this Deuteronomic ritual, and this text makes no mention of any feast of Unleavened Bread. On the other hand, the novelty of this feast is strongly underlined: 'No Passover like this had ever been celebrated since the days of the Judges who ruled Israel, or during all the time of the kings of Israel and of Judah.' There is a much longer account of this Passover in 2 Ch 35: 1-18 but it tells us nothing more about the customs followed in the time of Josias: the additional information is inspired by practices in vogue during the Chronicler's day: the feast of Unleavened Bread is mentioned (v. 17) and the contradiction between the rules for the Passover and for the feast of Unleavened Bread (cf. Dt 16: 7-8) is suppressed. The Chronicler, too, insists that this feast was of quite a new kind: no Passover like that had ever been celebrated since the time of Samuel (2 Ch 35: 18).

In order to discover precisely how this was a new kind of feast, we must compare it with more ancient customs.

3. *The ancient religious calendars.* Of the religious calendars listed on pp. 471-473, the two most ancient ones speak of the feast of Unleavened Bread (Ex 23: 15; 34: 18), but not of the Passover. *Maṣṣôth* were to be eaten for seven days in the month of Abib, and this was one of the three feasts of pilgrimage, *ḥag* (cf. Ex 23: 14, 17; 34: 23). These were the three feasts on which Solomon officiated in person at the Temple (according to 1 K 9: 25), and they are mentioned by name (Unleavened Bread, Weeks, Tents) in the parallel passage in 2 Ch 8: 13; cf. Dt 16: 16.

The Passover is mentioned in Ex 34: 25, but this is not part of a calendar for pilgrimage feasts; the parallel cited in this verse would suggest that we ought to see a reference to the Passover in Ex 23: 18 as well; but the context of this verse, too, is not concerned with the three pilgrimages. However, since the word *ḥag* occurs in both verses, both must have been edited after Deuteronomy, when the Passover had become a pilgrimage (*ḥag*).

And this is precisely where the innovation of Deuteronomy and of Josias lay: they made the Passover a pilgrimage, for which men came to the one central sanctuary. It was a consequence of the centralization of worship. The Passover had previously been a family feast kept in each town and in each home (cf. Ex 12: 21-23 and Dt 16: 5); it was quite distinct from the pilgrimage of the *maṣṣôth*. The two feasts, however, fell at the same time and had (as we shall see) several features in common: hence they were eventually combined. But they were not combined in the time of Josias, and the first mention of them as one feast is to be found in Ez 45: 21 and in the Priests' traditions.

Yet, according to another text of Chronicles, Josias' feast was not so very novel an idea. A similar Passover had been held under Ezechias; under him, however, the time needed for the purification of the priests and for gathering all the faithful from the former Northern kingdom led to the postponement of the feast, and it was celebrated, by way of exception, on the 14th of the second month. It was, says 2 Ch 30: 26, a feast such as had not been seen in Israel since the time of Solomon. Attempts have recently been made to defend the historicity even of the details in this story, and the observance of the feast in the second month has been attributed to a discrepancy between the calendars followed in Ephraim and in Judah. It seems, however, that the reform of Ezechias is a product of the Chronicler's imagination: the Books of Kings make only a passing allusion to this reform, but the Chronicler has described it on the pattern of Josias' reform. He has even stated that it ended with a solemn Passover; his description of this feast, however, follows the rules laid down by the Priests' Code rather than those of Deuteronomy, for the feast of Unleavened Bread is unhesitatingly connected with the Passover. The idea of a Passover in the second month is also taken from the Priests' Code; it is inspired by Nb 9: 1-14, which mentions the two excusing causes advanced by the Chronicler (lack of purity, and a long journey). This rule in Nb 9: 1-14 is to be explained by the conditions in which the Jews found themselves after the Exile, and in particular by the relations between the community in Palestine and those who had stayed in Babylonia, or who were living in the Diaspora.

It must be granted, then, that the Passover celebrated under Josias according to the prescriptions of Deuteronomy was something new; but had it never been heard of before? Certain texts in the Bible would indicate rather that it was a return to an older custom which had long been neglected: 'since the time of the Judges' says 2 K 23: 22; 'since the time of Samuel', says 2 Ch 35: 18 (which comes to the same thing). But we must distinguish two questions, namely, the combination of the Passover with the feast of Unleavened Bread, and the obligation to celebrate the Passover (alone) at Jerusalem.

The text of Jos 5: 10-12 has been used to prove that these two feasts were already combined in ancient times: when the Israelites pitched their first camp in the Promised Land, at Gilgal, they celebrated the Passover on the evening of the 14th of the month; on 'this same day', 'the day after the Passover', they ate produce of the land, *maṣṣôth* and parched corn, and then the manna ceased to fall. This story, it is claimed, represents a tradition of the sanctuary at Gilgal, and both the Passover and the *maṣṣôth* commemorated the end of the Exodus and the entry into the Promised Land. To this, other writers object that since the feast of Unleavened Bread is placed on the day after the Passover, the narrative must depend on the Priestly tradition, and must therefore be a late account. This objection, however, is not valid, for the words 'the day after the Passover' are missing from the best witnesses of the Greek version, and they contradict the phrase next to them, 'this same day'; in all probability, they are a gloss. On the other hand, it is by no means certain that the text is referring to that feast of *maṣṣôth* which is described by the liturgical texts: the oldest liturgical texts say that the feast lasted seven days, and they do not mention parched corn. Rather, the general impression is that Jos 5: 10–12 represents an independent tradition which reflects a custom of the sanctuary at Gilgal; but this does not prove that, from the moment the Israelites settled in Canaan, the Passover and a feast of Unleavened Bread like that described in the other texts were combined. The earliest religious calendars mention the feast of Unleavened Bread, but not the Passover; the two feasts had not been combined when Deuteronomy was first made known; and the story of Josias' reform mentions only the Passover.

The other question concerns the obligation of keeping the Passover at Jerusalem, and here Deuteronomy does introduce something new. Before the institution of the monarchy, the Passover may well have been a common feast celebrated at the central sanctuary of the tribal federation,[1] as 2 K 23: 22 and 2 Ch 35: 18 assert; it certainly had been a tribal feast before the settlement. But the settlement led to a loosening of tribal bonds, and to a decentralization of cultic worship[2]; and so the Passover became a family feast. This would explain why it is not mentioned in the calendars of Ex 23 and 34, and it would also explain why such stress is placed on the details by the old Yahwistic ritual in Ex 12: 21–23. The feast of Unleavened Bread, on the other hand, would be one of the annual pilgrimages to the local sanctuaries. Deuteronomy, and Josias' Reform, made Jerusalem the centre for both feasts, and in the end they were combined.

Whatever one may think of the details of this history, the two feasts were certainly of different character and of different origin.

(b) *The origin of the Passover.* The Hebrew word for the Passover is *pesaḥ*. It seems impossible to draw any conclusions from the meaning of the word, for its etymology is warmly debated. The Bible connects it with the root *psḥ*, meaning 'to limp' (2 S 4: 4), 'to limp, to hobble, to jump' (1 K 18: 21); in the last plague of Egypt, Yahweh 'jumped over, left out' the houses where the Passover was being observed (Ex 12: 13, 23, 27); this is not the primary meaning, but an explanation added in later times. Others have compared it with the Akkadian word *pashâḥu*, meaning 'to appease'; but the Israelite Passover never had any expiatory purpose. According to a more modern theory, it is to be explained by the Egyptian: it is said to be a transcription of an Egyptian word meaning 'a stroke, a blow': the Passover would then be the 'blow' of the tenth plague (Ex 11: 1), in which Yahweh 'struck' the first-born of Egypt (Ex 12: 12, 13, 23, 27, 29). This too is not convincing: it is easy to allow that the Israelites gave an Egyptian name to a

1. Cf. p. 331.   2. Cf. p. 332.

custom borrowed from Egypt, but it is hard to admit that they gave an Egyptian name to a custom which was strictly their own and which was actually instituted against the Egyptians. In addition, this explanation looks for the origin and the meaning of the Passover in the plague of the first-born of Egypt, and this is a secondary feature of the feast.

If we leave etymology aside, the Passover is seen to be a rite practised by shepherds. It is the kind of sacrifice which nomads or semi-nomads offer, and no other sacrifice in all Israelite ritual is more like the sacrifices of the ancient Arabs: there is no priest, no altar, and the use of the blood is most important.[1] The Passover was the spring-time sacrifice of a young animal in order to secure fecundity and prosperity for the flock. The purpose of putting blood upon the stiles of the door (originally, on the tent-poles) was to drive away evil powers, the *mashhît* or Exterminator, who is mentioned in the Yahwistic tradition (Ex 12: 23), and also perhaps, in a disfigured text, in the Priestly tradition (Ex 12: 13). As we have suggested, it may have been a feast celebrated when the tribe struck camp before setting out for the spring pastures, but this is not the whole explanation: it was, in a more general way, an offering for the welfare of the flock, like the old Arab feast which fell in the month of Rajab, the first month of spring. The other details of the Passover stress still more that it was essentially a feast for nomads: the victim was roasted over a fire without any kitchen utensils; it was eaten with unleavened bread (which is still the normal bread of Bedouin to-day), and with bitter herbs (which does not mean vegetables grown in the garden, but the desert plants which Bedouin pick to season their food). The ritual prescribed that those eating it should have their belts already fastened, sandals on their feet (as if they were going to make a long journey on foot), and a shepherd's stick in one hand.

This pastoral feast was not an offering of the 'first-born' of the flock; this is nowhere stated, even in the most detailed texts about the choice of the victim or about the rites to be followed at the feast. Nevertheless, Ex 34: 19-20 has put the law about the first-born in between the regulation for the feast of Unleavened Bread and its natural conclusion in 20b (as a comparison with Ex 23: 15 shows): and Ex 13: 1-2, 11-16 connects the law about the first-born with the law about the Passover and Unleavened Bread. It is an artificial connection, to establish which the tenth plague is used; during the night of the Passover, God struck the first-born of Egypt and spared the houses marked with the blood of the Passover victim; and, says Ex 13: 15, that is why the first-born of animals are killed, and the first-born of men are redeemed. This connection, however, is not mentioned in the basic account: there is no reference to it in the Passover ritual, and the law about the first-born is given separately in the old Code of the Covenant (Ex 22: 28-29).

The only texts which fix the date of the Passover are the Priestly texts and

1. Cf. pp. 435-438.

Ez 45: 21: they fix it for the 14th-15th of the first month, *i.e.* at the full moon. This must have been the date of the Passover from the very beginning. Since it was kept in the night-time, and in the desert, it would be observed at the full moon, not necessarily because it was connected with the cult of the stars, but simply because it was the brightest night of the month. This common-sense explanation is itself sufficient to refute the suggestion that the Passover was at first celebrated on the night of the new moon. Since *ḥodesh* meant the 'new moon' before it came to mean 'a month', the following rendering of Dt 16: 1 has recently been suggested: 'Take care to observe the new moon (*ḥodesh*) of Abib, and to celebrate then a Passover for Yahweh thy God'; the rest of the verse, in which *ḥodesh* occurs again (this time certainly with the meaning 'month') would be an addition by the Priests. There is, however, a more serious objection against the idea that from ancient times the Passover was kept at the full moon: an ostrakon found at Elephantine has on it a letter which, it is suggested, should read: 'Let me know when you celebrate the Passover.' If this is the correct interpretation of the text (and it is a most attractive rendering), and if this document is earlier than the Passover Papyrus mentioned above (which is probable), it still does not necessarily mean that the Passover was not previously kept at the full moon in the Jewish colonies of Egypt: the writer might be in doubt as to the month in which the feast was to be held, if the year could have had an intercalary month.[1]

One fact, however, is certain: the Passover was a most ancient feast. It dated back to the time when the Israelites were still semi-nomads. It dated back even before the Exodus, if the feast which the Israelites wanted to celebrate in the desert (Ex 5: 1) was itself a Passover. It was the Israelite version of the spring-time feast which all the Semitic nomads kept, but in Israel it acquired a particular meaning, which we shall explain in a moment.

(c) *The origin of the feast of Unleavened Bread.* The word *maṣṣôth* means 'unleavened, or unfermented, bread'. The feast of the *maṣṣôth* marked the beginning of the barley harvest, which was the first crop to be gathered. The seven weeks to the Harvest feast (or 'the feast of Weeks') were counted 'from the moment when the sickle begins to cut the grain' (Dt 16: 9). For the first seven days of the barley harvest, only bread made with the new grain was eaten: it was eaten 'without leaven', *i.e.* without anything from the harvest of the previous year in it. It represented, therefore, a new beginning. Further, it was wrong to present oneself before Yahweh with empty hands (Ex 23: 15 and 34: 20, where this rule is separated from the rule about Unleavened Bread by the insertion of the law about the first-born). The characteristic feature of this feast lay, therefore, in a first offering of the first-fruits, and this trait was accentuated in the later ritual giving details for the offering of the first sheaf (Lv 23: 9-14). But the real feast to celebrate the

1. Cf. p. 189.

first-fruits of the harvest was the feast of Weeks, which marked the end of the cereal harvests; the feast of Unleavened Bread was merely a preparation for this second feast, and the two together marked the beginning and the end of harvest-time.

The feast of Unleavened Bread was, therefore, an agricultural feast, and was not observed until the Israelites had settled in Canaan (Lv 23: 10 states this explicitly when referring to the first sheaf). It is quite possible, then, that the Israelites adopted this feast from the Canaanites. In this context, we may recall the execution of Saul's descendants at the high place near Gibeon (2 S 21: 9-11): it took place 'at the beginning of the barley harvest', and the Gibeonites took their revenge in the form of a fertility rite (as a passage in the poems of Ras Shamra shows).[1] The two rituals have nothing in common, however, except the date, and, in Israel, the feast of Unleavened Bread was always bound up with the week: the feast lasted seven days (Ex 23: 15; 34: 18), from one sabbath to the next (Ex 12: 16, Dt 16: 8; Lv 23: 6-8). This is the justification for the insertion of the law about the sabbath after that about the *maṣṣôth* in Ex 34: 21, and for the added detail 'even at harvest-time' (which began with the feast of Unleavened Bread). This connection with the sabbath shows that the seven days consecrated to the feast were not reckoned haphazardly, though seven-days feasts are found outside Israel; in Israel, this feast was essentially tied up with the system of the week, and this is confirmed by the fact that the Harvest feast was fixed for seven weeks after the feast of Unleavened Bread (Lv 23: 15; Dt 16: 9). The feast of Unleavened Bread may have been adopted by the Israelites from the Canaanites; but since the week and the sabbath are not found outside Israel, this feast must have taken on, apparently from the moment of its adoption, a strictly Israelite character. Since it was an agricultural feast, it depended on the condition of the crops, and could not be dated more precisely than in 'the month of the ears of corn', i.e. the month of Abib; this is the only regulation in the calendars of Ex 23 and 34 and in Deuteronomy.

We have seen that the Passover was kept during this same month, and at the full moon. Deuteronomy and the reform of Josias made the Passover a pilgrimage feast, as the feast of Unleavened Bread already was, and the obvious move was to combine the two feasts. The old rubric about eating unleavened bread at the Passover (a rubric which has nothing to do with the feast of Unleavened Bread) favoured the combination, and so perhaps did local usages, like that followed in the sanctuary at Gilgal (Jos 5: 10-12). The date of the Passover was already fixed for the full moon, and this was left unchanged; the feast of Unleavened Bread was attached to it, and ordered to be kept during the following seven days. This is the rule laid down in Lv 23: 5-8. Now, if the date we suggested for the Law of Holiness is correct,

1. Cf. p. 442.

this took place after Josias' reform, but before the Exile; this would then explain why Ezechiel knew of and accepted these dates (Ez 45: 21). Unfortunately, the Passover was reckoned by the phases of the moon, and the Unleavened Bread by the days of the week; this led to an insoluble problem, for the Passover would not necessarily fall on the day before a sabbath, and the feast of Unleavened Bread had to begin on a sabbath. In practice, the connection of the feast of Unleavened Bread with the week was abandoned, and both feasts were fixed by the moon, with the feast of Unleavened Bread following immediately after the Passover, whether it was a sabbath day or not. But in later times, the Pharisees and the Boethuseans (a group of the Sadducees) argued, without reaching any conclusion, as to how one should interpret the sabbath of the *maṣṣôth* and the 'day after the sabbath' in Lv 23: 11, 15. This was the day on which the first sheaf was to be offered, and from which the seven weeks were to be counted before the feast of Weeks; the Boethuseans said it was the sabbath which fell during the week of the *maṣṣôth*, whereas the Pharisees claimed that it was the very day of the Passover.

(d) *Their connection with the history of salvation.* All the traditions of the Pentateuch connect the feast of Unleavened Bread (Ex 23: 15; 34: 18; Dt 16: 3), or the Passover (Dt 16: 1 and 6), or both the Passover and the feast of Unleavened Bread (Ex 12: 23-27 and 39 [Yahwistic tradition]; Ex 12: 12-13 and 17 [Priestly tradition]), with the Exodus from Egypt. The text which connects them most closely is Ex 12, in which the rites for both feasts are incorporated into the story of the Exodus; and the theme of this chapter is that the two rites were instituted to help in setting Israel free, and to commemorate this deliverance.

Some scholars, who see in cult the actualization of myths, look upon the first sixteen chapters of Exodus (Ex 1-15) as the 'legend' of the Passover feast, and claim that it is useless to try to find historical events behind them: these chapters, they hold, are nothing more than the cultic expression of a myth about Yahweh's struggle with his enemies. The culminating point of the story is that night which is relived on the Passover night, on which men keep vigil as Yahweh himself 'kept vigil' (Ex 12: 42). In the morning (Ex 14: 24) the Egyptians are defeated: this is Yahweh's triumph, celebrated in a victory hymn; and this hymn ends with the glorification of the Temple at Jerusalem, in which the feast is held, and in which Yahweh dwells for evermore (Ex 15: 17).

No one will deny that there are cultic elements in the story of Ex 12, for the text itself stresses them; and everyone admits that the rites for the Passover and for the feast of Unleavened Bread have influenced the presentation of history. But this does not mean that Ex 12 (much less Ex 1-15) is merely a sacred commentary on certain rites. There are other elements in these chapters besides ritual ones, and the entire section forms part of a larger whole, which claims to be an historical work. Once more we must insist that Israel's religion was an historical religion, and that the faith of Israel was based on God's interventions in the history of his people. There was a feast called the Passover, probably even before Israel became a people; there was also a feast of Unleavened Bread, adopted perhaps from the Canaanites, but adopted in the fullest sense by the Israelites; and these two feasts were celebrated in the spring-time. One spring time there had been a startling intervention of God: he had brought Israel out of Egypt, and this divine intervention marked the beginning of Israel's history as a people, as God's Chosen People: this period of liberation reached its consummation when they settled in the Promised Land. The feasts of the Passover and of Unleavened Bread commemorated this event, which dominated the history of salvation. Both feasts soon took on this meaning, but in the older traditions there are two separate feasts which commemorate the event independently; their common feature, however, made it almost inevitable that they should one day be combined.

2. The feast of Weeks

The second great feast of the year is called, in Ex 23: 16, the Harvest feast (qaṣîr), or, more strictly, the feast of the wheat harvest (as in Ex 34: 22). It was one of the main periods in the agricultural calendar of Palestine (Gn 30: 14; Jg 15: 1; 1 S 6: 13; 12: 17) and in the calendar of Gezer.[1] In Ex 34: 22, the feast is also called the feast of Weeks; the phrase is perhaps a gloss to underline the fact that it was the same feast as that mentioned in Dt 16: 9-10 (the ḥag of the shabu'ôth, i.e. the 'pilgrimage' of the 'weeks'). This last text gives an explanation of the name, and fixes the date precisely: the feast was celebrated seven weeks after the first cereals had been cut, i.e. seven weeks after the feast of the maṣṣôth. In Nb 28: 26 it is called both the 'feast of Weeks' and the 'feast of the first-fruits' (bikkûrîm). This was the real feast for the first-fruits of the harvest, and it was a joyful feast (cf. Dt 16: 11; Is. 9: 2).

The most detailed account of its ritual is found in Lv 23: 15-21: starting from the day after the sabbath on which the first sheaf was presented to Yahweh,[2] seven complete weeks were reckoned, which brings us to the day after the seventh sabbath, making fifty days in all. (Hence the Greek name for the feast: Πεντηκοστή, the 'fiftieth' day or Pentecost; it is first mentioned in 2 M 12: 31-32 and Tb 2: 1, along with the name 'feast of Weeks'.) These 'fifty' days between the beginning of the barley harvest and the end of the wheat harvest are probably connected with the periods given in an old system of reckoning for the use of farmers.[3] The ceremony was marked by the offering of two loaves made out of the new flour, baked with leaven, and this is the only instance in which the use of yeast is ritually prescribed

1. Cf. p. 184.   2. Cf. p. 492.   3. Cf. pp. 180 and 184.

for an offering to Yahweh. The unusual nature of the offering underlines the fact that it was a farmers' feast, and closely connected with the feast of the *maṣṣ̂ôth*: at the beginning of the harvest, unleavened bread was eaten as a sign that here was a new beginning; at the end of the wheat harvest, leavened bread was offered in sacrifice, because it was the ordinary bread of a farming population. It meant that the harvest-time was over; with this offering, ordinary customs were again observed. This connection with the feast of Unleavened Bread (and later with the Passover) explains why the Rabbis called this feast the closing '*aṣereth* (assembly) and even 'the '*aṣereth* of the Passover'.

The feast of Weeks was a feast for farmers living a settled life; Israel adopted it only after its entry into Palestine, and must have taken it from the Canaanites. (The custom of presenting to a god the first-fruits of the harvest is very widespread.) At first the date of the feast was not fixed (Ex 23: 16; 34: 22); the earliest text which states anything with precision is Dt 16: 9-10, but the dating is only relative, for it is reckoned from the feast of Unleavened Bread; and this latter feast was, at that period, dependent on the condition of the crops. Hence the date of Pentecost was not fixed until the Priests connected the feast of Unleavened Bread with the Passover. We have seen, however, that the interpretation of this ruling gave rise to disputes.[1] In the calendar followed by the Book of Jubilees and by the Qumran sect, in which the same feasts fall every year on the same days of the week,[2] the first sheaf, which had to be offered 'on the day after the sabbath', was presented on the Sunday following the octave of the Passover, *i.e.* on the 26th of the first month; the feast of Weeks fell, consequently, on the 15th of the third month.

Like the Passover, the feast of Weeks was eventually related to the history of salvation, but this connection was made at a far later date. Ex 19: 1 says that the Israelites reached Sinai in the third month after they had left Egypt: and since they had left Egypt in the middle of the first month, the feast of Weeks became the feast commemorating the Covenant at Sinai. 2 Ch 15: 10 mentions that under Asa, a religious feast was held in the third month to renew the Covenant, but it does not expressly state that this was the feast of Weeks. The first time the connection is openly mentioned is in the Book of Jubilees, which puts all the covenants it can discover in the Old Testament (from Noah to Sinai) on the day of the feast of Weeks. The Qumran sect, too, which called itself the community of the New Covenant, celebrated the renewal of the Covenant on the feast of Weeks, and this was the most important feast in its calendar.

Among orthodox Jews, however, the feast of Weeks always remained of secondary importance. It is omitted from the calendar of Ez 45: 18-25, and (apart from liturgical texts) it is mentioned only in late books of the Old

1. Cf. p. 492.   2. Cf. p. 188.

Testament, and only in connection with something else (2 M 12: 31-32 and Tb 2: 1). The Mishnah gives a complete treatise to all the annual feasts except this one, and the idea that it commemorated the day on which the Law was given on Sinai was not accepted by the Rabbis until the second century of our era.

The Christian feast of Pentecost had, from the first, a different meaning. According to Ac 2, it was marked by the gift of the Holy Spirit and by the calling of all nations into the new Church. The fact that it coincides with a Jewish feast shows that the old system of worship has passed away, and that the promises which that system foreshadowed are now fulfilled. But there is no connection between the Christian feast of Pentecost and the feast of Weeks as understood by the Qumran community or, in later days, by orthodox Judaism. The story in Acts contains no allusion to the Sinaitic Covenant nor to the New Covenant of which Christ is the mediator.

3. The feast of Tents

(a) *The names of the feast: its importance.* The third great feast of the year is called, in the English versions of the Bible, the feast of Tabernacles or Booths. 'Tabernacles' is a transliteration of the word used by the Vulgate, and means little to a modern reader. 'Booths' is just as meaningless, and it is not quite so familiar. 'Tents', which is a literal translation of the Latin *tabernacula*, tells the reader more, but it may also lead him into error: the feast never involved the erection of 'tents'. We shall, however, keep this term, for want of a more suitable word. In Hebrew, the feast is called *sukkôth*, and the correct translation of this is 'Huts'; but 'the feast of Huts' is not a very pretty phrase, and is just as likely to give a wrong impression as the rendering 'Tents', though for different reasons.

The name *sukkôth* first appears in the later religious calendars (Dt 16: 13, 16; Lv 23: 34) and in those later texts which depend on them (Esd 3: 4; Za 14: 16, 18, etc.); but the feast itself is certainly the same one as that referred to, in the two oldest calendars (Ex 23: 16 and 34: 22), as the 'feast of Ingathering' (*'asîph*).

It was the most important and the most crowded of the three annual pilgrimages to the sanctuary. Lv 23: 39 calls it 'the feast of Yahweh' (cf. Nb 29: 12). In Ez 45: 25 it is *the* feast, without further qualification, *i.e.* the feast *par excellence*, as it is in 1 K 8: 2, 65. It can be recognized too, in 'the feast of Yahweh which was held each year at Shiloh' (Jg 21: 19), and this, no doubt, was the occasion of Elqanah's annual visit to Shiloh (1 S 1: 3). Zacharias foretold that all the nations would come each year to worship Yahweh in Jerusalem, at the feast of Tents (Za 14: 16). Even in Josephus' time, it was 'the holiest and the greatest of Hebrew feasts' (*Ant.* VIII, iv. 1), and a pagan, Plutarch, uses an almost identical formula (*Quaest. conv.* IV, 6).

(b) *Its historical development*. The oldest texts leave us in no doubt about the character of the feast: it was a farmers' feast, the feast of Ingathering, when all the produce of the fields (Ex 23: 16), and all the produce of the threshing-floor and of the presses (Dt 16: 13), had been gathered in. When all the fruits of the earth had been gathered, and the olives and the grapes had been pressed, the farmers assembled to give thanks to God. It was a joyful feast, and Eli's suspicion that Anna was tipsy (1 S 1: 14-15) shows that heavy drinking of the new wine was not unknown.

Naturally, it was an occasion for popular rejoicing. Jg 21: 19-21 tells how the Benjamites, when they had been decimated, carried off young girls from Shiloh while they were dancing in the vineyards at the feast of Yahweh. A similar tradition is preserved in the Mishnah (*Taanith* IV, 8): on the 15th day of Ab (July-August), and on the Day of Atonement, the young girls of Jerusalem went out in white clothes, newly washed, to dance in the vineyards and to sing: 'Young man, raise your eyes and see whom you are going to choose. Do not look for beauty, but for good family.' We need not consider the dance in the month of Ab. The other could not possibly have taken place, as the text says, on the Day of Atonement, for this was the great day of penance. If (as it seems) the story records an ancient tradition, then it must refer to the feast of Tents, which was held a few days later. Dancing still took place at this feast even in New Testament times: good-living men, the leading figures in the community, would dance in the Temple court-yards, singing and brandishing lighted torches. It was a gala occasion, and the saying went: 'The man who has never seen the joy of the night of this feast has never seen real joy in all his life.'

Among the ancient liturgical texts, the first details about the ritual are to be found in Dt 16: 13-15, where the feast is called the feast of 'Huts' (*suk-kôth*) without further explanation; it is described as a pilgrimage to the one central sanctuary, Jerusalem, and it lasted seven days. If we leave aside the mention of huts, this is exactly how the dedication of Solomon's Temple is described (it coincided with the feast of Tents): the faithful, we are told, came from all over the kingdom, kept a feast for seven days, and on the eighth day, at the command of the king, returned home (1 K 8: 65-66): the whole passage comes from the Deuteronomic editors.

The ritual outlined in Lv 23: 33-43 is far more precise, but it also raises questions of literary criticism.[1] Verses 34-36 repeat the prescriptions of Deuteronomy, but they mention an eighth day after the seven days of feasting; on this eighth day, a day of rest from work, the people were to assemble for worship and sacrifice. Nb 29: 12-34 lays down what sacrifices were to be offered during the seven days (the number of the main victims, bulls, grows steadily less), and Nb 29: 35-38 lays down the sacrifices for the eighth day, which were far less numerous. This eighth day is everywhere

1. Cf. pp. 472-473.

mentioned apart from the seven days of the feast, and is obviously a conclusion or appendix. In the later ritual contained in the Mishnah, there is no mention of living in huts or keeping a feast at night; the only rule is that the people are to remain in Jerusalem; the eighth day then, the day after the feast, was a day of transition before the return to normal life. It is wrong, therefore, to emphasize the silence of Ez 45: 25, for this verse is a very concise text which is dealing only with the sacrifices offered by the prince during the seven days of the feast of Tents (just as the previous two verses deal with the sacrifices to be offered during the seven days of the Passover and the feast of Unleavened Bread, Ez 45: 23-24). This is how 2 Ch 7: 8-10 presents the celebration of the feast in Solomon's day, but it puts the feast of Tents after the feast for the dedication of the Temple; the writer imagined that there had been seven days' celebration for the dedication of the Temple, followed by a further seven days for the feast of Tents. This way of looking at the dedication has been introduced into 1 K 8: 65 by a gloss in the Hebrew text which is not found in the Greek version.

The account of the celebration of the feast under Esdras (Ne 8: 13-18), in connection with the reading of the Law, is obviously inspired by the text of Lv 23; but this chapter was by then in a second (though not the final) stage of its redaction. Ne 8: 14 refers to Lv 23: 42-43: for seven days, men are to live in huts, in memory of the huts in which Israel dwelt after the Exodus from Egypt. When the people heard this text read out, they went off to cut branches and to erect huts for their families, either on the roof-tops or in the Temple courts or in the squares of Jerusalem: the text adds 'The Israelites had never done anything like this since the days of Josue (Ne 8: 17). It is hard to say what was so new about this action. It cannot have been the building of the huts themselves, for this must have been a feature of the feast in ancient times, since the feast had this name before Deuteronomy; it seems rather that, for the first time, these huts were erected at Jerusalem itself (which Dt 16: 15 does not mention).

Nor is this contradicted by Os 12: 10: 'I shall make thee live under tents once again, as on the day of Meeting (mô'ed)'. Mô'ed can also mean 'a solemn feast' (so the argument runs). Osee, however, lived before the centralization of worship, and therefore he could only be referring to a feast celebrated at a local sanctuary. Yet even this is not the true interpretation for the text speaks of 'tents', not of 'huts', and it is referring to the golden age of the desert period, when Yahweh 'met' Israel.

Lv 23: 40-41 represents a third, and last stage in the redaction of the passage: men are to take 'good fruit' and branches and to rejoice for seven days. There is no mention of fruit in Ne 8: 13-18, and the fruit had nothing to do with the erection of the huts; rather it was carried round in a joyous procession. This we know from later historical texts: in 2 M 10: 6-8, the renovation of the Temple is said to have been celebrated 'like the feast of

Tents', and for eight days the Jews carried around thyrsus, green branches and palms; Josephus, too, tells a story about Alexander Jannaeus, that high priest and king who was so hated by the Pharisees and the people: at the feast of Tents, he was pelted with the citrons which the people had in their hands (Ant. XIII, xiv, 5). The ritual in the Mishnah says that a citron ('etrôg) was carried in one hand, and a lûlab (a supple palm) in the other; branches of myrtle and of willow were tied to the lûlab.

(c) *Its dates.* If we take the literal sense of the terms used,[1] the feast was celebrated at the beginning of the autumnal year (according to Ex 23: 16), or at the end of this year (according to Ex 34: 22). There is no need to see in these two texts either a contradiction or an evolution in the way the feast was fixed. They simply mean that the exact date was not fixed at the time when these two texts were written: it depended on how the crops were ripening, for it was the 'Feast of the Ingathering', and was therefore held when all the crops had been gathered in, just before, or just after, the beginning of the year. The old agricultural calendar from Gezer begins with two months of harvesting.[2] Nor is this contradicted by Dt 31: 10–11, which commands that the law be read out on the feast of Tents 'at the end (miqqeṣ) of seven years', in the sabbatical year; the text should not be translated 'at the end of the seventh year', but 'every seven years', and the reference to the feast of Tents is of secondary importance: it merely indicates the occasion when this reading is to take place. In Dt 16: 13, the date of the feast is determined only by the progress of work in the fields: it is to be held when the produce of the threshing-floor and of the presses has been gathered in.

Incidental references in the Books of Kings give more precise indications, but these same texts also raise difficult problems. The dedication of Solomon's Temple (which coincided with the feast of Tents) took place in the month of Ethanim, according to the Canaanite calendar: a later insertion has explained that this was the seventh month of the Babylonian calendar introduced by Josias (1 K 8: 2). But, according to 1 K 6: 38, the Temple was completed in the Canaanite month of Bul; and another later insertion explains that this was the eighth month of the later Babylonian calendar. If we grant that these identifications are correct (and there is no reason to doubt it), then we must admit either that the dedication took place a month before work on the building was finished, or that it did not take place until eleven months afterwards. If the second alternative is correct, then the delay could be explained by the fact that all the bronze furnishings were still being cast: the story of how they were made is, in fact, contained in 1 K 7: 13–51, i.e. between the time when the Temple building was finished (1 K 6: 38) and the day of its dedication (1 K 8: 2). A third possibility is that the feast of the dedication and of Tents fell in the last week of Ethanim, and that the eighth day was the 1st of the month Bul: this reconciles the two data, but it is

1. Cf. p. 190.   2. Cf. p. 184.

scarcely convincing. It is essential to remember that in those days the date of the feast depended entirely on the condition of the crops: in that particular year, the harvest was gathered in before the work on the Temple was completely finished. Hence, the feast of Tents, and the dedication, were held in the month of Ethanim, but it was not until the following month, Bul, that the Temple was finished 'in all its plan and all its arrangement' (1 K 6: 38).

The question becomes more complicated, however, if we take into account the short note in 1 K 12: 32-33 about the inauguration of the new sanctuary at Bethel by Jeroboam I: 'Jeroboam celebrated a feast in the eighth month, on the fifteenth day of the month, like the feast they kept in Judah, and he went up to the altar . . . on the fifteenth day of the month, the month which he had arbitrarily chosen.' Two interpretations of this text have been put forward. One says that the feast was originally held in the eighth month, even in Jerusalem itself, and the arguments in its favour are these. First, Jeroboam celebrated a feast 'like the one they kept in Judah'; secondly, he must have held his feast at the same time, since his object was to prevent his subjects from going up to the Temple at Jerusalem (cf. 1 K 12: 38); thirdly, this would harmonize with the statement of 1 K 6: 38 that the Temple was finished (and dedicated) in the eighth month. The accusation that Jeroboam chose this date arbitrarily would be a tendentious note of a redactor, inserted after the time when the feast in Jerusalem had been put forward from the eighth to the seventh month; and this note of his would be in harmony with the date given (the seventh month) in 1 K 8: 2. The other interpretation says that Jeroboam did in fact alter the liturgical calendar, or, more precisely, that he reintroduced an old North-Israelite calendar, in which the feasts were determined by the agricultural conditions in Ephraim, where the harvest was later than in Judah. His purpose was, of course, to introduce a rival calendar to the one followed in Jerusalem. To this we must object that there is no difference in the time of harvest between Bethel and Jerusalem, that there is no noticeable difference between Ephraim and Judah, and that, if there was any difference, Ephraim would be rather in advance of Judah: at the present day, the cereals, olives and grapes around Nablus ripen earlier than those around Bethlehem and Hebron.

The following remarks, however, tell against both interpretations. First, the passage was edited at a comparatively late date, and certainly after Deuteronomy, for the month is denoted by an ordinal number; indeed, it is later than Lv 23, for the feast is fixed for the 15th of the month. Secondly, the date of the feast would not be more precisely fixed under Jeroboam than it was under Solomon. Thirdly, if the feast really was held in the eighth month, this merely means that in that particular year the feast was celebrated in the eighth month, both at Bethel and at Jerusalem. Lastly, we may note that there is no evidence to show that this date was afterwards observed for the feast of Tents in the Northern kingdom.

The date was not fixed before Lv 23: 34 (cf. Nb 29: 12), which says that the feast is to begin on the 15th of the seventh month of a year beginning in spring, that it is to last seven days, and that it is to end on the eighth day. Ez 45: 25 gives the same date. Attempts have been made, however, to show that this calendar was not yet observed in the time of Esdras. Ne 8: 13-18 does not state on which days of the month the feast was held, and from this some authors argue that the reference in v. 14 alludes to a law not contained in the Pentateuch. Some have even tried to calculate the date on which Esdras' feast was held: on the 1st of the seventh month, he read the Law before the whole people until midday (Ne 8: 2); on the 2nd, the heads of families met to study the Law under Esdras' guidance (Ne 8: 13); there they found a law telling them to live in huts during the feast of the seventh month, and this ruling was at once put into force (Ne 8: 14f.). Therefore, it is said, the feast was observed from the 3rd to the 10th. This reasoning, however, is incorrect. The text states quite clearly that the people dispersed after the 1st of the month, and that only a limited number attended the meeting on the 2nd; it also states that they had to call together all the people of Jerusalem and of the other towns in order to prepare for the feast (Ne 8: 15). Consequently, the feast could not possibly have begun on the 3rd. Moreover, since the references in vv. 14 and 18 correspond with Lv 23: 36 and 42, they undoubtedly refer to these laws; therefore the feast must have been celebrated from the 15th to the 22nd, as Lv 23: 34 prescribes.

(d) *The origin of the feast.* Plutarch (*Quaest. conv.* IV, 6) saw a similarity between the Jewish feast of Tents and the cult of Bacchus at vintage-time. This unhappy suggestion has from time to time been taken up by a few modern writers. Another writer has seen a connection with the feast of Adonis-Osiris; the *sukkôth* would then be the equivalent of the arbour erected over the bier of Adonis. There is, however, only one reference to the practice of this rite, and it comes from Alexandria, at the Greek period: Theocritus (*Idyll.* XV) is the source, and he says that the arbour was erected over the (dead) god, not over his devotees: there is, therefore, no possible connection.

An idea which has met with a more favourable welcome is based on the notion that at certain times, and especially at the turn of the year, evil powers are active, and attack homes: to cheat them, and to escape these attacks, the people would pass these days in temporary shelters. This would explain both the feast and the rites followed. In particular, nomads who had just begun to live as farmers would look upon their new way of life as fraught with all kinds of dangers. Hence, it is said, the feast must date from the early years of the settlement in Canaan, and must have been influenced by these primitive notions.

The texts in the Bible itself offer no support whatever to this hypothesis; on the contrary, they provide all the elements of a far simpler and far more convincing solution. The ancient feast of Tents was an agricultural feast, as its other name (Ingathering) implies, and as the details added in Ex 23: 16 and 34: 22 show. Even when it had come to be known as the feast of Tents, it did not lose its agricultural character: the vague date in Dt 16: 13 and the precise date in Lv 23: 34 are both witnesses to this, and these features can be seen even in the most recent ritual, that ordering fruit to be carried in procession at the feast (Lv 23: 40). The feast, then, could not have been instituted until after the settlement in Canaan, and the presumption is that it was adopted from the Canaanites. This presumption is confirmed by Jg 9: 27: after the vintage, the people of Shechem held a joyful feast in the temple of their god. The story in Jg 21: 19-21, which is of ancient origin, shows the connection between the two feasts.

It is by no means so certain that we ought to connect it (as some authors do) with the story in Nb 25: 1-18: in the Plains of Moab, the Israelites took part in a licentious feast of Baal-Peor, and one of them was put to death for having taken a Midianite woman into his *qubbah*.[1] The word means 'a tent or an alcove' and it has been suggested that it is very like *sukkôth*. But this 'tent' was not a 'hut'; the word *qubbah* is found nowhere else in the Bible; and there is no proof that the feast in question was celebrated in the autumn, nor that it had any connection with the feast of Tents.

We can be certain that the feast of Tents was an agricultural feast: the rite about the *sukkôth* ought to find its explanation, then, in some present custom. Now from time immemorial until the present day, it has been the custom in Palestine to erect huts made out of tree-branches in the vineyards and orchards while the grapes and fruit are being gathered in: and this is still the most satisfactory explanation. Originally, the feast (or at least a part of it) was celebrated outside (cf. Jg 21: 19-21), and the feast of Ingathering could also be called the feast of the huts (*sukkôth*). Deuteronomy retained the name, and allowed huts to be erected in the orchards, but prescribed that, for the sacrifices, men should go to the central sanctuary, not to the local sanctuaries (Dt 16: 13-15). The last step (a consequence of the centralization of worship) was that similar shelters were eventually erected in Jerusalem itself, and so the 'huts' became an essential part of the feast (Lv 23: 42; Ne 8: 16).

Like the Passover before it, and the feast of Weeks in later times, the feast of Tents became connected with an event in the history of salvation: the Israelites are to live in huts, says the Bible, in memory of the 'huts' (*sukkôth*) in which Yahweh made their fathers live after the Exodus from Egypt (Lv 23: 43). But this cannot be the primary meaning, for the Israelites lived in tents, not huts, during their days in the desert. Huts represent a custom followed among settled populations, and the first time the word is found in the Bible is when Jacob is settling in Canaan after his return from Mesopotamia: 'He built a house and made huts (*sukkôth*) for his cattle; that is how the place came to be called Sukkoth' (Gn 33: 17).

1. Cf. pp. 296-297.

Nevertheless, one recent writer has attempted to justify the connection of the feast of Tents with the desert. He does not deny that it was an agricultural feast, or that it is connected with Canaanite customs; he claims, however, that when the Israelites were living as semi-nomads, they still had a feast of Tents: the regulations in Nb 2, about the arrangement of the camp around the Tent of Re-union, refer, he says, to this. Secondly, Dt 31: 9-13 prescribes that the Law be read out at the feast of Tents: therefore the feast must have been a feast for the renewal of the Covenant, celebrated, at first, at Shechem. It was later modified to correspond with the conditions of a settled life, and, under the influence of Canaanite cults, its connections with nature became the predominant feature; this is how it was celebrated at Shiloh. Once the monarchy was established, and the Temple built, there was no sense in recalling the wanderings in the desert: as Is 33: 20 (a late text, however) says, 'Sion, city of our feasts' is 'a tent which is never moved'. The feast would, therefore, have taken on a new meaning: it commemorated the choice of Jerusalem as Yahweh's home, and the Covenant of Yahweh with the house of David. This argument is not convincing. The ancient texts (down to, and including, Deuteronomy) stress only the agricultural aspect of the feast, and the explanation given in Lv 23: 43 is clearly not the primary one. There is no proof whatever that, in Old Testament times, the feast commemorated the Covenant, and Dt 31: 9-13 connects the reading of the Law primarily with the sabbatical year, and only secondarily with the feast of Tents in that year. And when, in later ages, the Covenant was commemorated on a feast, the feast chosen was not the feast of Tents, but the feast of Weeks.[1]

4. Was there a New Year feast?

Among the Jews, the New Year feast, the Rosh ha-Shanah, is one of the great feasts of the year. It was already so in New Testament times and the Mishnah devotes a special treatise to it. The feast was kept on the first of Tishri (the Babylonian name of the seventh month in a calendar beginning in spring);[2] a horn (shôphar) was sounded, and hymns of praise were sung.

Under this name, and with these rites, the feast never existed in Old Testament times. There is no mention of it in the liturgical texts, or in the pre-exilic historical texts. Ezechiel dates his vision of the future Temple at the rôsh hashshanah, on the 10th of the month (Ez 40: 1), and this is the only biblical text which uses the expression. In later Hebrew, it came to mean the New Year, but it cannot possibly have this meaning in Ezechiel; indeed it is surprising to find so many writers accepting, without the flicker of an eyelid, that New Year's Day was kept on the '10th day' of a month. In this verse, rôsh hashshanah means 'the beginning of the year', and, in fact, of a year which commenced in the spring. This is the only kind of dating

1. Cf. pp. 494-495.   2. Cf. pp. 186 and 192-193.

Ezechiel ever uses, and he must therefore be referring to the month of Nisan, not to the month of Tishri, in which the Rosh ha-Shanah was later observed. This reckoning of the year from the spring-time is emphasized by Ex 12: 2, which refers to a change of calendar: 'This month shall come at the head of the others; you shall make it the first month of the year.' In this text, which comes from the Priestly editors, there is no mention of a New Year feast either; it merely tells us that the victim for the Passover was to be chosen on the 10th of this month' (Ex 12: 3). It would be pointless to make the question still more complicated by comparing with the text of Ezechiel that of Lv 25: 9-10 (a late text) fixing the 10th day of the seventh month as the Day of Atonement (cf. Lv 23: 27) and the end of the Jubilee period.

Neither Ezechiel nor the Priests' Code knew of any New Year feast; nor did Esdras. On the 1st day of the seventh month, Esdras read out the Law until mid-day, and those listening wept as they heard him read. Esdras, however, told them rather to rejoice, and they did so (Ne 7: 72—8: 12); surely he would have mentioned the New Year feast, if it had been held on that same day?

This leaves only two texts, both of which belong to the last edition of the Pentateuch, after Esdras. Leviticus (Lv 23: 24-25) prescribes that the 1st day of the seventh month shall be kept as a day of rest, with sacrifices, a cultic assembly and acclamation (*t'rû'ah*).[1] This ruling is given in a more extended form in Nb 29: 1-6, which calls the feast 'The Day of Acclamation', and lays down what sacrifices are to be offered to it. But it is by no means clear that this feast on the 1st of the seventh month, Tishri, is there regarded as a New Year feast; in the calendar of Lv 23, and in the commentary on it in Nb 28-29, the religious year always begins at the Passover. The feast held on the 1st of the seventh month was simply an unusually solemn new moon, the first day of a month which, at that time, was full of feasts (the Day of Atonement on the 10th, and the feast of Tents, from the 15th to the 22nd); perhaps too, this feast perpetuated the memory of the old civil and religious year which used to begin in the autumn, about the time of the feast of Ingathering.

Those apocryphal books of the Old Testament which date from before the Christian era never mention any New Year feast; Josephus does not include it in his list of Jewish feasts; Philo, too (*De special. legibus* 11, 188), mentions ten Jewish feasts, among which we find the 1st Tishri, but he merely repeats what is said in Lv 23: 24-25 and Nb 29: 1-6: it is a 'feast of trumpets' at the beginning of the month of the great feasts, which he calls the sacred month (ἱερομηνία), using a Greek liturgical term. The Jewish feast of Rosh ha-Shanah adopted the rite of acclamation prescribed in the Priests' calendar for the new moon of the seventh month, but it is impossible to say at what time or under what influence this New Year feast was

1. Cf. pp. 254 and 259.

instituted. It is unlikely that it was due, as some have said, to the influence of the Syro-Macedonian calendar in which the year began in autumn, for, in their internal affairs, the Jews always kept to the Babylonian system of reckoning, which they had adopted shortly before the Exile.[1]

5. Was there a feast of the Enthronement of Yahweh?

For all this, a considerable number of scholars hold that the New Year feast had its equivalent in ancient times, in the feast of Ingatherings or of Tents. This feast was kept, as we have said, at the turn of the year; it would have provided the framework for a 'New Year feast of Yahweh' or 'a feast of Yahweh's enthronement' or 'a feast of Yahweh's kingship', according to the different ways in which the thesis is proposed. The principal arguments put forward are these:

(1) In Babylon, a New Year feast (Akitu) was celebrated during the first twelve days of the month of Nisan (the beginning of the spring year). The feast commemorated the renewal of creation and the kingship of Marduk. The epic of creation, of Marduk's struggle against chaos, was recited and re-enacted, and the god himself was acclaimed with the words 'Marduk is King!' The same elements, it is claimed, are found in Egypt; we may presume that they existed in Canaan, and we may therefore conclude that a similar drama was enacted at Jerusalem on the feast of Tents at the beginning (or the end) of the (autumnal) year.

(2) Traces of the same cultic customs are then sought for in the Old Testament, especially in the psalms about the reign of Yahweh (which include at least Pss 47, 93 and 96-99). The defenders of this thesis call them 'The Psalms of the Enthronement of Yahweh' and these psalms would have formed part of the liturgy for the feast of Tents.

(3) The two accounts of the transfer of the Ark (2 S 6: 1-23 and 1 K 8: 1-13) would also have been used in worship, during an annual procession at which Yahweh was installed in his sanctuary; this procession is said to have taken place during the feast of Tents (on the basis of 1 K 8: 2).

Working from this information, an ancient feast is reconstructed. It would have included (according to a relatively moderate partisan of this thesis): (a) the celebration of Yahweh's original triumph over the forces of chaos, his enthronement in the assembly of the gods, and the demonstration of his power, not only in the creation of the world, but also in the guidance of history; (b) a dramatic representation of the eschatological 'Day' when Yahweh would assert his power against the rebellious gods, and against the nations of the earth, when he would establish his kingship not only over nature, but also in the moral order; (c) a corresponding representation of the Messiah's (the earthly king's) descent into the lower world and of Yahweh's

1. Cf. p. 192.

deliverance of him from darkness and death; (d) a triumphal procession, in which the Ark, the symbol of Yahweh's presence, and the king, the true Messiah, were led to the Temple for the final act of enthronement, which marked the beginning of a new era. Other scholars are still bolder, and use the Mesopotamian liturgies of Tammuz and the poems of Ras Shamra to add to this already rich ritual the death and resurrection of the god, and the sacred marriage between the god and his consort (the rôle of the god being played, in this liturgical drama, by the deified king).

In spite of the authority of the scholars who put forward these theories, and in spite of the erudition with which they defend them, one cannot help expressing very serious doubts as to whether the theories are true:

(1) The ritual for the New Year feast at Babylon dates from the Neo-Babylonian period. In all likelihood, its origins go back further into history, and Assyrian and Hittite texts from the end of the second millennium B.C. prove that a New Year feast was kept in Assyria and in Asia Minor; this feast included at least a procession of the god, and the fixing of destinies for the year. These texts, however, contain nothing similar to the mythological drama which is drawn out of the Babylonian ritual. If this mythical and cultic scheme is to be extended to the entire Near East, including Israel, further arguments are needed.

(2) In the psalms about the reign of Yahweh, the formula *yhwh malak* does not mean 'Yahweh has become king': it is not a formula of enthronement, for it is impossible to see who, according to Israel's religious concepts, could have enthroned Yahweh, since he himself possesses all power. Secondly, even in the Babylonian texts, and in those Egyptian texts which can be compared with them, the words 'Marduk is King' are not a formula of enthronement either: they are an acclamation, a recognition of Marduk's power: he acts as king. The biblical formula has the same meaning; it too is an acclamation, like the cry 'Long live the king!', which was used at the crowning of kings in Israel; it did not make the man king; it merely acknowledged the royal character of the new Anointed of Yahweh.[1]

These psalms, then, are not 'Enthronement Psalms', but psalms about the kingship of Yahweh. The idea of Yahweh as King certainly existed from early times in Israel, but the Psalms of his Kingship are so closely connected with second Isaias that they must be dependent upon him, and must therefore be post-exilic. They cannot possibly have been composed, or used, for a feast held under the monarchy.

(3) The accounts in 2 S 6 and 1 K 8 are concerned with two different transfers of the Ark: in the first, it is taken to the tent erected by David, and in the second, to the Temple built by Solomon. This entry (or these entries) of Yahweh into his sanctuary are commemorated in Pss 24 and 132,[2] which certainly belong to the Temple liturgy, but we do not know on what

1. Cf. p. 106.   2. Cf. p. 309.

occasion they were sung. There are no positive arguments for connecting them with the feast of Tents or with any 'enthronement' of Yahweh.

In addition, there are further objections of a more general kind. This feast of the enthronement of Yahweh is said to have been connected with the feast of Tents; why, then, is there no trace of it either in the liturgical or in the historical texts of the Old Testament? The only plausible argument is the late text of Za 14: 16: 'All the survivors of all nations which have marched against Jerusalem will come, year by year, to bow in adoration before the King, Yahweh Sabaoth, and to celebrate the feast of Tents' (cf. vv. 17-18). The connection between the two terms, however, is merely accidental: the entire passage is devoted to the eschatological triumph, to that 'Day' when Yahweh will be king over the whole earth (v. 9), and the feast of Tents is mentioned only because it was the main feast for pilgrimage to Jerusalem. We have seen too, that the feast of Tents was from the very beginning, and always, remained, an agricultural feast; it is rather paradoxical to say (as some do) that this was not its primary feature, and that it had at first an 'historical' character, i.e. the celebration of creation, and of Yahweh's victory over chaos.

Moreover, when the Israelites decided to give an historical meaning to the feasts of Tents, late on in their history, they connected it not with a creation-myth, but with their days in the desert. Here we encounter once again a general characteristic of the Israelite cult;[1] whatever may be said of neighbouring religious, the cult practised in Israel was not the outward expression of myths, but the homage paid by man to a personal God, who had made a Covenant with the people he had saved, and who remained faithful to that Covenant.

1. Cf. p. 272.

CHAPTER EIGHTEEN

THE LATER FEASTS

URING the last centuries of Old Testament times, several new feasts were introduced into the liturgical calendar.[1] We shall restrict ourselves here to those which are still observed: the Day of Atonement, the Hanukkah and Purim.

1. The Day of Atonement

The Yom Kippur is still one of the most solemn feasts of the Jews. In the New Testament times, the *yôm hakkippurîm* or 'Day of Expiations' was already important enough to be called 'The Day', without further qualification, and this is its name in the treatise (*Yomah*) which the Mishnah devotes to it. It has always been observed on the 10th Tishri (September–October).

Before the Babylonian names were adopted for the months of the year, the Day of Atonement was fixed for the same date, i.e. for the 10th of the seventh month (Lv 23: 27-32; Nb 29: 7-11, both late Priestly texts). Details of the ritual are given in Lv 16, which is also a late text.

(a) *The ritual of expiation.* No work whatever was to be done on this day; instead, penance and fasting were enjoined, and there was to be a meeting in the Temple at which special sacrifices were to be offered, to make expiation for the sanctuary, the priests and the people. The ritual outlined in Lv 16 is evidently made up of various strata, for the text has been re-edited several times: there are a number of doublets (vv. 6 and 11, vv. 9*b* and 15, vv. 4 and 32); vv. 2 and 3 do not follow logically, and on the other hand, v. 4 should not come between vv. 3 and 5, etc.; there are two conclusions (vv. 29*a* and 24); and vv. 29*b*–34 are an addition commenting on the preceding rites, which reminds us of Lv 23: 27-32.

This ritual is a combination of two ceremonies which were different both in their spirit and in their origin. First, there is a Levitical ritual: the high priest offered a bull as a sacrifice for his own sinfulness and for that of his 'house', *i.e.* of the Aaronite priesthood; then he entered—the only occasion during the year—behind the veil which shut off the Holy of Holies, to incense the mercy-seat (*kapporeth*)[2] and to sprinkle it with the bull's blood (vv. 11-14). Next he offered a goat for the sin of the people; he took the

1. Cf. pp. 473-474.   2. Cf. pp. 300-301.

blood of the goat, too, behind the veil, where he sprinkled it over the mercy-seat, as he had sprinkled the bull's blood (v. 15). This expiation of the sins of the priesthood and of the people is linked, artificially, it seems, with an expiation for the sanctuary, and more particularly for the altar, which also had blood rubbed and sprinkled upon it (vv. 16-19). The two ceremonies of expiation are combined in the final addition (v. 33), but the order is inverted. This ritual contains those ideas about purity and the expiatory value of blood which are a characteristic of the rulings in Leviticus.[1]

(b) *The goat 'for Azazel'.* Into this ritual, however, another one has been inserted, which is based on other ideas. The community put forward two goats, and lots were cast: one was for Yahweh, and the other 'for Azazel'. The goat for Yahweh was used for the sacrifice for the sins of the people, which has just been described. When this ceremony was over the other goat, still alive, was set 'before Yahweh': the high priest placed his hands on the goat's head and transferred to it all the faults, deliberate and indeliberate, of the Israelites. A man then took this goat off into the desert, and it carried with it the sins of the people (vv. 8-10, 20-22). The man who took the goat away became impure by doing so, and could not rejoin the community until he had washed himself and his clothes (v. 26). Rabbinical tradition says that the goat was taken to Beth Ḥadûdû, or Beth Ḥadûdûn, the modern Khirbeth Khareidan, which overlooks the Kedron valley some three and a half miles away from Jerusalem.

It is interesting to compare with this a Babylonian rite which took place on the 5th day of the New Year feast, *i.e.* the 5th Nisan: a cantor, singing incantations, purified the sanctuaries of Bel and of Nabu with water, oil and perfumes; then someone else beheaded a sheep and rubbed the corpse against the temple of Nabu, to take away the impurities of the temple; the two men then carried the head and the body of the sheep to the Euphrates and threw them into the river; finally, they went off into the country and were not allowed to return to the town until the end of the feast, on the 12th Nisan. No one can deny that there is a marked similarity with the ritual of the 'scape-goat': the animal was taken away, loaded with impurity, and those who perform the ceremony become impure by contact with it. But in Babylon, the animal was killed and was used to purify the sanctuary; the Day of Atonement certainly included this rite, but the 'scapegoat' figured only in order to carry away the sins of the people (a feature which is not mentioned in the Babylonian ritual).

In their researches into primitive civilisation of folklore, scholars have collected evidence of many more or less similar rites about the transferring of guilt, stain or sickness to animals. But there is a very close analogy in the Bible itself: in the ritual for leprosy, a living bird was released in the country to carry the evil away, and the leper was declared clean.[2]

1. Cf. pp. 419 and 460-461.   2. Cf. p. 463.

In the ritual for the Day of Atonement, however, there is something more than this. The name 'scape-goat' is the common translation in our English Bible, but the Septuagint and Vulgate call it the 'goat sent out' (*caper emissarius*). In the Hebrew the goat is destined 'for '*aza'zel*'. One scholar has recently suggested that this is a common noun, as the Greek and Latin versions take it, but that it means 'the precipice' and is the name of the place to which the goat was taken. Whatever be the philological value of this suggestion, it does not really fit the text: the high priest drew lots between the goats, one 'for Yahweh' and the other 'for '*aza'zel*'. The translation 'for the Precipice' does not seem sufficient for a true parallelism, which demands that the second name, like the first, should be the name of a person. It is more probable, therefore, that Azazel is the name of a supernatural being, a devil, and this is how it is interpreted by the Syriac version, the Targum and even the Book of Henoch, which makes Azazel the prince of the devils, banished to the desert. (We may recall that the Israelites looked on desert places as the dwellings of devils: Is 13: 21; 34: 11-14; cf. Tb 8: 3 and Mt 12: 43.)

And yet it is important to remember that the transferring of sins and the expiation which results from it are said to be effective only because the goat is presented before Yahweh (v. 10): Yahweh brought about the transfer, and the expiation. The goat was not sacrificed to Azazel or to Yahweh because, once it had been charged with the sins of the people, it was impure, and therefore could not be used as a victim for sacrifice. The Levitical ritual has therefore incorporated an old custom of unknown origin into its liturgy, but it has at the same time exorcised it.

(c) *When was the feast instituted?* This does not mean, however, that the Day of Atonement and its ritual are of very ancient origin. On the contrary, the opposite would seem to be true, for we have already had occasion to note that the combination of Levitical customs with popular superstitions is a characteristic of the very latest rituals of purification.[1] There is no mention of the feast in any pre-exilic text, either historical or prophetical. Ezechiel foretold that on the 1st and the 7th of the first month[2] a bull would be offered in sacrifice: the blood of the first bull would be used for the purification of the Temple and of the altar, whereas the second would be offered for the indeliberate sins of the people; and the two together would constitute 'the expiation for the Temple' (Ez 45: 18-20). Though the intention is undoubtedly the same, this is not yet the Day of Atonement, for the latter was fixed for the 10th day of the seventh month, and the ceremony of the goat 'for Azazel' is not mentioned.

There is no mention of it in the books of Esdras and of Nehemias, though this raises a further problem which is made still more complicated by difficulties of literary criticism. Esd 3: 1-6 contains no mention of the Day

1. Cf. pp. 461-464.   2. Cf. p. 473.

of Atonement, but only of the feast of Tents, which was observed by the first groups to return from exile. Ne 8 (which is based on Esdras' memorandum, and is the sequel to Esd 8: 36) says that the Law was read out, and then studied, on the 1st and the 2nd of the seventh month; it then goes on to describe the feast of Tents, which must have been held from the 15th to the 22nd;[1] it makes no mention of a Day of Atonement, on the 10th of this month. One suggestion is that in this particular year, the preparation for the celebration of the feast of Tents in a new way (Ne 8: 14-15) led to the omission of the Day of Atonement; this explanation seems hardly satisfactory. On the other hand, Ne 9: 1 (immediately after the account of the feast of Tents) says that on 'the 24th day of this month' there was a fast and a penitential ceremony. It is therefore suggested that this day was the Day of Atonement, and that it was either postponed, in this particular year, to the 24th, or that at this time it was celebrated on the 24th and later put forward to the 10th. Neither of these solutions is convincing, for Ne 9: 1-2 does not form a sequel to the document in Ne 8: modern commentators connect Ne 9: 1-2 either with Esd 10: 17 (the mission of Esdras) or with Ne 10: 1f. (the mission of Nehemias). The reference in Ne 9: 1-2 is therefore useless, and so is the date which it gives: 'the 24th day of *this* month': we do not know to which year or to which month it is referring, and perhaps this feast had no connection at all with the Day of Atonement.

The argument from silence is not, of course, decisive, but it does furnish a presumption that the feast had not yet been instituted in the time of Esdras and Nehemias. We may add, too, that the ritual in Lv 23: 26-32 begins with the words 'And Yahweh spoke', which would indicate an addition; we may also note that this ritual makes no mention of the goat for Azazel, which is a distinctive feature of the celebration of the feast in Lv 16. The only possible conclusion is that the feast was instituted at a late date, though we cannot say precisely either when it was instituted or when the ritual of Lv 16 was first put into practice. The connection in Lv 16: 1 with an episode in the desert (the death of Nadab and Abihu) is quite artificial (cf. Lv 10: 1-6).

2. *The feast of the Hanukkah*

Most modern translations call this feast the feast of the Dedication. Its Greek name, Τὰ Ἐγκαίνια, means the 'inauguration' or 'the renewal', and this is a more literal rendering of the Hebrew *ḥanukkah*, the name which was given to the feast by the Rabbis and by which it is still known among the Jews. Josephus calls it the feast of Lights, after the rite which was its principal feature.

(a) *The origin and history of the feast.* The story of its institution is told in 1 M 4: 36-59. Antiochus Epiphanes, after desecrating the Temple of Jeru-

1. Cf. p. 500.

salem and its altar, erected, over the altar of holocausts, a pagan altar, the
Abomination of Desolation (1 M 1: 54; Dn 9: 27; 11: 31), and there offered
the first sacrifice to Zeus Olympios, on the 25th Kisleu (December), 167.
Three years later, Judas Maccabee, after his first victories, purified the
sanctuary, built a new altar and inaugurated it on the 25th Kisleu, 164, the
third anniversary of its profanation (2 M 10: 5). It was then decided that
the feast should be observed each year (1 M 4: 59).

It is questionable whether the feast could have been regularly observed
during the following years, for the Syrians occupied the Citadel and there
was fighting in Jerusalem. The situation would have changed once religious
freedom was regained, and once Jonathan was appointed high priest, in
152 B.C. The opening verses of the second book of Maccabees (2 M 1: 1-9)
contain a letter written to the Jews of Egypt in 124: in this letter, they are
recommended to keep the Hanukkah, and reference is made to a previous
letter sent in 143. This document bears all the marks of authenticity. It is
followed, however, by another letter, for which the same claims cannot be
made (2 M 1: 10—2: 18): this second letter is said to have been despatched at
the first feast of the Dedication, in 164, and it already contains some legendary
features. Like the first, it ends with an invitation to keep the Hanukkah. In
the body of the book itself, all the first part (2 M 2: 19—10: 8) is an historical
justification of the feast (cf. the author's preface, 2 M 2: 19, and conclusion,
2 M 10: 8). The second part of the book is parallel to the first, and gives the
events leading up to the feast of Nicanor, which was held on the 13th Adar
in memory of the defeat and death of this Syrian general (2 M 15: 36). The
feast of Nicanor was not observed for long, and we shall omit all further
mention of it.

The feast of the Hanukkah, however, continued to be observed. It is
mentioned in the New Testament (Jn 10: 22), under its Greek name (Τὰ
Ἐγκαίνια) and in Josephus (Ant. XII, vii, 7), under the name of the feast of
Lights. The Mishnah merely alludes to it here and there, but this can be
explained by the hostility of orthodox circles to the Hasmoneans; the Rabbis
had no desire to bestow their approval on a feast instituted by them. All the
same, it remained a popular feast, and later rabbinical treatises give some
casuistic solutions and some bizarre explanations of problems connected with
it. The feast was originally in memory of the renovation of the Temple, but
it survived the destruction of the Temple because the ritual of lights, as we
shall see, made it independent of the sanctuary and allowed it to take on a
new meaning. Even to-day, it is still one of the great Jewish feasts.

(b) *The rites: the Hanukkah and the feast of Tents*. The celebration of the
feast lasted eight days from the 25th Kisleu (December), and it was a most
joyful feast (1 M 4: 56-59). Apart from the sacrifices offered in the Temple,
thyrsus, green branches and palms were carried around, and hymns were
sung (2 M 10: 6-8; cf. 1 M 4: 54). The title of Ps 30 says it was to be sung at

the Dedication of the Temple, and it must have been used on this occasion. But the principal psalms sung were the Hallel (Pss 113-118), and the addition of v. 27 in Ps 118 probably refers to a rite of this feast: it can be translated as 'Bring your procession (*or*, your dance, *hag*), palms in hand, close to the horns of the altar'.

Apart from this procession with palms and the singing of the Hallel, the feast was characterized by the use of lights (Josephus, as we have said, calls it 'The feast of Lights'). The Mishnah and rabbinical writings tell us that lamps were lit in front of each house, and that the number increased by one a day until the last day of the feast. The oldest texts do not mention this rite explicitly: the lighting of lamps in 1 M 4: 50 refers to the reintroduction of the chandelier into the Temple, not to the inauguration of the altar. Nevertheless, there are allusions to the rite in the first letter of 2 M 1: 8, which quotes a previous letter in the words 'We have lit lamps'; the second letter (2 M 1: 18f.) connects the commemoration of the sacred fire, miraculously preserved, and found by Nehemias, with the feast of the Hanukkah; and Ps 118: 27 has, just before the verse about the palms, 'Yahweh is God, he is our light'.

The second book of Maccabees stresses the similarity between the Hanukkah and the feast of Tents. It was celebrated on the first occasion, 'in the way they kept the feast of Tents' (2 M 10: 6), and the letter of 124 B.C. calls it 'the feast of Tents in the month of Kisleu' (2 M 1: 9). The first book of Maccabees does not make this connection, but the second deliberately underlines its relation to one of the great traditional feasts, in order to secure it a favourable reception in the Egyptian Diaspora. It is, of course, possible that Judas Maccabee himself wanted it to be like the feast of Tents, for this was the date on which Solomon's Temple (1 K 8: 2, 65) and the altar which was erected after the Exile (Esd 3: 4) had been dedicated.

In fact, the two feasts both lasted eight days (if we include the closing day of the feast of Tents, Lv 23: 34-36), and palms were carried both at the Hanukkah and at the feast of Tents (according to the ritual then in force, Lv 23: 40-41). But this is where the resemblances end. Psalms were certainly sung at the feast of Tents, but there is no evidence that it was the Hallel; it seems rather that the Hallel was first sung at the Hanukkah and later extended to the feasts of the Passover, of Pentecost and of Tents. During the Hanukkah, no-one lived in huts, and the lights put out in front of the houses are only remotely connected with the illumination of the Temple on the nights of the feast of Tents. Josephus (*Ant.* XII, vii, 7) says the lights of the Hanukkah symbolized that freedom had 'shone' upon the Jews in a way that could never have been hoped for; in later times, they became the symbol of the Law, which, in Pr 6: 23 and Ps 119: 105, is called a light. We still have to explain, however, why one more lamp was lit on each succeeding day of the feast, and this brings us to the question of pagan influences on the festal rites.

(c) *Was there any pagan influence in the origin or the rites of the Hanukkah?*
The Hanukkah is the only Jewish feast whose institution is recorded in a late
text, and which is also connected with an undeniable historical event. For
some scholars, this seems too simple, and they have tried to show that the feast
originated outside Israel. They say it is the Jewish adaptation of a feast of
the winter solstice, and that the 'Hanukkah' should be connected with
Henoch, who lived 365 years (Gn 5: 23), *i.e.* the number of days in a solar
year. Other writers, leaving Henoch aside, have maintained with less im-
probability that the feast corresponds to that of the *Sol invictus*, which was
celebrated at Rome on the 25th December. Others again recall that during
the persecution of Antiochus Epiphanes, the Jews were ordered to wear
crowns of ivy and to take part in a procession in honour of Bacchus (2 M 6:
7), and that an old man from Athens (2 M 6: 1) was sent by the king to
instruct them in the new rites: they add that the assimilation of the Nabatean
god Dusares and Bacchus could have made these rites less foreign to the
Jews. But they forget to prove (and it cannot be proved) that the Dionysiac
rites took place on the 25th Kisleu at Jerusalem: we shall see that the text of
2 M 6: 7 implies rather that they fell at a different time. Lastly, other writers
maintain that an extra light was lit each day to symbolize the lengthening of
days after the winter solstice.

The objections which can be raised against these theories seems to be
decisive. We cannot admit that this Jewish feast was of pagan origin, because
all the information we possess about it shows that it was instituted, and
thereafter observed, only to commemorate the purification of the Temple
after it had been defiled by pagan customs, and the restoration of lawful
worship. Further, even if this most unlikely possibility were accepted, it is
impossible for a feast of the winter solstice, which is tied to the solar calendar,
to be a feast fixed on a definite day of a lunar year, however many corrections
one may introduce: the 25th Kisleu would fall on the day of the solstice only
on rare occasions.

Nevertheless, there may have been a connection between the Hanukkah
and certain pagan usages, but it is an indirect and an adverse connection.
Judas Maccabee inaugurated the new altar on the precise anniversary of the
profanation of the old one, the 25th Kisleu. Now Antiochus Epiphanes had
deliberately chosen this date for the first sacrifice to Zeus Olympios. It has
been suggested that in the year 167, the winter solstice fell on the 25th
Kisleu, but attempts to prove this by calculation have not yielded any
certain results. The texts themselves, however, indicate the answer: according
to 2 M 6: 7, the Jews were obliged to take part in the monthly sacrifice, on
the king's birthday; according to 1 M 1: 58-59, attacks were made every
month on recalcitrant Jews, and on the 25th of each month, a sacrifice was
offered on the pagan altar. In this last verse, both the grammar and the context show that the reference is not merely to the sacrifice of 25th Kisleu, 167,

but to a sacrifice which was repeated on the 25th of each month, *i.e.* to a monthly sacrifice offered for the king's birthday, as 2 M 6: 7 says. There is evidence of the custom in the Hellenistic East, and it continued in vogue in these same regions until after the establishment of the Roman Empire.

The feasts of Dionysus, in which the Jews were ordered to wear ivy crowns, are distinguished from this monthly sacrifice in 2 M 6: 7 and this is yet another reason for denying that the branches carried at the Hanukkah were connected with the cult of Bacchus. Nevertheless, brandishing these branches in honour of the true God may have been intended to do away with the memory of the pagan rite which faithful Jews had been forced to follow, and which Hellenizing Jews had freely adopted: the custom followed on the feast of Tents would provide a justification. The lighting of lamps in front of the houses could be intended to replace the incense which, under Antiochus Epiphanes, had been burnt at the house-doors and on the squares (1 M 1: 55). Why one more lamp should have been lit each day we do not know: there is no evidence of it in the earliest documents; but neither is there evidence to show that it was connected with the rising of the sun from its solstice. The rite may indicate merely the increasing solemnity of the feast, or it may merely mark its passing from day to day. Popular customs and liturgical rules love these gradations: to take one example in the Jewish ritual, the sacrificial code in Nb 29: 13-32 prescribes that from the first to the seventh day of the feast of Tents, the number of bulls sacrificed should be one less each day, until, on the seventh day, seven victims were offered. If these secondary contacts with pagan customs are well-founded, and if our interpretation of them is valid, then the fundamental character of the Hanukkah is thereby confirmed: it was a feast for the purification of all the defilement contracted under the domination of the wicked (cf. 1 M 4: 36). Hence 2 M 2: 16 and 10: 5 call it simply the day of 'the purification of the Temple'.

3. *The feast of Purim*

(a) *Its date and its rites.* Josephus (*Ant.* XI, vi, 13), writing in the first century of our era, says that the feast of Purim was held on the 14th and 15th Adar, to commemorate the revenge of the Jews of Persia upon their enemies. The ritual is described in rabbinical writings. The feast was preceded by a day's fasting, on the 13th Adar: in the evening, lamps were lit in all the houses, and everyone went to the synagogue. The 14th and 15th were days of rejoicing. Everyone went to the synagogue again, to listen to the reading of the book of Esther; while the story was being read, the congregation would interrupt with curses against Aman and the wicked in general, and the meeting closed with a solemn blessing of Mardochai, of Esther and of the Israelites. Apart from this reading, the feast was an occasion for the distribution of presents and of alms, and pious persons made these gifts with a religious intention; but otherwise, it was an utterly profane feast, taken up with banquets and amusements, and considerable liberty was allowed. The Rabbis allowed that anyone could go on drinking until he could no longer tell the difference between 'Cursed be Aman!' and 'Blessed be Mardochai!' Later, the custom of putting on disguises was introduced, and the feast of Purim became the Jewish carnival.

(b) *Purim and the Book of Esther*. Obviously, the Book of Esther had to be read, for the feast owed both its name and institution to this story. The final note in the Greek translation of the book calls it 'this letter about the Purim' (Est 10: 3). Est 3: 7 (completed with the aid of the Greek) and 9: 24 tell us that these days are called 'Purim' because Aman had cast lots (*pûr*) on the 14th of Adar to exterminate the Jews, and this wicked plot of his had turned against him, and he had been hanged. The word *pûr* is not Hebrew, and in both cases needed to be glossed by the Hebrew *gôral* (lot). Because of the background against which the story is told, attempts have been made to find a Persian etymology, but it is now certain that the word is Akkadian (*pûru* means 'lot' or 'destiny'); we shall return to this point later.

It is curious that this casting of lots does not have a more prominent place in the story, and that there is no reference to it in the feast which bears its name. Moreover, Est 3: 7 breaks the narrative, and the second mention of 'lots' is the section (Est 9: 20-32) which tells how Mardochai wrote to the Jews of the Diaspora telling them to keep the feast; the same passage alludes to a previous letter of Mardochai on the same subject, and ends by saying that Esther herself issued an order confirming what Mardochai had written. It would seem that Est 3: 7 and 9: 20-32 were inserted into the story to spread the feast and to fix its name as Purim.

The body of the book, however, is already a 'legend of a feast'. Everything in the story—Esther's elevation and the intervention of her uncle Mardochai, the hatred of Aman for the Jews, his punishment and the revenge of the Jews, thanks to the esteem in which Esther and Mardochai were held by the king—converges on the feast which took place on the day after the massacre, and the final verses are an attempt to explain why the feast lasted two days (the 14th and 15th Adar), 'amid joy and banquets, amid festivities and the exchange of presents' (Est 9: 16-19). It is quite possible that the story has an historical foundation in some unexpected deliverance of the Jews of Susa from the threat of extermination, but we know nothing of the circumstances, and this historical basis would then have been freely adapted until it became the 'legend' of a feast.

(c) *The origin of the feast*. The origin of this feast is utterly different from that of the Hanukkah. The Book of Esther undertakes to justify the feast of Purim, but it is not an historical book, and the feast which it seeks to justify is quite unlike any of the feasts we have so far examined: it was not a religious feast; it was not held (at least directly) in honour of the God of Israel (whose name is not even mentioned in the Hebrew book of Esther); it was not connected with the ancient history of the Chosen People; and it contained no cultic elements at all. It was a foreign feast, but its origins are obscure.

Attempts have been made to show that it came from Babylonia, and that it should be explained in terms of mythology: Mardochai-Esther would be the divine couple Marduk-Ishtar; Aman-Vashti would be the two Elamite divinities Uman-Mashti (though the present reading of this name is: Parti); and the story would be a symbol of the victory of the god of light over the god of darkness. Vashti's reign lasted one hundred and eighty days (*i.e.* throughout the winter) and Esther came to power with the coming of spring; the feast would then be connected with the New Year feast, in which 'lots' were cast. But there is nothing comparable to the feast of Purim in Babylonia, and to bring in the Persian and Babylonian feast of the Σακαῖα which was (or became) a popular feast in which masters changed place with their servants, and the king with a subject, is merely to add to the confusion: we do not know enough about the history or the meaning of the Σακαῖα to throw further light on the story of Esther.

There is a far more interesting connection with a story related at length by Herodotus (*Hist*. III, 68-79). After the death of Cambyses, the magus Gaumata usurped the throne by passing himself off as Smerdis, the brother of Cambyses, whom the latter had secretly put to death. The Pseudo-Smerdis was unmasked by a certain Otanes, assisted by his daughter, who was one of the royal harem. Gaumata was put to death, and the people turned against all the Magi, and massacred them. The Persians celebrated this event in a great feast called the Massacre of the Magi. The story is very similar to the story of Esther, and cuneiform texts prove that it has an historical basis, for they mention that this Gaumata did actually usurp the throne. But the cuneiform texts do not mention the feast itself. Nevertheless, other texts from Persia show that it had some connection with the New Year.

If we now return to the feast of Purim, the pronounced local colour in the Book of Esther and its correspondence with what we know of the ancient town of Susa and of the customs at the court of Xerxes (Assuerus) give us ground for thinking that the feast is of Persian origin. Nevertheless, there are certain Babylonian features: the name Mardochai= Marduk, and Esther= Ishtar, and the Akkadian word *pûru*, which gave the name to the feast (unless Esther is derived from the ancient Persian *star-*, meaning 'star'). We suggest, therefore, that the origin of the feast is not to be sought in one civilisation alone; but this reconstruction is largely hypothetical.

We can say for certain that the feast originated in the communities of the Eastern Diaspora, perhaps at Susa itself. It probably commemorates a pogrom from which the Jews escaped in a way which seemed to them miraculous; this may have taken place in the fourth century B.C. It is clear, on the other hand, that the feast preserves certain characteristics of a foreign New Year feast (the amusements, the banquets, the New Year gifts, the notion of a change which brings a renovation); it is possible, therefore, that the Jewish feast was modelled on a Persian New Year feast. From Persia, the feast would have spread first to Mesopotamia, and would there have taken on its Babylonian character; in particular, it would have acquired its name (*pûrîm*) from the casting of lots (*pûru*); this would fit in with the Babylonian idea that at the beginning of each year men's destinies were fixed, and it might also be an attempt to explain the Persian name for the first month of the year (Farvadin) by the Akkadian. The feast did not reach Palestine until long afterwards; Ben Sirach, writing about 190 B.C., does not mention Mardochai or Esther in his praise of Israel's ancestors (Si 44-50). The first mention of the feast is in 2 M 15: 36, where it is called the 'Day of Mardochai', and is fixed for the 14th Adar. The Hebrew text of Esther calls it 'the days of the Purim' (in the addition contained in Est 9: 28, 31), and under this name, distorted into φρουραί ('watches' or 'guards') it was introduced into Egypt, from Jerusalem, in 114 B.C. (Est 10: 3, Greek).

It is next mentioned in Josephus (*Ant.* XI, vi, 13), and so makes its definitive entry into history. It was a popular feast, of suspect origin, and we must ask the reader's pardon for so ending our study of the religious institutions of ancient Israel.

BIBLIOGRAPHY

ABBREVIATIONS

AASOR   *Annual of the American Schools of Oriental Research.*
AfO   *Archiv für Orientforschung.*
AJSL   *American Journal of Semitic Languages and Literatures.*
BASOR   *Bulletin of the American Schools of Oriental Research.*
BIFAO   *Bulletin de l'Institut Français d'Archéologie Orientale* (Cairo).
BJPES   *Bulletin of the Jewish Palestine Exploration Society.*
BJRL   *Bulletin of the John Rylands Library* (Manchester).
HTR   *Harvard Theological Review.*
HUCA   *Hebrew Union College Annual.*
IEJ   *Israel Exploration Journal.*
JAOS   *Journal of the American Oriental Society.*
JBL   *Journal of Biblical Literature.*
JNES   *Journal of Near Eastern Studies.*
JPOS   *Journal of the Palestine Oriental Society.*
JQR   *Jewish Quarterly Review.*
JTS   *Journal of Theological Studies.*
PEQ   *Palestine Exploration Quarterly.*
PJB   *Palästinajahrbuch.*
RB   *Revue Biblique.*
RHPR   *Revue d'Histoire et de Philosophie Religieuses.*
TLZ   *Theologische Literaturzeitung.*
VT   *Vetus Testamentum.*
ZA   *Zeitschrift für Assyriologie und verwandte Gebiete.*
ZAW   *Zeitschrift für die Alttestamentliche Wissenschaft.*
ZDMG   *Zeitschrift der Deutschen Morgenländischen Gesellschaft.*
ZDPV   *Zeitschrift der Deutschen Palästina-Vereins.*

INTRODUCTION

NOMADISM AND ITS SURVIVAL

On the tribal organization of the Arabs:

F. WÜSTENFELD, *Genealogische Tabellen der Arabischen Stämme und Familien*, Göttingen, 1852.

W. ROBERTSON SMITH, *Kinship and Marriage in Early Arabia*, London, 1885; 3rd edition, 1903. Very important review by TH. NOLDEKE, in *ZDMG*, XL, 1886, 148-87.

I. GOLDZIHER, 'Das Arabische Stämmewesen und der Islam', in his *Muhammedanische Studien*, I, Halle, 1889, 40-100.

A. JAUSSEN, *Coutumes Arabes au pays de Moab*, Paris, 1908; re-ed. 1948.

A. JAUSSEN, 'Coutumes des Fuqara', in A. JAUSSEN and R. SAVIGNAC, *Mission Archéologique en Arabie*, III, Paris, 1920.

A. MUSIL, *The Manners and Customs of the Rwala Beduins*, New York, 1928.

T. ASHKENAZI, *Tribus semi-nomades de la Palestine du Nord*, Paris, 1938.

H. CHARLES, *Tribus moutonnières du Moyen-Euphrate*, Damascus, 1939.

H. CHARLES, *La sédentarisation entre Euphrate et Balik*, Beyrouth, 1942.

M. VON OPPENHEIM, *Die Beduinen*, Leipzig-Wiesbaden. Three volumes have appeared; vol. V is to give a general résumé, but the author has already summarized his views in vol. I, 1939, 22-36. With this one should read the article by his collaborator E. BRAUNLICH, 'Beiträge zur Gesellschaftsordnung der arabischen Beduinenstämme', published in *Islamica*, VI, 1934, 68-111; 182-229.

R. MONTAGNE, *La civilisation du désert*, Paris, 1947.

B. COUROYER, 'Histoire d'une tribu semi-nomade de Palestine', in *RB*, LVIII, 1951, 75-91.

J. SONNEN, *Die Beduinen am See Genesareth*, Cologne, 1952.

J. R. KUPPER, *Les nomades en Mésopotamie au temps des rois de Mari*, Paris, 1957.

F. GABRIELI and others, *L'antica società beduina*, Roma, 1959.

H. CHARLES, art. 'Nomadisme', in *Dictionnaire de la Bible, Supplément*, VI, 1959, 541-50.

On the tribal organization of Israel:

A. Causse, *Du groupe ethnique à la communauté religieuse*, Strasbourg, 1937, ch. 1: 'La solidarité familiale et tribale'.
J. van der Ploeg, 'Sociale groepeeringen in het oude Israel', in *Jaarbericht Ex Oriente Lux*, VIII, 1942, 646-50.
C. Umhau Wolf, 'Terminology of Israel's Tribal Organization', in *JBL*, LXV, 1946, 45-9.
S. Nyström, *Beduinentum und Jahwismus*, Lund, 1946.
R. de Vaux, 'Les Patriarches hébreux et les découvertes modernes', in *RB*, LVI, 1949, 5-19.

On the system of the Twelve Tribes of Israel:

B. Luther, 'Die Israelitischen Stämme', in *ZAW*, XXII, 1901, 1-76.
Ed. Meyer and B. Luther, *Die Israeliten und ihre Nachbarstämme*, Halle, 1906.
M. Noth, *Das System der Zwölf Stämme Israels*, Stuttgart, 1930. (Specially valuable.)

On war:

P. Humbert, *La Terou'ah. Analyse d'un rite biblique*, Neuchâtel, 1946.
G. von Rad, *Der Heilige Krieg im Alten Israel*, Zürich, 1951.

On the right of asylum:

Quatremère, 'Mémoire sur les asiles chez les Arabes', in *Mémoires de l'Institut Royal, Académie des Inscriptions et Belles-Lettres*, XV, 2, Paris, 1845, 307-48.
M. Löhr, *Das Asylwesen im Alten Testament*, Halle, 1930.
N. M. Nikolsky, 'Das Asylrecht in Israel', in *ZAW*, XLVIII, 1930, 146-75.

On blood-vengeance:

O. Procksch, *Ueber die Blutrache bei den vorislamischen Arabern*, Leipzig, 1899.
H. Lammens, 'Le caractère religieux du târ ou vendetta chez les Arabes préislamiques', in *BIFAO*, XXVI, 1926, 83-127.
E. Merz, *Die Blutrache bei den Israeliten*, Leipzig, 1916.

On the 'nomadic ideal' of the Old Testament:

The expression is derived from K. Budde, 'Das nomadische Ideal im Alten Testament', in *Preussische Jahrbücher*, 1896; and his *Die Religion des Volkes Israel*, Giessen, 1899, 112f. The idea has often been repeated:
P. Humbert, 'Osée le prophète bédouin, in *RHPR*, I, 1921, 97-118.
P. Humbert, 'La logique de la perspective nomade chez Osée', in *Festschrift Marti*, Giessen, 1925, 158-66.
A. Causse, *Les 'pauvres d'Israël'*, Strasbourg, 1922, ch. V: 'Les Prophètes du VIIIᵉ siècle et l'idéal patriarcal'.
J. W. Flight, 'The Nomadic Idea and Ideal in the Old Testament', in *JBL*, XLIII, 1923, 158-226.
S. Nyström, *Beduinentum und Jahwismus*, Lund, 1946.

On the Rekabites:

Apart from dictionary articles there are only:
L. Gautier, 'À propos des Rékabites', in *Études sur la religion d'Israël*, Lausanne, 1927, 104-29.
S. Talmon, '1 Ch 2: 55', in *Eretz-Israel*, V, 1958 (Volume Mazar), 111-13 (in Hebrew with a summary in English).

I

FAMILY INSTITUTIONS

1

THE FAMILY

On the typical Israelite family, and general points:

W. Robertson Smith, *Kinship and Marriage*, London, 1885: 2nd ed. 1903.
V. Aptowitzer, 'Spuren des Matriarchats im jüdischen Schrifttum', in *HUCA*, IV, 1927, 207-405; V, 1928, 261-97.
P. Koschaker, 'Fratriarchat, Hausgemeinschaft und Mutterrecht in Keilschriftrecten', in *ZA*, XLI, 1933, 1-89.
C. H. Gordon, 'Fratriarchy in the Old Testament', in *JBL*, LIV, 1935, 223-31.

J. HENNINGER, 'Die Familie bei den heutigen Beduinen Arabiens und seiner Randgebiete', in *Internationales Archiv für Ethnologie*, XLII, 1943, 1-188.
J. PEDERSEN, *Israel, its Life and Culture*, I-II, London, re-ed. 1946, 46-60.
I. MENDELSOHN, 'The Family in the Ancient Near East', in *Biblical Archaeologist*, XI, 1948, 24-40.
R. PATAI, *Sex and Family in the Bible and the Middle East*, Garden City, New York, 1959.

On the development of family customs:

A. CAUSSE, 'La crise de la solidarité de famille et de clan dans l'Ancien Israël', in *RHPR*, X, 1930, 24-60.
A. CAUSSE, *Du groupe ethnique à la communauté religieuse*, Strasbourg, 1937, ch. II: 'L'évolution politique et culturelle et la désintégration des anciens groupes'.

2

MARRIAGE

On marriage in general:

J. NEUBAUER, *Beiträge zur Geschichte des bibl-talmudischen Eheschliessungsrechts* (*Mitteilungen der vorderasiatish-ägyptischen Gesellschaft*), XXIV-XXV, Leipzig, 1919-20.
S. BIALOBLOCKI, *Materialen zum islamischen und jüdischen Eherecht*, Giessen, 1928.
H. GRANQUIST, *Marriage Conditions in a Palestine Village*, I-II, Helsingfors, 1931-5.
R. DUSSAUD, 'Le "mohar" Israëlite', in *Comptes Rendus de l'Académie des Inscriptions et Belles-Lettres*, 1935, 142-51.
G. R. DRIVER and J. C. MILES, *The Assyrian Laws*, Oxford, 1935, 126-271.
M. BURROWS, *The Basis of Israelite Marriage*, New Haven, 1938.
L. M. EPSTEIN, *Marriage Laws in the Bible and the Talmud*, Cambridge, Mass., 1942.
E. NEUFELD, *Ancient Hebrew Marriage Laws*, London, 1944.
A. GELIN, 'Le passage de la polygamie à la monogamie', in *Mélanges Podechard*, Lyons, 1945, 135-40.
W. KORNFELD, 'L'adultère dans l'Orient antique', in *RB*, LVII, 1950, 92-109.
P. KOSCHAKER, 'Ehesschliessung und Kauf nach alten Rechten', in *Archiv Orientální*, XVIII, III, 1950 (Festschrift Hrozný), 210-96.
G. R. DRIVER and J. C. MILES, *The Babylonian Laws*, III, Oxford, 1952, 245-324.
D. R. MACE, *Hebrew Marriage*, London, 1953.
J. J. RABINOWITZ, 'Marriage Contracts in Ancient Egypt in the Light of Jewish Sources', in *HTR*, XLVI, 1953, 91-7.
W. KORNFELD, 'Mariage dans l'Ancien Testament', in *Supplément au Dictionnaire de la Bible*, Paris, V, 1954, 905-26.
A. VAN SELMS, *Marriage and Family Life in Ugaritic Literature*, London, 1954.
C. WIENER, 'Jérémie II, 2, "Fiançailles" ou "épousailles"?', in *Recherches de Science Religieuse*, XLIV, 1956, 403-7.
E. VOLTERRA, 'Osservazioni sul divorzio nei documenti aramaici', in *Studi Orientalistici in onore di Giorgio Levi della Vida*, Rome, 1956, 586-600.
R. YARON, 'On Divorce in Old Testament Times', in *Revue Internationale des Droits de l'Antiquité*, VI, 1957, 77f.
R. YARON, 'Aramaic Marriage Contracts from Elephantine', in *Journal of Semitic Studies*, III, 1958, 1-39.
S. LOWY, 'The Extent of Jewish Polygamy in Talmudic Times', in *Journal of Jewish Studies*, IX, 1958, 115-38.
J. J. RABINOWITZ, 'The "Great Sin" in Ancient Egyptian Marriage Contracts', in *JNES*, XVIII, 1959, 73.
R. YARON, 'Aramaic Marriage Contracts: Corrigenda and Addenda', in *Journal of Semitic Studies*, V, 1960, 66-70.
W. L. MORAN, 'The Scandal of the "Great Sin" at Ugarit', in *JNES*, XVIII, 1959, 280-1.

On the Assyro-Babylonian *tirḫatu*:

E. A. SPEISER, 'New Kirkuk Documents relating to Family Laws', in *AASOR*, X, 1930, especially 23f.
P. VAN DER MEER, 'Tirḫâtu', in *Revue d'Assyriologie*, XXXI, 1934, 121-3.
C. H. GORDON, 'The Status of Women as reflected in the Nuzi Tablets', in *ZA*, XLIII, 1936, 146-69, especially 157-8.

On *beena* marriage:

J. MORGENSTERN, 'Beena Marriage (Matriarchate) and its Historical Implications', in *ZAW*, N.F. VI, 1929, 91-110; VIII, 1931, 46-58.

On Samson's marriage:

A. JAUSSEN, 'Le ğôz musarrib', in *RB*, XIX, 1910, 237-49.
A. VAN SELMS, 'The Best Man and Bride', in *JNES*, IX, 1950, 65-75.

On Jacob's marriages:

C. H. GORDON, 'The Story of Jacob and Laban in the Light of the Nuzi Tablets', in *BASOR*, **66**, 1937, 25-7.
M. BURROWS, 'The Complaint of Laban's Daughters', in *JAOS*, LVII, 1937, 259-76.

On the levirate:

J. SCHEFTELOWITZ, 'Die Leviratsehe', in *Archiv für Religionswissenschaft*, XVIII, 1915, 250-6.
P. CRUVEILHIER, 'Le lévirat chez les hébreux et chez les assyriens', in *RB*, XXXIV, 1925, 524-46.
K. H. RENGSTORF, *Die Mischna, Traktat Jebamot*, Giessen, 1929, with historical introduction and commentary.
P. KOSCHAKER, 'Zum levirat nach hethitischem Recht', in *Revue hittite et asianique*, II, 1933, 77-89.
J. MITTELMANN, *Der altisraelitische Levirat*, Leipzig, 1934.
G. R. DRIVER and J. C. MILES, *The Assyrian Laws*, Oxford, 1935, 240-50.
M. BURROWS, 'Levirate Marriage in Israel', in *JBL*, LIX, 1940, 23-33.
M. BURROWS, 'The Ancient Oriental Background of Hebrew Levirate Marriage', in *BASOR*, **77**, 1940, 2-15.
M. BURROWS, 'The Marriage of Boaz and Ruth', in *JBL*, LIX, 1940, 445-54.
H. H. ROWLEY, 'The Marriage of Ruth', in *HTR*, XL, 1947, 77-99, reproduced in *The Servant of the Lord and Other Essays on the Old Testament*, London, 1952, 161-86.
A. F. PUUKKO, 'Die Leviratsehe in den altorientalischen Gesetze', in *Archiv Orientální*, XVII, II, 1949 (Festschrift Hrozný), 296-9.
M. TSEVAT, 'Marriage and Monarchical Legitimacy in Ugarit and in Israel', in *Journal of Semitic Studies*, III, 1958, 237-43.

On the impediments to marriage:

W. KORNFELD, *Studien zum Heligkeitsgesetz*, Vienna, 1952, 89-134.
K. ELLIGER, 'Das Gesetz Leviticus 18', in *ZAW*, LXVII, 1955, 1-25.

3

THE POSITION OF WOMEN

M. LÖHR, *Die Stellung des Weibes zu Yahve-Religion und Kult*, Leipzig, 1918.
G. BEER, *Die soziale und religiöse Stellung der Frau im israelitischen Altertum*, Tübingen, 1919.
J. DOLLER, *Das Weib in Alten Testament*, Münster i.W., 1920.
P. CRUVEILHIER, 'La droit de la femme dans la Genèse et dans le recueil de lois assyriennes', in *RB*, XXXVI, 1927, 350-76.
E. M. MACDONALD, *The Position of Women as reflected in Semitic Codes*, Toronto, 1931.
J. LEIPOLDT, *Die Frau in der antiken Welt und im Urchristentum*, Leipzig, 1954, 69-114.

4

CHILDREN

On the attitude to children, and general points:

A. MARGOLIUS, *Mutter und Kind im altbiblischen Schrifttum*, Berlin, 1936.
H. GRANQUIST, *Child Problems among the Arabs*, Helsingfors, 1950.

On birth:

H. GRANQUIST, *Birth and Childhood among the Arabs*, Helsingfors, 1947.

On the name:

G. B. GRAY, *Studies in Hebrew Proper Names*, London, 1896.
M. NOTH, *Die israelitischen Personennamen im Rahmen der gemeinsemitischen Namengebung*, Stuttgart, 1928.

On circumcision:

Nothing useful apart from dictionary articles. The latest, with bibliography, are: *Reallexicon für Antike und Christentum*, II, Stuttgart, 1954, 159-69; *Theologisches Wörterbuch zum Neuen Testament*, VI, Stuttgart, 1955, 72-80. The study by F. SIERKSMA, 'Quelques remarques sur la circoncision en Israël', in *Oudtestamentische Studiën*, IX, 1951, 136-69, is not very trustworthy.

On education:

The essential work is L. DÜRR, *Das Erziehungswesen im Alten Testament und im Antiken Orient (Mitteilungen der vorderasiatisch-ägyptischen Gesellschaft*, XXXVI, 2), Leipzig, 1932.

J. HEMPEL, '*Pathos und Humor in der israelitischen Erziehung*' in *Von Ugarit nach Qumran*, Festschrift Eissfeldt, Berlin, 1958, 63-81.

On the rights of the eldest son:

I. MENDELSOHN, 'On the Preferential Status of the Eldest Son' in *BASOR*, 156, Dec. 1959, 38-40.

On adoption:

L. KÖHLER, 'Die Adoptionsform von Rt 4, 16', in *ZAW*, XXIX, 1909, 312-14.

M. DAVID, *Die Adoption im althabylonischen Recht*, Leipzig, 1927.

S. FEIGIN, 'Some Cases of Adoption in Israel', in *JBL*, L, 1931, 186-200.

E. M. CASSIN, *L'adoption à Nuzi*, Paris, 1938.

W. II. RUSSELL, 'New Testament Adoption—Graeco-Roman or Semitic?', in *JBL*, LXXI, 1952, 233-4.

M. DAVID, 'Adoptie in het oude Israel', in *Mededeelingen d. kon. Nederl. Akad. v. Wetensch., Afd. Letterek.*, 18, 4, 1955.

S. KARDIMON, 'Adoption as a Remedy for Infertility in the Period of the Patriarchs', in *Journal of Semitic Studies*, III, 1958, 123-6.

5

SUCCESSION AND INHERITANCE

M. TSCHERNOWITZ, 'The Inheritance of Illegitimate Children according to Jewish Law', in *Jewish Studies in Memory of Isaac Abrahams*, New York, 1927, 402-15.

E. NEUFELD, *Ancient Hebrew Marriage Laws*, London, 1944, 259-65.

J. PEDERSEN, *Israel, its Life and Culture*, I-II, 2nd ed., London, 1946, 89-96.

6

DEATH AND FUNERAL RITES

H. J. ELHORTS, *Die israelitischen Trauerriten*, Giessen, 1914.

S. H. JAHNOW, *Das hebräische Leichenlied im Rahmen der Völkerdichtung*, Giessen, 1923.

G. QUELL, *Die Auffassung des Todes im Israel*, Leipzig, 1925.

P. HEINISCH, *Die Trauergebrauche bei den Israeliten*, Munster i.W., 1931.

P. HEINISCH, *Die Totenklage im Alten Testament*, Munster i.W., 1931.

B. ALFRINK, 'L'expression shâkab 'im âbôtâw, in *Oudtestamentische Studiën*, II, 1943, 106-18.

B. ALFRINK, 'L'expression neěšap el-'ammâw', in *Oudtestamentische Studiën*, V, 1948, 118-31.

W. F. ALBRIGHT, 'The High Place in Ancient Palestine', in *Volume du Congrès, Strasbourg, 1956* (Supplement to *VT*, IV), Leiden, 1957, 242-58.

II

CIVIL INSTITUTIONS

1

POPULATION

These questions have hardly ever been studied, for lack of evidence. Some incidental information and solutions will be found in the following works:

F. BUHL, *La société israélite d'après l'Ancien Testament*, Paris, 1904, 83-9.

W. F. ALBRIGHT, in *JPOS*, V, 1925, 20-5.

M. LURJE, *Studien zur Geschichte der wirtschaftlichen und sozialen Verhältnisse im israelitisch-jüdischen Reiche*, Giessen, 1927, 35-41.

R. ZIMMERMAN, 'Bevölkerungsdichte und Heereszahlen im Alt-Palästina', in *Klio*, XXI, 1927, 310-3.

S. W. BARON, 'La population israélite sous les rois' (in Hebrew), in *Abhandlungen zur Erinnerung an H. P. Chajes*, 1932, 76-136.

J. W. CROWFOOT, *The Buildings of Samaria*, London, 1942, 2 and 4.

W. F. ALBRIGHT, *The Excavations of Tell Beit Mirsim*, II (*AASOR*, XXI-XXII, 1941-3), 39.

A. UNGNAD, 'Die Zahl der von Sanherib deportierten Judäer', in *ZAW*, LIX, 1942-3, 199-202.

J. JEREMIAS, 'Die Einwohnerzahl zur Zeit Jesu', in *ZDPV*, LXVI, 1943, 24-31.

A. Lucas, 'The Number of Israelites at the Exodus', in *PEQ*, 1944, 164-8.
W. F. Albright, *The Biblical Period*, Pittsburgh, 1950, 2nd ed., 1955, 59-60, n. 75.
S. W. Baron, *A Social and Religious History of the Jews*, I, 1, 2nd ed., New York, 1952, 64 and 320-1, n. 2.
G. E. Mendenhall, 'The Census Lists of Numbers 1 and 26', in *JBL*, LXXVII, 1958, 52-66.

2

The Free Population : Its Divisions

On the dignitaries:

J. van der Ploeg, '*Le sens de gibbôr ḥail* in *RB*, L 1941 (= *Vivre et Penser*, I) 120-5.
C. U. Wolf, 'Traces of Primitive Democracy in Israel', in *JNES*, VI, 1947, 98-108.
J. van der Ploeg, 'Les chefs du people d'Israël et leurs noms', in *RB*, LVII, 1950, 40-61.
J. van der Ploeg, 'Les "nobles israélites"', in *Oudtestamentische Studiën*, IX, 1955, 49-64.
W. McKane, 'The *gibbor ḥayil* in the Israelite Community', in *Transactions of the Glasgow University Oriental Society*, XVII, 1957-8 (1959), 28-37.
E. Neufeld, 'The Emergence of a Royal-Urban Society in Ancient Israel', in *HUCA*, XXXI, 1960. 31-53.

On the 'people of the land':

M. Sulzberger, *Am ha-aretz, the Ancient Hebrew Parliament*, Philadelphia, 1909.
E. Klamroth, *Die jüdischen Exulanten in Babylonien*, Leipzig, 1912, Excursus, 99-101.
M. Sulzberger, 'The Polity of the Ancient Hebrews', in *JQR*, n.s. III, 1912-13, 1-81.
N. Slousch, 'Representative Government among the Hebrews and Phoenicians', in *JQR*, n.s. IV, 1913-14, 303-10.
E. Gillischewski, 'Der Ausdruck 'am haareṣ im Alten Testament', in *ZAW*, XL, 1922, 137-42.
S. Daiches, 'The Meaning of am ha-aretz in the Old Testament', in *JTS*, XXX, 1929, 245-9.
S. Zeitlin, 'The Am haarez', in *JQR*, n.s. XXIII, 1932-3, 45-61.
L. Rost, 'Die Bezeichnungen für Land und Volk im Alten Testament', in *Festschrift Procksch*, Leipzig, 1934, 125-48.
R. Gordis, 'Sectional Rivalry in the Kingdom of Judah', in *JQR*, n.s. XXV, 1934-5, 237-59.
P. Lemaire, 'Crise et effondrement de la monarchie davidique', in *RB*, XLV, 1936, 161-83.
E. Würthwein, *Der 'am ha'arez im Alten Testament*, Stuttgart, 1936.
I. D. Amussin, 'Le "Peuple du Pays"' (in Russian) in *Vestnik Drevnej Istorii*, 1955, 2, 14-36. A German summary in *Bibliotheca Classica Orientalis* (Berlin), I, 1956, 73-5.
L. A. Snijders, 'Het "Volk des Lands" in Juda', in *Nederlands Theologisch Tijdschrift*, XII, 1957-8, 241-56.

On the rich and the poor: the question has been studied chiefly from the religious angle. See in particular:

A. Kuschke, 'Arm und Reich im Alten Testament, mit besonderer Berücksichtung der nachexilischen Zeit', in *ZAW*, LVII, 1939, 31-57.
J. van der Ploeg, 'Les pauvres d'Israël et leur piété', in *Oudtestamentische Studiën*, VII, 1950, 236-70.
A. Gelin, *Les pauvres de Yahvé*, Paris, 1953, with critical bibliography.
C. van Leeuwen, *Le développement du sens social en Israël avant l'ère chrétienne*, Assen, 1955.

On the resident foreigners:

A. Bertholet, *Die Stellung der Israeliten und der Juden zu den Fremden*, Leipzig, 1896, 27-50.
M. Sulzberger, 'Status of Labor in Ancient Israel', in *JQR*, n.s. XIII, 1922-3, 397-459.
M. Weber, *Das Antike Judentum*, 2nd ed., Tübingen, 1923, 38-42.
J. van der Ploeg, 'Sociale groepeeringen in het Oude Israël', in *Jaarbericht van het Vooraziatisch-Egyptisch Gezelshap*, VII, 1942, 642-6.
J. Pedersen, *Israel, its Life and Culture*, I-II, London, 2nd ed., 1946, 39-43.
E. Marmorstein, 'The Origins of Agricultural Feudalism in the Holy Land', in *PEQ*, 1953, 111-17.

On the wage-earners:

K. Fuchs, *Die alttestamentliche Arbeitergesetzgebung im Vergleich zu CH, zum altassyrischen und hettitischen Recht*, Dissertation Heidelberg, 1935.
W. Lauterbach, *Der Arbeiter in Recht und Rechtspraxis des Alten Testament und des Alten Orients*, Dissertation Heidelberg, 1935.
W. Bienert, *Die Arbeit nach der Lehre der Bibel*, Stuttgart, 2nd ed., 1956, 88-96.

On the artisans:

I. Mendelsohn, 'Guilds in Babylonia and Assyria', in *JPOS*, LX, 1940, 68-72.
I. Mendelsohn, 'Guilds in Ancient Palestine', in *BASOR*, 80, 1940, 17-21.

On the merchants:

W. F. LEEMANS, *The Old Babylonian Merchant* (*Studia et Documenta ad jura Orientis pertinentia*, III), Leyde, 1950.

C. H. GORDON, 'Abraham and the Merchants of Ura', in *JNES*, XVII, 1958, 28-31.

3

SLAVES

General points:

P. HEINISCH, 'Das Sklavenrecht in Israel und im Alten Orient', in *Studia Catholica*, XI, 1934-5, 201-18.

I. MENDELSOHN, *Slavery in the Ancient Near East*, New York, 1949.

R. NORTH, *Sociology of the Biblical Jubilee*, Rome, 1954, with bibliography of older works, pp. xix-xxi; summary, pp. 135-57.

On slavery in the neighbouring countries:

A. BAKIR, *Slavery in Pharaonic Egypt*, Cairo, 1952.

G. R. DRIVER and J. C. MILES, *The Babylonian Laws*, I, Oxford, 1952, especially 105-8, 221-30, 478-90.

J. KLIMA, 'Einige Bemerkungen zum Sklavenrecht nach den vorhammurapischen Gesetzefragmenten', in *Archiv Orientální*, XXI, 1933, 143-51.

I. MENDELSOHN, 'On Slavery in Alakakh', in *IEJ*, V, 1955, 65-72.

On Israelite slaves:

I. MENDELSOHN, 'The Conditional Sale into Slavery of Free-Born Daughters in Nuzi and in the Law of Ex 21, 7-11', in *JAOS*, LV, 1935, 190-5.

H. M. WEIL, 'Gage et cautionnement dans la Bible', in *Archives de l'Histoire du Droit Oriental*, II, 1938, 68 pp.

R. SUGRANYES DE FRANCH, *Études sur le droit palestinien à l'époque évangélique*, Fribourg (Switzerland), 1946, 68-106.

On the 'Hebrew' slave:

A. ALT, *Die Ursprünge des israelitischen Rechts*, Leipzig, 1934, 19-23 = *Kleine Schriften*, I, Munich, 1953, 291-4.

A. JEPSEN, 'Die "Hebräer" und ihr Recht', in *AfO*, XV, 1945-51, 55-68.

On capture:

A. ALT, 'Das Verbot des Diebstahls im Dekalog', in *Kleine Schriften*, I, Munich, 1953, 333-40.

On the y^elid bayt:

F. WILLESEN, 'The Yalid in Hebrew Society', in *Studia Theologica*, XII, 1958, 192-210.

On emancipation:

M. DAVID, 'The Manumission of Slaves under Zedekiah', in *Oudtestamentische Studiën*, V, 1948, 63-79.

Z. W. FALK, 'The Deeds of Manumission in Elephantine', in *Journal of Jewish Studies*, V, 1954, 114-17.

Z. W. FALK, 'Manumission by Sale', in *Journal of Semitic Studies*, III, 1958, 127-8.

On the hofši:

I. MENDELSOHN, 'The Canaanite term for "Free Proletarian"', in *BASOR*, **83**, 1941, 36-9.

E. R. LACHEMAN, 'Note on the Word ḫupšu at Nuzi', in *BASOR*, **86**, 1942, 36-7.

J. GRAY, 'Feudalism in Ugarit and Early Israel', in *ZAW*, LXIV, 1952, 49-55.

I. MENDELSOHN, 'New Light on the ḫupšu', in *BASOR*, **139**, 1955, 9-11.

On public slaves:

A. BERTHOLET, *Die Stellung der Israeliten und der Juden zu den Fremden*, Leipzig, 1896, 50-3.

I. MENDELSOHN, 'State Slavery in Ancient Israel', in *BASOR*, 85, 1942, 14-17. Revised and developed in *Slavery in the Ancient Near East*, New York, 1949, 92-106.

M. HARAN, 'The Gibeonites, the Nethinim and the Servants of Solomon', in *Judah and Jerusalem*, 1957, 37-45.

4

THE ISRAELITE CONCEPT OF THE STATE

K. GALLING, *Die israelitische Staatsverfassung in ihrer vorder-orientalischen Umwelt* (*Der Alte Orient*, XXVIII, 3 4), Leipzig, 1929.

A. ALT, *Die Staatbildung der Israeliten in Palästina*, Reformations-program der Universität Leipzig 1930=*Kleine Schriften*, II, Munich, 1953, 1-65.
M. NOTH, *Das System der Zwölf Stämme Israels*, Stuttgart, 1930.
C. R. NORTH, 'The Old Testament Estimate of the Monarchy', in *AJSL*, XLVIII, 1931-2, 1-19.
A. ALT, 'Das Grossreich Davids', in *TLZ*, LXXV, 1950, 213-20=*Kleine Schriften*, II, 66-67.
M. NOTH, 'Gott, König, Volk im Alten Testament', in *Zeitschrift für Theologie und Kirche*, XLVII, 1950, 157-91.
A. ALT, 'Das Königtum in den Reichen Israel und Juda', in *VT*, I, 1951, 2-22=*Kleine Schriften*, II, 116-34.
K. GALLING, 'Das Königsgesetz im Deuteronomium', in *TLZ*, LXXVI, 1951, 133-8.
H. J. KRAUS, *Prophetie und Politik*, Munich, 1952.
A. ALT, *Der Stadstaat Samaria* (Berichte über die Verhandlungen der sachsischen Akademie der Wissenschaften zu Leipzig, Phil.-hist. Klasse, 101, 5), Berlin, 1954=*Kleine Schriften*, III, 258-302.
I. MENDELSOHN, 'Samuel's Denunciation of Kingship in the Light of the Akkadian Documents from Ugarit', in *BASOR*, 143, 1956, 17-22.

5

THE PERSON OF THE KING

On Eastern parallels, in general:

K. F. EULER, 'Königtum und Götterwelt in den altaramäischen Inschriften Nordsyriens', in *ZAW*, LVI, 1938, 272-313.
R. LABAT, *Le caractère religieux de la royauté assyro-babylonienne*, Paris, 1939.
I. ENGNELL, *Studies in Divine Kingship in the Ancient Near East*, Uppsala, 1943.
H. FRANKFORT, *Kingship and the Gods*, Chicago, 1948.
T. FISH, 'Some Aspects of Kingship in the Sumerian City and Kingdom of Ur', in *BJRL*, XXXIV, 1951-2, 37-43.
J. RYCKMANS, *L'institution monarchique en Arabie méridionale avant l'Islam*, Louvain, 1951.
J. GRAY, 'Canaanite Kingship in Theory and Practice', in *VT*, II, 1952, 193-220.
'Authority and Law in the Ancient Orient', Supplement 17 to *JAOS*, 1954: J. A. WILSON (Egypt); E. A. SPEISER (Mesopotamia); H. G. GÜTERBOCK (Hittites); I. MENDELSOHN (Canaan and Israel).

On the religious character of the king, in general:

S. MOWINCKEL, *Psalmenstudien*, II, *Das Thronbesteigungsfest Jahwäs und der Ursprung der Eschatologie*, Christiania, 1922.
C. R. NORTH, 'The Religious Aspects of Hebrew Kingship', in *ZAW*, L, 1932, 8-38.
S. H. HOOKE (Ed.), *Myth and Ritual. Essays on the Myth and Ritual of the Hebrews in Relation to the Culture Pattern of the Ancient East*, London, 1933.
S. MOWINCKEL, 'Urmensch und "Königsideologie"', in *Studia Theologica* (Lund), II, 1948, 71-89.
A. BENTZEN, 'King Ideology—"Urmensch"—"Troonsbestijgingsfeest"', in *Studia Theologica* (Lund), III, 1950, 143-57.
A. R. JOHNSON, 'Divine Kingship and the Old Testament', in *Expository Times*, LXII, 1950, 36-42.
M. NOTH, 'Gott, König, Volk im Alten Testament', in *Zeitschrift für Theologie und Kirche*, XLVII, 1950, 157-91=*Gesammelte Studien zum Alten Testament*, Munich, 1956, 188-229.
J. DE FRAINE, *L'aspect religieux de la royauté israélite. L'institution monarchique dans l'Ancien Testament et dans les textes mésopotamiens*, Rome, 1954.
G. WIDENGREN, *Sakrales Königtum im Alten Testament und in Judentum*, Stuttgart, 1955.
A. R. JOHNSON, *Sacral Kingship in Ancient Israel*, Cardiff, 1955.
S. MOWINCKEL, *He that Cometh* (English translation), Oxford, 1956, esp. pp. 21-95.
G. FOHRER, 'Der Vertrag zwischen König und Volk in Israel', in *ZAW*, LXXI, 1959, 1-22.
E. I. J. ROSENTHAL, 'Some Aspects of the Hebrew Monarchy', in *Journal of Jewish Studies*, IX, 1958, 1-18.
S. H. HOOKE (Editor), *Myth, Ritual and Kingship. Essays on the Theory and Practice of Kingship in the Ancient Near East, and in Israel*, 1958.
G. W. ALSTRÖM, 'Psalm 89. Eine Liturgie ans', in *Ritual des Leidenden Königs*, Lund, 1959.
A. GARDINER, 'The Baptism of Pharao', in *Journal of Egyptian Archaeology*, XXXVI, 1950, 3-12.
S. MOWINCKEL, 'General Orientai and Specific Israelite Elements in the Israelite Conception of the Sacral Kingdom', in *The Sacral Kingship* (Supplement IV to *Numen*), Leiden, 1959, 285-93.

On the coronation rites:

K. SETHE, *Dramatische Texte zu altägyptischen Mysterienspielen*, Leipzig, 1928.
K. F. MULLER, *Das assyrische Ritual. I. Texte zum assyrischen Königsritual* (Mitteilungen der vorderasiatisch-ägyptischen Gesellschaft, XLI, 3), Leipzig, 1937.
G. VON RAD, 'Das judaische Königsritual', in *TLZ*, LXXII, 1947, 211-16.

P. A. H. DE BOER, 'Vive le roi', in *VT*, V, 1955, 225-31.
M. NOTH, *Amt und Berufung im Alten Testament*, Bonn, 1958.
E. COTHENET, art. 'Onction', in *Dictionnaire de la Bible, Supplément*, VI, 1959, 701-32.
J. MORGENSTERN, 'David and Jonathan', in *JBL*, LXXVIII, 1959, 322-5.
Z. W. FALK, 'Forms of Testimony', in *VT*, XI, 1961, 88-91 (on 'edûth).

On the coronation names:

A. M. HONEYMAN, 'The Evidence for Royal Names among the Hebrews', in *JBL*, LXVII, 1948, 13-26.
A. ALT, 'Jesaja 8, 23-9, 6. Befreiungsnacht und Krönungstag', in *Festschrift Bertholet*, Tübingen, 1950, 29-49.=*Kleine Schriften*, II, 206-25.
I. GELB, 'The Double Name of Hittite Kings', in *Rocznyk Orientalistyczny*, Cracow, XVII, 1953 (*Memorial T. Kowalsky*), 146-54.
S. MORENZ, 'Aegyptische und davidische Königstitulatur', in *Zeitschrift für ägyptische Sprache und Altertumskunde*, LXXIX, 1954, 73-4.
H. CAZELLES, 'La titulature du roi David', in *Mélanges A. Robert*, 1957, 131-6.
L. M. VON PAKOZDY, "Elhanan, der frühere Name Davids?', in *ZAW*, LXVIII, 1956, 257-9.
R. BORGER, 'Mesopotamien in den Jahren 629-621 v. Chr.', in *Wiener Zeitschrift für die Kunde des Morgenlandes*, LV, 1959, 62-76 (Assurbanipal=Kandalanu).

On the enthronement psalms:

L. DÜRR, *Psalm 110 im Lichte der neueren alttestamentlischen Forschung*, Münster i.W., 1929.
G. VON RAD, 'Erwägungen zu den Königpsalmen', in *ZAW*, LXVIII, 1940-1, 216-22.
G. WIDENGREN, *Psalm 110 och det sakrale Kungedömet i Israel*, Uppsala, 1941.
A. BENTZEN, *Messias, Moses redivivus, Menschensohn*, Zurich, 1948, esp. pp. 11-32.
R. MURPHY, *A Study of Psalm 72*, Washington, 1948.
A. ROBERT, 'Considérations sur le messianisme du Ps 2', in *Recherches de Science Religieuse*, XXXIX, 1951-2, 88-98.
J. DE FRAINE, 'Quel est le sens exact de la filiation divine dans Ps 2, 7?', in *Bijdragen, Tijdschrift voor Philosophie en Theologie* (Louvain and Maastricht), XVI, 1955, 349-56.
J. COPPENS, 'La portée messianique du Ps CX', in *Ephemerides Theologicae Lovanienses*, XXXII, 1956, 5-23.
J. DE SAVIGNAC, 'Théologie Pharaonique et messianisme d'Israël', in *VT*, VII, 1957, 82-90.
R. PRESS, 'Jahwe und seine Gesalbten (Ps. 2)', in *Theologische Zeitschrift*, XIII, 1957, 321-34.
H. J. STOEBE, 'Erwägungen zu Psalm 110 auf dem Hintergrund von 1. Sam. 21', in *Festschrift F. Baumgärtel*, Erlangen, 1959, 175-91.
M. BIČ, 'Das erste Buch des Psalters, eine Thronbesteigungsfestliturgie', in *The Sacral Kingship* (Supplement IV to *Numen*), Leiden, 1959, 316-32.
J. COPPENS, 'Les apports du Psaume cx (Vulgate cix) à l'idéologie royale israélite', ibid., 333-48.

On the king as saviour:

G. WIDENGREN, *The King and the Tree of Life in Ancient Near Eastern Religion* (*King and Saviour IV*), Uppsala, 1951.
R. MEYER, 'Der Erlöserkönig des Alten Testaments', in *Münchener Theologische Zeitschrift*, III, 1952, 221-43, 367-84.
J. L. McKENZIE, 'Royal Messianism', in *Catholic Biblical Quarterly*, XIX, 1957, 27-52.

On the priesthood of the king:

A. R. JOHNSON, 'The Role of the King in the Jerusalem Cultus', in S. H. Hooke, *The Labyrinth*, London, 1935, 73-111.
J. MORGENSTERN, 'A Chapter in the History of the High Priesthood', in *AJSL*, LV, 1938, 5-13.
H. H. ROWLEY, 'Melchizedek and Zadok', in *Festschrift Bertholet*, Tübingen, 1950, 461-72.
J. DE FRAINE, 'Peut-on parler d'un véritable sacerdoce du roi en Israël?', in *Sacra Pagina*, I, Gembloux, 1959, 537-47.
H. J. KRAUS, 'Königtum und Kultus in Jerusalem, Excursus 6' in the author's *Psalmen*, II, Neukirche Kreis Moer, 1960, 879-83.

6

THE ROYAL HOUSEHOLD

Nothing exists except some special studies on particular questions.

On the harem:

E. WEIDNER, 'Hof- und Harems-Erlasse assyrischen Könige', in *AfO*, XVII, 1956, 257-93.
M. TSEVAT, 'Marriage and Monarchical Legitimacy in Ugarit and Israel', in *Journal of Semitic Studies*, III, 1958, 237-43.

On the Great Lady:

A. KAMPMANN, 'Tawannanaš, de Titel der hethietische Köningin', in *Jaarbericht Ex Oriente Lux*, II (numbers 6-8), 1940, 432-42.
A. CAQUOT, 'La déesse Shegal', in *Semitica*, IV, 1951-2, 55-8.
H. LEWY, 'Nitokris-Naqî'a', in *JNES*, XI, 1952, 264-86.
G. MOLIN, 'Die Stellung der Gebira im Staate Juda', in *Theologische Zeitschrift*, X, 1954, 161-75.
C. J. GADD, 'The Harran Inscriptions of Nabonidus', in *Anatolian Studies*, VIII, 1958, 35-92.
H. DONNER, 'Art und Herkunft des Amtes der Königinmutter im Alten Testament', in *Festschrift J. Friedrich*, 1959.

On the 'king's son':

H. GAUTHIER, 'Les "Fils royaux de Koush"', in *Recueil de Travaux relatifs à la philologie et à l'archéologie égyptiennes et assyriennes*, XXXIX, 1920, 178-237.
S. YEIVIN, art. 'ben hammèlèk', in *Encyclopaedia Biblica* (in Hebrew), Jerusalem, III, 1954, 160.

On the king's 'servants':

W. F. ALBRIGHT, 'The Seal of Eliakim and the Latest Pre-exilic History of Judah', in *JBL*, LI, 1932, 77-106, esp. 79-80.
A. BERGMAN, 'Two Hebrew Seals of the 'Ebed Class', in *JBL*, LV, 1936, 221-6.

On armour-bearers:

E. KLAUBER, *Assyrisches Beamtentum nach den Briefen aus der Sargonidenzeit (Leipziger Semitische Studien*, V, 3), Leipzig, 1910, 111-15: *Der šalšu*.
A. GOETZE, 'Hittite Courtiers and their Titles', in *Revue Hittite et asianique*, XII, fasc, 54, 1952, 1-7.

On the *saris*:

E. VON SCHULER, *Hethitische Dienstanweisungen für höhere Hof- und Staatsbeamte (AfO, Beihefte 10)*, 1957.

On the 'king's friend':

R. DE VAUX, 'Titres et fonctionnaires égyptiens à la cour de David et de Salomon', in *RB*, XLVIII, 1939, 403-5.
A. VAN SELMS, 'The Origin of the Title "the King's Friend"', in *JNES*, XVI, 1957, 118-23.

On the royal estate:

M. NOTH, 'Das Krongut der israelitischen Könige und seine Verwaltung', in *ZDPV*, L, 1927, 211-44; cf. *PJB*, XXVIII, 1932, 60-1.
A. ALT, 'Der Anteil des Königstum an der sozialen Entwicklung in den Reichen Israel und Juda', in *Kleine Schriften*, III, Munich, 1959, 348-72.
W. F. ALBRIGHT, incidentally in *JPOS*, XI, 1931, 249; *JBL*, LI, 1932, 82-4.
E. SELLIN, 'Die palästinischen Krughenkel mit den Konigsstempeln', in *ZDPV*, LXVI, 1943, 216-32.

7

THE PRINCIPAL OFFICIALS OF THE KING

E. KLAUBER, *Assyrisches Beamtentum nach den Briefen aus der Sargonidenzeit (Leipziger Semitische Studien*, V, 3), Leipzig, 1910.
K. GALLING, 'Die Halle des Schreibers', in *PJB*, XXVII, 1931, 51-7.
H. KEES, *Kulturgeschichte des Alten Orients*, I, *Aegypten (Handbuch der Altertumswissenschaft)*, Munich, 1933, 185-218.
R. DE VAUX, 'Le sceau de Godolias, maitre du palais', in *RB*, XLV, 1936, 96-102.
R. DE VAUX, 'Titres et fonctionnaires égyptiens à la cour de David et de Salomon', in *RB*, XLVIII, 1939, 394-405.
J. BEGRICH, 'Sopher und Mazkir. Ein Beitrag zur inneren Geschichte des davidisch-salomonischen Grossreiches und der Königreiches Juda', in *ZAW*, LVIII, 1940-1, 1-29.
B. MAISLER, 'Le scribe de David et le problème des grands officiers dans l'ancien royaume d'Israël' (in Hebrew), in *BJPES*, XIII, 1946-7, 105-14.
N. AVIGARD, 'The Epitaph of a Royal Steward from Siloam Village', in *IEJ*, III, 1953, 137-52.
A. ALT, 'Hohe Beamten in Ugarit', in *Studia Orientalia Ioanni Pedersen . . . dedicata*, Copenhagen, 1953, 1-11 = *Kleine Schriften*, III, 186-97.
J. R. KUPPER, 'Baḥdi-lim, préfet du Palais du Mari', in *Bulletin de la Classe des Lettres et des Sciences Morale et Politique de l'Académie Royale de Belgique*, 5th series, XL, 1954, 572-87.
H. J. KATSENSTEIN, 'The House of Eliakim, a Family of Royal Stewards', in *Eretz-Israel*, V, 1958 (Volume Mazar), 108-10 (in Hebrew, with a summary in English).

8

THE ADMINISTRATION OF THE KINGDOM

On Solomon's prefectures:

A. ALT, 'Israels Gaue unter Salomo', in *Alttestamentliche Studien R. Kittel . . . dargebracht*, Leipzig, 1913, 1–19= *Kleine Schriften*, II, Munich, 1953, 76–89.
W. F. ALBRIGHT, 'The Administrative Divisions of Israel and Juda', in *JPOS*, V, 1925, 17–54.
R. P. DOUGHERTY, 'Cuneiform Parallels to Solomon's Provisioning System', in *AASOR*, V, 1925, 23–46.
F. M. ABEL, *Géographie de la Palestine*, II, Paris, 1938, 79–83.
F. PUZO, 'La segunda prefectura salomónica', in *Estudios Biblicos*, VII, 1949, 43–73.
A. ALT, 'Menschen ohne Namen', in *Archiv Orientální*, XVIII, 1–2, 1950, 9–24= *Kleine Schriften*, III, 198–213.

On the districts of Judah:

A. ALT, 'Judas Gaue unter Josia', in *PJB*, XXI, 1925, 100–16= *Kleine Schriften*, II, Munich, 1953, 276–88.
S. MOWINCKEL, *Zur Frage nach dokumentarischen Quellen in Josua 13–19*, Oslo, 1946.
F. M. CROSS and G. E. WRIGHT, 'The Boundary and Province Lists of the Kingdom of Judah', in *JBL*, LXXV, 1956, 202–26.
Z. KALLAI-KLEINMANN, 'The Town Lists of Judah, Simeon, Benjamin and Dan', in *VT*, VIII, 1958, 134–60.
Y. AHARONI, 'The Province-List of Judah', in *VT*, IX, 1959, 225–46.

On the districts of Israel:

A. ALT, 'Eine galiläische Ortsliste in Josua 19', in *ZAW*, XLV, 1927, 59–81.
M. NOTH, 'Studien zur Geschichte der historisch-geographischen Dokumente des Josuabuches', in *ZDPV*, LVIII, 1935, 185–255, esp. 215–30.

On the cantons of Samaria:

W. F. ALBRIGHT, 'The Administrative Divisions of Israel and Judah', in *JPOS*, V, 1925, 17–54, esp. 38–43.
M. NOTH, 'Das Krongut der israelitischen Könige und seine Verwaltung', in *ZDPV*, L, 1927, 211–44, esp. 230–40.
M. NOTH, 'Der Beitrag der samaritischen Ostraka zur Lösung topographischen Fragen', in *PJB*, XXVIII 1932, 54–67.
F. M. ABEL, *Géographie de la Palestine*, II, Paris, 1938, 95–7.
B. MAISLER, 'The Historical Background of the Samaria Ostraka', in *JPOS*, XXI, 1948, 117–33
S. MOSCATI, *L'epigrafia ebraica antica 1935–1950*, Rome, 1951, 27–31.

On the local administration, for comparison:

F. CHARLES JEAN, *Les lettres de Ḫammurapi à Sin-Idinnam*, Paris, 1913.
J. R. KUPPER, 'Un gouvernement provincial dans le royaume de Mari', in *Revue d'Assyriologie*, XLI, 1947, 149–83.
J. R. KUPPER, *Correspondance de Kibri-Dagan, gouverneur de Tirqa* (*Archives Royales de Mari*, III), Paris, 1950.

9

FINANCE AND PUBLIC WORKS

No special work. Material will be found in the following:

F. BUHL, *La société israélite d'après l'Ancien Testament*, Paris, 1904, 185–94.
A. BERTHOLET, *Kulturgeschichte Israels*, Göttingen, 1919, 181–4.
J. PEDERSEN, *Israel, its Life and Culture*, III–IV², London, 1947, 66–71.
I. MENDELSOHN, *Slavery in the Ancient Near East*, New York, 1949, 97–9, and the long note, pp. 149–50.
H. CAZELLES, 'La dîme israélite et les texts de Ras-Shamra', in *VT*, I, 1951, 131–4.
J. NOUGAYROL, *Le palais royal d'Ugarit*, III, *Textes accadiens et hourrites . . .*, Paris, 1955, Index s.v. 'Franchises et Exemptions', 'Recettes fiscales', 'Services et corvées'.
I. MENDELSOHN, 'Samuel's Denunciation of Kingship in the Light of the Akkadian Documents from Ugarit', in *BASOR*, 143, 1956, 17–22.
Y. AHARONI, 'Hebrew Jar-Stamps from Ramat Rachel', in *Eretz-Israel*, VI, 1960 (in Hebrew, with a summary in English).

10

Law and Justice

General:

M. Noth, *Die Gesetze im Pentateuch. Ihre Voraussetzungen und ihr Sinn.* (Schriften der Königsberger Gelehrten Gesellschaft), Halle, 1940= *Gesammelte Studien zum Alten Testament*, Munich, 1957, 9-141.
G. Ostborn, *Tôrah in Old Testament*, Lund, 1945.
D. Daube, *Studies in Biblical Law*, Cambridge, 1947.
J. van der Ploeg, 'Studies in Biblical Law', in *Catholic Biblical Quarterly*, XII, 1950, 248-59; 416-27; XIII, 1951, 28-43; 164-71; 296-307.
H. Cazelles, 'Loi Israélite', in *Supplément au Dictionnaire de la Bible*, Paris, V, 1952-3, 497-530.

On the laws of the ancient East:

G. Landsberger, 'Die babylonischen Termini für Gesetz und Recht', in *Symbolae . . . P. Koschaker dedicatae*, Leyden, 1939, 219-34.
'Authority and Law in the Ancient Orient', Supplement 17 to *JAOS*, 1954: J. A. Wilson (Egypt); E. A. Speiser (Mesopotamia); H. G. Guterbock (Hittites); I. Mendelsohn (Canaan and Israel).
G. Boyer, 'La place des textes d'Ugarit dans l'histoire de l'ancien droit oriental', in J. Nougayrol, *Le Palais Royal d'Ugarit*, III, Paris, 1955, 283-308.
E. Szlechter, 'Les anciennes codifications en Mésopotamie', in *Revue Internationale des Droits de l'Antiquité*, IV, 1957, 73-92.
The most important texts, well translated and with a bibliography, are collected in J. B. Pritchard, *Ancient Near Eastern Texts relating to the Old Testament*, 2nd ed., Princeton, 1955, 159-98.

Other recent translations, with commentary:
E. Szlechter, 'Le code d'Ur-Nammu', in *Revue d'Assyriologie*, XLIX, 1955, 169-77.
J. P. Lettinga, 'Het sumerische wetboek van Lipitištar, koning van Isin', in *Jaarbericht Ex Oriente Lux* XII, 1951-2, 249-63.
E. Szlechter, 'Le code de Lipit-Ištar', in *Revue d'Assyriologie*, LI, 1957, 57-82.
A. Goetze, *The Laws of Eshnunna (AASOR*, XXXI, 1951-2), 1956.
G. R. Driver and J. C. Miles, *The Babylonian Laws*, Oxford, I, 1952; II, 1955.
G. R. Driver and J. C. Miles, *The Assyrian Laws*, Oxford, 1935.
E. Neufeld, *The Hittite Laws*, London, 1951.
J. Friedrich, *Die hethitischen Gesetze*, Leiden, 1959.

On the sources of Israelite law:

A. Jirku, *Das weltliche Recht im Alten Testament*, Gütersloh, 1927.
H. Schmökel, *Das angewandte Recht im Alten Testament*, Leipzig, 1930.
V. Korošec, *Hethitische Staatsverträge. Ein Beitrag zu ihrer juristichen Wertung*, Leipzig, 1931.
E. F. Weidner, 'Der Staatsvertrag Aššurnirâris VI. von Assyrien mit Mati'ilu von Sît-Agusi', in *AfO*, VIII, 1932-3, 17-34.
M. David, 'The Codex Hammurabi and its relations to the Provisions of Law in Exodus', in *Oudtestamentische Studiën*, VII, 1950, 149-78.
A. Alt, *Die Ursprünge des israelitischen Rechts*, Leipzig, 1934= *Kleine Schriften*, I, Munich, 1953, 278-332.
A. Dupont-Sommer, 'Une inscription araméenne inédite de Sfiré (stèle III)', in *Bulletin du Musée de Beyrouth*, XII, 1956, 23-41.
J. Nougayrol, *Le Palais d'Ugarit*, IV, Paris, 1956.
D. J. Wiseman, 'The Vassal-Treaties of Esarhaddon', in *Iraq*, XX, 1958, 1-99.
A. Dupont-Sommer, 'Les inscriptions araméennes de Sfiré (stèles I et II)', in *Mémoires présentés par divers savants à l'Académie des Inscriptions et Belles-Lettres*, XV, 1958.

On the characteristics of Israelite law:

A. Alt, 'Zur Talionsformel', in *ZAW*, III, 1934, 303-5= *Kleine Schriften*, I, Munich, 1953, 341-4.
J. Begrich, 'Berit. Ein Beitrag zur Erfassung einer alttestamentlichen Denkform', in *ZAW*, LX, 1944, 1-11.
B. Gemser, 'The Importance of the Motive Clause in Old Testament Law', in *Congress Volume Copenhagen*, Supplement I to *VT*, 1953, 50-66.
M. Noth, 'Das alttestamentliche Bundschliessen im Lichte eines Mari-Textes', in *Mélanges Isidore Lévy (Annuaire de l'Institut de Philologie et d'Histoire Orientales et Slaves)*, XIII, 1953, 433-44= *Gesammelte Studien zum Alten Testament*, Munich, 1957, 142-54.
G. E. Mendenhall, *Law and Covenant in Israel and the Ancient Near East*, Pittsburgh, 1955, Reprinted from *Biblical Archaeologist*, XVII, 1954, 26-46; 49-76.
F. Horst, 'Recht und Religion im Bereich des Alten Testaments', in *Evangelische Theologie*, XVI, 1956, 49-74.
A. S. Diamond, 'An Eye for an Eye', in *Iraq*, XIX, 1957, 151-5.

E. Würthwein, 'Der Sinn des Gesetzes im Alten Testament', in *Zeitschrift für Theologie und Kirche*, LV, 1958, 255-70.
W. Zimmerli, 'Das Gesetz im Alten Testament', in *TLZ*, LXXXV, 1960, 481-98.

On the legislative and judicial power of the king:

M. Noth, *Die Gesetze im Pentateuch, op. cit.*, pp. 9-22; 33-29=*Gesammelte Studien* . . . , pp. 23-42; 58-67.
M. Noth, 'Das Amt des "Richters Israels"', in *Festschrift A. Bertholet*, Tübingen, 1950, 404-17.
H. W. Hertzberg, 'Die Kleinen Richter', in *TLZ*, LXXIX, 1954, 285-90.
G. Widengren, 'King and Covenant', in *Journal of Semitic Studies* (Manchester), II, 1957, 1-32.

On the courts of justice:

A. Walther, *Das altbabylonische Gerichtswesen* (*Leipziger Semitische Studien*, VI, 4-6), Leipzig, 1917.
J. van der Ploeg, 'Shapaṭ et Mishpaṭ', in *Oudtestamentische Studiën*, II, 1943, 144-55.
H. Liebesny, 'The Administration of Justice in Nuzi', in *JAOS*, LXIII, 1943, 128-44.
K. Pfluger, 'The Edict of King Haremhab', in *JNES*, V, 1946, 260-8.
W. F. Albright, 'The Reform of Jehoshaphat', in *Alexander Mark Jubilee Volume*, New York, 1950, 61-82.
E. Seidl, *Einführung in die ägyptische Rechtsgeschichte bis zum Ende des Neun Reiches*, I, Juristischer Teil, Gluckstadt-Hamburg, 2nd ed., 1951.
L. Köhler, *Der hebräische Mensch*, Tübingen, 1953. Appendix, pp. 143-71; 'Die hebräische Rechtsgemeinde'.
J. van der Ploeg, 'Les šōṭerim d'Israél, in *Oudtestamentische Studiën*, X, 1954, 185-96.
W. Helck, 'Das Dekret des Königs Haremhab', in *Zeitschrift für Aegyptische Sprache und Altertumskunde*, LXXX, 1955, 109-36.
A. Falkenstein, *Die neusumerischen Gerichtsurkunden* (Bayerische Akademie der Wissenschaften, Phil.-Hist. Klasse, Abhandlungen, N.F. 39), Munich, 1956.
E. Seidl, *Aegyptische Rechtsgeschichte der Saiten- und Perserzeit*, Gluckstadt-Hamburg, 1956.
H. Klengel, 'Zu den šibūtum in alt-babylonischer Zeit', in *Orientalia*, XXIX, 1960, 357-75.

On procedure:

L. Köhler, *Deuterojesaja stilkritisch untersucht* (Supplement to *ZAW*, 37), Giessen, 1923, 110-20.
H. Liebesny, 'Evidence in Nuzi Legal Procedure', in *JAOS*, LXI, 1941, 130-42.
B. Gemser, 'The Rîb-Pattern in Hebrew Mentality', in *Wisdom in Israel and in the Ancient Near East—Rowley Volume* (Supplement III to *VT*, 1955, 120-37).
D. Daube, 'Rechtsgedanken in der Erzählungen des Pentateuchs', in *Von Ugarit nach Qumran* (*Festschrift Eissfeldt*), Berlin, 1958, 32-41.
H. D. Huffman, 'The Covenant Lawsuit in the Prophets', in *JBL*, LXXVIII, 1959, 285-95.

On the judgment of God:

R. Press, 'Ordal im alten Israel', in *ZAW*, LI, 1933, 121-40; 227-55.
C. H. Gordon, 'Elohim in its Reputed Meaning of Rulers, Judges', in *JBL*, LIV, 1935, 139-44.
G. R. Driver and J. C. Miles, 'The Assyrian Laws', Oxford, 1935, 86-106.
G. Dossin, 'Un cas d'ordalie par le dieu Fleuve d'après une lettre de Mari', in *Symbolae* . . . *P. Koschaker dedicatae*, Leyden, 1939, 112-18.
G. R. Driver and J. C. Miles, *The Babylonian Laws*, I, Oxford, 1952, 63-5.
G. R. Driver and J. C. Miles, 'Ordeal by Oath at Nuzi', in *Iraq*, VII, 1940, 132-8.
A. Speiser, 'Nuzi Marginalia', in *Orientalia*, XXV, 1956, 15-23.
A. E. Draffkorn, 'Ilâni Elohim', in *JBL*, LXXVI, 1957, 216-24.
F. C. Fensham, 'New Light on Ex 21: 6 and 22: 7 from the Laws of Eshnunna', in *JBL*, LXXVIII, 1959, 160-1.
G. Dossin, 'L'ordalie à Mari', in *Comptes-rendus de l'Académie des Inscriptions et Belles Lettres* (Paris) 1958, 387-92.

On penalties:

Little exists apart from dictionaries and general works:

R. Sugranyes de Franch, *Etudes sur le droit palestinien à l'époque évangelique. La contrainte par corps*, Fribourg (Switzerland), 1946.
J. Gabriel, 'Die Todesstrafe im Licht des Alten Testaments', in *Theologische Fragen der Gegenwart*, Vienna, 1952, 69-79.

On the cities of refuge:

N. H. Nicolsky, 'Das Asylrecht in Israel', in *ZAW*, XLVIII, 1930, 146-75.
M. Löhr, *Das Asylwesen im Alten Testament*, Halle, 1930.
M. David, 'Die Bestimmungen über die Asylstädte in Josue XX', in *Oudtestamentische Studiën*, IX 1951, 30-48.

B. DINUR, 'The Religious Character of the Cities of Refuge and the Ceremony of Admission into them', in *Eretz-Israel*, III, 1954, 135-46 (in Hebrew, with English summary).
M. GREENBERG, 'The Biblical Conception of Asylum', in *JBL*, LXXVIII, 1959, 125-32.

11

ECONOMIC LIFE

On landed property:

G. DALMAN, *Arbeit und Sitte in Palästina*, II, *Der Ackerbau*, Gütersloh, 1932, 36-46.
R. CLAY, *The Tenure of Land in Babylonia and Assyria*, London, 1938.
H. LEWY, 'The Nuzian Feudal System', in *Orientalia*, XI, 1942, 1-40; 209-50; 297-349.
F. R. STEELE, *Nuzi Real Estate Transactions*, New Haven, 1943.
H. BUCKERS, *Die Biblische Lehre von Eigentum*, Bonn, 1947.
E. MARMORSTEIN, 'The Origin of Agricultural Feudalism in the Holy Land', in *PEQ*, 1953, 111-17.
K. H. HENRY, 'Land Tenure in the Old Testament', in *PEQ*, 1954, 5-15.
A. ALT, 'Der Anteil des Königstums an der sozialen Entwicklung in den Reichen Israel und Juda', in *Kleine Schriften*, III, Munich, 1959, 348-72.

On the formalities of transfer:

L. FISCHER, 'Die Urkunden in Jer. 32, 11-14 nach den Ausgrabungen und dem Talmud', in *ZAW*, XXX, 1910, 136-42.
L. WENGER, 'Signum (Doppelurkunden)', in PAULY-WISSOWA, *Real-Encyclopädie der classischen Altertumswissenschaft*, II, II, 1923, col. 2408-30.
E. R. LACHMAN, 'Note on Ruth 4, 7-8', in *JBL*, LVI, 1937, 53-6.
E. A. SPEISER, 'Of Shoes and Shekels', in *BASOR*, 77, February 1940, 15-18.

On interest:

J. HEJCL, *Das alttestamentliche Zinsverbot (Biblische Studien*, XII, 4), Freiburg i.Br., 1907.
S. STEIN, 'The Laws of Interest in the Old Testament', in *JTS*, n.s. IV, 1953, 161-70.
E. NEUFELD, 'The Rate of Interest and the Text of Nehemiah 5. 11', in *JQR*, n.s. XLIV, 1953-4, 194-204.
E. SZLECHTER, 'Le prêt dans l'Ancien Testament et dans les codes mésopotamiens d'avant Hammourabi', in *RHPR*, XXXV, 1955, 16-25.

On pledges and sureties:

P. KOSCHAKER, *Babylonisch-assyrisches Bürgschaftsrecht*, Leipzig, 1911.
A. ABELES, 'Der Bürge nach Biblischen Recht', in *Monatsschrift für Geschichte und Wissenschaft das Judentums*, LXVI, 1922, 279-94; LXVII, 1923, 35-53.
E. M. CASSIN, 'La caution à Nuzi', in *Revue d'Assyriologie*, XXXIV, 1937, 154-68.
H. M. WEIL, 'Gage et cautionnement dans la Bible', in *Archives d'Histoire du Droit Oriental*, II, 1938, 171-240.
H. M. WEIL, 'Exégèse de Jérémie 23, 33-40 et de Job 34, 28-33', in *Revue de l'Histoire des Religions*, CXVIII, 1938, 201-8.
M. DAVID, 'Deux anciens termes bibliques pour le gage', in *Oudtestamentische Studiën*, II, 1943, 79-86.

On the sabbatical and jubilee years:

C. H. GORDON, 'Parallèles nouziens aux lois et coutumes de l'Ancien Testament', in *RB*, XLIV, 1935, 38-41.
J. B. ALEXANDER, 'A Babylonian Year of Jubilee?' in *JBL*, LVII, 1938, 75-9.
V. TSCHERIKOWER and F. M. HEICHELHEIM, 'Jewish Religious Influence in the Adler Papyri', in *HTR*, XXV, 1942, 25-44.
M. DAVID, 'The Manumission of Slaves under Zedekiah', in *Oudtestamentische Studiën*, V, 1948, 63-79.
F. M. LEMOINE, 'Le jubilé dans la Bible', in *Vie Spirituelle*, LXXXI, 1949, 262-88.
G. LAMBERT, 'Jubilé biblique et jubilé chrétien', in *Nouvelle Revue Théologique*, LXXII, 1950, 234-51.
J. T. MILIK, 'De vicissitudinibus notionis et vocabuli jubilaei', in *Verbum Domini*, XXVIII, 1950, 162-7.
R. NORTH, 'Maccabean Sabbath Years', in *Biblica*, XXXIV, 1953, 505-15.
R. NORTH, 'Yad in the Shemittah Law', in *VT*, IV, 1954, 196-9.
R. NORTH, *Sociology of the Biblical Jubilee*, Rome, 1954.
J. LEWY, 'The Biblical Institution of Deror in the Light of Akkadian Documents', in *Eretz-Israel*, V (Volume Mazar), 1958, 21-31.
J. J. RABINOWITZ, 'A Biblical Parallel to a Legal Formula from Ugarit', in *VT*, VIII, 1958, 95.
E. NEUFELD, 'Socio-Economic Background of Yobel and Semiṭṭa', in *Rivista degli Studi Orientali*, XXXIII, 1958, 53-124.
D. CORRENS, *Die Mischna . . . , I, 5, Schebiit (Vom Sabbatjahr)*, Berlin, 1960.

12

DIVISIONS OF TIME

On the ancient Eastern calendars:

B. LANDSBERGER, Der kultischer Kalendar der Babylonier und Assyrer (Leipziger Semitische Studien, VI, 1-2), Leipzig, 1915

L. BORCHARDT, Die altägyptische Zeitmessung, Berlin, 1920.

R. W. SLOLEY, 'Primitive Methods of Measuring Time, with Special Reference to Egypt', in Journal of Egyptian Archaeology, XVII, 1931, 166-78.

S. LANGDON, Babylonian Menologies and the Semitic Calendars, London, 1935.

L. BORCHARDT, Das Mittel zur zeitlichen Festlegung von Punkten der ägyptischen Geschichte und ihre Anwendung, Cairo, 1935

C. H. GORDON and E. R. LACHEMAN, 'The Nuzu Menology', in Archiv Orientální, X, 1938, 51-64.

H. and J. LEWY, 'The Origin of the Week and the Oldest Asiatic Calendar', in HUCA, XVII, 1942-3, 1-155.

R. A. PARKER and W. H. DUBBERSTEIN, Babylonian Chronology, 626 B.C.-A.D. 45, Chicago, 2nd ed., 1946.

S. SCHOTT, Altagyptische Festdaten (Abhandlungen der Akademie der Wissenschaften und der Literatur in Mainz), Wiesbaden, 1950.

R. A. PARKER, The Calendars of Ancient Egypt, Chicago, 1950.

A. GARDINER, 'The Problems of the Month-Names', in Revue d'Égyptologie, X, 1955, 9-31.

M. HÖFNER, 'Die altsüdarabischen Monatsnamen', in Festschrift V. Christian, Vienna, 1956, 46-54.

On the Israelite day:

J. MORGENSTERN, 'Supplementary Studies in the Calendars of Ancient Israel', in HUCA, X, 1935, 15-28.

P. J. HEADWOOD, 'The Beginning of the Jewish Day', in JQR, n.s. XXXVI, 1945-6, 393-401.

S. ZEITLIN, 'The Beginning of the Jewish Day during the Second Commonwealth', in JQR, n.s. XXXVI, 1945-6, 403-14.

S. IWRY, 'The Qumran Isaiah and the End of the Dial of Achaz', in BASOR, 147, October 1957, 27-33.

Y. YADIN, 'The Dial of Achaz', in Eretz-Israel, V (Volume Mazar), 1958, 83-90 (in Hebrew with a summary in English).

J. M. BAUMGARTEN, 'The Beginning of the Day in the Calendar of Jubilees', in JBL, LXXVII, 1958, 355-60.

S. ZEITLIN, 'The Beginning of the Day in the Calendar of Jubilees', in JBL, LXXVIII, 1959, 153-6 (with a reply by Baumgarten, 157).

On the month and the week:

S. GANDZ, 'Studies in the Hebrew Calendar', in JQR, n.s. XXXIX, 1948-9, 259-80; LX, 1949-50, 157-72, 251-77.

N. H. TUR-SINAI, 'Sabbat und Woche', in Bibliotheca Orientalis, VIII, 1951, 14-24.

E. AUERBACH, 'Die babylonische Datierung im Pentateuch und das Alter des Priester-Kodex', in VT, II, 1952, 334-42.

A. JAUBERT, 'Le calendrier des Jubilés et de la secte de Qumrân. Ses origines bibliques', in VT, III, 1953, 250-64.

Y. KAUFMAN, 'Der Kalender und das Alter des Priester-Kodex', in VT, IV, 1954, 307-13.

J. MORGANSTERN, 'The Calendar of the Book of Jubilees, its Origin and its Character', in VT, V, 1955, 34-76.

A. JAUBERT, 'Le calendrier des Jubilés et les jours liturgiques de la semaine', in VT, VII, 1957, 35-61.

J. B. SEGAL, 'Intercalation and the Hebrew Calendar', in VT, VII, 1957, 250-307.

A. JAUBERT, Le date de la Cène. Calendrier biblique et liturgie chrétienne, Paris, 1957.

E. R. LEACH, 'A Possible Method of Intercalation in the Calendar of the Book of Jubilees', in VT, VII, 1957, 392-9.

S. TALMON, 'Divergences in Calendar Reckoning in Ephraim and Juda', in VT, VIII, 1958, 48-74.

S. TALMON, 'The Calendar Reckoning of the Sect from the Judaean Desert', in Aspects of the Dead Sea Scrolls (Scripta Hierosolymitana, IV), Jerusalem, 1958, 161-99.

A. JAUBERT, 'Jésus et le calendrier de Qumrân', in New Testament Studies, VII, 1960-1, 1-30.

E. KUTSCH, 'Der Kalender des Jubiläenbuches und das Alte und das Neue Testament', in VT, XI, 1961, 39-47.

On the year and its beginning: the eras:

J. BEGRICH, Die Chronologie der Könige von Israel und Juda, Tübingen, 1929, 66-94.

J. A. MONTGOMERY, 'The Year-Eponymate in the Hebrew Monarchy', in JBL, XLIX, 1930, 311-19.

J. MORGENSTERN, 'The New Year for Kings', in Gaster Anniversary Volume, London, 1936, 439-56.

N. H. SNAITH, The Jewish New Year Festival, its Origin and Development, London, 1947.

J. MORGENSTERN, 'The Chanukkah Festival and the Calendar of Ancient Israel.—The History of the Calendar of Israel during the Biblical Period', in *HUCA*, XXI, 1948, 365-496, with references to many of the author's previous works.

E. R. THIELE, *The Mysterious Numbers of the Hebrew Kings*, Chicago, 1951, 14-41.

S. MOWINCKEL, *Zum israelitischen Neujahr und zur Deutung der Thronbesteigungspsalmen*, Oslo, 1952, 5-38.

S. H. HORN and L. H. WOOD, 'The Fifth Century Jewish Calendar in Elephantine', in *JNES*, XIII, 1954, 623-46.

S. GANDZ, 'The Calendar of Ancient Israel', in *Homenaje Millás Vallícroza*, I, 1954, 1-20.

J. SCHAUMBERGER, 'Die neue Seleukidenliste BM 35603 und die makkabäische Chronologie', in *Biblica*, XXXVI, 1955, 423-5.

E. R. THIELE, 'New Evidence on the Chronology of the Last Kings of Judah', in *BASOR*, 143, 1956, 22-7.

E. AUERBACH, 'Der Wechsel des Jahres-Anfangs in Juda', in *VT*, IX, 1959, 113-21.

E. AUERBACH, 'Die Umschaltung vom judäischen auf dem babylonischen Kalendar', in *VT*, X, 1960, 69-70.

13

WEIGHTS AND MEASURES

On metrology:

A. G. BARROIS, 'La métrologie dans la Bible', in *RB*, XL, 1931, 185-213; XLI, 1932, 50-76. Summarized with some modifications in *The Interpreter's Bible*, I, New York, 1952, 152-7, and in *Manuel d'Archéologie Biblique*, II, Paris, 1953, 243-58.

H. LEWY, 'Assyro-Babylonian and Israelite Measures of Capacity and Rates of Seeding', in *JAOS*, LXIV, 1944, 65-73.

A. SEGRÈ, 'A Documentary Analysis of Ancient Palestine Units of Measure', in *JBL*, LXIV, 1945, 357-75.

C. C. WYLIE, 'On King Solomon's Molten Sea', in *Biblical Archaeologist*, XII, 1949, 86-90.

O. EISSFELDT, 'Die Menetekel-Inschrift und ihre Deutung (Dn 5 25)', in *ZAW*, LXIII, 1951, 105-14.

B. N. WAMBACQ, 'De 'ponderibus in S. Scriptura', in *Verbum Domini*, XXIX, 1951, 341-50.

O. TUFNELL, *Lachish III, The Iron Age*, London, 1953, 313-15 and 340-57.

N. AVIGAD, 'Another bath le-melekh Inscription', in *IEJ*, III, 1953, 121-2.

B. N. WAMBACQ, 'De mensuris in S. Scriptura', in *Verbum Domini*, XXXII, 1954, 266-74; 325-34.

H. OTTEN, 'Zum Hethitischen Gewichtsystem', in *AfO*, XVII, 1954-6, 128-31.

J. TRINQUET, 'Métrologie biblique', in *Supplément au Dictionnaire de la Bible*, V, Paris, 1957, col. 1212-50, with detailed bibliography.

R. B. Y. SCOTT, 'The Hebrew Cubit', in *JBL*, LXXVII, 1958, 295-14.

A. I. LEBOWITZ, 'A Note on R. B. Y. Scott's "The Hebrew Cubit"', in *JBL*, LXXVIII, 1959, 75-7.

R. B. Y. SCOTT, 'The Shekel Sign on Stone Weights', in *BASOR*, 153, February 1959, 32-5.

N. GLUECK, 'A Seal Weight from Nebi Rubin', in *BASOR*, 153, February, 1959, 35-8.

R. B. Y. SCOTT, 'Weights and Measures of the Bible', in *Biblical Archaeologist*, XXII, 1959, 22-40.

J. T. MILIK, 'Deux jarres inscrites provenant d'une grotte de Qumrân', in *Biblica*, XL, 1959, 985-91.

R. B. Y. SCOTT, 'Postscript on the Cubit', in *JBL*, LXXIX, 1960, 368.

Y. YADIN, 'Ancient Judaean Weights and the Date of the Samaria Ostraca', in *Studies in the Bible* (Studia Hierosolymitana, VIII), 1960, 1-17.

On coinage:

J. BABELON, 'Monnaie', in *Supplément au Dictionnaire de la Bible*, V, Paris, 1957, col. 1346-75, with long bibliography.

Consult also:

A. REIFENBERG, *Ancient Jewish Coins*, Jerusalem, 2nd ed., 1947.

B. KANAEL, 'The Beginning of Maccabean Coinage', in *IEJ*, I, 1950-1, 170-5.

A. REIFENBERG, *Israel's History in Coins from the Maccabees to the Roman Conquest*.

D. SCHLUMBERGER, *L'argent grec dans l'empire achéménide*, Paris, 1953.

L. KADMAN, 'A Coin Find at Masada', in *IEJ*, VII, 1957, 61-5.

Publications of the Israel Numismatic Society, I. Recent Studies and Discoveries in Ancient Jewish and Syrian Coins, Jerusalem, 1954.

Publications of the Israel Numismatic Society, II. The Dating and Meaning of Ancient Jewish Coins and Symbols, Jerusalem, 1958.

B. N. WAMBACQ, 'De Nummis in Sacra Scriptura', in *Verbum Domini*, XXXVIII, 1960, 156-72.

L. KADMAN, *The Coins of the Jewish War of 66-73 (Corpus Nummorum Palestinensium, III)*, Jerusalem, 1960.

III

MILITARY INSTITUTIONS

I

THE ARMIES OF ISRAEL

On armies in the Ancient Near East:

B. MEISSNER, *Babylonien und Assyrien*, I, Heidelberg, 1920, 80-114.
O. R. GURNEY, *The Hittites*, London, 1952, 104-16.
R. O. FAULKNER, 'Egyptian Military Organization', in *Journal of Egyptian Archaeology*, XXXIX, 1953, 32-47.

On the people under arms:

S. TOLKOWSKY, 'Gideon's 300', in *JPOS*, V, 1925, 69-74.
Y. SUKENIK (YADIN), 'Let the young men, I pray thee, arise and play before us', in *JPOS*, XXI, 1948, 110-16.
F. M. ABEL, 'Stratagèmes dans le livre de Josué', in *RB*, LVI, 1949, 321-39.
A. MALAMAT, 'The War of Gideon and Midian. A Military Approach', in *PEQ*, 1953, 61-5.
G. E. MENDENHALL, 'The Census Lists of Numbers 1 and 26', in *JBL*, LXXVII, 1958, 52-66.
R. DE VAUX, 'Les combats singuliers dans l'Ancien Testament', in *Studia Biblica et Orientalia*, I. *Vetus Testamentum*, Rome, 1959, 361-74= *Biblica*, XL, 1959, 495-508.

On the professional army:

(a) Mercenary troops:

K. ELLIGER, 'Die dreissig Helden Davids', in *PJB*, XXXI, 1935, 29-75.
J. VAN DER PLOEG, 'Le sens de *gibbôr ḥail*', in *Vivre et Penser*, I (*Revue Biblique*, L), 1941, 120-5.
F. WILLESEN, 'The *Yālīd* in Hebrew Society', in *Studia Theologica*, XII, 1958, 192-210.

(b) The chariot force:

M. LÖHR, 'Aegyptische Reiterei im Alten Testament?', in *Orientalistische Literaturzeitung*, XXXI, 1928, 923-8.
A. MOORTGAT, 'Der Kampf zu Wagen in der Kunst des alten Orients', in *Orientalistische Literaturzeitung*, XXXIII, 1930, 842-54.
W. F. ALBRIGHT, 'Mitannian maryannu "Charriot-Warrior" and the Canaanite and Egyptian Equivalents', in *AfO*, VI, 1930-1, 217-22.
J. WIESNER, 'Fahren und Reiten in Alteuropa und im Alten Orient' (*Der Alte Orient*, XXXVIII, 2-4), Leipzig, 1939.
R. T. O'CALLAGHAN, 'New Light on the Maryannu as "Charriot-Warrior"', in *Jahrbuch für kleinasiatische Forschung*, I, 1950-1, 309-21.
A. SALONEN, 'Die Landsfahrzeuge des alten Mesopotamien' (*Annales Acad. Scient. Fennicae*, ser. B, 72/73), Helsinki, 1951.
H. VON DEINES, 'Die Nachrichten über das Pferd und den Wagen in den ägyptischen Texten', in *Mitteilungen des Instituts für Orientforschung* (Berlin), I, 1953, 3-15.
A. ALT, 'Bemerkungen zu den Verwaltungs- und Rechtsurkunden von Ugarit und Alalakh', in *Die Welt des Orients*, II, 1, 1954, 10-15; II, 4, 1956, 234-7.
F. HANČAR, *Das Pferd in prähistorischer und früher historischer Zeit*, Vienna, 1956, 472-535.
A. SALONEN, 'Hippologica Akkadica' (*Annales Acad. Scient. Fennicae*, ser B, 100), Helsinki, 1956.
A. R. SCHULMAN, 'Egyptian Representations of Horsemen and Riding in the New Kingdom', in *JNES*, XVI, 1957, 263-71.

On the conscript army:

B. GRAY, 'The meaning of the Hebrew Word *dègèl*', in *JQR*, XI, 1899, 92-101.
E. JUNGE, *Der Wiederaufbau des Heerwesens des Reiches Juda unter Josia*, Stuttgart, 1937.
R. O. FAULKNER, 'Egyptian Military Standards', in *Journal of Egyptian Archaeology*, XXVII, 1941, 12-18.
Y. YADIN, 'The reorganization of the Army of Judah under Josiah', in *BJPES*, XV, 1949-50, 86-98 (in Hebrew).
J. R. KUPPER, 'Le recensement dans les textes de Mari', in A. PARROT, *Studia Mariana*, Leiden, 1950, 99-110.
J. VAN DER PLOEG, 'Les *šoterim* d'Israël', in *Oudtestamentische Studiën*, X, 1954, 185-96.
E. A. SPEISER, 'Census and Ritual Expiation in Mari and Israel', in *BASOR*, 149, 1958, 17-25.

2
FORTIFIED CITIES AND SIEGE WARFARE

On the fortified cities of Israel:

G. BEYER, 'Das Festungssystem Rehabeams', in *ZDPV*, LIV, 1931, 113-34.
E. JUNGE, *Der Wiederaufbau des Heerwesens des Reiches Juda unter Josia*, Stuttgart, 1937, 60-73.
A. ALT, 'Festungen und Levitenorte im Lande Juda', in *Kleine Schriften*, II, Munich, 1953, 306-15.

On fortifications:

The main source of information is archaeology, cf. A. G. BARROIS, *Manuel d'Archéologie Biblique*, I, Paris, 1939, ch. IV: 'La fortification'.

In addition, recent reports:

R. S. LAMON and G. M. SHIPTON, *Megiddo I*, Chicago, 1939, 28-32; 74-83.
W. F. ALBRIGHT, 'The Excavations of Tell Beit Mirsim', III (*Annual of the American Schools of Oriental Research*, XXI-XXII), New Haven, 1943, §§ 5-8; 26-31.
C. C. MCCOWN, *Tell en-Naṣbeh*, I, Berkeley, 1947, 182-205.
G. LOUD, *Megiddo II*, Chicago, 1948, 46-57.
B. MAISLER, *The Excavations at Tell Qasîle. Preliminary Report*, Jerusalem, 1951, 39-41 = *IEJ*, I, 1950-1, 200-2.
O. TUFNELL, *Lachish III. The Iron Age*, London, 1953, 87-102.
Y. AHARONI, 'Excavations at Rameth Raḥel', in *IEJ*, VI, 1956, 138-41.
Y. YADIN, 'Solomon's City Wall and Gate at Gezer', in *IEJ*, VIII, 1958, 80-6.

In addition:

J. SIMONS, 'Topographical and Archaeological Elements in the Story of Abimelech', in *Oudtestamentische Studiën*, II, 1943, 35-78.
L. KÖHLER, *Kleine Lichter*, Zürich, 1945, 6. 'Wohnturm statt Palast', 30-32.
Y. AHARONI, 'The Date of the Casemate Walls in Judah and Israel and their Purpose', in *BASOR*, 154, 1959, 35-9.
Y. YADIN, *Hazor, I: An Account of the First Season of Excavations*, 1955, Jerusalem, 1958.
L. A. SINCLAIR, 'An Archaeological Study of Gibeah (Tell el-Ful)', in *AASOR*, XXXIV-XXXV, 1954-6 (1960), 1-52.

On siege warfare:

R. P. DOUGHERTY, 'Sennacherib and the Walled Cities of Palestine', in *JBL*, XLIX, 1930, 160-71.
Y. SUKENIK (YADIN), '"Engines invented by Skilful Men" (2 Ch 26: 15)', in *BJPES*, XIII, 1946-7, 19-24 (in Hebrew).

On the water supply:

The archaeological information and bibliographical references can be found in A. G. BARROIS, *Manuel d'Archéologie Biblique*, I, Paris, 1939, ch. V: 'Installations hydrauliques'.

In addition:

O. TUFNELL, *Lachish III. The Iron Age*, London, 1953, 92-3 and 158-63.
J. B. PRITCHARD, 'The Water System at Gibeon', in *The Biblical Archaeologist*, XIX, 1956, 66-75.

3
ARMAMENTS

H. BONNET, *Die Waffen der Völker des Alten Orients*, Leipzig, 1926.
E. A. SPEISER, 'On Some Articles of Armor and their Names', in *JAOS*, LXX, 1950, 47-9.
J. T. MILIK and F. M. CROSS, 'Inscribed Javelin-Heads from the Period of the Judges', in *BASOR*, 134, 1954, 5-15.
O. EISSFELDT, 'Zwei verkannte militär-technische Termini', in *VT*, V, 1955, 232-8.
Y. YADIN, 'Goliath's Javelin and the *meꞵôr 'orgîm*', in *PEQ*, 1955, 58-69.
Y. YADIN, *The Scroll of the War of the Sons of Light against the Sons of Darkness*, Jerusalem 1956 (in Hebrew).
J. T. MILIK, 'An Unpublished Arrow-Head with Phoenician Inscription of the 11th-10th Century B.C.', in *BASOR*, 143, 3-6.
F. M. CROSS and J. T. MILIK, 'A Typological Study of the El Khadr Javelin- and Arrow-Heads', in *Annual of the Department of Antiquities of Jordan*, III, 1956, 15-23.
G. MOLIN, 'What is a Kidon?', in *Journal of Semitic Studies*, I, 1956, 334-7.
F. WILLESEN, 'The Philistine Corps of the Scimitar of Gath', in *Journal of Semitic Studies*, III, 1958, 327-35.

4

WAR

On the wars of Israel:
See the various histories of Israel, and add:

F. M. Abel, 'Topographie des campagnes maccabéennes', in *RB*, XXXII, 1923, 495-521; XXXIII, 1924, 201-17, 371-87; XXXIV, 1925, 194-216; XXXV, 1926, 206-22, 510-33.

G. E. Wright, 'The Literary and Historical Problem of Joshua 10 and Judges 1', in *JNES*, V, 1946, 105-14.

A. Malamat, 'The Last Wars of the Kingdom of Juda', in *JNES*, IX, 1950, 105-14.

A. Malamat, 'Introduction à l'histoire militaire d'Israël', in *Athidôt*, IV, 12, 1951, 1-11 (in Hebrew).

On the conduct of war:

S. B. Finesinger, 'The Shofar', in *HUCA*, VIII-IX, 1931-2, 193-228.

G. Dossin, 'Signaux lumineux au pays de Mari', in *Revue d'Assyriologie*, XXXV, 1938, 174-86.

P. Humbert, *La 'terou'a'. Analyse d'un rite biblique*, Neuchâtel, 1946.

S. Yeivin, 'Canaanite and Hittite Strategy in the Second Half of the Second Millenary B.C.', in *JNES*, IX, 1950, 101-7.

Y. Yadin, 'Some Aspects of the Strategy of Achab and David', in *Biblica*, XXXVI, 1955, 322-51.

A. Malamat, 'Military Rationing in Papyrus Anastasi I and the Bible', in *Mélanges Bibliques rédigés en l'honneur de André Robert*, Paris, 1957, 114-21.

On the consequences of war:

W. J. Martin, 'Tribut und Tributleistungen bei den Assyrern' (*Studia Orientalia*, VIII, 1), Helsinki, 1936.

H. Kruse, 'Ethos Victoriae in Vetere Testamento', in *Verbum Domini*, XXX, 1952, 3-13, 65-80, 143-53.

A. Aymard, 'Le partage des profits de la guerre dans les traités d'alliance antiques', in *Revue Historique*, CCXVII, 1957, 233-49.

M. Noth, 'Das alttestamentliche Bundschliessen im Lichte eines Mari-Textes', in *Mélanges Isidore Lévy*, Brussels, 1955, 433-44 = *Gesammelte Studien zum Alten Testament*, Munich, 1957, 142-54.

5

THE HOLY WAR

F. Schwally, *Semitische Kriegsaltertümer*. I, *Der heilige Kreig im alten Israel*, Leipzig, 1901.

E. Bickermann, *Der Gott der Makkabäer*, Berlin, 1937.

H. Fredriksson, *Jahwe als Krieger*, Lund, 1945.

P. Humbert, *La 'terou'a'. L'épithète divine Jahvé Seba'ot*, Neuchâtel, 1946

B. N. Wambacq, *L'épithète divine Jahvé Seba'ot*, Bruges, 1948.

O. Eissfeldt, 'Jahwe Zebaoth', in *Miscellanea Academica Berolinensia*, Berlin, 1950, 128-50.

H. Kruse, 'Conceptus interdicti in Levitico 27: 28-29', in *Verbum Domini*, XXVIII, 1950, 43-50.

G. von Rad, *Der Heilige Krieg im alten Israel*, Zürich, 1951.

Y. Yadin, *The Scroll of the War of the Sons of Light against the Sons of Darkness*, Jerusalem, 1955 (in Hebrew).

A. Dupont-Sommer, '"Règlement de la Guerre des Fils de Lumière", traduction et notes', in *Revue de l'Histoire des Religions*, CXLVIII, 1955-II, 25-43, 141-80.

G. von Rad, 'The Origin of the Concept of the Day of Yahweh', in *Journal of Semitic Studies*, IV, 1956, 97-108.

J. van der Ploeg, 'La guerre sainte dans la "Règle de la Guerre" de Qumrân', in *Mélanges Bibliques rédigés en l'honneur de André Robert*, Paris, 1957, 326-33.

J. Carmignac, *La Règle de la Guerre des Fils de Lumière contre les Fils de Ténèbres*, Paris, 1958.

J. van der Ploeg, 'Le Rouleau de la Guerre', translated and annotated with an introduction (*Studies on the Texts of the Desert of Judah*, II), Leiden, 1959.

C. H. W. Brekelmann, *De herem in het Oude Testament*, Nijmegen, 1959.

IV

RELIGIOUS INSTITUTIONS

INTRODUCTORY

See, in addition to works on biblical theology:

W. Zimmerli, 'Das zweite Gebot', in *Festschrift Bertholet*, Tübingen, 1950, 550-63.

S. Mowinckel, *Religion und Kultus*, Göttingen, 1953.
K. H. Bernhardt, *Gott und Bild*, Berlin, 1956.
J. Hempel, *Das Bild in Bibel und Gottesdienst*, Tübingen, 1957.
C. R. North, 'The Essence of Idolatry', in *Von Ugarit nach Qumran (Festschrift Eissfeldt)*, Berlin, 1958, 151-60.
S. H. Hooke (ed.), *Myth, Ritual and Kingship*, Oxford, 1958, especially the essay by G. Widengren, 'Early Hebrew Myths and their Interpretation', 149-203.
A. S. Herbert, *Worship in Ancient Israel*, London, 1959.

I

Semitic Sanctuaries

On the sacred territory and its privileges:

M.-J. Lagrange, *Études sur les religions sémitiques²*, Paris, 1905, 180-7.
G. Dalman, 'Der Gilgal der Bibel und die Steinkreise Palästinas', in *PJB*, XV, 1919, 5-30.
M. Gaudefroy-Demombynes, *Le pèlerinage à La Mekke*, Paris, 1923.
T. Canaan, *Mohammedan Saints and Sanctuaries*, London, 1927.
J. d'A. Waechter, 'The Excavations at Wadi Dhobaï', in *JPOS*, XVIII, 1938, p. 174, pl. XLIII.

On waters, trees and heights with a sacred character:

W. W. Baudissin, 'Heilige Gewässer, Bäume und Höhen bei den Semiten, insbesondere bei den Hebräern', in his *Studien zur semitischen Religionsgeschichte*, II, Leipzig, 1878, 145-269.
M.-J. Lagrange, *Études sur les religions sémitiques²*, Paris, 1905, 158-80.
H. Danthine, *Le palmier-dattier et les arbres sacrés dans l'iconographie de l'Asie Occidentale ancienne*, Paris, 1937.
N. Perrot, *Les représentations de l'arbre sacré sur les monuments de Mésopotamie et d'Élam*, Paris, 1937.

On Saphon:

J. Jeremias, *Der Gottesberg*, Gütersloh, 1919.
O. Eissfeldt, *Baal Zaphon, Zeus Casios und der Durchzug der Israeliten durchs Meer*, Halle, 1932.
B. Alfrink, 'Der Versammlungsberg in äussersten Norden', in *Biblica*, XIV, 1933, 41-57.
R. de Langhe, *Les Textes de Ras-Shamra-Ugarit et leurs Rapports avec le Milieu Biblique de l'Ancien Testament*, Gembloux, 1945, II, 217-45.
W. F. Albright, 'Baal-Zaphon', in *Festschrift Bertholet*, Tübingen, 1950, 1-14.

On Hermon:

R. Mouterde, 'Antiquités de l'Hermon et de la Beqā'', in *Mélanges de l'Université S. Joseph* (Beirut), XXIX, 1951-3, 22-37.

On Thabor:

O. Eissfeldt, 'Der Gott Tabor und seine Verbreitung', in *Archiv für Religionswissenschaft*, XXXI, 1934, 14-41.
J. Boehmer, 'Der Gottesberg Tabor', in *Biblische Zeitschrift*, XXIII, 1935-6, 333-41.
J. Lewy, 'Tabor, Tibar, Atabyros', in *HUCA*, XXIII, 1, 1950-1, 357-86.

On Carmel:

R. de Vaux, 'Les prophètes de Baal sur le mont Carmel', in *Bulletin du Musée de Beyrouth*, V, 1941, 7-20.
M. Avi-Yonah, 'Mount Carmel and the God of Baalbek', in *IEJ*, II, 1952, 118-24.
K. Galling, 'Der Gott Karmel und die Ächtung der fremden Götter', in *Geschichte und Altes Testament (Festschrift Alt)*, Tübingen, 1953, 105-25.
O. Eissfeldt, 'Der Gott Karmel' (*Sitzungsberichte der deutschen Akademie*, Berlin), 1953.
H. H. Rowley, 'Elijah on Mount Carmel', in *BJRL*, XLIII, 1960-1, 190-210.

On ziggurats:

Th. Dombart, 'Der babylonische Turm' (*Der Alte Orient*, XXIX, 2), Leipzig, 1930.
W. Andrae, *Das Gotteshaus und die Urformen des Bauens im Alten Orient*, Berlin, 1930.
H. J. Lenzen, 'Die Entwicklung der Ziggurat von ihren Anfängen bis zur Zeit der II. Dynastie von Ur' (*Ausgrabungen in Uruk-Warka*, IV), Leipzig, 1941.
L.-H. Vincent, 'De la Tour de Babel au Temple', in *RB*, LIII, 1946, 403-40.
A. Parrot, *Ziggurats et Tour de Babel*, Paris, 1949.
A. Parrot, *La Tour de Babel*, Neuchâtel-Paris, 1953.
P. Amiet, 'Ziggurats et culte en hauteur', in *Revue d'Assyriologie*, XLVIII, 1953, 23-33.
R. Ghirshman, 'Cinquième campagne de fouilles à Tchoga-Zanbil, près Suse', in *Comptes Rendus de l'Académie des Inscriptions* (Paris), 1956, 335-44.

On temples:

W. ANDRAE, *Das Gotteshaus und die Urformen des Bauens im Alten Orient*, Berlin, 1930.
W. ANDRAE, 'Kultbau im Alten Orient', in *Mélanges Syriens offerts à M. R. Dussaud*, II, Paris, 1939, 867-71.
H. H. NELSON, L. OPPENHEIM, G. E. WRIGHT, "The Significance of the Temple in the Ancient Near East', in *The Biblical Archaeologist*, VII, 1944, 41-63, 66-77.
M. AVI-YONAH and S. YEIVIN, *The Antiquities of Israel* (in Hebrew), I, Tel-Aviv, 1955, ch. II: 'Places of Worship and Sanctuaries', 145-204.

On the cult of the 'high places':

H. INGHOLT, 'Le sens du mot ḥammân', in *Mélanges Syriens offerts à M. R. Dussaud*, II, Paris, 1939, 795-802.
K. ELLIGER, 'Chammânim—Masseben?', in *ZAW*, LVII, 1939, 256-65.
W. F. ALBRIGHT, *Archaeology and the Religion of Israel*, Baltimore, 1942, 105-7, 202-4.
K. ELLIGER, 'Der Sinn des Worthes Chammân', in *ZDPV*, LXVI, 1943, 129-39.
G. LOUD, *Megiddo II*, Chicago, 1948, 73-81.
L.-H. VINCENT, 'La notion biblique du haut lieu', in *RB*, LV, 1948, 245-78, 438-45.
D. NEIMAN, 'Pgr, A Canaanite Cult-Object in the Old Testament', in *JBL*, LXVII, 1948, 55-60.
C. C. McCOWN, 'Hebrew High-Places and Cult Remains', in *JBL*, LXIX, 1950, 205-19.
R. AMIRAN, 'Excavations in the Tumuli West of Jerusalem', in *Bulletin of the Israel Exploration Society*, XVIII, 1954, 44-59 (in Hebrew, with a summary in English).
S. YEIVIN, art. '*bamah*', in *Encyclopaedia Biblica* (in Hebrew), II, Jerusalem, 1954.
F. HVIDBERG, 'The Massebah and the Holy Seed (Is 6: 13)', in *Interpretationes ad Vetus Testamentum pertinentes (Festschrift Mowinckel)*, Oslo, 1955, 96-9.
M. DOTHAN, 'Excavations at Nahariyah', in *IEJ*, VI, 1956, 14-25.
A. DUPONT-SOMMER, 'Les autels à encens de Lakish', in *Mélanges Isidore Lévy (Annuaire de l'Institut de Philologie et d'Histoire Orientales et Slaves*, XIII), 1955, 135-52.
W. F. ALBRIGHT, 'The High Place in Ancient Palestine', in *Volume du Congrès, Strasbourg* (Supplement to VT IV), Leiden, 1957, 242-58.
S. IWRY, 'Massebāh and Bāmāh in 1Q Isaiah^A 6: 13', in *JBL*, LXXVI, 1957, 225-32.
R. AMIRAN, 'The Tumuli West of Jerusalem', in *IEJ*, VIII, 1958, 205-27.

2

THE FIRST ISRAELITE SANCTUARIES

Two monographs, both old and insufficient:

A. VON GALL, *Altisraelitische Kultstätten*, Giessen, 1898
G. WESTPHAL, *Jahwes Wohnstätten nach den Anschuungen der alten Hebräer*, Giessen, 1908.

On Shechem:

A. ALT, 'Die Wallfahrt von Sichem nach Bethel', in his *Kleine Schriften*, I, Munich, 1953, 79-88.
E. NIELSEN, *Shechem, A Traditio-Historical Investigation*, Copenhagen, 1955.
C. A. KELLER, 'Über einige alttestamentliche Heiligtumslegendes, I, A. *Die Legenden um Sichem*', in *ZAW*, LXVII, 1955, 143-54.
W. HARRELSON, B. W. ANDERSON, G. E. WRIGHT, 'Shechem, "Navel of the Land"', in *The Biblical Archaeologist*, XX, 1957, 2-32.
J. T. MILIK, 'Le sanctuaire de Ba'al Berit à Sichem', in *RB*, LXVI, 1959, 560-2.

On Bethel:

O. EISSFELDT, 'Der Gott Bethel', in *Archiv für Religionswissenschaft*, XXVIII, 1930, 1-30.
J. P. HYATT, 'The Deity Bethel and the Old Testament', in *JAOS*, LIX, 1939, 81-98.
K. GALLING, 'Bethel und Gilgal', in *ZDPV*, LXVI, 1943, 140-55; LXVII, 1944-5, 21-45.
C. A. KELLER, 'Über einige alttestamentliche Heilgtumslegendes, I, C. Die Legende von Bethel', in *ZAW*, LXVII, 1955, 162-8.

On Mambre:

R. DE VAUX, art. 'Mambré', in *Dictionnaire de la Bible, Supplément*, V, 1957, 753-8.
E. MADER, *Mambre, Die Ergebnisse der Ausgrabungen im heiligen Bezirk Râmet el Ḥalîl in Südpalästina*, Freiburg i. Breisg., 1957.

On Beersheba:

W. ZIMMERLI, *Geschichte und Tradition von Beerseba im Alten Testament*, Giessen, 1932.

On the Tent and the Ark:

H. GRESSMANN, *Die Lade Jahves und das Allerheiligste des salomonischen Tempels*, Leipzig, 1920.

H. LAMMENS, 'Le culte des bétyles et les processions religieuses chez les Arabes pré-islamiques', in *BIFAO*, XVII, 1920, 39-101.

H. SCHMIDT, 'Kerubenthron und Lade', in *Eucharistèrion Gunkel*, I, Göttingen, 1923, 120-44.

H. G. MAY, 'The Ark—A Miniature Tempel', in *AJSL*, LII, 1935-6, 215-34.

H. INGHOLT, 'Inscriptions and Sculptures from Palmyra', in *Berytus*, III, 1936, 83-8.

H. DANTHINE, 'L'imagerie des trônes vides et des trônes porteurs de symboles dans le Proche Orient ancien', in *Mélanges Syriens offerts à M. R. Dussaud*, I, Paris, 1939, 857-66.

O. EISSFELDT, 'Lade und Stierbild', in *ZAW*, LVIII, 1940-1, 190-215.

J. MORGENSTERN, 'The Ark, the Ephod and the "Tent of Meeting"', in *HUCA*, XVII, 1942-3, 153-266; XVIII, 1943-4, 1-52.

F. M. CROSS, 'The Tabernacle', in *The Biblical Archaeologist*, X, 1947, 45-68.

A. BENTZEN, 'The Cultic Use of the Story of the Ark in Samuel', in *JBL*, LXVII, 1948, 37-53.

A. KUSCHKE, 'Die Lagervorstellung der priesterlichen Erzählung', in *ZAW*, LXII, 1951, 74-105.

J. JOMIER, *Le Mahmal et la caravane égyptienne du pèlerinage de la Mecque*, Le Caire, 1953.

CH. PICARD, 'Le trône vide d'Alexandre dans la cérémonie de Cyinda et le culte du trône vide à travers le monde gréco-romain', in *Cahiers Archéologiques*, VII, 1954, 1-17.

M. HARAN, 'The Ark of the Covenant and the Cherubs', in *Eretz-Israel*, V (*Volume Mazar*), 1958, 83-9 (in Hebrew, with a summary in English).

G. VON RAD, 'Zelt und Lade', in *Neue Kirchliche Zeitschrift*, XLII, 1931, 476-98 = *Gesammelte Studien zum Alten Testament*, Munich, 1958, 100-29.

M. HARAN, 'The Ark and the Cherubim. Their Symbolic Significance in Biblical Ritual', in *IEJ*, IX, 1959, 30-8.

D. W. GOODING, *The Account of the Tabernacle. Translation and Textual Problems of the Greek Exodus*, Cambridge, 1959.

L. ROST, 'Die Wohnstätte des Zeugnisses', in *Festschrift F. Baumgärtel*, Erlangen, 1959, 158-65.

M. HARAN, 'The Nature of the *'ōhel mō'ēdh* in Pentateuchal Studies', in *Journal of Semitic Studies*, V, 1960, 50-65.

E. NIELSEN, 'Some Reflections on the History of the Ark', in *Congress Volume, Oxford, 1959* (Supplement VII to *VT*), Leiden, 1960, 61-74.

E. KUTSCH, art. 'Lade Jahwes', in *Religion in Geschichte und Gegenwart*[2], 1960, 197-9.

On Gilgal:

K. GALLING, 'Bethel und Gilgal', in *ZDPV*, LXVI, 1943, 140-55; LXVII, 1944-5, 21-5, 34-43.

A. GEORGE, 'Les récits de Gilgal en Josué v. 2-15', in *Mémorial Chaine* (Bibliothèque de la Faculté Catholique de Théologie de Lyon, 5), 1950, 159-86.

F. M. ABEL, 'Galgala qui est aussi le Dodecalithon', *ibid.*, 29-34.

H. J. KRAUS, 'Gilgal, ein Beitrag zur Kultusgeschichte Israels', in *VT*, I, 1951, 181-9.

F. M. ABEL, 'L'apparition du chef de l'armée de Yahweh à Josué, Jos. v. 13-15', in *Miscellanea Biblica et Orientalia R. P. A. Miller oblata*, Rome, 1951, 109-13.

C. A. KELLER, 'Über einige alttestamentliche Heiligtumslegenden, II, D. Der Hieros Logos von Gilgal', in *ZAW*, LXVIII, 1956, 85-94.

On Shiloh:

O. EISSFELDT, 'Silo und Jerusalem', in *Volume du Congrès, Strasbourg* (Supplement to VT, IV), Leiden, 1957, 138-47.

On Mispah:

H. W. HERTZBERG, 'Mizpa', in *ZAW*, XLVII, 1929, 161-96.

J. MUILENBURG, in C. C. McCOWN, *Tell en-Naṣbeh*, I, New Haven, 1947, 3-49.

On Gibeon:

A. BRUNO, *Gibeon*, Leipzig, 1923.

H. CAZELLES, 'David's Monarchy and the Gibeonite Claim, II Sam. XXI 1-14', in *PEQ*, 1956, 155-75.

J. DUS, 'Gibeon, eine Kultstätte des Šmš und die Stadt des benjaminitischen Schicksals', in *VT*, X, 1960, 353-74.

On Ophra:

C. A. KELLER, 'Über einige alttestamentliche Heiligtumslegenden, I, B. Die Legenden um Ophra', in *ZAW*, LXVII, 1955, 154-62.

E. KUTSCH, 'Gideons Berufung und Altarbau, Jdc 6, 11-24', in *TLZ*, LXXXI, 1956, 75-84.

On Dan:

A. FERNANDEZ, 'El santuario de Dan', in *Biblica*, XV, 1934, 237-64.

A. MURTONEN, 'Some Thoughts on Judges XVII sq.', in *VT*, I, 1951, 233-4.

Ch. Hauret, 'Aux origines du sacerdoce danite', in *Mélanges Bibliques ... A. Robert*, Paris, 1957, 105-13.

On Jerusalem:

H. S. Nyberg, 'Studien zum Religionskampf im Alten Testament', in *Archiv für Religionswissenschaft*, XXXV, 1938, 329-87.
H. H. Rowley, 'Zadok and Nehustan', in *JBL*, LVIII, 1939, 113-41.
A. Bentzen, 'The Cultic Use of the Story of the Ark in Samuel', in *JBL*, LXVII, 1948, 37-53.
M. Noth, 'Jerusalem und die israelitische Tradition', in *Oudtestamentische Studiën*, VIII, 1950, 28-46= *Gesammelte Studien zum Alten Testament*, Munich, 1958, 172-87.
H. H. Rowley, 'Melchizedek and Zadok', in *Festschrift Bertholet*, Tübingen, 1950, 461-72.
L.-H. Vincent, 'Abraham à Jérusalem', in *RB*, LVIII, 1951, 360-71.
J. R. Porter, 'The Interpretation of 2 Samuel VI and Psalm CXXXII', in *JTS*, n.s. V, 1954, 161-73.
H. Schmidt, 'Jahwe und die Kulttradition von Jerusalem', in *ZAW*, LXVII, 1955, 147-97.
O. Eissfeldt, 'Silo und Jerusalem', in *Volume du Congrès, Strasbourg* (Supplement to VT, IV), 195 Leiden, 138-47.
G. Ahlström, 'Natan och tempelbygget', in *Svensk Exegetisk Årsbok*, XXV, 1960, 5-22.

3

THE TEMPLE AT JERUSALEM

General works:

K. Moehlenbrink, *Der Tempel Salomos*, Stuttgart, 1932.
A. Parrot, *Le Temple de Jérusalem*, Neuchâtel-Paris, 1954.
L.-H. Vincent and A.-M. Steve, *Jérusalem de l'Ancien Testament*, II-III, Paris 1956, 373-610.

On Solomon's Temple and its plan:

K. Galling, 'Das Allerheiligste in Salomos Tempel', in *JPOS*, XII, 1932, 43-6.
S. Smith, 'Timber and Brick or Masonry Construction', in *PEQ*, 1941, 5-17.
L. Waterman, 'The Damaged "Blueprints" of the Temple of Solomon', in *JNES*, II, 1943, 284-94.
R. de Vaux, 'Notes sur le Temple de Salomon', in *Qedem*, II, 1945, 48-58 (in Hebrew).
L. Waterman, 'The Treasuries of Solomon's Private Chapel', in *JNES*, VI, 1947, 161-3.
G. E. Wright, 'Dr. Waterman's View concerning the Solomonic Temple', in *JNES*, VII, 1948, 53.
L. Waterman, 'A Rebuttal', *ibid.*, 54-5.
P. L. Garber, 'Reconstructing Solomon's Temple', in *The Biblical Archaeologist*, XIV, 1951, 2-24.
G. E. Wright, 'The Steven's Reconstruction of the Solomonic Temple', in *The Biblical Archaeologist*, XVIII, 1955, 41-4.
P. L. Garber, 'Reconsidering the Reconstruction of Solomon's Temple', in *JBL*, LXXVII, 1958, 116-29.
W. F. Albright and G. E. Wright, 'Comments on Professor Garber's Article', *ibid.*, 129-33.

On the bronze pillars:

R. B. Y. Scott, 'The Pillars Jachin and Boaz', in *JBL*, LVIII, 1939, 143-9.
W. F. Albright, 'Two Cressets from Marissa and the Pillars of Jachin and Boaz', in *BASOR*, 85, 1942, 18-27.
H. G. May, 'The Two Pillars before the Temple of Solomon', in *BASOR*, 88, 1942, 19-27.
S. Yeivin, 'Jachin and Boaz', in *Eretz-Israel*, V (Volume ... Mazar), 1958, 97-104 (in Hebrew with a summary in English).

For the analogies with, and influences on, Solomon's Temple:

C. W. McEwan, 'The Syrian Expedition of the Oriental Institute of the University of Chicago', in *American Journal of Archaeology*, XLI, 1937, 9-13 (Tell Tainat).
A. Alt, 'Verbreitung und Herkunft des syrischen Tempeltypus', in *PJB*, XXXV, 1939, 83-99= *Kleine Schriften*, II, Munich, 1955, 100-15.
L. Wooley, *Alalakh, An Account of the Excavations at Tell Atchana*, London, 1955, 82-9.
Y. Yadin, 'Excavations at Hazor, 1957', in *IEJ*, VIII, 1958, 11-14.

On the identification of the site:
The best expositions of the two opposing theses are:

H. Schmidt, *Der heilige Fels in Jerusalem*, Tübingen, 1933 (second thesis).
L.-H. Vincent and A.-M. Steve, *Jérusalem de l'Ancien Testament*, II-III, Paris, 1956, 587-95 (first thesis).

On the cherubim:

P. Dhorme and L.-H. Vincent, 'Les Chérubins', in *RB*, XXXV, 1926, 328-58, 481-95.

W. F. ALBRIGHT, 'What were the Cherubins?', in *The Biblical Archaeologist*, I, 1938, 1-3.
M. HARAN, 'The Ark of the Covenant and the Cherubs', in *Eretz-Israel*, V (*Volume Mazar*), 1958, 83-90 (in Hebrew, with a summary in English).
J. TRINQUET, art. 'Kerub', in *Dictionnaire de la Bible*, Supplément, V, 1957.
M. HARAN, 'The Ark and the Cherubim', in *IEJ*, IX, 1959, 30-8, 89-94.

On the furnishings:
W. F. ALBRIGHT, *Archaeology and the Religion of Israel*, Baltimore, 1942, 142-55.
L.-H. VINCENT, 'Les bassins roulants du Temple de Salomon', in *Miscellanea Biblica B. Ubach*, Montserrat, 1953, 147-59.

On the character of the Temple:
K. GALLING, 'Königliche und nichtkönigliche Stifter beim Tempel von Jerusalem', in *ZDPV*, LXVIII, 1946-51, 134-42.
L.-H. VINCENT, 'Le caractère du Temple de Salomon', in *Mélanges Bibliques . . . A. Robert*, Paris, 1957, 137-48.
B. MAZAR, 'Jerusalem—"King's Chapel" and "Royal City"', in *Judah and Jerusalem*, Jerusalem, 1957, 25-32 (in Hebrew, with a summary in English).

On the Temple of Ezechiel:
Apart from commentaries on Ezechiel:
A. LODS, 'Les cuisines du Temple de Jérusalem', in *Revue de l'Histoire des Religions*, CXXVII, 1944-A, 30-4.
L.-H. VINCENT, 'L'autel des holocaustes et le caractère du Temple d'Ézéchiel', in *Analecta Bollandiana*, LXVII, 1949 (*Mélanges Paul Peeters*), 7-20.
K. ELLIGER, 'Die grossen Tempelsakristeien im Verfassungsentwurf des Ezechiel', in *Geschichte und Altes Testament (Festschrift Alt)*, Tübingen, 1953, 79-104.
TH. CHARY, *Les Prophètes et le culte à partir de l'Exil*, Paris-Tournai, 1955, chap. I-III.
H. GESE, *Der Verfassungsentwurf des Ezechiel (Kap. 40-48)*, Tübingen, 1958.

On the post-exilic Temple:
J. JEREMIAS, 'Hesekieltempel und Serubbabeltempel', in *ZAW*, LII, 1934, 109-12.
R. DE VAUX, 'Les décrets de Cyrus et de Darius sur la reconstruction du Temple', in *RB*, XLVI, 1937, 29-57.
E. BICKERMAN, 'The Edict of Cyrus in Ezra 1', in *JBL*, LXV, 1946, 249-75.
S. SMITH, 'Foundations: Ezra IV, 12; V, 16; VI, 3', in *Essays Presented to J. H. Hertz*, 1946, 385-96.
E. BIKERMAN, 'Une proclamation séleucide relative au Temple de Jérusalem', in *Syria*, XXV, 1946-8, 67-85.
J. BRAND, 'Some Observations on the Second Temple Edifice', in *Tarbiz*, XXIX, 1959-60, 210-17 (in Hebrew).
M. AVI-YONA, *Reply to the Article by J. Brand, ibid.*, 218-221 (in Hebrew).

On the theology of the Temple:
Fr. JEREMIAS, 'Das orientalische Heiligtun', in *ΑΓΓΕΛΟΣ, Archiv für neutestamentliche Zeitgeschichte*, IV, 1932, 56-69.
W. J. PHYTHIAN-ADAMS, *The People and the Presence*, London, 1942.
J. DANIÉLOU, *Le Signe du Temple ou de la Présence de Dieu*, Paris, 1942.
W. F. ALBRIGHT, *Archaeology and the Religion of Israel*, Baltimore, 1942, 142-55.
R. PATAI, *Man and Temple in Ancient Jewish Myth and Ritual*, London, 1947.
M. SCHMIDT, *Prophet und Tempel. Eine Studie zum Problem der Gottesnähe im Alten Testament*, Zollikon-Zürich, 1948.
G. FOHRER, 'Jeremias Tempelwort, 7, 1-15', in *Theologische Zeitschrift*, V, 1949, 401-17.
M. SIMON, 'La prophétie de Nathan et le Temple', in *RHPR*, XXXII, 1952, 41-58.
J. DANIÉLOU, 'Le symbolisme cosmique du Temple de Jérusalem', in *Symbolisme cosmique et Monuments religieux*, Paris, 1953, 61-4.
TH. CHARY, *Les Prophètes et le culte à partir de l'Exil*, Paris-Tournai, 1955.
M. J. CONGAR, *Le Mystère du Temple ou l'Économie de la Présence de Dieu à sa créature, de la Genèse à l'Apocalypse*, Paris, 1958.
E. L. EHRLICH, *Kultsymbolik im Alten Testament und im nachbiblischen Judeutum*, Stuttgart, 1959, 24-33.
G. WIDENGREN, 'Aspetti simbolici dei templi e luoghi di culto nel Vicino Oriente Antico', in *Numen*, VII, 1960, 1-25.

4

THE CENTRALIZATION OF THE CULT

On Jeroboam's schism, and Bethel:
O. EISSFELDT, 'Lade und Stierbild', in *ZAW*, LVIII, 1940-1, 190-215.

R. DE VAUX, 'Le schisme religieux de Jéroboam Ier', in *Angelicum*, XX, 1943=*Biblica et Orientalia R. P. Vosté dicata*, 77-91.
M. BIČ, 'Bet'el. Le sanctuaire du roi', in *Archiv Orientální*, XVII, 1, 1949, 46-63.

On the reforms of Ezechias and Josias, and Deuteronomy:

F. HORST, 'Die Kultusreform des Königs Josia', in *ZDMG*, LXXVII, 1923, 220-38.
K. BUDDE, 'Das Deuteronomium und die Reform König Josias', in *ZAW*, XLIV, 1926, 177-224.
A. C. WELCH, *The Work of the Chronicler*, London, 1939, ch. v.: 'Hezekiah's Reform'.
G. VON RAD, *Studies in Deuteronomy*, London, 1953.
H. H. ROWLEY, 'The Prophet Jeremiah and the Book of Deuteronomy', in *Studies in Old Testament Prophecy presented to Th. H. Robinson*, Edinburgh, 1950, 157-74.
H. CAZELLES, 'Jérémie et le Deutéronome', in *Recherches de Science Religieuse*, XXXVIII, 1951, 5-36.
H. JUNKER, 'Die Entstehungszeit des Ps 78 und das Deuteronomium', in *Biblica*, XXXIV, 1953, 487-500.
A. ALT, 'Die Heimat des Deuteronomiums', in *Kleine Schriften*, II, Munich, 1953, 250-75.
V. MAAG, 'Erwägungen zur deuteronomischen Kultzentralisation', in *VT*, VI, 1956, 10-18.
F. DUMERMUTH, 'Zur deuteronomischen Kulttheologie', in *ZAW*, LXX, 1958, 59-98.
A. JEPSEN, 'Die Reform des Josia', in *Festschrift F. Baumgärtel*, Erlangen, 1959, 97-108.

On the temple at Elephantine:

A. VINCENT, *La religion des judéo-araméens d'Éléphantine*, Paris, 1937, ch. VII.
E. G. KRAELING, *The Brooklyn Museum Aramaic Papyri*, New Haven, 1953, 76-119.
C. H. GORDON, 'The Origin of the Jews in Elephantine', in *JNES*, XIV, 1955, 56-8.
P. GRELOT, 'Le papyrus pascal d'Éléphantine et le problème du Pentateuque', in *VT*, V, 1955, 250-65.

On the temple at Leontopolis:

E. SCHÜRER, *Geschichte des jüdischen Volkes zur Zeit Jesu Christi*, III, Leipzig, 1909, 144-8.
M.-J. LAGRANGE, *Le Judaïsme avant Jésus-Christ*, Paris, 1931, 490-3.
A. FEUILLET, 'L'oracle d'Isaïe XIX (vv. 16-25) sur la conversion de l'Égypte', in *Recherches de Science religieuse*, XXXIX (*Mélanges Lebreton*, I), 1951, 65-87.
V. A. TCHERIKOVER and A. FUKS, *Corpus Papyrorum Judaicarum*, I, Jerusalem, 1957, 44-6.
A. BARUCQ, art. 'Léontopolis', in *Dictionnaire de la Bible, Supplément*, V, 1957, 359-72.

On the Samaritan temple:

E. BIKERMAN, 'Un document relatif à la persécution d'Antiochus IV Épiphane', in *Revue de l'Histoire des Religions*, CXV, 1937-A, 188-223.
P. ANTOINE, art. 'Garizim', in *Dictionnaire de la Bible, Supplément*, III, Paris, 1938, 535-61.
H. H. ROWLEY, 'Sanballat and the Samaritan Temple', in *BJRL*, XXXVIII, 1955-6, 166-98.

On the origin of synagogues:

K. GALLING, 'Erwägungen zur antiken Synagoge', in *ZDPV*, LXXII, 1956, 163-78.
J. MORGENSTERN, 'The Origin of the Synagogue', in *Studi Orientalistici in onore di G. Levi Della Vida*, II, Rome, 1956, 192-201.
V. A. TCHERIKOVER and A. FUKS, *Corpus Papyrorum Judaicarum*, I, Jerusalem, 1957, especially pp. 7-8.
E. L. EHRLICH, *Die Kultsymbolik im Alten Testament und im nachbiblischen Judentum*, Stuttgart, 1959, 85-96.

5

THE PRIESTLY OFFICE

On the priesthood in general:

There are no great modern works, but the following must still be consulted:

W. W. VON BAUDISSIN, *Die Geschichte des alttestamentlichen Priesterthums*, Leipzig, 1889.
A. VAN HOONACKER, *Le sacerdoce lévitique dans la loi et dans l'histoire des Hébreux*, London-Louvain, 1899.
G. HÖLSCHER, art. 'Levi', in PAULY-WISSOWA, *Real-Encyclopädie ...*, XII 2, Stuttgart, 1925, 2155-208.
G. B. GRAY, *Sacrifice in the Old Testament. Its Theory and Practice*, Oxford, 1925, 179-270.

On the assumption of office:

E. LOHSE, *Die Ordination in Spätjudentum und in Neuen Testament*, Göttingen, 1951.
M. NOTH, *Amt und Berufung im Alten Testament*, Bonn, 1958.

On priests and divine oracles in general:

F. KÜCHLER, 'Das priesterliche Orakel in Israel und Juda', in *Abhandlungen zur semitischen Religionskunde und Sprachwissenschaft (Festschrift Baudissin)*, Giessen, 1918, 285-301.

J. Döller, *Die Wahrsagerei im Alten Testament*, Münster i. W., 1923.
J. Begrich, 'Das priesterliche Heilsorakel', in *ZAW*, LII, 1934, 81-92.

On the ephod:

E. Sellin, 'Das israelitische Ephod', in *Orientalische Studien Th. Nöldeke . . .*, II, Giessen, 1906, 699-717.
W. R. Arnold, *Ephod and Ark* (Harvard Theological Studies, 3), Cambridge, Mass., 1917.
K. Budde, 'Ephod und Lade', in *ZAW*, XXXIX, 1921, 1-42.
J. Gabriel, *Untersuchungen über das alttestamentliche Priestertum, mit besonderer Berücksichtigung des hohen-priesterlichen Ornates*, Vienna, 1933, 44-70.
E. Sellin, 'Ephod und Terafim', in *JPOS*, XIV, 1934, 185-94.
H. Thiersch, *Ependytes und Ephod. Gottesbild und Priesterkleid im Alten Vorderasien*, Stuttgart, 1936.
E. Sellin, 'Zu Efod und Terafim', in *ZAW*, LV, 1937, 296-8.
H. G. May, 'Ephod and Ariel', in *AJSL*, LVI, 1939, 44-52.
W. F. Albright, 'Are Ephod and Terafim mentioned in the Ras Shamra Texts?', in *BASOR*, 83, 1941, 39-42.
J. Morgenstern, 'The Ark, the Ephod and the Tent of Meeting', in *HUCA*, XVIII, 1943-4, 1-17.
M. Haran, 'L'éphod d'après les sources bibliques' (in Hebrew), in *Tarbiz*, XXIV, 1955, 381-91.
K. Elliger, 'Ephod und Choschen', in *VT*, VIII, 1958, 19-35.

On the Urim and Thummim:

R. Press, 'Das Ordal im Alten Testament', II, in *ZAW*, LI, 1933, 227-31.
A. Jirku, 'Die Mimation in den nordsemitischen Sprachen und einige Bezeichnungen der altisraelitis-chen Mantik', in *Biblica*, XXXIX, 1953, 78-80.
J. Lindblöm, 'Lottdragning och Lottkastning i Gammeltestamentliga Texter', in *Septentrionalia et Orientalia Studia B. Karlgren dedicata*, Lund, 1960, 262-9.

On priests and teaching:

J. Begrich, 'Die priesterliche Tora', in *Werden und Wesen des Alten Testaments*, Berlin, 1936, 63-88.
G. Östborn, *Tora in the Old Testament*, Lund, 1945.
O. Plöger, 'Priester und Prophet', in *ZAW*, LXIII, 1951, 157-92.
H. W. Wolff, '"Wissen um Gott" bei Hosea als Urform von Theologie', in *Evangelische Theologie*, XII, 1952-3, 533-54.

On priests and sacrifice:

L. Gautier, 'Pretre ou sacrificateur?' in *Études sur la religion d'Israël*, Lausanne, 1927, 247-76.
A. E. J. Rawlinson, 'Priesthood and Sacrifice in Judaism and Christianity', in *Expository Times*, LX, 1949, 115-21.

On the priest as mediator:

A. Robert, art. 'Médiation dans l'Ancien Testament', in *Dictionnaire de la Bible, Supplément*, V, Paris, 1957, 1004-8.

6

THE LEVITES

Etymology:
Apart from the classical dictionaries (with references), see:

M. Noth, 'Remarks on the Sixth Volume of Mari Texts', in *Journal of Semitic Studies*, I, 1956, 327.
L. Kopf, 'Arabische Etymologien und Parallelen zum Bibelwörterbuch', in *VT*, VIII, 1958, 181-2.

On the Levitical tradition:

G. Hölscher, art. 'Levi', in Pauly-Wissowa, *Real-Encyclopädie . . .*, XII 2, 1925, 2155-208.
K. Möhlenbrink, 'Die levitischen Überlieferungen des Alten Testaments', in *ZAW*, LII, 1934, 184-231.
A. Lefèvre, 'Notes d'exégèse sur les généalogies des Qehatites', in *Recherches de Science religieuse*, XXXVII, 1950, 287-92.

On the historical development:

J. Goettsberger, 'Das alttestamentliche Priestertum und Ezechiel', in *Episcopus, Festgabe Faulhaber*, Regensburg, 1949, 1-19.
M. Greenberg, 'A New Approach to the History of the Israelite Priesthood', in *JAOS*, LXX, 1950, 41-6.
G. E. Wright, 'The Levites in Deuteronomy', in *VT*, IV, 1954, 325-30.
E. Nielsen, *Shechem. A Traditio-Historical Investigation*, Copenhagen, 1955, 264-86.
Ch. Hauret, 'Aux origines du sacerdoce danite, à propos de Jud. 18, 30-1', in *Mélanges Bibliques . . . A. Robert*, Paris, 1957, 105-13.

On Levitical towns:

W. F. ALBRIGHT, 'The List of Levitic Cities', in *Louis Ginzberg Jubilee Volume*, I, New York, 1945, 49-73.
A. ALT, 'Bemerkungen zu einigen judäischen Ortslisten des Alten Testaments', in *Beiträge zur biblischen Landes- und Altertumskunde (= ZDPV)*, LXVII, 1951, 193-210= *Kleine Schriften*, II, Munich, 1953, 289-305.
A. ALT, 'Festungen und Levitenorte im Lande Juda', in *Kleine Schriften*, II, Munich, 1953, 306-15.
M. HARAN, 'The Levitical Cities: Utopia and Historical Reality', in *Tarbiz*, XXVII, 1957-8, 421-39 (in Hebrew, with a summary in English).
B MAZAR, 'The Cities of the Priests and Levites', in *Congress Volume, Oxford, 1959* (Supplement VII to *VT*), Leiden, 1960, 193-205.

On the origin of the Levites:

H. GRIMME, 'Der südarabische Levitismus und sein Verhältnis zum Levitismus in Israel', in *Museon*, XXXVII, 1924, 169-99.
L. WATERMAN, 'Some Determining Factors in the Northward Progress of Levi', in *JAOS*, LVII, 1937, 375-80.
TH. J. MEEK, 'Moses and the Levites', in *AJSL*, LVI, 1939, 113-20.
H. H. ROWLEY, 'Early Levite History and the Question of the Exodus', in *JNES*, III, 1944, 73-8.
S. YEIVIN, 'The Exodus', in *Tarbiz*, XXX, 1960-1, 1-7 (in Hebrew).

7

THE PRIESTHOOD OF JERUSALEM UNDER THE MONARCHY

On Sadoq and the Sadoqites:

TH. MEEK, 'Aaron and the Sadocides', *AJSL*, XLV, 1928-9, 149-66.
E. AUERBACH, 'Die Herkunft der Sadokiden', in *ZAW*, XLIX, 1931, 327-8.
A. BENTZEN, *Studier over det Zadokidiske Praesterkabs historie*, Copenhagen, 1931.
A. BENTZEN, 'Zur Geschichte der Sadoiķden', in *ZAW*, LI, 1933, 173-6.
K. BUDDE, 'Die Herkunft Şadok's', in *ZAW*, LII, 1934, 42-50, cf. 160.
H. H. ROWLEY, 'Zadok and Nehustan', in *JBL*, LVIII, 1939, 113-41.
H. H. ROWLEY, 'Melchizedek and Zadok', in *Festschrift Bertholet*, Tübingen, 1950, 461-72.

On the priestly hierarchy:

J. MORGENSTERN, 'A Chapter in the History of the High Priesthood', in *AJSL*, LV, 1938, 1-24, 183-97, 360-77.

On the revenues of the priests:

O. EISSFELDT, *Erstlinge und Zehnten*, Leipzig, 1917.

On the lower-ranking staff:

M. LÖHR, *Die Stellung des Weibes zu Yahwe-Religion und -Kult*, Leipzig, 1908.
G. B. GRAY, *Sacrifice in the Old Testament. Its Theory and Practice*, Oxford, 1925, 184-93.
B. D. EERDMANS, 'Thoda-Songs and Temple-Singers', in *Oudtestamentische Studiën*, I 2, 1942, 162-75.
W. F. ALBRIGHT, *Archaeology and the Religion Of Israel*, Baltimore, 1942, 125-8.
M. HARAN, 'The Gibeonites, the Nethinim and the Servants of Salomon', in *Judah and Israel*, Jerusalem, 1957, 37-45 (in Hebrew, with a summary in English).

On the cult prostitutes:

B. S. BROOKS, 'Fertility Cult Functionaries in the Old Testament', in *JBL*, LX, 1941, 227-53.
J. P. ASMUSSEN, 'Bemerkungen zur sakralen Prostitution im Alten Testament', in *Studia Theologica*, XI, 1957, 167-92.

On cultic prophets:

S. MOWINCKEL, *Psalmenstudien III: Kultprophetie und prophetische Psalmen*, Kristiania (Oslo), 1923.
A. R. JOHNSON, *The Cultic Prophet in Ancient Israel*, Cardiff, 1944.
A. HALDAR, *Associations of Cult Prophets among the Ancient Semites*, Uppsala, 1945.
N. W. PORTEOUS, 'Prophet and Priest in Israel', in *Expository Times*, LXII, 1950-1, 4-9.
O. PLÖGER, 'Priester und Prophet', in *ZAW*, LXIII, 1951, 157-92.
E. WURTHWEIN, 'Ursprung der prophetischen Gerichtsrede', in *Zeitschrift für Theologie und Kirche*, XLIX, 1952, 1-16.
F. HESSE, 'Wurzelt die prophetische Gerichtsrede im israelitischen Kult?', in *ZAW*, LXV, 1953, 45-53.
R. HENTSCHKE, *Die Stellung der vorexilischen Schriftpropheten zum Kultus*, Berlin, 1957.
H. H. ROWLEY, 'Ritual and the Hebrew Prophets', in S. H. HOOKE (ed.), *Myth, Ritual and Kingship*, Oxford, 1958, 236-60.

8

THE PRIESTHOOD AFTER THE EXILE

On the priests and the Levites:

G. VON RAD, *Das Geschichtsbild des chronistischen Werkes*, Stuttgart, 1930.
R. MEYER, 'Levitische Emancipazionsbestrebungen in nach-exilischen Zeit', in *Orientalistische Literaturzeitung*, XLI, 1938, 721-8.
A. C. WELCH, *The Work of the Chronicler, Its Purpose and its Date*, London, 1939.
A. ALT, 'Bemerkungen zu einigen judäischen Ortslisten des Alten Testaments', in *Beiträge zur biblischen Landes- und Altertumskunde* (= *ZDVP*), LXVIII, 1951, 193-210= *Kleine Schriften*, II, Munich, 1953, 289-305.

On the line of Aaron and the line of Sadoq:

M. NOTH, *Überlieferungsgeschichte des Pentateuch*, Stuttgart, 1948, 195-9.
F. S. NORTH, 'Aaron's Rise in Prestige', in *ZAW*, LXVI, 1954, 191-9.
H. G. JUDGE, 'Zadok and Abiathar', in *JTS*, n.s. VII, 1956, 70-4.

On the high priest:

J. GABRIEL, *Untersuchungen über das alttestamentliche Hohepriestertum*, Vienna, 1933.
J. MORGENSTERN, 'A Chapter in the History of the High Priesthood', in *AJSL*, LV, 1938, 16-24; 183-97; 360-77.
F. STUMMER, 'Gedanken über die Stellung des Hohenpriesters in der alttestamentlichen Gemeinde', in *Episcopus, Festgabe Faulhaber*, Regensburg, 1949, 19-49.
A. DE BUCK, 'La fleur au front du Grand Prêtre', in *Oudtestamentische Studiën*, IX, 1951, 18-29.
S. ZEITLIN, 'The Titles High Priest and the Nasi of the Sanhedrin', in *JQR*, XLVIII, 1957-8, 1-5.
M. NOTH, *Amt und Berufung im Alten Testament*, Bonn, 1958, 11-16.
J. JEREMIAS, *Jerusalem zur Zeit Jesu*², Stuttgart, 1958 (almost exactly the same as the 1923 edition). See especially B 3-59.
E. COTHENET, art. 'Onction', in *Dictionnaire de la Bible, Supplément*, VI, Paris, 1959, 701-32.

On the revenues of the clergy:

There is no modern monograph, but the following should still be consulted:

E. SCHURER, *Geschichte des jüdischen Volkes im Zeitalter Jesu-Christi*, II, Leipzig, 1907, 297-317.
O. EISSFELDT, *Erstlinge und Zehnten im Alten Testament*, Leipzig, 1917.
M. A. BEEK, 'Hasidic Conceptions of Kingship in the Maccabean Period', in *The Sacral Kingship* (Supplement IV to *Numen*), Leiden, 1959, 349-55.

9

ALTARS

J. DE GROOT, *Die Altäre des salomonischen Tempelhofes*, Stuttgart, 1924.
K. GALLING, *Der Altar in den Kulturen des Alten Orients*, Berlin, 1924.
G. B. GRAY, *Sacrifice in the Old Testament. Its Theory and Practice*, Oxford, 1925, 96-178.
H. M. WIENER, *The Altars of the Old Testament*, Leipzig, 1927.
M. LÖHR, *Das Räucheropfer im Alten Testament. Eine archäologische Untersuchung*, Halle, 1927.
W. F. ALBRIGHT, *Archaeology and the Religion of Israel*², Baltimore, 1946, 150-2.
L.-H. VINCENT, 'L'autel des holocaustes et le caractère du Temple d'Ézéchiel', in *Analecta Bollandiana*, LXVII, 1949 (*Mélanges Paul Peeters*), 7-20.
R. DE LANGHE, *Het gouden altaar in de Israëlitische eredienst*, Brussels, 1952.
A. PARROT, 'Autels et installations cultuelles à Mari', in *Congress Volume, Copenhagen* (Supplement to *VI*, I), Leiden, 1953, 112-19.
R. DE LANGHE, 'L'autel d'or du temple de Jérusalem', in *Studia Biblica et Orientalia*, I. *Vetus Testamentum*, Rome, 1959, 342-60= *Biblica*, XL, 1959, 476-94.

10

THE RITUAL OF SACRIFICE

On sacrifices in general:

G. B. GRAY, *Sacrifice in the Old Testament. Its Theory and Practice*, Oxford, 1925.
A. WENDEL, *Das Opfer in der altisraelitischen Religion*, Leipzig, 1927.
W. O. E. OESTERLEY, *Sacrifices in Ancient Israel. The Origin, Purposes and Development*, London, 1937.

On certain particular rites:

A. VINCENT, 'Les rites de balancement (tenoûphâh) et de prélèvement (teroûmâh) dans le sacrifice de communion de l'Ancien Testament', in *Mélanges Syriens offerts à M. R. Dussaud*, I, Paris, 1939, 267-72.

W. B. STEVENSON, 'Hebrew 'olaḥ and zebach Sacrifices', in *Festschrift Bertholet*, Tübingen, 1950, 109-18.

G. R. DRIVER, 'Three Technical Terms in the Pentateuch' (for 'azkârah and tᵉnûphah), in *Journal of Semitic Studies*, I, 1956, 97-105.

N. H. SNAITH, 'Sacrifices in the Old Testament' (for zèbaḥ, minḥah, ḥaṭṭa'th), in *VT*, VII, 1957, 308-17.

L. MORALDI, 'Terminologia cultuale Israelitica', in *Rivista degli Studi Orientali*, XXXII, 1957 (*Scritti in onore di Giuseppe Furlani*, I), 321-37.

L. ROST, 'Erwägungen zum israelitischen Brandopfer', in *Von Ugarit nach Qumran* (*Festschrift Eissfeldt*), Berlin, 1958, 177-83.

A. CHARBEL, 'Virtus sanguinis non expiatoria in sacrificiis šᵉlamîm', in *Sacra Pagina*, I (*Vetus Testamentum*), Gembloux, 1959, 366-76.

On expiatory sacrifices:

D. SCHÖTZ, *Schuld- und Sündopfer im Alten Testament*, Breslau, 1930.

P. SAYDON, 'Sin-Offering and Trespass-Offering', in *Catholic Biblical Quarterly*, VIII, 1946, 393-9.

L. MORALDI, *Espiazione sacrificiale e riti espiatori nell'ambiente biblico e nell'Antico Testamento*, Rome, 1956.

On incense-offerings:

M. LÖHR, *Das Räuchopfer im Alten Testament. Eine archäologische Untersuchung*, Halle, 1927.

A. VINCENT, *La religion des judéo-araméens d'Éléphantine*, Paris, 1937, 212-23.

M. HARAN, 'The Use of Incense in the Ancient Israelite Ritual', in *VT*, X, 1960, 113-29.

11

THE HISTORY OF SACRIFICE IN ISRAEL

The bibliography is the same as for the preceding chapter, but add:

R. HENTSCHKE, *Die Stellung der vorexilischen Schriftpropheten zum Kultus*, Berlin, 1957.

G. W. VAN BECK and A. JAMME, 'An Inscribed South Arabian Clay Stamp from Bethel', in *BASOR*, 151, 1958, 9-16.

12

THE ORIGIN OF ISRAELITE RITUAL

On sacrifice among the Assyrians and Babylonians:

G. FURLANI, *Il sacrificio nella religione dei Semiti di Babilonia e Assiria*, Rome, 1932.

E. DHORME, 'Le sacrifice accadien à propos d'un ouvrage récent', in *Revue de l'Histoire des Religions*, CVI, 1932-A, 107-25.

F. BLOME, *Die Opfermaterie in Babylonien und Israel*, Rome, 1934.

G. FURLANI, *Riti babilonesi e assiri*, Udine, 1940.

E. DHORME, 'Les religions de Babylonie et d'Assyrie', in *Mana. Introduction à l'Histoire des Religions*, I II, Paris, 1945, 220-33.

R. LABAT, 'Le sort des substituts royaux en Assyrie au temps des Sargonides', in *Revue d'Assyriologie*, XL, 1945-6, 123-42.

G. GOOSSENS, 'Les substituts royaux en Babylonie', in *Ephemerides Theologicae Lovanienses*, XXV, 1949, 383-400.

J. GRAY, 'Royal Substitutes in the Ancient Near East', in *PEQ*, 1955, 180-2.

W. VON SODEN, 'Beiträge zum Verständnis der assyrischen Briefe über die Ersatzkönigsriten', in *Festschrift V. Christian*, Vienna, 1956, 100-7.

W. G. LAMBERT, 'A Part of the Ritual of the Substitute King', in *AfO*, XVIII, 1, 1957, 109-12.

On sacrifice among the ancient Arabs:

J. WELLHAUSEN, *Reste arabischen Heidenthums*², Berlin, 1897.

J. HENNINGER, 'Das Opfer in den altsüdarabischen Hochkulturen', in *Anthropos*, XXXVII-XL, 1942-4, 779-810.

J. HENNINGER, 'Le sacrifice chez les Arabes', in *Ethnos* (Stockholm), XII, 1948, 1-16.

G. RYCKMANS, 'Le sacrifice DBH dans les inscriptions safaïtiques', in *HUCA*, XXXIII 1, 1950-1, 431-8.
G. RYCKMANS, *Les religions arabes préislamiques²*, Louvain, 1951.
J. HENNINGER, 'Ist der sogenannte Nilus-Bericht eine brauchbare religionsgeschichtliche Quelle?', in *Anthropos*, L, 1955, 81-148.
J. CHELHOD, *Le sacrifice chez les Arabes*, Paris, 1955.
J. HENNINGER, 'Zur Frage des Haaropfers bei den Semiten', in *Die Wiener Schule der Völkerkunde, Festschrift zum 25jährigen Bestand, 1929-1954*, Vienna, 1956, 359-68.

On Canaanite sacrifice:

TH. H. GASTER, 'The Service of the Sanctuary: a Study in Hebrew Survivals', in *Mélanges Syriens offerts à M. R. Dussaud*, II, Paris, 1939, 577-82.
R. DUSSAUD, *Les origines cananéennes du sacrifice israélite²*, Paris, 1941.
R. DUSSAUD, *Les découvertes de Ras Shamra et l'Ancien Testament²*, Paris, 1941.
D. M. L. URIE, 'Sacrifice among the West Semites', in *PEQ*, 1949, 67-82.
J. GRAY, 'Cultic Affinities between Israel and Ras Shamra', in *ZAW*, LXII, 1949-50, 207-20.
A. DE GUGLIELMO, 'Sacrifices in the Ugaritic Texts', in *Catholic Biblical Quarterly*, XVII, 1955, 76-96.
J. G. FÉVRIER, 'Le vocabulaire sacrificiel punique', in *Journal Asiatique*, CCXLIII, 1955, 49-63.
J. GRAY, 'The Legacy of Canaan' (Supplement to *VT*, V), Leiden, 1957.
J. G. FÉVRIER, 'Remarques sur le grand tarif dit de Marseilles', in *Cahiers de Byrsa*, VIII, 1958-9, 35-40.

On connections with Greek sacrifice:

R. K. YERKES, *Sacrifice in Greek and Roman Religions and Early Judaism*, New York, 1952.
L. ROST, 'Erwägungen zum israelitischen Brandopfer', in *Von Ugarit nach Qumran (Festschrift Eissfeldt)*, Berlin, 1958, 177-83.

On human sacrifice:

A. GEORGE, 'Le sacrifice d'Abraham', in *Études de Critique et d'Histoire Religieuses (Mélanges Vaganay)*, Lyons, 1948, 99-110.
F. M. TH. BÖHL, 'Das Menschenopfer bei den alten Sumerern', in his *Opera Minora*, Groningen, 1953, 162-73, 488-90.
H. CAZELLES, 'David's Monarchy and the Gibeonite Claim, II Sam. XXI, 1-14', in *PEQ*, 1955, 165-75.
A. S. KAPELRUD, 'King and Fertility, A Discussion of II Sam. 21: 1-14', in *Interpretationes ad Vetus Testamentum pertinentes S. Mowinckel . . . missae*, Oslo, 1955, 113-22.
J. HENNINGER, 'Menschenopfer bei den Arabern', in *Anthropos*, LIII, 1958, 721s, 776s.

On 'sacrifice to Moloch':

O. EISSFELDT, *Molk als Opferbegriff im Punischen und Hebräischen und das Ende des Gottes Moloch*, Halle a. Saale, 1935.
R. DUSSAUD, 'Précisions épigraphiques touchant les sacrifices puniques d'enfants', in *Comptes Rendus de l'Académie des Inscriptions et Belles-Lettres* (Paris), 1946, 371-87.
W. KORNFELD, 'Der Moloch, eine Untersuchung zur Theorie O. Eissfeldts', in *Wiener Zeitschrift für die Kunde des Morgenlandes*, LI, 1952, 287-313.
J. G. FÉVRIER, 'Molchomor', in *Revue de l'Histoire des Religions*, CXLIII, 1953-A, 8-18.
R. CHARLIER, 'La nouvelle série des stèles puniques de Constantine et la question des sacrifices dits "molchomor" en relation avec l'expression "bšrm btm"', in *Karthago*, VI, 1953, 3-48.
J. G. FÉVRIER, 'Le vocabulaire sacrificiel punique', in *Journal Asiatique*, CCXLIII, 1955, 49-63.
J. G. FÉVRIER, 'Un sacrifice d'enfants chez les Numides', in *Annuaire de l'Institut de Philologie et d'Histoire Orientales et Slaves*, XIII (*Mélanges Isidore Lévy*), Brussels, 1955, 161-71.
E. DHORME, 'Le dieu Baal et le dieu Moloch dans la tradition biblique', in *Anatolian Studies*, VI, 1956, 57-61.
H. CAZELLES, art. 'Molok', in *Dictionnaire de la Bible, Supplément*, V, Paris, 1957, 1337-46.
J. HOFTIJZER, 'Eine Notiz zum punischen Kinderopfer', in *VT*, VIII, 1958, 288-92.

13

THE RELIGIOUS VALUE OF SACRIFICE

For the general bibliography, see chapter X. In addition:

A. BERTHOLET, 'Zum Verständnis des alttestamentlichen Opfergedankens', in *JBL*, XLIX, 1930, 218-33.
A. METZINGER, 'Die Substitutionstheorie und das alttestamentliche Opfer', in *Biblica*, XXI, 1940, 159-87; 247-72; 353-77.
J. E. COLERAN, 'Origins of the Old Testament Sacrifice', in *Catholic Biblical Quarterly*, II, 1940, 130-44.
R. DUSSAUD, *Les origines cananéennes du sacrifice israélite²*, Paris, 1941.
H. WHEELER ROBINSON, 'Hebrew Sacrifice and Prophetic Symbolism', in *JTS*, XLVIII, 1942, 129-39.
A. BERTHOLET, 'Der Sinn des kultischen Opfers', in *Abhandlungen der preussischen Akademie der Wissenschaften*, 1942, Phil.-hist. Klasse, 2, Berlin, 1942.

H. H. Rowley, 'The Meaning of Sacrifice in the Old Testament', in *BJRL*, XXXIII, 1950-1, 74-110.
G. Van der Leeuw, *Phänomenologie der Religion²*, Tübingen, 1956, 393-406.
W. Herrmann, 'Götterspeise und Göttertrank in Ugarit und Israel', in *ZAW*, LXXII, 1960, 205-16.

On polemic against sacrifice:

P. Volz, 'Die radikale Ablehnung der Kultreligion durch die alttestamentlichen Propheten', in *Zeitschrift für systematische Theologie*, XIV, 1937, 63-85.
C. Lattey, 'The Prophets and Sacrifice: a Study in Biblical Relativity', in *JTS*, XLII, 1941, 155-65.
J. E. Coleran, 'The Prophets and Sacrifice', in *Theological Studies*, V, 1944, 411-38.
N. H. Snaith, 'The Prophets and Sacrifice and Salvation', in *Expository Times*, LVIII, 1946-7, 152-3.
H. H. Rowley, 'The Prophets and Sacrifice', in *Expository Times*, LVIII, 1946-7, 305-7.
H. W. Hertzberg, 'Die prophetische Kritik am Kult', in *TLZ*, LXXV, 1950, 219-26.
J. M. Baumgartner, 'Sacrifice and Worship among the Jewish Sectarians of the Dead Sea (Qumrân) Scrolls', in *Harvard Theological Review*, XLVI, 1953, 141-59.
H. Kruse, 'Die "dialektische Negation" als semitisches Idiom', in *VT*, IV, 1954, 385-400.
Th. Chary, *Les prophètes et le culte à partir de l'Exil*, Paris-Tournai, 1955.
J. Carmignac, 'L'utilité ou l'inutilité des sacrifices sanglants dans la "Règle de la Communauté" de Qumrân', in *RB*, LXIII, 1956, 524-32.
R. Hentschke, *Die Stellung der vorexilischen Schriftpropheten zum Kultus*, Berlin, 1957.
R. Press, 'Die Gerichtspredigt der vorexilischen Propheten und der Versuch einer Steigerung der kultischen Leistung', in *ZAW*, LXX, 1958, 181-4.
R. Dobbie, 'Deuteronomy and the Prophetic Attitude to Sacrifice', in *Scottish Journal of Theology*, XII, 1959, 68-82.

14

SECONDARY ACTS OF THE CULT

On prayer:

N. Johansson, *Parakletoi, Vorstellungen von Fürsprechern*, Lund, 1940.
P. A. H. De Boer, *De voorbede in het Oud Testament = Oudtestamentische Studiën*, III, 1943.
E. Peterson, 'Die geschichtliche Bedeutung der jüdischen Gebetsrichtung', in *Theologische Zeitschrift*, III, 1947, 1-15 = *Frühkirche, Judentum und Gnosis*, Rome-Freiburg, 1959, 1-14.
N. B. Johnson, 'Prayer in the Apocrypha and Pseudepigrapha: a Study of the Jewish Concept of God' (*JBL*, Monograph Series, III), Philadelphia, 1948.
D. R. Ap-Thomas, 'Notes on Some Terms Relating to Prayer', in *VT*, VI, 1956, 225-41.

On rites of purification and consecration:

J. Döller, *Die Reinheits- und Speisegesetze des Alten Testaments*, Münster i. W., 1917.
J. Scheftelowitz, 'Das Opfer der roten Kuh (Num 19)', in *ZAW*, XXXIX, 1922, 113-23.
W. H. Gispen, 'Clean and Unclean', in *Oudtestamentische Studiën*, V, 1948, 190-7.
L. Koehler, 'Aussatz', in *ZAW*, LXVII, 1955, 290-1.
J. Bowman, 'Did the Qumran Sect burn the Red Heifer?', in *Revue de Qumrân*, I, 1958, 73-84.
P. Reymond, 'L'eau, sa vie et sa signification dans l'Ancien Testament' (*Supplement to VT*, VI), Leiden, 1958.

On vows and the Nazirites:

M. Jastrow, 'The "nazir" Legislation', in *JBL*, XXXIII, 1914, 265-85.
H. Salmanowitch, *Das Naziräat in Bibel und Talmud*, Wilna, 1931.
A. Wendel, *Das israelitisch-jüdische Gelübde*, Berlin, 1932.
J. Pedersen, *Israel, its Life and Culture*, III-IV, London, 1947, 264-6.
J. Henninger, 'Zur Frage des Haaropfers bei den Semiten', in *Die Wiener Schule der Völkerkunde*, *Festschrift zur 25jährigen Beistand 1929-1954*, Vienna, 1956, 359-68.

15

THE LITURGICAL CALENDAR

On the ordinary services in the Temple:

E. Schürer, *Geschichte des jüdischen Volkes im Zeitalter Jesu-Christi*, II⁴, Leipzig, 1907, 336-57.

On the liturgical calendars:

No one has yet made a comparative study of the liturgical calendars. We can only refer to the bibliography given in later chapters for the different feasts, and to general studies of Israelite feasts, in particular:

I. ELBOGEN, 'Die Feier der drei Wallfahrtsfeste im zweiten Tempel', in *46. Bericht der Hochschule für die Wissenschaft des Judentums in Berlin*, Berlin, 1929, 25-46.
I. ELBOGEN, *Der jüdische Gottesdienst in seiner geschichtlichen Entwicklung*, Leipzig, 1931, 107-54.
E. AUERBACH, 'Die Feste im alten Israel', in *VT*, VIII, 1958, 1-18.
E. KUTSCH, 'Feste und Feiern. II, in Israel', in *Die Religion in Geschichte und Gegenwart*[3], II, Leipzig, 1958, 910-17.
E. L. EHRLICH, *Kultsymbolik im Alten Testament und im nachbiblischen Judentum*, Stuttgart, 1959, 52-82.
J. VAN GOUDOEVER, *Biblical Calendars*, Leiden, 1959.

16

THE SABBATH DAY

J. MEINHOLD, *Sabbat und Woche im Alten Testament*, Göttingen, 1905.
J. HEHN, 'Siebenzahl und Sabbat' (*Leipziger semitische Studien*, II 5), Leipzig, 1907.
J. MEINHOLD, 'Die Entstehung des Sabbats', in *ZAW*, XXIX, 1909, 81-112.
J. MEINHOLD, 'Zur Sabbatfrage', in *ZAW*, XXXVI, 1916, 108-10.
T. J. MEEK, 'The Sabbath in the Old Testament', in *JBL*, XXXIII, 1914, 201-12.
B. B. EERDMANS, 'Der Sabbat', in *Vom Alten Testament* (*Festschrift Marti*), Giessen, 1925, 79-83.
K. BUDDE, 'The Sabbath and the Week', in *JTS*, XXX, 1929, 1-15.
J. MEINHOLD and K. BUDDE, 'Zur Sabbatfrage', in *ZAW*, XLVIII, 1930, 121-45.
W. W. CANNON, 'The Weekly Sabbath', in *ZAW*, XLIX, 1931, 325-7.
E. J. KRAELING, 'The Present Status of the Sabbath Question', in *AJSL*, XLIX, 1932-3, 218-28.
S. LANGDON, *Babylonian Menologies and the Semitic Calendars*, London, 1935.
G. SCHRENK, 'Sabbat oder Sonntag ?', in *Judaica*, II, 1946-7, 169-89.
H. M. FÉRET, 'Les sources bibliques', in *Le Jour du Seigneur* (Congrès de Pastorale Liturgique, Lyon), Paris, 1948, 41-404.
N. H. TUR-SINAI, 'Sabbat und Woche', in *Bibliotheca Orientalis*, VIII, 1951, 14-24.
H. H. ROWLEY, 'Moses and the Decalogue', in *BJRL*, XXXIV, 1951-2, 81-118.
G. J. BOTTERWECK, 'Der Sabbat im Alten Testament', in *Theologische Quartalschrift*, CXXXIV, 1954, 134-47; 448-57.
TH. H. GASTER, 'Le jour du repos', in *Évidences*, 43, Nov. 1954, 43-8.
R. NORTH, 'The Derivation of Sabbath', in *Biblica*, XXXVI, 1955, 182-201.
E. JENNI, *Die theologische Begründung des Sabbatgebotes im Alten Testament*, Zürich, 1956.
E. VOGT, 'Hat "sabbat" im AT den Sinn von "Woche" ?', in *Biblica*, XL, 1959, 1008-11.
D. GILAT, 'The Thirty-nine Classes of Work forbidden on the Sabbath', in *Tarbiz*, XXIX, 1959-60, 222-8 (in Hebrew).
E. LOHSE, art. *Σάββατον* in *Theologisches Wörterbuch zum Neuen Testament*, VII, 1960, 1-34.
A. CAQUOT, 'Remarques sur la fête de la "néoménie" dans l'ancien Israël', in *Revue de l'Histoire des Religions*, CLVIII, 1960-ii, 1-28.

17

THE ANCIENT FEASTS OF ISRAEL

On the Passover and the feast of Unleavened Bread:

G. BEER, *Pesachim* (*Die Mischna . . .*, II, 3), Giessen, 1912.
F. HORST, *Das Privilegrecht Yahves. Rechtsgeschichtliche Untersuchungen zum Deuteronomium*, Göttingen, 1930.
JEREMIAS, *Die Passahfeier der Samaritaner und ihre Bedeutung für das Vertständnis der altt. Passahüberlieferung*, Giessen, 1932.
J. PEDERSEN, 'Passahfest und Passahlegende', in *ZAW*, LII, 1934, 161-75.
J. PEDERSEN, *Israel. Its Life and Culture, III-IV*, London, 1940. Appendix I: 'The Crossing of the Dead Sea and the Paschal Legend', 728-37.
L. ROST, 'Weidewechsel und altisraelitischer Festkalender', in *ZDPV*, LXVI, 1943, 205-16.
A. DUPONT-SOMMER, 'Sur la fête de Pâque dans les documents araméens d'Éléphantine', in *Revue des Études Juives*, CVII, 1946-7, 39-51.
TH. H. GASTER, *Passover. Its History and Traditions*, New York, 1949.
J. HENNINGER, 'Les fêtes du printemps chez les Arabes et leurs implications historiques', in *Revista do Museu Paulista* (São Paulo); IV, 1950, 389-432.
H. J. KRAUS, 'Gilgal', in *VT*, I, 1951, 181-99.

S. Mowinckel, 'Die vermeintliche "Passahlegende", Ex 1-15', in *Studia Theologica*, V, 1951, 66-88.
I. Engnell, 'Paesaḥ-Maṣṣot and the Problem of "Patternism"', in *Orientalia Suecana*, I, 1952, 39-50.
P. Grelot, 'Études sur le "Papyrus Pascal" d'Éléphantine', in *VT*, IV, 1954, 348-84.
H. Haag, 'Ursprung und Sinn der alttestamentlichen Paschafeier', in *Luzerner Theologische Studien*, I, 1954, 17-46.
P. Grelot, 'Le Papyrus Pascal d'Éléphantine et le problème du Pentateuque', in *VT*, V, 1955, 250-65.
B. Couroyer, 'L'origine égyptienne du mot "Pâque"', in *RB*, LXII, 1955, 481-96.
T. Henninger, 'Zum Verbot des Knochenzerbrechens bei den Semitern', in *Studi Orientalistici in onore di G. Levi della Vida*, I, Rome, 1956, 448-58.
H. J. Kraus, 'Zur Geschichte des Passah-Massot-Festes im Alten Testament,' in *Evangelische Theologie*, XVIII, 1958, 47-67.
E. Kutsch, 'Erwägungen zur Geschichte der Passahfeier und des Massotfestes', in *Zeitschrift für Theologie und Kirche*, LV, 1958, 1-35.
H. Haag, art. 'Pâque', in *Dictionnaire de la Bible, Supplement*, VI, 1960, 1120-49.

On the feast of Weeks:

E. Brögelmann, 'Pfingsten in Altisrael', in *Monatschrift für Gottesdienst und kirchliche Kunst*, XLIV, 1939, 119-28.
K. H. Rengstorf, 'Christliches und jüdisches Pfingstfest', in *Monatschrift für Gottesdienst und kirchliche Kunst*, XLV, 1940, 75-8.
E. Lohse, 'Πεντηκοστή', in *Theologisches Wörterbuch zum Neuen Testament*, VI, 1954, 45-9.

On the feast of Tents:

R. Kittel, 'Osirismysterien und Laudhüttenfest', in *Orientalistische Literaturzeitung*, XXVII, 1924, 385-91.
J. A. Wensinck, 'Arabic New Year and the Feast of Tabernacles' (*Verhandelungen d. kon. Akad. v. Wetenskap, Letterkunde, N.R.*, XXV, 2), Leyden, 1925, 1-41.
L. I. Pap, *Das israelitische Neujahrfest*, Kampen, 933, 1933, 33-47.
H. Bornhäusen, *Sukka (Die Mischna . . .*, II, 6), Berlin, 1935.
J. Morgenstern, 'Amos Studies, II', in *HUCA*, XII-XIII, 1937-8, 20-34.
G. von Rad, *Das formgeschichtliche Problem des Hexateuchs*, Stuttgart, 1938, 30-7 = *Gesammelte Studien zum Alten Testament*, Munich, 1958, 41-8.
R. de Vaux, 'Le schisme religieux de Jéroboam Ier', in *Angelicum*, XX, 1943 = *Biblica et Orientalia R. P. Vosté dicata*, 77-91.
A. Alt, 'Zelte und Hütten', in *Alttestamentliche Studien (Festschrift Nötscher)*, Bonn, 1950, 16-25.
H. J. Kraus, *Gottesdienst in Israel. Studien zur Geschichte des Laubhüttenfest*, Munich, 1954.
S. Talmon, 'Divergences in Calendar-Reckoning in Ephraim and Juda', in *VT*, VIII, 1958, 48-74.
G. W. MacRae, 'The Meaning and Evolution of the Feast of Tabernacles', in *Catholic Biblical Quarterly*, XXII, 1960, 251-76.
See also the bibliography for the next two paragraphs.

On the New Year and the feast of Yahweh's enthronement:

Since the two problems are often treated together, we have combined the bibliography for the two paragraphs into one:

P. Volz, *Das Neujahrfest Yahwes*, Tübingen, 1912.
P. Fiebig, 'Rosch ha-schana' (*Die Mischna . . .*, II, 8), Giessen, 1914.
F. Thureau-Dangin, *Rituels akkadiens*, Paris, 1921.
S. Mowinckel, *Psalmenstudien*, II. *Das Thronbesteigungsfest Jahwäs und der Ursprung der Eschatologie*, Kristiania, 1922.
H. Schmidt, *Die Thronfahrt Jahves am Fest der Jahreswende im Alten Testament*, Tübingen, 1927.
L. I. Pap, *Das israelitische Neujahrsfest*, Kampen, 1933.
S. H. Hooke (ed.), *Myth and Ritual*, Oxford, 1933.
N. H. Snaith, *The Jewish New Year Festival. Its Origin and Development*, London, 1947.
A. Bentzen, 'The Cultic Use of the Story of the Ark in Samuel', in *JBL*, LXVII, 1948, 37-53.
R. Pettazzoni, 'Der babylonische Ritus des Akîtu und das Gedicht der Weltschöpfung', in *Eranos-Jahrbuch*, XIX, 1950, 403-30.
H. J. Kraus, *Die Königsherrschaft Gottes im Alten Testament. Untersuchungen zu den Liedern von Jahwes Thronbesteigung*, Tübingen, 1951.
A. Feuillet, 'Les Psaumes eschatologiques du Règne de Yahvé', in *Nouvelle Revue Théologique*, LXX, 1931, 244 60; 352-63.
F. Köcher, 'Ein mittelassyrisches Ritualfragment', in *ZA*, L, 1952, 192-202.
S. Mowinckel, *Zum israelitischen Neujahr und zur Deutung der Thronbesteigungspsalmen*, Oslo, 1952.
J. de Fraine, *L'aspect religieux de la royauté israélite*, Rome, 1954.
A. R. Johnson, *Sacral Kingship in Ancient Israel*, Cardiff, 1955.
G. Widengren, *Sakrales Königtum im Alten Testament und im Judentum*, Stuttgart, 1955.
S. Mowinckel, *He that Cometh*, Oxford, 1956.
D. Michel, 'Studien zu den sogenannten Thronbesteigungspsalmen', in *VT*, VI, 1956, 40-68.

H. OTTEN, 'Ein Text zum Neujahrsfest aus Boğazköy', in *Orientalistische Literaturzeitung*, LI, 1956, 101-5.

H. GROSS, 'Lässt sich in den Psalmen ein "Thronbesteigungsfest Gottes" nachweisen?' in *Trier theologische Zeitschrift*, LXV, 1956, 24-40.

E. AUERBACH, 'Neujahr- und Versöhnungs-Fest in den biblischen Quellen', in *VT*, VIII, 1958, 337-43.

S. H. HOOKE, *Myth, Ritual and Kingship*, Oxford, 1958.

H. CAZELLES, 'Nouvel An en Israël', in *Dictionnaire de la Bible, Supplément*, VI, Paris, 1959, 620-45.

18

THE LATER FEASTS

On the Day of Atonement:

J. G. FRAZER, *The Scapegoat*, London, 1913.

J. MEINHOLD, 'Joma' (*Die Mischna* . . ., II, 5), Giessen, 1913.

S. LANDERSDORFER, *Studien zum biblischen Versöhnungstag*, Münster i. W., 1924.

M. LÖHR, *Das Ritual von Lev. 16*, Berlin, 1925.

H. KAUPEL, *Die Dämonen im Alten Testament*, Augsburg, 1930, 81-91.

I. SCHUR, 'Versöhnungstag und Sündenbock' (*Soc. scient. Fennica, Comm. Hum. Litt.*, VI, 3), Helsingfors, 1934.

G. ORMANN, *Das Sündenbekenntnis des Versöhnungstag*, Bonn, 1935.

L. ROST, 'Weidewechsel und altisraelitischer Festkalendar', in *ZDPV*, LXVI, 1943, 205-16.

TH. C. VRIEZEN, 'The Term *hizza*: Lustration and Consecration', in *Oudtestamentische Studiën*, VII, 1950, 201-35.

J. MORGENSTERN, 'Two Prophecies from the Fourth Century B.C. and the Evolution of Yom Kippur', in *HUCA*, XXIV, 1952-3, 1-74.

G. R. DRIVER, 'Three Technical Terms in the Pentateuch' (for Azazel), in *Journal of Semitic Studies*, I, 1956, 97-8.

E. AUERBACH, 'Neujahrs- und Versöhnungs-Fest in den biblischen Quellen', in *VT*, VIII, 1958, 337-43.

On the Hanukkah:

H. HÖPFL, 'Das Chanukafest', in *Biblica*, II, 1922, 165-79.

O. S. RANKIN, *The Origins of the Festival of Hanukkah*, Edinburgh, 1930.

E. BICKERMANN, 'Ein jüdischer Brief vom Jahre 124 v. Chr. (II Macc. 1: 1-9)', in *Zeitschrift für die neutestamentliche Wissenschaft*, XXXII, 1933, 233-54.

O. S. RANKIN, 'The Festival of Hanukkah', in S. H. HOOKE (ed.), *The Labyrinth*, London, 1935, 159-209.

F.-M. ABEL, 'La fête de la Hanoucca', in *RB*, LIII, 1946, 538-46.

J. MORGENSTERN, 'The Chanukkah Festival and the Calendar of Ancient Israel', in *HUCA*, XX, 1947, 1-136; XXI, 1948, 365-496.

TH. H. GASTER, *Festivals of the Jewish Year²*, New York, 1955.

On the feast of Purim:

In addition to commentaries on the book of Esther, see:

N. S. DONIACH, *Purim, or the Feast of Esther. An Historical Study*, Philadelphia, 1933.

J. LEWY, 'The Feast of the 14th Day of Adar', in *HUCA*, XIV, 1939, 127-51.

V. CHRISTIAN, 'Zur Herkunft des Purim-Festes', in *Alttestamentliche Studien (Festschrift Nötscher)*, Bonn, 1950, 33-7.

J. LEWY, 'Old Assyrian *puru'um* and *purum*', in *Revue Hittite et Asianique*, V, 1939, 117-24.

A. BEA, 'De origine vocis *pûr*', in *Biblica*, XXI, 1940, 198-9.

Th. H. GASTER, *Purim and Hanukkah in Custom and Tradition*, New York, 1950.

H. RINGGREN, 'Esther and Purim', in *Svensk Exegetisk Årsbok*, XX, 1955, 5-24.

GENERAL INDEX

In this first index, the most important page-references are given first, and the sub-headings are arranged, as far as possible, in a logical order (e.g. historically).

INDEX TO PROPER NAMES

1. Jabesh, etc. For words beginning with J not listed here, see Y.

INDEX OF SEMITIC FORMS

(including a few Egyptian words)

INDEX OF BIBLICAL REFERENCES